International Relations Theory

THIRD EDITION

International Relations Theory

Realism, Pluralism, Globalism, and Beyond

Paul R. Viotti

Mark V. Kauppi

Allyn and Bacon

Boston ■ London ■ Toronto ■ Sydney ■ Tokyo ■ Singapore

Vice President and Editor-in-Chief: Paul E. Smith
Editorial Assistant: Kathy Rubino
Composition Buyer: Linda Cox
Editorial-Production Service: Susan McNally
Cover Administrator: Jenny Hart
Manufacturing Buyer: Megan Cochran
Marketing Manager: Susan Ogar

Copyright 1999, 1993, 1987 by Allyn & Bacon
A Viacom Company
160 Gould Street
Needham Heights, MA 02494

Internet: www.abacon.com

Library of Congress Cataloging-in-Publication Data

Viotti, Paul R.
    International relations theory : realism, pluralism, globalism /
Paul R. Viotti, Mark V. Kauppi.—3rd ed.
        p.   cm.
    Includes bibliographical references and index.
    ISBN 0-205-29253-4
    1. International relations. I. Kauppi, Mark V. II. Title.
JZ1305.V56 1998
327—dc21   98-26481
                                                        CIP

Printed in the United States of America
10   9   8   7   03   02

To Linda and Kathleen

CONTENTS

4 Globalism: Dependency and the Capitalist World-System   341

PREFACE

The idea for this book resulted from a conversation between the authors in 1982 as they strolled through the grounds of *Schloss Solitud*, located outside Stuttgart, Germany. The topic of discussion was the perennial problem of presenting in a relatively coherent manner a significant portion of the vast literature that comprises the field of international relations theory. After several years of classroom experimentation and numerous other conversations, the result was the first edition of this textbook, published in 1987. The fact that we have published this third edition is in no small measure due to feedback in North America, Europe, East Asia and elsewhere from former students, colleagues, and reviewers including Ronald J. Deibert, University of Toronto and Joseph Lepgold, Georgetown University—our thanks to all of you.

This book has five major objectives: (1) to discuss and illustrate what is meant by *theory* and why the theorizing enterprise is important; (2) to analyze and assess the underlying assumptions and images that influence scholarly work in the international relations field—images that we label *realism, pluralism* (referred to by many in the field as *liberalism*), and *globalism;* (3) to provide in the chapters and readings not an exhaustive list, but rather representative samples of theoretical works; (4) to introduce to the reader key concepts used in the international relations field (indicated in bold-face type)—hence an extensive glossary substantially expanded in this edition; and (5) to encourage the reader to scrutinize critically conceptual and theoretical works—historical and contemporary—dealing with international politics (for which we include at the end of each chapter in this edition an expanded, categorized list of additional readings).

The fifth purpose is of particular importance. If one is better equipped to analyze everyday events from a conceptual perspective, to ask the right questions, to recognize underlying assumptions of written works or public pronouncements of academics, government officials, and journalists, this would transcend any supposed achievement made by simply memorizing which author is associated with what theory.

Those who have read the earlier editions of this book will note that the subtitle has been modified: *Realism, Pluralism, Globalism,* **and Beyond.** This is recognition that recent theoretical work on international relations does not fit as neatly into a tripartite division of the field. Extension of the prefix *neo-* to modify *realism, liberalism,* and even *constructivism* and *structuralism*—terms that already cross the three images—is one indicator of practical problems associated with any effort to apply air-tight, mutually exclusive categorization. Fortunately, we have always viewed the three images and defined them more as pure or ideal types. Through this categorization we hope to make the field somewhat more intelligible—fully recognizing that the work of particular scholars (and the scholars themselves) oftentimes blend or cross from one image or category of thought to another. As such (and with these qualifications), the three-image categorization remains durable. Whether the field will move to some new synthesis worthy of additional and separate categorization remains to be seen.

Viewed as a whole, the field remains intellectually very vibrant. Journals and recently published books have been filled with important new theoretical work as well as challenges to already established understandings and responses from their defenders. Critical theory, post-modernism, cognitive theory, social constructivism, structuralism, feminism, liberal or neoliberal institutionalism, the English school, and normative theory on human rights are among the topics addressed at greater length in this edition. Given understandable constraints on the length of this volume, it is impossible to cover every topic as extensively as we might like, much less reprint every article suggested by colleagues, students, and reviewers.

Nevertheless, we hope that his book remains a useful starting point and reference in helping readers not only to understand current trends in a still very dynamic field, but also to gain an appreciation for the extent to which current theoretical work and debates rest so heavily upon the rich conceptual foundation of earlier years and across the millennia.

Paul R. Viotti
University of Denver
Graduate School of International Relations

Mark V. Kauppi
United States Department of Defense

International Relations Theory

Theory, Images, and International Relations: An Introduction

Why do wars occur? Is nationalism the primary cause? Or ideology? Or the lack of world government? Or misperception? Or are people innately aggressive? How can stability (if not peace) be achieved? Why is there such tremendous social and economic inequality between different regions of the world? These are the sorts of questions that have preoccupied scholars and statesmen at various times over the millennia, whether the political entity in question were an ancient city-state or a modern nation-state, a centralized empire or a decentralized feudal system, a socialist or a liberal democratic society. Nor are these questions the private preserve of intellectuals, diplomatic practitioners, and assorted political pundits and commentators. At one time or another, most citizens reflect on one or more of these important queries.

International relations as a field of inquiry addresses such questions. Despite the adjective *international,* the field is concerned with much more than relations between or among states. Other actors, such as international organizations, multinational corporations, environmental organizations, and terrorist groups, are all part of what could more correctly be termed **world politics.** Studies have also focused on factors internal to a state, such as bureaucratic governmental coalitions, interest groups, and decision making. The study of international relations, therefore, ranges from balance of power politics and economic structures at the international level to the ideological and perceptual predispositions of individual leaders.

Given the tremendous diversity and complexity of *what* is studied, it is not too surprising that there is a multiplicity of views concerning *how* one studies international relations. The possible avenues go well beyond the realms of history and political science. They include economics, psychology, social psychology, sociology, and anthropology. All this may seem rather intimidating to the student. If it is any consolation, it can also be intimidating to the professional in the field. As a result, many professionals tend to focus on one particular aspect of international relations, perhaps alliance behavior, the functioning of the United Nations and other international organizations, decision making in crisis situations, or the construction of **international regimes.**

No matter how ambitious or modest an international relations research project may be, however, every scholar approaches it from a particular point of view. Although some would argue that values ought to be central, most academics strive (or at least claim to strive) to reduce the impact of personal values when it comes to **empirical** research. Nevertheless, personal background and the nature of academic training inevitably influence the manner in which scholars interpret and examine international relations. As the German scholar Max Weber once argued: "All knowledge of cultural reality is always knowledge from particular points of view." How research is conducted will be "determined by the evaluative ideas that dominate the investigator and his age."[1] In other words, each individual's work will be influenced by a particular doctrine, image of the world, ideology, paradigm, or perspective. One may strive to be value free and objective, but at best, these goals can be achieved only imperfectly.

Different perspectives on international relations naturally generate debates. In the 1930s, **realists** and **idealists** argued over the nature of international politics and the possibility of peaceful change. In the 1960s, the so-called second great debate between **traditionalists** and **behavioralists** dealt with the question of appropriate **methodology.** Traditionalists emphasized the relative utility of history, law, philosophy, and other traditional methods of inquiry. Behavioralists argued in favor of social science conceptualization, quantification of variables, formal hypothesis testing, and causal model building. **Dialectical** approaches drawing on history and Marxist insights have been the subject of much discussion in certain journals in the field, although this debate is not widely reflected in the textbook literature. **Critical theory** perspectives raise doubts about the **epistemological** and **ontological** assumptions underlying much of the social science work on international relations. **Social constructivists** see states and nonstate actors not as mere products of the international system, but as actually playing a decisive role in shaping it. These actors influence, and are influenced by, the international norms and institutions they construct—activities that sustain or create new interests, values, and the ordering of foreign policy preferences.

In this book we emphasize three alternative images or perspectives of international relations we label **realism, pluralism,** and **globalism.**[2] We argue that these images have provided the basis for the development of many theoretical works that attempt to explain various aspects of international relations. The image that one has of international relations is of critical importance. Each image contains certain assumptions about world politics—whether or not explicitly recognized by the researcher—concerning critical actors, issues, and processes in world politics. These images lead one to ask certain questions, seek certain types of answers, and use certain methodological tools in the construction and testing of hypotheses and theories. The advantage is that such images bring order to the analytical effort and make it more manageable. A potential disadvantage, however, is that alternative perspectives and insights may be ignored or overlooked. Although the realist, pluralist, and globalist images are not mutually exclusive in all respects, the differences in point of view and emphasis are much greater than any apparent similarities. The resultant attempts at theory building, therefore, also vary considerably. Although some of these works fit neatly into one of the three categories or images we have identified, some efforts combine assumptions underlying different images. After all, theoretical work need not be constrained by preexisting taxonomies or organizing frameworks. Theorists are free to break out of or transcend existing categories, perhaps forging new syntheses. Indeed, the international relations field remains dynamic, with theorists continuing to break new ground.

In this chapter, we first address the question of what is meant by the term *theory*. We then briefly discuss the three images as alternative perspectives that influence the construction of international relations **theory.**

WHAT IS THEORY?

The word *theory* means different things to different people. It may even mean different things to the same person. In common parlance, for example, something may be true "in theory" but not in fact or in a particular case or set of circumstances. In this rather loose usage, "in theory" equates to "in principle" or "in the abstract."

Another meaning, somewhat more consistent with usage in this volume, views theory as a way of making the world or some part of it more intelligible or better understood. Theories dealing with international relations aspire to achieve this goal. Making things more intelligible may, of course, amount to nothing more than better or more precise *description* of the things we observe. Although accurate description is essential, theory is something more.

For many people, theory is *explaining* or *predicting*. One goes beyond mere description of phenomena observed and engages in **causal** explanation or prediction based on certain prior occurrences or conditions. Thus, whenever A is present, then B can be expected to follow. "If A, then B" as hypothesis may be subject to empirical test—that is, tested against real-world or factual data. "If states engage in arms races, then the likelihood of war increases" is an example of such a hypothesis. Indeed, formal statement and testing of hypotheses through the use of a statistical methodology is seen by many as central to the theory-building process. Others prefer to rely on nonquantitative case and comparative case studies, historical methods, and reasoned argument—the so-called traditional methods of theory building.

Whatever differences international relations scholars might have among themselves, they all agree on one thing—theory is necessary and unavoidable when it comes to explaining and attempting to foresee the future of international relations. As noted, theory is *unavoidable* in that all scholars approach their subject matter from what have been variously termed different perspectives, paradigms, metatheoretical constructs, or images. Theory is also *necessary* in that it tells us what to focus on and what to ignore in making sense of the world around us. Without theory, we would be overwhelmed and immobilized by an avalanche of mere facts. The sense we make of what we observe is informed by the perspectives and theories that we hold.

A theory, therefore, is an intellectual construct that helps one to select facts and interpret them in such a way as to facilitate explanation and prediction concerning regularities and recurrences or repetitions of observed phenomena. One can certainly think theoretically when it comes to explaining foreign policy processes in general or the foreign policy of a particular state. But international relations theorists tend to be interested in patterns of behavior *among* various international actors. In identifying patterns, the stage is set for making modest predictions about the possible nature and direction of change. To think theoretically, however, is not to engage in point predictions—"A will attack B the first week of the year"—however much foreign policy, national security, and intelligence analysts may aspire to such precision.[3]

To think theoretically is to be interested in central tendencies. As James Rosenau notes in the article that follows this chapter, the theorist views each event as an instance of a more encompassing class or pattern of phenomena. Fitting pieces into a larger whole makes theory building analogous to puzzle solving. In fact, for many theorists, the goal is not merely explanation of patterns of behavior, but explanations of patterns that at first glance seem counterintuitive or different from what one might expect.

Furthermore, the best theories are *progressive*—meaning they lead researchers to ask new and interesting questions—and are also *parsimonious*—explaining a great deal of behavior through the use of a relatively few concepts with relations among them clearly specified. By contrast, theories that lack this parsimony contain too many factors—quickly becoming as or more complex than the reality they purport to explain.

War continues to be a topic of considerable concern among international relations theorists using a wide variety of methodological approaches to developing better causal theory. War poses a substantial puzzle to theorists. The phenomenon persists even though wars are extremely costly in terms of lives and treasure lost. It may be that in the minds of decisionmakers, the expected benefit of going to war still outweighs expected costs in particular cases. Quincy Wright's *A Study of War* and Lewis Richardson's *Statistics of Deadly Quarrels* were pioneering efforts at trying to solve this puzzle. Kenneth Waltz's *Man, the State and War* examined causes in the context of three **levels of analysis.** Since the 1960s, J. David Singer and others sharing his preference for formal hypothesis testing through the use of statistical methods have been engaged extensively in studying the phenomenon of war. Bruce Bueno de Mesquita's *The War Trap* and Michael Doyle's *Ways of War and Peace* are examples of continuing efforts to gain better understanding of war by building better theory.[4]

One view is that the underlying cause of war is the absence of any world government or central authority vested with the capability to enforce rules, settle disputes, and maintain peace among states. It is this **anarchy** or lack of common government that poses no obstacle and thus permits war to occur. As such, anarchy is the *permissive* cause of war.[5] Misperception may be the immediate or direct cause of a given war. Or, by contrast, war may break out not so much as the result of misperception or misunderstanding but because of the hardheaded, **rational** calculation that the benefits of going to war appear to outweigh the costs.

Theory in a stronger or more formal sense will go beyond proposing the cause of war in such broad terms and will insist that the relations among **variables** be clearly specified and weighted with the precision one finds in an algebraic equation or set of related equations.[6] Such fully developed theory is not common in the social sciences, which are often said to be at a lesser level of progress than are the natural sciences.

General theories that would provide a complete account of the causes of war are less common than *partial*, or *middle-range*, theories that are more modest in the scope of what is to be explained or predicted. Part of the war puzzle addressed by such middle-range theorists, for example, involves crises and decision making in crises. Are partial theories about such things as crisis decision making like building blocks that can at some future date be assembled into a fully developed, general theory of war? Some theorists would say yes and that the most productive enterprise for the present is the development of better middle-range theories. Not everyone would agree; some would argue that formulating general theory comes first, with partial theories being deduced or flowing from it.

The world of theory is an abstract one. Theories may exist apart from facts. Mathematical theorists, for example, deal entirely in the realm of abstraction, whether or not their work has direct relevance to problems of the world in which we live. Practical application for the work of mathematical theorists is sometimes found years later, if ever. **Empirical** theories in the social or natural sciences, by contrast, relate to facts and provide explanation or prediction for observed phenomena. Hypotheses associated with these theories are subject to test against real-world data or facts. The theorist need not have any purpose in developing such empirical theories other than satisfying his or her intellectual curiosity, although many will seek to make their work "policy relevant."[7]

Policy-relevant theories may have explicit purposes that stem from the value preferences of the theorist, such as reducing the likelihood of war or curbing the arms race. Acting on such theories, of course, is the domain of the policymaker, a task separate from that of the empirical theorist. Theorists who become policymakers may well make choices informed by what theories say will be the likely outcomes of implementing one or another alternative. Their choices may be informed by empirical theory or understanding of world events, but the decisions they make are still based on value preferences.

Normative theory deals precisely with values and value preferences. Unlike empirical theory, however, propositions in normative theory are not subject to empirical test as a means of establishing their truth or falsehood. Normative theory deals not with what *is*, the domain of empirical theory. Rather, normative theory deals explicitly with what *ought* to be—the way the world should be ordered and the value choices decisionmakers *should* make. Although the bulk of the effort in this volume is allocated to empirical theory within the context of separate images of world politics, we consider normative theory to be an important and policy-relevant, if often neglected, enterprise. Chapter 5 deals explicitly with normative theories relevant to international relations and foreign policy choices. We also identify normative preferences often associated with the three images of international relations theory that are at the core of our effort.

ALTERNATIVE IMAGES

This section provides an overview of the two most striking or immediately apparent distinctions among the three images of international relations under consideration: (1) the key *actors*, or *units*, and (2) the *assumptions* made about them. In the succeeding chapters, we go well beyond this brief examination of actors and underlying assumptions. The discussion of realism, for example, focuses on the concepts of power and the balance of power, the chapter on pluralism emphasizes decision making and transnationalism, and the treatment of globalism stresses the concept of dependency in a world capitalist context. We also discuss the intellectual precursors of these images and philosophical and conceptual issues such as **determinism, voluntarism, system,** and system change. Although normative assumptions and implications of the three images are treated explicitly in Chapter 5, they are also woven throughout the discussion in earlier chapters.

We begin this introductory overview with a discussion of *realism*. As will become apparent, proponents of the other two perspectives have to a certain degree been forced to come to terms with this long-established tradition. Indeed, many of their arguments are addressed directly to the strengths and weaknesses of work by realists.

Realism—Major Actors and Assumptions

Realism is based on four key assumptions. First, *states are the principal or most important actors*. States represent the key **unit of analysis,** whether one is dealing with ancient Greek city-states or modern nation-states. The study of international relations is the study of relations among these units. Realists who use the concept of system defined in terms of interrelated parts usually refer to an international system of states. What of nonstate actors? International organizations such as the United Nations may aspire to the status of independent actor, but from the realist perspective, this aspiration has not in fact been achieved to any significant degree. Multinational corporations, terrorist groups, and other transnational and international organizations are frequently acknowledged by realists, but the position of these nonstate actors is always one of lesser importance. States are the dominant actors.

Second, the state is viewed as a *unitary actor*. For purposes of analysis, realists view the state as being encapsulated by a metaphorical hard shell. A country faces the outside world as an integrated unit. A common assumption associated with realist thought is that political differences within the state are ultimately resolved authoritatively such that the government of the state speaks with one voice for the state as a whole. The state is a unitary actor in that it is usually assumed by realists to have one policy at any given time on any particular issue. To be sure, exceptions occur from time to time, but to the realists, these are exceptions that demonstrate the rule and that actually support the general notion of the state as an integrated, unitary actor.

Even in those exceptional cases in which, for example, a foreign ministry expresses policies different from policy statements of the same country's defense ministry, corrective action is taken in an attempt to bring these alternative views to a common and authoritative statement of policy. "End running" of state authorities by bureaucratic and nongovernmental, domestic, and transnational actors is also possible, but it occurs unchecked by state authorities in only those issues in which the stakes are low. From the realist perspective, if the issues are important enough, higher authorities will intervene to preclude bureaucratic end running or action by nongovernmental actors that are contrary to centrally directed policy.

Third, given this emphasis on the unitary state-as-actor, realists usually make the further assumption that *the state is essentially a rational actor*. A rational foreign policy decision-making process would include a statement of objectives, consideration of all feasible alternatives in terms of existing capabilities available to the state, the relative likelihood of attaining these objectives by the various alternatives under consideration, and the benefits or costs associated with each alternative. Following this rational process, governmental decisionmakers evaluate each alternative, selecting the one that maximizes utility (maximizing benefit or minimizing cost associated with attaining the objectives sought). The result is a rank ordering of preferences.

As a practical matter, the realist is aware of the difficulties in viewing the state as a rational actor. Governmental decisionmakers may not have all the factual information or knowledge of cause and effect they need to make value-maximizing decisions. The process may well be clouded by considerable uncertainty as decisionmakers grope for the best solution. They also have to deal with the problem of human bias and misperception that may lead them astray. In any event, the choice made—if not always the *best* or value-maximizing choice in fact—is at least perceived to be a satisfactory one. It is a **satisficing** or suboptimal choice—less than a value-maximizing choice, but still good enough in terms of the objectives sought. The assumption of the unitary, rational actor is particularly important in **game theory** and many works on **deterrence** theory.

Fourth, realists assume that within the hierarchy of international issues, *national security* usually tops the list. Military and related political issues dominate world politics. A realist focuses on actual or potential conflict between state actors and the use of **force,** examining how international stability is attained or maintained, how it breaks down, the utility of force as a means to resolve disputes, and the prevention of the violation of territorial integrity. **Power,** therefore, is a key concept. To the realist, military security or strategic issues are sometimes referred to as **high politics,** whereas economic and social issues are viewed as less important or **low politics.** Indeed, the former is often understood to dominate or set the environment within which the latter occurs.

Pluralism—Major Actors and Assumptions

The pluralist image (often referred to as **liberalism** or as a *liberal* construct) consists of a different set of assumptions. First, *nonstate actors* are important entities in international relations that cannot be ignored. International organizations, for example, can be independent actors in their own right. The organization's own decisionmakers, bureaucrats, and other associated groups have considerable influence in areas such as agenda setting—determining which issues are most important politically. International organizations are more than simply arenas within which sovereign states compete. Organizational power and autonomy are neither absolute nor nonexistent but something in between, varying from organization to organization. Similarly, other nongovernmental actors, such as environmental organizations and multinational corporations (MNCs), cannot be dismissed as being of merely marginal importance, given an increasingly **interdependent** world economy. Indeed, in some cases, they are even capable of circumventing the authority of the state.

Second, for the pluralist, *the state is not a unitary actor.* Indeed, the realist view of the state as unitary actor is an abstraction that masks the essence of politics that is found principally within the state. The state is not some **reified** entity—an abstraction to be treated as if it were a physical being that acts with single-minded determination, always in a coherent manner. It is, rather, composed of individual bureaucracies, interest groups, and individuals that attempt to formulate or influence foreign policy. Competition, coalition building, conflict, and compromise among these actors are the stuff of politics. To speak of "the foreign policy" of the United Kingdom or the United

States, for example, is really to speak of a number of foreign policy decisions determined by competition among a number of actors. Foreign policy preferences, therefore, are not set in stone. Pluralists disaggregate the state—break it into its component parts. They reject the notion of the state as an integrated entity, impermeable to outside forces. Both governmental and nongovernmental actors pass through this soft outer shell, sometimes taking actions with policy implications contrary to preferences of central state authorities. These are not just exceptional cases from the pluralist perspective. In fact, focusing on the state as if it were a unitary actor again misses the essence of politics. This is not only in terms of interactions *within* the state; equally important, it is the **transnational** dimension of state and nonstate actors that operates *across* national borders. The pluralist image thus offers greater complexity than the relatively simpler image of states as unitary actors interacting with one another.

Third, pluralists *challenge* the utility of the realist assumption of *the state as rational actor.* This follows logically from the pluralist image of the disaggregated state in which the foreign policy decision-making process is the result of clashes, bargaining, and compromise between and among different actors. In some cases, a particular policy may be suggested in order to enhance the bureaucratic power, prestige, and standing of one organization at the expense of others. Although this may seem rational from the perspective of an individual bureaucracy, it can lead to poor, if not disastrous, foreign policies. The pursuit of individual, value-maximizing strategies at the organization level can lead to collective disaster at the nation-state level. Moreover, the decision-making process is typically one of coalition and countercoalition building, bargaining, and compromising that may not yield a best or optimal decision. Attempting to establish a consensus or at least a **minimum winning coalition** is a process far different in kind from the earlier simple description of what is usually meant by the term **rational.** Misperception on the part of decisionmakers as a result of incomplete information, bias, stress, and uncertainty about cause and effect is also a key focus of attention for some pluralist scholars. All such factors undercut the idea of a rational decision-making process.

Finally, for the pluralist, *the agenda of international politics is extensive.* The pluralist rejects the notion that the agenda of international politics is dominated primarily by military-security issues. Foreign affairs agendas have expanded and diversified over recent decades such that economic and social issues are often at the forefront of foreign policy debates. Former Secretary of State Henry Kissinger, himself a realist, noted as far back as 1975 that

> progress in dealing with the traditional agenda is no longer enough. A new and unprecedented kind of issue has emerged. The problems of energy, resources, environment, pollution, the uses of space and the seas now rank with questions of military security, ideology, and territorial rivalry which have traditionally made up the diplomatic agenda.[8]

Not surprisingly, such a statement was made at a time of détente, or relatively relaxed tensions, between East and West. It may be that as international tensions decrease, economic and social, or **welfare,** issues tend to come to the forefront of international debate.

Globalism—Major Actors and Assumptions

Globalism, as we use the term, is a third perspective, fundamentally different from both the realist and the pluralist images. In the 1970s, debate within the international relations discipline tended to focus on the realists and pluralists. Only recently has attention been paid to the globalist perspective. Globalists typically assume that the starting point of analysis for international relations is *the global context within which states and other entities interact*. Globalists emphasize the overall structure of the international system or, more colloquially, the "big picture." To explain behavior, one must first grasp the essence of the global environment within which such behavior takes place. This is a dominant theme within the globalist image, although some realists and pluralists also share this perspective. To understand the external behavior of states requires more than merely examining factors internal to a state. One must first grasp how the structure of the system conditions and predisposes certain actors to act in certain ways.

Second, globalists assume that it is not only useful but also imperative to *view international relations from a historical perspective*. It is only through an examination of history that one can understand the current environment within which world politics takes place. For many globalists, Marxists as well as non-Marxists, the defining characteristic of the international system is that it is **capitalist.** This requires the study of the rise of capitalism as it emerged in sixteenth-century Western Europe, its development, changes, and expansion to the point at which today we can speak of a **world capitalist system** that conditions and constrains the behavior of all states and societies. Some states and societies benefit from this capitalist system; others do not. Furthermore, the evolution of the world capitalist system supposedly accounts for the creation of states, not just their behavior. While realists and many pluralists tend to see states as a given, utilizing them as *independent variables,* some globalists view states as *dependent* variables—that which is to be explained.

Third, although globalists recognize the importance of states-as-actors, international organizations, and transnational actors and coalitions, the particular focus of their analysis is on how these and other factors act as *mechanisms of domination* by which some states, classes, or elites manage to benefit from this capitalist system at the expense of others. More specifically, globalists are typically concerned with the development and maintenance of **dependency** relations among northern, industrialized states (in North America, Europe, Japan) and the poor, underdeveloped, or industrially backward Third World or less developed countries (LDCs) of Latin America, Africa, and Asia. The basic argument is that these latter states and societies are underdeveloped not because they have failed to develop capitalist economic systems or because they are poorly integrated into the world capitalist system. On the contrary, it is not a matter of too little capitalism but of too much. Far from being placed outside the mainstream of the world capitalist system, LDCs have become an integral part of it. The structure of the global political economy has developed in such a manner—intentionally and unintentionally—as to keep the Third World countries underdeveloped and dependent on the rich northern states. The LDCs play a crucial role in the economic well-being of the United States and other advanced industrial countries by providing cheap labor, raw

materials necessary to fuel the American economy, and markets for American manufactured goods. As part of the world capitalist system, LDCs cannot choose their own
path toward economic and political development. Autonomous development in these
circumstances is not possible.

Finally, as should now be apparent, globalists emphasize to a greater extent than
either realists or pluralists the critical *importance of economic factors* when it comes to
explaining the dynamics of the international system. Realists, you will recall, subordinate economic factors to those of a political-military nature. Pluralists argue that this
is an open question; they typically reject this high versus low politics dichotomy. Social
and economic issues to pluralists are at least as important as the security concerns of the
realists. Globalists, however, start with the assumption that economics is the key to
understanding the creation, evolution, and functioning of the contemporary world

**TABLE 1.1   Alternative Images of International Relations:
Underlying Assumptions**

	Realism	Pluralism	Globalism
Analytic Unit(s)	1. State is the principal actor	1. State and nonstate actors are important	1. Classes, states and societies, and nonstate actors operate as part of world capitalist system
View of Actor(s)	2. State is unitary actor	2. State disaggregated into components, some of which may operate transnationally	2. International relations viewed from historical perspective, especially the continuous development of world capitalism
Behavioral Dynamic	3. State is rational actor seeking to maximize its own interest or national objectives in foreign policy	3. Foreign policymaking and transnational processes involve conflict, bargaining, coalition, and compromise—not necessarily resulting in optimal outcomes	3. Focus is on patterns of dominance within and among societies
Issues	4. National security issues are most important	4. Multiple agenda with socioeconomic or welfare issues as, or more, important than national security questions	4. Economic factors are most important

system. Although the pluralist and globalist would seem to share common ground because both place importance on economic and social questions, they differ fundamentally in the ways in which they deal with them. The more fragmented pluralist image of multiple actors bargaining, compromising, and building coalitions within and across national borders contrasts sharply with the structural image of the globalist. The globalist would tell a pluralist that the outcome of bargaining among various actors is in most cases predetermined if it involves a **North–South** issue. Such interactions take place within the context of an exploitative and dependent relation that works, at the most general level, to the benefit of maintaining the world capitalist system and, more specifically, to the benefit of particular groups or classes.

Images of International Relations: Some Qualifications

We find the threefold division of realism, pluralism, and globalism to be a useful way to view the diverse images on which many theoretical efforts are based in the field of international relations. We are the first to admit that this classification scheme also has its limitations. Accordingly, we offer several qualifications and clarifications.

First, each image should be viewed as an **ideal** or **pure type** in that each image emphasizes what a number of seemingly diverse theoretical approaches have in common.[9] For example, there are substantial differences in the works of Kenneth Waltz, Stanley Hoffmann, and the late Hans J. Morgenthau, but all three scholars share core assumptions of the realist perspective. What unites them as international relations theorists is more important for our purposes than what divides them.

Second, the overview of key assumptions of each of the three perspectives might give the impression that the three images are mutually exclusive in all respects. This is not the case. Realists such as Robert Gilpin and Stephen Krasner are prominent contributors to work on international political economy. In underscoring the importance of economic factors in international relations, they differ from some other scholars who put relatively more emphasis on political-military factors. Gilpin, Krasner, and other theorists who share their orientation to the international political economy focus on the *political* determinants or influences on international economic relations. They ask such questions, for example, as how do changes in the distribution of power among states affect the degree of openness in the international trading system?

Such globalists as Immanuel Wallerstein also recognize the significance of the state in international relations but prefer to emphasize economic trends and class relations. Similarly, many interdependence theorists of pluralist orientation do not deny the importance of the state as a key international actor, but they prefer to examine non-state actors as well as transnational, socioeconomic factors that they see as having reduced the autonomy of the state-as-actor. Even if the three images are not mutually exclusive in every respect, and even if every observer of international relations can agree that sensitivity to alternative perspectives on world politics is commendable, the reader may want to keep in mind how difficult it is to combine three images with so very different underlying assumptions from which all subsequent analyses, hypotheses, and theories derive.

Third, we readily confess that not all international relations specialists can be assigned conveniently to one particular image. Bruce Russett, for example, has written on dependency, the democratic peace, and conflict between states-as-actors—each subject associated, respectively, with globalist, pluralist, and realist images. Robert Jervis has bridged two camps in his pluralist examination of psychological factors in foreign policy decision making and in his realist focus on national security questions associated with deterrence, arms races, and how the anarchical international system provides the environment within which wars occur. Robert Keohane was a prominent contributor in the 1970s to pluralist works on transnationalism and interdependence that reflected a **liberal** understanding of a world politics composed of multiple kinds of both state and such nonstate actors as international organizations, corporations, bureaucracies, and even individuals and small groups. Interest by Keohane and others in how international **regimes** and associated institutions influence, and are influenced by, both competition and cooperation among states led them to adapt the realist analytical assumption of the rational, unitary state as the starting point for work referred to as **neoliberal institutionalism**. Neoliberals understand the continuing importance of nonstate actors but are not about to ignore states that continue to play a prominent and often decisive role.

Although we believe that the vast majority of writers within the international relations discipline tends to be associated with one of the three perspectives, notable exceptions do not, in our estimation, undermine the utility of the tripartite division of the field that we employ in this volume. We acknowledge a certain amount of conceptual eclecticism by scholars in the study of international relations, perhaps reflecting the absence of a single, dominant perspective. For some, conceptual diversity is to be applauded; for others, it is a source of despair. Be that as it may, our focus is primarily on ideas, trends, and generalized images of international relations and only secondarily on the work of particular authors. Indeed, our references to work in the international relations field are meant to be representative of the images we discuss, not encyclopedic in scope. Just as it is hoped that the reader will come to appreciate the strengths and weaknesses of each of the three perspectives, so too do many specialists in the field weigh the relative utility of these alternative images in generating insights helpful in answering particular theoretical questions they may be asking.[10] Moreover, it is not surprising to find a certain amount of conceptual eclecticism in the work of a number of theorists whose interests have changed over the years.[11]

Fourth, the images tend to focus more on *what* is studied than on *how* to conduct such studies. A central argument we make is that quantitative and nonquantitative approaches to the study of international politics are methods that transcend the three images we have identified. Statistical methods, formal hypothesis testing, and **causal modeling** find their adherents within each of the perspectives, as do the more traditional, nonquantitative, historical, philosophical, legal, case study, and comparative case study methods. Our point remains that these are *methods*, not images of international relations or world politics. Images may influence the choice of methods, but images and methods are not one and the same.

Although it has been the subject of endless debates and much bloodletting in academic circles, the behavioralist—traditionalist (or the "science"—traditionalist) dichotomy is not particularly useful for our purposes. One can argue over the relative merits of particular methods for answering political questions, but a more fundamental concern is the conceptual framework within which those methods are used. Are these methods informed by realist, pluralist, or globalist images of international politics, and how useful are these alternative images by which we order or make some sense of what we observe?[12]

Efforts to predict global futures through complex modeling, for example, reflect one or another of the three images we identify.[13] An image of international or world politics influences the selection of units or processes examined and **variables** identified and operationalized. Thus, for realists, states and state interactions are of key importance; for pluralists, transnational interactions to include communications flows across national borders may well be the central focus; and for globalists, patterns of class or North–South relations of dominance or dependence are perhaps most important.

Similarly, methods associated with the literature on **decision-making** and **public choice theory**—economic models applied to political decision making—transcend the three world images we identify.[14] Assumptions made about actors and processes are informed by realist, pluralist, and globalist images and color the use a particular method is given. Thus, **public** or **collective goods theory, game theory, econometrics,** and other approaches identified with the rapidly growing interdisciplinary field of **political economy** find their adherents among scholars holding diverse images and thus are not the exclusive preserve of realists, pluralists, or globalists.

Finally, we wish to state explicitly that the three images we identify are not *theories* of international relations.[15] Rather, they represent general perspectives on international relations out of which particular theories *may* develop. Assumptions of an image may become part of a theory (such as the realist assumptions of a unified, rational, state-as-actor in some realist works), but more often than not, they simply help to orient a scholar's research by highlighting certain units of analysis for investigation in the construction of a theory and help to determine what constitutes evidence in the testing of hypotheses.

THE LEVELS OF ANALYSIS

It is necessary to address further the question every scholar of international relations must first ask no matter what image or perspective one holds: Where should one focus one's research efforts? Let us assume that we are rather ambitious and wish to explain the causes of war between states. Does one deal with individual decisionmakers or small groups of individuals engaged in the policy process? How important, for example, are such factors as the correctness of individual perceptions or bargaining skill in determining the decision to go to war? On the other hand, if one looks outside the individual or small decision-making group to the entire state apparatus, society as a whole, or the international political system of states, one is acknowledging the importance of external or environmental factors as well.

Work by Kenneth N. Waltz in the 1950s on the causes of war represented a path-breaking effort due to his identification of distinct **levels of analysis** and his attempt to specify the relations among these levels[16] (an excerpt is provided in one of the readings that follows in Chapter 2). Was the cause of war to be found in the nature of individuals? (Are humans innately aggressive?) Or in the nature of states and societies? (Are some types of states more aggressive than others?) Or in the nature of the international system of states? Each answer reflects a different level of analysis—individual, state and society, or international (see Figure 1.1). Waltz's conclusion was that the *permissive* cause of war is the condition of anarchy in the international political system of states, whereas the *efficient* causes of any given war can be found as well at the other levels of analysis (individual or state and societal levels). Whether or not one agrees with his conclusion, the important point is that his analysis of the problem of war was at different levels. In 1961, the importance of the question of levels of analysis to the study of international relations was further discussed in detail in an often-cited article by J. David Singer. Singer argued that one's choice of a particular level of analysis determines what one will and will not see. Different levels tend to emphasize different actors and processes.[17]

For example, it is quite common for the levels of analysis to include (1) the international system (distribution of power among states, geography, technology, and other factors); (2) the state (often treated as a unified actor) and society (democratic, authoritarian, etc.); (3) groups as in bureaucratic politics; (4) individuals as in psychology and individuals in the context of the groups of which they are a part as in social psychology. It is also quite typical for these various levels to be used to explain the foreign policy behavior of states—the **dependent** variable. The state, in other words, is often the **unit of analysis,** and explaining its behavior could entail taking into account factors at all of these levels of analysis.

But *which* level of analysis, one may ask, is most important? To take a specific example, let us assume that the foreign policies of most states exhibit relative constancy, or slowness to change. How is this constancy to be explained? Some scholars

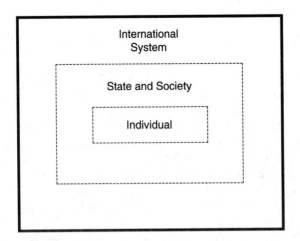

FIGURE 1.1   Levels of Analysis

point to external factors such as the balance of power among states that is relatively slow to change in any major way. Others emphasize relatively constant factors within the state—the same decisionmakers or decision-making processes, with incremental or small changes being the rule.

Another example: How are arms races explained? Some scholars point to international factors such as the military expenditures and hostility of other states that lead to an increase in the production of weapons. Other researchers emphasize the importance of domestic factors such as bureaucratic competition between branches of the military services and budgetary processes that encourage a steady increase in expenditures.[18]

The easy answer to the question of which level of analysis should be emphasized is that all levels of analysis should be considered. Such a response is not particularly useful because it suggests that we have to study everything under the sun. Few scholars would even attempt such a task,[19] and the resulting theory would hardly be parsimonious. Hence, a great deal of the literature on international relations is constantly posing the questions of *what* should be examined *within* each level of analysis, and *how* actors, structures, and variables relate to one another across levels of analysis and over time.

This issue of levels of analysis also subtly pervades the three images. What have been termed **neorealists,** for example, note how the overall structure of the international system influences the behavior of states or the perception of decisionmakers. Hence, neorealist analysis emphasizes the systems level. Similarly, certain globalists, as we have noted, examine how the historical development of the capitalist world economy generates state actors. Despite their differences, both neorealists and *world-system theorists* emphasize the systems level. Those authors associated with the pluralist image, however, who examine bureaucracies, interest groups, and individuals tend to emphasize the state-societal and individual levels of analysis. Some pluralists, however, are also interested in how the development and spread of international norms influence state behavior—a system-level focus.

There is a final important issue that should be mentioned in conjunction with the levels of analysis but that goes well beyond the latter as it raises basic philosophy-of-science questions concerning the so-called *agent–structure* problem. As summarized by one author, the problem

> emerges from two uncontentious truths about social life: first, that human agency is the only moving force behind the actions, events, and outcomes of the social world; and second, that human agency can be realized only in concrete historical circumstances that condition the possibilities for action and influence its course. "People make history," observed Marx in an often-quoted aphorism, "but not in conditions of their own choosing." These truths impose two demands on our scientific explanations: first, that they acknowledge and account for the powers of agents; and second, that they recognize the causal relevance of "structural factors," that is, the conditions of action. The "agent–structure problem" refers to the difficulties of developing theory that successfully meets both demands.[20]

This problem is usually viewed as a matter of **ontology,** the branch of metaphysics concerned with the nature of being. In this case, the ontological issue deals with the nature of both agents (very often viewed as the state) and structures (as in the international system), and relations between them. As we will see in the following chapters, a constant theme is how authors deal with the relative importance of human agents and "structural factors," or what we call the issue of **voluntarism** and **determinism.** Very often unstated, one's position on this issue heavily influences how one goes about explaining international politics as well as assessing the possibilities and means of peaceful change.

SCIENTIFIC UNDERSTANDING

Positivism

All three images discussed in this book essentially reflect a positivist approach to understanding international relations. **Positivism** involves a commitment to a unified view of science, meaning a belief that it is possible to adopt the methodologies of the natural sciences to explain the social world, which includes international relations. Positivists believe that objective knowledge of the world is possible and, hence, have a faith and commitment to the Enlightenment's rationalist tradition. The so-called great debates of the international relations discipline—realism versus idealism and traditionalism versus behavioralism—have given way to debates on **epistemology**—how one knows or acquires knowledge. Accordingly, we undertake here a discussion of these epistemological issues, including the vigorous critiques of mainstream international relations theorizing by postpositivists, critical theorists, and postmodernists.

Positivism has been under assault for its attempts to separate facts from values, to define and **operationalize** concepts into precisely and accurately measurable variables, and to test truth claims in the form of hypotheses drawn from theories. Whether using quantitative or statistical methods or such nonquantitative (or "qualitative") methods as case and comparative-case studies, those who have tried to be scientific have been criticized for ignoring or taking insufficient account of the personal or human dimension of scholarship. What we observe in either the natural or the social sciences is heavily influenced by the **interpretive understanding** we have of the concepts we employ, not to mention causal relations we infer when we specify the relations among variables, theories, hypotheses, and the observed behavior of states and nonstate actors in the political and social milieu in which they are immersed.

It was the Scottish writer David Hume (1711–1776) who objected to causal inferences drawn too readily. A skeptic at heart, Hume recognized that causality is itself not directly observable but merely a construct used by human beings to make what they observe around them understandable or even predictable. To Hume, causality is no more than an inference human beings draw from the conjunction of impressions about the things we observe. For example, when we perceive that some factor or event (X) precedes another (Y), our minds may be prone to think that X is the cause of Y. Consistent with Hume and also influenced by the positivism of the French philosopher, Auguste Comte (1798–1857), John Stuart Mill (1806–1873) developed formal canons of induction that would allow both natural and social scientists to arrive at causal truth claims by applying systematically one or another of five specified tests or methods to observed phenomena.[21]

The **empiricism** of these earlier writers was adopted by scholars in the "Vienna circle" of the 1930s who developed a somewhat extreme scientific form called **logical positivism**—the pursuit of a pure science that would separate fact from value and achieve the precision of mathematics. Among members of the Vienna circle were such luminaries as Moritz Schlick, Otto Neurath, and Rudolf Carnap. They were also influenced by the earlier work of their contemporary, Ludwig Wittgenstein, whose *Tractatus Logico-Philosophicus* (1921) related the thought and ideas we have to the words we use, focusing on the necessary logic and precision of language applied to observations about the world. Following Wittgenstein, the Vienna circle and its followers would seek both logical precision and clarity in scientific language.

In the post–World War II period, a broad, somewhat watered-down application of positivist premises to the social sciences—an approach that also included incorporation of statistical methodologies and the use of mathematical equations to specify causal relations among variables—resulted in a highly critical reaction to this "modernist" epistemology. Taking various critiques into account, refinement of positivist epistemology continued during the 1950s and 1960s.

Carl Hempel, for example, set forth a **deductive-nomological** schema for scientific explanation. He referred to "laws invoked in a scientific explanation" as **covering laws.** Thus, what is to be explained—the explanandum—is preceded by certain explanatory sentences—an explanans that "consists of general laws" and "other statements" concerning "particular facts."[22] Hempel applied this formalized deductive approach in the formulation of both universal and probabilistic law-like statements.

In the mid-1930s, Karl Popper had addressed empirical tests of **hypotheses** drawn from theories. To "prove" empirically that a certain hypothesis or universal proposition is true is virtually impossible since to do so in an absolute sense would mean submitting it to an infinite number of tests in space and time. Popper argued that to be scientific, claims or propositions have to be stated in falsifiable form. Falsifiability means simply that if a proposition is false, it must be possible empirically to show that it is false. To Popper, **scientific propositions** must be falsifiable. With varying degrees of confidence based on logical consistency and available evidence, one can accept a falsifiable proposition at least until, by experiment or other scientific means, one shows it to be false.[23]

One example in the study of international relations of a positivist social science at work is the effort of Kenneth Waltz to offer a more formal theory of international politics. To Waltz, "theories explain laws."[24] Waltz identifies a power-based structure of the international system that purportedly explains the behavior of states as the system's principal actors. Having stated "the theory being tested," one proceeds to

infer hypotheses from it; subject the hypotheses to experimental or observational tests; . . . use the definitions of terms found in the theory being tested; eliminate or control perturbing variables not included in the theory under test; devise a number of distinct and demanding tests; if a test is not passed, ask whether the theory flunks completely, needs repair and restatement, or requires a narrowing of the scope of its explanatory claims.[25]

The positivism Waltz owes to Popper is clear in the last comment that underscores the importance of falsifiability in the testing of theories and hypotheses drawn therefrom.[26]

Interpretive Understanding, Critical Theory, and a Postmodernist Critique of International Relations Theory

If the central question of *epistemology* is how we know what we think we know, critical and postmodernist theorists set aside the abstract universalist claims of logical positivists, focusing instead on the human perception and understandings that give diverse meanings to the concepts and theories we formulate and the behavior we observe.

That facts, concepts, and theories may not be separated from values stems from their observation and construction by human **agency.** To post-modernists, what we see, what we choose to see or measure, and the mechanisms or methods we employ are all of human construction that essentially rely on **perception** and **cognitive processes** influenced as well by prior understandings and meanings. Even the language we use constitutes an embedded set of values that are an integral part of any culture.

Thomas S. Kuhn's effort in his identification of "scientific revolutions" focused on the natural sciences,[27] but it has perhaps had even greater impact on understanding in the social sciences. Arguing that **paradigms,** or frameworks of understanding, influence the way we observe and make sense of the world around us, Kuhn was criticized for his alleged **relativism**—a direct challenge to the positivist school. To some of his opponents, knowledge was understood to be empirically grounded and not so arbitrary as to be based on such preexisting or newly discovered frameworks of understanding. To be fair, Kuhn did not reject empirically based claims as such. He argued only that when theories and component concepts associated with a particular paradigm are challenged empirically or theoretically, holders of this paradigm may be forced through some modification to accommodate the new finding or insight or give way to a new paradigm.

Thus, the Ptolomeic idea of Earth as center of the universe—an understanding also closely tied to and reinforcing certain underlying religious beliefs—was toppled by the Copernican revolution in human understanding of the heavens, a paradigm shift developed further from the empirical observations of Galileo. A highly complex, Earth-central, Ptolomeic astronomy (still used in celestial navigation) was replaced by a vision that portrayed Earth as merely one among a number of planets revolving around the Sun— the solar system. Similarly, it was Einstein's theory of relativity that challenged the Newtonian understanding of gravity and the laws of motion, effectively reducing Newtonian mechanics to Earth-based, observable laws not as directly applicable either to the macrouniversal domain of astrophysics or to the microdomain concerning motion of subatomic particles in quantum mechanics. Of course, even these new paradigms are subject to challenge in an eternally skeptical, scientific approach to knowledge.

There is substantial debate within the social sciences generally, and in particular fields such as international relations, as to whether these fields are developed sufficiently to justify identification of paradigms. Setting this issue aside, the important point in Kuhn's thesis is that knowledge, even in the natural sciences, is grounded in human understanding in the form of paradigms that influence observation and the construction of concepts and theories. At least as much or even more so, such interpretive understanding or agreed meaning would seem to apply to the social sciences that deal with human behavior in all its forms.

Hermeneutics is a linguistic study of the meanings human beings hold that contribute to, and flow from, the languages they construct and use. Emphasis in hermeneutics is on how we interpret or draw meaning. In Wittgenstein's later work, he became critical of earlier claims in his highly formal *Tractatus,* which is mentioned in the discussion above for its influence on the Vienna circle. Indeed, Wittgenstein's *Philosophical Investigations* (1953) paint a picture more prone to coping with ambiguities that come from the context of language use.[28]

Both Weber (for his concept of **Verstehen,** or *interpretive understanding*) and the later Wittgenstein are among those figures whose ideas have influenced formation of epistemological challenges to modernist, scientific thought. These challenges have come from more recent **critical** and **postmodernist** theorists—Jürgen Habermas and his associates in what is commonly referred to as the Frankfurt school of critical theory and, separately, postmodernist French scholars Michel Foucault, Jacques Derrida, and others. In the extreme, a few postmodernists deny the possibility of any empirically based truth claims, thus underscoring their total rejection of positivism.

Some critical theorists argue that beliefs held by theorists necessarily bias their truth claims and may well be part of global ideological schemes to legitimate particular world orders. In supporting an alleged agenda of domination, it may be convenient to advance ideologies often masquerading as scientifically based theories. One of the tasks of critical theorists is to unmask such deceptions, probe for deeper understandings or meanings, and expose the class or other interests these ideologies or alleged theories are designed to serve. Power is a core concept for critical theorists.

The present-day Frankfurt school is in some respects an outgrowth of the critical work of an earlier generation within this "school" of thought that included Theodor Adorno, Max Horkheimer, and Herbert Marcuse. Indeed, the development of critical theory has included rather diverse philosophical influences: escaping from ideological constraints, as in the revolutionary spirit of Rousseau; searching for universal moral principles with the universality of application found in Kant; identifying the oppression of class or other socioeconomic structures observed by Marx; understanding the role of human psychologies in relationships of dominance, drawn from the work of Freud; and rejecting determinism in favor of a more Gramsci-style Marxism that adopts a normative, but practical, approach to challenging and overthrowing structures of domination.

One example of criticism applied to a positivist understanding of international relations is Richard Ashley's comment on Waltz's structural explanation summarized in the previous section. Although we are not classifying Ashley as a critical theorist, the influence of critical theory in the following passage is apparent. Referring to Waltz and the "poverty of neorealism," Ashley asserts:

> What emerges is a positivist structuralism that treats the given order as the natural order, limits rather than expands political discourse, negates or trivializes the significance of variety across time and place, subordinates all practice to an interest in control, bows to the ideal of a social power beyond responsibility, and thereby deprives political interaction of those

practical capacities which make social learning and creative change possible. What emerges is an ideology that anticipates, legitimizes, and orients a totalitarian project of global proportions: the rationalization of global politics.[29]

Critical theory may be viewed separately from postmodernism since most critical theorists retain strict methodological criteria to guide their work. Nevertheless, some critical theory does overlap with, or can be understood more broadly, as part of a postmodernist understanding. In this regard, postmodernist ontology[30] is prone to find the **subtexts** and to **deconstruct**—unpack and take apart—the meanings embedded in what we say or write and even in the ways we act. Human beings are essentially subjective creatures; to postmodernists, claims made to empirically based, objective truth are necessarily hollow. Our understandings and meanings are, after all, humanly constructed. In the extreme, no knowledge or truth is possible apart from the motivations and purposes people put into their construction. From this perspective, truth is entirely relative.

These are, to say the least, significant challenges to "modernist" science more generally and to international relations theory in particular. It is difficult, however, so quickly to deny or dismiss scientific methodologies that have produced so much accumulated knowledge in so many diverse fields of human inquiry. Defenders of positivism see critical and postmodernist thinkers as misrepresenting science which, after all, retains an inherently skeptical orientation to truth claims and demands continued and unending empirical tests of such propositions. Just as it has historically accommodated empirical, theoretical, and philosophical critiques by modifying its methods and understandings, science remains open to critical, postmodernist, and other challenges.

What critical and postmodernist perspectives do contribute to theorizing in international relations is an ever-increased epistemological sensitivity to, and caution concerning, the fragility of what we think to be true. Normative theory may well influence the interpretive understanding that leads us to formulate the concepts we adopt.[31]

Interpretive understanding thus has its place in international relations theorizing—an enterprise captured by realist, pluralist, and globalist images specified in this volume and in the ongoing search for new syntheses in human understandings of the political world that will take us beyond these categories.

Feminism and International Relations Theory

Although some feminists are critical theorists or postmodernists, others remain positivists. Accordingly, we place feminism as another, separate critique of conventional international relations theory that offers an alternative perspective and starting point for both theory and practice.

Feminist understandings have had and likely will continue to have substantial impact on a global scale concerning human rights to equal treatment and the empowerment of women, allowing them the same opportunities that traditionally and historically have been reserved in most cultures to men. Some feminists note that empowering women will also give them the means to limit family size voluntarily, thus reducing population growth rates to economically sustainable levels. Women are also seen by many feminists as more prone to constructive, peaceful approaches to the many conflictual issues on the global agenda. They are underrepresented in these efforts.

At the risk of pushing gender stereotypes too far, we can summarize a feminist perspective in international relations[32] theory as being more prone to see human beings coming together constructively and collaboratively in various organizational forms. Human relationships matter. Rather than adopt a cold, abstract analysis of the inter-action of states and nonstate actors as, for example, **structural-** or **neorealists** often do, the feminist perspective underscores the **constructivist** potential of people. Multi-lateral rather than unilateral or hegemonic models enhance this human potential for building peaceful relationships and positive, interdependent linkages across national borders. Pluralist **liberal institutionalism** and regime construction are consistent with this perspective.

It is not as if men are incapable of such thoughts or that women cannot be hard-headed realists or any more or less aggressive than men. Indeed, it may be that many women have adopted what some feminist theorists have labeled "masculine" under-standings, perhaps in order to be taken seriously in a male-dominated world that extends to academic communities.

Advocates of the feminist perspective in international relations theory, however, identify a feminist perspective not tied by gender to particular individuals, but rather generally associated with women across cultures due to both genetic and environmen-tal factors. Although not all would agree, a few point to traditional family and com-munity-building roles that women have historically played as informing the feminist perspective. Having said that, however, feminist perspectives are not in any way restricted to women. Indeed, many men engaged in theorizing are quite capable of (and often have adopted) what are labeled feminist perspectives.

SUMMATION

For the realist, states are the principal or most important actors on the international political stage and represent the key unit of analysis. States are viewed as unitary actors that behave in a generally rational manner. National security issues dominate the hier-archy of the international agenda. For the pluralist, by contrast, nonstate actors are also important entities. The state is disaggregated into its component parts and is continu-ally subjected to outside elements, including state as well as nonstate actors. The hier-archy of world issues is also subject to change and is not always dominated by matters of military security. For the globalist, all actors must be viewed within the context of an overarching global structure. The defining characteristic of this structure is its capital-ist nature; it must be viewed in a historical context with a particular emphasis on the role of dominant classes that transcend the particular confines of any one state. To understand the mechanisms of dependency whereby rich, industrialized states main-tain poor LDCs in a subordinate position within this world capitalist system requires an appreciation of the paramount role played by economic factors.

We now turn to a more comprehensive discussion of the three images of inter-national relations, giving in subsequent chapters summaries of major actors and assumptions, intellectual precursors and influences, key concepts and representative theoretical works, and criticisms.

NOTES

1. Max Weber, *Methodology of the Social Sciences,* trans. and ed. E. A. Shils and H. A. Finch (New York: Free Press, 1949), pp. 81, 84.

2. Such categorizations are popular, in part reflecting a desire to bring some degree of order to the theoretical chaos of the field. See, for example, James N. Rosenau, "Order and Disorder in the Study of World Politics," in *Globalism Versus Realism: International Relations' Third Debate,* ed. Ray Maghroori and Bennett Ramberg (Boulder, CO: Westview Press, 1982), pp. 1–7.

3. For one argument on the importance of developing "generic knowledge" about international relations, see Alexander L. George, "Is Research on Crisis Management Needed?" in *Avoiding War: Problems of Crisis Management,* ed. Alexander L. George (Boulder, CO: Westview Press, 1991), p. 5. Cf. Kenneth N. Waltz, "Realist Thought and Neorealist Theory," *Journal of International Affairs,* 44, 1 (Spring/Summer 1990): 21–37.

4. Quincy Wright, *A Study of War* (Chicago: University of Chicago Press, 1942); Lewis F. Richardson, *Statistics of Deadly Quarrels* (Chicago: Quadrangle Books, 1960); Kenneth N. Waltz, *Man, the State and War* (New York: Columbia University Press, 1959). See also Bruce Bueno de Mesquita, *The War Trap* (New Haven, CT: Yale University Press, 1981); John A. Vasquez, *The War Puzzle* (Cambridge, England: Cambridge University Press, 1993); J. David Singer and P. F. Diehl, *Measuring the Correlates of War* (Ann Arbor: University of Michigan Press, 1993); Michael W. Doyle, *Ways of War and Peace* (New York: W. W. Norton, 1997).

5. Waltz, *Man, the State and War,* pp. 232–38. Consistent with this view, anarchy is also a *necessary* condition for war to occur, but it is by no means *sufficient* as a sole cause of the phenomenon. The distinction between underlying and immediate causes of war can be traced back to Thucydides, a 5th century B.C. Greek historian.

6. For a discussion on how to approach the study of international conflict, see the articles by Bruce Bueno de Mesquita, Stephen Krasner, and Robert Jervis in *International Studies Quarterly* 29, no. 2 (June 1985): 121–54. Bueno de Mesquita in particular calls for the development of rigorous, deductive, axiomatic theory.

7. For arguments challenging the supposed ability to determine in an objective manner what constitutes "facts," let alone "the real world," see Richard J. Bernstein, *The Restructuring of Social and Political Theory* (New York: Harcourt Brace Jovanovich, 1976).

8. Henry A. Kissinger, "A New National Partnership," *Department of State Bulletin,* 72 (17 February 1975): 199, cited in Robert O. Keohane and Joseph S. Nye, *Power and Interdependence: World Politics in Transition* (Boston: Little, Brown, 1977), p. 3.

9. On ideal types, see Weber, *Methodology,* pp. 90–93. Cf. Max Weber, *Basic Concepts in Sociology,* trans. H. P. Secher (Westport, CT: Greenwood Press, 1962, 1969), pp. 52–55.

10. Whether different images of the world lead to the formulation of different questions or whether the questions themselves have resulted in these different mental constructs for dealing with them is arguable and may depend on the particular theorist.

11. It is one thing to produce a work that is purposely eclectic, drawing on insights from a wide variety of sources, but this is different from attempting to reconcile underlying assumptions reflecting fundamentally divergent perspectives on world politics without relaxing one or more of these critical assumptions. For attempts at reconciliation, see Joseph S. Nye, Jr., "Neorealism and Neoliberalism, *World Politics* 40, 2 (January 1988): 235–51; Richard K. Ashley, *The Political Economy of War and Peace* (London: Frances Pinter, 1980); Nazli Choucri and Robert C. North, *Nations in Conflict: National Growth and International Violence* (San Francisco: W. H. Freeman, 1975); Richard W. Mansbach and John A. Vasquez, *In Search of Theory: A New Paradigm for Global Politics* (New York: Columbia University Press, 1981). See also John Gerard Ruggie, "Continuity and Transformation in the World Polity: Toward a Neorealist Synthesis," *World Politics*

35, no. 2 (January 1983): 261–85; and Alan C. Lamborn, "Theory and the Politics in World Politics," *International Studies Quarterly* 41, no. 2 (June 1997): 187–214. He argues that many of the competing research programs share a core set of metatheoretical assumptions.

12. See the articles in Klaus Knorr and James N. Rosenau, eds., *Contending Approaches to International Politics* (Princeton, NJ: Princeton University Press, 1969). See also G. David Garson, "Marxism as Methodology," in his *Handbook of Political Science Methods,* 2d ed. (Boston: Holbrook Press, 1976), pp. 9–20.

13. The dominant image among most world modelers, however, is a pluralist one informed by what Ashley calls "liberal positivist commitments." See Richard K. Ashley, "The Eye of Power: The Politics of World Modeling," *International Organization* 37, no. 3 (Summer 1983): 500.

14. See, for example, Bruno S. Frey, "The Public Choice View of International Political Economy," *International Organization* 38, no. 1 (Winter 1984): 199–223; Mancur Olson, *The Rise and Decline of Nations* (New Haven, CT: Yale University Press, 1982) and *The Logic of Collective Action* (Cambridge, MA: Harvard University Press, 1965). See also "Symposium: Mancur Olson on the Rise and Decline of Nations," *International Studies Quarterly* 27, no. 1 (March 1983): 3–37; and John A. C. Conybeare, "Public Goods, Prisoners' Dilemmas, and the International Political-Economy," *International Studies Quarterly* 28, no. 1 (March 1984): 5–22.

15. Nor are the images equivalent to the research program discussed by Imre Lakatos. Such a research program, if formulated for international relations, would be more specific than the images discussed in this book but more general than any particular theory we mention. See Imre Lakatos, "Falsification and the Methodology of Scientific Research Programmes," in *Criticism and the Growth of Knowledge,* ed. Imre Lakatos and Alan Musgrave (Cambridge: Cambridge University Press, 1970). Lakatos is attempting to refute what he sees as the relativism of Thomas Kuhn's influential *The Structure of Scientific Revolutions* (Chicago: University of Chicago Press, 1962).

16. Kenneth N. Waltz, *Man, the State and War* (New York: Columbia University Press, 1959).

17. J. David Singer, "The Level-of-Analysis Problem in International Relations," in *International Politics and Foreign Policy,* ed. James N. Rosenau (New York: Free Press, 1969), pp. 20–29.

18. The literature on arms races is extensive. For reviews, see Urs Luterbacher, "Arms Race Models: Where Do We Stand? *European Journal of Political Research* 3, no. 2 (June 1975): 199–217, and Kendall D. Moll and Gregory M. Luebbert, "Arms Races and Military Expenditure Models: A Review," *Journal of Conflict Resolution* 24, no. 1 (March 1980): 153–85. A preliminary test of an external model of arms races is Thomas R. Cusack and Michael D. Ward, "Military Spending in the United States, Soviet Union, and the People's Republic of China," *Journal of Conflict Resolution* 25, no. 3 (September 1981): 429–69. See also Matthew Evangelista, *Innovation and the Arms Race* (Ithaca, N.Y.: Cornell University Press, 1988).

19. See, however, the series of books by Rudolph J. Rummel under the title *Understanding Conflict and War.* The first of the series is subtitled *The Dynamic Psychological Field* (Beverly Hills, CA: Sage Publications, 1975).

20. David Dessler, "What's at Stake in the Agent–Structure Debate?" *International Organization* 43, no. 3 (Summer 1989): 443. See also Alexander E. Wendt, "The Agent–Structure Problem in International Relations Theory," *International Organization* 41, no. 3 (Summer 1987): 335–70; John S. Dryzek, Margaret L. Clark, and Garry McKenzie, "Subject and System in International Interaction," *International Organization* 43, no. 3 (Summer 1989): 475–504.

21. We have simplified Mill's canons of induction as follows: The cause or independent variable (X) that explains the dependent variable (Y) can be inferred by the: (1) *method of agreement*—X is always present whenever Y is also present; (2) *method of difference*—X is always absent whenever Y is also absent; (3) *joint method of agreement and difference*—when X and Y are both present in one set but not in another, as in controlled experiments when X is put in one experiment to see if Y appears, but X is omitted from the other experiment in the expectation that Y will not appear; (4) *method of concomitant variation*—when X and Y both vary in relation to one another either in the same or opposite directions (e.g., a positive or direct relation—as X increases (or decreases), Y also increases (or decreases))—or a negative or inverse relation—as X increases, Y decreases, or as X decreases, Y increases; (5) *method of residues*—as when, in a statistical analysis of the percentage of explained and unexplained variance, a certain independent variable (X) or certain

independent variables (X_1, X_2, etc.) have been identified as accounting for some of the variations in Y, the remaining variation can be accounted for as due to other independent variables present even if they have not been identified as such. See the discussion and specification of these canons in A. James Gregor, *An Introduction to Metapolitics: A Brief Inquiry into the Conceptual Language of Political Science* (New York: Free Press, 1971), pp. 146–50.

22. Carl G. Hempel, *Philosophy of Natural Science* (Englewood Cliffs, N.J.: Prentice Hall, 1966), p. 51.
23. See Karl Popper, *The Logic of Scientific Discovery* (New York: Basic Books, 1959). Metaphysical, nonfalsifiable statements such as religious beliefs about an afterlife or predictions about the end of the world may well be true, but they are in any event beyond the domain of a science that is limited by human or machine-assisted observations. If they are true, the truth of these claims will only be known when they occur. If they are false, we will never know because their occurrence can always be anticipated as coming, but not yet experienced. That is why to followers of Popper, such statements, whatever their truth may be, are inherently metaphysical, not scientific.
24. Kenneth N. Waltz, *Theory of International Politics* (Reading, MA: Addison-Wesley, 1979), p. 6.
25. *Ibid.*, p. 13.
26. In his text, Waltz also refers directly to Popper's influence on his thinking. *Ibid.*, p. 123.
27. See Thomas S. Kuhn, *The Structure of Scientific Revolutions*, 2nd ed. (Chicago: University of Chicago Press, 1962, 1970).
28. For an excellent treatment of the impact of Wittgenstein on social and political thought, see Hanna Fenichel Pitkin, *Wittgenstein and Justice* (Berkeley: University of California Press, 1972).
29. See Richard K. Ashley, "The Poverty of Neorealism," in *Neorealism and Its Critics*, ed. Robert O. Keohane (New York: Columbia University Press, 1986), p. 258.
30. For one of the most balanced, easily read, and focused treatments of postmodernism, see Pauline Marie Rosenau, *Post-Modernism and the Social Sciences: Insights, Inroads, and Intrusions* (Princeton, NJ: Princeton University Press, 1992). Another useful source concerning critical and postmodernist critiques of international relations theory is Jim George, *Discourses of Global Politics: A Critical (Re)Introduction to International Relations* (Boulder, CO: Lynne Rienner, 1994). For a critique of post-modernism, see Aram Hessami, *Postmodern Thinking & Democracy*, doctoral dissertation, the George Washington University, 1994.
31. For a very helpful treatment of normative theory and its relation to empirical theory and concepts, see Mervyn Frost, *Ethics in International Relations: A Constitutive Theory* (Cambridge, England: Cambridge University Press, 1996).
32. A list of sources drawn from a very extensive feminist literature is included among the Selections for Reading and Reference sections at the end of this chapter. For overviews, see Christine Sylvester, *Feminist Theory and International Relations in a Postmodern Era* (Cambridge, England: Cambridge University Press, 1994); J. Ann Tickner, *Gender in International Relations: Feminist Perspectives on Achieving Global Security* (New York: Columbia University Press, 1992); and Peter R. Beckman and Francine D'Amico, eds., *Women, Gender, and World Politics* (Westport, CT: Bergin and Garvey, 1994). Cf. Craig N. Murphy, "Seeing Women, Recognizing Gender, Recasting International Relations," *International Organization* 50, No. 3 (Summer 1996): 513–18 and Robert O. Keohane, "International Relations Theory: Contributions of a Feminist Standpoint," *Millennium* 18, No. 2 (1989): 245–53. See also Francis A. Beer and Robert Hariman eds., *Post-Realism: The Rhetorical Turn in International Relations* (East Lansing, MI: Michigan State University Press, 1996).

SELECTIONS FOR FURTHER READING AND REFERENCE

General

Caporaso, James A. "Across the Great Divide: Integrating Comparative and International Politics." *International Studies Quarterly* 41, 4 (December 1997): 536–91.

Ferguson, Yale H., and Richard W. Mansbach. "Between Celebration and Despair: Constructive Suggestions for Future International Theory." *International Studies Quarterly* 35, 4 (December 1991): 363–496.

————. *The Elusive Quest: Theory and International Politics.* Columbia: University of South Carolina Press, 1988.

Groom, A. J. R., and Margot Light, eds. *Contemporary International Relations: A Guide to Theory.* London: Pinter Publishers, 1994.

Hoffmann, Stanley. *Janus and Minerva: Essays in the Theory and Practice of International Politics.* Boulder, CO: Westview Press, 1987.

Hollis, Martin, and Steve Smith. *Explaining and Understanding International Relations.* Oxford, England: Clarendon Press, 1990.

Lamborn, Alan C. "Theory and the Politics in World Politics." *International Studies Quarterly* 41, 2 (June 1997): 187–214.

Neuman, Stephanie G., ed. *International Relations Theory and the Third World.* New York: St. Martin's Press, 1998.

Olson, William C., and A. J. R. Groom. *International Relations Then and Now: Origins and Trends in Interpretation.* London: Harper Collins, 1991.

Rothstein, Robert L. *The Evolution of Theory in International Relations.* Columbia: University of South Carolina Press, 1991.

Smith, Steve, Ken Booth, and Marysia Zalewski, eds. *International Theory: Positivism and Beyond.* Cambridge, England: Cambridge University Press, 1996.

Thompson, Kenneth W. *Schools of Thought in International Relations.* Baton Rouge: Louisiana State University Press, 1996.

On History, Intellectual History, and International Relations

Carr, E. H. *What Is History?* Harmondsworth, England: Penguin Books, 1964.

Howard, Michael. *The Lessons of History.* New Haven: Yale University Press, 1991.

Kauppi, Mark V., and Paul R. Viotti. *The Global Philosophers: World Politics in Western Thought.* New York/San Francisco: Lexington/Jossey Bass, 1992.

"Symposium: History and Theory." *International Security* 22, 1 (Summer 1997): 5–85.

Other Overviews of the Field

Art, Robert J., and Robert Jervis. *International Politics: Enduring Concepts and Contemporary Issues.* New York: Harper Collins, 1992.

Booth, Ken, and Steve Smith, eds. *International Relations Theory Today.* University Park: Pennsylvania State University Press, 1995.

Crane, George T., and Abla Amawi. *The Theoretical Evolution of International Political Economy: A Reader.* New York: Oxford University Press, 1991, 1997.

Dougherty, James E., and Robert L. Pfaltzgraff, Jr. *Contending Theories of International Relations,* 4th ed. New York: Longman, 1997.

Doyle, Michael W., and G. John Ikenberry. *New Thinking in International Relations Theory.* Boulder, CO: Westview, 1997.

Kegley, Charles W., ed. *Controversies in International Relations Theory: Realism and the Neoliberal Challenge.* New York: St. Martin's, 1995.

Morgan, Patrick M. *Theories and Approaches to International Politics.* New Brunswick, NJ: Transaction Books, 1986.

Neumann, Iver B., and Ole Weaver, eds. *The Future of International Relations.* London: Routledge, 1997.

Positivism, Social Science, and International Relations

Brodbeck, May. *Readings in the Philosophy of the Social Sciences.* New York: Macmillan, 1968.

Bronowski, Jacob. *The Origins of Knowledge and Imagination.* New Haven: Yale University Press, 1978.

Bueno de Mesquita, Bruce, Stephen D. Krasner, and Robert Jervis. "Symposium: Methodological Foundations of the Study of International Conflict." *International Studies Quarterly* 29, 2 (June 1985): 121–49.

Coleman, James S. *Foundations of Social Theory.* Cambridge, MA: Harvard University Press, 1990.

Green, Donald P. and Ian Shapiro. *Pathologies of Rational Choice Theory.* New Haven, Conn.: Yale University Press, 1994.

Gregor, A. James. *An Introduction to Metapolitics: A Brief Inquiry into the Conceptual Language of Political Science*. New York: Free Press, 1971.

Holsti, K. J. "Mirror, Mirror on the Wall, Which Are the Fairest Theories of All?" *International Studies Quarterly* 33, 3 (September 1989): 255–61.

Kaplan, Abraham. *The Conduct of Inquiry*. New York: Harper & Row, 1964.

King, Gary, Robert O. Keohane, and Sidney Verba. *Designing Social Inquiry: Scientific Inference in Qualitative Research*. Princeton, NJ: Princeton University Press, 1994.

Knorr, Klaus, and James N. Rosenau, eds. *Contending Approaches to International Politics*. Princeton, NJ: Princeton University Press, 1969.

Kuhn, Thomas S. *The Structure of Scientific Revolutions*. Chicago: University of Chicago Press, 1962.

Lakatos, Imre. *The Methodology of Scientific Research Programmes*. Cambridge, England: Cambridge University Press, 1978.

Lakatos, Imre, and A. Musgrave, eds. *Criticism and the Growth of Knowledge*. Cambridge, England: Cambridge University Press, 1970.

Miller, Richard W. *Fact and Method*. Princeton, NJ: Princeton University Press, 1987.

Nagel, Ernest. *The Structure of Scientific Explanation*. New York: Harcourt Brace Jovanovich, 1961.

Olson, Mancur. *The Logic of Collective Action*. Cambridge, MA: Harvard University Press, 1965.

———. *The Rise and Decline of Nations*. New Haven, CT: Yale University Press, 1982.

Popper, Karl R. *The Logic of Scientific Discovery*. London: Hutchinson, 1959.

Rapoport, Anatol. "Various Meanings of Theory." *American Political Science Review* 52, 4 (December 1958): 972–88.

Rosenau, James N., and Mary Durfee. *Thinking Theory Thoroughly: Coherent Approaches to an Incoherent World*. Boulder, CO: Westview Press, 1995.

Simon, Herbert A. *Models of Thought*. New Haven, CT: Yale University Press, 1979.

Singer, J. David. *Models, Methods, and Progress in World Politics*. Boulder, CO: Westview, 1990.

Stinchcombe, Arthur. *Constructing Social Theories*. New York: Harcourt Brace Jovanovich, 1968.

Toulmin, Stephen. *Foresight and Understanding: An Inquiry into the Aims of Science*. New York: Harper & Row, 1963.

Van Evera, Stephen. *Guide to Methods for Students of Political Science*. Ithaca, NY: Cornell University Press, 1998.

Waltz, Kenneth N. "Evaluating Theories." *American Political Science Review* 91, 4 (December 1997): 913–17.

———. "Reflections on *Theory of International Politics:* Response to My Critics." In *Neorealism and Its Critics,* ed. Robert O. Keohane. New York: Columbia University Press, 1986.

———. *Theory of International Politics*. New York: McGraw Hill/Addison Wesley, 1979. [especially chs. 1–4]

———. "Theory of International Relations." In *Handbook of Political Science*, Vol. 8, ed. Nelson W. Polsby and Fred I. Greenstein. Reading, MA: Addison-Wesley, 1975.

Weber, Max. *The Methodology of the Social Sciences*. New York: Free Press, 1949.

Interpretive Understanding, Critical Theory, and Postmodernism

Alker, Hayward R., ed. *Rediscoveries and Reformations: Humanistic Methodologies for International Studies*. New York: Cambridge University Press, 1996.

Ashley, Richard K. "The Geopolitics of Geopolitical Space: Toward a Critical Social Theory of International Politics." *Alternatives* 12, 4 (October 1987): 403–34.

Ashley, Richard K. and R. B. J. Walker, eds. *Speaking the Language of Exile—Dissidence in International Studies*. Special Issue of *International Studies Quarterly* 34, 3 (September 1990): 259–417.

Beer, Francis A., and Robert Hariman. *Post-Realism: The Rhetorical Turn in International Relations*. East Lansing: Michigan State University Press, 1996.

Berger, Peter L., and Thomas Luckmann. *The Social Construction of Reality: A Treatise in the Sociology of Knowledge*. New York: Doubleday, 1966.

Bronner, Stephan Eric, and Douglas MacKay Kellner, eds. *Critical Theory and Society: A Reader*. New York: Routledge, 1989.

Der Derian, James, ed. *International Theory: Critical Investigations.* New York: New York University Press, 1995.

Der Derian, James, and Michael J. Shapiro, eds. *International/Intertextual Relations: Postmodern Readings of World Politics.* Lexington, MA: Lexington Books, 1989.

Frost, Mervyn. *Ethics in International Relations: A Constitutive Theory.* Cambridge: Cambridge University Press, 1996. [especially chs. 1 and 2 on relation of normative theory to positivism, interpretive understanding, postmodernism, critical theory, etc.]

Goertz, Gary. *Contexts of International Politics.* Cambridge, England: Cambridge University Press, 1994.

Habermas, Jürgen. *The Past as Future.* Lincoln: University of Nebraska Press, 1994.

Hollinger, Robert. *Post-Modernism and the Social Sciences.* Thousand Oaks, CA: SAGE Publications, 1994.

Keat, Russell. *The Politics of Social Theory: Habermas, Freud and the Critique of Positivism.* Chicago: University of Chicago Press, 1981.

Klein, Bradley. *Strategic Studies and World Order.* Cambridge, England: Cambridge University Press, 1994.

Lapid, Yosef. "The Third Debate: On the Prospects of International Theory in a Post-Positivist Era." *International Studies Quarterly* 33, 3 (September 1989): 235–54.

Lapid, Yosef, and Friedrich Kratochwil. *The Return of Culture and Identity in IR Theory.* Boulder, CO: Lynne Rienner, 1996.

Linklater, Andrew. *Beyond Realism and Marxism: Critical Theory and International Relations.* New York: St. Martin's, 1990.

Morrow, Raymond A. *Critical Theory and Methodology.* Thousand Oaks, CA: Sage Publications, 1994.

Neufeld, Mark. *The Restructuring of International Relations Theory.* Cambridge, England: Cambridge University Press, 1995.

Onuf, Nicholas G. *World of Our Making: Rules and Rule in Social Theory and International Relations.* Columbia: University of South Carolina Press, 1989.

Rosenau, James N., ed. *Global Voices: Dialogues in International Relations.* Boulder, CO: Westview Press, 1993.

Smith, Steve, Ken Booth, and Marysia Zalewski, eds. *International Theory: Positivism and Beyond.* Cambridge, England: Cambridge University Press, 1996.

Feminism

Beckman, Peter R., and Francine D'Amico, eds. *Women, Gender, and World Politics: Perspectives, Policies, and Politics.* Westport, CT: Bergin and Garvey, 1994.

Charlesworth, Hilary, Christine Chinkin, and Shelley Wright. "Feminist Approaches to International Law." *American Journal of International Law* 85 (1991): 613–45. [Reprinted in Beck, Robert J., Anthony Clark Arend, and Robert D. Vander Lugt.] *International Rules.* New York: Oxford University Press, 1996.

Charlton, Sue Ellen. *Women in Third World Development.* Boulder, CO: Westview Press, 1984.

Charlton, Sue Ellen, Jana Everett, and Kathleen Staudt, eds. *Women, the State, and Development.* Albany, NY: SUNY Press, 1989.

Enloe, Cynthia. *Bananas, Beaches, and Bases: Making Feminist Sense of International Relations.* Berkeley: University of California Press, 1990.

———. *The Morning After: Sexual Politics at the End of the Cold War.* Berkeley: University of California Press, 1993.

Grant, Rebecca, and Kathleen Newland, eds. *Gender and International Relations.* Bloomington: Indiana University Press, 1991.

Keohane, Robert O. "International Relations Theory: Contributions of a Feminist Standpoint." *Millennium* 18, 2 (1989): 245–53.

Murphy, Craig N. "Seeing Women, Recognizing Gender, Recasting International Relations." *International Organization* 50, 3 (Summer 1996): 513–38.

Peterson, V. Spike, ed. *Gendered States: Feminist (Re)Visions of International Relations Theory.* Boulder, CO: Lynne Rienner, 1992.

Rosenau, James N., ed. *Global Voices: Dialogues in International Relations*. Boulder, CO: Westview Press, 1993.

Sylvester, Christine. *Feminist Theory and International Relations in a Postmodern Era*. Cambridge, England: Cambridge University Press, 1994.

Tessler, Mark, and Ina Warriner. "Gender, Feminism, and Attitudes Toward International Conflict." *World Politics* 49, 2 (January 1997): 250–81.

Tickner, J. Ann. *Gender in International Relations: Feminist Perspectives on Achieving Global Security*. New York: Columbia University Press, 1992.

———. "You Just Don't Understand: Troubled Engagements between Feminists and IR Theorists." *International Studies Quarterly* 41, 4 (December 1997): 611–32. [See also the dialogue in the subsequent issue, Vol. 42, No. 1 (March 1998).]

Warren, Carol A. B. *Gender Issues in Field Research*. Newberry Park, CA: SAGE Publications, 1988.

Whitworth, Sandra. *Feminism and International Relations*. New York: St. Martin's, 1994.

Thinking Theory Thoroughly

JAMES N. ROSENAU

James Rosenau addresses creative theorizing and develops nine principles to guide those who would engage in this enterprise. Indeed, not everyone is prone automatically to think theoretically.

It rarely happens, but now and again in academic life one is jolted into returning to fundamentals, into ascertaining whether one has unknowingly strayed from one's organizing premises. This happened to me recently when a graduate student inquired whether she should take an "independent reading" course under my direction. Noting that my competence was limited, I responded by asking what topics or problems she planned to investigate. Her answer startled me, perhaps partly because it was ungrammatical but mainly because I found it pedagogically challenging. Her answer was simple: "I would like you to teach me to think theory!" I agreed to take on the role of advisor.

At this writing, some eleven weeks, many conversations and much reflection later, I still find the assignment challenging, though now I am beginning to wonder whether the capacity to think theoretically, the inclination to perceive and assess the course of events as suggestive or expressive of larger forces, is a talent that can be taught. It may be, instead, a cast of mind, a personality trait, or a philosophical perspective that some acquire early in life and others do not.

If this is so, there is not much that a professor can do to teach students how to think theoretically. They can be introduced to the nature of theories, taught the various purposes theories can serve, exposed to the controversies over the relative worth of different theories, and instructed on the steps required for the construction of viable theories. And, to solidify the learning of these lessons, they can then be given assignments in which they have to formulate concrete hypotheses and tie them together into an actual theoretical framework. The learning of these skills underlying the design of theories is not, however, the equivalent of learning how to think theoretically. Or, more accurately, it is not the equivalent of what I understood my student as wanting me to teach her. In fact, she may only have been asking instruction on the dos and don'ts of theoretical design. But because of the way she worded her request I interpreted her as seeking more than an introduction to the procedures and techniques essential to creative theorizing. It seemed to me she was looking to acquire not a set of skills, but rather a set of predispositions, a cluster of habits, a way of thinking, a mental lifestyle—or whatever may be the appropriate label for that level of intellectual existence that governs the use of skills and the application of values—that she did not possess and that she thought she valued enough to want to make part of her orientation toward interna-

From James N. Rosenau. *The Scientific Study of Foreign Policy,* rev. ed. London: Frances Pinter, 1980, pages 19–31. Reprinted by permission.

tional phenomena. It is this more fundamental dimension of the life of the mind that I now suspect may not be teachable or learnable, a caveat that needs emphasis at the outset because the ensuing analysis amounts to nothing less than a pronouncement on how to think theoretically.

Nine Pre-Conditions for Creative Theorizing

It follows that the task of disciplining ourselves and our students to think theoretically consists, first, of identifying the cognitive inclinations and perceptual impulses from which creative theory springs and, second, of then forming intellectual habits which assure the prevalence of these inclinations and impulses whenever we turn to theory-building endeavors. The central question examined in this paper follows: what are the mental qualities that best enable one to "think theory" and how can their acquisition be best assured? Nine such qualities strike me as especially conducive to the development of good theorists. Each of the nine seems equally important and there is some overlap among them. Accordingly, the sequence of their elaboration here should not be interpreted as implying a rank ordering.

> To think theoretically one has to avoid treating the task as that of formulating an appropriate definition of theory.

So as to clarify what is involved in thinking theoretically, let me start with the proposition that the task is not one of developing a clear-cut definition of theory. On balance, it is probably preferable to have a precise conception of the nature of theory rather than a vague one, but definitional exactness is not the only criterion of thinking theoretically and it may not even be a necessary requirement for such thought. I can readily imagine a young student thinking theoretically about international phenomena well before his or her first course on the subject turns to the question of what constitutes theory and the various uses to which it can be put. Indeed, I

have had the good fortune of encountering a few students who were, so to speak, born theoreticians. From their very first comments in class as freshmen it was clear that they thought theoretically even though they have never had any methodological training or any exposure to the history of international relations.

Most of us are not so lucky. Most of us have to be trained to think theoretically and then we have to engage in the activity continuously in order to achieve and sustain a genuinely theoretical perspective. Hence, the fact that a few among us can maintain such a perspective without training and practice is a useful reminder that definitional clarity is not a prerequisite to creative theorizing.

The reminder is important because many of us tend to exaggerate the importance of exact definitions. To be clear about the nature of theory is not to guarantee the formulation of meaningful theory. Such clarity can be misleading. It can provide a false sense of security, a misguided confidence that one needs only to organize one's empirical materials in the proper way if one is equipped with a clear-cut definition of theory. It is my impression that much of the writing in our field derives from this premise that good definitions automatically yield good theories, as if the definitions somehow relieve the observer of the need to apply imagination and maintain philosophical discipline.

To be sure, much of the writing also suffers from loose and ambiguous conceptions of theory or from a confusion between theory and method. Such research would, obviously, be more valuable if it proceeded from a tighter and clearer notion of what the theoretical enterprise entails. So, to repeat, I am not arguing against definitional clarity. On the contrary, I believe it is highly appropriate to help students achieve such clarity by introducing them to the vast array of articles and books now available on the dynamics, boundaries, uses, and abuses of theory in the international field. But I am arguing for more than definitional clarity. I am arguing for caution and restraint in the use of definitions: in digesting the literature on theory and building a more elaborate conception of what it involves, one has to be careful not to lean too heavily on definitions and guidance. Also needed is a cast of mind, a mental set that focuses application of the definitions and facilitates creative theorizing.

> To think theoretically one has to be clear as to whether one aspires to empirical theory or value theory.

Progress in the study of international affairs depends on advances in both empirical and value theory. But the two are not the same. They may overlap; they can focus on the same problem; and values always underlie the selection of the problems to which empirical theories are addressed. Yet they differ in one overriding way: empirical theory deals essentially with the "is" of international phenomena, with things as they are if and when they are subjected to observation, while value theory deals essentially with the "ought" of international phenomena, with things as they should be if and when they could be subjected to manipulation. This distinction underlies, in turn, entirely different modes of reasoning, a different rhetoric, and different types of evidence.

The habit of making the necessary analytic, rhetorical, and evidential distinctions between empirical and value theory can be difficult for young students to develop. Indeed, it can be weak and elusive for any of us who have strong value commitments and a deep concern for certain moral questions. The more intensive are our values, the more are we tempted to allow our empirical inquiries to be guided by our beliefs rather than by our concern for observation. For this reason I have found that helping students become habituated to the is–ought distinction is among the most difficult pedagogical tasks. They can understand the distinction intellectually and they can even explain and defend it

when pressed; but practicing it is another matter and often their empirical analyses slip into moral judgments without their being aware of it. It is as if they somehow fear that their values and the policy goals they want to promote will be undermined if they allow themselves to focus on observable phenomena. Such, of course, is not the case. On the contrary, moral values and policy goals can be well served, even best served, by putting them aside and proceeding detachedly long enough to enlarge empirical understanding of the obstacles that hinder realization of the values and progress toward the goals.

This is the one line of reasoning on behalf of thinking theoretically that my most value-committed students find persuasive. If empirical theory is posited as a tool of moral theory, they can approach it instrumentally and see virtue in habituating themselves to distinguishing between the two. It takes a while, however, before the perceived virtues of habituation are translated into actual habits and, in fact, some never manage to make the transition, hard as they may try. Impatient with the need for change, convinced that time is too scarce to afford the slow pace of empirical inquiry, many simply give up and dismiss the is–ought distinction as one of those picayune obsessions to which some academics fall prey.

It is my impression that impatience with empirical theorizing is likely to be especially intense among Third World students of international relations. The newly developed consciousness of the long-standing injustices built into First World–Third World relationships, the lure of dependency theory, and perhaps a frustration over the central tendencies of social science in the First World have made Third World theorists particularly resistant to detached empirical theorizing. Their resistance gives a First World scholar pause: is his insistence on habituating oneself to the is–ought distinction yet another instance of false superiority, of projecting onto the developing world practices that have worked in industrial societies? It could be.

Of late I have become keenly aware of the biases that may underlie my intellectual endeavors and thus I am not prepared merely to brush aside the idea that the is–ought distinction may be inappropriate to theorizing in much of the world. In this particular instance, however, I cannot even begin to break the habit. The relevance of the distinction strikes me as global, as independent of any national biases, as necessary to thinking theoretically wherever and whenever enlarged comprehension is sought. Empirical theory is not superior to moral theory; it is simply preferable for certain purposes, and one of these is the end of deepening our grasp of why international processes unfold as they do.

Aware that my own expertise, such as it may be, lies in the realm of empirical theory, the ensuing discussion makes no pretense of being relevant to thinking theoretically in the moral context. All the precepts that follow are concerned only with those mental qualities that may render us more thoroughgoing in our empirical theorizing.

> To think theoretically one must be able to assume that human affairs are founded on an underlying order.

A prime task of empirical theory is to explain why international phenomena are structured as they are and/or behave as they do. To perform this task one must assume that each and every international phenomenon is theoretically explicable, that deeper understanding of its dynamics could be achieved if appropriate instruments for measuring it were available. To assume that everything is potentially explicable is to presume that nothing happens by chance, capriciously, at random, that for every effect there must be a cause. That is, there must be an underlying order out of which international relations springs. If this were not the case, if events could occur for no reason, there would be little point in theorizing. If some events are inherently inexplicable, efforts to build creative

theory are bound to fall short to the extent that they embrace phenomena that may occur at random. Indeed, in the absence of the assumption of an underlying order, attempts to fashion theory are futile, pointless exercises, a waste of time that could be better spent writing poetry, playing tennis, or tending the garden.

This is *not* to say that thought only acquires the status of theory when it purports to account for every event. As indicated below, theory is also founded on the laws of probability. Hence it only purports to account for central tendencies, but this claim is unwarranted if an assumption of underlying order is not made. That is, to think theoretically one must presume that there is a cause for every effect even though one does not seek to explain every effect.

I have found that most students have a difficult time becoming habituated to the assumption of an underlying order. They see it as a denial of their own freedom. To presume there is a cause for everything, they reason, is to deprive people of free will, perhaps even to relieve them of responsibility for their actions. The assumption of an underlying order does not, of course, have such implications. One's freedom of choice is not lessened by the fact that the choices made are not random and, instead, derive from some source. Yet, fearful about compromising their own integrity, many students cannot accept this subtlety and insist on the premise that people have the capacity to cut themselves off from all prior experience and to act as they please for no reason whatsoever. To support their resistance to the assumption of an underlying order, they will often cite instances of international history when the unexpected occurred or when a highly deviant, impetuous, and irrational action was undertaken, as if somehow irrationality and impetuosity are capricious and do not stem from any sources.

Besides patiently reassuring dubious students that there are no insidious threats in the assumption of an underlying order, resistance to the idea can be lessened, even broken in some instances, by pointing out how the assumption offers hope for greater understanding and deeper comprehension. To presume that there is a cause of every effect is to assume that everything is potentially knowable, that inquiry can pay off, that one is not necessarily destined to go down an intellectual path that dead ends, leads nowhere. The assumption of an underlying order, in other words, is pervaded with hope. We do not make it to allow ourselves to be hopeful, but it has that consequence. It enables us to view ourselves as totally in charge of our own investigations, limited only by our imaginations and the resources at our disposal. It allows us to approach the chaos we perceive in the world around us as a challenge, as an orderliness that has yet to be identified and traced. It permits us to dare to think theory thoroughly because the affairs of people are patterned and the patterns are susceptible to being uncovered.

> To think theoretically one must be predisposed to ask about every event, every situation, or every observed phenomenon, "Of what is it an instance?"

Of all the habits one must develop to think theoretically, perhaps none is more central than the inclination to ask this question at every opportunity. It must be a constant refrain, a melody that haunts every lurch forward in the process of moving from observations to conclusions. For to see every event as an instance of a more encompassing class of phenomena is to sustain the search for patterns and to avoid treating any phenomenon as inherently unique. To think theoretically is to be at home with abstractions, to generalize, to discern the underlying order that links otherwise discrete incidents, and such a mode of thinking cannot be achieved and maintained unless every observed phenomenon is approached as merely one instance of a recurring sequence.

Again students appear to have a hard time building up this habit. They are inclined to probe for the special meaning of an event, to explore it for what sets it apart from all other events, rather than to treat it as an instance of a larger pattern. They want to understand the Iranian revolution, not revolutions as a social process, and to the extent this is their preference, to that extent do they resist building up the impulse to always reach for more general theoretical insights. Indeed, I have had many students who simply do not know where to begin when asked to indicate of what pattern some event they regard as important is an instance. Their faces turn blank and their tongues turn silent. They are paralyzed. They do not know what it means to treat the event as merely an instance of something, as just part of a larger category. And so they stumble, mumble, or otherwise resist thinking in those elementary terms out of which theorizing springs.

My response here is twofold. First, I try to portray the pleasure, the sheer joy, to be had from taking steps up the ladder of abstraction. Fitting pieces into larger wholes offers, I believe, a special sense of satisfaction, a feeling of accomplishment not unlike that which accompanies solving a puzzle or resolving a mystery. Indeed, theory building can readily be viewed as puzzle solving, as uncovering the dynamics embedded deep in the interstices of human relationships, and there are few students who are not intrigued by the challenge of solving puzzles.

If appealing thus to the curiosity of students does not succeed in getting them to ask habitually "Of what is this an instance?" (and often it is not a sufficient incentive), I revert to a second line of reasoning which, in effect, amounts to an attempt to shame them into the habit. This involves pointing out the implications of stumbling and mumbling, of not being able to discern any larger class of phenomena of which the observed phenomenon is an instance. The implications are unmistakable: to be paralyzed by the question "Of what is this an instance?" is not to know what one is interested in, to be lacking questions that generate and guide one's inquiry, to be confused by the phenomena one claims to be worthy of investigation. Based on the presumption of an underlying order, I believe that no phenomenon exists in isolation, unique only unto itself, and thus I believe that we always have an answer to the of-what-is-this-an-instance question, whether we know it or not. Accordingly, the task is not one of figuring out an answer presently unknown to us; it is rather that of explicating an answer that we have already acquired but have yet to surface. I am arguing, in other words, that we do not get interested in an international phenomenon for no reason, that our interest in it stems from a concern about a more encompassing set of phenomena, and that there is therefore no need to be paralyzed by the question if we press ourselves to move up the ladder of abstraction on which our intellectuality is founded. Once shamed into acknowledging that their concerns are not confined to the lowest rung on the ladder, most students are willing to begin to venture forth and approach the phenomena they observe as mere instances of something else.

> To think theoretically one must be ready to appreciate and accept the need to sacrifice detailed descriptions for broad observations.

One cannot begin to mount the rungs of the ladder of abstraction if one is unable to forgo the detailed account, the elaborated event, the specific minutia. As indicated, the theoretical enterprise is committed to the teasing out of central tendencies, to encompassing ever greater numbers of phenomena, to moving up the ladder of abstraction as parsimoniously as possible. Thus theory involves generalizing rather than particularizing and, in so doing, it requires relinquishing, subordinating, and/or not demonstrating much of one's impulse to expound everything one knows. It means, in effect, that one must discipline one's self to accept simple explanations over complex ones.

These are not easy tasks. Most of us find comfort in detail. The more details we know, the more are we likely to feel we have mastered our subject. To forgo much of the detail, on the other hand, is to opt for uncertainties, to expose ourselves to the criticisms of those who would pick away at our generalizations with exceptions. The temptations to fall back on details are thus considerable and much concentration on the upper rungs of the ladder of abstraction is required if the temptations are to be resisted.

Happily this is less of a problem for beginning students than more mature ones who are introduced late to the theoretical enterprise. The former have yet to acquire extensive familiarity with details and they are therefore not likely to feel threatened by the loss of their knowledge base. They want to focus on the unique, to be sure, but at least it is possible to expose them to the case of theorizing before they find security in endless minutiae. Exactly how more mature scholars accustomed to the comforts of detail can be persuaded to be theoretically venturesome is, I confess, a problem for which I have yet to find anything resembling a solution.

> To think theoretically one must be tolerant of ambiguity, concerned about probabilities, and distrustful of absolutes.

To be concerned about central tendencies one needs to be accepting of exceptions, deviations, anomalies, and other phenomena that, taken by themselves, run counter to the anticipated or prevailing pattern. Anomalies ought not be ignored and often explorations of them can lead to valuable, path-breaking insights; but neither can anomalies be allowed to undermine one's focus on central tendencies. Empirical theories deal only with probabilities and not with absolutes, with how most phenomena are likely to respond to a stimulus and not with how each and every phenomenon responds. Theorists simply do not aspire to account for every phenomenon. They know there will be anomalies and exceptions; indeed, they are suspicious on those unlikely occasions when no exceptions are manifest. Rather their goal is to build theories in which the central tendencies encompass the highest possible degree of probability, with certainties and absolutes being left for ideologues and zealots to expound.

Although they engage in it continuously in their daily lives, students tend to be resistant to the necessity of thinking probabilistically when they turn to theorizing. More accurately, they tend to be reluctant to ignore the ambiguity, to be restless with anything less than perfect certainty, as if any exception to the anticipated central tendencies constitutes a negation of their reasoning. I have found this low tolerance of ambiguity difficult to contest. Many students, fearful of uncertainty, seem to get fixated on the exception, and it is very hard at that point to recapture their interest in central tendencies. The very rhetoric of their everyday language— that things are "completely" the case or that an observation is "absolutely" accurate—reinforces their inclinations to be intolerant of deviations. In this mood they recognize only the "whole truth" as valid and regard central tendencies as a partial rather than a legitimate form of knowledge.

I confess to perplexity over how to handle this obstacle to theorizing on the part of students. I have tried elaborating on the many ways in which probabilistic thinking underlies their daily lives. I have tried making analogies between the physicist and the political scientist, pointing out that the former does not aspire to account for the behavior of every atom any more than the latter aspires to accounting for every voter. I have tried sarcasm, stressing the noxious values that derive from a concern with absolutes. Neither alone nor in combination, however, do such techniques seem to have any effect on many students. Whatever its sources, their intolerance of ambiguity is apparently too deep-seated to yield to reasoning or persuasion. So, reluctantly, I have concluded that students with a low tolerance of ambiguity and a high need for certainty are unlikely to ever think theory thoroughly and that it is probably wasted energy to try to teach them to do so.

> To think theoretically one must be playful about international phenomena.

At the core of the theorizing process is a creative imagination. The underlying order of world affairs is too obscure and too complex to yield to pedestrian, constricted, or conventional minds. Only deep penetration into a problem, discerning relationships that are not self-evident and might even be the opposite of what seems readily apparent, can produce incisive and creative theory. Thus to think theoretically one must allow one's mind to run freely, to be playful, to toy around with what might seem absurd, to posit seemingly unrealistic circumstances and speculate what would follow if they were ever to come to pass. Stated differently, one must develop the habit of playing and enjoying the game of "as if"—that is, specifying unlikely conditions and analyzing them as *if* they prevailed.

Put in still another way, it has always seemed to me that good theory ought never be embarrassed by surprises, by unanticipated events that have major consequences for the system on which the theory focuses. A Hitler–Stalin pact, a Nixon resignation, or a Sadat peace initiative should not catch the creative theorist unawares because part of his or her creativity involves imagining the unimaginable. One imagines the unimaginable by allowing one's variables to vary across the entire range of a continuum even if some of its extreme points seem so unlikely as to be absurd. To push one's thinking beyond previously imagined extremes of a continuum is to play the game of "as if," and it involves a playfulness of mind that mitigates against surprises as well as facilitates incisive theorizing.

How one teaches playfulness is, of course, another matter. In some important sense it is an intellectual quality that cannot be taught. One acquires—or perhaps inherits—creativity early in life and no amount of subsequent training can greatly enhance the imaginative powers of those with tunnel vision and inhibited mentalities. On the other hand, encouragement to playfulness can bring out previously untapped talents in some students. Many have become so used to being told what to think that their creative impulses have never been legitimated and, accordingly, they have never even heard of the existence of the "as if" game. So no harm can be done by pressing our students (not to mention ourselves) to be playful and flexible in their thinking, and just conceivably such an emphasis may produce some unexpected results.

To think theoretically one must be genuinely puzzled by international phenomena.

Creative use of the imagination requires humility toward international phenomena. One must be as concerned about asking the right questions about the order underlying world affairs as finding the right answers. To focus only on answers is to be sure about the questions one wants to probe and this, in turn, is to impose unnecessary limits on one's capacity to discern and integrate the deeper structures of global politics. If, on the other hand, one is genuinely puzzled by why events unfold as they do, one is committed to always asking why they occur in one way rather than another and, in so doing, pressing one's theoretical impulses as far as possible.

I do not use the notion of "genuine puzzles" casually. They are not simply open-ended questions but refer, rather, to perplexity over specific and patterned outcomes. To be genuinely puzzled about the declining capacity of governments to govern effectively, for example, one does not ask, "Why do governments do what they do?" Rather, one asks, say, "Why are most governments unable to control inflation?" or "Why do they alter their alliance commitments under specified conditions?" Genuine puzzles, in other words, are not idle, ill-framed, or impetuous speculations. They encompass specified dependent variables for which adequate explanations are lacking. I do not see how one can begin to think theoretically if one does not discern recurrent outcomes that evoke one's curiosity and puzzlement. Some analysts believe they are starting down the road to theory when they start asking what the outcomes are, but such a line of inquiry leads only to deadends, or worse, to endless mazes, because one never knows when one has come upon a relevant outcome. Genuine puzzles can lead us down creative paths, however, because they discipline us to focus on particular patterns.

One cannot teach others to be puzzled. Again it is very much a matter of whether curiosity has been repressed or allowed to flourish at an early age. It is possible, however, to keep after students and colleagues with the simple question, "What genuinely puzzles you about international affairs?" Hopefully repetition of the question will prove to be sufficiently challenging to facilitate a maximum expression of whatever may be the curiosity potential students may possess.

To think theoretically one must be constantly ready to be proven wrong.

Perhaps nothing inhibits the ability to be intellectually puzzled and playful more than the fear of being embarrassed by the inaccuracies of one's theorizing. Many of us have fragile egos that are so sensitive to error as to lead us to prefer sticking close to conventional wisdom rather than risking speculation that may be erroneous. It is as if our stature as students depends upon the soundness of our observations.

Fragile egos are not readily bolstered and some students may never be capable of venturing forth. In my experience, however, there is one line of reasoning that some students find sufficiently persuasive to lessen their fears of appearing ridiculous. It involves the thought that our comprehension of international phenomena can be substantially advanced even if our theories about them prove to be woefully wrong. Such progress can occur in two ways. One is that falsified theory has the virtue of indicating avenues of inquiry which no longer need be traversed. Doubtless egos are best served by theoretical breakthroughs but if one presumes that knowledge is at least partly developed through a process of elimination, there is some satisfaction to be gained from having narrowed the range of inquiry through theory that subsequently proves fallacious.

Secondly, unsound theory can facilitate progress by provoking others into demonstrating its falsity and attempting to show how and why it went astray. Indeed, assuming that the erroneous theory focuses on significant matters, often the more outrageous the theory is, the more it is likely to provoke further investigation. Thus even if one cannot negotiate a theoretical breakthrough on one's own, one can serve one's ego by the possibility that one's errors may sustain the knowledge-building process. This is surely what one astute analyst had in mind when he observed, "it is important to err importantly."[1]

Conclusion: Bringing It All Together

Plainly, there is no easy way to evolve the habit of thinking theoretically. Indeed, if the foregoing nine precepts are well founded, it can be readily argued that theorizing is the hardest of intellectual tasks. Clearing away the confusion of day-to-day events and teasing out their underlying patterns is not merely a matter of applying one's mental skills. Sustained, disciplined, and uninhibited work is required, and even then theory can be elusive, puzzles difficult to identify, details hard to ignore, and probabilities tough to estimate. And the lures and practices of non-theoretical thinking are always present, tempting us to forgo the insecurities and ambiguities of high levels of abstraction in favor of the comfortable precision available at low levels.

Yet the payoffs for not yielding to the temptations and persisting to think theoretically are considerable. There is an exhilaration, an exquisiteness, to be enjoyed in the theoretical enterprise that virtually defies description. Stimulated by the rarified atmosphere, energized by the freedom to roam uninhibitedly across diverse realms of human experience, one gets giddy at high levels of abstraction. It is that special kind of giddiness that comes from the feeling that one is employing all the resources and talents at one's command, moving beyond anything one has done before. And if one should be so fortunate as actually to achieve a theoretical breakthrough, then the exhilaration, the excitement, and the sense of accomplishment can approach the thrill of discovery that Darwin, Einstein, Freud, and the other great explorers of underlying order must have experienced at their moments of breakthrough.

For all the difficulties it entails, then, thinking theoretically is, on balance, worth the effort. And so, therefore, is the effort to teach others to think thoroughly in this way. The habits of theoretical thinking may not always be teachable, and they may not even be teachable at all; but if our efforts successfully manage to reach only a few students, they are worth undertaking. And it is even conceivable that in trying to teach others to think theoretically, we may refine and enlarge our own capacities for comprehending the underlying order that sustains and alters the human condition.

Note

1. Marion J. Levy, " 'Does It Matter If He's Naked?' Bawled the Child," in Klaus Knorr and James N. Rosenau (eds.), *Contending Approaches to International Relations* (Princeton, NJ: Princeton University Press, 1969), p. 93.

Positivism and Beyond

S T E V E   S M I T H

The author takes up the essential critique of positivism and empiricism—the impossibility of "pure unvarnished perception" or "objective observation." He then examines alternatives to positivism: scientific realism, looking for "structures and things of the world that make science possible"; critical theory, drawn from the Frankfurt School—"that there can be no such thing as true empirical statements" apart from "knowledge-constitutive interest in control and prediction"; feminist epistemology that identifies the dominance of male perspective to the virtual exclusion of feminine understanding; and postmodernism that observes how knowledge is "dependent on underlying power structures" and focuses on "the fundamental problem" of "how to match the subjective self, or knower, with an 'objective' or external world." The author concludes that "epistemological concerns are absolutely salient for contemporary international theory," but that these problems do "not mean accepting a less rigorous epistemological warrant" than positivism has offered.

For the last forty years the academic discipline of International Relations has been dominated by positivism. Positivism has involved a commitment to a unified view of science, and the adoption of methodologies of the natural sciences to explain the social world. The so-called "great debates" in the discipline's history, between idealism and realism, traditionalism and behaviouralism, or between transnationalism and state-centrism, have not involved questions of epistemology. The discipline has tended to accept implicitly a rather simple and, crucially, an uncontested set of positivist assumptions which have fundamentally stifled debate over both what the world is like and how we might explain it. This is not true of those who worked either in the so-called "English school" or at the interface between international relations and political theory, because these writers never

bought into the positivist assumptions that dominated the discipline. But it has been the dominance of positivism that has accounted for both the character, and more importantly, the content of the central debates in international theory.

Viewed in this light, even the inter-paradigm debate of the 1980s looks very narrow, because all three paradigms, (realism, pluralism and globalism/structuralism) were working under positivist assumptions. This helps explain just why they could be seen as three versions of one world, rather than three genuine alternative views of international relations. Similarly, the current "debate" between neo-realism and neo-liberalism becomes much clearer when it is realised that both approaches are firmly positivist. My central claim here will be that positivism's importance has been not so much that it

Reprinted by permission from Steve Smith, Ken Booth, and Marysia Zalewski (eds.), *International Theory: Positivism and Beyond* (Cambridge, England: Cambridge University Press, 1996).

has given international theory a method but that its empiricist epistemology has determined what could be studied because it has determined what kinds of things exist in international relations. ... The one feature that the new "critical" approaches to international theory have in common is a rejection of the assumptions of what is loosely described as positivism. By "critical" here is meant the work of post-modernists, Critical Theorists (in the Frankfurt School sense), feminist theorists and post-structuralists. There can be little doubt both that these various approaches represent a massive attack on traditional or mainstream international theory, and that this traditional or mainstream theory has been dominated by positivist assumptions. ...

It is because of these two features of contemporary international theory that Lapid writes of the current period constituting the "post-positivist era" of international theory; indeed he adds that the debate between traditional and post-positivist theory is so important that it is the third "discipline-defining debate" in international relations' history (1989, pp. 235–9), following the two earlier debates between idealism and realism in the 1930s and 1940s, and between traditional and scientific approaches to studying the discipline in the 1960s. In essence, then, because much contemporary "critical" international theory self-consciously portrays itself as being *post*-positivist, this makes it rather important to be clear as to what positivism means and what might be involved in speaking of a post-*positivist* international theory.

The stakes are high in such a debate. This much is clear from the way that mainstream theorists have responded to the rise of the approaches that Lapid groups together as post-positivist (and which I above called "critical theories"). One particularly important response has been that of Robert Keohane, who, in his Presidential Address to the International Studies Association in 1988, spoke of the need to evaluate the rival research paradigms of rationalist

(i.e. traditional neo-realism and neo-liberalism) and reflective (i.e. what I termed "critical") approaches in terms of their "testable theories", without which "they will remain on the margins of the field . . . [since] . . . it will be impossible to evaluate their research program" (1989, pp. 173–4). As is noted below, this form of response reveals the dominance of positivism, since Keohane issues the challenge on grounds that are themselves positivist. Thus, positivism is precisely what is at issue in what Lapid calls the third debate because of its role in underpinning theory and, ultimately, serving as the criterion for judging between theory. Crucially, Keohane's central move is to propose that judgement between rationalist and reflective theories takes place on criteria that not only favour rationalism, but, more importantly, are exactly the criteria that reflective accounts are attacking. But note that a failure to come up to the (positivist) mark will result in reflective work being confined to the margins. Important consequences follow, then, from whether or not theories are positivist, and these consequences are not confined to questions as to what counts as knowledge but also involve the standing of theories and theorists within academia. All of this makes it very important to be clear as to how positivism operates in international theory, and to show how it is seen not merely as one explicit alternative among many but rather as the implicit "gold standard" against which all approaches are evaluated.

But the stakes are also high because of the links between theory and practice. International theory underpins and informs international practice, even if there is a lengthy lag between the high-point of theories and their gradual absorption into political debate. Once established as common sense, theories become incredibly powerful since they delineate not simply what can be known but also what it is sensible to talk about or suggest. Those who swim outside these safe waters risk more than simply the judgement that their theories are wrong; their entire ethical or moral stance may be ridiculed or seen as dangerous just because their theoretical assumptions are deemed unrealistic. Defining common sense is therefore the ultimate act of political power. In this sense what is at stake in debates about epistemology is very significant for political practice. Theories do not simply explain or predict, they tell us what possibilities exist for human action and intervention; they define not merely our explanatory possibilities but also our ethical and practical horizons. In this Kantian light epistemology matters, and the stakes are far more considerable than at first sight seem to be the case.

Having pointed out just how much is at stake in any discussion of epistemology in international theory, it is necessary, before examining the present debate about whether we can characterise the current situation in international theory as one of "positivism *and* beyond", or simply "beyond positivism", to look at the history of positivism in the social sciences and then to examine various alternative epistemological positions. This will provide the intellectual context for the debates in international theory, as well as serve as an introduction to the language and contexts of these wider philosophy of social science debates.

The History of Positivism

Positivism has a long history in the social sciences. There are three main chronological variants of positivism in the history of the social sciences, with the third of these being the most relevant for international relations. What unites them is a strong commitment to a specific way of gaining knowledge about the world, as will be discussed in more detail below.

The first variant is that developed by Auguste Comte in the early nineteenth century (indeed it was Comte who coined the word "positivism", as well as "sociology"). Comte's aim was to develop a science of society, based on the *methods* of the natural sciences, namely observation. Its aim was to reveal the "evolu-

tionary causal laws" that explained observable phenomena. For Comte, positive science was a distinct third stage in the development of knowledge, which progressed first from theological to metaphysical knowledge and then to positivist knowledge. He saw the sciences as hierarchically arranged, with mathematics at the base and sociology at the top, and thought that each of the sciences passed through the three stages of knowledge. Crucially, he therefore thought that all sciences (including the sciences dealing with society) would eventually be unified methodologically. This view was enormously important in the development of the social sciences throughout the nineteenth century, fundamentally influencing writers as diverse as Marx and Engels, and Durkheim. It is an assumption that still dominates the discipline of International Relations insofar as scholars search for the same kinds of laws and regularities in the international world as they assume characterise the natural world.

The second variant is that of logical positivism (or as it is sometimes called logical empiricism), which emerged in the 1920s in what was known as the Vienna Circle. This variant dominated English-speaking philosophy into the late 1960s, and is the starkest variant of the three summarised here. The central shared proposition of the members of this circle was that science was the only true form of knowledge and that there was nothing that could be known outside of what could be known scientifically. Hence, statements were only cognitively meaningful if they could be falsified or verified by experience. Moral and aesthetic statements were seen therefore as cognitively meaningless since they could not be in principle verified or falsified by experience. Such statements are merely expressions of preferences or feelings and emotions, but they are not knowledge. Thus, for instance, logical positivists rejected Comte's notion of causal laws explaining observable phenomena as metaphysical and therefore unscientific. In international relations, such a view would mean that it was simply not possible to speak of unobservables such as the structure of the international system or the "objective" laws of human nature.

The third variant is the one that has been most influential in the social sciences in the last fifty years. It emerged out of logical positivism, but moved away from its extremely stark criteria for what counts as knowledge and its reductionist view (contra Comte) that all cognitive knowledge should be based on the principles of physics. Christopher Lloyd has summarised its four main features as follows (1993, pp. 72–3): first, *logicism,* the view that the objective confirmation of scientific theory should conform to the canons of deductive logic; second, *empirical verificationism,* the idea that only statements that are either empirically verifiable or falsifiable (synthetic) or true by definition (analytic) are scientific; third, *theory and observation distinction,* the view that there is a strict separation between observations and theories, with observations being seen as theoretically neutral; finally, *the Humean theory of causation,* the idea that establishing a causal relationship is a matter of discovering the invariant temporal relationship between observed events.

This view was extremely important in the social sciences, where the orthodoxy of the 1950s and 1960s was one of trying to apply the ideas of the main proponents of this view, Carnap, Nagel, Hempel and Popper, to the fledgling social science disciplines. Particularly important was the work of Carl Hempel (especially 1966 and 1974) because he developed an extremely influential account of what is involved in explaining an event. He argued that an event is explained by "covering" it under a general law. Usually this takes the form of a deductive argument whereby (1) a general law is postulated, (2) antecedent conditions are specified, and (3) the explanation of the observed event deduced from (1) and (2). This model is known as the "deductive-nomological" model, and Hempel argued famously that it could be applied to the social sciences and to history

(1974). He also put forward an alternative, the "inductive-statistical" model, whereby statistical or probabilistic laws are established inductively and are used to show how a specific event is highly likely given the established law (1966, p. 11).

This third variant underpins much of the literature of international relations since the 1950s. Its features seem to me to have become somewhat detached from their philosophical roots as they have taken hold in international relations. In my judgement, positivism in international theory has had four underlying and very often deeply implicit assumptions, which deal with many of the points raised in Lloyd's four-point summary noted above but in an altogether less philosophically conscious and explicit way. The first is a belief in the unity of science (including the social sciences). This was especially influential in international relations, and many would argue continues to be so. Accordingly, the slow pace of development of international theory could be explained by comparing it to the development of physics, which took centuries to create powerful theories. In short, the same methodologies and epistemologies apply to all realms of enquiry. In philosophical language this is known as naturalism, of which there are strong and weak versions; the strong view is that there is no fundamental difference between the social and the "natural" worlds; the weaker version is that despite differences between the two realms the methods of the natural sciences can still be used for the analysis of the social world. In international relations an example of the strong version might be the view that the international system is essentially the same as the systems of the natural world; the weaker version is illustrated by the claim that scientific methods can be used to understand the beliefs of decision-makers even though this does not mean that these beliefs follow some (strong) laws of behaviour.

The second influential assumption is the view that there is a distinction between facts and values, and, moreover, that "facts" are theory neutral. This fitted particularly well into the rush towards behaviouralist quantification in the 1960s, and was a position very much to the fore in the USA during the debates over US involvement in Vietnam. In philosophical terms this is an objectivist position, one that sees objective knowledge of the world as possible despite the fact that observations may be subjective. Thirdly, there has been a powerful belief in the existence of regularities in the social as well as the natural world. This, of course, licenses both the "deductive-nomological" and the "inductive-statistical" forms of covering law explanation. Again, in international relations terms, this kind of assumption lies at the heart of debates about polarity and stability, or about long cycles in world history. Finally, there has been a tremendous reliance on the belief that it is empirical validation or falsification that is the hallmark of "real" enquiry, a position we have already seen explicitly taken by Keohane; in philosophical language this is the adoption of an empiricist epistemology.

The impact of positivism on international theory has been surprisingly unreflective, with the canon of positivism significantly shaping the discipline since the 1950s. But there has been little in the way of a discussion of what positivism actually means. . . .[T]he terms "positivism" and "empiricism" are conflated and confused in international relations. . . . But it is certainly evident that in international relations positivism has tended to involve a commitment to a natural science methodology, fashioned on an early twentieth-century view of physics; that is to say a physics before the epistemologically revolutionary development of quantum mechanics in the 1920s, which fundamentally altered the prevailing view of the physical world as one which could be accurately observed. Accordingly, positivism in international relations, as in all the social sciences, has essentially been a methodological commitment, tied to an empiricist epistemology: together these result in a very re-

stricted range of permissible ontological claims. Thus whilst the terms "positivism" and "empiricism" are used interchangeably, in both the philosophy of social science and the philosophy of natural science, I think that it is absolutely necessary to maintain a conceptual distinction between the two. However, this is not easy to do because whereas for the logical positivists (or logical empiricists) positivism operated as an epistemological warrant about what kinds of knowledge claims might be made, in the third variant of Hempel, Popper *et al.* summarised above, positivism was much more than just a commitment to an empiricist epistemology. If it is difficult to differentiate between the use of the terms in the philosophy of natural and social science, in international relations and the other social sciences the two terms are virtually synonymous.

An answer to the question "what does positivism mean in international relations?" can now be given. Positivism is a methodological view that combines naturalism (in either its strong (ontological and methodological) or its weak (methodological) sense, and a belief in regularities. It is licensed by a strict empiricist epistemology itself committed to an objectivism about the relationship between theory and evidence. Whilst the usage of terms such as "epistemology", "methodology" and "ontology" may be various and inconsistent it is important that we separate "epistemology" conceptually from both "ontology" and "methodology", and then separate positivism from empiricism. Thus, as to the latter, I do not accept the view that empiricism = positivism = epistemology + methodology; rather positivism is a methodological position reliant on an empiricist epistemology which grounds our knowledge of the world in justification by (ultimately brute) experience and thereby licensing methodology and ontology in so far as they are empirically warranted.

As to the separation of epistemology, methodology and ontology, the three are indeed fundamentally interrelated. Methodology (why use that method?) needs the warrant of an epistemology (answer: because this method discriminates between "true" and "false" within the range of what we could know to be "true" or "false"); whereas ontological claims (what is the world like and what is its furniture?) without an epistemological warrant is dogma and will not itself license a methodology. . . . My argument should not be taken as meaning that just because I have come to this point in this chapter via an analysis of empiricism this means I think the epistemological warrant is or should be empiricism, although this is the assumption that has underpinned much of the literature of international relations for the last forty years. But I do maintain that epistemology matters because it determines of what we can have knowledge; moreover, it is not possible to wish it away, or undermine its importance, by arguing, as is fashionably the case amongst post-modernist philosophers and (philosophical) realists, that ontology is prior to epistemology. All of this is very tricky ground but my main claim is simply that I see neither ontology nor epistemology as prior to the other, but instead see the two of them as mutually and inextricably interrelated. Thus, just as epistemology is important in determining what can be accepted ontologically, so ontology affects what we accept epistemologically. In this light, prioritising one or the other, as has certainly been the case in work on the philosophy of knowledge (prioritising epistemology) and in post-modernist work (which prioritises ontology), misses the point because such a move sets up a false distinction between the two and implies that one is separable from the other. . . .

Empiricism, as noted above, is the view that the only grounds for justified belief are those that rest ultimately on observation. Based upon the work of philosophers such as David Hume and John Locke, its central premise is that science must be based on a phenomenalist nominalism, that is to say the notion that only statements about phenomena which can be directly experi-

enced can count as knowledge and that any statements that do not refer to independent atomised objects cannot be granted the status of justified knowledge (Kolakowski, 1972, pp. 11–17). Empiricists believe that science can rest on a bedrock of such pure observation, and from this bedrock can be established, by induction, the entire scientific structure. Put simply, basic beliefs, warranted by direct perception, provide the basis for induction so that we can move away from a very narrow foundation for knowledge to much wider inductive generalisations. Of course, it is much more complicated than this. . . . The key point, however, is the simple one that if one grants that such a bedrock, however narrow, exists, then one can see how there might be an empirical foundation to knowledge.

But there are serious, and in my view insuperable, limitations to an empiricist epistemology. I will simply outline three fundamental ones. The first is that the epistemological warrant offered by empiricism is very narrow indeed, if in the end it has to be based on direct observation. Such a warrant rules out any consideration of (unobservable) things like social or international structures, or even social facts (to use Durkheim's phrase which refers to those shared social concepts and understandings such as crime, which he believed should be treated "as things"). Thus, many philosophers point out that a strict empiricism actually allows us to *know* very little about only a very restricted amount of "reality". The second limitation is that, strictly speaking, empiricism does not allow us to talk about causes since these are unobservable. The best we can do, following Hume, is to talk about "constant conjunctions", and therefore eschew notions of necessity. Causation is thus reduced to mere correlation, and our enquiry is therefore limited to that of *prediction* and cannot involve *explanation*. Hempel's covering law model, for example, can tell us what we might expect to happen, but not why it happens. Moreover, the logical structure of the covering law model allows us to make correct predictions from false premises. Overall, then, the kind of knowledge we can gain from an empiricism that refuses discussion of unobservables such as causes is very limited indeed.

But it is the final problem that really undermines empiricism most fundamentally: put simply it is the objective that the kind of pure unvarnished perception talked of by empiricists is simply impossible. There can be no "objective" observation, nor any "brute experience". Observation and perception are always affected by prior theoretical and conceptual commitments. Empiricism, in other words, underestimates the amount of theory involved in perception or observation. To describe what we experience we have to use concepts, and these are not dictated by what we observe; they are either *a priori* in the mind, or they are the result of a prior theoretical language. The problems for empiricism arising out of its underestimation of the role of theory have been most clearly expressed in Quine's famous essay "Two Dogmas of Empiricism" (1961), in which he disputed both aspects of the empiricist view of the relationship between theory and facts. First, he noted that there was no easy distinction between analytic and synthetic statements, and that even analytical statements (that is those deemed true by convention) are susceptible to revision by experience. For empiricists this matters because they treat theory (or, in Hume's phrase the "relations of ideas") as "merely" a series of tautologies, or to use Martin Hollis's phrase (1994, p. 52) a "filing system"; no truths about the world can come from this filing system, such truths can only come from observation (or again to use Hume's phrase, from "matters of fact"). Quine's first objection, then, punctures the neat distinction between analytic and synthetic statements that is central to the empiricist view of the role of theories.

His second objection is equally fundamental. Whereas empiricism rests on pure observation, Quine argues that this is simply not possible, since theory is involved in all empirical observation. Even the most simple acts of "pure"

observation involve a web of belief which is both far removed and far more complex than the individual act of observation. Our senses cannot give us access to "the truth" since there is no way of describing experience independently of its interpretation. There are, therefore, no brute facts, no facts without interpretation, and interpretation always involves theory. Thus, whereas the empiricist view of knowledge clearly implies that if experience differs from our prior beliefs then we should change our beliefs (since these can never reveal any truths about the world), Quine shows that the web of belief in which individual acts of observation occur can give us reasons to think that it is our interpretation of observation that is mistaken. Any individual observation, therefore, can be revised or redefined. Theories define what the "facts" are, and it is always an alternative to reject the "facts" and thereby save the theory. Facts are always theory dependent, and not independent as empiricism maintains. To quote Quine "it is misleading to speak of the empirical content of an individual statement. . . . Any statement can be held true come what may. . . . Conversely . . . no statement is immune to revision" (1961, p. 43).

These are absolutely fundamental objections to the empiricism that has dominated international theory, and, despite protests to the contrary by many contemporary empiricists, I think they apply to much of the work currently being undertaken in international relations. . . .

Contemporary Epistemological Debates

If, as I have claimed, positivism and its epistemological foundation, empiricism, are seriously flawed, if rationalism (empiricism's long-standing rival) is currently out of favour, and if pragmatism seems to run into a series of objections from those who want to retain notions of a foundational truth, then maybe there are other positions that might be of interest to those international theorists attempting to locate their work in an epistemology other than empiricism.

Broadly speaking there are *five* alternatives in the philosophy of knowledge that look particularly promising for post-positivist international theory. These are (a) scientific realism, (b) hermeneutics, (c) Critical Theory (in its Frankfurt School sense, hence the capital C and T to differentiate it from the more generic notion of "critical theories" which is used to refer to all post-positivist approaches), (d) feminist standpoint epistemology, and (e) post-modernist epistemology. Some of these are related to the approaches mentioned above: notably, both scientific realism and Critical Theory share much with rationalism, and hermeneutics, feminist standpoint and post-modernism have close links to pragmatism.

The central claim of *scientific realism* is that it makes sense to talk of a world outside of experience; that is to say, it is interested in uncovering the structures and things of the world that make science possible. Accordingly, the empiricist conception of the role of theories (as heuristic) is entirely wrong in that the existence of theoretical concepts such as electrons or classes are to be treated in the same way as so-called "facts". As a result, its epistemology is nonempiricist, with epistemology being the transitive objects of science which we create to represent and account for intransitive objects such as the structures and furniture of the world. Bhaskar distinguishes between the real, the actual and the empirical: the first refers to what entities and mechanisms make up the world, the second to events, and the third to that which we experience. The problem with empiricism is that it has looked at the third of these as a way of explaining the other two so that it reduces questions about what is (ontology) to questions about how we know what is (epistemology). As Bhaskar puts it: "It is important to avoid the epistemic fallacy . . . [which] consists in confusing the ontological order with the epistemic order, priority in being with priority in deciding claims to being" (1978, p. 250). Similarly, Bhaskar rejects rationalism since it too reduces

ontology to epistemology by its reliance on the role of theoretically necessary conceptual truths to make sense of the world. In contrast, realist science is an attempt to describe and explain the structures and processes of the world that exist independently of our perception of them. Indeed, for science to be possible, the world *must* be made up of real structures and processes. Bhaskar fundamentally disputes the primacy given to epistemology by both rationalism and empiricism, since they reduce ontology to epistemology. For Bhaskar, ontology is primary, but is nothing like as flexible as the pragmatists imply; in this sense scientific realism disputes the primacy of epistemology over ontology in rationalism and empiricism, yet sees pragmatism as mistaken in its claim (or more accurately its implication) that what is true is only what is "good in the way of belief".

Hermeneutics develops out of the work of Dilthey, Husserl, Weber, Heidegger, Wittgenstein and Gadamer. Its central claim is antinaturalist in that it does not see the social world as in any sense amenable to the kind of treatment that empiricism, and especially positivism, assumes. Developing out of textual analysis, hermeneutics, as developed by Dilthey in the nineteenth century, starts from the premise that the analysis of nature and the analysis of the mind are very different enterprises. For Dilthey, each required a very different form of analysis, contra positivism, and these forms of analysis are what we now call explaining and understanding. Hermeneutics can at first sight be seen as a concern with how to understand a text or an actor, and the work of Collingwood (1946) and Skinner (see especially, Tully, 1988), are primarily concerned with this essentially methodological hermeneutics. However, the much more radical work of particularly Heidegger (1962), and Gadamer (1994) raises ontological questions about the nature of being: what does it mean for us to interpret and understand the world? Crucially, hermeneutics reverses the argument of traditional epistemology and instead of a being interpreting a world sees a being formed by tacit know-how which is prior to the interpretation of facts, events, or data. Individuals are caught up in a hermeneutic circle whereby we can only understand the world by our being caught up in a web of significance. Hermeneutics, in short, has ontological significance, which means that the traditional concerns of epistemology are inappropriate for understanding and making sense of our beliefs, since they posit the interpretive or observing subject as in some way prior to questions about the nature of being. In its place, Gadamer stresses the importance of the embeddedness of all analysis in language and history; individuals analyse and act within what Gadamer refers to as an "horizon", by which he means their beliefs, preconceptions and situatedness and which both enables and constrains them. Crucially, for Gadamer, this embeddedness means that notions of truth and reason are themselves historically constituted, so that the kinds of claims about objective knowledge that have dominated epistemological discussions between rationalism and empiricism are fundamentally mistaken. What Gadamer proposes is an ontology of knowledge, reason and truth which shows how they are embedded in history rather than being above it. Epistemology, in its traditional sense discussed above, can therefore never be something prior, neutral, foundational or decisive, but instead has to be seen as secondary to ontology.

Critical Theory has a more recent history, emerging out of the work of the Frankfurt School in the inter-war years. Its most influential thinker has been Jürgen Habermas. The main implication for epistemology has derived from his work on a broader conception of reason than the instrumental view which dominates Western science and his development of a non-positivist methodology for the social sciences. In his book *Knowledge and Human Interests* (1987, first published in 1968), Habermas puts forward the view that there are three types of knowledge: empirical-analytical (the natural

sciences), historical-hermeneutic (concerned with meaning and understanding), and critical sciences (concerned with emancipation). Habermas claims that each of these types of knowledge has its own set of "cognitive interests", respectively, those of a technical interest in control and prediction, a practical interest in understanding, and an emancipatory interest in enhancing freedom. The epistemological implication of this transcendental claim is that there can be no such thing as true empirical statements, for example in the realm of the natural sciences, independent of the knowledge-constitutive interest in control and prediction. Since the late 1960s, Habermas has moved away from this rather restricted notion of knowledge-constitutive interests towards the development of what he terms a theory of communicative action (1984; 1987), in which he is concerned with developing an epistemology based on the notion of universal pragmatics or discourse ethics, whereby he sees knowledge emerging out of a consensus theory of truth. Central to this is his idea of an "ideal speech situation", which he sees as implicit in the act of communication, and as rationally entailing ethical and normative commitments. The "ideal speech situation" is based upon the notion that acts of communication necessarily presuppose four things: that statements are comprehensible, true, right and sincere. It is not that Habermas thinks that the ideal speech situation is something that is commonly found in communicative actions, only that it is presumed by the very acts themselves. Habermas believes that we could in principle reach a consensus on the validity of each of these four claims, and that this consensus would be achievable if we envisaged a situation in which power and distortion were removed from communication so that the "force of the better argument prevails" (Outhwaite, 1994, p. 40). Thus, his epistemological position is one which seeks to avoid the simple objectivism of positivism whilst at the same time stopping short of embracing the kind of relativism implicit in traditional hermeneutics.

He proposes that the social sciences cannot proceed as do the natural sciences, and instead must see action from the perspective of the actor involved; but he maintains that this does not mean that the social sciences cannot criticise these perspectives on theoretical and ethical grounds. Crucially, Habermas's emphasis on the existence of foundations for making judgements between knowledge claims places his work as a direct descendant of the Kantian enlightenment project, a position that has been both a major source of criticism from post-modernists and yet a great source of strength to those who want to link foundational knowledge to emancipation.

Feminist work on epistemology is diverse, and only one variant of it will be dealt with here. . . . Sandra Harding (1986) has noted three main strands in feminist work on epistemology: feminist empiricism, feminist standpoint and feminist post-modernism. The first of these ultimately rests on the kind of empiricist epistemology discussed above, while the third has much to do with the work on post-modern epistemology discussed in the next section. The central claim of feminist standpoint epistemology is well expressed in the work of Nancy Hartsock (1983), who set out to "explore some of the epistemological consequences of claiming that women's lives differ structurally from those of men" (1983, p. 284). For Hartsock, the male (and Western, and white) domination of science and knowledge has produced knowledge which is partial and which excludes or marginalises women. Developing the Hegelian notion of the master–slave relationship, standpoint feminists argue that this marginality can be turned to epistemic advantage since women can have a better knowledge of male-dominated science than can the men involved; thus feminist standpoint knowledge will have both explanatory and emancipatory potential for greater than that created by feminist empiricists. The implication of feminist standpoint analysis for epistemology is enormous since it requires us to challenge the traditional epistemological assumption that the identity of the knower was irrelevant in the process of knowing, an assumption found in both rationalism and empiricism. Indeed, not only is a feminist standpoint epistemology corrosive of such a claim, but so is feminist empiricism, since each is claiming that there can be no "master" narrative and that the situatedness of the mind is irrelevant. Moreover, feminist work on epistemology has made it abundantly clear that the knowing mind of traditional epistemology is axiomatically a male mind. This has radical consequences, since it requires us to abandon the idea of a disinterested and detached knowing subject, a move which is equally problematic for both rationalism and empiricism; in its place feminists propose the idea that knowledge is a social activity. In this light, the knowledge produced by this process cannot but fail to be influenced by the social location of those who construct it. The fundamental question for epistemology therefore becomes "whose knowledge?"

Post-modern work on epistemology is extraordinarily diverse, and defies easy summary . . . because its central tenet is one which seeks nothing less than the overthrow of virtually all preceding positions on epistemology. There are extensive debates over what is post-modernism and how it differs from post-structuralism, let alone quite what a post-modern epistemology looks like. It is a genre of work that has been attacked and dismissed, usually by people who have not bothered to engage with the complex issues involved (and maybe without reading the texts either!). . . .

The central implication of Foucault's work for epistemology comes from his concern with the historically specific conditions in which knowledge is generated. In his book *The Order of Things* (1970), he undertook "an archaeology of the human sciences" to show how the human sciences were not "natural" modes of enquiry but rather were made possible by an underlying structure of thought. His work on prisons

(1977), on the rise of "modern" medicine (1975) and on madness (1967) was concerned not so much with the content of the knowledge generated in these areas but rather on the relationship between knowledge and practice—that is to say on the relationship between power and knowledge—a relationship so intertwined that he referred to it as power/knowledge; each is always involved in the operation of the other. His later work on genealogy (1986) sought to show how specific academic "discourses" emerged not as a neutral result of scholarly enquiry, but as the direct consequence of power relations. In short, power is implicated in all knowledge systems, such that notions like reason or truth are the products of specific historical circumstances. The concept of truth has to alter accordingly, since it can no longer refer to an underlying or foundational notion of truth, but rather to the idea of multiple truths. Epistemology is therefore decidedly not the centrepiece of philosophical enquiry, but is instead dependent on underlying power structures. This is a very radical move away from empiricism, rationalism or even pragmatism; it was also a source of considerable dispute between Foucault and Habermas. Finally, Foucault saw the concept of truth not as an empirically valid concept but rather as a tool for resisting power. Accordingly, the central feature of epistemology, a concern with the criteria for determining the truth, is replaced by a much more practical notion of truth-as-tool.

Derrida's work can be seen as an attack on one central assumption of traditional work on epistemology, what he calls the "metaphysics of presence". His claim is anti-essentialist and anti-foundationalist in that he refuses to see the knower as a given, and instead as merely one more construction of language and culture. Accordingly, he sees as flawed the central tenet of empiricist and rationalist epistemology, namely that the fundamental problem of epistemology is how to match the subjective self, or knower, with an "objective" or external world. His work on deconstruction forces us to examine the "reason-

ableness of reason", since he locates it within a specific cultural and historical setting of thinking and writing. His meticulous examinations of specific pieces of writing (see as examples, 1976, 1978, 1982) show how arbitrary and particular are the logocentric structures which mark language and thought; it is this which removes the foundations from rationalism and empiricism, since it completely subverts the idea of a prior presence (the metaphysics of presence). Instead, the knower is always caught up in a language and mode of thinking which, far from interpreting a world, instead constructs it. . . .

Positivism in International Theory

Having mapped out the terrain of the debate in the social sciences, this section will look at positivism in international theory, and the next will speculate about the possibilities open for developing a post-positivist international theory. The first question is whether international theory is currently dominated by positivism, or whether instead it has in some way moved *beyond* positivism.

At the outset I want to stress just how ill-defined "positivism" is in international theory. Basically there are three common ways of using the term. The *first* treats positivism as essentially the same thing as empiricism, which is to say that each is seen as an *epistemology*. An epistemology deals with how it is that we might know something about the world. A *second* uses positivism in a *methodological* way, by which is meant a set of rules for the actual practice of science or study. *Thirdly*, positivism is often equated with *behaviouralism*, by which is meant a very restrictive reliance on quantitative data, and a disregard for what goes on inside actors' heads, as the basis for knowledge claims. Usually, it is the first of these uses that has characterised international relations, but the overlap of usages has been especially marked, and it is quite common to be able to discern more than one of the above usages in any given enquiry.

Within philosophy the term involves a series of different kinds of commitments. As Martin Hollis shows, . . . positivism is usually seen by philosophers as entailing both empiricism (an epistemology) and naturalism (the view that the natural and social worlds are one and the same kind of thing, a view which has both ontological and methodological consequences); positivism thereby entails methodological, ontological and epistemological assumptions and commitments. Indeed Andrew Sayer has remarked that the terms positivism and empiricism are so contested that he chooses not to use them in his (philosophical) realist rejection of these two associated positions (1992, p. 7).

The problem is not just that international theorists have tended to use the term in very free and easy ways, unaware of the depths of the philosophical waters involved, but, more importantly, that the vast majority of international relations research over the last 30 years has rested *implicitly* on positivist assumptions. Thus, while many of the leading behaviouralists were aware of their commitment to positivism and indeed in many cases were powerful advocates of its strengths (see Hoole and Zinnes, 1976, which includes a particularly robust and tetchy defence by Singer), many others adopted an unthinking positivism, and worked within a Kuhnian normal science thereby foreclosing debate or theoretical and philosophical self-consciousness. This has been especially problematic when the interrelationship of the epistemological, methodological and ontological entailments of positivism are ignored, and when theorists are unaware of the consequences of these. Moreover, there has been little in the way of discussion as to what an alternative to positivism might look like. It is often erroneously assumed either that "we are all positivists now" or that positivism is now much more sophisticated than it once was, and that this "neo-positivism" overcomes the inadequacies of the positivism-as-behaviouralism that characterised international

theory in the 1950s and 1960s (such a position is well illustrated by Hermann, Kegley and Rosenau, 1987, pp. 18–22). In short, mainstream international theory has never really bothered to examine its positivist assumptions, nor what alternatives are available. Keohane's response to one such move to develop an alternative illustrates this poverty of imagination.

However, there have been notable exceptions to this silence about the role of positivism, but at first sight these seem to have been relatively ineffective in altering the orientation of the mainstream discipline. But on reflection such a view may simply reflect a massive (and very common) underestimation of the hold that positivism has had over international relations. One seemingly important reaction came in the so-called "great debate" of the mid-1960s, when Hedley Bull attacked the "scientists" for their methodological assumptions (see Knorr and Rosenau, 1969, for a collection of the main papers dealing with this "debate"); in place of "science" Bull proposed more traditional and historical analysis. Now the problem with the debate was that it ignored both epistemology and ontology; it was instead a very narrow dispute about what methods were appropriate for the study of international relations. A second celebrated debate came in the late 1960s with the induction/deduction dispute between Oran Young and Bruce Russett (see Young, 1969 and Russett, 1969); this was essentially a debate about whether enquiry was led by observation or by theory. But again this, although it seemed more important at the time, was really only another debate about the appropriateness of different methods. A third, and much more substantive, response was the critique of Charles Reynolds (1973, 1992), which noted the weaknesses of empiricism and in its place proposed a form of Collingwoodian history whereby the task of the theorist was to understand events as perceived by the individuals involved in them. But this too was largely ignored in the mainstream literature. The reason seems to me to be that the mainstream was simply too wedded to positivism, and crucially, wedded in an implicit rather than an explicit way. On an anecdotal level, I recall many discussions with leading specialists in my own research area at the time (foreign policy analysis) who denied outright that they were positivists, associating it with a crude form of behaviourism which had failed 'to produce the goods'. This was very evident in the mid-1970s when the comparative foreign policy movement lost its impetus (see Kegley, 1980, Rosenau, 1976 and Smith, 1986). The response was *not* to abandon positivism, since this seemed untouched by the problems facing this sub-field of the discipline, but rather to reject the excessive reliance on quantitative data characteristic of behaviouralism, and also to question the belief in an inductive route to general theory. But, of course, neither of these moves involved a rejection of positivism, only one component of it, and a rather extreme one at that.

More recently, a series of post-modernist writers (most notably Jim George 1988, pp. 67–70 and 74–85; 1994, pp. 41–68) and Richard Ashley (1984) have written about the limitations of positivism. But their work has been largely ignored by many traditionalists precisely because they write from theoretical positions that traditionalists do not accept as capable of providing "real" or "proper" knowledge. Kenneth Waltz's (1986) response to Ashley's (1984) critique, John Mearsheimer's quite amazingly confused comments on "critical theory" (1995), Kal Holsti's (1993) worries that such interventions do not lead to "progress", Roy Jones's (1994) reaction to Rob Walker's work, and Kal Holsti's (1989) and Tom Biersteker's (1989) responses to Lapid's article on post-positivism discussed above, are very clear examples of the reaction to post-structural or post-modern attacks on positivism. Rare indeed is the attempt to engage with these criticisms. . . . Yet again the reaction is essentially that writers such as Ashley and George are not doing "proper" international

relations. Part of the reason for this quite consistent rejection of attacks on positivism in international relations is, as stated above, that many international relations specialists tend to think of it in a very narrow sense; in this light, the critiques mentioned above "do not apply to them". But there is more to it than that, and in my judgement the explanation lies in the epistemological and ontological features of positivism. Thus the methodological aspects of positivism can be rejected as unduly quantitative or behaviouralist, but doing so does not mean that positivism's epistemological basis, and thereby its range of possible statements about what exists (its ontological realm), are also rejected. Positivism-as-methodology may be rejected but all too often positivism-as-epistemology continues to play the same role as before.

My basic argument, then, is that positivism is usually equated with a specific epistemological position, but almost always involved methodological commitments; together these result in a very limited range of possible ontological claims. It is precisely this linkage that lies at the heart of Keohane's view of what is at stake in the rationalist/reflective debate; and it is this linkage that explains just why his proposed test of the alternatives is so problematic. Keohane accepts as settled exactly the kind of epistemological and methodological questions that non-positivists want to problematise, and therefore his proposed test results in only a small range of ontological statements being deemed acceptable. Positivism is therefore used in a variety of ways, lacks a common definition, conflates and confuses very distinct philosophical concepts (so that positivism is sometimes used to refer to an epistemology and at others to refer to a methodology), is implicitly and explicitly powerful, and through the 1980s has come to be increasingly criticised. All of which begs the question of whether we can move beyond positivism, and what might such theories look like; or, perhaps whether there can now only be post-positivist theory?

Positivism and Beyond

At the outset I want to claim that there is really no such thing as *a* post-positivist approach, only post-positivist approaches. I have written about this before (Smith, 1995), pointing out that there were two main debates concerning post-positivist international theory, between explanatory and constitutive theory and between foundational and anti-foundational theory. I called traditional international theory as overwhelmingly explanatory in character, and post-positivist theory as constitutive, and among post-positivist approaches saw critical theory, historical sociology, and some feminist theory as foundational and post-modernism and some feminist theory as anti-foundational. This classification can now be improved on so as to take account of the fact that the various post-positivist approaches operate within very different epistemological positions.

My claim is that whilst the vast bulk of international theory is indeed explanatory because it is positivist, and though a lot of post-positivist work is constitutive (or reflective to use Keohane's term), the post-positivist accounts are working with distinctively different epistemologies. It is this which explains why there is no prospect of them constituting an alternative. Rather, historical sociology, despite the fact that it has been central in undermining the realist concept of the state, seems to me now to be largely working within an empiricist epistemology, if not an outright positivism. The epistemological positions of the other three sets of approaches seem to fit within at least three of the five alternative epistemological stances summarised above. Thus, although the post-positivist approaches are united in an opposition to traditional international theory, one of them works within the same epistemology as traditional theory, and the others are operating in distinctly different epistemologies to each other.

To illustrate these differences I will broaden my recent division of approaches into founda-

tionalist and anti-foundationalist. In its place I will use four criteria, those of *objectivism, empiricism, naturalism* and *behaviouralism,* to assess the precise commitments of the alternative epistemologies. Following Martin Hollis's definitions of these . . . *objectivism* can be defined as referring to the view that objective knowledge of the world is possible; *naturalism* as meaning that there is a single scientific method which can analyse both the "natural" and the social worlds; *empiricism* as involving the claim that knowledge has finally to be justified by experience; and *behaviouralism* as meaning that we do not need to worry about what actors think they are doing to explain their behaviour. . . .

Although the five views have been influential in developing post-positivist international theory, it is interesting to note that some have been much more influential than others. Scientific realism has been used very little (see Wendt, 1987; Dessler, 1989), which is rather surprising given that it has enormous potential for those who wish to construct an account of the influence of unobservable structures (such as the international system or the society of states?) on behaviour. Similarly, hermeneutics, as distinct from work on perceptions, has been little used, despite its obvious implications for the study of decision-making (for one important exception see Shapcott, 1994; see also the essays in Little and Smith, 1988). Feminist standpoint epistemology has been supported by Keohane (1991) as offering additional insights (to those of the mainstream), and used by Tickner (1992) in her book on international relations, but, as Zalewski (1993) argues, has otherwise been largely ignored in international theory. The other two epistemological perspectives, Critical Theory and post-modernism have been far more widely incorporated into international theory (for paradigmatic examples see, respectively, Cox, 1981, 1987; Hoffman, 1987; Linklater, 1990, 1992; and George, 1994; Ashley, 1987; Walker, 1993; Der Derian, 1987; Campbell, 1992). There is evidently still a large amount of epistemological space for the development of post-positivist approaches in international theory.

In conclusion, my task has been to show that positivism has had an enormous influence in international theory primarily because it has critically influenced what the discipline could talk about; in this sense it matters because its epistemological assumptions have had enormous ontological consequences. International theory now has a number of post-positivist approaches, which are opening up space not merely for other ways of thinking about international relations but also for other international realities. But there is no hope of a (single) post-positivist approach because some very distinctly different and mutually exclusive epistemological positions underlie post-positivist international theories. My aim has been to say something about both the nature of positivism and its traditional alternatives, and about the kinds of epistemological positions open to those who want to move beyond positivist international theory. This does not mean, however, that anything goes epistemologically, or that one can adopt a pick and mix approach to these alternative epistemological positions. Indeed, my main argument is that epistemological concerns are absolutely salient for contemporary international theory and to claim that the move away from positivism does not mean accepting a less rigorous epistemological warrant for theory. In my judgement, the weaknesses of positivism are so fundamental that the positivist project cannot be resurrected. At the same time, positivism's dominance of the discipline has been, and continues to be, so great that it has come to be seen as almost common sense. But more important still has been positivism's role in determining, in the name of science, just what counts as the subject matter of international relations. Its epistemology has had enormous ontological effects, and these have affected not only the study but also the practice of international relations. In positivism's place, international theory needs to develop strong post-positivist theories

based on a variety of epistemologies because much more than epistemology is at stake.

References

Ashley, Richard (1984), 'The Poverty of Neorealism', *International Organization*, 38 (2), pp. 225–86.

—— (1987), 'The Geopolitics of Geopolitical Space: Toward a Critical Social Theory of International Politics', *Alternatives*, 12 (4), pp. 403–34.

Bhaskar, Roy (1978), *A Realist Theory of Science* (Brighton: Harvester).

—— (1979), *The Possibility of Naturalism: A Philosophical Critique of the Contemporary Human Sciences* (Brighton: Harvester).

—— (1989), *Reclaiming Reality: A Critical Introduction to Contemporary Philosophy* (London: Verso).

Biersteker, Thomas (1989), 'Critical Reflections on Post-Positivism in International Relations', *International Studies Quarterly*, 33 (3), pp. 263–8.

Campbell, David (1992), *Writing Security: United States Foreign Policy and the Politics of Identity* (Manchester: Manchester University Press).

Collingwood, R. G. (1946), *The Idea of History* (London: Oxford University Press).

Cox, Robert (1981), 'Social Forces, States and World Orders: Beyond International Relations Theory', *Millennium: Journal of International Studies*, 10 (2), pp. 126–55.

—— (1987), *Production, Power and World Order: Social Forces in the Making of History* (New York: Columbia University Press).

Der Derian, James (1987), *On Diplomacy: A Genealogy of Western Estrangement* (Oxford: Blackwell).

Derrida, Jacques (1976), *Of Grammatology* (translated with an introduction by Gayatri Spivak) (Baltimore MD: Johns Hopkins University Press).

—— (1978), *Writing and Difference* (translated with an introduction by Alan Bass) (London: Routledge).

—— (1982), *Margins of Philosophy* (translated with additional notes by Alan Bass) (Brighton: Harvester).

Dessler, David (1989), 'What's At Stake in the Agent-Structure Debate?', *International Organization*, 43 (3), pp. 441–73.

Foucault, Michel (1967), *Madness and Civilisation: A History of Insanity in the Age of Reason* (first published 1961) (London: Tavistock Publications).

—— (1970), *The Order of Things: An Archaeology of the Human Sciences* (first published 1966) (New York: Random House).

—— (1975), *The Birth of the Clinic: An Archaeology of Medical Perception* (first published 1963) (New York: Vintage Books).

(1977), *Discipline and Punish: The Birth of the Prison* (first published 1975) (Harmondsworth: Allen Lane).

(1986), 'Neitzsche, Genealogy, History', in Paul Rabinow (ed.), *The Foucault Reader* (Harmondsworth: Peregrine Books), pp. 76–100.

Gadamer, Hans-Georg (1994), *Truth and Method,* 2nd revised edition (New York: Continuum Books).

George, Jim (1988), 'The Study of International Relations and the Positivist/Empiricist Theory of Knowledge: Implications for the Australian Discipline', in Richard Higgott (ed.), *New Directions in International Relations* (Canberra: Australian National University), pp. 65–142.

(1994), *Discourses of Global Politics: A Critical (Re)Introduction to International Relations* (Boulder, CO: Lynne Reinner).

George, Jim and Campbell, David (1990), 'Patterns of Dissent and the Celebration of Difference: Critical Social Theory and International Relations', *International Studies Quarterly,* 34 (3), pp. 269–93.

Habermas, Jürgen (1987), *Knowledge and Human Interests* (first published 1968) (Cambridge: Polity).

(1984 [1991]), *The Theory of Communicative Action Vol. 1: Reason and the Rationalisation of Society* (Cambridge: Polity Press).

(1987 [1987]), *The Theory of Communicative Action Vol. 2: The Critique of Functionalist Reason* (Cambridge: Polity).

Harding, Sandra (1986), *The Science Question in Feminism* (Milton Keynes: Open University Press).

(1991), *Whose Science? Whose Knowledge?* (Milton Keynes: Open University Press).

Harding, Sandra (ed.) (1987), *Feminism and Methodology* (Milton Keynes: Open University Press).

Hartsock, Nancy (1983), 'Feminist Standpoint: Developing the Ground for a Specifically Feminist Historical Materialism', in Sandra Harding and Merrill Hintikka (eds.), *Discovering Reality: Feminist Perspectives on Epistemology, Metaphysics, Methodology and Philosophy of Science* (Dordrecht, Holland: Reidel), pp. 283–310.

Heidegger, Martin (1962), *Being And Time* (Oxford: Blackwell).

Hempel, Carl (1966), *Philosophy of Natural Science* (Englewood Cliffs, NJ: Prentice-Hall).

(1974), 'Reasons and Covering Laws in Historical Explanation', in Patrick Gardiner (ed.), *The Philosophy of History* (Oxford: Oxford University Press), pp. 90–105.

Hermann, Charles, Kegley, Charles and Rosenau, James (eds.) (1987), *New Directions in the Study of Foreign Policy* (London: Allen & Unwin).

Hoffman, Mark (1987), 'Critical Theory, and the Inter-Paradigm Debate', *Millennium: Journal of International Studies,* 16 (2), pp. 231–49.

Hollis, Martin (1994), *The Philosophy of Social Science: An Introduction* (Cambridge: Cambridge University Press).

Hollis, Martin and Smith, Steve (1990), *Explaining and Understanding International Relations* (Oxford: Clarendon Press).

(1991), 'Beware of Gurus: Structure and Action in International Relations', *Review of International Studies,* 17 (4), pp. 394–410.

(1992), 'Structure and Action: Further Comment', *Review of International Studies,* 18 (2), pp. 187–8.

(1994), 'Two Stories About Structure and Agency', *Review of International Studies,* 20 (3), pp. 241–51.

(forthcoming, 1996), 'Why Epistemology Matters in International Theory', *Review of International Studies,* 22 (1).

Holsti, Kal (1989), 'Mirror, Mirror on the Wall Which are the Fairest Theories of All?', *International Studies Quarterly,* 33 (3), pp. 255–61.

(1993), 'International Relations at the End of the Millennium', *Review of International Studies,* 19 (4), pp. 401–8.

Hoole, Francis and Zinnes, Dina (eds.) (1976), *Quantitative International Politics: An Appraisal* (New York: Praeger).

Jones, Roy (1994), 'The Responsibility to Educate', *Review of International Studies,* 20 (3), pp. 299–311.

Kegley, Charles (1980), *The Comparative Study of Foreign Policy: Paradigm Lost?* (Columbia, SC: University of South Carolina).

Keohane, Robert (1989), *International Institutions and State Power: Essays in International Relations Theory* (Boulder, CO: Westview).

(1991), 'International Relations Theory: Contributions of a Feminist Standpoint', in Rebecca Grant and Kathleen Newland (eds.), *Gender and International Relations* (Milton Keynes: Open University Press), pp. 41–50.

King, Gary, Keohane, Robert and Verba, Sidney (1994), *Designing Social Enquiry: Scientific Inference in Qualitative Research* (Princeton, NJ: Princeton University Press).

Knorr, Klaus and Rosenau, James (eds.) (1969), *Contending Approaches to International Politics* (Princeton, NJ: Princeton University Press).

Kolakowski, Leszek (1972), *Positivist Philosophy* (Harmondsworth: Penguin Books).

Kuhn, Thomas (1970), *The Structure of Scientific Revolutions,* 2nd edition (Chicago: University of Chicago Press).

Lapid, Yosef (1989), 'The Third Debate: On the Prospects of International Theory in a Post-Positivist Era', *International Studies Quarterly*, 33 (3), pp. 235–54.

Linklater, Andrew (1990), *Beyond Realism and Marxism: Critical Theory and International Relations* (Basingstoke: Macmillan).

— (1992), 'The Question of the Next Stage in International Relations Theory: A Critical-Theoretical Point of View', *Millennium: Journal of International Studies*, 21 (1), pp. 77–98.

Lloyd, Christopher (1993), *The Structures of History* (Oxford: Blackwell).

Mearsheimer, John (1995), 'The False Promise of International Institutions', *International Security*, 19 (3), pp. 5–49.

Outhwaite, William (1987), *New Philosophies of Social Science: Realism, Hermeneutics and Critical Theory* (Basingstoke: Macmillan).

— (1994), *Habermas: A Critical Introduction* (Cambridge: Polity).

Quine, W. V. O. (1961), 'Two Dogmas of Empiricism', in his *From a Logical Point of View*, 2nd edition (Cambridge, MA: Harvard University Press), pp. 20–46.

Reynolds, Charles (1973), *Theory and Explanation in International Politics* (Oxford: Martin Robertson).

— (1992), *The World of States: An Introduction to Explanation and Theory* (Aldershot: Edward Elgar Publishing).

Rorty, Richard (1980), *Philosophy and the Mirror of Nature* (Oxford: Blackwell).

— (1989), *Contingency, Irony, and Solidarity* (Cambridge: Cambridge University Press).

— (1991), *Objectivity, Relativism and Truth: Philosophical Papers, Vol. 1* (Cambridge: Cambridge University Press).

— (1993), 'Human Rights, Rationality, and Sentimentality', in Stephen Shute and Susan Hurley (eds.), *On Human Rights: The Oxford Amnesty Lectures 1993* (New York: Basic Books), pp. 111–34.

Rosenau, James (1976), 'Puzzlement in Foreign Policy', *Jerusalem Journal of International Relations*, 1 (1), pp. 1–10.

Russett, Bruce (1969), 'The Young Science of International Politics', *World Politics*, 22 (1), pp. 87–94.

Sayer, Andrew (1992), *Method in Social Science: A Realist Approach*, 2nd edition (London: Routledge).

Smith, Steve (1986), 'Theories of Foreign Policy: An Historical Overview', *Review of International Studies*, 12 (1), pp. 13–29.

— (1994a), 'Rearranging the Deckchairs on the Ship Called Modernity: Rosenberg, Epistemology and Emancipation', *Millennium: Journal of International Studies*, 23 (2), pp. 395–405.

— (1994b), 'Foreign Policy Theory and the New Europe', in Walter Carlsnaes and Steve Smith (eds.), *European Foreign Policy: The EC and Changing Perspectives in Europe* (London: Sage Publications), pp. 1–20.

— (1995), 'The Self-Images of a Discipline: A Genealogy of International Relations Theory', in Ken Booth and Steve Smith (eds.), *International Relations Theory Today* (Cambridge: Polity), pp. 1–37.

Stanley, Liz and Wise, Sue (1993), *Breaking Out Again: Feminist Ontology and Epistemology* (London: Routledge).

Sylvester, Christine (1994), *Feminist Theory and International Relations in a Postmodern Era* (Cambridge: Cambridge University Press).

Tickner, J. Ann (1992), *Gender in International Relations: Feminist Perspectives on Achieving Global Security* (New York: Columbia University Press).

Tully, James (ed.) (1988), *Meaning and Context: Quentin Skinner and his Critics* (Cambridge: Polity Press).

Vasquez, John (1995), 'The Post-Positivist Debate: Reconstructing Scientific Enquiry and International Relations Theory After Enlightenment's Fall', in Ken Booth and Steven Smith (eds.), *International Relations Theory Today* (Cambridge: Polity), pp. 217–40.

Walker, Rob (1993), *Inside/Outside: International Relations as Political Theory* (Cambridge: Cambridge University Press).

Waltz, Kenneth (1986), 'Reflections on Theory of International Politics: A Response to My Critics', in Robert Keohane (ed.), *Neorealism and its Critics* (New York: Columbia University Press), pp. 322–45.

Wendt, Alexander (1987), 'The Agent–Structure Problem in International Relations Theory', *International Organization*, 41 (3), pp. 335–70.

— (1992), 'Anarchy is What States Make of It: A Social Construction of Power Politics', *International Organization*, 46 (2), pp. 391–425.

Wiggershaus, Rolf (1994), *The Frankfurt School* (Cambridge: Polity).

Young, Oran (1969), 'Professor Russett: Industrious Tailor to a Naked Emperor', *World Politics*, 21 (3), pp. 586–611.

Zalewski, Marysia (1993), 'Feminist Standpoint Theory Meets International Relations Theory: A Feminist Version of David and Goliath?', *The Fletcher Forum of World Affairs*, 17 (2), pp. 13–32.

2 Realism: The State, Power, and the Balance of Power

MAJOR ACTORS AND ASSUMPTIONS: A SUMMARY

In the previous chapter, we stated that realism is an image of international relations that is based on four assumptions. Scholars or policymakers who identify themselves as realists, however, do not all perfectly match the realism ideal type. We find, however, that the four assumptions identified with this perspective are useful as a general statement of the main lines of realist thought and the basis on which hypotheses and theories are developed.

To recapitulate, for the realist, *states are the principal actors,* and the study of international relations focuses on these units. Nonstate actors, such as multinational corporations and other **transnational** organizations are decidedly less important. International organizations, such as the United Nations or NATO (the North Atlantic Treaty Organization), do not have independent standing because they are composed of sovereign, independent, or autonomous states that determine what these international organizations will do. In short, for the realist, the focus is on states and interstate (or international) relations.

What, then, is the nature of this actor that is at the core of international relations? For purposes of analysis, the realist views the state as both *unitary* and *rational*. The state is said to be unitary because any differences of view among political leaders or bureaucracies within the state are ultimately resolved so that the state speaks with one voice. If there are exceptions in practice (as when one agency of government adopts a foreign policy line different from that of another agency of the same government), these cases either deal with trivial issues or are corrected in due course by the leadership. In any event, exceptions are precisely that—exceptions or marginal cases that in effect demonstrate the general rule that unitary states are the principal actors in world politics.

Realists also assume that states are rational actors. Given particular goals, states consider feasible alternatives to achieve these goals in light of their existing capabilities. Realists recognize problems of lack of information, uncertainty, bias, and misperception, but it is assumed by realists that decisionmakers strive to achieve the best possible decision even with these constraints.

One may well ask if this characterization of the formulation of foreign policy is accurate. Could one not just as easily argue that history is better characterized as a "march of folly"?[1] Was it wise, for example, for Germany to invade Poland in 1939? Was it in Japan's interest to attack Pearl Harbor in 1941? Was the American conduct of the Vietnam war an example of rationality at work?

From the standpoint of **methodology,** the image of a unified, rational state is a realist *assumption,* not a description of the actual world. Assumptions, it is sometimes argued, should be viewed not in terms of descriptive accuracy but, rather, in terms of how fruitful they are in generating insights and valid generalizations about international politics. From this point of view, assumptions are neither true nor false; they are more or less useful in helping the theorist derive testable propositions or hypotheses about international relations. Once hypotheses are developed, they are tested against the real world. The image of the unified, rational state is, therefore, the starting point for realist analysis, not a concluding statement. Hans J. Morgenthau has explained the utility of the rational, unitary actor assumption as follows:

> We put ourselves in the position of a statesman who must meet a certain problem of foreign policy under certain circumstances, and we ask ourselves what the rational alternatives are from which a statesman may choose . . . and which of these rational alternatives this particular statesman, acting under these circumstances, is likely to choose. It is the testing of this rational hypothesis against the actual facts and their consequences that gives meaning to the facts of international politics and makes a theory of politics possible.[2]

Game theory involves the use of such simplifying assumptions as an aid to developing hypotheses and theories about the causes of various international political phenomena, including war, arms races, the formation and maintenance of international organizations, and so on. Many works on **deterrence** also use the rational, unitary actor assumptions.[3] Rationalist explanations of international conflict are widespread. The dominant theoretical approach in contemporary international relations theorizing, **neorealism,** depends on rationalist assumptions. The same is true of the **expected utility model** of international politics, whose starting point is that war may occur when two states each estimate that the expected benefits of using force outweigh the expected costs. In other words, war can be rational if both sides have positive expected utilities for fighting—the expected utility of war (expected benefits minus costs) is greater than the expected utility of remaining at peace.

Finally, realists typically assume that among the array of world issues, *national security* tops the list for states. Military and political issues dominate the agenda and are referred to as high politics. States act to maximize what is often called the **national interest,** which at times may require the use of **force.** Put another way, states try to maximize the likelihood that they will achieve whatever objectives they have set. These objectives include high-political concerns of assuring state survival—security matters— as well as the more mundane or low-political objectives in such fields as trade, finance, monetary exchange, and health. States use the power they have to serve their interests or achieve their objectives. To most realists, the struggle for (or use of) power among states is at the core of international relations. In the words of Morgenthau: "International politics, like all politics, is a struggle for power. Whatever the ultimate aims of international politics, power is always the immediate aim."[4]

As an image of politics, therefore, realism is concerned with power and power politics among states. Differences exist, of course, among realists. Neorealists such as Kenneth Waltz, John Mearsheimer, and Christopher Layne emphasize the overall distribution of power among states and are highly skeptical of the extent to which international norms and international institutions can ameliorate competition among states.[5] Traditional realists such as Morgenthau, E. H. Carr, and Arnold Wolfers and their present-day followers, however, have had a more inclusive approach. While recognizing the importance of balance of power, they also have argued for the serious consideration of how norms and institutions influence international relations and whether the state is revisionist or status quo oriented. Hence, as with other images discussed in this book, an adherence to basic realist assumptions can still result in different interpretations and readings based on these assumptions.

Where did these assumptions of contemporary realist thought come from? They obviously did not appear out of thin air following World War II. Rather, they represent the culmination of thinking about international relations over the centuries. We now turn to some of the more notable intellectual precursors who have had a significant impact on the writings of contemporary realists.

INTELLECTUAL PRECURSORS AND INFLUENCES

Thucydides

Thucydides (471–400 B.C.) is usually credited with being the first writer in the realist tradition as well as the founding father of the international relations discipline.[6] Anyone who has taken a class in political philosophy would probably agree that the profound insights of many ancient Greek writers are not easily grasped on first reading. One might initially find this less a problem with Thucydides' *The Peloponnesian War* because this famous work chronicles twenty-one of the twenty-eight years of war between Athens and Sparta (and their respective allies) in the fifth century B.C. Taken simply as history, it is a masterful account of this era, filled with tales of heroism and brutality, victory and defeat, brilliance and stupidity, honor and deceit. These human traits are certainly exhibited not only in one particular war but in all wars throughout the ages. This is what makes *The Peloponnesian War* such a classic.

The task Thucydides set for himself, however, was much more ambitious than simply describing what was occurring. Particular events were dealt with in great and vivid detail, but his goal was to say something significant not only about the events of his own time, but also about the nature of war and why it continually recurs. For Thucydides, the past was the guide for the future. He was less interested in the immediate causes of the Peloponnesian War than he was in the underlying forces at work. Leaders might point to a particular event to justify a policy, but for Thucydides, this simply obscured more profound factors that operate throughout history. At heart, *The Peloponnesian War* is a study of the struggle for military and political power.

Thucydides was younger than Socrates and Sophocles and older than Aristophanes. In 424 B.C., during the eighth year of the Peloponnesian War, he was elected an Athenian general. While stationed in Thrace, he failed to prevent the Spartan capture of a city and was punished with twenty years of exile. Athens might have lost a general, but the world gained a historian.

As a member of one of the more notable Athenian families, Thucydides spent the rest of the war observing events, traveling, and interviewing participants. As an exile, he was detached from, yet obsessed with politics. Although concerned with accuracy, he gave precedence to understanding the motives and policies of the leaders on all sides of the conflict and used the technique of liberally reconstructing speeches and episodes. His purpose was to draw historical lessons for future statesmen who might read his work.[7] By analyzing the particular, he hoped to illuminate the general.

Why did war break out between Athens and Sparta? Thucydides states:

> I propose first to give an account of the causes of complaint which they had against each other and of the specific instances where their interests clashed [i.e., the immediate causes of the war]: this is in order that there should be no doubt in anyone's mind about what led to this great war falling upon the Hellenes. But the real reason for the war is, in my opinion, most likely to be disguised by such argument. What made war inevitable was the growth of Athenian power and the fear which this caused in Sparta [i.e., this was the underlying cause of the war].[8]

Thus, according to Thucydides, the real or underlying cause of the war was *fear* associated with a shift in the balance of power. Sparta was afraid of losing its preeminent role in the Hellenic world and therefore took countermeasures to build up its military strength and enlist the support of allies. Athens responded in kind. In the ensuing analysis, the situations, events, and policies Thucydides described lend themselves to comparison with such familiar notions as arms races, deterrence, balance of power, alliances, diplomacy, strategy, concern for honor, and perceptions of strengths and weaknesses.

Thucydides' emphasis on fear as a cause of the Peloponnesian War, fear that resulted from the increase in Athenian power relative to that of Sparta, is echoed throughout history. As statesmen perceive the balance of power to be shifting in their disfavor, they make efforts to rectify the situation that in turn causes fear, suspicion, and distrust on the part of their rivals. One could quite easily substitute for Athens and Sparta other historical examples such as France and Britain in the seventeenth and eighteenth centuries, Napoleonic France and the rest of Europe in the early nineteenth century, Germany and Britain after the Franco-Prussian War of 1870, and the Soviet Union and the United States in the four decades following World War II. In all such historical examples, a good case can be made that fear is a dominant characteristic and a motivating factor for arms races and war itself.

One reason Thucydides is deemed a scholar of international relations, however, is that the cause of fear he identifies is not so much innate or basic human nature as it is the nature of interstate politics. In a world in which no superordinate or central authority exists to impose order on all states—whether ancient city-states or modern states often encompassing large expanses of territory—"the strong do what they have the power to do and the weak accept what they have to accept."[9] Although fear may lead to war, power and capabilities relative to that of others determine the outcome.

Thucydides is sometimes unfairly criticized as an advocate of harsh and brutal wartime policies, one who rationalized such events as he described in the famous Melian dialogue. Thucydides, however, favored the democracy of the Golden Age of Pericles. In fact, the second half of *The Peloponnesian War* is a description of the degeneration of Athenian democracy and the resulting fanaticism that turned the war from a defensive effort to a war of conquest. The Melian dialogue reflects the latter phase of the war and should not be viewed as a personal preference on the part of Thucydides.

Machiavelli

By his own admission, the Italian political philosopher Niccolò Machiavelli (1469–1527) drew heavily from his study of ancient, especially Roman writings. In some respects, the situation in sixteenth-century Italy, divided as the peninsula was into separate city-states, was similar to the Hellenic world of Thucydides. Machiavelli worked as a civil servant and diplomat until the Republic of Florence fell in 1512. During his enforced idleness, he put his time to good use by reflecting on the chaos and political instability of Italy.

Like Thucydides, Machiavelli wrote of power, balance of power, formation of alliances and counteralliances, and the causes of conflict between different city-states. His primary focus, however, was on what present-day writers refer to as national security. For Machiavelli, survival of the state (identified with the ruling prince) was paramount. The prince could lose his state by not coping effectively with both internal and external threats to his rule. The German term **Realpolitik,** so central to realist thought, refers to power and power politics among states. Machiavelli's most famous work, *The Prince,* is a practical manual on how to gain, maintain, and expand power.[10] It is dedicated to the ruler of Florence at that time, Lorenzo di Medici.

One of the more controversial parts of Machiavelli's thesis is the notion that the security of the state is so important that it may justify certain acts by the prince that would be forbidden to other individuals not burdened by the princely responsibility of assuring that security. The end—security of the state—is understood to justify any means necessary to achieve that end. **Machiavellianism** (or **Machiavellism**) has been condemned by many who consider such a view to be immoral. Others have argued, however, that the actions of statesmen do (and should) follow a code of conduct different from that of the average citizen. Thus, it has been observed that there are two separate and distinct ethics: first, conventional religious morality concerned with such matters as individual salvation (the ethics of ultimate ends) and, second, by contrast, the moral obligations of rulers who must take actions to provide for national security (the ethics of responsibility).[11] Following this interpretation, one can understand Machiavelli's view that rulers should be good if they can (good in the conventional sense) but be willing to practice evil *if necessary* (consistent with their obligations as rulers).

Another point of view is that Machiavelli wrote of the world as it *is,* not the world as it *should* or *ought* to be. Ethics and politics are divorced from each other. His advice to the prince, following this interpretation, was based on an analysis of history, and of what actually occurs in the political realm, not on abstract ethical principles:

> Many have imagined republics and principalities which have never been seen or known to exist in reality; for how we live is so far removed from how we ought to live, that he who abandons what is done for what ought to be done, will rather learn to bring about his own ruin than his preservation. A man who wishes to make a profession of goodness in everything must necessarily come to grief among so many who are not good.[12]

This is not so much an endorsement of human behavior in politics as it is a statement of what he understands it actually to be. The realism in Machiavelli is a focus on what *is* rather than on what *ought to be.* For Machiavelli, in an amoral (if not immoral) world, what meaning, after all, does the preaching of conventional morality have? Indeed, an extreme statement of realist thinking is that considerations of power and power politics are the *only* relevant factors.

In the modern world, a convenient way to discredit an opponent is to accuse him or her of being Machiavellian. Nevertheless, it must be emphasized that Machiavelli did not encourage rulers to use violence for its own sake. In numerous passages, he advises the prince not to be needlessly cruel because this may eventually undermine his rule.[13] The yardstick one should use is how a particular policy contributes to the security and stability of the state.

Hobbes

The political philosophy of the Englishman Thomas Hobbes (1588–1679) was developed during the first fifty, turbulent years of the seventeenth century. After attending university in Oxford, Hobbes became a tutor to the son of a nobleman, and throughout his life, he remained associated with the family. A Royalist, Hobbes left for France in 1641 at a time when Parliament was asserting its power against the monarchy. For three years, he tutored the son of Charles I, the latter eventually being executed in 1649 during the English civil war. Hobbes returned to England in 1652, pledging loyalty to the republican regime.

Hobbes's famous work *Leviathan,* which was the first general theory of politics in English, was published that same year.[14] Like Machiavelli, Hobbes had a pessimistic view of human nature. His primary focus was domestic politics, and his goal was to make the strongest case possible for the necessity of a powerful, centralized political authority. To illustrate his philosophical points, Hobbes posited that prior to the creation of society, human beings lived in a "state of nature"—a condition of war of "every one against every one." There was "a continual fear and danger of violent death; and the life of man, solitary, poor, nasty, brutish, and short."[15]

Hobbes did not argue that such a state of nature had ever really existed. To him, the state of nature was the result of a thought experiment—imagining what the world would be like without governmental authority or any other social structure. Accordingly, he was interested in showing how people could escape from this hypothetical situation by agreeing to place all power in the hands of a sovereign or Leviathan (a state authority, or supreme ruler) that would maintain order and end the anarchy of the state of nature. If governmental authority did not already exist, it would have to be created. In his words: "There must be some coercive power to compel men equally to the performance of their covenants, by the terror of some punishment, greater than the benefit they expect by the breach of their covenant."[16] Without order, he argued, civilization and all its benefits are impossible—no economic development, art, knowledge, or anything else of value.

Hobbes's impact on the realist view of international relations stems from this image of individuals in a mythical state of nature. His description is equally applicable to relations among states because in the state of nature as well as in international politics, there is no Leviathan or superordinate power to impose order. It is a condition of **anarchy**—the absence of central or superordinate authority over states that claim individually to be **sovereign** with a *right* to be independent or autonomous with respect to one another. In Hobbes's words:

> In all times, kings, and persons of sovereign authority, because of their independency, are in continual jealousies, and in the state and posture of gladiators; having their weapons pointing, and their eyes fixed on one another; that is, their forts, garrisons, and guns upon the frontiers of their kingdoms; and continual spies upon their neighbours; which is a posture of war.[17]

As anarchy prevails in the state of nature, so too is anarchy a dominant characteristic of international politics. Without a Leviathan (or, in the language of contemporary international relations literature, a **hegemonic** power or world state), suspicion, distrust, conflict, and war are seemingly inevitable. In the absence of any **social contract** among (or authority over) them, there are no moral obligations to govern the relations of states.

Grotius

Hugo Grotius (1583–1645), a Dutch contemporary of Thomas Hobbes, offered a different view of international relations from that associated with Hobbes and Machiavelli. Grotius dealt with the essential anarchy of international relations by calling for the establishment (or acknowledging the existence) of laws or rules accepted by states as binding. That the relations of states *ought* to conform to such rules is a central tenet of the Grotian tradition in international relations. To Grotians, values or norms, particularly when recognized as international law, are important in maintaining order among states.

Grotius dealt with the problems of international relations (including commercial transactions) from a very practical point of view. Given the importance of trade to his native Holland as a seafaring nation, he addressed this subject in his *Law of Prize and Booty* (1604–1605) and questions of freedom of navigation and territorial seas in his *Freedom of the Seas* (1609). Probably his most important work was his *Law of War and Peace* (1625), three volumes that dealt with war and questions of national security—central themes in much realist writing then and now.

What are the sources of international law? Grotius looked to the use of reason and the "natural law" for general principles. He also looked to customary practice and to rules agreed on by governments that would be binding on states. Such treaties or formal covenants would be binding (in Latin, *pacta sunt servanda*) in the sense that states are obligated to follow them even in the absence of central authority to enforce their adherence. Changing circumstances might lead to the alteration of rules, but the important point is that to Grotians, order in international relations and matters of war and peace involve both power *and* values. In this regard, some contemporary realists owe as much to Grotius and the Grotian tradition as they do to Thucydides, Machiavelli, and Hobbes.[18] Similarly, the Grotian emphasis on norms and laws leads pluralists to claim him as one of their own as does the *English school* of theory.

Clausewitz

Carl von Clausewitz (1780–1831), a Prussian officer who rose to the rank of general and who served in the Napoleonic wars, thought the military element of a state's power to be extremely important but subordinate always to the political. Consistent with the writings of Machiavelli on war, Clausewitz argued in an oft-quoted phrase that war is "a continuation of political activity by other means."[19]

Much of Clausewitz's writing took place in the interwar period between the defeat of Napoleon in 1815 and Clausewitz's recall to duty in 1830 for service in East Prussia. Clausewitz died in 1831, never having completed his magnum opus, *On War*. His legacy, nevertheless, remains a central contribution to the realist school. Clausewitz identified the uncertainty that attends decisionmaking in battlefield conditions—the "fog of war." He was also well aware that rationally made plans often run into obstacles or "friction" when actually implemented. These are the kinds of observations one readily finds in present-day strategic literature in the realist genre that owes much to Clausewitz. As significant as his view that the military is properly a political means was his exposition of societal (including social and economic) dimensions of national capabilities. At the same time, his focus on national security problems places him in the mainstream of realist thought.

Carr

Many students of international relations consider Edward Hallett Carr's *The Twenty Years' Crisis, 1919–1939* already a classic. Although Carr can be viewed as an intellectual precursor for realists and a forerunner of the present-day **English school,** his work transcends narrow classification in that he has also been influential, as has Grotius, on the thinking of certain authors whom we would label pluralist.

The writings of Thucydides, Machiavelli, Hobbes, Grotius, and Clausewitz illustrate how great works are often written during the most difficult times. *The Twenty Years' Crisis* is no exception in that it was completed in the summer of 1939 with the shadow of war looming over Europe. As with other authors we have discussed, Carr was less interested in apportioning blame to particular leaders for the imminent onset of World War II than he was in attempting "to analyse the underlying and significant, rather than the immediate and personal, causes of the disaster."[20] Unless this were done, he argued, we would fail to understand how war could break out twenty short years after the signing of the Versailles Treaty in 1919. He dedicated his book "to the makers of the coming peace."

In attempting to understand "the more profound causes of the contemporary international crisis," echoes of Thucydides can be discerned. Carr, for example, placed a great deal of emphasis on the role of fear in explaining World War I.[21] Similarly, he also argued (and quoted Machiavelli and Hobbes to this effect) that "the exercise of power always appears to beget the appetite for more power. . . . Wars, begun for motives of security, quickly become wars of aggression and self-seeking."[22] Just as Thucydides saw Athens at the outset of the Peloponnesian War claim "self-defense" and then turn into a more ambitious, aggressive power, so too Carr noted that during the course of World War I

> nearly every country participating . . . regarded it initially as a war of self-defense; and this belief was particularly strong on the Allied side. Yet during the course of the war, every Allied government in Europe announced war aims which included the acquisition of territory from the enemy powers. In modern conditions, wars of limited objective have become almost as impossible as wars of limited liability.[23]

Throughout *The Twenty Years' Crisis,* Carr refers to the impact of Machiavelli and Hobbes on realist thinking. Although his work is best known as a critique of **utopian** or **idealist** thought, Carr also evaluates the more extreme versions of realism that posit the divorce of morality from politics in international relations. He argues that

> any sound political thought must be based on elements of both utopia [i.e., values] and reality [i.e., power]. Where utopianism has become a hollow and intolerable sham, which serves merely as a disguise for the interests of the privileged, the realist performs an indispensable service in unmasking it. But pure realism can offer nothing but a naked struggle for power which makes any kind of international society impossible.[24]

Hence, for Carr, politics is made up of two elements, inextricably intertwined: utopia and reality, values and power.

More than a third of the book is devoted to such Grotian topics as the role of morality in international relations, the foundations of law, the sanctity of treaties, the judicial settlement of international disputes, peaceful change, and the prospects for a new international order. Because Carr critically estimated the strengths and weaknesses of utopianism as well as realism, he can be viewed as an important influence on many contemporary international relations theorists, both realists and nonrealists.

Others in the **English school,** which relies on more traditional insights drawn from history, philosophy, and law, include such luminaries as the late Martin Wight and his follower, Hedley Bull. International relations occur in an anarchical *society* of sovereign states. Order in this anarchical society doesn't just occur on its own. Statesmen create balances of power, establish rules of customary behavior out of enlightened self-interest, or subscribe to universal norms based on common moral understandings. Concerning power and balance of power, one turns to Machiavelli or Hobbes; for the regulation offered by international law or other rules as in international regimes, one sees the philosophical and historical influence of Grotius and Grotian thought; and in the quest for universals as normative bases of state behavior in global society, one invokes the aspirations of Kant and other moral philosophers. That ideas and values or norms play a part in international relations alongside interest and power considerations constitutes a blend, but also a tension between *realist* and *idealist* understandings.

This brief overview of the intellectual precursors of realism illustrates a distinct realist preoccupation with war. A concern with the causes and consequences of conflict helps to explain why the realist perspective is held by statesmen throughout the world; over the centuries leaders have engaged in the very battles and struggles described by authors from Thucydides to Carr. Realism, from the statesman's point of view, is indeed realistic because it tends to correspond to personal experiences.

Among realists, there are two basic concepts that traditionally have been the foci of analysis at the state and international levels: **power** and **system.** In the following pages, we discuss how realists have attempted to define these terms. We then give examples of how theorists have used these concepts in generating insights and explanations of the causes of war. This is followed by a discussion of how realists deal with the concepts of **interdependence** and *change*. We conclude with a critique of the realist image of international relations.

POWER

Definitions

In discussing several of the more important intellectual precursors of realism, the concept of power was mentioned time and again. Any attempt to give the reader a more complete understanding of the realist image of international relations starts with a discussion of this crucial term. Power is the core concept for realists.

Having said this, it is rather ironic that even among realists, there is no clear consensus on how to define the term *power*. Some realists understand power to be the sum of military, economic, technological, diplomatic, and other *capabilities* at the disposal of the state. Others see power not as some absolute value determined for each state as if it were in a vacuum but, rather, as capabilities *relative* to the capabilities of other states. Thus, the power of the United States is evaluated in terms of its capabilities relative to the capabilities of other states.

Both of these definitions—whether treating capabilities of a state in isolation or relative to the capabilities of other states—assume a *static* view of power. Power is an attribute of the state that is the sum of its capabilities whether considered alone or relative to other states. An alternative, *dynamic* definition of power focuses on the interactions of states. A state's influence (or capacity to influence or coerce) is not only determined by its capabilities (or relative capabilities) but also by (1) its willingness (and perceptions by other states of its willingness) to use these capabilities and (2) its control or influence over other states. Power can thus be inferred by observing the behavior of states as they interact. The relative power of states is most clearly revealed by the *outcomes* of their interactions.

Examples of diverse views of power are the following definitions drawn from the literature: power as the capacity of an individual, group, or nation "to influence the behavior of others in accordance with one's own ends," power as "man's control over the minds and actions of other men," and power as "the ability to prevail in conflict and overcome obstacles."[25]

Measurement

Given these definitional and conceptual disputes, it follows that attempts to measure power will also be divergent. If one understands power as being equivalent to capabilities, one looks for some way to measure military, economic, and other component elements. If one views power as actual control or influence, some measurement of capabilities may still be a useful "first cut" if one is engaged in predicting the outcome of interactions between or among states.

Even if one assumes that it is possible to measure these capabilities adequately through such indicators as defense expenditures or gross national product, the further problems of weighting and aggregating or adding up such diverse capabilities into a common measure of power remains. How should one weight different component capabilities? Which, for example, is the more important—military or economic capabilities—and how much more important? How does one measure geographic, technological, or diplomatic factors with any degree of precision? What about the unity and strength of a society, which one scholar claims is the "forgotten dimension of strategy"?[26] And, if capabilities are difficult to measure, are not *relative* capabilities between and among states even more difficult to specify?

Scholars who focus on power in the international system are well aware of these difficulties. Nevertheless, in order to use power as an analytical concept, certain measurements have been suggested. A. F. K. Organski, for example, has argued that gross national product, or national income, is perhaps the best yardstick of national capability. J. David Singer and his associates emphasize military, industrial, and demographic capacities as the critical variables required to indicate overall national capabilities.[27]

We must remember that the purpose in devising such formulas is not trivial. Measuring the power or capabilities of states is a critical step in attempts to explain the behavior of states and the functioning of the international system with regard to matters of war and peace. Such concerns are evident in the Correlates of War project headed by Singer, in which state power is a key variable. Similarly, Bruce Bueno de Mesquita uses Singer's national capabilities scores as key elements of his expected utility theory, which seeks to explain the causes and outcomes of wars. The theory logically assumes that decisionmakers attempt to calculate the power capabilities of a rival before initiating armed conflict. The probability of success is a function of each state's relative power adjusted for such factors as alliance commitments. Bueno de Mesquita found, for example, that between 1816 and 1974, states with a positive expected utility score who initiated a war won 83 percent of the conflicts.[28]

Some would say that the view of power as a unitary concept calculated by aggregating component capabilities or relative capabilities misses the key point, which is that the power of a state is dependent on the *issue* involved. Consider, for example, the argument that some states, such as Japan, have substantial economic power but are militarily weak. Hence, in a particular area, the Japanese are powerful. Opponents of this disaggregation of power into its component capabilities note that persuasive as it may be on the surface, it is misleading because it overlooks the relations among the various power components. Thus, the *economic* capabilities of Japan as a global trader are said to be related to its *military* ties with the United States that assure Japan's freedom to engage in commerce. From this perspective, whether addressing the power of Japan, Europe, or Third World countries, one cannot understand economic, military, political, or other component capabilities of power as if they were factors independent of one another. Much as military ties and divisions among states may define the framework within which economic relations take place, so military capabilities of states are bolstered (or weakened) by the strength or relative strength of their economies.

SYSTEM

In the preceding section, we discussed the concept of power and attempts to measure state power. Using that discussion as a basis, we now move on to a discussion of the concept of system.

When applied to international relations, the term *system* has currency within each of the three images we have identified—realism, pluralism, and globalism. As one might expect, however, there is considerable diversity among theorists on both the *definition* of the term and the *uses* to which it should be put in the construction of international relations theory.

Thus, for neorealists, the defining characteristic of a system is the various distributions of power or capabilities among states—unipolar, bipolar, multipolar. The polarity of the system is measured by the number of Great Powers, and polarity is a significant explanatory variable for neorealists. Others speak of international economic and social systems. Still others understand system to be the set of interactions among states and other nonstate actors, a behavioral definition.

However system may be defined, the uses to which the concept is put vary considerably. Some theorists are content to use systems as mere **taxonomies,** frameworks for organizing knowledge about international relations. Others are more ambitious. Beyond **heuristic** purposes—that is, contributing to common understanding of the subject—they may see utility in actually using the system concept to explain and predict outcomes of international relations.[29]

Some scholars view the concept of system as an abstraction. Systems are mental images that may help to describe, explain, or predict international phenomena. They are, in effect, superimposed on the real world by a scholar in order to make the real world more intelligible and easier to understand. Other theorists go beyond this and ascribe such properties to systems as **equilibrium,** or balance, of their component parts (such as among states). Critics, however, find little use in such notions as "equilibrating tendencies." Treating a system as if it were a concrete or tangible entity and ascribing properties to it is of questionable validity from this point of view. To do so, according to critics, is to be guilty of the methodological error of **reification**—treating abstractions as if they were real and had a life of their own.[30]

A response by some system theorists to this line of criticism is that dealing in abstractions is useful in the generation of propositions or **hypotheses** about international relations. These, in turn, can be tested **empirically** to determine whether or not they have factual support. To the extent, then, that use of the systems concept enables the theorist to describe, explain, or predict international phenomena, the use of the concept is justified.

The reader may or may not wish to visualize international relations or world politics as a system that is defined in terms of patterns of interactions, polarity, equilibrating tendencies, or some other characteristics. We do note, however, that the systems concept as an approximation to the nature of world politics is present within the mainstream of contemporary realist thought, even if some realists avoid its use.

Speaking of abstractions, this discussion has been rather abstract. To lend substance to the concept of system, we next examine two ways in which the concept of system has been used by realists: *system* as patterns of interactions, and *system* as anarchy plus the distribution of capabilities. In each case, the intention of scholars has been to explain some aspect of international relations concerning such matters as instability, conflict, and war. In each case, the state and state power have been a key focus of analysis and investigation.

System as Interactions

Traditional realists emphasize the relative distribution of capabilities between specific states or alliances and how shifts in these capabilities influence state behavior, interactions, and, hence, the probability of war. Scholars who have a behavioralist orientation emphasize system as interactions.

Two examples of viewing the international system as sets or patterns of interactions are to be found in the works of Rudolph J. Rummel and Charles A. McClelland, published in the 1960s and 1970s during the heyday of the behavioralist ascendance in international relations theorizing. In his Dimensionality of Nations (DON) Project, Rummel attempted to explain and predict the behavior of states. In doing so, he identified recurrent patterns of behavior by using **factor analysis,** a statistical tool designed to identify patterns of variation in the data being analyzed. In one study, ninety-four **variables** falling into such categories as military, international conflict, international collaboration, colonialism, communication, and international organization were selected for factor analysis. The analysis involved eighty-two countries. According to Rummel, tentative findings included first, that conflict is not a necessary consequence of a nation's increased involvement in foreign affairs (which would seem to be counterintuitive, or contrary to what one might expect); and second, that the genesis of foreign conflict behavior lies outside the state, not internal to it (one answer to the questions raised in the discussion of the problem of levels of analysis). Such conflict behavior "is a *relational* phenomenon depending on the degree of economic, social, and political similarity between nations, the geographic distance between them, and their power parity." This latter point—that conflict is primarily relational—is the basis for Rummel's extensive work in what is termed *field theory*.[31]

Charles McClelland focused on international transactions and interactions between states in his World Event/Interaction Survey (WEIS) project. The data base consisted of the actions and responses of states over a number of years as reported in the press. Events were coded and placed in specific categories. Quantitative analyses of the data were meant to reveal patterns of behavior between and among states, the basis for prediction. Although the major focus was on conflict behavior and periods of high tension (particularly international crises), the data were not limited to this type of state action. The underlying assumption was that the past behavior of a state is a source for the prediction of its current and future behavior. The major results of the WEIS project were reported in a number of articles.[32]

System as Anarchy and the Distribution of Capabilities

Many realist writers have emphasized anarchy and the distribution of capabilities, or power, among states as critical components of the international system. These so-called system-level, or **structural,** attributes are viewed as crucial because they act as constraints on decisionmakers. As we will see, the condition of international anarchy is seen by realists as contributing to the amount of distrust and conflict among states. Realists have also been concerned whether particular distributions of capabilities involving various balances of power make war between states more or less likely. We will first take up the concept of anarchy and related terms.

Anarchy.   The word *anarchy* brings forth images of violence, destruction, and chaos. For realists, however, anarchy simply refers to the absence of any authority above states. States are **sovereign.** They claim a right to be independent or autonomous from other states, and they claim a right to exercise complete authority over their own territories. Although states differ in terms of the power they possess or are able to exercise, none may claim the *right* to dominate another sovereign state.[33]

We wish to be clear on the term *anarchy* and the difference between **authority** and **power.** When we use the term *anarchy,* we are referring to the absence of any hierarchy of authority. There *is* hierarchy of power in international politics, but there is not a hierarchy of authority. Some states are clearly more powerful than others, but there is no recognized authority higher than that of any state.

Anarchy, so understood, is the defining characteristic of the environment within which sovereign states interact. Violence and war may be evident but so too are periods of relative peace and stability. This absence of any superordinate or central authority over states (such as a world government with authority to enforce rules and to maintain order) is fundamentally different from domestic societies, where an authority exists to maintain order and to act as an arbiter of disputes except in cases of total government collapse or in civil wars when legitimate authority may be unclear.[34]

Realists argue that the absence of a central and overriding authority helps to explain why states come to rely on power, seeking to maintain or increase their power positions relative to other states. For one thing, the condition of anarchy is usually accompanied by a lack of trust among states in this environment. Each state faces a **self-help** situation in which it is dangerous to place the security of one's own country in the hands of another. What guarantee is there against betrayal, however solemn another state's promises may be to an ally? Consistent with the world described by Hobbes, there is really nothing to keep a supposed ally from reneging on a security agreement or any other international pact. There is no world governmental authority to enforce covenants or agreements among states. In such a world, it is logical, rational, and prudent to look out for number one. Indeed, this was the same counsel reported by Thucydides when he noted Athenian advice to the Melians not to place their hope for survival in the hands of the Spartans and their allies.

Given international anarchy and the lack of trust in such a situation, states find themselves in what has been called a **security dilemma**.[35] The more one state arms to protect itself from other states, the more threatened these states become and the more prone they are to resort to arming themselves to protect their own national security interests. The dilemma is that even if a state is sincerely arming only for defensive purposes, it is rational in a self-help system to assume the worst in an adversary's intentions and keep pace in any arms buildup. How can one know for certain that a rival is arming strictly for defensive purposes? This is the stuff of arms races. Isn't it best to hedge one's bets by devoting more resources to match a potential adversary's arms buildup? Because a state may not have sufficient resources to be completely self-reliant, it may join an alliance in an attempt to deter aggression by any would-be adversaries.

Given an understanding of the anarchic condition of international politics, one can more easily grasp certain dynamics of arms races. All sides involved may sincerely desire peace, but the anarchical nature of international politics leads states to be suspicious of one another and engage in worst-case analyses of one another's intentions. This realist insight, it is argued, is just as applicable to understanding the ancient competition between Sparta and Athens as it is to understanding contemporary international relations. It is a system-level explanation in that the emphasis is placed on the anarchic structure of international politics as a whole, not on the *internal* nature of a particular state. An example of an explanation that relies on internal factors is the claim that a given country keeps building more and more weapons because of demands from its own military-industrial complex or because of the nature of a national mentality that reflects its regional or global ambitions. *External* factors such as the anarchic structure of the system or the actions and reactions of other states are ignored.

Even realists, however, disagree on how much weight to accord anarchy as a contributing factor to international conflict. So-called *defensive realists,* for example, while recognizing the importance of anarchy, caution that analysts should not overstate its importance. They argue that security is readily available, particularly if states adopt defensive strategies. The assumption is made that the international system provides incentives for cautious and restrained behavior on the part of states and that reckless, expansionist behavior is the result of domestic factors, not of systemic conditions such as anarchy.[36]

Finally, an anarchical, self-help system obviously makes cooperation among states difficult to achieve. How are states to act in such a world? Is it inevitable that they will be self-seeking, attempting to maximize their short-term individual or self-interests? Or is it possible that states can upgrade their common (perhaps enlightened) self-interests over both the short and long term? What is the rational thing to do? The informing image for some realists is provided by the allegory of the stag hunt, taken from the writings of the Geneva-born, eighteenth-century philosopher Jean Jacques Rousseau.[37]

Each of five individuals in the state of nature—a world without government or any other form of social structure—has to decide (1) whether to collaborate in the hunting of a stag necessary to meet the hunger needs of all five or (2) to defect from the group to capture a hare. To choose the latter course of action would be to serve one's own self-interest at the expense of the group (see Figure 2.1).

If the individual prefers to serve the common interest (go after the stag), can he or she trust the others to do so? And if one can't trust the others, is it not rational to go for the hare and defect from the group before any of the others do? Or is it possible to develop the basis for collaboration on a continuing basis by all five?[38] Scholars who deal with **game theory** attempt to answer such questions. Game theory is an approach to determining rational choice or optimum strategy under conditions of uncertainty. As such, game theory has direct relevance to the study of foreign policy choice and to much scholarly work on deterrence as a means of avoiding war.

How one understands Rousseau's stag hunt fable has a great deal to do with how one sees states interacting in world politics. Some tend to see the state as serving only narrow self-interest. Pessimists point to the number, duration, and intensity of wars. Those of a more optimistic bent note that in many cases states live in peace and harmony for years, and there is, indeed, great potential for collaboration among states.

For international relations theorists, however, it is not simply a matter of a pessimistic or optimistic nature. Aside from the assumptions that states are unitary and rational actors, neorealists also tend to make the analytical assumption that states are largely concerned with *relative* rather than just *absolute gains*. What is the difference? If

	Individual interests: pursue the hare	Group/collective interests: pursue the stag
Short run	Serve immediate self-interest	May provide basis for possible future collaboration
Long run	No apparent basis for collaborative behavior	Serve long-term common interest

FIGURE 2.1   The Stag Hunt Fable: A Dilemma of Rational Choice

a state is concerned with individual, absolute gains, it is indifferent to the gains of others—"As long as I'm doing better, I don't care if others are also increasing their wealth or military power." If, however, a state is concerned with relative gains, it is not satisfied with simply increasing its power or wealth but is concerned with how much those capabilities have kept pace with, or increased, relative to other states. Differing assumptions about a state's preferences lead to different expectations about the prospects for international conflict and cooperation. For neorealists, the relative gains assumption makes international cooperation in an anarchic world difficult to attain. More optimistic about the prospects for international cooperation, **neoliberal institutionalists** assume that states may well be satisfied with absolute gains.[39]

The Distribution of Capabilities: Balance of Power. Unless one state or some sort of superordinate international authority comes to dominate the world, anarchy will continue to be a defining characteristic of the international system. Within this anarchical environment, however, various distributions of capabilities or power among states are possible. Anarchy plus the distribution of capabilities among states define for many realists the international system at any one time.

As we have seen, many realists begin with the security dilemma in an anarchic world. Where does order come from under such conditions? What keeps states from continually attacking one another? One answer—associated with the thought of Hugo Grotius and the English school of international relations—is the development of international norms as codified in international law. Another answer offered by realists is that states find it expedient to band together and pool their capabilities whenever one state or group of states appears to be gathering a disproportionate amount of power, thus threatening to dominate the world, or even a portion of it.

This reasoning—the need to maintain a **balance of power** to avoid the triumph of a dominant power—is a realist concern dating back to the works of Thucydides. It is also found in a report of the British Foreign Office written before World War I:

> History shows that the danger threatening the independence of this or that nation has generally arisen, at least in part, out of the momentary predominance of a neighboring State at once militarily powerful, economically efficient, and ambitious to extend its frontiers or spread its influence. . . . The only check on the abuse of political predominance derived from such a position has always consisted in the opposition of an equally formidable rival, or a combination of several countries forming leagues of defense. The equilibrium established by such a grouping of forces is technically known as the balance of power, and it has become almost an historical truism to identify England's secular policy with the maintenance of this balance by throwing her weight now in this scale and now in that, but ever on the side opposed to the political dictatorship of the strongest single State or group at a given time.[40]

A **bipolar** balance of power (two states with relatively equal power) or a **multipolar** balance of power (three or more states engaging in checks and balances) are two realist categorizations of particular distributions of capabilities. Such power configurations have occurred in the aftermath of major European wars—the Peace of Westphalia in 1648 following the Thirty Years' War, the Congress of Vienna in 1815 following the defeat of Napoleon, and the settlements following both twentieth-century world wars. Although the post-World War I arrangements bought only twenty years of peace, the Congress of Vienna was more successful in establishing a basis for maintaining a balance of power without general or major war for almost a century. Assessing the efforts of the diplomats at Vienna and subsequent meetings, Henry Kissinger concluded: "Their goal was stability, not perfection, and the balance of power is the classic expression of the lesson of history that no order is safe without physical safeguards against aggression." In short, according to Kissinger, a "new international order came to be created with a sufficient awareness of the connection between power and morality; between security and legitimacy."[41]

Two questions are subject to debate among realist scholars: (1) Do balances of power automatically occur, or are they created by statesmen? and (2) Which balance of power—bipolar or multipolar—is more likely to maintain international stability?

As to the first question, Kissinger's view emphasizes **voluntarism**—the balance of power is a foreign policy creation or construction of statesmen; it doesn't just occur automatically. Makers of foreign policy do not act as automatons, prisoners of the balance of power and severely constrained by it. Rather, they are its creators and those charged with maintaining it. They are free to exercise their judgment and their will as agents for their states in the conduct of foreign policy with the expectation that they can have some constructive effect on outcomes.

In contrast to this voluntarist conception is that of Kenneth Waltz, who sees the balance of power as an attribute of the system of states that will occur whether it is willed or not.[42] Given the assumptions that the state is a rational and a unitary actor that will use its capabilities to accomplish its objectives, states inevitably interact and conflict in the competitive environment of international politics. The outcome of state actions and interactions is a tendency toward equilibrium, or balance of power. Balance of power from this point of view, then, is a systemic tendency that occurs whether or not states seek to establish such a balance. Indeed, states may be motivated to improve their own positions so as to dominate others, but such attempts will likely be countered by other states similarly motivated. Thus, a balance of power more often than not occurs as states tend to balance against a rising power as opposed to joining its bandwagon. Balance-of-power theory so viewed can be used to account for arms races, alliances and counteralliances, coalitions and countercoalitions, and other forms of competitive behavior among states.

This image of the balance of power, therefore, refers to a recurrent phenomenon characteristic of international relations. It seems to matter little whether the states are democratic or authoritarian; the systemic tendency toward balance, or equilibrium, is always the same. It is as if states were billiard balls colliding with one another.[43] The faster and larger balls (the major powers) knock the smaller balls (the lesser powers) out of the way, although their own paths may also be deflected slightly by these collisions. These interactions, it is argued, tend toward international equilibrium or stability just as billiard balls eventually come to rest, at least until the balance is upset once again. But then the same tendency toward equilibrium repeats itself, only to be upset again. And so forth. The actors involved in this timeless drama remain the same: states. Actor combinations involving two or more states can be observed as the mechanical workings of the balance of power: multipolar prior to World War II, bipolar (the United States and the Soviet Union) in the years following the war. Post-Cold War descriptions of polarity vary among realists with some focusing on American unipolarity. Others depict a multipolarity (or an emerging multipolarity), albeit one skewed asymmetrically or unevenly for the time being at least in favor of the United States.

Kenneth Waltz observes that in international relations, "the freedom of choice of any one state is limited by the actions of all the others." Moreover, he argues that "the balance of power is not so much imposed by statesmen on events as it is imposed by events on statesmen."[44] For Waltz, the statesman has much less freedom to maneuver, much less capability to affect the workings of international politics, than Kissinger would allow. In a sense, then, Kissinger and Waltz represent alternative ends of a spectrum of contemporary realists conversant with balance-of-power thinking. Realists such as Waltz who emphasize balance of power as a system tendency have been labelled as "structural realists" or "neorealists" because they have allegedly departed from a realist tradition that granted the statesman or policymaker greater freedom from constraint and thus greater ability to affect international events.[45]

Some critics of balance of power as a system tendency reject this mode of thinking precisely because of its mechanistic quality. One such critic, Ernst B. Haas, who finds little if any use in realist notions of balance of power, rejects "this formulation" because of its "system-dominant automaticity."[46] In other words, this mode of balance-of-power theory is too **deterministic;** individual policymakers can do little to affect events, much less have constructive impact on the system as a whole. Haas is even more explicit in later writings, criticizing determinists who

> see the components [of systems, i.e., states] as relatively unchangeable and arrange them in an eternal preprogrammed dance; the rules of the dance may be unknown to the actors and are specified by the theorist. The recurrent patterns discovered by him constitute a super-logic which predicts the future state of the system.[47]

The voluntarism-determinism debate is comparable in some ways to theological dispute over determinism and free will. As we use the term, *voluntarism* does not refer to freedom of choice only but to the ability of human beings to influence the course of events. How free are individuals to determine their own fates? How much effective choice do they have? How much are events *determined* by factors independent of human will exercised by statesmen? In the context of international relations, the question is whether states or their decisionmakers can affect their environment or whether their actions are severely constrained by other states interacting in a system of states. How much is free? How much is determined? Put another way, how much is the behavior of states and other units driven by the international system or its structure and how much is socially constructed by human volition—statesmen and diplomats, institutions and groups, and other human actors?

Kissinger's position is closer to the voluntarist pole, but he definitely would not argue that foreign policymakers are totally free of external constraints. Indeed, their ability to maneuver within these constraints is at least partly a function of their diplomatic skills. Similarly, Waltz would reject the idea that he is in any way a determinist. Nevertheless, his views are far removed from the purely voluntarist pole. The implication of his view of the balance of power is that individual decisionmakers and their states have much less freedom or capability to affect the course of events than others such as Kissinger would assert.

In some respects, the writings of Hans J. Morgenthau are an attempt to combine the two perspectives, thus inviting wrath by proponents of both. Morgenthau acknowledged the balance of power as a tendency within international politics while, at the same time, prescribing what statesmen should do to maintain the balance. He argued that "the balance of power and policies aiming at its preservation are not only inevitable but are an essential stabilizing factor in a society of sovereign nations."[48] Quite apart from the apparent determinism in this statement, Morgenthau assigned to diplomats not just the task of maintaining the balance of power; he also charged them to "create the conditions under which it will not be impossible from the outset to establish a world state."[49]

In short, for Morgenthau, escape from the balance of power and the voluntarist creation of a new world order remained possibilities worthy of pursuit. At the same time, his detractors have noted that, on the one hand, to argue that the balance of power is an inevitable system tendency and, on the other hand, to prescribe what should be done to maintain a balance or transform the system itself is to argue in contradictory terms. Be that as it may, Morgenthau's thinking represents a middle ground between realists who tend toward voluntarist or determinist poles. The present theoretical debate between structuralists and **social constructivists** is a more recent manifestation of this continuing controversy.

Balance of Power and System Stability

We conclude this discussion of the realist's use of the system concept with reference to a long-standing realist debate: Is a bipolar or a multipolar balance of power more conducive to the stability of the international system? Stated another way, is war more likely to occur in a bipolar or a multipolar world?

The best-known statements on this matter are by Kenneth Waltz on the one hand and J. David Singer and Karl Deutsch on the other.[50] All three have agreed that the amount of uncertainty about the consequences of a particular action taken by a decisionmaker increases as the number of international actors increases. The logic of this assumption is that as the number increases, a decisionmaker has to deal with a greater quantity of information; more international actors mean more information is generated that has to be taken into account in the formulation of foreign policy. Therefore, all three authors have agreed that as an international system moves from being bipolar to being multipolar, the amount of overall uncertainty in the system increases. So far, so good.

Where they part company is on the matter of whether an increase in the number of actors (and hence uncertainty) makes war more or less likely. Waltz argues that greater uncertainty makes it *more* likely that a decisionmaker will misjudge the intentions and actions of a potential foe. Hence, a multipolar system, given its association with higher levels of uncertainty, is less desirable than a bipolar system because multipolarity makes uncertainty and thus the probability of war greater. Singer and Deutsch, however, make the opposite argument. They believe a multipolar system is more conducive to stability because uncertainty breeds caution on the part of decisionmakers. Caution means following tried and true policies of the past, avoiding deviations. Fur-

thermore, they argue that "the increase in number of independent actors diminishes the share [of attention] that any nation can allocate to any other single actor."[51] This, it is argued, also reduces the probability of war because a state's attention is allocated to a larger number of actors.

Both arguments seem logical. But if *both* cannot be correct, it is still possible that *neither* one is correct. This is a proposition put forth by Bruce Bueno de Mesquita. For example, he challenges the assumption that uncertainty is greater in a multipolar world, arguing that "if the system's structure—be it bipolar or multipolar—does not change, there will be little uncertainty" because "learned patterns from prior behavior will aid decision makers to anticipate the likely consequences of similar behaviors under similar circumstances." Hence, "the level of systemic uncertainty, by itself, neither increases nor decreases the likelihood of war. Consequently, neither the number of blocs, nor the magnitude of change in the number of blocs in the system is expected to be associated with the likelihood of war."[52] Bueno de Mesquita goes on to discuss a number of other propositions dealing with such matters as the relation between the increase in overlapping interests of states (détente) and war, and the relation between the tightening and loosening of alliances and the probability of war. He found, for example, that since the early nineteenth century, the amount of war tended to rise as commitments within a bloc became more tight-knit. This was particularly true for the twentieth century. Bueno de Mesquita's work is an example of explicitly stating commonly held and sometimes conflicting assumptions and hypotheses about the causes of war and then subjecting them to formal empirical tests. Others have continued this quantitative work on the causes of war and on the phenomenon of militarized disputes.[53]

Leaving aside the question of uncertainty, other arguments have been advanced concerning the relative stability of bipolar and multipolar worlds. This is of more than passing interest, given the fact that with the demise of the Soviet Union and the economic rise of Japan and Germany, there is a consensus that the world will become increasingly multipolar. Waltz now concurs with those who see a shift taking place in the distribution of capabilities among states. Since the 1960s, Waltz had argued that the international system was still bipolar—counter to what was a commonplace view that the world already had become (or was becoming) multipolar. While agreeing that the relative power position of the United States had changed from the late 1940s and early 1950s, when European states and Japan were still suffering the devastation wrought by World War II, Waltz pointed to both economic and military indicators that put the United States and the Soviet Union as superpowers so far above Germany, Japan, or any other state as to make the world still very much bipolar. Responding to changes he has observed in the 1980s and 1990s, Waltz now sees the structure of the international system as becoming multipolar, perhaps in the first decade of the new millennium. Although the decline and breakup of the Soviet Union leaves the United States for the short term as the single most powerful global actor, Waltz contends that the principal poles in the new multipolar world that is emerging likely will be the United States, Germany (or "Europe" if it unites), Japan, and Russia (which likely will reassume its historical position as a defensive great power).[54]

For Waltz, this change in systemic structure is not without significant behavioral consequences. Relations in a bipolar system between superpowers were relatively simple and predictable, resulting in a relatively stable world order in which direct conflicts between superpowers usually were avoided, thus reducing the likelihood of general war. By contrast, Waltz still contends that the uncertainties attendant to calculations in a more complex, multipolar world make relations somewhat less predictable. From Waltz's view, we may come to regret the passing of what was a stable, bipolar world. Based upon Waltz's logic, one scholar has deduced a sobering scenario for Europe.[55] Other realist work, however, goes beyond neorealism's concept of polarity and addresses two other dimensions at the systemic level of analysis—disparities in capabilities among poles, and whether the relative capability growth rates of states are static or dynamic regionally or across the system as a whole.[56]

Other works examine different factors at the state-societal level of analysis, such as the economy and concern for domestic political stability that may influence foreign policy choices. Such a focus is a welcome corrective to traditional work on alliances that tends to assume that the distribution of capabilities virtually alone determines a state's international alignment.[57] Similarly, Stephen Walt has recast balance of power theory (states align against the most powerful states), arguing that a balance of threat theory offers more historically correct explanations. Hence, intentions need to be taken into account (states balance against states that are not only powerful but also threatening). More recently, he has used this theoretical adjustment to realism to analyze how revolutionary domestic changes can increase the risk of international war by intensifying international security competition.[58]

Ambitious attempts also have been made to integrate societal and system-level variables (such as polarity, technology, and geography) in the hope of gaining insight on how to explain and predict alliance strategies.[59]

INTERDEPENDENCE

To this point, we have discussed some of the intellectual precursors of realism and have then examined two concepts important to the realist analysis of world politics: power and system. In the next two sections, we discuss the realist view on two ongoing concerns within the international relations discipline: interdependence and accounting for system change. As will become apparent in Chapter 3, the concept of interdependence is an important one to many scholars whom we would classify as pluralists. It is useful, therefore, to present the realist view of this concept, a view that is derived from the realist emphasis on power in the international system.

Interdependence and Vulnerability

To realists, interdependence is not necessarily such a good thing. Rather than being a symmetric relation between coequal parties—which is how many people view the term—interdependence is, realists argue, usually dominance–dependence, with the dependent party particularly vulnerable to the choices of the dominant party. Interdependence does not mean equality. Interdependence connotes some degree of vulnerability by one party to another. Indeed, interdependence as vulnerability is a source of power of one state over another. To reduce this vulnerability, realists have argued that it is better for the state to be independent or, at least, to minimize its dependency. For example, the state needing to import oil is vulnerable to an embargo or price rise engineered by the state or states exporting the commodity. To reduce this vulnerability would require reducing oil imports—by finding an alternative source, for example.

To realists, interdependence does not affect all states equally. Although the economies of most oil-importing countries were affected by the quadrupling of oil prices in 1973–1974, they were not all equally vulnerable. Vulnerability is in part a question of what alternatives are available. For example, as a matter of policy, the United States has tried to increase domestic production, create a strategic oil reserve to be drawn from only in emergencies, find other foreign sources of oil, and substitute alternative forms of energy whenever feasible. Given these measures, the United States has attempted to reduce somewhat its vulnerability to a new oil embargo; however, as a practical matter, the United States remains heavily dependent on imported oil. Not all oil-importing countries have been able to develop even this degree of protection against the oil embargo risk. In short, in any given issue area, not all states are equally vulnerable. Therefore, the realist is suspicious of such blanket statements as "the entire world is interdependent" to the extent that such claims are supposedly *equally* applicable to all states.

Realists thus tend to see interdependence as being between or among states. Therefore, the balance of power is a kind of interdependence. To be sure, some realists of a more eclectic sort acknowledge interdependence involving nonstate actors such as multinational corporations and try to take them into account. But at the core of realist thought is the image of states interacting like billiard balls. This captures the essential meaning of interdependence for the realist, which is a fundamentally different view of interdependence from that held by either pluralists or globalists.

Interdependence and Economics

Economic factors, as we noted earlier, are important to realists to the extent that they reflect or affect national power or capabilities. Industrial countries that effectively combine technology with capital, skilled labor, and raw materials not only enjoy a higher standard of living but also tend to have more leverage in their relations with other states. In addition to trade, financial, and monetary influence that flows from a strong economy, military capabilities are usually greatest in states with advanced industrial economies. This is particularly true in modern military establishments that rely so heavily on technology and on a relatively large pool of skilled labor.

As is clear from reading Machiavelli, the relation between socioeconomic and military capabilities was also acknowledged in earlier, preindustrial times. But the realist has tended to see the economy as subordinate to political choice. If grand strategy, alliance theory, and national and international security are the stuff of high politics, then trade, finance, monetary exchange, fishing rights, and other socioeconomic and humanitarian issues have traditionally been viewed by the realist as somewhat less important—low politics.

On the other hand, realists do understand that maintenance of access to oil and other natural resources is essential to national security. Some economic issues, for example, have been elevated to the status of high politics, as was true following the 1973 oil embargo and the subsequent rise in the real price of petroleum. Maintaining access to oil supplies was a core objective of the multistate coalition that forced Iraq to withdraw from Kuwait in 1991. In the broadest sense, the continued viability of national economies and global markets in which commercial, investment, and other financial transactions take place is also a concern of realists who understand the power and relative power of states as closely tied to these factors.

Conceiving of world politics in terms of separate issue areas or, in the words of one realist, alternative "chessboards," is one example of awareness among realists of the importance to the state of socioeconomic and other nonmilitary issues.[60] If a state wants to be more powerful, however, it avoids or minimizes economic dependency on other states just as it avoids political or military dependency on other states if this amounts to a reduction of its relative power position. Dependency on others is to be minimized, whereas dependency of others on one's own state may be desirable to the extent that it increases one's leverage over those other states.

Interdependence, Peace, and Hegemony

Interdependence, according to realists, may or may not enhance prospects for peace. Conflict, not cooperation, could just as easily result. Just as in households or community conflicts, one way to establish peace is to eliminate or minimize contact among opponents or potential adversaries. Separation from other units, if that were possible, would mean less contact and thus less conflict.[61]

Some realists, however, do have something to say about the conditions under which international cooperation in nonmilitary issues may be enhanced. In the 1970s, several scholars argued that leadership exercised by one state or another is conducive to stability even if this "leadership" becomes hegemonic. According to the theory of **hegemonic stability,** the hegemon, or dominant power, assumes leadership, perhaps for the entire globe, in dealing with a particular issue. Thus, Britain was seen as offering leadership in international monetary matters in the nineteenth and early twentieth centuries. The gold standard associated with the international exchange of money was managed from London by the Bank of England. After World War II, the leadership role was finally assumed by the United States.[62]

The absence of hegemony, or leadership, may result in chaos and instability, as happened in the 1930s when the United States was unwilling to assume leadership of the world economy and Britain, given its weakened position, was unable to do so.[63] Competitive depreciation of currencies, erection of trade barriers, and a drastic reduction in the volume of trade were the outcome.

Although not all realists would subscribe to the view, stability is therefore seen by some as enhanced by a concentration of power in international politics; there is virtue in inequality among states. The hegemonic state or states benefit, but so too do other, less powerful states. By contrast, the decline of hegemony and the consequent fragmentation of power in international politics is said to produce disorder—a breakdown or unraveling of previously constructed international agreements. Leadership provided by hegemonic states is understood as facilitating achievement of collaboration among states.

Theoretical and empirical controversy in the 1980s and 1990s over whether the United States was a hegemon in decline was sparked primarily by the work of the historian Paul Kennedy, who examined the rise and fall of great powers over some five hundred years.[64] The debate influenced (and was influenced by) discussion already under way mainly among neorealists on the stabilizing role performed by global hegemons, a view originally set forth by the economic historian Charles Kindleberger and developed by others. Thus, Joseph Lepgold examined American adaptation to hegemonic decline.[65] Other writers challenged the whole notion of U.S. decline in any absolute sense.[66] After all, U.S. "decline" was *relative* only to the rise of other actors such as Germany and Japan. Notwithstanding all of America's economic problems at the time, this gradual "leveling" of relative standings still left the United States effectively in first position. Moreover, the breakup of the Soviet Union resulted in the United States, at least for a short term, being the only global superpower—a "unipolar" structure to some theorists, however multipolar the world might eventually become.

Perhaps because of its intuitive plausibility—not to mention the issue of the relative "decline" of American power and the problem of international cooperation "after hegemony"[67]—the theory of hegemonic stability has been applied to a wide range of issue areas during various historical periods. The hegemon influences states to cohere and establish the rules by which international relations are to be conducted in various issue areas such as the exchange of money, trade, finance, health, environment, communications, air transportation, and fishing and navigation on the high seas. Using the concept of hegemonic stability is one approach among several dealing with the emergence and functioning of **international regimes** governing these issue areas, regimes having become a major empirical and theoretical focus in recent years. Regimes have been defined as "implicit or explicit principles, norms, rules and decision-making procedures around which actors' expectations converge in a given area of international relations."[68] Hence, an international regime can be viewed as a **dependent variable**—something to be explained—and an **independent variable**—a possible influence on the behavior of states. Those realists who apply the theory of hegemonic stability to the question of regime development begin with the assumption that the structure of the international system—particularly the distribution of capabilities—defines the possibilities of cooperation. Other realists, using game theory and its attendant assumptions of unified, rational state actors, try to explain how cooperation in an anarchic international system can be achieved.[69]

In sum, the realist view of interdependence challenges many conventional ideas of the concept: (1) Interdependence is not necessarily a good thing for any one particular state if interdependence is defined in terms of vulnerability; (2) increasing interdependence may produce conflict as opposed to peace; and (3) in an interdependent world, there are certain virtues in having a hegemonic power capable of enforcing stability in a number of different issue areas.

CHANGE

Realists stress the continuity of international relations. Many of the insights of Thucydides are deemed to be as relevant today as they were 2,500 years ago. Balance of power involving states, whether viewed as a policy or a recurrent outcome, has existed at least since the fifteenth and sixteenth centuries. Although continuity is the watchword for realists, this does not mean that they are uninterested in change. For many theorists of international relations, understanding the evolution of the international system and predicting its future should be the preeminent research goals. The methods for discovering global patterns may vary. Some scholars have applied quantitative measures to historical data, as in the Correlates of War project.[70] Others have approached the issue of international political change by attempting to discern cycles of national power and their relation to the outbreak of war.

Lewis Richardson's now-classic *Statistics of Deadly Quarrels* stands as one of the earliest systematic and quantitative studies of interactions resulting in either avoidance or the actual use of force. Among other things, he found that, contrary to what might have been expected, "world population increases seem not to have been accompanied by a proportionate increase in the frequency or severity of war." He also found empirically that such factors as "similarity of language" and "common religion" had little bearing on the incidence of war or the maintenance of peace. Incidence of war was empirically more associated with territorial contiguity of states than other factors.[71] Later work in this genre—using statistical methods in the Correlates of War project under J. David Singer and his associates—found "that big powers have participated in more wars, that major powers undergoing rapid growth in capabilities are more likely to fight with other major powers, and that international disputes between larger countries tend to escalate to war if there has been an arms race between them."[72]

To illustrate how realists have dealt with the issue of change, we will also briefly discuss the works of Robert Gilpin, Lewis Richardson, J. David Singer, and George Modelski. As the title of his book suggests, Gilpin is interested in developing a framework for thinking about *War and Change in World Politics*. He believes "it is possible to identify recurrent patterns, common elements, and general tendencies in the major turning points in international history." International political change is the result of efforts of political actors "to change the international system in order to advance their own interests," however these interests may be defined (security, economic gain, ideological goals, etc.).[73] Gilpin lists five assumptions concerning the behavior of states that will guide his analysis. For example, the realist emphasis on the unified, rational actor state is revealed in the second assumption: "A state will attempt to change the international system if the expected benefits exceed the expected costs (i.e., if there is an expected net gain)."[74]

Various periods of history are marked by equilibrium (such as after the Congress of Vienna in 1815) or disequilibrium. As long as the system can adjust to the demands of its constituent states, stability is maintained. What accounts for change and the undermining of the status quo? The key factor, originally identified by Thucydides, "is the tendency in an international system for the powers of member states to change at different rates because of political, economic, and technological developments. In time, the differential growth in power of the various states in the system causes a fundamental redistribution of power in the system."[75] A state with ever-increasing power may determine that the costs involved in attempting to change the nature of the system are outweighed by the benefits if such an endeavor is successful. What has been the principal mechanism of change throughout history? War, because wars determine which states will govern the system. The peace settlement after the war codifies the new status quo. This equilibrium reflects the new distribution of power in the international system until eventually the differential growth in the power of states leads to another attempt to change the system.

Like balance of power theory, therefore, power transition theory is a systems-level theory. Realist adherents to both theories claim that the distribution of power among states is the key to understanding international relations. Power transition theorists, however, see the international system as hierarchically ordered, with the most powerful state dominating the rest, which are classified as satisfied or dissatisfied with the ordering of the system. But while balance of power theorists argue that the equality of power leads to peace, power transition theorists such as Gilpin claim that war may be more likely when states are relatively equal, particularly when the differential growth in two states' economies brings a challenger close to the reigning hegemon's power.

George Modelski has argued that the global political system goes through distinct and identifiable historical cycles or recurrent patterns of behavior.[76] The global political system dates from about A.D. 1500, and over the years, various world powers have helped to shape and maintain the system. According to Modelski, since A.D. 1500, four states have played dominant roles, each one corresponding to a "long cycle": Portugal (1500 to the end of the sixteenth century), the Netherlands (the seventeenth century), Great Britain (early eighteenth century to the Napoleonic Wars, and a second cycle from 1815 to 1945), and the United States (1945 to the present). As in the case of Gilpin's analysis, war tends to mark the end of one cycle and the beginning of another.

What produces these cycles? Two conditions are critical: (1) the urge of a power to create a global order, and (2) particular properties and weaknesses of the global system. Modelski notes that, as with long-term business cycles, world order is also subject to decay. The dominant power is inevitably faced with the growth of rival power centers, and attempts to maintain territorial control around the globe prove to be a costly task that drains the vitality and energy of the home country. Each cycle, therefore, exhibits a particular nation-state in an ascending and then a descending phase. As Modelski notes, following a major war, one world power

> emerges from that conflict in an advantageous position and organizes the world even as the struggle still goes on and then formalizes its position in the global layer in the peace settlement. For the space of another generation that new power maintains basic order and is the mainspring of world institutions, often taking transnational forms. But the time comes when the energy that built this order begins to run down. . . . The prominent role of world power attracts competitors (other great powers) . . . ; the system moves into multipolarity. Rivalries among the major powers grow fiercer and assume the characteristics of oligopolistic competition. Gradually, as order dissolves, the system moves toward its original point of departure, that of minimal order and a Babel of conflicting and mutually unintelligible voices.[77]

Modelski and Gilpin, therefore, both present a dynamic view of the international system. Patterns of behavior are evident throughout history. Periods of rapid change alternate with periods of relative stability. Given the emphasis on the importance of war in changing the structure of the system, are we currently experiencing a lull before some sort of global cataclysm? Both Gilpin and Modelski would undoubtedly find such a question too pessimistic. As Modelski notes, it is possible that the international system may be "propelled in a new direction. We have no means of predicting what that new direction might be except that it could be moved away from the present system that relies too heavily on the steady, if long-spaced-out, progression of global wars."[78] Work continues by Modelski and his associates on the "rhythm of global politics." To those using this mode of analysis, long cycles "organize international relations in the past and they clarify the future."[79]

There is a growing body of literature emphasizing how changes in the power positions of states—some of which are in an ascending phase and some in a descending trend relative to other states—contribute to the outbreak of war.[80] This "power transition" work on war has been criticized on historical, empirical, and conceptual grounds.[81] Nevertheless, given the ongoing shifts in the distribution of world power and the increase in the number of democracies, it can be expected that scholars will devote even more attention to specifying the links between the international and domestic levels of analysis in order to understand better the dynamics of peace and stability.[82]

REALISTS AND THEIR CRITICS: AN OVERVIEW

Realism: The Term Itself

What is perhaps most impressive about the realist image of international politics is its longevity. Although modifications, clarifications, additions, and methodological innovations have been made down through the years, the core elements have remained basically intact.

If realism represents a "realistic" image of international politics, what does that say about competing images? Are they by definition "unrealistic"? In debate and discourse, labels are important. A good example of this involves the interwar years, during which realists were challenged by advocates of the League of Nations, world federalism, or peace through international law. Many of these individuals came to be known as "idealists" or "utopians."

The very labels attached to these competing images of world order obviously put the so-called idealists at a disadvantage. Realists could claim that they were dealing with the world as it actually functioned. The idealists, on the other hand, were supposedly more concerned with what *ought* to be. "Yes," a realist might say, "I too wish the world were a more harmonious place, but that unfortunately is not the case." Those persons who were placed in the idealist camp certainly did not choose this particular label for themselves. Who did? The realists. By so doing, the opposition was stripped of a certain amount of legitimacy. Idealism conjured up images of wooly-headed professors, unsophisticated peace advocates, and impractical, utopian schemes.

Realists would respond that *realism* should be taken at face value; it is an appropriate term precisely because its basic tenets in fact closely approximate the world as it is. This is nothing of which to be ashamed. The longevity of the realist tradition is not simply a function of the expropriation of a particular label but a result of realism's inherent descriptive, explanatory, and predictive strengths.

Another reason for the longevity of realism is that this particular image of the world most closely approximates the image held by practitioners of statecraft. Realism has always had strong policy-prescriptive components, as we have already noted. Machiavelli's *The Prince,* for example, was expressly presented as a guide for the ruler. Nor is it mere coincidence that two of the best known American academics who held high positions in the U.S. foreign policy establishment in the 1970s, Henry A. Kissinger and Zbigniew Brzezinski, are both self-professed realists. Their successors in the 1980s and 1990s have largely sustained the same tradition. Indeed, the realist as academic speaks much the same language as the realist as statesman: power, force, national interest, and diplomacy.

It has been argued, however, that some realist writers help to perpetuate the very world they analyze. By describing the world in terms of violence, duplicity, and war, and then providing advice to statesmen as to how statesmen should act, such realists are justifying one particular conception of international relations. Realism becomes a self-fulfilling prophecy. Even efforts to place realism on a stronger theoretical foundation (referred to as "structural realism" or "neorealism") that favor explanation over policy prescription have the same effect. Critics contend that such realists suffer from a lack of imagination and an inability to consider seriously alternative conceptions of world politics and how these might be achieved.

The realist response is that there is nothing inherently wrong with being policy relevant and helping leaders navigate through dangerous waters. Advice based on wishful thinking and questionable assessments of international forces and trends could lead to disastrous policies, particularly if one is the lone "idealist" leader in a world of realists. Moreover, most criticism is understood to be based on a selective reading of realists, ignoring their genuine concern not only with the causes of war but also with how peace can be achieved or maintained. Finally, not all realists would claim to be particularly interested in providing advice to statesmen. They would rather use realist assumptions and insights to develop better theories of international politics. Being policy relevant or ingratiating oneself with political leaders is not the goal for these realists who merely entertain the scholarly goal of explaining how the world functions.

The System and Determinism

As we have seen, the concept of system is critical to many realist writers. Whether the rather simple notion of anarchy or the more elaborate formulations devised by contemporary realist authors, the system is deemed important for its impact on international actors. It is charged, however, that recent realist writers portray the system as having a life of its own. The system is seemingly independent of the wishes and actions of states, even though it is the result of the preferences and powers of the constituent states. Statesmen are granted too little autonomy and too little room to maneuver, and the decision-making process is seemingly devoid of human volition. Human agents are pawns of a bloodless system that looms over them, a structure whose functioning they do not understand and the mechanics of which they only dimly perceive. Statesmen are faced with an endless array of constraints and few opportunities. It is as if they are engaged in a global game, a game called power politics, and they are unable to change the rules even if they so desire. In sum, critics claim there is a fatalistic, deterministic, and pessimistic undercurrent to much of the realist work. As a result, some of these critics have turned to the sociology discipline in search of more dynamic conceptions of structure that emphasize the reciprocal influence of structure and human agents.[83]

Realists differ among themselves as to how much explanatory emphasis is to be given the international system. There is disagreement as to what extent the system functions as an independent variable in influencing state behavior. For neorealists, the system is more than the aggregation of state interactions. Rather, it represents a material structure that does indeed influence the behavior of states that are part of the system. It is these scholars who have drawn the most criticism, but they reject the charge that they are structural determinists who ignore actors operating at the unit, or state, level of analysis. One realist who argues that a systemic theory of international politics is composed of "the structure of the system and its interacting units," notes that

> if structure influences without determining, then one must ask how and to what extent the structure of a realm accounts for outcomes and how and to what extent the units [i.e., states] account for outcomes. Structure has to be studied in its own right as do units.[84]

Another realist categorically states that "no neorealist that I have read argues that political structure determines all behavior."[85] Consistent with Wolfers, Morgenthau, Kissinger, and others, traditional realists have often made the distinction between imperialist, revolutionary, or revisionist states on the one hand, and status-quo powers interested in maintaining their own position in a relatively constant regional or global order on the other. More recently, so-called *modified structural realists*, while appreciating the insights of neorealism, have attempted to incorporate international institutions and explanatory factors at the state-society level of analysis.[86] Similarly, still other realists have examined relations among states (or the interactions level of analysis) that analytically fall between the level of system structure and the level of state and society— high versus low security dilemmas, arms racing and arms control, alliance behavior (balancing, bandwagoning). Such factors, it is argued, will affect the stability of either bipolar or multipolar systems and, consequently, the possibility of moving toward a more peaceful world.[87]

Realists therefore differ on the extent to which statesmen impose themselves on events, or vice versa. No realist is completely determinist or voluntarist. It is not a matter of either-or but varying assessments as to how strong are the constraints placed on statesmen and how much room leaders have to maneuver.[88]

Realists and the State

The state is the centerpiece of realist work. Few persons would disagree as to the importance of the state in international affairs. The criticism, however, is that realists are so obsessed with the state that they ignore other actors and other issues not directly related to the maintenance of state security. Other nonstate actors—multinational corporations, banks, terrorists, and international organizations—are either excluded, downplayed, or trivialized in the realist perspective. Furthermore, given the national security prism through which realists view the world, other concerns such as the socioeconomic gap between rich and poor societies or international pollution rarely make the realist agenda. At best, such issues are dealt with in a derivative manner. A preoccupation with national security and the state by definition relegates other issues to secondary importance or bans them entirely from the realist agenda.

Realists counter that simply because nonstate actors are not dealt with in depth does not mean that they are considered irrelevant. Political scientists, one realist notes, should avoid slipping "into thinking that what an author fails to concentrate his attention upon, he takes to be inconsequential."[89] Similarly, another realist has stated that to argue "that the state . . . is the principal actor in international relations does not deny the existence of other individual and collective actors."[90]

Second, realists contend that theories are constructed to answer certain questions and to explain certain types of international behavior and outcomes. As a result, they purposely limit the type of actors analyzed. A theory concerned with explaining state behavior naturally focuses on states, not multinational corporations or terrorist groups. Similarly, a concern with national security issues by definition makes it unlikely that global welfare and humanitarian issues will receive the same degree of attention.

Finally, it can be argued that focusing on the state is justified on normative grounds. Many scholars, for example, are concerned with how unbridled arms races and military spending contribute to international tension, devastating regional wars, and socioeconomic deprivation. Because it is almost exclusively states that spend this money to buy or produce military hardware, it makes sense to focus on them as the unit of analysis. Hence, far from being enamored of states, many realists are critical of these political entities that are deemed too important to be ignored.

Realists and the Balance of Power

Given the emphasis on the state and the concern with national security issues, we have seen how the concept of balance of power has played a dominant role in realist thought and theory. Although balance of power has been a constant theme in realist writings down through the centuries, it has also come in for a great deal of abuse. Balance of power has been criticized for creating definitional confusion. Hans Morgenthau, a realist himself, discerned at least four definitions: (1) a policy aimed at a certain state of affairs; (2) an objective or actual state of affairs; (3) an approximately equal distribution of power, as when a balance of power exists between the United States and the Soviet Union; and (4) any distribution of power including a preponderance of power, as when the balance of power shifts in favor of either superpower. One critic has found eight meanings of the term.[91] If the balance of power means so many different things, does it mean anything?

Balance of power has also been criticized for leading to war as opposed to preventing it, serving as a poor guide for statesmen, and functioning as a propaganda tool to justify defense spending and foreign adventures. Despite these constant attacks and continual reformulations of the meaning of the term, balance of power remains a crucial concept in the realist vocabulary.

At times, it has appeared that the harshest critics of balance of power as a concept have been the realists themselves. All of these criticisms have been acknowledged and some deemed valid. Attempts have been made, however to clear up misconceptions and misinterpretations of balance of power, placing it on a more solid conceptual footing. One such effort has been made by Kenneth Waltz.[92] Even his formulation, however, is not without its critics. In fact, the debate between Waltz and his critics has been ongoing since the late 1970s.

Realism and Change

Given the realist view of the international system, the role of the state, and balance of power politics, critics suggest that very little possibility for the fundamental and peaceful transformation of international politics is left. Realists, claim the critics, at best offer analysis aimed at understanding how international stability is achieved but nothing approaching true peace. Realist stability reflects a world bristling with weapons, forever on the verge of violent conflict and war. Alternative world futures—scenarios representing a real alternative to the dismal Hobbesian world—are rarely discussed or taken seriously. The timeless quality of international politics, its repetitive nature and cycles of war, and a world in which the strong do as they will and the weak do as they must, dominate the realist image. We are given little information, let alone any hope, say the critics, as to how meaningful and peaceful change can occur and help us escape from the security dilemma.

Realists, it is argued, simply assume state interests, but tell us little about how states come to define their interests, or the processes by which those interests are redefined. Interests are not simply "out there" waiting to be discovered, but are constructed through social interaction.[93]

The issue of change, of course, is intimately connected to that of determinism and to what was referred to in Chapter 1 as the *agent-structure* problem. Although power politics and the state are central to all realist analyses, this does not mean that fundamental change is impossible or that change is limited to war and the cyclical rise and fall of states. Robert Gilpin argues that

> the state is the principal actor in that the nature of the state and the patterns of relations among states are the most important determinants of the character of international relations at any given moment. This argument does not presume that states need always be the principal actors, nor does it presume that the nature of the state need always be the same and that the contemporary nation-state is the ultimate form of political organization.[94]

Another realist has held out the possibility of diplomacy leading to a world state.[95] What separates realists from some other writers on the question of system change, however, is a belief that "if the nation-state is to disappear . . . it will do so through age-old political processes and not as idealists would wish through a transcendence of politics itself."[96] Hence, realists claim that fundamental change *is* possible and is taken into consideration in their work. Once again, however, the strength of this view varies depending on the author under consideration.

Realism: The Entire Enterprise

Critics of realism have always felt that they have been faced with a difficult task because the image comes close to approaching an impregnable edifice seemingly unscathed by years of criticism. Indeed, scholars who at one time in their careers struggled to devise alternative approaches based on alternative images of international politics have in some instances given up the quest, become converts, or resigned themselves to modifying existing realist explanatory frameworks.

Critics are faced with several problems. First, as noted earlier, given realism's affinity to the real world of policy making, this particular image of the world is automatically imbued with a certain degree of attractiveness and legitimacy. It represents the world out there, not some ivory tower perspective on human events. Not only is the realist perspective the accepted wisdom of the Western foreign policy establishments, but even in the Third World, leaders more often than not speak the language of realism as a result of concern over the survival of their regimes and states. Within the halls of academe, realism also has great attractiveness; "peace studies" programs sometimes find it advantageous to change the title to "security and conflict studies" in order to generate student interest. Realism can be as seductive to the academic professional as it can be to the student.

Second, realism is also seductive in that it has been given an increasingly scientific face. Earlier criticisms of the realist literature were very often based on the contention that such concepts as balance of power had less to do with theory building and more to do with ideology and self-justification of one particular approach to conducting international relations. Much of the realist work was, therefore, considered "unscientific." But at least some realists have cast their hunches and insights in the form of hypotheses, testable either quantitatively or with nonquantitative indicators.[97] The work is better grounded scientifically and placed within the context of the **positivist** view of how we comprehend reality. The positivist approach to knowledge still reigns in the natural and social sciences. As a result, any image of international politics that can be presented in the cloak of positivism is immediately granted a certain stature.

Realism has a lot going for it: It has a venerable tradition, is often policy relevant, addresses the big issues of war and peace, is intuitively plausible, and has more recently aspired to truly scientific status.

More recent formulations of realism, however, have actually been criticized for violating the realist tradition, particularly by ignoring the value sensitivity of the realist legacy as represented by E. H. Carr and Hans J. Morgenthau. In a sweeping attack on those he calls *neorealists*, Richard Ashley argues that their work presents a "self-enclosed, self-affirming" view of the world biased toward the existing state-centric order, subordinates all issues to a concern for control and survival of this state system, presents a historically homogeneous view of world history, trivializes alternative conceptions of world order, and dismisses the possibilities of fundamental change and peaceful transformation of the international system.[98] Neorealism, it is claimed, represents the new orthodoxy of the international relations discipline, and hence "students must prepare themselves to retell and carry forward yet another lore."[99] Neorealists reject these charges.

In conclusion, a comment is in order on criticism in general. One may wish to be wary of sweeping criticisms concerning an entire image, whether it be realist, pluralist, or globalist. It is not particularly difficult to find fault with the work of individual theorists, compile a list of their shortcomings, and then present the results as criticisms of the image as a whole. Such selectivity can be misleading. As this chapter illustrates, although realists may find common ground in terms of basic assumptions and key international actors, they also differ in a number of important respects, such as methods they use, levels of analysis they choose, and what they assume about the ability of decisionmakers to influence international outcomes. That is why it is imperative for the serious student of the international relations literature to go to the original sources, evaluate the validity of such criticisms, and assess the value of each image as the basis for a mode of thinking about international relations.

NOTES

1. See Barbara W. Tuchman, *The March of Folly* (New York: Knopf, 1984).
2. Hans J. Morgenthau, *Politics Among Nations*, 4th ed. (New York: Knopf, 1966), p. 5.
3. Some works assume *procedural* rationality or omniscience on the part of actors. Other works simply assume *instrumental* rationality or choice, meaning given two or more alternatives, the actor will choose the one likely to yield the preferred outcome. Logically consistent preference orders can exist despite incomplete and erroneous information. See Frank C. Zagare, "Rationality and Deterrence," *World Politics* 42, no. 2 (January 1990): 238–60.
4. Morgenthau, *Politics Among Nations*, p. 25.
5. Kenneth N. Waltz, *Theory of International Politics* (Reading, MA: Addison-Wesley, 1979); John J. Mearsheimer, "The False Promise of International Institutions," *International Security* 19, no. 3 (Winter 1994/95): 5–49; Christopher Layne, "The Unipolar Illusion: Why Great Powers Will Rise," *International Security* 17, no. 4 (Spring 1993): 5–51.
6. For a discussion of what type of realist Thucydides may have been, see Michael W. Doyle, "Thucydides: A Realist?" in *Hegemonic Rivalry: From Thucydides to the Nuclear Age,* eds. Richard Ned Lebow and Barry S. Strauss (Boulder, CO: Westview Press, 1991), pp. 169–88. On Thucydides' importance to current theory, see Mark V. Kauppi, "Contemporary International Relations Theory and the Peloponnesian War," in Lebow and Strauss, pp. 101–24. See also George Modelski, "Kautilya: Foreign Policy and International System in the Ancient Hindu World," *American Political Science Review* 58 (September 1964): 549–60.
7. See John H. Finley's introduction to *The Complete Writings of Thucydides* (New York: Modern Library, 1951), pp. ix–x.
8. See Thucydides, *History of the Peloponnesian War,* trans. Rex Warner (Harmondsworth, England, and New York: Penguin Books, 1982), p. 49. Cf. Finley, *Complete Writings,* p. 15.
9. See "The Melian Dialogue" in Thucydides, *History,* p. 402. The idea that "it has always been a rule that the weak should be subject to the strong" is discussed earlier in the same work in "The Debate at Sparta and Declaration of War," pp. 80–81.
10. In his lengthier work, *The Discourses,* Machiavelli's republican preferences are apparent. Given the audience for which he wrote *The Prince* (the Medicis), Machiavelli does not emphasize there this republican orientation as he does in *The Discourses*. For a discussion of Machiavelli's thought, see the introduction by Max Lerner in Nicolò Machiavelli, *The Prince* and *The Discourses* (New York: Modern Library, 1950), pp. xxv–xxvi.
11. The distinction between the ethics of "responsibility" and "ultimate ends" is drawn by Max Weber, "Politics As a Vocation," in *From Max Weber: Essays in Sociology,* eds. H. H. Gerth and C. Wright Mills (New York: Oxford University Press, 1946, 1978), p. 120.

12. See Machiavelli, *The Prince,* Chapter XV, p. 56.

13. For example, Machiavelli argues in Chapter XVIII that the prince "should not deviate from what is good, if possible, but be able to do evil if constrained." Indeed, "it is well" for the prince "to seem merciful, faithful, humane, sincere, religious, and also to be so." *The Prince,* p. 65.

14. See William Ebenstein, *Great Political Thinkers: Plato to the Present,* 4th ed. (New York: Holt, Rinehart and Winston, 1969), p. 364.

15. Thomas Hobbes, *Leviathan,* edited by Michael Oakeshott (New York and London: Collier Macmillan, 1974). These classic citations are drawn from Book 1, Chapter 13.

16. Ibid., Book 1, Chapter 15, p. 113.

17. Ibid., Book 1, Chapter 13, p. 101.

18. One such realist is Hedley Bull. See his *The Anarchical Society: A Study of Order in World Politics* (New York: Columbia University Press, 1977).

19. Carl von Clausewitz, *On War,* ed. and trans. Michael Howard and Peter Paret (Princeton, NJ: Princeton University Press, 1976), p. 87. See also Peter Paret, "The Genesis of *On War,*" Michael Howard, "The Influence of Clausewitz," and Bernard Brodie, "The Continuing Relevance of *On War*" and "A Guide to the Reading of *On War,*" all in *On War,* pp. 3–58 and 641–711. For an extension of Clausewitzian ideas on the importance of societal factors, see Michael Howard, "The Forgotten Dimensions of Strategy," *Foreign Affairs* 57, no. 5 (Summer 1979): 975–86.

20. Edward Hallett Carr, *The Twenty Years' Crisis, 1919–1939* (London: Macmillan and Co., 1962), p. ix.

21. Ibid., pp. 111–12.

22. Ibid., p. 112.

23. Ibid., p. 112–13.

24. Ibid., p. 93.

25. A. F. K. Organski, *World Politics,* 2d ed. (New York: Knopf, 1968), p. 104; Morgenthau, *Politics Among Nations,* p. 26; Karl Deutsch, *The Analysis of International Relations* (Englewood Cliffs, NJ: Prentice Hall, 1967), p. 22.

26. Howard, "The Forgotten Dimensions of Strategy."

27. Organski, *World Politics,* p. 358; and J. David Singer, Stuart Bremer, and John Stuckey, "Capability Distribution, Uncertainty, and Major Power War, 1820–1965," in *Peace, War, and Numbers,* ed. Bruce Russett (Beverly Hills, CA: Sage Publications, 1972), pp. 21–27. See also Klaus Knorr, *Military Power and Potential* (Cambridge, MA: D. C. Heath, 1970).

28. Bruce Bueno de Mesquita, *The War Trap* (New Haven, CT: Yale University Press, 1981), p. 153. J. David Singer and associates, *Explaining War: Selected Papers from the Correlates of War Project* (Beverly Hills, CA: Sage Publications, 1979).

29. See the discussion in Ernst B. Haas, "On Systems and International Regimes," *World Politics* 27, no. 2 (January 1975), especially pp. 149–155. For examples of the use of the concept of system, see Morton Kaplan, *System and Process in International Politics* (New York: Wiley, 1957) and Richard Rosecrance, *Action and Reaction in World Politics* (Boston: Little, Brown, 1962).

30. For a number of supposed fallacies, including reification, see Marion J. Levy, Jr., " 'Does it Matter If He's Naked?' Bawled the Child," in *Contending Approaches to International Politics,* ed. Klaus Knorr and James N. Rosenau (Princeton, NJ: Princeton University Press, 1969), pp. 87–106.

31. Rudolph J. Rummel, "Some Dimensions in the Foreign Behavior of States," in James N. Rosenau (ed.), *International Politics and Foreign Policy* (New York: The Free Press, 1969), p. 612. A pioneering work on field theory is Quincy Wright, *The Study of International Relations* (New York: Appleton-Century-Crofts, 1955).

32. Charles A. McClelland and Gary D. Hoggard, "Conflict Patterns in the Interactions Among Nations," in *International Politics and Foreign Policy,* ed. James N. Rosenau, pp. 711–24. Also Charles A. McClelland, "Warnings in the International Events Flow: EFI and Roz as Threat Indicators," *International Interactions* 5, nos. 2 and 3 (1978): 135–204; "The Acute International Crisis," in *The International System: Theoretical Essays,* ed. Klaus Knorr and Sidney Verba (Princeton, NJ: Princeton University Press, 1961), pp. 77–92; "The Anticipation of International Crises: Prospects for Theory and Research," *International Studies Quarterly* 21, no. 1 (March 1977): 15–30. For another example of system as interaction, see K. J. Holsti, *International Politics: A Framework for Analysis,* 4th ed. (Englewood Cliffs, NJ: Prentice Hall, 1983), p. 27.

33. See. J. L. Brierly, *The Law of Nations: An Introduction to the International Law of Peace* (New York: Oxford University Press, 1963), p. 47.

34. For an excellent critique of the concept of anarchy and the argument that the dichotomy between domestic and international politics is overdrawn by neorealists, see Helen Milner, "The Assumption of Anarchy in International Relations Theory: A Critique," *Review of International Studies* 17, no. 1 (January 1991): 67–85.

35. See John H. Herz, "Idealist Internationalism and the Security Dilemma," *World Politics* 5, no. 2 (January 1950): 157–80.

36. See Charles Glaser, "Realists as Optimists: Cooperation as Self-Help," *International Security* 19, no. 3 (Winter 1994/95): 50–90; Jack Snyder, *Myth of Empire: Domestic Politics and International Ambition* (Ithaca: Cornell University Press, 1991). For an argument that states seek influence-maximization rather than mere survival, see Fareed Zakaria, "Realism and Domestic Politics: A Review Essay," in *The Perils of Anarchy: Contemporary Realism and International Security,* eds. Michael E. Brown, Sean M. Lynn-Jones, and Steven E. Miller (Cambridge, MA: MIT Press, 1995).

37. Kenneth N. Waltz develops the stag hunt allegory in his *Man, the State and War* (New York: Columbia University Press, 1959), pp. 165–71. For a critique of Waltz's interpretation of Rousseau, see Stanley Hoffmann, "Rousseau on War and Peace," *American Political Science Review* 57, no. 2 (June 1963): 317–33. Cf. J. J. Rousseau, "A Discussion on the Origins of Inequality," in *The Social Contract and Discourses,* trans. G. D. H. Cole (New York: E. P. Dutton and Co., 1950), pp. 235–38.

38. A nonrealist, Ernst B. Haas, argues that such collaboration is indeed possible. Although collaboration is not an inevitable outcome, even "if the cooperative hunting of the stag is demonstrated to be impossible," a likely possibility would be for the hunters to "make informal rules regulating the separate or cooperative hunting of hares." See Haas, *Beyond the Nation-State* (Stanford, CA: Stanford University Press, 1964), pp. 69–71. An important work that has influenced the use of game theory in international relations is John von Neumann and Oskar Morgenstern, *Theory of Games and Economic Behavior* (Princeton, NJ: Princeton University Press, 1944, 1953). See also Martin Shubik, *Games for Society, Business, and War: Towards a Theory of Gaming* (New York: Elsevier, 1975); Barry R. Schlenker and Thomas V. Bonoma, "Fun and Games: The Validity of Games for the Study of Conflict," *Journal of Conflict Resolution* 22, no. 1 (March 1978): 1–28; Anatol Rapoport and A. M. Ghammah, *Prisoner's Dilemma* (Ann Arbor: University of Michigan Press, 1965). On bargaining, see Thomas C. Schelling, *The Strategy of Conflict* (Cambridge, MA: Harvard University Press, 1960). For a discussion of games such as stag hunt, prisoner's dilemma, deadlock, and chicken, see Robert Axelrod and Robert O. Keohane, "Achieving Cooperation Under Anarchy," *World Politics* 38, no. 1 (October 1985): 226–54.

39. See Robert Powell, "Absolute and Relative Gains in International Relations Theory," *American Political Science Review* 85 (1991): 1303–1320; Joseph Grieco, Robert Powell, and Duncan Snidal, "The Relative Gains Problem for International Cooperation," *American Political Science Review* 87 (1993): 729–743.

40. See "Memorandum by Sir Eyre Crowe on the Present State of British Relations with France and Germany, January 1, 1907" in G. P. Gooch and H. Temperly, eds., *British Documents on the Origin of the War, 1898–1914* (London: H. M. Stationery Office, 1928), 5, no. 3, pp. 402–7 and 414–20. Reprinted in Fred A. Sondermann, David S. McClellan, and William C. Olson, eds., *The Theory and Practice of International Relations,* 5th ed. (Englewood Cliffs, NJ: Prentice Hall, 1979), p. 120.

41. See Henry A. Kissinger, *A World Restored: The Politics of Conservatism in a Revolutionary Age* (New York: Grosset & Dunlap, 1964), pp. 317–18.

42. Waltz, *Theory of International Politics.* The use of the term *voluntarism* differs somewhat from the technical use of the term by many philosophers. See Paul Edwards, ed., *Encyclopedia of Philosophy* 5, nos. 7 and 8 (New York: Free Press, 1972), pp. 270–72.

43. The billiard ball metaphor for the balance of power is generally attributed to Arnold Wolfers, "The Actors in International Politics," in *Theoretical Aspects of International Relations,* ed. William T. R. Fox (Notre Dame, IN: Notre Dame University Press, 1959), pp. 83–106.

44. See Waltz, *Man, the State and War,* pp. 204, 209.
45. Richard K. Ashley, "The Poverty of Neorealism," *International Organization* 38, no. 2 (Spring 1984): 225–86.
46. See pluralist Ernst B. Haas, *Beyond the Nation–State,* p. 70.
47. See Ernst B. Haas, "On Systems and International Regimes," *World Politics* 27, no. 2 (January 1975), p. 151.
48. Morgenthau, *Politics Among Nations,* p. 161.
49. Ibid., p. 519.
50. Kenneth N. Waltz, "The Stability of a Bipolar World," *Daedalus* 93 (Summer 1964): 881–909; Karl W. Deutsch and J. David Singer, "Multipolar Power Systems and International Stability," *World Politics* 16, no. 3 (April 1964): 390–406.
51. Deutsch and Singer, "Multipolar Power Systems," p. 400.
52. Bruce Bueno de Mesquita, "Systemic Polarization and the Occurrence and Duration of War," *Journal of Conflict Resolution* 22, no. 2 (June 1978): 245, 246. See also Michael D. Wallace, *War and Rank Among Nations* (Lexington, MA: D. C. Heath, 1973).
53. See, for example, Melvin Small and J. David Singer, eds., *International War: An Anthology and Study Guide* (Homewood, IL: Dorsey Press, 1985); John A. Vasquez, *The War Puzzle* (Cambridge: Cambridge University Press, 1993); Manus I. Midlarsky, ed., *Handbook of War Studies* (Boston: Unwin Hyman, 1989); Midlarsky, *The Onset of War* (Boston: Unwin Hyman, 1988); and Jack S. Levy, "Theories of General War," *World Politics,* 37, no. 3 (April 1985): 344–74.
54. Kenneth N. Waltz, "The New World Order," *Millennium* 22, no. 2 (Summer 1993): 187–95.
55. Waltz, *Theory of International Politics,* pp. 165–70; John J. Mearsheimer, "Back to the Future: Instability in Europe after the Cold War," *International Security* 15, no. 1 (Summer 1990): 5–56. See also Glenn Snyder, "The Security Dilemma in Alliance Politics," *World Politics* 36, no. 4 (July 1984): 461–95.
56. See, for example, Randall L. Schweller, *Deadly Imbalances: Tripolarity and Hitler's Strategy of World Conquest* (New York: Columbia University Press, 1997); Edward Mansfield, *Power, Trade, and War* (Princeton: Princeton University Press, 1994); Nazli Choucri and Robert C. North, *Nations in Conflict: National Growth and International Violence* (San Francisco: W. H. Freeman, 1975); Dale C. Copeland, "Neorealism and the Myth of Bipolar: Stability Toward a New Dynamic Realist Theory of Major War," *Security Studies* 5, no. 3 (Spring 1996): 29–89. Discussion and references to power transition and power cycle theories are later in this chapter.
57. See, for example, Michael N. Barnett and Jack S. Levy, "Domestic Sources of Alliances and Alignments: The Case of Egypt, 1962–73," *International Organization* 45, no. 3 (Summer 1991): 369–95; Steven R. David, "Explaining Third World Alignment," *World Politics* 43, no. 2 (January 1991): 233–55.
58. Stephen Walt, *The Origins of Alliances* (Ithaca: Cornell University Press, 1987) and *Revolutions and War* (Ithaca: Cornell University Press, 1996).
59. See, for example, Thomas J. Christensen and Jack Snyder, "Chain Gangs and Passed Bucks: Predicting Alliance Patterns in Multipolarity," *International Organization* 44, no. 2 (Spring 1990): 137–68.
60. Stanley Hoffmann, "Weighing the Balance of Power," *Foreign Affairs* 50, no. 4 (July 1972): 618–43.
61. Steven L. Spiegel and Kenneth N. Waltz, eds., *Conflict in World Politics* (Cambridge, MA: Winthrop, 1971), pp. 454–74.
62. Robert O. Keohane, "The Theory of Hegemonic Stability and Changes in International Economic Regimes, 1967–1977," in Ole R. Holsti, Randolph M. Siverson, and Alexander L. George, eds., *Change in the International System* (Boulder, CO: Westview Press, 1980), pp. 131–62. For a critique and citations of the literature, see Arthur A. Stein, "The Hegemon's Dilemma: Great Britain, the United States, and the International Economic Order," *International Organization* 38, no. 2 (Spring 1984): 355–86; Susan Strange, "The Persistent Myth of Lost Hegemony," *International Organization* 41, no. 4 (Autumn 1987): 551–74; Isabelle Grunberg, "Exploring the 'Myth' of Hegemonic Stability," *International Organization* 44, no. 4 (Autumn 1990): 431–77.

63. Charles P. Kindleberger, *The World in Depression, 1929–1939* (Berkeley: University of California Press, 1973); Robert Gilpin, *U.S. Power and the Multinational Corporation* (New York: Basic Books, 1975); and Stephen Krasner, "State Power and the Structure of International Trade," *World Politics* 28, no. 3 (April 1976): 317–47.

64. Paul Kennedy, *The Rise and Fall of the Great Powers* (New York: Random House, 1987). Cf. the earlier work of the economist Mancur Olson, *The Rise and Decline of Nations* (New Haven: Yale University Press, 1982).

65. Kindleberger, *The World in Depression;* Joseph Lepgold, *The Declining Hegemon: The United States and European Defense, 1960–1990* (New York: Praeger, 1990).

66. For example, see Henry R. Nau, *The Myth of America's Decline* (New York: Oxford University Press, 1990); Joseph S. Nye, Jr., *Bound to Lead: The Changing Nature of American Power* (New York: Basic Books, 1990); and Samuel P. Huntington, "The U.S.—Decline or Renewal?" *Foreign Affairs* 67, 2 (Winter 1988/89): 76–96.

67. Robert Keohane, *After Hegemony: Cooperation and Discord in the World Political Economy* (Princeton: Princeton University Press, 1984).

68. Stephen Krasner, "Structural Causes and Regime Consequences: Regimes as Intervening Variables," in Krasner, ed., *International Regimes* (Ithaca: Cornell University Press, 1983), pp. 1–21.

69. See the special issue of *World Politics* 38, no. 1 (October 1985), edited by Kenneth Oye; R. Harrison Wagner, "The Theory of Games and the Problem of International Cooperation," *American Political Science Review* 70, no. 2 (June 1983): 330–46; Robert Jervis, "Realism, Game Theory, and Cooperation," *World Politics* 40, no. 3 (April 1988): 317–49; Robert Axelrod, *The Evolution of Cooperation* (New York: Basic Books, 1984); Michael Taylor, *Anarchy and Cooperation* (New York: Wiley, 1976). For an overview of the various approaches to regimes, see Stephen Haggard and Beth A. Simmons, "Theories of International Regimes," *International Organization* 41, no. 3 (Summer 1987): 491–517.

70. For works associated with the Correlates of War project, see "Suggested Readings" for this chapter under Singer's name. For an overview, see Vasquez, *The War Puzzle.*

71. This summary is drawn from Karen A. Feste, "Behavioral Theories" in *Women, Gender, and World Politics,* eds. Peter R. Beckman and Francine D'Amico (Westport, CT: Bergin & Garvey, 1994), p. 48. Cf. Lewis F. Richardson, *Statistics of Deadly Quarrels* (Chicago: Quadrangle Books, 1960) and David Wilkinson, *Deadly Quarrels: Lewis F. Richardson and the Statistical Study of War* (Berkeley: University of California Press, 1980).

72. *Ibid.,* p. 45.

73. Robert Gilpin, *War and Change in World Politics* (New York: Cambridge University Press, 1981), pp. 3, 10.

74. *Ibid.,* p. 10.

75. *Ibid.,* p. 13. The implications of the uneven growth of power were also addressed in Lenin's concept of "uneven development."

76. George Modelski, "The Long Cycle of Global Politics and the Nation-State," *Comparative Studies in Society and History* 20, no. 2 (April 1978): 214–35. Notice that Modelski does not describe the international system as being anarchic. Although a central authority is lacking, order and authority do exist. See his comments in "Long Cycles and the Strategy of the U.S. International Economic Policy," in *America in a Changing World Political Economy,* eds. William P. Avery and David P. Rapkin (White Plains, NY: Longman, 1982), p. 99.

77. Modelski, "The Long Cycle of Global Politics," p. 217. It is Modelski's emphasis on the primacy of political factors that places him within the context of the realist as opposed to globalist image.

78. *Ibid.,* p. 235.

79. George Modelski, ed., *Exploring Long Cycles* (Boulder, CO: Lynne Rienner Publishers, 1987), p. ix. See also George Modelski and William R. Thompson, *Seapower in Global Politics, 1494–1993* (Seattle: University of Washington Press, 1988). Cf. Nathaniel Beck, "The Illusion of Cycles in International Relations," and Joshua S. Goldstein, "The Possibility of Cycles in International Relations," *International Studies Quarterly* 35, no. 4 (December 1991): 455–80.

80. Aside from Robert Gilpin and George Modelski, other authors who deal with power cycles include Charles F. Doran, *The Politics of Assimilation* (Baltimore: Johns Hopkins University Press, 1971);

Charles F. Doran and Wes Parsons, "War and the Cycle of Relative Power," *American Political Science Review* 74, no. 4 (December 1980): 947–65; Mancur Olson, *The Rise and Decline of Nations* (New Haven, CT: Yale University Press, 1982); A. F. K. Organski and Jacek Kugler, *The War Ledger* (Chicago: University of Chicago Press, 1980); Jacek Kugler and Douglas Lemki, *Parity and War* (Ann Arbor: University of Michigan Press, 1996). William C. Wohlforth, "Realism and the End of the Cold War," *International Security* 19, no. 3 (Winter 1994/95): 91–129.

81. See, for example, Jack S. Levy, "Theories of General War," *World Politics* 37, no. 3 (April 1985): 344–74.

82. For example, see Randall L. Schweller, "Domestic Structure and Preventive War: Are Democracies More Pacific?" *World Politics* 44, no. 2 (January 1992): 235–69.

83. Anthony Giddens' theory of structuration has been particularly influential. See, among other works, *A Contemporary Critique of Historical Materialism* (Berkeley: University of California Press, 1981); Giddens, *Central Problems in Social Theory* (Berkeley: University of California Press, 1979).

84. See Kenneth N. Waltz, "Letter to the Editor," *International Organization* 36, no. 3 (Summer 1982): 680, which cites his *Theory of International Politics*, p. 78.

85. Robert G. Gilpin, "The Richness of the Tradition of Political Realism," *International Organization* 38, no. 2 (Spring 1984): 302.

86. See Randall L. Schweller and David Priess, "A Tale of Two Realisms: Expanding the Institutions Debate," *Mershon International Studies Review* 41, supplement 1 (May 1997): 1–33.

87. Glenn H. Snyder, "Process Variables in Neorealist Theory," in *Realism: Restatements and Renewal*, ed. Benjamin Frankel, special issue of *Security Studies* 5, no. 3 (Spring 1996): 167–192; Barry Buzan discusses what he terms "interaction capacity," systemic but nonstructural factors that "not only affect the ability and willingness of units to interact, but also determine what types and levels of interaction are possible and desired." See Barry Buzan, Charles Jones, and Richard Little, *The Logic of Anarchy: Neorealism to Structural Realism* (New York: Columbia University Press, 1993), pp. 69–80. See also Thomas J. Christensen and Jack Snyder, "Chain Gangs and Passed Bucks: Predicting Alliance Behavior in Multipolarity," *International Organization* 44, no. 2 (Spring 1990): 137–168.

88. In a review of Kenneth Waltz's *Theory of International Politics*, Richard Rosecrance suggests Waltz's work is heavily determinist. Rosecrance, "International Relations Theory Revisited," *International Organization* 35, no. 4 (Autumn 1981): 691–713. Waltz rejects this charge in his "Letter to the Editor," p. 680.

89. Waltz, "Letter to the Editor," p. 680.

90. Gilpin, "Richness of Political Realism," p. 300.

91. Morgenthau, *Politics Among Nations*, p. 161; and Ernst B. Haas, "The Balance of Power: Prescription, Concept or Propaganda?" *World Politics* 5, no. 2 (July 1953): 442–77.

92. Waltz, *Theory of International Politics*.

93. See Martha Finnemore, *National Interests in International Society* (Ithaca: Cornell University Press, 1996).

94. Gilpin, "Richness of Political Realism," p. 300.

95. Morgenthau, *Politics Among Nations*, p. 548.

96. Gilpin, "Richness of Political Realism," p. 299; Morgenthau, *Politics Among Nations*, p. 9.

97. See, for example, P. Terrence Hopmann, Dina A. Zinnes, and J. David Singer, *Cumulation in International Relations Research* (Denver, CO: University of Denver, Graduate School of International Studies, 1981).

98. Richard K. Ashley is criticizing such authors as Kenneth Waltz, Robert Gilpin, Stephen Krasner, George Modelski, Robert Tucker, and Charles Kindleberger. See Ashley's "The Poverty of Neorealism," *International Organization* 38, no. 2 (Spring 1984): 225–86, p. 228. Also see Ashley, "Political Realism and Human Interests," *International Studies Quarterly* 25, no. 2 (June 1984): 204–35; Ashley, "Three Modes of Economism," *International Studies Quarterly* 27, no. 4 (December 1983): 463–96.

99. Ashley, "Poverty of Neorealism," p. 230. See also Robert Keohane, *Neorealism and Its Critics* (New York: Columbia University Press, 1986).

SELECTIONS FOR FURTHER READING AND REFERENCE

General

Brecher, Michael. *Crises in World Politics*. Oxford: Pergamon Press, 1993.

Brooks, Stephen G. "Dueling Realisms." *International Organization* 51, 3 (Summer 1997): 445–77.

Doyle, Michael W. *Ways of War and Peace*. New York: W. W. Norton, 1997. [Part One addresses Realism.]

Huntington, Samuel. *The Clash of Civilizations and the Remaking of the World Order*. New York: Simon & Schuster, 1996.

Jervis, Robert, and Jack Snyder, eds. *Dominoes and Bandwagons*. New York: Oxford University Press, 1991.

Kegley, Charles W., Jr., and Gregory A. Raymond. *A Multipolar Peace? Great-Power Politics in the Twenty-first Century*. New York: St. Martin's 1994.

Kissinger, Henry. *Diplomacy*. New York: Simon & Schuster, 1994.

Lebow, Richard Ned, and Thomas Risse-Kappen. *International Relations Theory and the End of the Cold War*. New York: Columbia University Press, 1995.

Levy, Jack S. "Prospect Theory, Rational Choice, and International Relations." *International Studies Quarterly* 41, 1 (March 1997): 87–112.

Liska, George. *The Ways of Power*. Cambridge, England: Basil Blackwell, 1990.

Modelski, George, and W. R. Thompson. *Leading Sectors and World Powers*. Columbia: University of South Carolina Press, 1996.

Sullivan, Michael P. *Power in Contemporary International Politics*. Columbia: University of South Carolina Press, 1990. [An example of a mathematical and statistical approach.]

Tucker, Robert W., and David C. Hendrickson. *The Imperial Temptation*. New York: Council on Foreign Relations Press, 1992.

Walt, Stephen M. *The Origins of Alliances*. Ithaca, NY: Cornell University Press, 1987.

———. "The Progressive Power of Realism." *American Political Science Review* 91, 4 (December 1997): 931–35.

———. "Why Alliances Endure or Collapse." *Survival* 39, 1 (Spring 1997): 156–79.

Waltz, Kenneth N. "The Emerging Structure of International Politics." *International Security* 17 (Fall 1993): 33–79.

———. "The New World Order." *Millennium* 22 (1993): 187–95.

———. "Realist Thought and Neorealist Theory." *Journal of International Affairs* 44 (Spring/Summer 1990): 21–37.

———. *Theory of International Politics*. New York: McGraw Hill/Addison Wesley, 1979.

———. "Theory of International Relations." In *Handbook of Political Science*, Vol. 8, ed. Nelson W. Polsby and Fred I. Greenstein. Reading, MA: Addison-Wesley, 1975.

Wendt, Alexander and Michael N. Barnett. "Dependent State Formation and Third World Militarization." *Review of International Studies,* Vol. 19 (1993): 321–47.

The "English School" in International Relations Theory

Best, Geoffrey. *War and Law Since 1945*. New York: Oxford University Press, 1994.

Booth, Ken, and Steve Smith, eds. *International Relations Theory Today*. University Park: Pennsylvania State University Press, 1995.

Bull, Hedley. *The Anarchical Society: A Study of Order in World Politics*. New York: Columbia University Press, 1977.

———. *The Control of the Arms Race*. New York: Praeger, 1961, 1965.

Bull, Hedley, and Adam Watson, eds. *The Expansion of International Society*. Oxford: Clarendon Press, 1984.

Buzan, Barry. "From International System to International Society: Structural Realism and Regime Theory Meet the English School," *International Organization* 47 (1983): 327–52.

———. *People, States and Fear*. 2nd ed. London: Harvester Wheatsheaf, 1991.

Buzan, Barry, Ole Waever, and Jaap de Wilde, *Security: A New Framework for Analysis*. Boulder, CO: Lynne Rienner, 1997.

Buzan, Barry, Richard Little, and Charles Jones. *The Logic of Anarchy: Neorealism to Structural Realism*. New York: Columbia University Press, 1993.

Carr, E. H. *The Twenty Years' Crisis, 1919–39*. New York: Harper & Row, 1964.

Gong, Gerrit W. *The Standard of Civilization in International Society*. Oxford, England: Clarendon Press, 1984.

Hinsley, F. H. *Power and the Pursuit of Peace*. Cambridge, England: University of Cambridge Press, 1963.

———. *Sovereignty*. Cambridge, England: Cambridge University Press, 1966, 1986.

Holsti, K. J. "America Meets the 'English School': State Interests in International Society." *International Studies Quarterly* 41, Supplement 2 (November 1997): 275–80.

Howard, Michael. *The Causes of War and Other Essays*. Cambridge, MA: Harvard University Press, 1983.

———. *The Lessons of History*. New Haven: Yale University Press, 1991.

———. *War and the Liberal Conscience*. New Brunswick, NJ: Rutgers University Press, 1978.

Watson, Adam. *The Evolution of International Society: A Comparative Historical Analysis*. London: Routledge, 1992.

Wight, Martin. "An Anatomy of International Thought." *Review of International Studies* 13 (1987): 222–47.

———. *International Theory: The Three Traditions*. ed. Gabriele Wight and Brian Porter. London: Leicester University Press, 1991 and New York: Holmes & Meier, 1992.

———. *Power Politics*. New York: Holmes and Meier, 1946, 1978.

———. *Systems of States*. ed. Hedley Bull. Leicester, England: Leicester University Press, 1977.

On Anarchy and Cooperation under Anarchy

Brown, Michael E., Sean M. Lynn-Jones, and Steven E. Miller, eds. *The Perils of Anarchy: Contemporary Realism and International Security*. Cambridge, MA: MIT Press, 1995.

Bull, Hedley. *The Anarchical Society: A Study of Order in World Politics*. New York: Columbia University Press, 1977.

Buzan, Barry, Richard Little, and Charles Jones. *The Logic of Anarchy: Neorealism to Structural Realism*. New York: Columbia University Press, 1993.

Grieco, Joseph M. "Anarchy and the Limits of Cooperation." *International Organization* 42, 3 (Summer 1988): 485–506.

———. *Cooperation among Nations*. Ithaca, NY: Cornell University Press, 1990.

Oye, Kenneth A., ed. *Cooperation under Anarchy*. Princeton, NJ: Princeton University Press, 1986.

Stein, Arthur. *Why Nations Cooperate: Circumstance and Choice in International Relations*. Ithaca, NY: Cornell University Press, 1993.

On Empires

Doyle, Michael. *Empires*. New York: Cornell University Press, 1986.

Kupchan, Charles A. *The Vulnerability of Empire*. Ithaca, NY: Cornell University Press, 1994.

Snyder, Jack. *Myths of Empire: Domestic Politics and International Ambition*. Ithaca, NY: Cornell University Press, 1991.

On War, Its Causes and Remedies

GENERAL REFERENCE

Aron, Raymond. *On War*. London: Secker and Warburg, 1958.

———. *Peace and War*. Garden City, NY: Doubleday, 1966.

Brodie, Bernard. *War and Politics*. New York: Macmillan, 1973.

Brown, Seyom. *The Causes and Prevention of War*. New York: St. Martin's, 1987.

Doyle, Michael W. *Ways of War and Peace*. New York: W. W. Norton, 1997.

Fearon, James D. "Rationalist Explanations for War." *International Organization* 49, 3 (Summer 1995): 379–414.

George, Alexander L. *Bridging the Gap: Theory and Practice in Foreign Policy*. Washington, DC: U.S. Institute of Peace, 1993.

George, Alexander, and Richard Smoke. *Deterrence in American Foreign Policy*. New York: Columbia University Press, 1974.

Gilpin, Robert. *War and Change in World Politics*. Cambridge, England: Cambridge University Press, 1981.

Hoffmann, Stanley. *The State of War*. New York: Praeger, 1965.

Hoffmann, Stanley, and David Fidler. *Rousseau on International Relations*. Oxford, England: Clarendon Press, 1991.

Holsti, Kalevi J. *Peace and War: Armed Conflicts and International Order, 1648–1989*. New York: Cambridge University Press, 1991.

———. *The State, War, and the State of War*. New York: Cambridge University Press, 1996.

Howard, Michael. *The Causes of War and Other Essays*. Cambridge, MA: Harvard University Press, 1983.

———. *War and the Liberal Conscience*. New Brunswick, NJ: Rutgers University Press, 1978.

Lebow, Richard Ned. *Between Peace and War*. Baltimore: The Johns Hopkins University Press, 1981.

Mueller, John. *Quiet Cataclysm: Reflections on the Recent Transformation of World Politics*. New York: Harper Collins, 1995.

———. *Retreat from Doomsday: The Obsolescence of Major War*. New York: Basic Books, 1989.

Sagan, Scott, and Kenneth N. Waltz. *The Spread of Nuclear Weapons: A Debate*. New York: W. W. Norton, 1995. [Waltz presents a realist case and Sagan responds with more of a pluralist understanding that relies on organization theory.]

Schelling, Thomas S. *Arms and Influence*. New Haven, CT: Yale University Press, 1966.

———. *The Strategy of Conflict*. New York: Oxford University Press, 1960.

Stoessinger, John G. *Why Nations Go to War*. New York: St. Martin's, 1978.

Thompson, William R. *On Global War: Historical-Structural Approaches to World Politics*. Columbia: University of South Carolina Press, 1990.

Van Evera, Stephen. "Hypotheses on Nationalism and War." *International Security* 18, 4 (Spring 1994): 5–39.

Walt, Stephen M. *Revolution and War*. Ithaca, NY: Cornell University Press, 1996.

Waltz, Kenneth N. "Kant, Liberalism, and War." *American Political Science Review* 56 (June 1962): 331–40.

———. *Man, the State and War*. New York: Columbia University Press, 1959.

Wright, Quincy. *A Study of War*. Chicago: University of Chicago Press, 1964.

MATHEMATICAL AND STATISTICAL WORK

Bueno de Mesquita, Bruce. *The War Trap*. New Haven, CT: Yale University Press, 1981.

———. "The War Trap Revisited: A Revised Expected Utility Model." *American Political Science Review* 79, 1 (March 1985): 156–73.

Bueno de Mesquita, Bruce, and David Lalman. *War and Reason: Domestic and International Imperatives*. New Haven: Yale University Press, 1992.

Bueno de Mesquita, Bruce, and Randolph M. Siverson. "War and the Survival of Political Leaders." *American Political Science Review* 89, 4 (December 1995): 841–55.

Bueno de Mesquita, Bruce, Randolph M. Siverson, and Gary Woller. "War and the Fate of Regimes." *American Political Science Review* 86 (1992): 638–46.

Bueno de Mesquita, Bruce, et al., "Capabilities, Perception and Escalation." *American Political Science Review* 91, 1 (March 1997): 15–27.

Choucri, Nazli, and Robert C. North. *Nations in Conflict*. San Francisco: W. H. Freeman, 1975.

Cioffi-Revilla, Claudio. *The Scientific Measurement of International Conflict*. Boulder, CO: Lynne Rienner, 1990.

Hagan, Joe D. "Domestic Political Systems and War Proneness." *Mershon International Studies Review* 38 (1994): 183–207.

Kugler, Jacek, and Douglas Lemke, eds. *Parity and War: Evaluations and Extensions of the War Ledger*. Ann Arbor: University of Michigan Press, 1996.

Levy, Jack S. "The Diversionary Theory of War" in Midlarsky, *Handbook of War Studies*. (See below under Midlarsky.)

———. "Theories of General War." *World Politics* 37, 3 (April 1985): 344–74.

Mansfield, Edward D. *Power, Trade, and War*. Princeton, NJ: Princeton University Press, 1994.

Midlarsky, Manus, ed. *Handbook of War Studies*. Boston: Unwin Hyman, 1989.

———. *The Onset of World War*. Boston: Unwin Hyman, 1988.

Rapoport, Anatol. *The Origins of Violence*. New Brunswick, NJ: Transaction Publishers, 1989, 1995.

Richardson, Lewis F. *Arms and Insecurity*. Pittsburg, PA: Boxwood, 1960.

———. *Statistics of Deadly Quarrels*. Chicago: Quadrangle Books, 1960.

Rummel, Rudolph. *Dimensions of Nations*. Beverly Hills, CA: Sage Publications, 1972.

———. *Understanding Conflict and War* (5 volumes). Beverly Hills, CA: Sage Publications, 1975–81.

Singer, J. David, and P. F. Diehl. *Measuring the Correlates of War*. Ann Arbor: University of Michigan Press, 1993.

Singer, J. David, and Melvin Small. *The Wages of War, 1816–1965*. New York: John Wiley, 1972.

Small, Melvin, and J. David Singer, eds. *International War: An Anthology and Study Guide*. Homewood, IL: Dorsey Press, 1985.

Vasquez, John A. "The Steps to War: Toward a Scientific Explanation of the Correlates of War Findings." *World Politics* 40, 1 (October 1987): 108–45.

———. *The War Puzzle*. Cambridge, England: Cambridge University Press, 1993.

On International Political Economy

Gilpin, Robert. *The Political Economy of International Relations*. Princeton, NJ: Princeton University Press, 1987.

———. *U.S. Power and the Multinational Corporation*. New York: Basic Books, 1975.

Katzenstein, Peter J. *Small States in World Markets*. Ithaca, NY: Cornell University Press, 1985.

Kindleberger, Charles P. *World Economic Primacy, 1500–1900*. New York: Oxford University Press, 1996.

Knorr, Klaus. *The Power of Nations: The Political Economy of International Relations*. New York: Basic Books, 1975.

Krasner, Stephen D. *Structural Conflict: The Third World against Global Liberalism*. Berkeley: University of California Press, 1985.

Mastanduno, Michael. "Do Relative Gains Matter? America's Response to Japanese Industrial Policy." In *Neorealism and Neoliberalism*. Ed. David Baldwin. New York: Columbia University Press, 1993: 250–66.

Olson, Mancur. *The Rise and Decline of Nations*. New Haven, CT: Yale University Press, 1982.

Rosecrance, Richard. *The Rise of the Trading State*. New York: Basic Books, 1986.

Strange, Susan. *States and Markets*. London: Pinter, 1988, 1994.

Zysman, John. *Governments, Markets and Growth*. Ithaca, NY: Cornell University Press, 1983.

On Leadership, Hegemony, and Hegemonic Stability

Keohane, Robert O. *After Hegemony: Cooperation and Discord in the World Political Economy*. Princeton, NJ: Princeton University Press, 1984.

Lebow, Richard Ned, and Barry S. Strauss, eds. *Hegemonic Rivalry: From Thucydides to the Nuclear Age*. Boulder, CO: Westview Press, 1991.

Lepgold, Joseph. *The Declining Hegemon*. New York: Praeger, 1990.

Nau, Henry. *The Myth of America's Decline*. New York: Oxford University Press, 1990.

Nye, Joseph S. *Bound to Lead: The Changing Nature of American Power*. New York: Basic Books, 1990.

Strange, Susan. "The Persistent Myth of Lost Hegemony." *International Organization* 41, 4 (Autumn 1987): 551–74.

On Long Cycles, History, and International Relations Theory

Goldstein, Joshua S. *Long Cycles: Prosperity and War in the Modern Age*. New Haven: Yale University Press, 1988.

———. "The Possibility of Cycles in International Relations." *International Studies Quarterly* 35, 4 (December 1991): 477–80.

Kennedy, Paul. *The Rise and Fall of the Great Powers*. New York: Random House, 1987.

Modelski, George. *Exploring Long Cycles*. Boulder, CO: Lynne Rienner, 1987.

Modelski, George, and William R. Thompson. *Seapower in Global Politics, 1494–1993*. Seattle: University of Washington Press, 1988.

Rasler, Karen A., and William R. Thompson. *The Great Powers and Global Struggle, 1490–1990*. Lexington: University Press of Kentucky, 1994.

Rosecrance, Richard. "Long Cycle Theory in International Relations." *International Organization* 41, 2 (Spring 1987): 283–301.

Thompson, William R. "Long Waves, Technological Innovation, and Relative Decline." *International Organization* 44, 2 (Spring 1990): 201–33.

Other Earlier Work in the Field

Claude, Inis. *Power and International Relations*. New York: Random House, 1962.

Herz, John. *Political Realism and Political Idealism*. Chicago: University of Chicago Press, 1951.

———. "Political Realism Revisited." *International Studies Quarterly* 25, 2 (June 1981): 182–241.

Hoffmann, Stanley. "Raymond Aron and the Theory of International Relations." *International Studies Quarterly* 29, 1 (March 1985): 13–27.

Ikle, Fred C. *How Nations Negotiate*. New York: Harper & Row, 1964.

Kaplan, Morton. *System and Process in International Politics*. New York: John Wiley, 1957.

Kissinger, Henry. *A World Restored*. New York: Grosset and Dunlap, 1964.

Liska, George. *Nations in Alliance*. Baltimore: Johns Hopkins University Press, 1968.

Mackinder, Halford J. "The Round World and the Winning of the Peace." *Foreign Affairs* 21, 4 (July 1943): 595–605.

Morgenthau, Hans. J. *In Defense of the National Interest*. New York: Knopf, 1951.

———. *Politics among Nations*, 5th ed. New York: Knopf, 1978.

Osgood, Robert E. *Alliances and American Foreign Policy*. Baltimore: Johns Hopkins University Press, 1967.

Osgood, Robert E., and Robert W. Tucker. *Force, Order and Justice*. Baltimore: Johns Hopkins University Press, 1967.

Riker, William H. *A Theory of Political Coalitions*. New Haven, CT: Yale University Press, 1962.

Rosecrance, Richard. *Action and Reaction in World Politics*. Boston: Little, Brown, 1963.

Russett, Bruce M. *International Regions and the International System*. Chicago: Rand McNally, 1967.

Tucker, Robert W. *The Inequality of Nations*. New York: Basic Books, 1977.

Waltz, Kenneth N. *Foreign Policy and Democratic Politics*. Boston: Little, Brown, 1967.

Wolfers, Arnold. *Discord and Collaboration*. Baltimore: Johns Hopkins University Press, 1962.

Wright, Quincy. *The Study of International Relations*. New York: Appleton-Century-Crofts, 1955.

Realist Critiques, Challenges, and Modifications

Ashley, Richard K. "Political Realism and Human Interests." *International Studies Quarterly* 25, 2 (June 1981): 204–36.

Baldwin, David A., ed. *Neorealism and Neoliberalism: The Contemporary Debate*. New York: Columbia University Press, 1993.

Beer, Francis A. and Robert Hariman, eds. *Post-Realism: The Rhetorical Turn in International Relations*. East Lansing, MI: Michigan State University Press, 1996.

Grieco, Joseph M. "Anarchy and the Limits of Cooperation: A Realist Critique of the Newest Liberal Institutionalism." *International Organization* 42, 3 (Summer 1988): 485–506.

———. *Cooperation among Nations*. Ithaca, NY: Cornell University Press, 1990.

———. "The Relative-Gains Problem for International Cooperation." *American Political Science Review* 87, 3 (September 1993): 729–35.

Haas, Ernst B. "The Balance of Power: Prescription, Concept or Propaganda?" *World Politics* 5, 4 (July 1953): 442–77.

Hoffmann, Stanley. "Obstinate or Obsolete? The Fate of the Nation-State and the Case of Western Europe." *Daedalus* 95 (Summer 1966): 862–915.

Kegley, Charles W., ed. *Controversies in International Relations Theory: Realism and the Neoliberal Challenge.* New York: St. Martin's, 1995.

Keohane, Robert O. *After Hegemony: Cooperation and Discord in the World Political Economy.* Princeton, NJ: Princeton University Press, 1984.

———. *International Institutions and State Power.* Boulder, CO: Westview, 1989.

———. ed. *Neorealism and Its Critics.* New York: Columbia University Press, 1986.

———. "The Theory of Hegemonic Stability and Changes in International Economic Regimes." In *Change in the International System,* ed. Ole Holsti, Randolph M. Siverson, and Alexander George. Boulder, CO: Westview, 1980.

———. "Theory of World Politics: Structural Realism and Beyond." In *Political Science: State of the Discipline,* ed. Ada W. Finifter. Washington, DC: American Political Science Association, 1983.

Keohane, Robert O., and Joseph S. Nye. *Power and Interdependence.* Boston: Little, Brown, 1977.

Lyons, Gene M., and Michael Mastanduno, eds. *Beyond Westphalia: State Sovereignty and International Intervention.* Baltimore: Johns Hopkins University Press, 1995.

Nye, Joseph S. "Neorealism and Neoliberalism." *World Politics* 40, 2 (January 1988): 235–51.

Powell, Robert. "Absolute and Relative Gains in International Relations Theory." *American Political Science Review* 85 (1991): 1303–20.

———. "Anarchy in International Relations Theory: The Neorealist-Neoliberal Debate." *International Organization* 48 (1994): 313–44.

Rapoport, Anatol. *Strategy and Conscience.* New York: Schocken Books, 1969.

Rosecrance, Richard, and Arthur Stein. *The Domestic Bases of Grand Strategy.* Ithaca, NY: Cornell University Press, 1993.

Snidal, Duncan. "Relative Gains and the Pattern of International Cooperation." *American Political Science Review* 85, 3 (September 1991): 701–26.

Spruyt, Hendrik. *The Sovereign State and Its Competitors.* Princeton, NJ: Princeton University Press, 1994.

Vasquez, John A. "The Realist Paradigm and Degenerative versus Progressive Research Programs: An Appraisal of Neotraditional Research on Waltz's Balancing Proposition." *American Political Science Review* 91, 4 (December 1997): 899–912.

———. *The War Puzzle.* Cambridge, England: Cambridge University Press, 1993.

Waltz, Kenneth N. "Reflections on *Theory of International Politics:* Response to My Critics." In Keohane, *Neorealism and Its Critics,* cited above.

Wendt, Alexander E. "The Agent-Structure Problem in International Relations Theory." *International Organization* 41, 3 (Summer 1987): 335–70.

The Melian Dialogue

THUCYDIDES

This classic contains the essential ingredients of the realist perspective described by Thucydides in perhaps its boldest and most extreme form. The Athenians have no interest in whether the demands they make on the Melians are just or moral. In a classic statement, the Athenians emphasize the overriding importance of power: "The strong do what they have the power to do, and the weak accept what they have to accept." Other important concepts and notions such as honor, perception, neutrality, self-interest, alliances, balance of power, capabilities, and the uncertainty of power calculations are also discussed.

Next summer Alcibiades sailed to Argos with twenty ships and seized 300 Argive citizens who were still suspected of being pro-Spartan. These were put by the Athenians into the nearby islands under Athenian control.

The Athenians also made an expedition against the island of Melos. They had thirty of their own ships, six from Chios, and two from Lesbos; 1,200 hoplites, 300 archers, and twenty mounted archers, all from Athens; and about 1,500 hoplites from the allies and the islanders.

The Melians are a colony from Sparta. They had refused to join the Athenian empire like the other islanders, and at first had remained neutral without helping either side; but afterwards when the Athenians had brought force to bear on them by laying waste their land, they had become open enemies of Athens.

Now the generals Cleomedes, the son of Lycomedes, and Tisias, the son of Tisimachus, encamped with the above force in Melian territory and, before doing any harm to the land, first of all sent representatives to negotiate. The Melians did not invite these representatives to speak before the people, but asked them to make the statement for which they had come in front of the governing body and the few. The Athenian representatives then spoke as follows:

"So we are not to speak before the people, no doubt in case the mass of the people should hear once and for all and without interruption an argument from us which is both persuasive and incontrovertible, and should so be led astray. This, we realize, is your motive in bringing us here to speak before the few. Now suppose that you who sit here should make assurance doubly sure. Suppose that you, too, should refrain from dealing with every point in detail in a set speech, and should instead interrupt us whenever we say something controversial and deal with that before going on to the next point? Tell us first whether you approve of this suggestion of ours."

The Council of the Melians replied as follows:

From Thucydides, *History of the Peloponnesian War,* translated by Rex Warner. Penguin Classics, 1954, pages 400–408. Reprinted by permission of Penguin Books Ltd.

"No one can object to each of us putting forward our own views in a calm atmosphere. That is perfectly reasonable. What is scarcely consistent with such a proposal is the present threat, indeed the certainty, of your making war on us. We see that you have come prepared to judge the argument yourselves, and that the likely end of it all will be either war, if we prove that we are in the right, and so refuse to surrender, or else slavery."

Athenians: If you are going to spend the time in enumerating your suspicions about the future, or if you have met here for any other reason except to look the facts in the face and on the basis of these facts to consider how you can save your city from destruction, there is no point in our going on with this discussion. If, however, you will do as we suggest, then we will speak on.

Melians: It is natural and understandable that people who are placed as we are should have recourse to all kinds of arguments and different points of view. However, you are right in saying that we are met together here to discuss the safety of our country and, if you will have it so, the discussion shall proceed on the lines that you have laid down.

Athenians: Then we on our side will use no fine phrases saying, for example, that we have a right to our empire because we defeated the Persians, or that we have come against you now because of the injuries you have done us—a great mass of words that nobody would believe. And we ask you on your side not to imagine that you will influence us by saying that you, though a colony of Sparta, have not joined Sparta in the war, or that you have never done us any harm. Instead we recommend that you should try to get what it is possible for you to get, taking into consideration what we both really do think; since you know as well as we do that, when these matters are discussed by practical people, the standard of justice depends on the equality of power to compel and that in fact the strong do what they have the power to do and the weak accept what they have to accept.

Melians: Then in our view (since you force us to leave justice out of account and to confine ourselves to self-interest)—in our view it is at any rate useful that you should not destroy a principle that is to the general good of all men—namely, that in the case of all who fall into danger there should be such a thing as fair play and just dealing, and that such people should be allowed to use and to profit by arguments that fall short of a mathematical accuracy. And this is a principle which affects you as much as anybody, since your own fall would be visited by the most terrible vengeance and would be an example to the world.

Athenians: As for us, even assuming that our empire does come to an end, we are not despondent about what would happen next. One is not so much frightened of being conquered by a power which rules over others, as Sparta does (not that we are concerned with Sparta now), as of what would happen if a ruling power is attacked and defeated by its own subjects. So far as this point is concerned, you can leave it to us to face the risks involved. What we shall do now is to show you that it is for the good of our own empire that we are here and that it is for the preservation of your city that we shall say what we are going to say. We do not want any trouble in bringing you into our empire, and we want you to be spared for the good both of yourselves and of ourselves.

Melians: And how could it be just as good for us to be the slaves as for you to be the masters?

Athenians: You, by giving in, would save yourselves from disaster; we, by not destroying you, would be able to profit from you.

Melians: So you would not agree to our being neutral, friends instead of enemies, but allies of neither side?

Athenians: No, because it is not so much your hostility that injures us; it is rather the case that, if we were on friendly terms with you, our subjects would regard that as a sign of weakness in us, whereas your hatred is evidence of our power.

Melians: Is that your subjects' idea of fair play—that no distinction should be made between people who are quite unconnected with you and people who are mostly your own colonists or else rebels whom you have conquered?

Athenians: So far as right and wrong are concerned they think that there is no difference between the two, that those who still preserve their independence do so because they are strong, and that if we fail to attack them it is because we are afraid. So that by conquering you we shall increase not only the size but the security of our empire. We rule the sea and you are islanders, and weaker islanders too than the others; it is therefore particularly important that you should not escape.

Melians: But do you think there is security for you in what we suggest? For here again, since you will not let us mention justice, but tell us to give in to your interests, we, too, must tell you what our interests are and, if yours and ours happen to coincide, we must try to persuade you of the fact. Is it not certain that you will make enemies of all states who are at present neutral, when they see what is happening here and naturally conclude that in course of time you will attack them too? Does not this mean that you are strengthening the enemies you have already and are forcing others to become your enemies even against their intentions and their inclinations?

Athenians: As a matter of fact we are not so much frightened of states on the continent. They have their liberty, and this means that it will be a long time before they begin to take precautions against us. We are more concerned about islanders like yourselves, who are still unsubdued, or subjects who have already become embittered by the constraint which our empire imposes on them. These are the people who are most likely to act in a reckless manner and to bring themselves and us, too, into the most obvious danger.

Melians: Then surely, if such hazards are taken by you to keep your empire and by your subjects to escape from it, we who are still free would show ourselves great cowards and weaklings if we failed to face everything that comes rather than submit to slavery.

Athenians: No, not if you are sensible. This is no fair fight, with honour on one side and shame on the other. It is rather a question of saving your lives and not resisting those who are far too strong for you.

Melians: Yet we know that in war fortune sometimes makes the odds more level than could be expected from the difference in numbers of the two sides. And if we surrender, then all our hope is lost at once, whereas, so long as we remain in action, there is still a hope that we may yet stand upright.

Athenians: Hope, that comforter in danger! If one already has solid advantages to fall back upon, one can indulge in hope. It may do harm, but will not destroy one. But hope is by nature an expensive commodity, and those who are risking their all on one cast find out what it means only when they are already ruined; it never fails them in the period when such a knowledge would enable them to take precautions. Do not let this happen to you, you who are weak and whose fate depends on a single movement of the scale. And do not be like those people who, as so commonly happens, miss the chance of saving themselves in a human and practical way, and, when every clear and distinct hope has left them in their adversity, turn to what is blind and vague, to prophecies and oracles and such things which by encouraging hope lead men to ruin.

Melians: It is difficult, and you may be sure that we know it, for us to oppose your power and fortune, unless the terms be equal. Nevertheless we trust that the gods will give us fortune as good as yours, because we are standing for what is right against what is wrong; and as for what we lack in power, we trust that it will be made up for by our alliance with the Spartans, who are bound, if for no other reason, than for honour's sake, and because we are their kinsmen, to come to our help. Our confidence, therefore, is not so entirely irrational as you think.

Athenians: So far as the favour of the gods is concerned, we think we have as much right to that as you have. Our aims and our actions are perfectly consistent with the beliefs men hold about the gods and with the principles which govern their own conduct. Our opinion of the gods and our knowledge of men lead us to conclude that it is a general and necessary law of nature to rule whatever one can. This is not a law that we made ourselves, nor were we the first to act upon it when it was made. We found it already in existence, and we shall leave it to exist forever among those who come after us. We are merely acting in accordance with it, and we know that you or anybody else with the same power as ours would be acting in precisely the same way. And therefore, so far as the gods are concerned, we see no good reason why we should fear to be at a disadvantage. But with regard to your views about Sparta and your confidence that she, out of a sense of honour, will come to your aid, we must say that we congratulate you on your simplicity but do not envy you your folly. In matters that concern themselves for their own constitution the Spartans are quite remarkably good; as for their relations with others, that is a long story, but it can be expressed shortly and clearly by saying that of all people we know the Spartans are most conspicuous for believing that what they like doing is honourable and what suits their interests is just. And this kind of attitude is not going to be of much help to you in your absurd quest for safety at the moment.

Melians: But this is the very point where we can feel most sure. Their own self-interest will make them refuse to betray their own colonists, the Melians, for that would mean losing the confidence of their friends among the Hellenes and doing good to their enemies.

Athenians: You seem to forget that if one follows one's self-interest one wants to be safe, whereas the path of justice and honour involves one in danger. And, where danger is concerned, the Spartans are not, as a rule, very venturesome.

Melians: But we think that they would even endanger themselves for our sake and count the risk more worth taking than in the case of others, because we are so close to the Peloponnese that they could operate more easily, and because they can depend on us more than on others, since we are of the same race and share the same feelings.

Athenians: Good will shown by the party that is asking for help does not mean security for the prospective ally. What is looked for is a positive preponderance of power in action. And the Spartans pay attention to this point even more than others do. Certainly they distrust their own native resources so much that when they attack a neighbour they bring a great army of allies with them. It is hardly likely therefore that, while we are in control of the sea, they will cross over to an island.

Melians: But they still might send others. The Cretan sea is a wide one, and it is harder for those who control it to intercept others than for those who want to slip through to do so safely. And even if they were to fail in this, they would turn against your own land and against those of your allies left unvisited by Brasidas. So, instead of troubling about a country which has nothing to do with you, you will find trouble nearer home, among your allies, and in your own country.

Athenians: It is a possibility, something that has in fact happened before. It may happen in your case, but you are well aware that the Athenians have never yet relinquished a single siege operation through fear of others. But we are somewhat shocked to find that, though you announced your intention of discussing how you could preserve yourselves, in all this talk you have said absolutely nothing which could justify a man in thinking that he could be preserved. Your chief points are concerned with what you hope may happen in the future, while your actual resources are too scanty to give you a chance of survival against the forces that are opposed to you at this moment. You will therefore be showing an extraordinary lack of common sense if, after you have asked us to retire from this meeting, you still fail to reach a conclusion wiser than anything you have mentioned so far. Do not be led astray by a false sense of honour—a thing which often brings men to ruin when they are faced with an obvious danger that somehow affects their pride. For in many cases men have still been able to see the dangers ahead of them, but this thing called dishonour, this word, by its own force of seduction, has drawn them into a state where they have surrendered to an idea, while in fact they have fallen voluntarily into irrevocable disaster, in dishonour that is all the more dishonourable because it has come to them from their own folly rather than their misfortune. You, if you take the right view, will be careful to avoid this. You will see that there is nothing disgraceful in giving way to the greatest city in Hellas when she is offering you such reasonable terms—alliance on a tribute-paying basis and liberty to enjoy your own property. And, when you are allowed to choose between war and safety, you will not be so insensitively arrogant as to make the wrong choice. This is the safe rule—to stand up to one's equals, to behave with deference towards one's superiors, and to treat one's inferiors with moderation. Think it over again, then, when we have withdrawn from the meeting, and let this be a point that constantly recurs to your minds—that you are discussing the fate of your country, that you have only one country, and that its future for good or ill depends on this one single decision which you are going to make.

The Athenians then withdrew from the discussion. The Melians, left to themselves, reached a conclusion which was much the same as they had indicated in their previous replies. Their answer was as follows:

"Our decision, Athenians, is just the same as it was at first. We are not prepared to give up in a short moment the liberty which our city has enjoyed from its foundation for 700 years. We put our trust in the fortune that the gods will send and which has saved us up to now, and in the help of men—that is, of the Spartans; and so we shall try to save ourselves. But we invited you to allow us to be friends of yours and enemies to neither side, to make a treaty which shall be agreeable to both you and us, and so to leave our country."

The Melians made this reply, and the Athenians, just as they were breaking off the discussion, said:

"Well, at any rate, judging from this decision of yours, you seem to us quite unique in your ability to consider the future as something more certain than what is before your eyes, and to see uncertainties as realities, simply because you would like them to be so. As you have staked most on and trusted most in Spartans, luck, and hopes, so in all these you will find yourselves most completely deluded."

The Athenian representatives then went back to the army, and the Athenian generals, finding that the Melians would not submit, immediately commenced hostilities and built a wall completely round the city of Melos, dividing the work out among the various states. Later they left behind a garrison of some of their own and some allied troops to blockade the place by land and sea, and with the greater part of their army returned home. The force left behind stayed on and continued with the siege.

About the same time the Argives invaded Phliasia and were ambushed by the Phliasians and the exiles from Argos, losing about eighty men.

Then, too, the Athenians at Pylos captured a great quantity of plunder from Spartan territory. Not even after this did the Spartans renounce the treaty and make war, but they issued a proclamation saying that any of their people who wished to do so were free to make raids on the Athenians. The Corinthians also made some attacks on the Athenians because of private quarrels of their own, but the rest of the Peloponnesians stayed quiet.

Meanwhile the Melians made a night attack and captured the part of the Athenian lines opposite the market-place. They killed some of the troops, and then, after bringing in corn and everything else useful that they could lay their hands on, retired again and made no further move, while the Athenians took measures to make their blockade more efficient in the future. So the summer came to an end.

In the following winter the Spartans planned to invade the territory of Argos, but when the sacrifices for crossing the frontier turned out unfavourably, they gave up the expedition. The fact that they had intended to invade made the Argives suspect certain people in their city, some of whom they arrested, though others succeeded in escaping.

About this same time the Melians again captured another part of the Athenian lines where there were only a few of the garrison on guard. As a result of this, another force came out afterwards from Athens under the command of Philocrates, the son of Demeas. Siege operations were now carried on vigorously and, as there was also some treachery from inside, the Melians surrendered unconditionally to the Athenians, who put to death all the men of military age whom they took, and sold the women and children as slaves. Melos itself they took over for themselves, sending out later a colony of 500 men.

On Princes and the Security of Their States

NICCOLÒ MACHIAVELLI

In this selection from The Prince, *Machiavelli makes a number of his famous observations on how a prince should rule. Although a prince may not wish to be hated, Machiavelli argues "it is much safer to be feared than to be loved, if one must choose." Although the prince may be criticized for being harsh, this is acceptable to Machiavelli so long as the prince keeps his subjects united and loyal. These are the sorts of argument that have given Machiavellianism a negative connotation, but followers of Machiavelli would respond that the ultimate goal meant to justify particular policies is the security of the state, not just the security of an individual ruler.*

On Things for Which Men, and Particularly Princes, Are Praised or Blamed

We now have left to consider what should be the manners and attitudes of a prince toward his subjects and his friends. As I know that many have written on this subject I feel that I may be held presumptuous in what I have to say, if in my comments I do not follow the lines laid down by others. Since, however, it has been my intention to write something which may be of use to the understanding reader, it has seemed wiser to me to follow the real truth of the matter rather than what we imagine it to be. For imagination has created many principalities and republics that have never been seen or known to have any real existence, for how we live is so different from how we ought to live that he who studies what ought to be done rather than what is done will learn the way to his downfall rather

From Niccolò Machiavelli, *The Prince,* translated and edited by Thomas G. Bergin. Reprinted by permission.

than to his preservation. A man striving in every way to be good will meet his ruin among the great number who are not good. Hence it is necessary for a prince, if he wishes to remain in power, to learn how not to be good and to use his knowledge or refrain from using it as he may need.

Putting aside then the things imagined as pertaining to a prince and considering those that really do, I will say that all men, and particularly princes because of their prominence, when comment is made of them, are noted as having some characteristics deserving either praise or blame. One is accounted liberal, another stingy, to use a Tuscan term—for in our speech avaricious (*avaro*) is applied to such as are desirous of acquiring by rapine whereas stingy (*misero*) is the term used for those who are reluctant to part with their own—one is considered bountiful, another rapacious; one cruel, another tender-hearted; one false to his word, another trustworthy; one effeminate and pusillanimous, another wild and spirited; one humane, another haughty; one lascivious, another chaste; one a man of integrity and another sly; one tough and another pliant; one serious and another frivolous; one religious and another skeptical, and so on. Everyone will agree, I know, that it would be a most praiseworthy thing if all the qualities accounted as good in the above enumeration were found in a Prince. But since they cannot be so possessed nor observed because of human conditions which do not allow of it, what is necessary for the prince is to be prudent enough to escape the infamy of such vices as would result in the loss of his state; as for the others which would not have that effect, he must guard himself from them as far as possible but if he cannot, he may overlook them as being of less importance. Further, he should have no concern about incurring the infamy of such vices without which the preservation of his state would be difficult. For, if the matter be well considered, it will be seen that some habits which appear virtuous, if adopted would signify ruin, and others that seem vices lead to security and the well-being of the prince.

Cruelty and Clemency and Whether It Is Better to Be Loved or Feared

Now to continue with the list of characteristics. It should be the desire of every prince to be considered merciful and not cruel, yet he should take care not to make poor use of his clemency. Cesare Borgia was regarded as cruel, yet his cruelty reorganized Romagna and united it in peace and loyalty. Indeed, if we reflect, we shall see that this man was more merciful than the Florentines who, to avoid the charge of cruelty, allowed Pistoia to be destroyed.[1] A prince should care nothing for the accusation of cruelty so long as he keeps his subjects united and loyal; by making a very few examples he can be more truly merciful than those who through too much tender-heartedness allow disorders to arise whence come killings and rapine. For these offend an entire community, while the few executions ordered by the prince affect only a few individuals. For a new prince above all it is impossible not to earn a reputation for cruelty since new states are full of dangers. Virgil indeed has Dido apologize for the inhumanity of her rule because it is new, in the words:

> Res dura et regni novitas me talia cogunt Moliri
> et late fines custode tueri.

Nevertheless a prince should not be too ready to listen to talebearers nor to act on suspicion, nor should he allow himself to be easily frightened. He should proceed with a mixture of prudence and humanity in such a way as not to be made incautious by overconfidence nor yet intolerable by excessive mistrust.

Here the question arises; whether it is better to be loved than feared or feared than loved. The answer is that it would be desirable to be both but, since that is difficult, it is much safer to be feared than to be loved, if one must choose. For on men in general this observation may be made: they are ungrateful, fickle, and deceitful, eager to avoid dangers, and avid for gain, and while you are useful to them they are all with you, offering you their blood, their property, their lives, and their sons so long as danger is remote, as we noted above, but when it approaches they turn on you. Any prince, trusting only in their words and having no other preparations made, will fall to his ruin, for friendships that are bought at a price and not by greatness and nobility of soul are paid for indeed, but they are not owned and cannot be called upon in time of need. Men have less hesitation in offending a man who is loved than one who is feared, for love is held by a bond of obligation which, as men are wicked, is broken whenever personal advantage suggests it, but fear is accompanied by the dread of punishment which never relaxes.

Yet a prince should make himself feared in such a way that, if he does not thereby merit love, at least he may escape odium, for being feared and not hated may well go together. And indeed the prince may attain this end if he but respect the property and the women of his subjects and citizens. And if it should become necessary to seek the death of someone, he should find a proper justification and a public cause, and above all he should keep his hands off another's property, for men forget more readily the death of their father than the loss of their patrimony. Besides, pretexts for seizing property are never lacking, and when a prince begins to live by means of rapine he will always find some excuse for plundering others, and conversely pretexts for execution are rarer and are more quickly exhausted.

A prince at the head of his armies and with a vast number of soldiers under his command should give not the slightest heed if he is esteemed cruel, for without such a reputation he will not be able to keep his army united and ready for action. Among the marvelous things told of Hannibal is that, having a vast army under his command made up of all kinds and races of men and waging war far from his country, he never allowed any dissension to arise either as between the troops and their leaders or among the troops themselves, and this both in times of good fortune and bad. This could only have come about through his most inhuman cruelty which, taken in conjunction with his great valor, kept him always an object of respect and terror in the eyes of his soldiers. And without the cruelty his other characteristics would not have achieved this effect. Thoughtless writers have admired his actions and at the same time deplored the cruelty which was the basis of them. As evidence of the truth of our statement that his other virtues would have been insufficient let us examine the case of Scipio, an extraordinary leader not only in his own day but for all recorded history. His army in Spain revolted and for no other reason than because of his kind-heartedness, which had allowed more license to his soldiery than military discipline properly permits. His policy was attacked in the Senate by Fabius Maximus, who called him a corrupter of the Roman arms. When the Locrians had been mishandled by one of his lieutenants, his easy-going nature prevented him from avenging them or disciplining his officer, and it was à propos of this incident that one of the senators remarked, wishing to find an excuse for him, that there were many men who knew better how to avoid error themselves than to correct it in others. This characteristic of Scipio would have clouded his fame and glory had he continued in authority, but as he lived under the government of the Senate, its harmful aspect was hidden and it reflected credit on him.

Hence, on the subject of being loved or feared I will conclude that since love depends on the subjects, but the prince has it in his own hands to create fear, a wise prince will rely on what is his own, remembering at the same time that he must avoid arousing hatred, as we have said.

Note

1. By unchecked rioting between opposing factions (1502).

Of the Natural Condition of Mankind

THOMAS HOBBES

Hobbes analyzes why conflict and violence between individuals or states are to be expected. Although his focus in Leviathan *is on domestic societies, his observations are also relevant to international politics and have had a major impact on realism. In the absence of a sovereign or central, superordinate authority, the world described by Hobbes is a rather dismal one in which the life of the individual is "solitary, poor, nasty, brutish, and short" and "kings . . . because of their independency, are in continual jealousies, and in the state and posture of gladiators."*

Men by Nature Equal. Nature hath made men so equal, in the faculties of the body, and mind; as that though there be found one man sometimes manifestly stronger in body, or of quicker mind than another; yet when all is reckoned together, the difference between man, and man, is not so considerable, as that one man can thereupon claim to himself any benefit, to which another may not pretend, as well as he. For as to the strength of body, the weakest has strength enough to kill the strongest, either by secret machination, or by confederacy with others, that are in the same danger with himself.

And as to the faculties of the mind, setting aside the arts grounded upon words, and especially that skill of proceeding upon general, and infallible rules, called science; which very few have, and but in few things; as being not a native faculty, born with us; nor attained, as prudence, while we look after somewhat else, I find yet a greater equality amongst men, than that of strength. For prudence, is but experience; which equal time, equally bestows on all men, in those things they equally apply themselves unto. That which may perhaps make such equality incredible, is but a vain conceit of one's own wisdom, which almost all men think they have in a greater degree, than the vulgar; that is, than all men but themselves, and a few others, whom by fame, or for concurring with themselves, they approve. For such is the nature of men, that howsoever they may acknowledge many others to be more witty, or more eloquent, or more learned; yet they will hardly believe there be many so wise as themselves; for they see their own wit at hand, and other men's at a distance. But this proveth rather that men are in that point equal, than unequal. For there is not ordinarily a greater sign of the equal distribution of any thing, than that every man is contented with his share.

From Equality Proceeds Diffidence. From this equality of ability, ariseth equality of hope in the attaining of our ends. And therefore if any two men desire the same thing, which nevertheless they cannot both enjoy they become enemies; and in the way to their end, which is principally their own conservation, and sometimes their delectation only, endeavour to destroy, or subdue one another. And from hence it comes to pass, that where an invader hath no more to fear, than another man's single power; if one plant, sow, build, or possess a convenient seat, others may probably be expected

From Thomas Hobbes, *Leviathan,* introduction by Richard S. Peters. New York: Macmillan/Collier Books, 1962.

to come prepared with forces united, to dispossess, and deprive him, not only of the fruit of his labour, but also of his life, or liberty. And the invader again is in the like danger of another.

From Diffidence War.   And from this diffidence of one another, there is no way for any man to secure himself, so reasonable, as anticipation; that is, by force, or wiles, to master the persons of all men he can, so long, till he see no other power great enough to endanger him: and this is no more than his own conservation requireth, and is generally allowed. Also because there be some, that taking pleasure in contemplating their own power in the acts of conquest, which they pursue farther than their security requires; if others, that otherwise would be glad to be at ease within modest bounds, should not by invasion increase their power, they would not be able, long time, by standing only on their defence, to subsist. And by consequence, such augmentation of dominion over men being necessary to a man's conservation, it ought to be allowed him.

Again, men have no pleasure, but on the contrary a great deal of grief, in keeping company, where there is no power able to overawe them all. For every man looketh that his companion should value him, at the same rate he sets upon himself: and upon all signs of contempt, or undervaluing, naturally endeavours, as far as he dares, (which amongst them that have no common power to keep them in quiet, is far enough to make them destroy each other), to extort a greater value from his contemners, by damage; and from others, by the example.

So that in the nature of man, we find three principal causes of quarrel. First, competition; secondly, diffidence; thirdly, glory.

The first, maketh men invade for gain; the second, for safety; and the third, for reputation. The first use violence, to make themselves masters of other men's persons, wives, children, and cattle; the second, to defend them; the third, for trifles, as a word, a smile, a different opinion, and any other sign of undervalue, either direct in their persons, or by reflection in their kindred, their friends, their nation, their profession, or their name.

Out of Civil States, There Is Always War of Every One against Every One.   Hereby it is manifest, that during the time men live without a common power to keep them all in awe, they are in that condition which is called war; and such a war, as is of every man, against every man. For WAR, consisteth not in battle only, or the act of fighting; but in a tract of time, wherein the will to contend by battle is sufficiently known: and therefore the notion of *time,* is to be considered in the nature of war; as it is in the nature of weather. For as the nature of foul weather, lieth not in a shower or two of rain; but in an inclination thereto of many days together: so the nature of war, consisteth not in actual fighting; but in the known disposition thereto, during all the time there is no assurance to the contrary. All other time is PEACE.

The Incommodities of Such a War.   Whatsoever therefore is consequent to a time of war, where every man is enemy to every man; the same is consequent to the time, wherein men live without other security, than what their own strength, and their own invention shall furnish them withal. In such condition, there is no place for industry; because the fruit thereof is uncertain: and consequently no culture of the earth; no navigation, nor use of the commodities that may be imported by sea; no commodious building; no instruments of moving, and removing, such things as require much force; no knowledge of the face of the earth; no account of time; no arts; no letters; no society; and which is worst of all, continual fear, and danger of violent death; and the life of man, solitary, poor, nasty, brutish, and short.

It may seem strange to some man, that has not well weighed these things; that nature should thus dissociate, and render men apt to invade, and destroy one another; and he may therefore, not trusting to this inference, made from the passions, desire perhaps to have the same confirmed by experience. Let him therefore consider with himself, when taking a journey, he arms himself, and seeks to go well accompanied; when going to sleep, he locks his doors; when even in his house he locks his chests; and this when he knows there be laws, and public officers, armed, to revenge all injuries shall be done him; what opinion he has of his fellow-subjects, when he rides armed; of his fellow citizens, when he locks his doors; and of his children, and servants, when he locks his chests. Does he not there as much accuse mankind by his actions, as I do by my words? But neither of us accuse man's nature in it. The desires, and other passions of man, are in themselves no sin. No more are the actions, that proceed from those passions, till they know a law that forbids them: which till laws be made they cannot know: nor can any law be made, till they have agreed upon the person that shall make it.

It may peradventure be thought, there was never such a time, nor condition of war as this; and I believe it was never generally so, over all the world: but there are many places, where they live so now. For the savage people in many places of America, except the government of small families, the concord whereof dependeth on natural lust, have no government at all; and live at this day in the brutish manner, as I said before. Howsoever, it may be perceived what manner of life there would be, where there were no common power to fear, by the manner of life, which men that have formerly lived under a peaceful government, use to degenerate into, in a civil war.

But though there had never been any time, wherein particular men were in a condition of war one against another; yet in all times, kings,

and persons of sovereign authority, because of their independency, are in continual jealousies, and in the state and posture of gladiators; having their weapons pointing, and their eyes fixed on one another; that is, their forts, garrisons, and guns upon the frontiers of their kingdoms; and continual spies upon their neighbours; which is a posture of war. But because they uphold thereby, the industry of their subjects; there does not follow from it, that misery, which accompanies the liberty of particular men.

In Such a War Nothing Is Unjust.   To this war of every man, against every man, this also is consequent; that nothing can be unjust. The notions of right and wrong, justice and injustice have there no place. Where there is no common power, there is no law: where no law, no injustice. Force, and fraud, are in war the two cardinal virtues. Justice, and injustice are none of the faculties neither of the body, nor mind. If they were, they might be in a man that were alone in the world, as well as his senses, and passions. They are qualities, that relate to men in society, not in solitude. It is consequent also to the same condition, there be no propriety, no dominion, no *mine* and *thine* distinct; but only that to be every man's, that he can get: and for so long, as he can keep it. And thus much for the ill condition, which man by mere nature is actually placed in; though with a possibility to come out of it, consisting partly in the passions, partly in his reason.

The Passions that Incline Men to Peace.   The passions that incline men to peace, are fear of death; desire of such things as are necessary to commodious living; and a hope by their industry to obtain them. And reason suggesteth convenient articles of peace, upon which men may be drawn to agreement.

The State of War: Confederation as Means to Peace in Europe

JEAN JACQUES ROUSSEAU

Rousseau observes that "man is naturally peaceful and shy." He takes issue with the Hobbesian view of man's nature, contesting the idea that it could be so negative. At the same time, it is the "liberty" that states have in relation to one another that results in "accidental and specific wars." He portrays states as unitary and rational (purposive) actors that may come into conflict, engaging in warfare with one another. War does not depend upon the nature of man. No, to Rousseau war is the product of a social context within which the state (or body politic) finds itself—one in which there is no authority higher than the state itself. Rousseau does not reject the view that a European confederation could produce peace, but considers it unlikely that such a restructuring of politics will be achieved. This selection is key to understanding realist and neo-realist views. Along with Rousseau's other works, this selection has influenced such present-day writers as Kenneth Waltz, Stanley Hoffmann, Michael Doyle, and many others.

I open my books about rights and morals, I listen to scholars and legal experts, and inspired by their suggestive discourses, I deplore the miseries of nature, admire the peace and justice established by the civil order, bless the wisdom of public institutions, and find consolation for being a man by seeing myself as a citizen. Well instructed as to my duties and my happiness, I close the books, leave the lecture room, and look around me. There I see a miserable people groaning under an iron yoke, the whole human race crushed by a handful of oppressors, and an enraged mob overwhelmed by pain and hunger whose blood and tears the rich drink in peace. And everywhere the strong are armed against the weak with the formidable power of the law.

All of this happens peacefully and without resistance. With a tranquility like that of Odysseus's imprisoned companions waiting to be devoured by the Cyclops, we can only groan and be quiet. But I must draw a veil over these horrors. I lift my eyes and look into the distance. There I see fires and flames, deserted countrysides, pillaged villages. Monstrous men, where are you dragging these poor creatures? I hear a terrible noise, an uproar, screams! I draw near. Before me is a panorama of murder—ten thousand slaughtered men, the dead piled up in heaps, the dying trampled by horses—and everywhere the sight of death and agony. And yet all of this is the fruit of peaceful institutions. Pity and indignation rise up from the depths of my heart. Barbarous philosopher, come read us your book on a battlefield!

What human soul would not be sickened by such painful scenes? But one is no longer a man if one pleads the cause of humanity. Justice and truth must be twisted in the interest of the strongest. That is now the rule. The poor cannot provide pensions or employment, they do not grant academic honors or endow university chairs, so why should we protect them? Magnanimous princes, I speak in the name of the literary class: oppress the people in sound conscience. It is from you alone that we expect everything; the people can give us nothing.

How then will a feeble voice make itself heard above so many selfish clamors? Must I simply keep quiet? Cannot a voice from the heart break through these oppressive silences? No. Without entering into horrifying details that would be considered satirical if only because they are true, I will limit myself, as I have always done, to examining human institutions by means of their principles; to correcting, if it is possible, the false ideas given about them by self-interested authors; and, at the very least, to ensuring that injustice and violence do not shamelessly take on the names of right and equity.

When I reflect upon the condition of the human race, the first thing that I notice is a manifest contradiction in its constitution. As individuals we live in a civil state and are subject to laws, but as nations each enjoys the liberty of nature. The resulting continual vacillation makes our situation worse than if these distinctions were unknown. For living simultaneously in the social order and in the state of nature, we are subjected to the evils of both without gaining the security of either. The perfections of the social order consists, it is true, in the conjunction of force and law. But for this it is necessary that law direct force. According to the notion that princes must be absolutely independent, however, force alone, which appears as law to its own citizens and "raison d'état" to foreigners, deprives the latter of the power and the former of the will to resist, so that in the end the vain name of justice serves only to safeguard violence.

As for what is called the law of nations, it is clear that without any real sanction these laws are only illusions that are more tenuous even than the notion of natural law. The latter at least addresses itself to the heart of individuals, whereas decisions based on the law of nations, having no other guarantee than the utility of the one who submits to them, are respected only as long as those decisions confirm one's own self-interest. In the double condition in which we find ourselves, by doing too much or too little for whichever of the two systems we happen to prefer, we in fact have done nothing at all, and thereby have put ourselves in the worst possible position. This, it seems to me, is the true origin of public calamities.

For a moment let us put these ideas in opposition to the horrible system of Hobbes. We will find, contrary to his absurd doctrine, that far from the state of war being natural to man, war is born out of peace, or at least out of the precautions men have taken to assure themselves of peace. . . .

Who could imagine without shuddering the insane system of a natural war of every man against every man? What a strange animal this man must be who believes that his own well-being depends upon the destruction of his species! And how could anyone think that this species, so monstrous and detestable, could last even two generations? But it is to extremes such as these that the desire, or rather the fury, to establish despotism and passive obedience has led one of the greatest geniuses that ever lived. Such an insidious theory was surely worthy of its underlying purpose.

The social state that governs all our natural inclinations cannot, however, eliminate them. In spite of our prejudices and in spite of ourselves, our natural inclinations speak to us from the depths of our hearts and often lead us back to the truth that we have abandoned as fantasy. If a destructive and mutual enmity were essential to our constitution, it would make itself felt even more and would burst forth, unopposed, from within every social bond. The fierce hatred of humanity would eat away at the heart of man.

He would mourn at the birth of his children, rejoice at the death of his brothers, and kill every sleeping man he happened to come across.

The benevolence that enables us to share in the happiness of our fellow men, the compassion that identifies us with those who suffer and that touches us with their pain, would be unknown sentiments and contrary to nature. A sensitive and sympathetic man would be considered a monster, and we would be naturally that which we have taken great pains to become in the midst of the corruption that surrounds us.

In vain could our sophist argue that this mutual enmity might not be innate and immediate but that it is founded on an inevitable competition resulting from the right of each for all things. For the sentiment of this alleged right is no more natural to man than the war that it gives birth to.

I have said before and cannot repeat too often that the error of Hobbes and the *philosophes* is to confuse natural man with the man that they have before their eyes, and to transport into one system a being which could only exist in another. Man wishes for his own well-being and for all that can contribute to it—this is incontestable. But by nature the well-being of man is limited to physical necessity. For when he has a healthy soul and his body is not in pain, what does his natural constitution lack to make him happy? He who has nothing desires few things; he who commands no one has few ambitions. But surplus awakens greed: The more one accumulates, the more one desires. Those who have much want to have all, and the mad passion for universal monarchy has only tormented the hearts of great kings. This is in the nature of things—this is how the passions expand. A superficial philosopher observes souls that are endlessly kneaded and allowed to ferment in the yeast of society and believes he has observed man. But in order to know man well, he must know how to separate out the natural growth of the sentiments. And it is not among

city dwellers that he must search to find nature's first imprint on the human heart.

Thus, this analytic method offers only mystery and abyss where those who are most wise understand the least. Let someone ask the *philosophes* why morals are corrupted in proportion to the enlightenment of minds. Being unable to find the cause, they will have the audacity to deny the fact. Let someone ask them why primitive people brought among us share neither our passions nor our pleasures and do not worry about the things that we desire with so much fervor. Either the *philosophes* will never explain this or they will explain it with the principles put forth by me. They know only what they see, and they have never seen nature. They may very well know a bourgeois from Paris or London, but they will never know man.

But even if it were true that this unlimited and uncontrollable greed had developed in every man to the extent that Hobbes presumes, still it would not bring on that state of universal war of each against all that he has described in such odious terms. For the frenzied desire to appropriate everything for oneself is incompatible with the desire to destroy one's fellow men. The victor in such a war would face the world alone, and having gained everything he would enjoy nothing. What good are riches if they cannot be exchanged? What good would it be to possess the whole universe if one were its only survivor? Can one man's belly devour all the earth's fruit? Who would harvest for him all the world's crops? Who would carry the word of his empire to the vast wastelands where he himself could never live? What would he do with his treasures, who would consume his commodities, before whose eyes would he display his power? I know: Instead of massacring everyone, he would put them all in chains and then he at least would own some slaves. And this of course would immediately change things, for as soon as destruction itself is no longer the issue, the state of war as such disappears. May the reader here suspend his judgment; I will return to this point.

Man is naturally peaceful and shy; at the slightest danger his first movement is to flee. He only becomes emboldened by force of habit and experience. Honor, self-interest, prejudice, vengeance—all the passions that can make him brave the perils of death—are far from him in the state of nature. It is only after having associated with one man that he determines to kill another. He only becomes soldier after having been citizen. It is not in natural man that one finds the great propensities for war. But I need not dwell on a system that is as revolting as it is absurd, and that has been refuted a thousand times.

In the state of nature there is thus no general war of every man against every man; the human race was not created simply to destroy itself. But it still remains for us to consider those accidental and specific wars that might arise between two or several individuals.

If natural law were inscribed only on human reason, it would hardly be capable of directing most of our actions. But it is also indelibly engraved in the human heart. It is from the heart that natural law speaks to man more powerfully than all the precepts of philosophers. It is from there that it cries out to him that he may not sacrifice the life of his fellow man except to save his own, and that even when he sees himself obliged to do so, he cannot but feel a sense of horror at the idea of killing in cold blood. . . .

Concerning Civil Society

We now enter into a new order of things where we see men united by an artificial accord coming together to cut one another's throats, and where all the horrors of war arise from the efforts that were taken to prevent it. But first of all it is important to formulate more exact notions that we have up until now about the essence of this body politic. . . .

The state . . . since it is an artificial body, has no fixed measure and is never sure of its proper size. It can always expand, and yet it always feels weak as long as there are other states that are stronger than itself. Its security, its defense, demand that it try to appear more powerful than its neighbors; and it can only grow, feed itself, and test its strength at their expense. Even if it does not actually need to seek its subsistence beyond its own borders, it is ceaselessly on the lookout for new members who might give it a more stable base. For the inequality of men has limits put in place by the hands of nature, but the inequalities of states can grow incessantly, until one alone absorbs all the others.

Its power thus being purely relative, the political body is forced ceaselessly to compare itself in order to know itself. It depends on its surroundings, and must take an interest in all that happens there. For in vain might it wish simply to keep to itself without risking gain or loss; whether a state becomes small or great, weak or strong, depends on whether its neighbor expands or pulls back, adds to its forces or reduces them. Finally even political stability, insofar as it results in a more systematic foreign policy, can give an added forcefulness to a state's actions and thus make its conflicts more severe. . . .

For the state to survive it is thus necessary that the intensity of its passions supplement the intensity of its actions, and that its will become animated to the extent that its strength becomes slack. This is the law of self-preservation that nature herself established among the species and which sustains them all in spite of their inequality. It is also, I must say in passing, the reason why smaller states have in proportion more vigor than larger ones. For public vitality does not increase with territory. The further a society extends itself, the weaker grows its will, and the great body that is overburdened with its own weight soon sinks down, falls into decline, and perishes.

After having seen the earth become covered with new states, after having discovered among them a general relationship which tends toward their mutual destruction, it remains for us to see what exactly it is that constitutes their existence, their well-being, and their life, in order then to identify the kinds of hostilities by which they are able to attack and harm one another.

It is from the social pact that the body politic receives its unity and its "*moi commun.*" The government and the laws determine the robustness of its constitution, the hearts of its citizens give it its life, their courage and their customs determine its durability, and the only actions that it undertakes freely and that it can be accountable for are those dictated by the general will. It is by these actions that we can judge whether the being that produced them is well or poorly constituted.

Thus as long as there exists a common will to observe the social pact and its laws, the social pact will continue to survive; and as long as this will manifests itself as external acts, the state is not destroyed. But without ceasing to exist, the state can find itself at a point of vigor or decline from which—weak, healthy, or ill, and tending either to destroy itself or to assert itself—its power can grow or alter in an infinite number of ways, almost all of which are contingent upon its well-being. . . .

The General Idea of War between State and State

The life principle of the body politic, and, if I may say so, the heart of the state, is the social pact, which, if harmed in any way, immediately dies, falls apart, and dissolves. But this pact is not a charter made out of parchment that can simply be torn apart into shreds. It is written into the general will, where it is not at all easy to get rid of.

Unable at first to be broken up all at once, the social pact can be attacked part by part. If the body is invulnerable, its separate members can be struck at one by one. If its life cannot be taken, at least its health can be altered. If the source of its life cannot be reached, that which maintains it—the government, laws, customs, holdings, possessions, men—can still be destroyed. When everything that preserves it is annihilated, the state will finally die.

All these means are used or can be used in a war of one power against another, and they are also often the conditions imposed by the conquerors as a way further to harm a disarmed and defeated state. For the objective of all the harm inflicted on one's enemy at war is to force him to accept those things that he will have to suffer even more from when at peace. . . .

What the State of War Is

Although these two words war and peace appear to be exactly correlative, the second contains a broader significance, since peace can be troubled or interrupted in many different ways without leading to war. Repose, unity, concord, and all the notions of benevolence and mutual affection seem contained in the sweet name of peace. It brings to one's soul a fullness of sentiment that makes us love simultaneously our own existence and that of others; it represents the tie among beings that unites them into a universal system. Its full meaning is to be found in the spirit of God, whom nothing can harm and who desires the preservation of all the beings that he has created.

The constitution of this universe does not permit all the sensible beings that compose it to concur at the same time in their mutual happiness. Instead, the happiness of one is the misfortune of another, and thus according to the law of nature each gives himself preference, both when he works to his own advantage and when he works to the disadvantage of others. As soon as peace is upset on the side of the one who suffers, then not only is it natural to rebuff the hurt that is directed at us, but, in cases when an intelligent being sees that this hurt comes from the ill will of someone else, it is natural to get angry and seek to counter it. From this arises discord, quarrels, sometimes conflicts, but still not war.

Finally, when things have arrived at the point where a rational being is convinced that the care for its own preservation is incompatible not only with the well-being of another but with that other's existence, then this being takes up arms and seeks to destroy the other with the same ardor with which it seeks to preserve itself, and for the same reason. The one that is attacked, sensing that the security of its existence is incompatible with the existence of the aggressor, attacks in turn with all its strength the life of the one who is after him. This manifest will to destroy each other and all the actions that it gives rise to produce between the two enemies a relation that is called war.

From the above it follows that war does not consist of one or a few unpremeditated conflicts, or even of homicide or murder as long as they are committed in a brief fit of anger. Instead, war consists in the constant, reflected, and manifest will to destroy one's enemy. For in order to judge that the existence of this enemy is incompatible with our well-being, one needs coolness and reason—both of which produce a lasting resolve; and in order for the relationship to be mutual, the enemy in turn, knowing that its life is in jeopardy, must have the intention to defend its own life at the risk of ours. All these ideas are contained in the word war.

The public effects of this will reduced into acts are called hostilities. But whether or not there are hostilities, the relation of war, once established, can only cease by means of a formal peace. Otherwise, each of the two enemies, having no proof that the other has ceased resenting its existence, cannot or should not cease defending its own life at the cost of the other's.

These differences lead to a certain distinction in terminology. When both sides continue to engage in acts of hostility, there is what is properly called the *waging of war*. On the other hand, when two self-declared enemies remain stationary and take no offensive actions against each other, the relationship has not in any way changed, but so long as there are no actual effects there is what is called only a *state of war*. Long wars that people get tired of but that they cannot end ordinarily produce this state. Sometimes, far from being lulled into inaction, the animosity needs only to wait for a favorable moment to surprise the enemy, and then often the state of war that produces this release is more dangerous than war itself.

It has been argued whether a truce, a suspension of arms, a "Peace of God" are a state of war or peace. It is clear from the preceding notions that they all constitute a modified state of war in which the two enemies tie their own hands without losing or disguising the will to harm each other. They make preparations, pile up weapons and materials for a siege, and all the nonspecified military operations continue apace....

I thus define war between one power and another the effect of a mutual, constant, and manifest intention to destroy the enemy state, or at least to weaken it by all possible means. This intention carried into action is war properly so called; but as long as it does not come into effect it is only the state of war....

On the Perpetual Peace Project

Just as there is no greater nor more beautiful and useful project for the human spirit to reflect upon than one which aims at a perpetual and universal peace among all the peoples of Europe, so there is no author who better deserves the attention of the public than one who proposes the means for putting this project into effect. It is even difficult for a sane and virtuous person not to become enthusiastic about such a project, for in this case I am not sure whether the dreams of a truly human heart whose own zeal makes everything seem easy are not to be preferred to that cold and calculating reason which always finds in its indifference to the public good the first obstacle to everything that might benefit it.

I do not doubt that many readers are armed in advance skeptically to resist persuasion in these matters, and I pity them for so stubbornly mistaking hard-headedness as realism. But I hope that at least a few good souls will share the gratifying feelings with which I take up my pen on a subject so vital to humanity. I am about to see, at least in my mind, men coming together and loving each other; I am about to imagine a sweet and peaceful society of brothers, living in an eternal concord, all led by the same beliefs, all content with common pleasures; and, realizing in myself such a touching scene, the image of a happiness which does not exist will allow me to enjoy a few moments of one that does.

I could not withhold my sentiments from these first lines, but now let us reason realistically. Determined to put forth nothing that I cannot prove, I believe I can ask the reader in turn to deny nothing that he cannot refute. For it is not the true polemicists whom I fear so much as those who, while refusing to accept any proofs, yet have no objections to bring to them.

It is not necessary to have thought long about the means of perfecting any government to perceive the difficulties and obstacles that arise less from its constitution than from its foreign policy—to the extent that we are forced to give over to our defense most of the attention that should be devoted to enforcing the law and to think more about being in a state of readiness to resist others than about perfecting the government itself. Indeed, if our social order were, as it is claimed to be, the work of reason rather than of the passions, would we have taken so long to see that as far as our well-being is concerned we have accomplished either too much or too little; that each one of us being both in the civil state with his fellow citizens and in the state of nature with the whole rest of the world, we have prevented private wars only so as to set off public wars, which are a thousand times worse; and that by uniting with a few men we have really become the enemies of mankind?

If there is any means of removing these dangerous contradictions it can only be by a form of confederative government, which, by uniting nations with ties similar to those which unite individuals, submits each of them equally to the authority of laws. This form of government, moreover, appears preferable to any other in that it combines at the same time the advantages of both large and small states. It is externally secure because of its power, internally sound because of its laws, and it is the only form which is able to include subjects, leaders, and foreigners on an equal basis. . . .

All the powers of Europe constitute among themselves a sort of system in which they are united by a common religion, by a common sense of the customary laws governing the relations among states [*droit des gens*], by manners, literature, and commerce, and by a sort of equilibrium which is the necessary effect of all that, and which, without anyone consciously maintaining it, would nevertheless not be as easy to disturb as many people might think. This society of European peoples has not always existed, but the particular causes that gave birth to it serve to maintain it still. Indeed, before the conquests of the Romans all the peoples of this part of the world, barbarous and unknown to one another, had nothing in common except their quality as human beings—a quality which, greatly suppressed at that time by slavery, hardly differentiated them spiritually from beasts. The Greeks, with their rationalism and vanity, thus came to distinguish two kinds of humanity—one (their own), which was made to command, and the other (which comprised the rest of the world), simply to serve. The result of this principle was that to the Greeks a Gaul or an Iberian meant no more than a Kaffir or an American, nor did the barbarians have any more affinity among themselves than the Greeks had for any of them.

But when this naturally sovereign people had been subjected to the Romans who had been its slaves, and when one whole part of the known world had suffered under the same yoke, a political and civil union gradually developed among all the members of the common Empire. This union was held together by the either quite wise or quite foolish practice of bestowing on the conquered peoples all the rights of the conquerors, and above all by the famous decree of Claudius, which incorporated all the subjects of Rome into the ranks of her citizens.

The political network that thus united all the members into one body was reinforced by civil institutions and laws that determined in an equitable, clear, and precise manner (at least as much as was possible in such a vast empire) the duties and reciprocal rights of the prince and of his subjects and of the citizens among themselves. . . . This . . . greatly slowed down the decline of the Empire and preserved for it a sort of authority even over the barbarians who eventually became the cause of its ruin.

A . . . tie, stronger than the preceding ones, was that of religion, and no one can deny that it is, above all, to Christianity that Europe even today owes the kind of society that has been perpetuated among its members—to the extent that one who has not adopted the sentiment of the others on this point remains a stranger among them. Christianity, so maligned at its birth, served finally as a refuge for its detractors. After having persecuted Christianity so cruelly and so vainly, the Roman Empire found in it the resources that it could no longer find among its own forces. The Empire came to value conversion more than victory, it sent bishops to repair the mistakes of generals, and it triumphed with priests when its soldiers were defeated. It is thus that the Franks, the Goths, the Bourguignons, the Lombards, the Avares, and thousands of others finally recognized the authority of the Empire after having subjugated it, and in appearance at least, received with the law of the Gospel the law of the prince who had had it preached to them. . . .

All these factors together make Europe not just an idealized collection of peoples who have only a name in common, like Asia or Africa, but a real society with its own religion, manners, customs, and even laws, from which no single nation composing it could withdraw without immediately causing problems for the others. When we see, on the other hand, the endless conflicts, violence, usurpations, revolts, wars, and murders that daily lay waste to this respectable abode of the wise, this brilliant haven for the sciences and the arts; when we compare our elegant speeches with our horrifying procedures, the humanity of our maxims with the cruelty of our actions, the gentleness of our religion with the brutality of our prejudices, the wisdom of our politics in theory with its harshness in practice, our benevolent leaders with our miserable people, our moderate governments with our cruel wars—then we hardly know how to reconcile such strange contradictions, and the so-called fraternity of the peoples of Europe seems nothing more than a name of derision to express with irony their mutual hate.

In all this, however, things are only following their natural course. Any society without leaders or without laws, its union formed or maintained by chance, must necessarily degenerate into quarrels or dissension at the first change in circumstance. The ancient union of the peoples of Europe has complicated their interests and their rights in a thousand ways; they overlap at so many points that the slightest movement of some cannot help but trouble the others; their divisions are all the more deadly as their ties are more intimate; and their frequent quarrels have almost the same cruelty as civil wars.

Let us agree then that the relative state of the powers of Europe is properly speaking a state of war, and that all the partial treaties among certain of these powers are but temporary truces rather than true states of peace—either because such treaties commonly have no other guarantee than the contracting parties themselves or because the rights of each of them are never determined in any fundamental way—and thus that these half-stifled rights (or the claims substituted for them between powers that recognize no superior) will infallibly become the source of new wars as soon as different circumstances have given new strengths to the claimants.

International public law, moreover, having never been established or authorized in concert, having no general principles, and varying incessantly according to time and place, is full of contradictory rules that can only be tested by the right of the strongest. With reason having no definite guide and in questionable matters always leaning toward personal self-interest, war thus becomes inevitable even when each side would like to be just. With all good intentions, all that can be done is to settle these kinds of problems by means of arms, or to assuage them by temporary treaties. . . .

Everyone can see that society is formed by common interests; that discord arises out of opposing ones; that since a thousand fortuitous events can change and modify these interests, then once there is a society it is necessary to have a coercive force to organize and coordinate the movements of its members so that the common interests and reciprocal ties are given the solidity they would not be able to have by themselves.

It would be a great error, however, to hope that the violent state of things could ever change simply by the force of circumstances and without the help of art. The European system has precisely the degree of solidity that can maintain it in a perpetual agitation without overthrowing it completely. . . .

Therefore let us not think that such a highly praised equilibrium was established by anyone or that anyone has purposely done anything to preserve it. It is found to exist, and those who do not feel in themselves enough strength to break it apart hide their particular views under the pretext of sustaining it. But whether one thinks about it or not, this equilibrium subsists, and needs nothing but itself to survive, without interference from anyone; and when it disintegrates for a moment on one side, it soon reestablishes itself on the other—to the extent that if the princes whom we accuse of aspiring to universal monarchy really did aspire to it, they would thereby demonstrate more ambition than talent. For how could one envisage such a plan for one moment without immediately perceiving its folly? How can anyone avoid seeing that there is no power in Europe superior enough ever to become its master? Conquerors who have succeeded in overthrowing states have always appeared with unexpected military forces or with strangely armed foreign troops before peoples who were either disarmed or divided or completely lacking in discipline. But where could a European prince, aiming to overthrow all the others, find such an unprecedented force, since the most powerful state is still such a small part of the whole and since the others would be on their guard against such an attack? Could he have more soldiers than all of them? He could not—or would all the sooner be ruined, or his soldiers would be less effective by virtue of their greater number. Could he have troops that were better trained? He would have proportionately fewer of them. Besides, discipline is everywhere pretty much the same, or quickly becomes so. Would he have more money? The sources of funds are common to all, and in any case, money alone has never been the cause of great victories. Could he make a sudden invasion? Famine or fortresses would slow his pace. Would he gain power step by step? He would then give his enemies the means to unite to resist him; his time, his money, and his men would soon disappear. Would he divide the other powers in order to conquer them one by one? The European ethos would make this policy useless, and even the most narrow-minded prince would not give in to this ploy. In sum, because no single one of them could gain exclusive command over resources, the resistance would, in the long run, equal the effort, and time would soon repair the sudden accidents of fortune, if not for each prince in particular, at least for the general constitution.

Shall we now whimsically suppose that two or three powers could agree to subject all the rest? These three powers, whichever they were, could not together make up half of Europe. Moreover, the other half would certainly unite against them, and the aggressors would have to overcome something stronger than themselves. I will add that the views of each one would be too opposed to those of the others and that there would reign too great a jealousy among them for them to be able to form such a plan. I also will add that if they were able to form the plan, to execute it, and to have any kind of success, this success in itself would seed discord among them: It would not be possible for the spoils to be so fairly divided that each one would be equally satisfied with his own share; and the least happy would soon oppose the progress of the others, who, for a similar reason, would quickly become divided among themselves. Indeed, I doubt whether, since the world has existed, there have ever been three or even two great powers well enough united to subjugate others without fighting among themselves over the responsibilities or the profits of war, and without soon providing, by their misunderstandings, additional resources for the weaker powers. Thus, however one looks at it, it is not likely that any prince or league could henceforth change in any considerable or permanent way the present status of things among us.

This is not to say that the Alps, the Rhine, the sea, the Pyrenees, are insurmountable obstacles to ambition, but that these obstacles are fortified by others that reinforce them or that restore states back to the same limits when temporary attempts have been made to transgress them. What provides the real basis of the European system is certainly in part the interplay of negotiations, which almost always ends up in a mutual balance. But the system has another, even more solid support. This is the body of Germanic states placed in the center of Europe, which demands respect from all the others and serves perhaps much more for the maintenance of its neighbors than for that of its own mem-

bers. A body that is formidable to outsiders on account of its size and its population, it is also useful to everyone else on account of its constitution, which by denying the means and the will to conquer creates an obstruction for conquerors. Despite the defects of this constitution, it is certain that as long as it lasts the equilibrium of Europe will never be broken, that no prince will have to fear being dethroned by another, and that the Treaty of Westphalia will perhaps forever be the basis of the political system among us. Thus the public law that the Germans study with so much care is yet more important than they think and is not only the Germanic public law but in certain respects the public law of all of Europe.

But if the present system is unshakable, it is by the same token all the more violent, for there is among the European powers an action and reaction which, while not dislodging them completely, hold them in a continual agitation. Such efforts are always futile and always recurring, like the currents of the sea that ceaselessly agitate the surface without ever changing its level, and the people are incessantly devastated, without any visible rewards for the sovereigns.

It would be easy for me to deduce the same truth from the individual interests of all the courts of Europe, for I could easily show that these interests coincide in a way that could hold all their forces in mutual respect, except that the ideas of commerce and money have produced a kind of political fanaticism that makes the apparent interests of princes change every day. Since everything now depends on the rather bizarre economic theories that happen to pass through the heads of ministers, it has become impossible to form any firm convictions about princes' true interests. Nevertheless, commerce does tend on a daily basis to move toward an equilibrium: By depriving certain powers of the exclusive advantage that they might gain from it, commerce deprives them at the same time of one of the great means that they have to make others obey them.

If I have insisted on the equal distribution of power that results in Europe from its present situation, it was to point to a consequence that is important for the establishment of any more general association. For, in order to form a solid and durable confederation, it would be necessary to put all the members in such a mutual dependence not only that no one singly would be in a condition to resist all the others, but also that particular associations that might be harmful to the whole would meet in it obstacles sufficient to prevent their execution. Without such mutual dependence the confederation would be useless, and each one while appearing to be subjected, would really remain independent. Now, if these obstacles are such as I have described them above, when at present all the powers are in complete liberty to form leagues and offensive treaties with each other, just imagine what they might be if there were a great armed league, always ready to intervene against those who would like to start to destroy it or resist it. This suffices to show that such an association would not consist simply of futile deliberations that each participant could ignore at will; instead, it would give rise to an effective power capable of forcing ambitious men to keep within the limits of the general treaty.

Three incontestable truths result from this exposition. First, that except for Turkey there reigns among all the peoples of Europe a social bond that is imperfect but tighter than the general and loose ties of humanity; second, that the imperfection of this society makes the condition of those who compose it worse than it would be were there no social structures at all; third, that the original bonds that make this society harmful simultaneously make it easy to perfect: All of its members could draw their happiness from that which at present causes their misery and could change into an eternal peace the state of war that now reigns among them.

Now let us see how this great work, begun by chance, could be achieved by reason, and how, by taking on the force and the solidity of a true body politic, the free and voluntary society that unites all the European states could change into a real Confederation. By giving to this association the perfection it now lacks, it is clear that such an institution would destroy its present abuses, extend its advantages, and force all its members to cooperate for the common good. But for that it is necessary that this Confederation be so general that no considerable power could refuse it; that it have a judiciary tribunal to establish laws and regulations that would be binding on its members; that it have a compulsory and coercive force to constrain each state to submit to the common deliberations, whether by taking action or abstaining from action; finally, that it be firm and durable, to prevent members from seceding from it at will the moment they believe their particular interests to be contrary to the general interest. These are the sure signs that will show whether or not the institution is wise, useful, and sound. . . .

The first question is whether the proposed Confederation would be sure to attain its purpose and would be sufficient to give Europe a solid and perpetual peace.

The second is whether it is in the interest of the sovereigns to establish this confederation and to purchase a continual peace at this price. . . .

Let us consider the motives that cause princes to take up arms. These motives are either to make conquests, or to defend oneself from an invasion, or to weaken a too-powerful neighbor, or to uphold one's rights when those rights have been infringed upon, or to settle a difference that cannot be settled amicably, or, finally, to fulfill the responsibilities of a treaty. There has never been a cause or pretext for war that does not fall under one of these six headings. Now, it is evident that not one of these six motives could exist in the proposed new state of things.

First, any form of invasion would have to be renounced because of the impossibility of its success. Any invader would be sure to be stopped in his tracks by forces much greater than those he could muster alone, and by risking all, he would be powerless to gain anything. An ambitious prince who wishes to gain power in Europe usually does two things. He begins by fortifying himself with good alliances, and then he tries to take his enemy by surprise. But individual alliances will serve no purpose against a more powerful and permanent alliance; and without any real reason for being armed, no prince would be able to do so without being noticed, warned, and punished by the Confederation, which would always be in a state of preparedness.

The same reason that deprives each prince of all hope of invasion relieves him at the same time of all fear of being attacked. And not only would his states be guaranteed by the whole of Europe and made as secure to him as the personal possessions of citizens in a well-regulated nation are, but as much more so than if he were their sole and only protector as Europe as a whole is stronger than he alone.

There is no reason to want to weaken a neighbor from whom one no longer has anything to fear, and there is not even a temptation to do so when one has no hope of succeeding.

Regarding the protection of one's rights, it is first of all necessary to say that an infinite number of quibbles and obscure pretensions and quarrels would be eliminated. . . .

But, within the terms of the Confederation, no one could infringe on my rights by force without incurring the ban of the assembly. Thus it would no longer be by force that I now should defend those rights. The same can be said of insults, damages, reparations, and all the different unforeseen events that can arise between two sovereigns. The same power that must defend their rights must also settle their grievances.

As for the last motive for going to war, the solution offered by the Confederation is right before our eyes. First we can see that, no longer having any aggressor to fear, there would be no longer any need for defensive treaties, and that

since one could not devise a treaty that was more solid and more secure than the great Confederation, any others would be useless, illegitimate, and consequently nil.

It would thus be impossible that the Confederation, once established, could let fall a single seed of war between the Confederates, and that the objective of perpetual peace could not be perfectly fulfilled by carrying out the proposed system.

It now remains for us to examine the other question, which has to do with the advantages for the contracting parties, for it is obvious that it would be futile to speak of the public self-interest to the detriment of private self-interest. Proving that peace is in general preferable to war says nothing to someone who believes that he has reasons to prefer war over peace; indeed, showing him the means of establishing a durable peace is only going to arouse his opposition.

Such a person will argue, in effect, that with this plan you are taking away the sovereigns' right to determine justice for themselves—that is to say, their precious right to be unjust when they please. You are taking away their power to grow at the expense of their neighbors, you are making them give up the apparatus of power and of terror with which they love to frighten the world—that glory of conquest from which they derive their honor; finally you are forcing them to become equitable and peaceful. How will they be compensated for such cruel deprivations?

Here I would not dare to reply, as the Abbé de Saint-Pierre does, that the true glory of princes consists in procuring the happiness of their subjects and the well-being of the public; that the whole of their self-interest is subordinate to their reputation and that their reputation among sensible men is measured by how much good they have done for the people; that the institution of a perpetual peace, being the greatest initiative that had ever been undertaken, would be the most capable of covering its author with an everlasting glory; that this same initiative, while being the most advantageous for the people, still would be the most honorable for the sovereigns—the only one, moreover, that is not tainted with blood, rape, tears, and curses; and finally that the most certain means of standing out from the crowd of kings would be to work for the welfare of the public. In the offices of ministers such lofty words may have brought ridicule to the Abbé and his projects, but let us not be mistaken like them about his underlying reasoning. Whatever may be true about the virtues of princes, let us speak only in terms of their own self-interest.

All the powers of Europe have rights or claims relative to one another. However, these rights are inherently unable to be elucidated in any absolute way, both because there is no common or constant rule with which to judge them and because they are often founded on ambivalent or uncertain facts. Nor can the conflicts that they cause ever be completely settled in any permanent way—as much because of the lack of any competent arbiter as because each prince will heedlessly take any chance he can get to revoke the concessions that were forced upon him, either by treaties made by the more powerful or by his defeat in a bitter way. . . .

If every king has not yet renounced the lust for conquest, it seems that the wiser of them are at least beginning to see that wars cost more than they are worth. In this regard, without entering into a thousand distinctions that would lead us too far afield, we can say in general that a prince, who, to extend his frontiers, loses as many former subjects as he acquires new ones, thus becomes weaker through his desire to grow. With a greater territory to defend, he no longer has any defenders. Moreover, we cannot ignore that, in the manner in which war is waged today, it is not in the armies that the greatest fatalities occur. It is there that we may find the most apparent and obvious losses, but at the same time throughout the state the increase in the number of those who will never be born, the rise in taxes, the interruption of commerce, the

desertion of the countryside, and the abandonment of agriculture all cause a more serious and irreparable harm than the loss of men who die. Such evils, while perhaps not immediately evident, make themselves known painfully later on, and it is then that people are surprised at being so weak after supposedly making themselves so strong.

What also makes conquest less tempting is that it is now known how to double or triple one's power not only without extending one's territory but sometimes by contracting it, as was done very wisely by the emperor Hadrian. It is clear that men alone constitute the force of kings, and a proposition that follows from what I have just said is that of two states that nourish the same number of inhabitants, the one occupying the least territory is really the more powerful. It is by means of good laws, wise policies, and economic foresight that a judicious sovereign, without leaving anything to chance, can thus add to his strength. The real victories that he will gain over his neighbors will be whatever beneficial institutions he develops in his own states. The number of new subjects born under him are worth as much as the number of enemies that he might have killed.

It would be useless to object here that I am proving too much and that if things were really the way I represent them and each sovereign had a true common interest in maintaining peace, then peace would be established by itself and would last forever without any confederation. This would be to engage in very poor reasoning in the present situation. For although it would be much better for everyone always to be at peace, the common lack of security in this respect makes it so that each one, lacking any assurance of being able to avoid war, tries at least to begin it with an advantage in case the occasion presents itself, and to anticipate his neighbor—who in turn does not miss any favorable occasion to anticipate him. Hence many wars, even offensive wars, result less from the desire to usurp the interests of others than from the unjust precautions that each side takes to make its own interests secure. However worthy a commitment to the public good might be in general, given the objectives that are followed in politics and even in morality, it is certain that these commitments become dangerous to anyone who persists in practicing them with others when no one else practices them with him. . . .

I know that it would not be agreeable to all sovereigns to disband their troops and be completely without armed forces on hand to stifle unexpected uprisings or to push back a sudden invasion; I know also that they would have to furnish a contingent to the Confederation, both to guard the frontiers of Europe and to maintain the Confederative army intended to defend, if need be, the decrees of the assembly. But once these expenses had been paid and the contingencies of war forever done away with, there would remain still more than half the usual military expenses to be divided between the needs of the people and the treasury of the prince. In this way the people would pay much less; the prince, being much richer, would be able to stimulate commerce, agriculture, the arts, and to develop useful institutions that would further increase the people's wealth and his own; and the state would thus have a much more perfect security than that which it could gain from armies and from the whole apparatus of war, which never ceases to weaken it even in times of peace.

One might argue that the countries on the frontiers of Europe would thereby be in a more disadvantageous position and might correspondingly have wars to sustain either with Turkey or with Africa or with the Tartars.

To this I answer (1) that those countries are in the same position today and that consequently it would not be citing a positive disadvantage but simply one less advantage and an inevitable inconvenience that their situation exposes them to; (2) that freed from all uneasiness from the European side, they would be in a much better position to resist an external threat;

(3) that getting rid of all the defenses in the interior of Europe and the costs necessary to maintain them would put the Confederation in a position to establish a large number of defenses on the frontiers with no extra burden on the confederates; (4) that these defenses—constructed, maintained, and commissioned at common expense—would similarly provide defenses and savings for the powers at the borders whose states were being guarded; (5) that the armies of the Confederation, distributed within the confines of Europe, would always be ready to repel an aggressor; (6) and, finally, that a body as formidable as the European Republic would discourage foreigners from the desire to attack any of its members—just as the Germanic body, though infinitely less powerful, still is powerful enough to make itself respected by its neighbors and to protect effectively all the princes that compose it.

One might also argue that if Europeans were to have no more wars among themselves, the art of military strategy might fall gradually into oblivion, that troops would lose their courage and their disciplines, and that there would be no more generals or soldiers, and Europe would remain at the mercy of the first foreign invader. . . .

Once they are carefully examined, all the so-called inconveniences of the status of confederation can be reduced to nothing. We now ask whether anyone on earth would dare to say as much for the inconveniences that result from the present manner of settling differences between princes by the right of the strongest—that is, from the state of anarchy and war that is necessarily brought on by each sovereign's absolute and mutual independence within the imperfect social context that holds sway among us in Europe. . . .

If we have reasoned well in the exposition of this project, it is demonstrated, first, that the establishment of perpetual peace depends solely on the consent of sovereigns and presents no difficulty other than their resistance; second, that this establishment would be useful to them in every way and that there is no comparison even for them between its inconveniences and its advantages; third, that it is reasonable to suppose that their will accords with their self-interest; finally, that this establishment, once it is developed according to the proposed plan, would be solid and durable and would fulfill its objective perfectly. Doubtless this is not to say that sovereigns will adopt this project (who can speak for the reasoning of others?) but only that if they were to adopt it, they would be acting with respect to their own true interests. For it must be observed that we have not been considering men such as they ought to be—good, generous, disinterested, and loving the public well-being from a humanitarian standpoint—but such as they are—unjust, greedy, and looking to their own self-interest above all else. The only thing that we have assumed about them is that they are both rational enough to perceive what is useful to them and courageous enough to work toward their own happiness. If, despite all this, the project remains unfulfilled, it is not therefore because it is too idealistic; rather, it is because men are insane and because it is a sort of folly to remain wise in the midst of those who are mad. . . .

Critique of the Perpetual Peace Project

As the most worthy cause to which a good man might devote himself, the *Project for Perpetual Peace* must also have been, among all the projects of the Abbé de Saint-Pierre, the one that he thought about the most and the one that he pursued with the greatest obstinacy. For how else could one explain the missionary zeal with which he clung to this project—despite the obvious impossibility of its success, the ridicule that it brought upon him every day, and the hostility that he was made continually to suffer. It seems that this humane soul was so single-mindedly focused on the public good that he measured the efforts that he gave things solely on the basis of their usefulness, without ever letting himself be discouraged by obstacles and without ever thinking about his own personal self-interest.

If ever a moral truth has been demonstrated, it seems to me that it is the general and the specific usefulness of this project. The advantages that would result from its formation both for each prince and for each nation, as well as for Europe as a whole, are immense, clear, and uncontestable. One cannot imagine anything more solid and more precise than the arguments with which the author supports his case. Indeed, so much would the experience allow each individual to gain from the common good, that to realize the European Republic for one day would be enough to make it last forever. However, these same princes who would defend the European Republic with all their might once it existed would now be opposed even to its being set up, and they would invariably prevent it from being established with just as much energy as they would prevent it from being destroyed. The work of the Abbé de Saint-Pierre thus would seem both ineffectual for producing peace and superfluous for maintaining it. Some impatient reader will say that it is therefore nothing but vain speculation. No, it is a solid and sensible book, and it is very important that it exists.

Let us begin by examining the difficulties of those who do not judge arguments with reason but only with events and who have nothing to object to in this project other than that it has not been tried. In effect, they doubtlessly will say, if the advantages are so real, why have the sovereigns of Europe not adopted them already? Why do they neglect their own self-interest, if this self-interest has now been made so clear? Do we see them rejecting all the other ways of increasing their revenues and their power? If this project were as good for that purpose as is claimed, is it plausible that they would be less impressed with it than with those which have failed them so many times before, or that they would prefer a thousand risky chances to one sure gain?

Clearly, all this is plausible unless we pretend that the wisdom of all these sovereigns is equal to their ambition and that the more strongly they desire their own advantages the better they can see them. Instead, the great penalty for excessive *amour propre* is forever to resort to the means that abuse it, and the very heat of the passions is what almost always prevents them from reaching their goal. We must distinguish, then, in politics as well as in morality, real interest from apparent interest. The first is to be found in perpetual peace—that has been demonstrated in the *Project*. The second can be found in the condition of absolute independence that draws sovereigns away from the rule of law in order to submit them to the rule of chance—like a mad sailor who, to show off his knowledge and intimidate his crew, would prefer to drift dangerously among the reefs during a storm than to secure his ship with an anchor. . . .

We must add, in considering the great commercial advantages that would result from a general and perpetual peace, that while they are obviously in themselves certain and incontestable, being common to all they would not be relative advantages to anyone. Since advantage is usually only sensed by virtue of difference, to add to one's relative power one must seek out only exclusive gains.

Ceaselessly deceived by the appearance of things, princes will therefore reject this peace when judging it by their own self-interest. Just think, then, what will happen when they leave such judgments to their ministers, whose interests are always opposed to those of the people and almost always opposed to those of the prince. Ministers need war to make themselves necessary, to precipitate the prince into crises that he cannot get out of without them, and to cause the loss of the state, if it is necessary, rather than the loss of their jobs. They need war to harass the people in the guise of public safety, to find work for their protégés, to make money on the markets, and to form a thousand corrupt monopolies in secret. They need it to satisfy their passions and to push each other out of office. They need it to preoccupy the prince and remove him from the court while dangerous intrigues arise among them. Such resources would all be lost to them if there were a perpetual peace. And the public keeps on demanding why, if the project is possible, it has not been adopted! They fail to see that there is nothing impossible about the project except its adoption. And what will the ministers do to oppose it? What they have always done—they will turn it to ridicule.

Nor is it possible to believe along with the Abbé de Saint-Pierre that, even with the good will which neither princes nor ministers will ever have, it would be easy to find a favorable moment to set this system in motion. For that it would be necessary that the sum of individual interests would not outweigh the common interest, and that each one would believe that he had found in the good of all the greatest good that he could hope for for himself. Now this would require a convergence of wisdom among so many different minds and a convergence of aims among so many different interests that one could hardly hope to get the happy agreement of all these necessary circumstances simply by chance. The only way to make up for the failure of this agreement to come about by chance would be to make it come about by force. Then it would no longer be a question of persuading but of compelling, and then what would be needed is not to write books but to levy troops.

Thus, although the project was very wise, the means of putting it into effect reflect the naiveté of the author. He innocently imagined that all you would need to do is to assemble a committee, propose his articles, have everyone sign them, and that would be it. We must conclude that, as with all the projects of this good man, he could envision quite well the effect of things after they had been established, but he judged with too little sophistication the methods for getting them established in the first place. . . .

We may not say, therefore, that if his system has not been adopted, it is because it was not good; on the contrary, we must say that it was too good to be adopted. For evil and abuse, which so many men profit from, happen by themselves, but whatever is useful to the public must be brought by force—seeing as special interests are almost always opposed to it. Doubtless perpetual peace is at present a project that seems absurd. . . .

We will not see federative leagues establishing themselves except by revolution, and, on this principle, who would dare to say whether this European league is to be desired or to be feared? It would perhaps cause more harm in one moment than it could prevent for centuries to come.

Does Order Exist in World Politics?

HEDLEY BULL

The late Professor Bull identifies three traditions of thought—Hobbesian (or realist), Kantian (or universalist), and Grotian (or internationalist). Bull's own work is a blend of the Hobbesian and Grotian traditions in that order in world politics rests, in his view, on both the balance of power and agreed-on rules or norms. Hedley Bull's work and that of his predecessor and mentor, Martin Wight, are core to the present-day "English school" that focuses not just on the state system, but also on various aspects of international society.

Order in world politics may one day take the form of the maintenance of elementary goals of social life in a single world society or great society of all mankind. . . . It cannot be seriously argued, however, that the society of all mankind is already a going concern. In the present phase we are still accustomed to thinking of order in world politics as consisting of domestic order, or order within states, and international order, or order among them.

No one would deny that there exists within some states a high degree of domestic or municipal order. It is, however, often argued that international order does not exist, except as an aspiration, and that the history of international relations consists simply of disorder or strife. To many people the idea of international order suggests not anything that has occurred in the past, but simply a possible or desirable future state of international relations, about which we might speculate or which we might work to bring about. To those who take this view a study of international order suggests simply a design for a future world, in the tradition of Sully, Cruce, St. Pierre and other irenists or peace theorists.

This present study takes as its starting-point the proposition that, on the contrary, order is part of the historical record of international relations; and in particular, that modern states have formed, and continue to form, not only a system of states but also an international society. To establish this proposition I shall begin by showing first that there has always been present, throughout the history of the modern states system, an idea of international society, proclaimed by philosophers and publicists, and present in the rhetoric of the leaders of states. . . .

The Idea of International society

Throughout the history of the modern states system there have been three competing traditions of thought: the Hobbesian or realist tradition, which views international politics as a state of war; the Kantian or universalist tradition, which sees at work in international politics a potential community of mankind; and the Grotian or internationalist tradition, which views international politics as taking place within an international society.[1] Here I shall state what is essential to the Grotian or internationalist idea of international society, and what divides it from the Hobbesian or realist tradition on the one hand, and from the Kantian or universalist tradition on the other. Each of these traditional patterns of thought embodies a description of the nature of international politics and a set of prescriptions about international conduct.

The Hobbesian tradition describes international relations as a state of war of all against all, an arena of struggle in which each state is pitted against every other. International relations, on the Hobbesian view, represent pure conflict between states and resemble a game that is wholly distributive or zero-sum: the interests of each state exclude the interests of any other. The particular international activity that, on the Hobbesian view, is most typical of international activity as a whole, or best provides the clue to it, is war itself. Thus peace, on the Hobbesian view, is a period of recuperation from the last war and preparation for the next.

The Hobbesian prescription for international conduct is that the state is free to pursue its goals in relation to other states without moral or legal restrictions of any kind. Ideas of morality and law, on this view, are valid only in the context of a society, but international life is beyond the bounds of any society. If any moral or legal goals are to be pursued in international

politics, these can only be the moral or legal goals of the state itself. Either it is held (as by Machiavelli) that the state conducts foreign policy in a kind of moral and legal vacuum, or it is held (as by Hegel and his successors) that moral behaviour for the state in foreign policy lies in its own self-assertion. The only rules or principles which, for those in the Hobbesian tradition, may be said to limit or circumscribe the behaviour of states in their relations with one another are rules of prudence or expediency. Thus agreements may be kept if it is expedient to keep them, but may be broken if it is not.

The Kantian or universalist tradition, at the other extreme, takes the essential nature of international politics to lie not in conflict among states, as on the Hobbesian view, but in the transnational social bonds that link the individual human beings who are the subjects or citizens of states. The dominant theme of international relations, on the Kantian view, is only apparently the relationship among states, and is really the relationship among all men in the community of mankind—which exists potentially, even if it does not exist actually, and which when it comes into being will sweep the system of states into limbo.[2]

Within the community of all mankind, on the universalist view, the interests of all men are one and the same; international politics, considered from this perspective, is not a purely distributive or zero-sum game, as the Hobbesians maintain, but a purely cooperative or non-zero-sum game. Conflicts of interest exist among the ruling cliques of states, but this is only at the superficial or transient level of the existing system of states; properly understood, the interests of all peoples are the same. The particular international activity which, on the Kantian view, most typifies international activity as a whole is the horizontal conflict of ideology that cuts across the boundaries of states and divides human society into two camps—the trustees of the immanent community of mankind and those who stand in its way, those who are of the true faith and the heretics, the liberators and the oppressed.

The Kantian or universalist view of international morality is that, in contrast to the Hobbesian conception, there are moral imperatives in the field of international relations limiting the action of states, but that these imperatives enjoin not coexistence and cooperation among states but rather the overthrow of the system of states and its replacement by a cosmopolitan society. The community of mankind, on the Kantian view, is not only the central reality in international politics, in the sense that the forces able to bring it into being are present; it is also the end or object of the highest moral endeavour. The rules that sustain coexistence and social intercourse among states should be ignored if the imperatives of this higher morality require it. Good faith with heretics has no meaning, except in terms of tactical convenience; between the elect and the damned, the liberation and the oppressed, the question of mutual acceptance of rights to sovereignty or independence does not arise.

What has been called the Grotian or internationalist tradition stands between the realist tradition and the universalist tradition. The Grotian tradition describes international politics in terms of a society of states or international society.[3] As against the Hobbesian tradition, the Grotians contend that states are not engaged in simple struggle, like gladiators in an arena, but are limited in their conflicts with one another by common rules and institutions. But as against the Kantian or universalist perspective the Grotians accept the Hobbesian premise that sovereigns or states are the principal reality in international politics; the immediate members of international society are states rather than individual human beings. International politics, in the Grotian understanding, expresses neither complete conflict of interest between states nor complete identity of interest; it resembles a game that is partly distributive but also partly productive. The particular international activity which, on the Grotian view, best typifies international activity as a whole is neither war between states, nor horizontal conflict cutting across the boundaries of states, but trade—or, more generally, economic and social intercourse between one country and another.

The Grotian prescription for international conduct is that all states, in their dealings with one another, are bound by the rules and institutions of the society they form. As against the view of the Hobbesians, states in the Grotian view are bound not only by rules of prudence or expediency but also by imperatives of morality and law. But, as against the view of the universalists, what these imperatives enjoin is not the overthrow of the system of states and its replacement by a universal community of mankind, but rather acceptance of the requirements of coexistence and cooperation in a society of states.

Each of these traditions embodies a great variety of doctrines about international politics, among which there exists only a loose connection. In different periods each pattern of thought appears in a different idiom and in relation to different issues and preoccupations. This is not the place to explore further the connections and distinctions within each tradition. Here we have only to take account of the fact that the Grotian idea of international society has always been present in thought about the states system. . . .

My contention is that the element of a society has always been present, and remains present, in the modern international system, although only as one of the elements in it, whose survival is sometimes precarious. The modern international system in fact reflects all three of the elements singled out, respectively, by the Hobbesian, the Kantian, and the Grotian traditions; the element of war and struggle for power among states, the element of transnational solidarity and conflict, cutting across the divisions among states, and the element of cooperation and regulated intercourse among states. In different historical phases of the states system, in different geographical theatres of its operation, and in the policies of different states and statesmen, one of these three elements may predominate over the others. . . .

Notes

1. This threefold division derives from Martin Wight. The best published account of it is his "Western Values in International Relations," in *Diplomatic Investigations*, ed. Herbert Butterfield and Martin Wight (London: Allen and Unwin, 1967). The division is further discussed in my "Martin Wight and the Theory of International Relations. The Second Martin Wight Memorial Lecture," *British Journal of International Studies* 2, no. 2 (1976).

2. In Kant's own doctrine there is of course ambivalence as between the universalism of *The Idea of Universal History from a Cosmopolitan Point of View* (1784) and the position taken up in *Perpetual Peace* (1795), in which Kant accepts the substitute goal of a league of 'republican' states.

3. I have myself used the term 'Grotian' in two senses: (i) as here, to describe the broad doctrine that there is a society of states; (ii) to describe the solidarist form of this doctrine, which united Grotius himself and the twentieth-century neo-Grotians, in opposition to the pluralist conception of international society entertained by Vattel and later positivist writers. See "The Grotian Conception of International Society," in *Diplomatic Investigations*.

Explaining War

KENNETH N. WALTZ

In this article excerpted from Man, the State and War, *Professor Waltz provides a causal explanation of war that combines three levels of analysis: individual, state and society, and international system. The permissive cause (providing no obstacle to war) is systemic anarchy; efficient or proximate causes of a given war may also be found at other levels. The systemic argument presented here is the foundation for structural realism developed some twenty years later in his* Theory of International Politics.

Introduction

Asking who won a given war, someone has said, is like asking who won the San Francisco earthquake. That in wars there is no victory but only varying degrees of defeat is a proposition that has gained increasing acceptance in the twentieth century. But are wars also akin to earthquakes in being natural occurrences whose control or elimination is beyond the wit of man? Few would admit that they are, yet attempts to eliminate war, however nobly inspired and assiduously pursued, have brought little more than fleeting moments of peace among states. There is an apparent disproportion between effort and product, between desire and result. The peace wish, we are told, runs strong and deep among the Russian people; and we are convinced that the same can be said of Americans. From these statements there is some comfort to be derived, but in the light of history and of current events as well it is difficult to believe that the wish will father the condition desired.

Social scientists, realizing from their studies how firmly the present is tied to the past and

This condensation originally appeared in John F. Reichart and Steven R. Sturm, eds., *American Defense Policy*, 5th ed. (Baltimore, MD: Johns Hopkins University Press, 1982), pp. 8–18. From *Man, the State and War* by Kenneth N. Waltz, copyright 1954 and 1959, Columbia University Press, New York. Used by permission from the publisher and consent of the author.

how intimately the parts of a system depend upon each other, are inclined to be conservative in estimating the possibilities of achieving a radically better world. If one asks whether we can now have peace where in the past there has been war, the answers are most often pessimistic. Perhaps this is the wrong question. And indeed the answers will be somewhat less discouraging if instead the following questions are put: Are there ways of decreasing the incidence of war, of increasing the chances of peace? Can we have peace more often in the future than in the past?

Peace is one among a number of ends simultaneously entertained. The means by which peace can be sought are many. The end is pursued and the means are applied under varying conditions. Even though one may find it hard to believe that there are ways to peace not yet tried by statesmen or advocated by publicists, the very complexity of the problem suggests the possibility of combining activities in different ways in the hope that some combination will lead us closer to the goal. Is one then led to conclude that the wisdom of the statesman lies in trying first one policy and then another, in doing what the moment seems to require? An affirmative reply would suggest that the hope for improvement lies in policy divorced from analysis, in action removed from thought. Yet each attempt to alleviate a condition implies some idea of its causes: to explain how peace can be more readily achieved requires an understanding of the causes of war. It is such an understanding that we shall seek in the following pages.

The First Image: International Conflict and Human Behavior

> There is deceit and cunning and from these wars arise.
>
> Confucius

According to the first image of international relations, the focus of the important causes of war is found in the nature and behavior of man. Wars result from selfishness, from misdirected aggressive impulses, from stupidity. Other causes are secondary and have to be interpreted in the light of these factors. If these are the primary causes of war, then the elimination of war must come through uplifting and enlightening men or securing their psychic-social readjustment. This estimate of causes and cures has been dominant in the writings of many serious students of human affairs from Confucius to present-day pacifists. It is the leitmotif of many modern behavioral scientists as well.

Prescriptions associated with first-image analyses need not be identical in content, as a few examples will indicate. Henry Wadsworth Longfellow, moved to poetic expression by a visit to the arsenal at Springfield, set down the following thoughts:

Were half the power that fills the world with terror,
Were half the wealth bestowed on camps and courts,
Given to redeem the human mind from error,
There were no need of arsenals or forts.

Implicit in these lines is the idea that the people will insist that the right policies be adopted if only they know what the right policies are. Their instincts are good, though their present gullibility may prompt them to follow false leaders. By attributing present difficulties to a defect in knowledge, education becomes the remedy of war. The idea is widespread. Beverly Nichols, a pacifist writing in the 1930s, thought that if Norman Angell "could be made educational dictator of the world, war would vanish like the morning mist, in a single generation."[1] In 1920, a conference of Friends, unwilling to rely upon intellectual development alone, called upon the people of the world to replace self-seeking with the spirit of sacrifice, cooperation, and trust.[2] Bertrand Russell, at about the same time and in much the same vein, saw a decline in the possessive instincts as a prerequisite to peace.[3] By others, increasing the chances of peace has been said to require not so much a change in "instincts" as a channeling of energies that are presently expended in the destructive folly of war. If there were something that men would rather do than fight, they would cease to fight altogether. Aristophanes saw the point. If the women of Athens would deny themselves to husbands and lovers, their men would have to choose between the pleasures of the couch and the exhilarating experiences of the battlefield. Aristophanes thought he knew the men, and women, of Athens well enough to make the outcome a foregone conclusion. William James was in the same tradition. War, in his view, is rooted in man's bellicose nature, which is the product of centuries-old tradition. His nature cannot be changed or his drives suppressed, but they can be diverted. As alternatives to military service, James suggests drafting the youth of the world to mine coal and man ships, to build skyscrapers and roads, to wash dishes and clothes. While his estimate of what diversions would be sufficient is at once less realistic and more seriously intended than that of Aristophanes, his remedy is clearly the same in type.[4]

The prescriptions vary, but common to them all is the thought that in order to achieve a more peaceful world men must be changed, whether in their moral-intellectual outlook or in their psychic-social behavior. One may, however, agree with the first-image analysis of causes without admitting the possibility of practicable prescriptions for their removal. Among those who accept a first-image explanation of war there are both optimists and pessimists, those who think the possibilities of progress so great that wars will end before the next generation is dead and those who think that wars will continue to occur though by them we may all die.

The Second Image: International Conflict and the Internal Structure of States

> However conceived in an image of the world, foreign policy is a phase of domestic policy, an inescapable phase.
>
> Charles Beard, *A Foreign Policy for America*

The first image did not exclude the influence of the state, but the role of the state was introduced as a consideration less important than, and to be explained in terms of, human behavior. According to the first image, to say that the state acts is to speak metonymically. We say that the state acts when we mean that the people in it act, just as we say that the pot boils when we mean that the water in it boils. The preceding [section] concentrated on the contents rather than the container; the present [section] alters the balance of emphasis in favor of the latter. To continue the figure: Water running out of a faucet is chemically the same as water in a container, but once the water is in a container, it can be made to "behave" in different ways. It can be turned into steam and used to power an engine, or, if the water is sealed in and heated to extreme temperatures, it can become the instrument of a destructive explosion. Wars would not exist were human nature not what it is, but neither would Sunday schools and brothels, philanthropic organizations and criminal gangs. Since everything is related to human nature, to explain anything one must consider more than human nature. The events to be explained are so many and so varied that human nature cannot possibly be the single determinant.

The attempt to explain everything by psychology meant, in the end, that psychology succeeded in explaining nothing. And adding sociology to the analysis simply substitutes the error of sociologism for the error of psychologism. Where Spinoza, for example, erred by leaving out of his personal estimate of cause all reference to the causal role of social structures, sociologists have, in approaching the problem of war and peace, often erred in omitting all reference to the political framework within which individual and social actions occur. The conclusion is obvious: to understand war and peace political analysis must be used to supplement and order the findings of psychology and sociology. What kind of political analysis is needed? For possible explanations of the occurrence or nonoccurrence of war, one can look to international politics (since it is in the name of the state that the fighting is actually done). The former approach is postponed [until the next section]; according to the second image, the internal organization of states is the key to understanding war and peace.

One explanation of the second-image type is illustrated as follows. War most often promotes the internal unity of each state involved. The state plagued by internal strife may then, instead of waiting for the accidental attack, seek the war that will bring internal peace. Bodin saw this clearly, for he concludes that "the best way of preserving a state, and guaranteeing it against sedition, rebellion, and civil war is to keep the subjects in amity one with another, and to this end, to find an enemy against whom they can make common cause." And he saw historical evidence that the principle had been applied, especially by the Romans, who "could find no better antidote to civil war, nor one more certain in its effects, than to oppose an enemy to the citizens."[5] Secretary of State William Henry Seward followed this reasoning when, in order to promote unity within the country, he urged upon Lincoln a vigorous foreign policy, which included the possibility of declaring war on Spain and France.[6] Mikhail Skobelev, an influential Russian military officer of the third quarter of the nineteenth century, varied the theme but slightly when he argued that the Russian monarchy was doomed unless it could produce major military successes abroad.[7]

The use of internal defects to explain those external acts of the state that bring war can take many forms. Such explanation may be related to a type of government that is thought to be generically bad. For example, it is often thought that the deprivations imposed by despots upon their subjects produce tensions that may find expressions in foreign adventure. Or the explanation may be given in terms of defects in a government not itself considered bad. Thus it has been argued that the restrictions placed upon a government in order to protect the prescribed rights of its citizens act as impediments to the making and executing of foreign policy. These restrictions, laudable in original purpose, may have the unfortunate effect of making difficult or impossible the effective action of that government for the maintenance of peace in the world.[8] And, as a final example, explanation may be made in terms of geographic or economic deprivation or in terms of deprivations too vaguely defined to be labeled at all. Thus a nation may argue that it has not attained its "natural" frontiers, that such frontiers are necessary to its security, that war to extend the state to its deserved compass is justified or even necessary.[9] The possible variations on this theme have been made familiar by the "have-not" arguments so popular in this century. Such arguments have been used both to explain why "deprived" countries undertake war and to urge the satiated to make the compensatory adjustments thought necessary if peace is to be perpetuated.[10]

The examples just given illustrate in abundant variety one part of the second image, the idea that defects in states cause wars among them. But in just what ways should the structure of states be changed? What definition of the "good" state is to serve as a standard? Among those who have taken this approach to international relations there is a great variety of definitions. Karl Marx defines "good" in terms of ownership of the means of production; Immanuel Kant in terms of abstract principles of right; Woodrow Wilson in terms of national self-determination and modern democratic organization. Though each definition singles out different items as crucial, all are united in asserting that if, and only if, substantially all states reform will world peace result. That is, the reform prescribed is considered the sufficient basis for world peace. This, of course, does not exhaust the subject. Marx, for example, believed that states would disappear shortly after they became socialist. The problem of war, if war is defined as violent conflict among states, would then no longer exist. Kant believed that republican states would voluntarily agree to be governed in their dealings by a code of law drawn up by the states themselves. Wilson urged a variety of requisites to peace, such as improved international understanding, collective security and disarmament, a world confederation of states. But history proved to Wilson that one cannot expect the steadfast cooperation of undemocratic states in any such program for peace.

For each of these men, the reform of states in the ways prescribed is taken to be the *sine qua non* of world peace. The examples given could be multiplied. Classical economists as well as socialists, aristocrats and monarchists as well as democrats, empiricists and realists as well as transcendental idealists—all can furnish examples of men who have believed that peace can be had only if a given pattern of internal organization becomes widespread. Is it that democracies spell peace, but we have had wars because there have never been enough democracies of the right kind? Or that the socialist form of government contains within it the guarantee of peace, but so far there have never been any true socialist governments?[11] If either question were answered in the affirmative, then one would have to assess the merits of different prescriptions and try to decide just which one, or which combination, contains the elusive secret formula for peace. The import of our criticism, however, is that no prescription for international relations written entirely in terms of the second image can be valid, that the approach itself is faulty. Our criticisms of the liberals apply to all theories that would rely on the generalization of one pattern of state and society to bring peace to the world.

Bad states lead to war. As previously said, there is a large and important sense in which this is true. The obverse of this statement, that good states mean peace in the world, is an extremely doubtful proposition. The difficulty, endemic with the second image of international relations, is the same in kind as the difficulty encountered in the first image. There the statement that men make the societies, including the international society, in which they live was criticized not simply as being wrong but as being incomplete. One must add that the societies they live in make men. And it is the same in international relations. The actions of states, or, more accurately, of men acting for states, make up the substance of international relations. But the international political environment has much to do with the ways in which states behave. The influence to be assigned to the internal structure of states in attempting to solve the war – peace equation cannot be determined until the significance of the international environment has been reconsidered.

The Third Image: International Conflict and International Anarchy

> For what can be done against force without force?
>
> Cicero, *The Letters to His Friends*

With many sovereign states, with no system of law enforceable among them, with each state judging its grievances and ambitions according to the dictates of its own reason or desire—conflict, sometimes leading to war, is bound to occur. To achieve a favorable outcome from such conflict a state has to rely on its own devices, the relative efficiency of which must be its constant concern. This, the idea of the third image, is to be examined [here]. It is not an esoteric idea; it is not a new idea. Thucydides implied it when he wrote that it was "the growth of the Athenian power, which terrified the Lacedaemonians and forced them into war."[12] John Adams implied it when he wrote to the citizens of Petersburg, Virginia, that "a war with France, if just and necessary, might wean us from fond and blind affections, which no Nation ought ever to feel towards another, as our experience in more than one instance abundantly testifies."[13] There is an obvious relation between the concern over relative power position expressed by Thucydides and the admonition of John Adams that love affairs between states are inappropriate and dangerous. This relation is made explicit in Frederick Dunn's statement that "so long as the notion of self-help persists, the aim of maintaining the power position of the nation is paramount to all other considerations."[14]

In anarchy there is no automatic harmony. The three preceding statements reflect this fact. A state will use force to attain its goals if, after assessing the prospects for success, it values those goals more than it values the pleasures of peace. Because each state is the final judge of its own cause, any state may at any time use force to implement its policies. Because any state may at any time use force, all states must constantly be ready either to counter force with force or to pay the cost of weakness. The requirements of state action are, in this view, imposed by the circumstances in which all states exist.

In a manner of speaking, all three images are a part of nature. So fundamental are man, the state, and the state system in any attempt to understand international relations that seldom does an analyst, however wedded to one image, entirely overlook the other two. Still, emphasis on one image may distort one's interpretation of the others. It is, for example, not uncommon to find those inclined to see the world in terms of either the first or the second image countering the oft-made argument that arms breed not war but security, and possibly even peace, by pointing out that the argument is a compound of dishonest myth, to cover the interests of politicians, armament makers, and others, and honest illusion entertained by patriots sincerely interested in the safety of their states. To dispel the illusion, Cobden, to recall one of the many who have argued this way, once pointed out that doubling armaments, if everyone does it, makes no state more secure and, similarly, that none would be endangered if all military establishments were simultaneously reduced by, say, 50 percent.[15] Putting aside the thought that the arithmetic is not necessarily an accurate reflection of what the situation would be, this argument illustrates a supposedly practical application of the first and second images. Whether by educating citizens and leaders of the separate states or by improving the organizations of each of them, a condition is sought in which the lesson here adumbrated becomes the basis for the policies of states. The result?—disarmament, and thus economy, together with peace, and thus security, for all states. If some states display a willingness to pare down their military establishments, other states will be able to pursue similar policies. In emphasizing the interdependence of the policies of all states, the argument pays heed to the third image. The optimism is, however, the result of ignoring some inherent difficulties. [Here Waltz takes up Rousseau's view of man in the early state of nature.—*Ed.*]

In the early state of nature, men were sufficiently dispersed to make any patterns of cooperation unnecessary. But finally the combination of increased numbers and the usual natural hazards posed, in a variety of situations, the proposition: cooperate or die. Rousseau illustrates the line of reasoning with the simplest example. The example is worth reproducing, for it is the point of departure for the establishment of government and contains the basis for his explanation of conflict in international relations as well. Assume that five men who have acquired a rudimentary ability to speak and to understand each other happen to come together at a time when all of them suffer from hunger. The hunger of each will be satisfied by the fifth part of a stag, so they "agree" to cooperate in a project to trap one. But also the hunger of any one of them will be satisfied by a hare, so, as a hare comes within reach, one of them grabs it. The defector obtains the means of satisfying his hunger but in doing so permits the stag to escape. His immediate interest prevails over consideration for his fellows.[16]

The story is simple; the implications are tremendous. In cooperative action, even where all agree on the goal and have an equal interest in the project, one cannot rely on others. Spinoza linked conflict causally to man's imperfect reason. Montesquieu and Rousseau counter Spinoza's analysis with the proposition that the sources of conflict are not so much in the minds of men as they are in the nature of social activity. The difficulty is to some extent verbal. Rousseau grants that if we knew how to receive the true justice that comes from God, "we should need neither government nor laws."[17] This corresponds to Spinoza's proposition that "men in so far as they live in obedience to reason, necessarily live always in harmony one with another."[18] The idea is a truism. If men were perfect, their perfection would be reflected in all of their calculations and actions. Each could rely on the behavior of others, and all decisions would be made on principles that would preserve a true harmony of interests. Spinoza emphasizes not the difficulties inherent in mediating conflicting interests but the defectiveness of man's reason that prevents their consistently making decisions that would be in the interest of each and for the good of all. Rousseau faces the same problem. He imagines how men must have behaved as they began to depend on one another to meet their daily needs. As long as each provided for his own wants, there could be no conflict; whenever the combination of natural obstacles and growth in population made cooperation necessary, conflict arose. Thus in the stag-hunt example the tension between one man's immediate interest and the general interest of the group is resolved by the unilateral action of the one man. To the extent that he was motivated by a feeling of hunger, his act is one of passion. Reason would have told him that his long-run interest depends on establishing, through experience, the conviction that cooperative action will benefit all of the participants. But reason also tells him that if he forgoes the hare, the man next to him might leave his post

to chase it, leaving the first man with nothing but food for thought on the folly of being loyal.

The problem is now posed in more significant terms. If harmony is to exist in anarchy, not only must I be perfectly rational but I must be able to assume that everyone else is too. Otherwise there is no basis for rational calculation. To allow in my calculation for the irrational acts of others can lead to no determinate solutions, but to attempts to act on a rational calculation without making such an allowance may lead to my own undoing. The latter argument is reflected in Rousseau's comments on the proposition that "a people of true Christians would form the most perfect society imaginable." In the first place he points out that such a society "would not be a society of men." Moreover, he says, "For the state to be peaceable and for harmony to be maintained, all the citizens without exception would have to be [equally] good Christians; if by ill hap there should be a single self-seeker or hypocrite . . . he would certainly get the better of his pious compatriots."[19]

If we define cooperative action as rational and any deviation from it irrational, we must agree with Spinoza that conflict results from the irrationality of men. But if we examine the requirements of rational action, we find that even in an example as simple as the stag hunt we have to assume that the reason of each leads to an identical definition of interest, that each will draw the same conclusion as to the methods appropriate to meet the original situation, that all will agree instantly on the action required by any chance incidents that raise the question of altering the original plan, and that each can rely completely on the steadfastness of purpose of all the others. Perfectly rational action requires not only the perception that our welfare is tied up with the welfare of others but also a perfect appraisal of details so that we can answer the question: Just how in each situation is it tied up with everyone else's? Rousseau agrees with Spinoza in refusing to label the act of the rabbit-snatcher either good or bad; unlike Spinoza, he also refuses to label it either rational or irrational. He has noticed that the difficulty is not only in the actors but also in the situations they face. While by no means ignoring the part that avarice and ambition play in the birth and growth of conflict,[20] Rousseau's analysis makes clear the extent to which conflict appears inevitably in the social affairs of men.

In short, the proposition that irrationality is the cause of all the world's troubles, in the sense that a world of perfectly rational men would know no disagreements and no conflicts, is, as Rousseau implies, as true as it is irrelevant. Since the world cannot be defined in terms of perfection, the very real problem of how to achieve an approximation to harmony in cooperative and competitive activity is always with us and, lacking the possibility of perfection, it is a problem that cannot be solved simply by changing men. Rousseau's conclusion, which is also the heart of his theory of international relations, is accurately though somewhat abstractly summarized in the following statement: That among particularities accidents will occur is not accidental but necessary.[21] And this, in turn, is simply another way of saying that in anarchy there is no automatic harmony.

If anarchy is the problem, then there are only two possible solutions: (1) to impose an effective control on the separate and imperfect states; (2) to remove states from the sphere of the accidental, that is, to define the good state as so perfect that it will no longer be particular. Kant tried to compromise by making states good enough to obey a set of laws to which they have volunteered their assent. Rousseau, whom on this point Kant failed to follow, emphasizes the particular nature of even the good state and, in so doing, makes apparent the futility of the solution Kant suggests.[22] He also makes possible a theory of international relations that in general terms explains the behavior of all states, whether good or bad.[23]

In the stag-hunt example, the will of the rabbit-snatcher was rational and predictable from his own point of view. From the point of view of the rest of the group, it was arbitrary and capricious. So of any individual state, a will perfectly good for itself may provoke the violent resistance of other states.[24] The application of Rousseau's theory to international politics is stated with eloquence and clarity in his commentaries on Saint-Pierre and in a short work entitled *The State of War*. His application bears out the preceding analysis. The states of Europe, he writes, "touch each other at so many points that no one of them can move without giving a jar to all the rest; their variances are all the more deadly, as their ties are more closely woven." They "must inevitably fall into quarrels and dissensions at the first changes that come about." And if we ask why they must "inevitably" clash, Rousseau answers: Because their union is "formed and maintained by nothing better than chance." The nations of Europe are willful units in close juxtaposition with rules neither clear nor enforceable to guide them. The public law of Europe is but "a mass of contradictory rules which nothing but the right of the stronger can reduce to order: so that in the absence of any sure clue to guide her, reason is bound, in every case of doubt, to obey the promptings of self-interest—which in itself would make war inevitable, even if all parties desired to be just." In this condition, it is foolhardy to expect automatic harmony of interest and automatic agreement and acquiescence in rights and duties. In a real sense there is a "union of the nations of Europe," but "the imperfections of this association make the state of those who belong to it worse than it would be if they formed no community at all."[25]

The argument is clear. For individuals the bloodiest stage of history was the period just prior to the establishment of society. At that point they had lost the virtues of the savage without having acquired those of the citizen. The late stage of the state of nature is necessarily a state of war. The nations of Europe are precisely in that stage.[26]

What then is cause: the capricious acts of the separate states or the system within which they exist? Rousseau emphasizes the latter:

Every one can see that what unites any form of society is community of interests, and what disintegrates [it] is their conflict; that either tendency may be changed or modified by a thousand accidents; and therefore that, as soon as a society is founded, some coercive power must be provided to co-ordinate the actions of its members and give to their common interests and mutual obligations that firmness and consistency which they could never acquire of themselves.[27]

But to emphasize the importance of political structure is not to say that the acts that bring about conflict and lead to the use of force are of no importance. It is the specific acts that are the immediate causes of war,[28] the general structure that permits them to exist and wreak their disasters. To eliminate every vestige of selfishness, perversity, and stupidity in nations would serve to establish perpetual peace, but to try directly to eliminate all the immediate causes of war without altering the structure of the "union of Europe" is utopian.

What alteration of structure is required? The idea that a voluntary federation, such as Kant later proposed, could keep peace among states, Rousseau rejects emphatically. Instead, he says, the remedy for war among states "is to be found only in such a form of federal Government as shall unite nations by bonds similar to those which already unite their individual members, and place the one no less than the other under the authority of the Law."[29] Kant made similar statements only to amend them out of existence once he came to consider the reality of such a federation. Rousseau does not modify his principle, as is made clear in the following quotation, every point of which is a contradiction of Kant's program for the pacific federation:

The Federation [that is to replace the "free and voluntary association which now unites the States of Europe"] must embrace all the important Powers in its membership; it must have a Legislative Body, with powers to pass laws and ordinances binding upon all its members; it must have a coercive force capable of compelling every State to obey its common resolves whether in the way of command or of prohibition; finally, it must be strong and firm enough to make it impossible for any member to withdraw at his own pleasure the moment he conceives his private interest to clash with that of the whole body.[30]

It is easy to poke holes in the solution offered by Rousseau. The most vulnerable point is revealed by the questions: How could the federation enforce its law on the states that comprise it without waging war against them? and How likely is it that the effective force will always be on the side of the federation? To answer these questions Rousseau argues that the states of Europe are in a condition of balance sufficiently fine to prevent any one state or combination of states from prevailing over the others. For this reason, the necessary margin of force will always rest with the federation itself. The best critical consideration of the inherent weakness of a federation of states in which the law of the federation has to be enforced on the states who are its members is contained in the *Federalist Papers*. The arguments are convincing, but they need not be reviewed here. The practical weakness of Rousseau's recommended solution does not obscure the merit of his theoretical analysis of war as a consequence of international anarchy.

Conclusion

The third image, like the first two, leads directly to a utopian prescription. In each image a cause is identified in terms of which all others are to be understood. The force of the logical relation between the third image and the world-government prescription is great enough to cause some to argue not only the merits of world government but also the ease with which it can be realized.[31] It is of course true that with world government there would no longer be international wars, though with an ineffective world government there would no doubt be civil wars. It is likewise true, reverting to the first two images, that without the imperfections of the separate states there would not be wars, just as it is true that a society of perfectly rational beings, or of perfect Christians, would never know violent conflict. These statements are, unfortunately, as trivial as they are true. They have the unchallengeable quality of airtight tautologies: perfectly good states or men will not do bad things; within an effective organization highly damaging deviant behavior is not permitted. The near perfection required by concentration upon a single cause accounts for a number of otherwise puzzling facts: the pessimism of St. Augustine, the failure of the behavioral scientists as prescribers for peace, the reliance of many liberals on the forces of history to produce a result not conceivably to be produced by the consciously directed efforts of men, the tendency of socialists to identify a corrupting element every time harmony in socialist action fails to appear. It also helps to explain the often rapid alternation of hope and despair among those who most fully adopt a single-cause approach to this or to almost any other problem. The belief that to make the world better requires changing the factors that operate within a precisely defined realm leads to despair whenever it becomes apparent that changes there, if possible at all, will come slowly and with insufficient force. One is constantly defeated by the double problem of demonstrating how the "necessary changes" can be produced and of substantiating the assertion that the changes described as necessary would be sufficient to accomplish the object in view.

The contrary assertion, that all causes may be interrelated, is an argument against assuming that there is a single cause that can be isolated by analysis and eliminated or controlled by wisely constructed policy. It is also an argument against working with one or several hypotheses without bearing in mind the interrelation of all causes. The prescriptions directly derived from a single image are incomplete because they are based upon partial analyses. The partial quality of each image sets up a tension that drives one toward inclusion of the others. With the first image the direction of change, representing Locke's perspective as against Plato's, is from men to societies and states. The second image catches up both elements. Men make states, *and* states make men; but this is still a limited view. One is led to a search for the more inclusive nexus of causes, for states are shaped by the international environment as are men by both the national and international environments. Most of those whom we have considered in preceding [sections] have not written entirely in terms of one image. That we have thus far been dealing with the consequences arising from differing degrees of emphasis accounts for the complexity of preceding [sections] but now makes somewhat easier the task of suggesting how the images can be interrelated without distorting any one of them.

The First and Second Images in Relation to the Third

It may be true that the Soviet Union poses the greatest threat of war at the present time. It is not true that were the Soviet Union to disappear the remaining states could easily live at peace. We have known wars for centuries; the Soviet Union has existed only for decades. But some states, and perhaps some forms of the state, are more peacefully inclined than others. Would not the multiplication of peacefully inclined states at least warrant the hope that the period between major wars might be extended? By emphasizing the relevance of the framework of action, the third image makes clear the misleading quality of such partial analyses and of the hopes that are often based upon them. The act that by individual moral standards would be applauded may, when performed by a state, be an invitation to the war we seek to avoid. The third image, taken not as a theory of world government but as a theory of the conditioning effects of the state system itself, alerts us to the fact that so far as increasing the chances of peace is concerned there is no such thing as an act good in itself. The pacification of the Hukbalahaps was a clear and direct contribution to the peace and order of the Philippine state. In international politics a partial "solution," such as one major country becoming pacifistic, might be a real contribution to world peace; but it might as easily hasten the coming of another major war.

The third image, as reflected in the writings of Rousseau, is based on an analysis of the consequences arising from the framework of state action. Rousseau's explanation of the origin of war among states is, in broad outline, the final one so long as we operate within a nation–state system. It is a final explanation because it does not hinge on accidental causes—irrationalities in men, defects in states—but upon his theory of the framework within which *any* accident can bring about a war. That state A wants certain things that it can get only by war does not explain war. Such a desire may or may not lead to war. My wanting a million dollars does not cause me to rob a bank, but if it were easier to rob banks, such desires would lead to much more bank robbing. This does not alter the fact that some people will and some will not attempt to rob banks no matter what the law enforcement situation is. We still have to look to motivation and circumstance in order to explain individual acts. Nevertheless one can predict that, other things being equal, a weakening of law enforcement agencies will lead to an increase in crime. From this point of view it is social structure—institutionalized restraints and institutionalized methods of altering and adjusting interests—that counts. And it counts in a way different from the ways usually associated with the word "cause." What causes a man to

rob a bank are such things as the desire for money, a disrespect for social proprieties, a certain boldness. But if obstacles to the operation of these causes are built sufficiently high, nine out of ten would-be bank robbers will live their lives peacefully plying their legitimate trades. If the framework is to be called cause at all, it had best be specified that it is a permissive or underlying cause of war.

Applied to international politics this becomes, in words previously used to summarize Rousseau, the proposition that wars occur because there is nothing to prevent them. Rousseau's analysis explains the recurrence of war without explaining any given war. He tells us that war may at any moment occur, and he tells us why this is so. But the structure of the state system does not directly cause state A to attack state B. Whether or not that attack occurs will depend on a number of special circumstances—location, size, power, interest, type of government, past history and tradition—each of which will influence the actions of both states. If they fight against each other it will be for reasons especially defined for the occasion by each of them. These special reasons become the immediate, or efficient, causes of war. These immediate causes of war are contained in the first and second images. States are motivated to attack each other and to defend themselves by the reason and/or passion of the comparatively few who make policies for states and of the many more who influence the few. Some states, by virtue of their internal conditions, are both more proficient in war and more inclined to put their proficiency to the test. Variations in the factors included in the first and second images are important, indeed crucial, in the making and breaking of periods of peace—the immediate causes of every war must be either the acts of individuals or the acts of states.

If every war is preceded by acts that we can identify (or at least try to identify) as cause, then why can we not eliminate wars by modifying individual or state behavior? This is the line of thinking followed by those who say: To end war, improve men; or: To end war, improve states. But in such prescriptions the role of the international environment is easily distorted. How can some of the acting units improve while others continue to follow their old and often predatory ways? The simplistic assumption of many liberals, that history moves relentlessly toward the millennium, is refuted if the international environment makes it difficult almost to the point of impossibility for states to behave in ways that are progressively more moral. Two points are omitted from the prescriptions we considered under the first and second images: (1) If an effect is produced by two or more causes, the effect is not permanently eliminated by removing one of them. If wars occur because men are less than perfectly rational and because states are less than perfectly formed, to improve only states may do little to decrease the number and intensity of wars. The error here is in identifying one cause where two or more may operate. (2) An endeavor launched against one cause to the neglect of others may make the situation worse instead of better. Thus, as the Western democracies became more inclined to peace, Hitler became more belligerent. The increased propensity to peace of some participants in international politics may increase, rather than decrease, the likelihood of war. This illustrates the role of the permissive cause, the international environment. If there were but two loci of cause involved, men and states, we could be sure that the appearance of more peacefully inclined states would, at worst, not damage the cause of world peace. Whether or not a remedy proposed is truly a remedy or actually worse than none at all depends, however, on the content and timing of the acts of all states. This is made clear in the third image.

War may result because state A has something that state B wants. The efficient cause of the war is the desire of state B; the permissive cause is the fact that there is nothing to prevent state B from undertaking the risks of war. In a different circumstance, the interrelation of efficient and permissive causes becomes still closer. State A may fear that if it does not cut state B down a peg now, it may be unable to do so ten years from now. State A becomes the aggressor in the present because it fears what state B may be able to do in the future. The efficient cause of such a war is derived from the cause that we have labeled permissive. In the first case, conflicts arise from disputes born of specific issues. In an age of hydrogen bombs, no single issue may be worth the risk of full-scale war. Settlement, even on bad grounds, is preferable to self-destruction. The use of reason would seem to require the adoption of a doctrine of "non-recourse to force." One whose reason leads him down this path is following the trail blazed by Cobden when in 1849 he pointed out "that it is almost impossible, on looking back for the last hundred years, to tell precisely what any war was about," and thus implied that Englishmen should never have become involved in them.[32] He is falling into the trap that ensnared A. A. Milne when he explained the First World War as a war in which ten million men died because Austria-Hungary sought, unsuccessfully, to avenge the death of one archduke.[33] He is succumbing to the illusion of Sir Edward Grey, who, in the memoirs he wrote some thirty years ago, hoped that the horrors of the First World War would make it possible for nations "to find at least one common ground on which they should come together in confident understanding: an agreement that, in the disputes between them, war must be ruled out as a means of settlement that entails ruin."[34]

It is true that the immediate causes of many wars are trivial. If we focus upon them, the failure to agree to settlement without force appears to be the ultimate folly. But it is not often true that the immediate causes provide sufficient explanation for the wars that have occurred. And if it is not simply particular disputes that produce wars, rational settlement of them cannot eliminate war. For, as Winston Churchill has written, "small matters are only the symptoms of the dangerous disease, and are only important for that reason. Behind them lie the interests, the passions and the destiny of mighty races of men; and long antagonisms express themselves in trifles."[35] Nevertheless Churchill may be justified in hoping that the fear induced by a "balance of terror" will produce a temporary truce. Advancing technology makes war more horrible and presumably increases the desire for peace; the very rapidity of the advance makes for uncertainty in everyone's military planning and destroys the possibility of an accurate estimate of the likely opposing forces. Fear and permanent peace are more difficult to equate. Each major advance in the technology of war has found its prophet ready to proclaim that war is no longer possible. Alfred Nobel and dynamite, for example, or Benjamin Franklin and the lighter-than-air balloon. There may well have been a prophet to proclaim the end of tribal warfare when the spear was invented and another to make a similar prediction when poison was first added to its tip. Unfortunately, these prophets have all been false. The development of atomic and hydrogen weapons may nurture the peace wish of some, the war sentiment of others. In the United States and elsewhere after the Second World War, a muted theme of foreign-policy debate was the necessity of preventive war—drop the bomb quickly before the likely opponent in a future war has time to make one of his own. Even with two or more states equipped with similar weapon systems, a momentary shift in the balance of terror, giving a decisive military advantage temporarily to one state, may tempt it to seize the moment in order to escape from fear. And the temptation would be proportionate to the fear itself. Finally, mutual fear of big weapons may produce, instead of peace, a spate of smaller wars.

The fear of modern weapons, of the danger of destroying the civilizations of the world, is not sufficient to establish the conditions of peace identified in our discussions of the three images of international relations. One can equate fear with world peace only if the peace wish exists in all states and is uniformly expressed in their policies. But peace is the primary goal of few men or states. If it were the primary goal of even a single state, that state could have peace at any time—simply by surrendering. But, as John Foster Dulles so often warned, "Peace can be a cover whereby evil men perpetrate diabolical wrongs."[36] The issue in a given dispute may not be: Who shall gain from it? It may instead be: Who shall dominate the world? In such circumstances, the best course of even reasonable men is difficult to define; their ability always to contrive solutions without force, impossible to assume. If solutions in terms of none of the three images is presently—if ever—possible, then reason can work only within the framework that is suggested by viewing the first and second images in the perspective of the third, a perspective well and simply set forth in the *Federalist Papers*, especially in those written by Hamilton and Jay.

What would happen, Jay asks, if the thirteen states, instead of combining as one state, should form themselves into several confederations? He answers:

> Instead of their being "joined in affection" and free from all apprehension of different "interests," envy and jealousy would soon extinguish confidence and affection, and the partial interests of each confederation, instead of the general interests of all America, would be the only objects of their policy and pursuits. Hence, like most *bordering* nations, they would always be either involved in disputes and war, or live in the constant apprehension of them.[37]

International anarchy, Jay is here saying, is the explanation for international war. But not international anarchy alone. Hamilton adds that to presume a lack of hostile motives among states is to forget that men are "ambitious, vindictive, and rapacious." A monarchical state may go to war because the vanity of its king leads him to seek glory in military victory; a republic may go to war because of the folly of its assembly or because of its commercial interests. That the king may be vain, the assembly foolish, or the commercial interests irreconcilable: none of these is inevitable. However, so many and so varied are the causes of war among states that "to look for a continuation of harmony between a number of independent, unconnected sovereigns in the same neighborhood, would be to disregard the uniform course of human events, and to set at defiance the accumulated experience of the ages."[38]

Jay and Hamilton found in the history of the Western state system confirmation for the conclusion that among separate sovereign states there is constant possibility of war. The third image gives a theoretical basis for the same conclusion. It reveals why, in the absence of tremendous changes in the factors included in the first and second images, war will be perpetually associated with the existence of separate sovereign states. The obvious conclusion of a third-image analysis is that world government is the remedy for world war. The remedy, though it may be unassailable in logic, is unattainable in practice. The third image may provide a utopian approach to world politics. It may also provide a realistic approach, and one that avoids the tendency of some realists to attribute the necessary amorality, or even immorality, of world politics to the inherently bad character of man. If everyone's strategy depends upon everyone else's, then the Hitlers determine in part the action, or better, reaction, of those whose ends are worthy and whose means are fastidious. No matter how good their intentions, policy makers must bear in mind the implications of the third image, which can be stated in summary form as follows: Each state pursues its own interests, however defined, in ways it judges best. Force is a means of achieving the external ends of states because there exists no consistent, reliable process of reconciling the conflicts of interest that inevitably arise among

similar units in a condition of anarchy. A foreign policy based on this image of international relations is neither moral nor immoral, but embodies merely a reasoned response to the world about us. The third image describes the framework of world politics, but without the first and second images there can be no knowledge of the forces that determine policy; the first and second images describe the forces in world politics, but without the third image it is impossible to assess their importance or predict their results.

Notes

1. Beverly Nichols, *Cry Havoc!* (New York: Doubleday, Doran & Co., 1933), p. 164.

2. Margaret E. Hirst, *The Quakers in Peace and War* (London: Swarthmore Press, 1923), pp. 521–25.

3. Bertrand Russell, *Political Ideals* (New York: Century Co., 1917), p. 42. In one way or another the thought recurs in Lord Russell's many writings on international relations.

4. William James, "The Moral Equivalent of War," in *Memories and Studies* (New York: Longmans, Green and Co., 1912), pp. 262–72, 290.

5. Jean Bodin, *Six Books of the Commonwealth*, abridged and trans. M. J. Tooley (Oxford: Basil Blackwell, n.d.), p. 168.

6. "Some Thoughts for the President's Consideration," Apr. 1, 1861, in *Documents of American History*, ed. Henry Steele Commager, 3d ed. (New York: F. S. Crofts & Co., 1946), p. 392.

7. Hans Herzfeld, "Bismarck und die Skobelewespisode," *Historische Zeitschrift* 142 (1930): 279–302.

8. Cf. Robert E. Sherwood, *Roosevelt and Hopkins* (New York: Harper and Brothers, 1948), pp. 67–68, 102, 126, 133–36, 272, and esp. 931; and Secretary of State Hay's statement in Henry Adams, *The Education of Henry Adams* (New York: Book League of America, 1928), p. 374. Note that in this case the fault is one that is thought to decrease the ability of a country to implement a peaceful policy. In the other examples, the defect is thought to increase the propensity of a country to go to war.

9. Cf. Bertrand Russell, who in 1917 wrote: "There can be no good international system until the boundaries of states coincide as nearly as possible with the boundaries of nations" (*Political Ideals*, p. 146).

10. Frank H. Simonds and Brooks Emery, *The Great Powers in World Politics* (New York: American Book Co.,

1939), passim; W. S. Thompson, *Danger Spots in World Population* (New York: Alfred A. Knopf, 1930), esp. the Preface and chaps. 1 and 13.

11. Cf. Vladimir Dedijer, "Albania, Soviet Pawn," *Foreign Affairs* 30(1961): 104: Socialism, but not Soviet Union state capitalism, means peace.

12. Thucydides, *History of the Peloponnesian War*, trans. B. Jowett, 2d ed. (London: Oxford University Press, 1900), bk. 1, par. 23.

13. John Adams to the citizens of the town of Petersburg, Virginia, June 6, 1798, reprinted in the program for the visit of William Howard Taft, Petersburg, May 19, 1909.

14. Frederick S. Dunn, *Peaceful Change* (New York: Council on Foreign Relations, 1937), p. 13.

15. Richard Cobden, esp. *Speeches on Peace, Financial Reform, Colonial Reform and Other Subjects Delivered during 1849* (London: James Gilbert, n.d.), p. 135.

16. Jean Jacques Rousseau, *The Social Contract and Discourses*, trans. G.D.H. Cole, Everyman's Library Edition (New York: E. P. Dutton and Co., 1950); see esp. *Inequality*, pp. 234 ff.

17. Ibid., p. 34.

18. Benedict de Spinoza, *The Chief Works of Benedict de Spinoza*, trans. R.H.M. Elwes, 2 vols. (New York: Dover Publications, 1951), *Ethics*, pt. 4, prop. 35, proof.

19. Rousseau, *The Social Contract and Discourses*, pp. 135–36 (bk. 4, chap. 8), italics added. The word "equally" is necessary for an accurate rendering of the French text but does not appear in the translation, cited.

20. Jean Jacques Rousseau, *A Lasting Peace through the Federation of Europe and the State of War*, trans. C. E. Vaughan (London: Constable and Co., 1917), p. 72.

21. This parallels Hegel's formulation: "It is to what is by nature accidental that accidents happen, and the fate whereby they happen is thus a necessity" [G.W.F.] Hegel, *Philosophy of Right*, trans. T. M. Knox (Oxford: Clarendon Press, 1942), sec. 324.

22. Kant is more willing to admit the force of this criticism than is generally realized.

23. This is not, of course, to say that no differences in state behavior follow from the different constitutions and situations of states. This point raises the question of the relation of the third image to the second, which will be discussed below.

24. Rousseau, *The Social Contract and Discourses*, pp. 290–91.

25. Rousseau, *A Lasting Peace*, pp. 46–48, 58–59.

26. Ibid., pp. 38, 46–47. On p. 121, Rousseau distinguishes between the "state of war," which always exists among states, and war proper, which manifests itself in the settled intention to destroy the enemy state.

27. Ibid., p. 49.

28. In ibid., p. 69, Rousseau presents his exhaustive list of such causes.

29. Ibid., pp. 38–39.

30. Ibid., pp. 59–60.

31. Cf. Karl Popper, *The Open Society and Its Enemies* (Princeton: Princeton University Press, 1950), pp. 158–59; and William Esslinger, *Politics and Science* (New York: Philosophical Library, 1955), passim.

32. Richard Cobden, *Speeches on Questions of Public Policy*, 2 vols., ed. John Bright and James E. Thorold Rogers (London: Macmillan & Co., 1870), 2: 165.

33. A. A. Milne, *Peace and War* (New York: E. P. Dutton & Co., 1934), p. 11.

34. Edward Grey, *Twenty-Five Years*, 2 vols. (New York: Frederick A. Stokes Co., 1925), 2: 285.

35. Winston Churchill, *The World Crisis*, 1911–1914, 4 vols. (New York: Charles Scribner's Sons, 1923–29), 1: 52.

36. "Excerpts from Dulles Address on Peace," Washington, D.C., Apr. 11, 1955, in *New York Times*, Apr. 12, 1955, p. 6.

37. Alexander Hamilton, John Jay, and James Madison, *The Federalist* (New York: Modern Library, 1941), pp. 23–24 (no. 5).

38. Ibid., pp. 27–28 (no. 6); cf. p. 18 (no. 4, Jay) and pp. 34–40 (no. 7, Hamilton).

War and Change in World Politics

ROBERT GILPIN

Professor Gilpin outlines key factors to explain the rise and decline of states. States are rational actors that seek expected benefits as exceeding expected costs. Power and the distribution of power in the international system are key explanatory factors. Peaceful change is possible, as in the aftermath of the Cold War; however, historically, the principal mechanism of change has been through war with reordering of the international system through a peace settlement that creates a new systemic equilibrium.

During the 1970s and early 1980s a series of dramatic events signaled that international relations were undergoing a significant upheaval. Long-established and seemingly stable sets of relationships and understandings were summarily cast aside. Political leaders, academic observers, and the celebrated "man in the street" were suddenly conscious of the fact that the energy crisis, dramatic events in the Middle East, and tensions in the Communist world were novel developments of a qualitatively different order from those of the preceding decade. These developments and many others in the political, economic, and military realms signaled far-reaching shifts in the international distribution of power, an unleashing of new sociopolitical forces, and the global realignment of diplomatic relations. Above all, these events and developments revealed that the relatively stable international system that the world had known since the end of World War II was entering a period of uncertain political changes.

Ours is not the first age in which a sudden concatenation of dramatic events has revealed underlying shifts in military power, economic interest, and political alignments. In the twentieth century, developments of comparable magnitude had already taken place in the decades preceding World War I and World War II. This awareness of the dangers inherent in periods of political instability and rapid change causes profound unease and apprehension. The fear grows that events may get out of hand and the world may once again plunge itself into a global conflagration. Scholars, journalists, and others turn to history for guidance, asking if the current pattern of events resembles the pattern of 1914 and 1939.[1]

These contemporary developments and their dangerous implications raise a number of questions regarding war and change in international relations: How and under what circumstances does change take place at the level of international relations? What are the roles of political, economic, and technological developments in producing change in international systems? Wherein lies the danger of intense military conflict during periods of rapid economic and political upheaval? And, most important of all, are answers that are derived from examination of the past valid for the contemporary world? In other words, to what extent have social, economic, and technological developments such as increasing economic interdependence of nations

From Robert Gilpin, *War and Change in World Politics* (1981), pp. 1–15 and 39–44. Reprinted by permission of Cambridge University Press.

and the advent of nuclear weapons changed the role of war in the process of international political change? Is there any reason to hope that political change may be more benign in the future than it has been in the past?

The purpose of this book is to explore these issues. In this endeavor we shall seek to develop an understanding of international political change more systematic than the understanding that currently exists. We do not pretend to develop a general theory of international relations that will provide an overarching explanatory statement. Instead, we attempt to provide a framework for thinking about the problem of war and change in world politics. This intellectual framework is intended to be an analytical device that will help to order and explain human experience. It does not constitute a rigorous scientific explanation of political change. The ideas on international political change presented are generalizations based on observations of historical experience rather than a set of hypotheses that have been tested scientifically by historical evidence; they are proposed as a plausible account of how international political change occurs.[2]

To this end we isolate and analyze the more obvious regularities and patterns associated with changes in international systems. However, we make no claim to have discovered the "laws of change" that determine when political change will occur or what course it will take.[3] On the contrary, the position taken here is that major political changes are the consequences of the conjuncture of unique and unpredictable sets of developments. However, the claim is made that it is possible to identify recurrent patterns, common elements, and general tendencies in the major turning points in international history. As the distinguished economist W. Arthur Lewis put it, "The process of social change is much the same today as it was 2,000 years ago . . . We can tell how change will occur if it occurs; what we cannot foresee is what change is going to occur."[4]

The conception of political change presented in this book, like almost all social science, is not predictive. Even economics is predictive only within a narrow range of issues.[5]

Most of the alleged theories in the field of political science and in the sub-field of international relations are in fact analytical, descriptive constructs; they provide at best a conceptual framework and a set of questions that help us to analyze and explain a type of phenomenon.[6] Thus, Kenneth Waltz, in his stimulating book, *Man, the State and War*, provided an explanation of war in general terms, but not the means for predicting any particular war.[7] In similar fashion, this study seeks to explain in general terms the nature of international political change.

The need for a better understanding of political change, especially international political change, was well set forth by Wilbert Moore in the latest edition of the *International Encyclopedia of the Social Sciences*: "Paradoxically, as the rate of social change has accelerated in the real world of experience, the scientific disciplines dealing with man's actions and products have tended to emphasize orderly interdependence and static continuity."[8]

Moore's judgment concerning the inadequate treatment of political change by social scientists is borne out by analyses of international-relations textbooks and theoretical works. Although there are some recent outstanding exceptions,[9] few of these books have addressed the problem of political change in systematic fashion. As David Easton rightly commented, "students of political life have . . . been prone to forget that the really crucial problems of social research are concerned with the patterns of change."[10]

It is worth noting, as Joseph Schumpeter pointed out, that the natural development of any science is from static analysis to dynamic analysis.[11] Static theory is simpler, and its propositions are easier to prove. Unfortunately, until the statics of a field of inquiry are sufficiently well developed and one has a good grasp of repetitive processes and recurrent phenomena, it is difficult if not impossible to proceed to the study of dynamics. From this perspective, systematic study of international relations is a young field, and much of what passes for dynamics is in reality an effort to understand the statics of interactions of particular international systems: diplomatic bargaining, alliance behavior, crisis management, etc. The question whether or not our current understanding of these static aspects is sufficiently well advanced to aid in the development of a dynamic theory poses a serious challenge to the present enterprise.

A second factor that helps to explain the apparent neglect, until recent years, of the problem of political change is what K. J. Holsti called the decline of "grand theory."[12] The political realism of Hans Morgenthau, the systems theory of Morton Kaplan, and the neofunctionalism of Ernst Haas, as well as numerous other "grand theories," have one element in common: the search for a general theory of international politics. Each in its own way, with varying success, has sought, in the words of Morgenthau, "to reduce the facts of experience to mere specific instances of general propositions."[13] Yet none of these ambitious efforts to understand the issues (war, imperialism, and political change) has gained general acceptance. Instead, "the major preoccupations of theorists during the past decade have been to explore specific problems, to form hypotheses or generalizations explaining limited ranges of phenomena, and particularly, to obtain data to test those hypotheses."[14] In brief, the more recent emphasis on so-called middle-range theory, though valuable in itself, has had the unfortunate consequence of diverting attention away from more general theoretical problems.[15]

A third reason for neglect of the study of political change is the Western bias in the study of international relations. For a profession whose intellectual commitment is the understanding of the interactions of societies, international relations as a discipline is remarkably parochial and ethnocentric. It is essentially a study of the Western state system, and a sizable fraction of the existing literature is devoted to developments since the end of World War II. Thus the profession has emphasized recent developments within that particular state system. Although there are exceptions, the practitioners of this discipline have not been forced to come to terms with the dynamics of this, or any other, state system.[16] As Martin Wight suggested, international relations lacks a tradition of political theorizing. In large measure, of course, this is because of the paucity of reliable secondary studies of non-Western systems.[17] This situation in itself is a formidable obstacle to the development of a theory of international political change.

A fourth reason for neglect of the theoretical problem of political change is the widespread conviction of the futility of the task. Prevalent among historians, this view is also held by many social scientists.[18] The search for "laws of change" is held to be useless because of the uniqueness and complexity of historical events. Thus the search for generalizations or patterns in human affairs is regarded as a hopeless enterprise. Such a position, if taken at face value, denies the very possibility of a science or history of society; yet one should note its admonitions that there are no immutable laws of change and that although repetitive patterns may exist, social change is ultimately contingent on unique sets of historical events.

Finally, the development of a theory of political change has been inhibited by ideology and emotion. In part this is due to a conservative bias in Western social science. Most academic social scientists have a preference for stability or at least a preference for stability or at least a preference for orderly change. The idea of radical changes that threaten accepted values and interests is not an appealing one. This issue is especially acute for the theorist of international political change, who must confront directly the fundamental problem of international relations: war. The inhibiting effect of this dreadful issue has been well put by John Burton in a sweeping indictment of contemporary international-relations scholarship:

> The chief failure of orthodoxy has been in relation to change. The outstanding feature of reality is the dynamic nature of International Relations. No general theory is appropriate which cannot take into consideration the rapidly changing technological, social and political environment in which nations are required to live in peace one with the other. But the only device of fundamental change which is possible in the context of power politics is that of war, for which reason war is recognized as a legitimate instrument of national policy. It is not surprising that International Relations has tended to be discussed in static terms, and that stability has tended to be interpreted in terms of the maintenance of the *status quo*. A dynamic approach to International Relations would immediately confront the analyst with no alternative but to acknowledge war as the only available mechanism for change.[19]

Burton's challenge to orthodox theory of international relations goes to the heart of the present study. In recent years theorists of international relations have tended to stress the moderating and stabilizing influences of contemporary developments on the behavior of states, especially the increasing economic interdependence among nations and the destructiveness of modern weapons. These important developments have encouraged many individuals to believe that peaceful evolution has replaced military conflict as the principal means of adjusting relations among nation-states in the contemporary world. This assumption has been accompanied by a belief that economic and welfare goals have triumphed over the traditional power and security objectives of states. Thus, many believe that the opportunity for peaceful economic intercourse and the constraints im-

posed by modern destructive warfare have served to decrease the probability of a major war.

In the present study we take a very different stance, a stance based on the assumption that the fundamental nature of international relations has not changed over the millennia. International relations continue to be a recurring struggle for wealth and power among independent actors in a state of anarchy. The classic history of Thucydides is as meaningful a guide to the behavior of states today as when it was written in the fifth century B.C. Yet important changes have taken place. One of the subthemes . . . , in fact, is that modern statecraft and premodern statecraft differ in significant respects, a situation first appreciated by Montesquieu, Edward Gibbon, and other earlier writers on the subject. Nevertheless, we contend that the fundamentals have not been altered. For this reason, the insights of earlier writers and historical experience are considered relevant to an understanding of the ways in which international systems function and change in the contemporary era.

Thus although there is obviously an important element of truth in the belief that contemporary economic and technological development have altered relations among states, events in Asia, Africa, and the Middle East in the 1970s and early 1980s force us once again to acknowledge the continuing unsolved problem of war and the role of war in the process of international political change. Even more than in the past, in the last decades of the twentieth century we need to understand the relationship of war and change in the international system. Only in this way can we hope to fashion a more peaceful alternative. As E. H. Carr reminded us, this is the basic task of the study of international relations: "To establish methods of peaceful change is . . . the fundamental problem of international morality and of international politics."[20] But if peace were the ultimate goal of statecraft, then the solution to the problem of peaceful change would be easy. Peace may always be had by surrender to the aggressor state. The real task for the peaceful state is to seek a peace that protects and guarantees its vital interests and its concept of international morality.

The Nature of International Political Change

An international system is established for the same reason that any social or political system is created; actors enter social relations and create social structures in order to advance particular sets of political, economic, or other types of interests. Because the interests of some of the actors may conflict with those of other actors, the particular interests that are most favored by these social arrangements tend to reflect the relative powers of the actors involved. That is, although social systems impose restraints on the behavior of all actors, the behaviors rewarded and punished by the system will coincide, at least initially, with the interests of the most powerful members of the social system. Over time, however, the interests of individual actors and the balance of power among the actors do change as a result of economic, technological, and other developments. As a consequence, those actors who benefit most from a change in the social system and who gain the power to effect such change will seek to alter the system in ways that favor their interests. The resulting changed system will reflect the new distribution of power and the interests of its new dominant members. Thus, a precondition for political change lies in a disjuncture between the existing social system and the redistribution of power toward those actors who would benefit most from a change in the system.

This conception of political change is based on the notion that the purpose or social function of any social system, including the international system, may be defined in terms of the benefits that various members derived from its operation.[21]

As in the case with domestic society, the nature of the international system determines whose interest are being served by the function-

ing of the system. Changes in the system imply changes in the distribution of benefits provided to and costs imposed on individual members of the system. Thus the study of international political change must focus on the international system and especially on the efforts of political actors to change the international system in order to advance their own interests. Whether these interests are security, economic gain or ideological goals, the achievement of state objectives is dependent on the nature of the international system (i.e., the governance of the system, the rules of the system, the recognition of rights, etc.). As is the case in any social or political system, the process of international political change ultimately reflects the efforts of individuals or groups to transform institutions and systems in order to advance their interests. Because these interests and the powers of groups (or states) change, in time the political system will be changed in ways that will reflect these underlying shifts in interest and power. The elaboration of this approach for the understanding of international political change is the purpose of the subsequent discussion.

A Framework for Understanding International Political Change

The conceptualization of international political change to be presented [here] rests on a set of assumptions regarding the behavior of states:

1. An international system is stable (i.e., in a state of equilibrium) if no state believes it profitable to attempt to change the system.
2. A state will attempt to change the international system if the expected benefits exceed the expected costs (i.e., if there is an expected net gain).
3. A state will seek to change the international system through territorial, political, and economic expansion until the marginal costs of further change are equal to or greater than the marginal benefits.

4. Once an equilibrium between the costs and benefits of further change and expansion is reached, the tendency is for the economic costs of maintaining the status quo to rise faster than the economic capacity to support the status quo.
5. If the disequilibrium in the international system is not resolved, then the system will be changed, and a new equilibrium reflecting the redistribution of power will be established.

Obviously these assumptions are abstractions from a highly complex political reality. They do not describe the actual decision processes of statesmen, but as in the case of economic theory, actors are assumed to behave as if they were guided by such a set of cost/benefit calculations. Moreover, these assumptions are not mutually exclusive; they do overlap. Assumptions 2 and 4 are mirror images of one another, assumption 2 referring to a revisionist state and assumption 4 referring to a status quo state.

On the basis of these assumptions, the conceptualization of international political change to be presented here seeks to comprehend a continuing historical process. Because history has no starts and stops, one must break into the flow of history at a particular point. The following analysis of political change begins with an international system in a state of equilibrium as shown in Figure 1. An international system is in a state

of equilibrium if the more powerful states in the system are satisfied with the existing territorial political, and economic arrangements. Although minor changes and adjustments may take place, an equilibrium condition is one in which no powerful state (or group) believes that a change in the system would yield additional benefits commensurate with the anticipated costs of bringing about a change in the system.[22] Although every state and group in the system could benefit from particular types of change, the costs involved will discourage attempts to seek a change in system. As one writer has put it, "a power equilibrium represents a stable political configuration provided there are no changes or returns to conquest."[23] Under these conditions, where no one has an incentive to change the system, the status quo may be said to be stable.

In the more traditional language of international relations, the international status quo is held to be a legitimate one, at least by the major states in the system. The meaning of legitimacy was defined by Henry Kissinger as follows:

> [Legitimacy] implies the acceptance of the framework of the international order by all major powers, at least to the extent that no state is so dissatisfied that, like Germany after the Treaty of Versailles, it expresses its dissatisfaction in a revolutionary foreign policy. A legitimate order does not make conflicts impossible, but it limits their

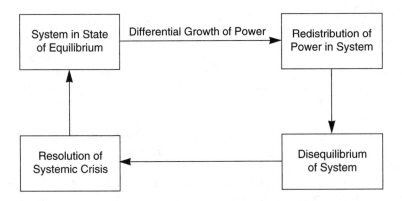

FIGURE 2.1   Diagram of International Political Change

scope. Wars may occur, but they will be fought *in the name of* the existing structure and the peace which follows will be justified as a better expression of the "legitimate," general consensus. Diplomacy in the classic sense, the adjustment of differences through negotiations, is possible only in "legitimate international orders."[24]

What this quotation suggests is that an international system or order exists in a condition of homeostatic or dynamic equilibrium. Like any other system, it is not completely at rest; changes at the level of interstate interactions are constantly taking place. In general, however, the conflicts, alliances, and diplomatic interactions among the actors in the system tend to preserve the defining characteristics of the system. Thus, as Kissinger demonstrated, the legitimate order or equilibrium created by the Congress of Vienna (1814) survived limited conflicts and diplomatic maneuvering until it finally collapsed in response to the profound economic, technological, and political upheavals of the latter part of the nineteenth century. This issue of legitimacy will be discussed later.

In every international system there are continual occurrences of political, economic, and technological changes that promise gains or threaten losses for one or another actor. In most cases these potential gains and losses are minor, and only incremental adjustments are necessary in order to take account of them. Such changes take place within the existing international system, producing a condition of homeostatic equilibrium. The relative stability of the system is, in fact, largely determined by its capacity to adjust to the demands of actors affected by changing political and environmental conditions. In every system, therefore, a process of disequilibrium and adjustment is constantly taking place. In the absence of large potential net benefits from change, the system continues to remain in a state of equilibrium.

If the interests and relative powers of the principal states in an international system remained constant over time, or if power relations

changed in such a way as to maintain the same relative distribution of power, the system would continue indefinitely in a state of equilibrium. However, both domestic and international developments undermine the stability of the status quo. For example, shifts in domestic coalitions may necessitate redefinition of the "national interest." However, the most destabilizing factor is the tendency in an international system for the powers of member states to change at different rates because of political, economic, and technological developments. In time, the differential growth in power of the various states in the system causes a fundamental redistribution of power in the system.

The concept of power is one of the most troublesome in the field of international relations and, more generally, political science. Many weighty books have analyzed and elaborated the concept. In this book, power refers simply to the military, economic, and technological capabilities of states. This definition obviously leaves out important and intangible elements that affect the outcomes of political actions, such as public morale, qualities of leadership, and situational factors. It also excludes what E. H. Carr called "power over opinion."[25] These psychological and frequently incalculable aspects of power and international relations are more closely associated with the concept of prestige. . . .

As a consequence of the changing interests of individual states, and especially because of the differential growth in power among states, the international system moves from a condition of equilibrium to one of disequilibrium. Disequilibrium is a situation in which economic, political, and technological developments have increased considerably the potential benefits or decreased the potential costs to one or more states of seeking to change the international system. Forestalling one's losses or increasing one's gains becomes an incentive for one or more states to attempt to change the system. Thus there develops a disjuncture between the existing international system and the potential gains to particular states from a change in the international system.

The elements of this systemic disequilibrium are twofold. First, military, technological, or other changes have increased the benefits of territorial conquest or the benefits of changing the international system in other ways. Second, the differential growth in power among the states in the system has altered the cost of changing the system. This transformation of the benefits and/or the costs of changing the system produces an incongruity or disjuncture among the components of the system (Table 1). On the one hand, the hierarchy of prestige, the division of territory, the international division of labor, and the rules of the system remain basically unchanged; they continue to reflect primarily the interests of the existing dominant powers and the relative power distribution that prevailed at the time of the last systemic change. On the other hand, the international distribution of power has undergone a radical transformation that has weakened the foundations of the existing system. It is this disjuncture between the several components of the system and its implications for relative gains and losses among the various states in the system that cause international political change.

This disjuncture within the existing international system involving the potential benefits and losses to particular powerful actors from a change in the system leads to a crisis in the international system. Although resolution of a crisis

Table 1   Mechanisms of Control (Components of System)

Government[a]	Dominance of great power[b]
Authority	Hierarchy of prestige
Property rights	Division of territory
Law	Rules of the system
Domestic economy	International economy

[a]Based on distribution of power among domestic groups, coalitions, classes, etc.

[b]Based on distribution of power among states in the system.

through peaceful adjustment of the systemic disequilibrium is possible, the principal mechanism of change throughout history has been war, or what we shall call hegemonic war (i.e., a war that determines which state or states will be dominant and will govern the system). The peace settlement following such a hegemonic struggle reorders the political, territorial, and other bases of the system. Thus the cycle of change is completed in that hegemonic war and the peace settlement create a new status quo and equilibrium reflecting the redistribution of power in the system and the other components of the system.

Notes

1. Miles Kahler, "Rumors of War: The 1914 Analogy," *Foreign Affairs* 58 (1979–80), pp. 374–396.

2. However, in principle, these ideas are translatable into specific testable hypotheses. At least we would argue that this is possible for a substantial fraction of them. The carrying out of this task, or part of it, would require another volume.

3. The term "law" . . . is to be interpreted as a general tendency that may be counteracted by other developments. This conception of law is taken from Jean Baechler, *Les Origines du Capitalisme* (Paris: Editions Gallimard, 1971). English edition (Oxford: Basil Blackwell, 1975), p. 52.

4. W. Arthur Lewis, *The Theory of Economic Growth* (New York: Harper & Row, 1970), pp. 17–18.

5. F. S. C. Northrop, *The Logic of the Sciences and the Humanities* (New York: Macmillan, 1947), pp. 243–45.

6. Stanley Hoffmann (ed.), *Contemporary Theory in International Relations* (Englewood Cliffs, N.J.: Prentice Hall, 1960), p. 40.

7. Kenneth N. Waltz, *Man, the State and War* (New York: Columbia University Press, 1959), p. 232.

8. Wilbert E. Moore, "Social Change" in *International Encyclopedia of the Social Sciences*, vol. 14, ed. by David Sills (New York: Crowell Collier and Macmillan, 1968), p. 365.

9. Nazli Choucri and Robert C. North, *Nations in Conflict* (San Francisco: W. H. Freeman, 1975); Robert O. Keohane and Joseph S. Nye, *Power and Interdependence* (Boston: Little, Brown, 1977); Kenneth N. Waltz, *Theory of International Politics* (Reading, MA: Addison-Wesley, 1979).

10. David Easton, *The Political System* (New York: Alfred A. Knopf, 1953), p. 42. It is symptomatic of this continued general neglect that the *Handbook of Poli-*

tical Science does not contain a section devoted to the problem of political change. Nor does the entry "political change" appear in its cumulative index. See Fred I. Greenstein and Nelson W. Polsby, eds., *Handbook of Political Science* (Reading, Mass.: Addison-Wesley, 1975).

11. Joseph Schumpeter, *History of Economic Analysis* (New York: Oxford University Press, 1954), p. 964.

12. K. J. Holsti, "Retreat from Utopia," *Canadian Journal of Political Science*, Vol. 4 (1971), pp. 165–177.

13. *Ibid.*, p. 167.

14. *Ibid.*, p. 171.

15. Several important books have recently indicated revival of interest in general theory. See Choucri and North, *Nations in Conflict*; Hedley Bull, *The Anarchical Society* (New York: Columbia University Press, 1977); Keohane and Nye, *Power and Interdependence*; Stanley Hoffmann, *Primacy or World Order* (New York: McGraw-Hill, 1978); Ralph Pettman, *State and Class* (London: Croom Helm, 1979); Kenneth N. Waltz, *Theory of International Politics* (Reading, Mass.: Addison-Wesley, 1979). Marxist scholars, of course, never lost interest in "grand theory."

16. Three recent exceptions are Evan Luard, *Types of International Society* (New York: Free Press, 1976); Robert G. Wesson, *The Imperial Order* (Berkeley: University of California Press, 1967); Martin Wight, *Systems of States*, ed. Hedley Bull (Leicester, England: Leicester University Press, 1977).

17. Martin Wight, "Why Is There No International Theory?" in Herbert Butterfield and Martin Wight (eds.), *Diplomatic Investigations* (London: George Allen and Unwin, 1966), pp. 17–34.

18. Albert O. Hirschman, "The Search for Paradigms as a Hindrance to Understanding," *World Politics*, Vol. 22 (1970), pp. 329–43.

19. John Burton, *International Relations: A General Theory* (Cambridge, MA: Cambridge University Press, 1965), pp. 71–72.

20. E. H. Carr, *The Twenty Years' Crisis* (London: Macmillan, 1951).

21. John Harsanyi, "Rational-Choice Models of Political Behavior vs. Functionalist and Conformist Theories," *World Politics*, Vol. 21 (1969), pp. 513–38.

22. R. L. Curry Jr. and L. L. Wade, *A Theory of Political Exchange* (Englewood Cliffs, N.J.: Prentice Hall, 1968), p. 49; and Lance E. Davis and Douglass C. North, *Institutional Change and American Economic Growth* (Cambridge England: Cambridge University Press, 1971), p. 40.

23. Trout Rader, *The Economics of Feudalism* (New York: Gordon and Breach, 1971), p. 50.

24. Henry A. Kissinger, *A World Restored* (Boston: Houghton Mifflin, 1967), pp. 1–2.

25. Carr, *Twenty Years' Crisis*, p. 132.

Theory of World Politics: Structural Realism and Beyond

ROBERT O. KEOHANE

The author surveys and critically evaluates the work of realists and "structural realists." Keohane argues that structural realism helps us understand world politics by focusing on its systemic aspects that establish the context for state action. On the other hand, to explain state behavior and outcomes, Keohane looks not just to international political structure but also to its relation to domestic politics and decision making, internal–external interactions, and the workings of international institutions.

From *Political Science: The State of the Discipline*, ed. Ada W. Finifter (Washington, DC: American Political Science Association, 1983). Reprinted by permission of the APSA.

For over 2000 years, what Hans J. Morgenthau dubbed "Political Realism" has constituted the principal tradition for the analysis of international relations in Europe and its offshoots in the New World (Morgenthau, 1966). Writers of the Italian Renaissance, balance of power theorists, and later adherents of the school of *Machtpolitik* all fit under a loose version of the Realist rubric. Periodic attacks on Realism have taken place; yet the very focus of these critiques seems only to reconfirm the centrality of Realist thinking in the international political thought of the West.[1]

Realism has been criticized frequently during the last few years, and demands for a "new paradigm" have been made. Joseph S. Nye and I called for a "world politics paradigm" a decade ago, and Richard Mansbach and John A. Vasquez have recently proposed a "new paradigm for global politics." In both these works, the new paradigm that was envisaged entailed adopting additional concepts—for instance, "transnational relations," or "issue phases" (Keohane & Nye, 1972, esp. pp. 379–386; Mansbach & Vasquez, 1981, Chapter 4). Yet for these concepts to be useful as part of a satisfactory general theory of world politics, a theory of state action— which is what Realism purports to provide— is necessary. Understanding the general principles of state action and the practices of governments is a necessary basis for attempts to refine theory or to extend the analysis to non-state actors. Approaches using new concepts may be able to supplement, enrich, or extend a basic theory of state action, but they cannot substitute for it.[2]

The fixation of critics and reformers on the Realist theory of state action reflects the importance of this research tradition. In my view, there is good reason for this. Realism is a necessary component in a coherent analysis of world politics because its focus on power, interests, and rationality is crucial to any understanding of the subject. Thus any approach to international relations has to incorporate, or at least come to grips with, key elements of Realist

thinking. Even writers who are concerned principally with international institutions and rules, or analysts in the Marxist tradition, make use of some Realist premises. Since Realism builds on fundamental insights about world politics and state action, progress in the study of international relations requires that we seek to build on this core.

Yet as we shall see, Realism does not provide a satisfactory theory of world politics, if we require of an adequate theory that it provide a set of plausible and testable answers to questions about state behavior under specified conditions. Realism is particularly weak in accounting for change, especially where the sources of that change lie in the world political economy or in the domestic structures of states. Realism, viewed dogmatically as a set of answers, would be worse than useless. As a sophisticated framework of questions and initial hypotheses, however, it is extremely valuable.[3]

Since Realism constitutes the central tradition in the study of world politics, an analysis, like this one, of the current state of the field must evaluate the viability of Realism in the penultimate decade of the twentieth century. Doing this requires constructing a rather elaborate argument of my own, precluding a comprehensive review of the whole literature of international relations. I have therefore selected for discussion a relatively small number of works that fit my theme, ignoring entire areas of research, much of it innovative.[4] Within the sphere of work dealing with Realism and its limitations, I have focused attention on several especially interesting and valuable contributions. My intention is to point out promising lines of research rather than to engage in what Stanley Hoffmann once called a "wrecking operation" (Hoffmann, 1960, p. 171).

Since I have written on the subject of Realism in the past, I owe the reader an explanation of where I think my views have changed, and where I am only restating, in different ways, opinions that I have expressed before. This chapter deals more systematically and more sympathetically with Realism than does my previous work. Yet its fundamental argument is consistent with that of *Power and Interdependence*. In that book Nye and I relied on Realist theory as a basis for our structural models of international regime change (Keohane & Nye, 1977, pp. 42—46). We viewed our structural models as attempts to improve the ability of Realist or neo-Realist analysis to account for international regime change: we saw ourselves as adapting Realism, and attempting to go beyond it, rather than rejecting it.

Admittedly, Chapter 2 of *Power and Interdependence* characterized Realism as a descriptive ideal type rather than a research program in which explanatory theories could be embedded. Realist and Complex Interdependence ideal types were used to help specify the conditions under which overall structural explanations of change would or would not be valid; the term, "Realist," was used to refer to conditions under which states are the dominant actors, hierarchies of issues exist, and force is usable as an instrument of policy (Keohane & Nye, 1977, pp. 23–29). Taken as a full characterization of the Realist tradition this would have been unfair, and it seems to have led readers concerned with our view of Realism to focus excessively on Chapter 2 and too little on the attempt, which draws on what I here call structural realism, to account for regime change (Chapters 3–6).[5]

To provide criteria for the evaluation of theoretical work in international politics—Structural Realism, in particular—I employ the conception of a "scientific research programme" explicated in 1970 by the philosopher of science, Imre Lakatos (1970). Lakatos developed this concept as a tool for the comparative evaluation of scientific theories, and in response to what he regarded as the absence of standards for evaluation in Thomas Kuhn's (1962) notion of a paradigm.[6] Theories are embedded in research programs. These programs contain inviolable assumptions (the "hard core") and initial condi-

tions, defining their scope. For Lakatos, they also include two other very important elements: auxiliary, or observational, hypotheses, and a "positive heuristic," which tells the scientist what sorts of additional hypotheses to entertain and how to go about conducting research. In short, a research program is a set of methodological rules telling us what paths of research to avoid and what parts to follow.

Consider a research program, with a set of observational hypotheses, a "hard core" of irrefutable assumptions, and a set of scope conditions. In the course of research, anomalies are bound to appear sooner or later: predictions of the theory will seem to be falsified. For Lakatos, the reaction of scientists developing the research program is to protect the hard core by constructing auxiliary hypotheses that will explain the anomalies. Yet any research program, good or bad, can invent such auxiliary hypotheses on an *ad hoc* basis. The key test for Lakatos of the value of a research program is whether these auxiliary hypotheses are "progressive," that is, whether their invention leads to the discovery of *new facts* (other than the anomalous facts that they were designed to explain). Progressive research programs display "continuous growth": their auxiliary hypotheses increase our capacity to understand reality (Lakatos, 1970, pp. 116–122, 132–138, 173–180).

Lakatos developed this conception to assess developments in the natural sciences, particularly physics. If we took literally the requirements that he laid down for "progressive" research programs, all actual theories of international politics—and perhaps all conceivable theories—would fail the test. Indeed, it has been argued that much of economics, including oligopoly theory (heavily relied upon by Structural Realists), fails to meet this standard (Latsis, 1976). Nevertheless, Lakatos' conception has the great merit of providing clear and sensible criteria for the evaluation of scientific traditions, and of asking penetrating questions that may help us to see Realism in a revealing light. Lakatos' questions are relevant, even if applying them without modification could lead to premature rejection not only of Realism, but of our whole field, or even the entire discipline of political science.[7]

The stringency of Lakatos' standards suggests that we should supplement this test with a "softer," more interpretive one. That is, how much insight does Realism provide into contemporary world politics?

For this line of evaluation we can draw inspiration from Clifford Geertz's discussion of the role of theory in anthropology. Geertz argues that culture "is not a power, something to which social events, behaviors, institutions, or processes can be causally attributed; it is a context—something within which they can be intelligibly—that is, thickly—described" (1973, p. 14). The role of theory, he claims, is "not to codify abstract regularities but to make thick description possible, not to generalize across cases but to generalize within them" (*ibid.*, p. 26). This conception is the virtual antithesis of the standards erected by Lakatos, and could all too easily serve as a rationalization for the proliferation of atheoretical case studies. Nevertheless, culture as discussed by Geertz has something in common with the international system as discussed by students of world politics. It is difficult to generalize across systems. We are continually bedeviled by the paucity of comparable cases, particularly when making systemic statements—for example, about the operation of balances of power. Much of what students of world politics do, and what Classical Realism in particular aspires to, is to make the actions of states understandable (despite obfuscatory statements by their spokesmen): that is, in Geertz's words, to provide "a context within which they can be intelligibly described." For example, Morgenthau's discussion of the concept of interest defined in terms of power, quoted at length below, reflects this objective more than the goal of arriving at testable generalizations.

This essay is divided into four major sections. The first of these seeks to establish the basis for a dual evaluation of Realism: as a source of interpretive insights into the operation of world politics, and as a scientific research program that enables the investigator to discover new facts. I examine the arguments of Thucydides and Morgenthau to extract the key assumptions of Classical Realism. Then I discuss recent work by Kenneth N. Waltz, whom I regard as the most systematic spokesman for contemporary Structural Realism.

Section II addresses the question of interpretation and puzzle-solving within the Realist tradition. How successful are Realist thinkers in making new contributions to our understanding of world politics? In Section III, I consider the shortcomings of Realism when judged by the standards that Lakatos establishes, or even when evaluated by less rigorous criteria, and begin to ask whether a modified version of Structural Realism could correct some of these faults. Section IV carries this theme further by attempting to outline how a multi-dimensional research program, including a modified structural theory, might be devised; what its limitations would be; and how it could be relevant, in particular, to problems of peaceful change.

The conclusion emphasizes the issue of peaceful change as both a theoretical and a practical problem. Realism raises the question of how peaceful change could be achieved, but does not resolve it. Understanding the conditions under which peaceful change would be facilitated remains, in my view, the most urgent task facing students of world politics.

I. Structural Realism as Research Program

To explain the research program of Realism, I begin with two classic works, one ancient, the other modern: *The Peloponnesian War*, by Thucydides, and *Politics Among Nations*, by Morgenthau.[8] The three most fundamental Realist assumptions are evident in these books: that the most important actors in world politics are territorially organized entities (city–states or modern states); that state behavior can be explained rationally; and that states seek power and calculate their interests in terms of power, relative to the nature of the international system that they face.

The Peloponnesian War was written in an attempt to explain the causes of the great war of the Fifth Century B.C. between the coalition led by Athens and its adversaries, led by Sparta. Thucydides assumes that to achieve this purpose, he must explain the behavior of the major city–states involved in the conflict. Likewise, Morgenthau assumes that the subject of a science of international politics is the behavior of states. Realism is "state-centric."[9]

Both authors also believed that observers of world politics could understand events by imagining themselves, as rational individuals, in authoritative positions, and reflecting on what they would do if faced with the problems encountered by the actual decision-makers. They both, therefore, employ the method of *rational reconstruction*. Thucydides admits that he does not have transcripts of all the major speeches given during the war, but he is undaunted:

> It was in all cases difficult to carry [the speeches] word for word in one's memory, so my habit has been to make the speakers say what was in my opinion demanded of them by the various occasions, of course adhering as closely as possible to the general sense of what they really said. (Thucydides, Book I, paragraph 23 [Chapter I, Modern Library edition, p. 14]).

Morgenthau argues that in trying to understand foreign policy,

> We put ourselves in the position of a statesman who must meet a certain problem of foreign policy under certain circumstances, and we ask ourselves what the rational alternatives are from which a statesman may choose . . . and which of these rational alternatives this particular statesman, acting under these circumstances, is likely to choose. It is the testing of this rational hypothesis against the actual facts and their con-

sequences that gives meaning to the facts of international politics and makes a theory of politics possible. (Morgenthau, 1966, p. 5)

In reconstructing state calculation, Thucydides and Morgenthau both assume that states will act to protect their power positions, perhaps even to the point of seeking to maximize their power. Thucydides seeks to go beneath the surface of events to the power realities that are fundamental to state action:

> The real cause [of the war] I consider to be the one which was formally most kept out of sight. The growth in the power of Athens, and the alarm which this inspired in Lacedemon, made war inevitable. (Thucydides, Book I, paragraph 23, Chapter I, Modern Library Edition, p. 15)[10]

Morgenthau is even more blunt: "International politics, like all politics, is a struggle for power" (1966, p. 25, see also Morgenthau, 1946). Political Realism, he argues, understands international politics through the concept of "interest defined as power":

> We assume that statesmen think and act in terms of interest defined as power, and the evidence of history bears that assumption out. That assumption allows us to retrace and anticipate, as it were, the steps a statesman—past, present, or future—has taken or will take on the political scene. We look over his shoulder when he writes his dispatches; we listen in on his conversation with other statesmen: we read and anticipate his very thoughts. (1966, p. 5)

The three assumptions just reviewed define the hard core of the Classical Realist research program:

1. The *state-centric assumption:* states are the most important actors in world politics;

2. The *rationality assumption:* world politics can be analyzed as if states were unitary rational actors, carefully calculating costs of alternative courses of action and seeking to maximize their expected utility, although doing so under conditions of uncertainty and without necessarily having sufficient information about alternatives or resources (time or otherwise) to conduct a full review of all possible courses of action;[11]

3. The *power assumption:* states seek power (both the ability to influence others and resources that can be used to exercise influence); and they calculate their interests in terms of power, whether as end or as necessary means to a variety of other ends.

More recently, Kenneth N. Waltz (1959) has attempted to reformulate and systematize Realism on the basis of what he called, in *Man, the State and War*, a "third image" perspective. This form of Realism does not rest on the presumed iniquity of the human race—original sin in one form or another—but on the nature of world politics as an anarchic realm:

> Each state pursues its own interests, however defined, in ways it judges best. Force is a means of achieving the external ends of states because there exists no consistent, reliable process of reconciling the conflicts of interests that inevitably arise among similar units in a condition of anarchy. (p. 238)[12]

Even well-intentioned statesmen find that they must use or threaten force to attain their objectives.

Since the actions of states are conceived of as resulting from the nature of international politics, the paramount theoretical task for Realism is to create a *systemic* explanation of international politics. In a systemic theory, as Waltz explains it, the propositions of the theory specify relationships between certain aspects of the system and actor behavior (1979, pp. 67–73). Waltz's third-image Realism, for instance, draws connections between the distribution of power in a system and the actions of states: small countries will behave differently from large ones, and in a balance of power system, alliances can be expected to shift in response to changes in power relationships. Any theory will, of course, take into account the attributes of actors, as well as features of the system itself. But the key distinguishing characteristic of a systemic theory is that *the internal attributes of actors are given by assumption rather than treated as variables.* Changes in actor behavior, and system outcomes, are explained not on the basis of variations in these actor characteristics, but on the basis of changes in the attributes of the system itself. A good example of such a systemic theory is microeconomic theory in its standard form. It posits the existence of business firms, with given utility functions (such as profit maximization), and attempts to explain their behavior on the basis of environmental factors such as the competitiveness of markets. It is systemic because its propositions about variations in behavior depend on variations in characteristics of the system, not of the units (Waltz, 1979, pp. 89–91, 93–95, 98).

To develop a systemic analysis, abstraction is necessary: one has to avoid being distracted by the details and vagaries of domestic politics and other variables at the level of the acting unit. To reconstruct a systemic research program, therefore, Structural Realists must devise a way to explain state behavior on the basis of systemic characteristics, and to account for outcomes in the same manner. This needs to be a coherent explanation, although it need not tell us everything we would like to know about world politics.

Waltz's formulation of Structural Realism as a systemic theory seeks to do this by developing a concept not explicitly used by Morgenthau or Thucydides: the *structure* of the international system. Two elements of international structure are constants: (1) the international system is anarchic rather than hierarchic, and (2) it is characterized by interaction among units with similar functions. These are such enduring background characteristics that they are constitutive of what we mean by "international politics."[13] The third element of structure, the distribution of capabilities across the states in the system, varies from system to system, and over time. Since it is a variable, this element—the distribution of "power"—takes on particular importance in the theory. The most significant capabilities are those of the most powerful actors. Structures "are defined not by all of the actors that flourish within them but by the major ones" (Waltz, 1979, p. 93).

According to Waltz, structure is the principal determinant of outcomes at the systems level: structure encourages certain actions and discourages others. It may also lead to unintended consequences, as the ability of states to obtain their objectives is constrained by the power of others (1979, pp. 104–111).

For Waltz, understanding the structure of an international system allows us to explain patterns of state behavior, since states determine their interests and strategies on the basis of calculations about their own positions in the system. The link between system structure and actor behavior is forged by the rationality assumption, which enables the theorist to predict that leaders will respond to the incentives and constraints imposed by their environments. Taking rationality as a constant permits one to attribute variations in state behavior to variations in characteristics of the international system. Otherwise, state behavior might have to be accounted for by variations in the calculating ability of states; in that case, the systemic focus of Structural Realism (and much of its explanatory power) would be lost. Thus the rationality assumption—as we will see in examining Waltz's balance of power theory—is essential to the theoretical claims of Structural Realism.[14]

The most parsimonious version of a structural theory would hold that any international system has a single structure of power. In such a conceptualization, power resources are homogeneous and fungible: they can be used to achieve results on any of a variety of issues without significant loss of efficacy.[15] Power in politics becomes like money in economics: "in many respects, power and influence play the same role

in international politics as money does in a market economy" (Wolfers, 1962, p. 105).

In its strong form, the Structural Realist research program is similar to that of micro-economics. Both use the rationality assumption to permit inferences about actor behavior to be made from system structure. The Realist definition of interests in terms of power and position is like the economist's assumption that firms seek to maximize profits: it provides the utility function of the actor. Through these assumptions, actor characteristics become constant rather than variable, and systemic theory becomes possible.[16] The additional assumption of power fungibility simplifies the theory further: on the basis of a *single* characteristic of the international system (overall power capabilities), *multiple* inferences can be drawn about actor behavior and outcomes. "Foreknowledge"—that aspiration of all theory—is thereby attained (Eckstein, 1975, pp. 88–89). As we will see below, pure Structural Realism provides an insufficient basis for explaining state interests and behavior, even when the rationality assumption is accepted; and the fungibility assumption is highly questionable. Yet the Structural Realist research program is an impressive intellectual achievement: an elegant, parsimonious, deductively rigorous instrument for scientific discovery. The anomalies that it generates are more interesting than its own predictions; but as Lakatos emphasizes, it is the exploration of anomalies that moves science forward.

Richard K. Ashley has recently argued that Structural Realism—which he calls "technical realism"—actually represents a regression from the classical Realism of Herz or Morgenthau.[17] In his view, contemporary Realist thinkers have forgotten the importance of subjective self-reflection, and the dialectic between subjectivity and objectivity, which are so important in the writings of "practical," or "classical" Realists such as Thucydides and Morgenthau. Classical Realism for Ashley is interpretive: "a practical tradition of statesmen is the real subject whose language of experience the interpreter tries to make his own" (1981, p. 221). It is self-reflective and non-deterministic. It treats the concept of balance of power as a dialectical relation: not merely as an objective characterization of the international system but also as a collectively recognized orienting scheme for strategic action. Classical Realism encompasses the unity of opposites, and draws interpretive insight from recognizing the dialectical quality of human experience. Thus its proponents understand that the state system is problematic, and that "strategic artistry" is required to keep it in existence (Ashley, 1982, p. 22).

The problem with Classical Realism is that it is difficult to distinguish what Ashley praises as dialectical insight from a refusal to define concepts clearly and consistently, or to develop a systematic set of propositions that could be subjected to empirical tests. Structural Realism seeks to correct these flaws, and thus to construct a more rigorous theoretical framework for the study of world politics, while drawing on the concepts and insights of the older Realism. Structural Realism, as embodied particularly in the work of Waltz, is more systematic and logically more coherent than that of its Classical Realist predecessors. By its own standards, Structural Realism is, in Ashley's words, "a progressive scientific redemption of classical realism" (Ashley, 1982, p. 25). That is, it sees itself, and Classical Realism, as elements of a continuous research tradition.

Ashley complains that this form of Realism objectifies reality, and that in particular it regards the state as unproblematic. This leads, in his view, to some pernicious implications; that the interests expressed by dominant elites must be viewed as legitimate, that economic rationality is the highest form of thought, and that individuals are not responsible for the production of insecurity (1982, pp. 34–41). But Structural Realists need not make any of these claims. It is true that Structural Realism seeks to understand

the limits of, and constraints on, human action in world politics. It emphasizes the strength of these constraints, and in that sense could be considered "conservative." But an analysis of constraints, far from implying an acceptance of the *status quo*, should be seen as a precondition to sensible attempts to change the world. To be self-reflective, human action must take place with an understanding of the context within which it occurs. Structural Realists can be criticized, as we will see, for paying insufficient attention to norms, institutions, and change. But this represents less a fault of Structural Realism as such than a failure of some of its advocates to transcend its categories. Structural Realism's focus on systemic constraints does not contradict Classical Realism's concern with action and choice. On the contrary, Classical Realism's emphasis on *praxis* helps us to understand the origins of Structural Realism's search for systematic understanding, and—far from negating the importance of this search—makes it seem all the more important.

I have argued thus far that Structural Realism is at the center of contemporary international relations theory in the United States; that it constitutes an attempt to systematize Classical Realism; and that its degree of success as a theory can be legitimately evaluated in part according to standards such as those laid down by Lakatos, and in part through evaluation of its capacity to generate insightful interpretations of international political behavior. Two distinct tests, each reflecting one aspect of this dualistic evaluative standard, can be devised to evaluate Structural Realism as a research program for international relations:

1. How "fruitful" is the Realist paradigm for puzzle-solving and interpretation of world politics (Toulmin, 1963)? That is, does current work in the Realist tradition make us see issues more clearly, or provide answers to formerly unsolved puzzles? Realism was designed to provide

insights into such issues, and if it remains a live tradition, should continue to do so.

2. Does Realism meet the standards of a scientific research program as enunciated by Lakatos? To answer this question, it is important to remind ourselves that the hard core of a research program is irrefutable within the terms of the paradigm. When anomalies arise that appear to challenge Realist assumptions, the task of Realist analysts is to create auxiliary theories that defend them. These theories permit explanation of anomalies consistent with Realist assumptions. For Lakatos, the key question about a research program concerns whether the auxiliary hypotheses of Realism are "progressive." That is, do they generate new insights, or predict new facts? If not, they are merely exercises in "patching up" gaps or errors on an ad hoc basis, and the research program is degenerative.

Realism cannot be judged fairly on the basis of only one set of standards. Section II addresses the question of fruitfulness by examining works in the central area of Realist theory: the study of conflict, bargaining, and war. Section II then judges Realism by the more difficult test of Lakatos, which (as noted above) is better at asking trenchant questions than at defining a set of standards appropriate to social science. We will see that in one sense, Realism survives these tests, since it still appears as a good starting point for analysis. But it does not emerge either as a comprehensive theory or as a progressive research program in the sense employed by Lakatos. Furthermore, it has difficulty interpreting issues, and linkages among issues, outside of the security sphere: it can even be misleading when applied to these issues without sufficient qualification. It also has little to say about the crucially important question of peaceful change. The achievements of Realism, and the prospect that it can be modified further to make it even more useful, should help students of world politics to avoid unnecessary

self-deprecation. Yet they certainly do not justify complacency.

II. Progress within the Realist Paradigm: Three Achievements

The fruitfulness of contemporary Realist analysis is best evaluated by considering some of the finest work in the genre. Poor scholarship can derive from even the best research program; only the most insightful work reveals the strengths as well as the limits of a theoretical approach. In this section I will consider three outstanding examples of works that begin, at least, from Realist concerns and assumptions: Waltz's construction of balance of power theory in *Theory of International Politics* (1979); the attempt by Glenn Snyder and Paul Diesing in *Conflict Among Nations* (1977) to apply formal game-theoretic models of bargaining to sixteen case studies of major-power crises during the seventy-five years between Fashoda and the Yom Kippur "alert crisis" of 1973; and Robert Gilpin's fine recent book, *War and Change in World Politics* (1981). These works are chosen to provide us with one systematic attempt to develop structural Realist theory, one study of bargaining in specific cases, and one effort to understand broad patterns of international political change. Other recent works could have been chosen instead, such as three books on international conflict and crisis published in 1980 or 1981 (Brecher, 1980; Bueno de Mesquita, 1981; Lebow, 1981), or the well-known works by Nazli Choucri and Robert C. North (1975) or by Alexander George and Richard Smoke (1974). But there are limits on what can be done in a single chapter of limited size.

Balance of Power Theory: Waltz
Waltz has explicated balance of power theory as a central element in his Structural Realist synthesis: "If there is any distinctively political theory of international politics, balance of power

theory is it" (1979, p. 117). The realization that balances of power periodically form in world politics, is an old one, as are attempts to theorize about it. The puzzle that Waltz addresses is how to "cut through such confusion" as has existed about it: that is, in Kuhn's words, how to "achieve the anticipated in a new way" (1962, p. 36).

Waltz attacks this problem by using the concept of structure, which he has carefully developed earlier in the book, and which he also employs to account for the dreary persistence of patterns of international action (1979, pp. 66–72). Balance of power theory applies to "anarchic" realms, which are formally unorganized and in which, therefore, units have to worry about their survival: "Self-help is necessarily the principle of action in an anarchic order" (p. 111). In Waltz's system, states (which are similar to one another in function) are the relevant actors; they use external as well as internal means to achieve their goals. Relative capabilities are (as we saw above) the variable element of structure; as they change, we expect coalitional patterns or patterns of internal effort to be altered as well. From his assumptions, given the condition for the theory's operation (self-help), Waltz deduces "the expected outcome: namely, the formation of balances of power" (p. 118). His solution to the puzzle that he has set for himself is carefully formulated and ingenious.

Nevertheless, Waltz's theory of the balance of power encounters some difficulties. First, it is difficult for him to state precisely the conditions under which coalitions will change. He only forecasts that balances of power will periodically recur. Indeed, his theory is so general that it hardly meets the difficult tests that he himself establishes for theory. In Chapter 1 we are told that to test a theory, one must "devise a number of distinct and demanding tests" (1979, p. 13). But such tests are not proposed for balance of power theory: "Because only a loosely defined and inconstant condition of balance is pre-

dicted, it is difficult to say that any given distribution of power falsifies the theory" (p. 124). Thus rather than applying demanding tests, Waltz advises that we "should seek *confirmation* through observation of difficult cases" (p. 125, emphasis added). In other words, he counsels that we should search through history to find examples that conform to the predictions of the theory: he then proclaims that "these examples tend to confirm the theory" (p. 125). Two pages later, Waltz appears to change his view, admitting that "we can almost always find confirming cases if we look hard." We should correct for this by looking "for instances of states conforming to common international practices even though for internal reasons they would prefer not to" (p. 127). But Waltz is again making an error against which he warns us. He is not examining a universe of cases, in all of which states would prefer not to conform to "international practice," and asking how often they nevertheless do conform. Instead, he is looking only at the latter cases, chosen *because* they are consistent with his theory. Building grand theory that meets Popperian standards of scientific practice is inherently difficult; even the best scholars, such as Waltz, have trouble simultaneously saying what they want to say and abiding by their canons of scientific practice.

Waltz's theory is also ambiguous with respect to the status of three assumptions that are necessary to a strong form of Structural Realism. I have already mentioned the difficult problem of whether a structural theory must (implausibly) assume fungibility of power resources. Since this problem is less serious with respect to balance of power theory than in a broader context, I will not pursue it here, but will return to it in Section III. Yet Waltz is also, in his discussion of balances of power, unclear on the questions of rationality and interests.

Waltz argues that his assumptions do not include the rationality postulate: "The theory says simply that if some do relatively well, others will emulate them or fall by the wayside" (p. 118).

This evolutionary principle, however, can hold only for systems with many actors, experiencing such severe pressure on resources that many will disappear over time. Waltz undermines this argument by pointing out later (p. 137) that "the death rate for states is remarkably low." Furthermore, he relies explicitly on the rationality principle to show that bipolar balances must be stable. "Internal balancing," he says, "is more reliable and precise than external balancing. States are less likely to misjudge their relative strengths than they are to misjudge the strength and reliability of opposing coalitions" (p. 168). I conclude that Waltz does rely on the rationality argument, despite his earlier statement to the contrary.

The other ambiguity in Waltz's balance of power theory has to do with the interests, or motivations, of states. Waltz recognizes that any theory of state behavior must ascribe (by assumption) some motivations to states, just as microeconomic theory ascribes motivations to firms. It is not reductionist to do so as long as these motivations are not taken as varying from state to state as a result of their internal characteristics. Waltz specifies such motivations: states "at a minimum, seek their own preservation, and at a maximum, drive for universal domination" (p. 118).

For his balance of power theory to work, Waltz needs to assume that states seek self-preservation, since if at least some major states did not do so, there would be no reason to expect that roughly equivalent coalitions (i.e., "balances of power") would regularly form. The desire for self-preservation makes states that are behind in a struggle for power try harder, according to Waltz, and leads states allied to a potential hegemon to switch coalitions in order to construct balances of power. Neither of these processes on which Waltz relies to maintain a balance—intensified effort by the weaker country in a bipolar system and coalition formation against potentially dominant states in a multipolar system—could operate reliably without this motivation.

The other aspect of Waltz's motivational assumption—that states "at a maximum, drive for universal domination," is reminiscent of the implication of Realists such as Morgenthau that states seek to "maximize power." For a third-image Realist theory such as Waltz's, such an assumption is unnecessary. Waltz's defense of it is that the balance of power depends on the possibility that force may be used. But this possibility is an attribute of the self-help international system, for Waltz, rather than a reflection of the actors' characteristics. That some states seek universal domination is not a necessary condition for force to be used.

This ambiguity in Waltz's analysis points toward a broader ambiguity in Realist thinking: *Balance of power theory is inconsistent with the assumption frequently made by Realists that states "maximize power,"* if power is taken to refer to tangible resources that can be used to induce other actors to do what they would not otherwise do, through the threat or infliction of deprivations.[18] States concerned with self-preservation do not seek to maximize their power when they are not in danger. On the contrary, they recognize a trade-off between aggrandizement and self-preservation; they realize that a relentless search for universal domination may jeopardize their own autonomy. Thus they moderate their efforts when their positions are secure. Conversely, they intensify their efforts when danger arises, which assumes that they were not maximizing them under more benign conditions.

One might have thought that Realists would readily recognize this point, yet they seem drawn against their better judgment to the "power maximization" or "universal domination" hypotheses. In part, this may be due to their anxiety to emphasize the significance of force in world politics. Yet there may be theoretical as well as rhetorical reasons for their ambivalence. The assumption of power maximization makes possible strong inferences about behavior that would be impossible if we assumed only that states "sometimes" or "often" sought to aggrandize themselves. In that case, we would have to ask about competing goals, some of which would be generated by the internal social, political, and economic characteristics of the countries concerned. Taking into account these competing goals relegates Structural Realism to the status of partial, incomplete theory.

Waltz's contribution to the study of world politics is conceptual. He helps us think more clearly about the role of systemic theory, the explanatory power of structural models, and how to account deductively for the recurrent formation of balances of power. He shows that the international system shapes state behavior as well as vice versa. These are major contributions. But Waltz does not point out "new ways of seeing" international relations that point toward major novelties. He reformulates and systematizes Realism, and thus develops what I have called Structural Realism, consistent with the fundamental assumptions of his classical predecessors.

Game Theory, Structure, and Bargaining: Snyder and Diesing

Game theory has yielded some insights into issues of negotiations, crises, and limited war, most notably in the early work of Thomas Schelling (1960). Snyder and Diesing's contribution to this line of analysis, as they put it, is to "distinguish and analyze nine different kinds of bargaining situations, each one a unique combination of power and interest relations between the bargainers, each therefore having its own dynamics and problems" (1977, pp. 181–182). They employ their game-theoretic formulations of these nine situations, within an explicit structural context, to analyze sixteen historical cases.

This research design is consistent with the hard core of Realism. Attention is concentrated on the behavior of states. In the initial statement of the problem, the rationality assumption, in suitably modest form, is retained: each actor attempts "to maximize expected value across a given set of consistently ordered objectives given the information actually available to the actor or which he could reasonably acquire in the time available for decision" (p. 181). Interests are defined to a considerable extent in terms of power: that is, power factors are built into the game structure. In the game of "Protector," for instance, the more powerful state can afford to "go it alone" without its ally, and thus has an interest in doing so under certain conditions, whereas its weaker partner cannot (pp. 145–147). Faced with the game matrix, states, as rational actors, calculate their interests and act accordingly. The structure of world politics, as Waltz defines it, is reflected in the matrices and becomes the basis for action.

If Structural Realism formed a sufficient basis for the understanding of international crises, we could fill in the entries in the matrices solely on the basis of states' positions in the international system, given our knowledge of the fact that they perform "similar functions," including the need to survive as autonomous entities. Interests would indeed be defined in terms of power. This would make game theory a powerful analytic tool, which could even help us predict certain outcomes. Where the game had no unique solution (because of strategic indeterminacy), complete predictability of outcomes could not be achieved, but our expectations about the range of likely action would have been narrowed.

Yet Snyder and Diesing find that even knowledge of the values and goals of top leaders could not permit them to determine the interests of about half the decision-making units in their cases. In the other cases, one needed to understand intragovernmental politics, even when one ignored the impact of wider domestic political factors (pp. 510–511). The "internal-external interaction" is a key to the understanding of crisis bargaining.

As Snyder and Diesing make their analytical framework more complex and move into detailed investigation of their cases, their focus shifts toward concern with cognition and with the effects on policy of ignorance, misperception, and misinformation. In my view, the most creative and insightful of their chapters use ideas developed largely by Robert Jervis (1976) to analyze information processing and decision-making. These chapters shift the focus of attention away from the systemic-level factors reflected in the game-theoretic matrices, toward problems of perception, personal bias, and group decision-making (Snyder & Diesing, 1977, Chapters IV and V).

Thus Snyder and Diesing begin with the hard core of Realism, but their most important contributions depend on their willingness to depart from these assumptions. They are dissatisfied with their initial game-theoretic classificatory scheme. They prefer to explore information processing and decision-making, without a firm deductive theory on which to base their arguments, rather than merely to elucidate neat logical typologies.

Is the work of Snyder and Diesing a triumph of Realism or a defeat? At this point in the argument, perhaps the most that can be said is that it indicates that work in the Realist tradition, analyzing conflict and bargaining with the concepts of interests and power, continues to be fruitful, but it does not give reason for much confidence that adhering strictly to Realist assumptions will lead to important advances in the field.

Cycles of Hegemony and War: Gilpin

In *War and Change in World Politics*, Gilpin uses Realist assumptions to reinterpret the last 2400 years of Western history. Gilpin assumes that states, as the principal actors in world politics, make cost-benefit calculations about alternative courses of action. For instance, states attempt to change the international system as the expected benefits of so doing exceed the costs. Thus, the rationality assumption is applied explicitly, in a strong form, although it is relaxed toward the end of the book (1981, pp. 77, 202). Further-

more, considerations of power, relative to the structure of the international system, are at the core of the calculations made by Gilpin's states: "the distribution of power among states constitutes the principal form of control in every international system" (p. 29). Thus Gilpin accepts the entire hard core of the classical Realist research program as I have defined it.[19]

Gilpin sees world history as an unending series of cycles: "The conclusion of one hegemonic war is the beginning of another cycle of growth, expansion, and eventual decline" (p. 210). As power is redistributed, power relations become inconsistent with the rules governing the system and, in particular, the hierarchy of prestige: war establishes the new hierarchy of prestige and "thereby determines which states will in effect govern the international system" (p. 33).

The view that the rules of a system, and the hierarchy of prestige, must be consistent with underlying power realities is a fundamental proposition of Realism, which follows from its three core assumptions. If states, as the central actors of international relations, calculate their interests in terms of power, they will seek international rules and institutions that are consistent with these interests by maintaining their power. Waltz's conception of structure helps to systematize this argument, but it is essentially static. What Gilpin adds is a proposed solution to the anomalies (for static Realism) that institutions and rules can become inconsistent with power realities over time, and that hegemonic states eventually decline. If, as Realists argue, "the strong do what they can and the weak suffer what they must" (Thucydides, Book V, paragraph 90 [Chapter XVII, Modern Library edition, p. 331]), why should hegemons ever lose their power? We know that rules do not always reinforce the power of the strong and that hegemons do sometimes lose their hold, but static Realist theory cannot explain this.

In his attempt to explain hegemonic decline, Gilpin formulates a "law of uneven growth":

According to Realism, the fundamental cause of wars among states and changes in international systems is the uneven growth of power among states. Realist writers from Thucydides and MacKinder to present-day scholars have attributed the dynamics of international relations to the fact that the distribution of power in an international system shifts over a period of time: this shift results in profound changes in the relationships among states and eventually changes in the nature of the international system itself. (p. 94)

This law, however, restates the problem without resolving it. In accounting for this pattern, Gilpin relies on three sets of processes. One has to do with increasing, and then diminishing, marginal returns from empire. As empires grew, "the economic surplus had to increase faster than the cost of war" (p. 115). Yet sooner or later, diminishing returns set in: "the law of diminishing returns has universal applicability and causes the growth of every society to describe an S-shaped curve" (p. 159). Secondly, hegemonic states tend increasingly to consume more and invest less; Gilpin follows the lead of Carlo Cipolla in viewing this as a general pattern in history (Cipolla, 1970). Finally, hegemonic states decline because of a process of diffusion of technology to others. In *U.S. Power and the Multinational Corporation* (1975), Gilpin emphasized this process as contributing first to the decline of Britain, then in the 1970s to that of the United States. In *War and Change* he makes the argument more general:

> Through a process of diffusion to other states, the dominant power loses the advantage on which its political, military, or economic success has been based. Thus, by example, and frequently in more direct fashion, the dominant power helps to create challenging powers. (p. 176)

This third argument is systemic, and, therefore, fully consistent with Waltz's Structural Realism. The other two processes, however, reflect the operation of forces within the society, as well as international forces. A hegemonic power may suffer diminishing returns as a result of the expansion of its defense perimeter and the increased military costs that result (Gilpin, 1981, p. 191; Luttwak, 1976). But whether diminishing returns set in also depends on internal factors such as technological inventiveness of members of the society and the institutions that affect incentives for innovation (North, 1981). The tendency of hegemonic states to consume more and invest less is also, in part, a function of their dominant positions in the world system: they can force costs of adjustment to change onto others, at least for some time. But it would be hard to deny that the character of the society affects popular tastes for luxury, and, therefore, the tradeoffs between guns and butter that are made. Eighteenth-century Saxony and Prussia were different in this regard; so are contemporary America and Japan. In Gilpin's argument as in Snyder and Diesing's, the "external-internal interaction" becomes a crucial factor in explaining state action, and change.

Gilpin explicitly acknowledges his debt to Classical Realism: "In honesty, one must inquire whether or not twentieth-century students of international relations know anything that Thucydides and his fifth-century compatriots did not know about the behavior of states" (p. 227). For Gilpin as for Thucydides, changes in power lead to changes in relations among states: the *real* cause of the Peloponnesian War, for Thucydides, was the rise of the power of Athens and the fear this evoked in the Spartans and their allies. Gilpin has generalized the theory put forward by Thucydides to explain the Peloponnesian War, and has applied it to the whole course of world history:

> Disequilibrium replaces equilibrium, and the world moves toward a new round of hegemonic conflict. It has always been thus and always will be, until men either destroy themselves or learn to develop an effective mechanism of peaceful change. (p. 210)

This Thucydides–Gilpin theory is a systemic theory of change only in a limited sense. It explains the *reaction* to change systematically, in a rationalistic, equilibrium model. Yet at a more fundamental level, it does not account fully for the sources of change. As we saw above, although it is insightful about systemic factors leading to hegemonic decline, it also has to rely on internal processes to explain the observed effects. Furthermore, it does not account well for the rise of hegemons in the first place, or for the fact that certain contenders emerge rather than others.[20] Gilpin's systemic theory does not account for the extraordinary bursts of energy that occasionally catapult particular countries into dominant positions on the world scene. Why were the Athenians, in words that Thucydides attributes to Corinthian envoys to Sparta, "addicted to innovation," whereas the Spartans were allegedly characterized by a "total want of invention" (Thucydides, Book I, paragraph 70 [Chapter III, Modern Library edition, p. 40])? Like other structural theories, Gilpin's theory underpredicts outcomes. It contributes to our understanding but (as its author recognizes) does not explain change.

This is particularly true of peaceful change, which Gilpin identifies as a crucial issue: "The fundamental problem of international relations in the contemporary world is the problem of peaceful adjustment to the consequences of the uneven growth of power among states, just as it was in the past" (p. 230).

Gilpin's book, like much contemporary American work on international politics, is informed and propelled by concern with peaceful change under conditions of declining hegemony. Gilpin sympathetically discusses E. H. Carr's "defense of peaceful change as the solution to the problem of hegemonic war," written just before World War II (Gilpin, p. 206; Carr, 1939/1946). Yet peaceful change does not fit easily into Gilpin's analytical framework, since it falls, by and large, into the category of "interactions change," which does not entail alteration in the overall hierarchy of power and prestige in a system, and Gilpin deliberately avoids focusing on interactions change (p. 44). Yet after one puts down *War and Change*, the question of how institutions and rules can be developed *within* a given international system, to reduce the probability of war and promote peaceful change, looms even larger than it did before.

Thus Gilpin's sophisticated adaptation of Classical Realism turns us away from Realism. Classical Realism, with its philosophical roots in a tragic conception of the human condition, directs our attention in the twentieth century to the existential situation of modern humanity, doomed apparently to recurrent conflict in a world with weapons that could destroy life on our planet. But Realism, whether classical or structural, has little to say about how to deal with that situation since it offers few insights into the international rules and institutions that people invent to reduce risk and uncertainty in world affairs in the hope of ameliorating the security dilemma.[21] Morgenthau put his hopes in diplomacy (1966, Chapter 32). This is a practical art far removed from the abstractions of Structural Realism. But diplomacy takes place within a context of international rules, institutions, and practices, which affect the incentives of the actors (Keohane, 1982). Gilpin realizes this, and his gloomy argument—hardly alleviated by a more optimistic epilogue—helps us to understand their importance, although it does not contribute to an explanation of their creation or demise.

Conclusions

Realism, as developed through a long tradition dating from Thucydides, continues to provide the basis for valuable research in international relations. This point has been made by looking at writers who explicitly draw on the Realist tradition, and it can be reinforced by briefly examining some works of Marxist scholars. If they incorporate elements of Realism despite their general antipathy to its viewpoint, our conclusion that Realism reflects enduring realities of world politics will be reinforced.

For Marxists, the fundamental forces affecting world politics are those of class struggle and uneven development. International history is dynamic and dialectical rather than cyclical. The maneuvers of states, on which Realism focuses, reflect the stages of capitalist development and the contradictions of that development. Nevertheless, in analyzing the surface manifestations of world politics under capitalism, Marxists adopt similar categories to those of Realists. Power is crucial; world systems are periodically dominated by hegemonic powers wielding both economic and military resources.

Lenin defined imperialism differently than do the Realists, but he analyzed its operation in part as a Realist would, arguing that "there can be no other conceivable basis under capitalism for the division of spheres of influence, of interests, of colonies, etc. than a calculation of the *strength* of the participants in the division. . . ." (Lenin, 1916/1939, p. 119).

Immanuel Wallerstein provides another example of my point. He goes to some effort to stress that modern world history should be seen as the history of capitalism as a world system. Apart from "relatively minor accidents" provided by geography, peculiarities of history, or luck—which give one country an edge over others at crucial historical junctures—"it is the operations of the world-market forces which accentuate the differences, institutionalize them, and make them impossible to surmount over the long run" (1979, p. 21). Nevertheless, when his attention turns to particular epochs, Wallerstein emphasizes hegemony and the role of military force. Dutch economic hegemony in the seventeenth century was destroyed in quintessential Realist fashion, not by the operation of the world-market system, but by the force of British and French arms (Wallerstein, 1980, pp. 38–39).

The insights of Realism are enduring. They cross ideological lines. Its best contemporary exponents use Realism in insightful ways. Waltz

has systematized the basic assumptions of Classical Realism in what I have called Structural Realism. Snyder and Diesing have employed this framework for the analysis of bargaining; Gilpin has used the classical arguments of Thucydides to explore problems of international change. For all of these writers, Realism fruitfully focuses attention on fundamental issues of power, interests, and rationality. But, as we have seen, many of the most interesting questions raised by these authors cannot be answered within the Realist framework.

III. Explanations of Outcomes from Power: Hypotheses and Anomalies

A Structural Realist theory of interests could be used both for explanation and for prescription. If we could deduce a state's interest from its position in the system, via the rationality assumption, its behavior could be explained on the basis of systemic analysis. Efforts to define the national interest on an a priori basis, however, or to use the concept for prediction and explanation, have been unsuccessful. We saw above that the inability to define interests independently of observed state behavior robbed Snyder and Diesing's game-theoretical matrices of predictive power. More generally, efforts to show that external considerations of power and position play a dominant role in determining the "national interest" have failed. Even an analyst as sympathetic to Realism as Stephen D. Krasner has concluded, in studying American foreign economic policy, that the United States was "capable of defining its own autonomous goals" in a non-logical manner (1978, p. 333). That is, the systemic constraints emphasized by Structural Realism were not binding on the American government during the first thirty years after the Second World War.

Sophisticated contemporary thinkers in the Realist tradition, such as Gilpin, Krasner, and Waltz, understand that interests cannot be derived, simply on the basis of rational calculation, from the external positions of states, and that this is particularly true for great powers, on which, ironically, Structural Realism focuses its principal attentions (Gilpin, 1975; Waltz, 1967). Realist analysis has to retreat to a "fall-back position": that, *given state interests*, whose origins are not predicted by the theory, patterns of outcomes in world politics will be determined by the overall distribution of power among states. This represents a major concession for systemically-oriented analysts, which it is important not to forget. Sensible Realists are highly cognizant of the role of domestic politics and of actor choices within the constraints and incentives provided by the system. Since systemic theory cannot predict state interests, it cannot support deterministic conclusions (Sprout & Sprout, 1971, pp. 73–77). This limitation makes it both less powerful as a theory, and less dangerous as an ideology.[22] Despite its importance, it cannot stand alone.

When realist theorists say that, given interests, patterns of outcomes will be determined by the overall distribution of power among states, they are using "power" to refer to resources that can be used to induce other actors to do what they would not otherwise do, in accordance with the desires of the power-wielder. "Outcomes" refer principally to two sets of patterns: (1) the results of conflicts, diplomatic or military, that take place between states; and (2) changes in the rules and institutions that regulate relations among governments in world politics. This section focuses on conflicts, since they pose the central puzzles that Realism seeks to explain. Section IV and the Conclusion consider explanations of changes in rules and institutions.

Recent quantitative work seems to confirm that power capabilities (measured not only in terms of economic resources but with political variables added) are rather good predictors of the outcomes of wars. Bueno de Mesquita finds, for example, that countries with what he calls positive "expected utility" (a measure that uses composite capabilities but adjusts them for dis-

tance, alliance relationships, and uncertainty) won 179 conflicts while losing only 54 between 1816 and 1974, for a success ratio of over 75% (1981, especially p. 151; Organski & Kugler, 1980, Chapter 2).

The question of the fungibility of power poses a more troublesome issue. As I have noted earlier (see footnote 19), Structural Realism is ambiguous on this point; the desire for parsimonious theory impels Realists toward a unitary notion of power as homogeneous and usable for a variety of purposes, but close examination of the complexities of world politics induces caution about such an approach. In his discussion of system structure, for instance, Waltz holds that "the units of an anarchic system are distinguished primarily by their greater or lesser capabilities for performing similar tasks," and that the distribution of capabilities across a system is the principal characteristic differentiating international-political structures from one another (1979, pp. 97, 99). Thus each international political system has one structure. Yet in emphasizing the continued-role of military power, Waltz admits that military power is not perfectly fungible: "Differences in strength do matter, *although not for every conceivable purpose*"; "military power no longer brings political control, but then it never did" (1979, pp. 189, 191, emphasis added). This seems to imply that any given international system is likely to have *several* structures, differing by issue-areas and according to the resources that can be used to affect outcomes. Different sets of capabilities will qualify as "power resources" under different conditions. This leads to a much less parsimonious theory and a much more highly differentiated view of the world, in which what Nye and I called "issue-structure" theories play a major role, and in which military force, although still important, is no longer assumed to be at the top of a hierarchy of power resources (Keohane & Nye, 1977, chs. 3 and 6).

The status in a Structural Realist theory of the fungibility assumption affects both its power and the incidence of anomalies. A strong version of Structural Realism that assumed full fungibility of power across issues would predict that when issues arise between great powers and smaller states, the great powers should prevail. This has the advantage of generating a clear prediction and the liability of being wrong much of the time. Certainly it does not fit the American experience of the last two decades. The United States lost a war in Vietnam and was for more than a year unable to secure the return of its diplomats held hostage in Iran. Small allies such as Israel, heavily dependent on the United States, have displayed considerable freedom of action. In the U.S.-Canadian relationship of the 1950s and 1960s, which was virtually free of threats of force, outcomes of conflicts as often favored the Canadian as the American position although this was not true for relations between Australia and the United States (Keohane & Nye, 1977, Chapter 7).

In view of power theory in social science, the existence of these anomalies is not surprising. As James G. March observes, "there appears to be general consensus that either potential power is different from actually exerted power or that actually exerted power is variable." (1966, p. 57) That is, what March calls "basic force models," which rely, like Realist theory, on measurable indices of power, are inadequate tools for either prediction or explanation. They are often valuable in suggesting long-term trends and patterns, but they do not account well for specific outcomes: the more that is demanded of them, the less well they are likely to perform.

Lakatos' discussion of scientific research programs leads us to expect that, when confronted with anomalies, theorists will create auxiliary theories that preserve the credibility of their fundamental assumptions. Thus it is not surprising that Realists committed to the fungibility assumption have devised auxiliary hypotheses to protect its "hard core" against challenge. One of these is what David Baldwin calls the "conversion-process explanation" of unanticipated outcomes:

> The would-be wielder of power is described as lacking in skill and/or the "will" to use his power resources effectively: "The Arabs had the tanks but didn't know how to use them." "The Americans had the bombs but lacked the will to use them." (1979, pp. 163–164)

The conversion-process explanation is a classic auxiliary hypothesis, since it is designed to protect the assumption that power resources are homogeneous and fungible. If we were to accept the conversion-process account, we could continue to believe in a single structure of power, even if outcomes do not favor the "stronger" party. This line of argument encounters serious problems, however, when it tries to account for the discrepancy between anticipated and actual outcomes by the impact of intangible resources (such as intelligence, training, organization, foresight) not recognized until after the fact. The problem with this argument lies in its post hoc quality. It is theoretically degenerate in Lakatos' sense, since it does not add any explanatory power to structural Realist theory, but merely "explains away" uncomfortable facts.

Thus what March says about "force activation models" applies to Structural Realist theories when the conversion-process explanation relies upon sources of power that can be observed only after the events to be explained have taken place:

> If we observe that power exists and is stable and if we observe that sometimes weak people seem to triumph over strong people, we are tempted to rely on an activation hypothesis to explain the discrepancy. But if we then try to use the activation hypothesis to predict the results of social-choice procedures, we discover that the data requirements of 'plausible' activation models are quite substantial. As a result, we retreat to what are essentially degenerate forms of the activation model—retaining some of the form but little of

the substance. This puts us back where we started, looking for some device to explain our failures in prediction. (1966, p. 61)

A second auxiliary hypothesis designed to protect the fungibility assumption must be taken more seriously: that discrepancies between power resources and outcomes are explained by an asymmetry of motivation in favor of the objectively weaker party. Following this logic, John Harsanyi has proposed the notion of power "in a schedule sense," describing how various resources can be translated into social power. An actor with intense preferences on an issue may be willing to use more resources to attain a high probability of a favorable result than an actor with more resources but lower intensity. As a result, outcomes may not accurately reflect underlying power resources (Harsanyi, 1962).

To use this insight progressively rather than in a degenerate way, Realist theory needs to develop indices of intensity of motivation that can be measured independently of the behavior that theorists are trying to explain. Russett, George, and Bueno de Mesquita are among the authors who have attempted, with some success, to do this (Russett, 1963; George *et al.*, 1971; Bueno de Mesquita, 1981). Insofar as motivation is taken simply as a control, allowing us to test the impact of varying power configurations more successfully, Harsanyi's insights can be incorporated into Structural Realist theory. If it became a key variable, however, the effect could be to transform a systemic theory into a decision-making one.

An alternative approach to relying on such auxiliary hypotheses is to relax the fungibility assumption itself. Failures of great powers to control smaller ones could be explained on the basis of independent evidence that in the relevant issue-areas, the states that are weaker on an overall basis have more power resources than their stronger partners, and that the use of power derived from one area of activity to affect outcomes in other areas (through "linkages") is

difficult. Thus Saudi Arabia can be expected to have more impact on world energy issues than on questions of strategic arms control; Israel more influence over the creation of a Palestinian state than on the reconstruction of the international financial and debt regime.

Emphasizing the problematic nature of power fungibility might help to create more discriminating power models, but it will not resolve the inherent problems of power models, as identified by March and others. Furthermore, at the limit, to deny fungibility entirely risks a complete disintegration of predictive power. Baldwin comes close to this when he argues that what he calls the "policy-contingency framework" of an influence attempt must be specified before power explanations are employed. If we defined each issue as existing within a unique "policy-contingency framework," no generalizations would be possible. Waltz could reply, if he accepted Baldwin's view of power, that all of world politics should be considered a single policy-contingency framework, characterized by anarchy and self-help.[23] According to this argument, the parsimony gained by assuming the fungibility of power would compensate for the marginal mispredictions of such a theory.

This is a crucial theoretical issue, which should be addressed more explicitly by theorists of world politics. In my view, the dispute cannot be resolved a priori. The degree to which power resources have to be disaggregated in a structural theory depends both on the purposes of the theory and on the degree to which behavior on distinct issues is linked together through the exercise of influence by actors. The larger the domain of a theory, the less accuracy of detail we expect. Since balance of power theory seeks to explain large-scale patterns of state action over long periods of time, we could hardly expect the precision from it that we demand from theories whose domains have been narrowed.

This assertion suggests that grand systemic theory can be very useful as a basis for further theoretical development in international relations, even if the theory is lacking in precision, and it therefore comprises part of my defense of the Realist research program as a foundation on which scholars should build. Yet this argument needs immediate qualification.

Even if a large-scale theory can be developed and appropriately tested, its predictions will be rather gross. To achieve a more finely-tuned understanding of how resources affect behavior in particular situations, one needs to specify the policy-contingency framework more precisely. The domain of theory is narrowed to achieve greater precision. Thus the debate between advocates of parsimony and proponents of contextual subtlety resolves itself into a question of *stages*, rather than an either/or choice. We should seek parsimony first, then add complexity while monitoring the adverse effects that this has on the predictive power of our theory: its ability to make significant inferences on the basis of limited information.

To introduce greater complexity into an initially spare theoretical structure, the conception of an issue-area, developed many years ago by Robert A. Dahl (1961) and adapted for use in international relations by James N. Rosenau (1966), is a useful device. Having tentatively selected an area of activity to investigate, the analyst needs to delineate issue-areas at various levels of aggregation. Initial explanations should seek to account for the main features of behavior at a high level of aggregation—such as the international system as a whole—while subsequent hypotheses are designed to apply only to certain issue-areas.

In some cases, more specific issue-areas are "nested" within larger ones (Aggarwal, 1981; Snidal, 1981). For instance, North Atlantic fisheries issues constitute a sub-set of fisheries issues in general, which comprise part of the whole area of oceans policy, or "law of the sea." In other cases, specific issues may belong to two or more broader issues: the question of passage through straits, for example, involves questions of military security as well as the law of the sea.

Definitions of issue-areas depend on the beliefs of participants, as well as on the purposes of the investigator. In general, however, definitions of issue-areas should be made on the basis of empirical judgments about the extent to which governments regard sets of issues as closely interdependent and treat them collectively. Decisions made on one issue must affect others in the issue-area, either through functional links or through regular patterns of bargaining. These relationships of interdependence among issues may change. Some issue-areas, such as international financial relations, have remained fairly closely linked for decades; others, such as oceans, have changed drastically over the past 35 years (Keohane & Nye, 1977, Chapter 4, especially pp. 64–65; Simon, 1969; Haas, 1980).

When a hierarchy of issue-areas has been identified, power-structure models employing more highly aggregated measures of power resources can be compared with models that disaggregate resources by issue-areas. How much accuracy is gained, and how much parsimony lost, by each step in the disaggregation process? In my view, a variegated analysis, which takes some specific "snapshots" by issue-area as well as looking at the broader picture, is superior to either monistic strategy, whether assuming perfect fungibility or none at all.

This approach represents an adaptation of Realism. It preserves the basic emphasis on power resources as a source of outcomes in general, but it unambiguously jettisons the assumption that power is fungible across all of world politics. Disaggregated power models are less parsimonious than more aggregated ones, and they remain open to the objections to power models articulated by March and others. But in one important sense disaggregation is progressive rather than degenerative. Disaggregated models call attention to linkages among issue-areas, and raise the question: under what conditions, and with what effects, will such linkages arise? Current research suggests that understanding linkages systematically, rather than merely describing them on an ad hoc basis, will add significantly to our comprehension of world politics (Oye, 1979, 1983; Stein, 1980; Tollison and Willett, 1979). It would seem worthwhile, in addition, for more empirical work to be done on this subject, since we know so little about when, and how, linkages are made.

Conclusions

Structural Realism is a good starting point for explaining the outcomes of conflicts, since it directs attention to fundamental questions of interest and power within a logically coherent and parsimonious theoretical framework. Yet the ambitious attempt of Structural Realist theory to deduce national interests from system structure via the rationality postulate has been unsuccessful. Even if interests are taken as given, the attempt to predict outcomes from interests and power leads to ambiguities and incorrect predictions. The auxiliary theory attributing this failure to conversion-processes often entails unfalsifiable tautology rather than genuine explanation. Ambiguity prevails on the question of the fungibility of power: whether there is a single structure of the international system or several. Thus the research program of Realism reveals signs of degeneration. It certainly does not meet Lakatos' tough standards for progressiveness.

More attention to developing independent measures of intensity of motivation, and greater precision about the concept of power and its relationship to the context of action, may help to correct some of these faults. Careful disaggregation of power-resources by issue-area may help to improve the predictive capability of structural models, at the risk of reducing theoretical parsimony. As I argue in the next section, modified structural models, indebted to Realism although perhaps too different to be considered Realist themselves, may be valuable elements in a multi-level framework for understanding world politics.

Yet to some extent the difficulties encountered by Structural Realism reflect the inherent limitations of structural models which will not be corrected by mere modifications or the relaxation of assumptions. Domestic politics and decision-making, Snyder and Diesing's "internal-external interactions," and the workings of international institutions all play a role, along with international political structure, in affecting state behavior and outcomes. Merely to catalog these factors, however, is not to contribute to theory but rather to compound the descriptive anarchy that already afflicts the field, with too many independent variables, exogenously determined, chasing too few cases. As Waltz emphasizes, the role of unit-level forces can only be properly understood if we comprehend the structure of the international system within which they operate.

IV. Beyond Structural Realism

Structural Realism helps us to understand world politics as in part a systemic phenomenon, and provides us with a logically coherent theory that establishes the context for state action. This theory, because it is relatively simple and clear, can be modified progressively to attain closer correspondence with reality. Realism's focus on interests and power is central to an understanding of how nations deal with each other. Its adherents have understood that a systemic theory of international relations must account for state behavior by examining the constraints and incentives provided by the system; for this purpose to be accomplished, an assumption of rationality (although not of perfect information) must be made. The rationality assumption allows inferences about state behavior to be drawn solely from knowledge of the structure of the system.

Unfortunately, such predictions are often wrong. The concept of power is difficult to measure validly a priori; interests are underspecified by examining the nature of the international system and the position of various states in it; the view of power resources implied by overall structure theories is overaggregated, exaggerating the extent to which power is like money. The problem that students of international politics face is how to construct theories that draw on Realism's strengths without partaking fully of its weaknesses.

To do this we need a multi-dimensional approach to world politics that incorporates several analytical frameworks or research programs. One of these should be that of Structural Realism, which has the virtues of parsimony and clarity, although the range of phenomena that it encompasses is limited. Another, in my view, should be a modified structural research program, which relaxes some of the assumptions of Structural Realism but retains enough of the hard core to generate a priori predictions on the basis of information about the international environment. Finally, we need better theories of domestic politics, decision-making, and information processing, so that the gap between the external and internal environments can be bridged in a systematic way, rather than by simply adding catalogs of exogenously determined foreign policy facts to theoretically more rigorous structural models. That is, we need more attention to the "internal-external interactions" discussed by Snyder and Diesing.

Too much work in this last category is being done for me to review it in detail here. Mention should be made, however, of some highlights. Peter J. Katzenstein, Peter Gourevitch, and others have done pioneering work on the relationship between domestic political structure and political coalitions, on the one hand, and foreign economic policies, on the other (Katzenstein, 1978; Gourevitch, 1978). This line of analysis, which draws heavily on the work of Alexander Gerschenkron (1962) and Barrington Moore (1966), argues that the different domestic structures characteristic of various advanced industrialized countries result from different historical patterns of development; in particular, whether development came early or late, and what the position of the country was in the international political system at the time of its economic development (Kurth, 1979). Thus it

attempts to draw connections both between international and domestic levels of analysis, and across historical time. This research does not provide deductive explanatory models, and it does not account systematically for changes in established structures after the formative developmental period, but its concept of domestic structure brings order into the cacophony of domestic political and economic variables that could affect foreign policy, and therefore suggests the possibility of eventual integration of theories relying on international structure with those focusing on domestic structure.

Katzenstein and his associates focus on broad political, economic, and social patterns within countries, and their relationship to the international division of labor and the world political structure. Fruitful analysis can also be done at the more narrowly intragovernmental level, as Snyder and Diesing show. An emphasis on bureaucratic politics was particularly evident in the 1960s and early 1970s, although Robert J. Art has pointed out in detail a number of difficulties, weaknesses, and contradictions in this literature (1973). At the level of the individual decision-maker, insights can be gained by combining theories of cognitive psychology with a rich knowledge of diplomatic history, as in Jervis's work, as long as the investigator understands the systemic and domestic-structural context within which decision-makers operate.[24] This research program has made decided progress, from the simple-minded notions criticized by Waltz (1959) to the work of Alexander and Juliette George (1964), Alexander George (1980), Ole Holsti (1976), and Jervis (1976).[25]

Despite the importance of this work at the levels of domestic structure, intragovernmental politics, and individual cognition, the rest of my analysis will continue to focus on the concept of international political structure and its relevance to the study of world politics. I will argue that progress could be made by constructing a modified structural research program, retaining some of the parsimony characteristic of Structural

Realism and its emphasis on the incentives and constraints of the world system, while adapting it to fit contemporary reality better. Like Realism, this research program would be based on microeconomic theory, particularly oligopoly theory. It would seek to explain actor behavior by specifying a priori utility functions for actors, using the rationality principle as a "trivial animating law" in Popper's sense (Latsis, 1976, p. 21), and deducing behavior from the constraints of the system as modeled in the theory.

Developing such a theory would only be worthwhile if there were something particularly satisfactory both about systemic explanations and about the structural forms of such explanations. I believe that this is the case, for two sets of reasons.

First, systemic theory is important because we must understand the context of action before we can understand the action itself. As Waltz (1979) has emphasized, theories of world politics that fail to incorporate a sophisticated understanding of the operation of the system—that is, how systemic attributes affect behavior—are bad theories. Theoretical analysis of the characteristics of an international system is as important for understanding foreign policy as understanding European history is for understanding the history of Germany.

Second, structural theory is important because it provides an irreplaceable *component* for a thorough analysis of action, by states or non-state actors, in world politics. A good structural theory generates testable implications about behavior on an a priori basis, and, therefore, comes closer than interpretive description to meeting the requirements for scientific knowledge of neo-positivist philosophers of science such as Lakatos. This does not mean, of course, that explanation and rich interpretation—Geertz's "thick description" (1973)—are in any way antithetical to one another. A good analysis of a given problem will include both.[26]

The assumptions of a modified structural research program can be compared to Realist assumptions as follows:

1. The assumption that the principal actors in world politics are states would remain the same, although more emphasis would be placed on non-state actors, intergovernmental organizations, and transnational and transgovernmental relations than is the case in Realist analysis (Keohane & Nye, 1972).

2. The rationality assumption would be retained, since without it, as we have seen, inferences from structure to behavior become impossible without heroic assumptions about evolutionary processes or other forces that compel actors to adapt their behavior to their environments. It should be kept in mind, however, as is made clear by sophisticated Realists, that the rationality postulate only assumes that actors make calculations "so as to maximize expected value across a given set of consistently ordered objectives" (Snyder & Diesing, 1977, p. 81). It does not assume perfect information, consideration of all possible alternatives, or unchanging actor preferences.

3. The assumption that states seek power and calculate their interests accordingly, would be qualified severely. Power and influence would still be regarded as important state interests (as ends or necessary means), but the implication that the search for power constitutes an overriding interest in all cases, or that it always takes the same form, would be rejected. Under different systemic conditions states will define their self-interests differently. For instance, where survival is at stake efforts to maintain autonomy may take precedence over all other activities, but where the environment is relatively benign energies will also be directed to fulfilling other goals. Indeed, over the long run, whether an environment is malign or benign can alter the standard operating procedures and sense of identity of the actors themselves.[27]

In addition, this modified structural approach would explicitly modify the assumption of fungibility lurking behind unitary conceptions of "international structure." It would be assumed that the value of power resources for influencing behavior in world politics depends on the goals sought. Power resources that are well-suited to achieve certain purposes are less effective when used for other objectives. Thus power resources are differentially effective across issue-areas, and the usability of a given set of power resources depends on the "policy-contingency frameworks" within which it must be employed.

This research program would pay much more attention to the roles of institutions and rules than does Structural Realism. Indeed, a structural interpretation of the emergence of international rules and procedures, and of obedience to them by states, is one of the rewards that could be expected from this modified structural research program (Krasner, 1982; Keohane, 1982, Stein, 1982).

This research program would contain a valuable positive heuristic—a set of suggestions about what research should be done and what questions should initially be asked—which would include the following pieces of advice:

1. When trying to explain a set of outcomes in world politics, always consider the hypothesis that the outcomes reflect underlying power resources, without being limited to it;
2. When considering different patterns of outcomes in different relationships, or issue-areas, entertain the hypothesis that power resources are differently distributed in these issue-areas, and investigate ways in which these differences promote or constrain actor attempts to link issue-areas in order to use power-resources from one area to affect results in another;
3. When considering how states define their self-interests, explore the effects of international structure on self-interests, as well as the effects of other international factors and of domestic structure.

Such a modified structural research program could begin to help generate theories that are more discriminating, with respect to the sources of power, than is Structural Realism. It would be less oriented toward reaffirming the orthodox verities of world politics and more inclined to explain variations in patterns of rules and institutions. Its concern with international institutions would facilitate insights into processes of peaceful change. This research program would not solve all of the problems of Realist theory, but it would be a valuable basis for interpreting contemporary world politics.

Yet this form of structural theory still has the weaknesses associated with power analysis. The essential problem is that from a purely systemic point of view, situations of strategic interdependence do not have determinate solutions. No matter how carefully power resources are defined, no power model will be able accurately to predict outcomes under such conditions.[28]

One way to alleviate this problem without moving immediately to the domestic level of analysis (and thus sacrificing the advantages of systemic theory), is to recognize that what it is rational for states to do, and what states' interests are, depend on the institutional context of action as well as on the underlying power realities and state position upon which Realist thought concentrates. Structural approaches should be seen as only a basis for further systemic analysis. They vary the power condition in the system, but they are silent on variations in the frequency of mutual interactions in the system or in the level of information.

The importance of these non-power factors is demonstrated by some recent work on cooperation. In particular, Robert Axelrod has shown that cooperation can emerge among egoists under conditions of strategic interdependence as modelled by the game of prisoners' dilemma. Such a result requires, however, that these egoists expect to continue to interact with each other for the indefinite future, and that these expectations of future interactions be given sufficient weight in their calculations (Axelrod, 1981). This argument reinforces the practical wisdom of diplomats and arms controllers, who assume that state strategies, and the degree of eventual cooperation, will depend significantly on expectations about the future. The "double-cross" strategy, for instance, is more attractive when it is expected to lead to a final, winning move, than when a continuing series of actions and reactions is anticipated.

High levels of uncertainty reduce the confidence with which expectations are held, and may therefore lead governments to discount the future heavily. As Axelrod shows, this can inhibit the evolution of cooperation through reciprocity. It can also reduce the ability of actors to make mutually beneficial agreements at any given time, quite apart from their expectations about whether future interactions will occur. That is, it can lead to a form of "political market failure" (Keohane, 1982).

Information that reduces uncertainty is therefore an important factor in world politics. But information is not a systemic constant. Some international systems are rich in institutions and processes that provide information to governments and other actors; in other systems, information is scarce or of low quality. Given a certain distribution of power (Waltz's "international structure"), variations in information may be important in influencing state behavior. If international institutions can evolve that improve the quality of information and reduce uncertainty, they may profoundly affect international political behavior even in the absence of changes either in international structure (defined in terms of the distribution of power) or in the preference functions of actors.

Taking information seriously at the systemic level could stimulate a new look at theories of information-processing within governments, such as those of Axelrod (1976), George (1980), Jervis (1976), and Holsti (1976). It could also help us, however, to understand a dimension of the concept of complex interdependence (Keohane and Nye, 1977) that has been largely ignored. Complex interdependence can be seen as a condition under which it is not only difficult to use conventional power resources for certain purposes, but under which

information levels are relatively high due to the existence of multiple channels of contact among states. If we focus exclusively on questions of power, the most important feature of complex interdependence—almost its only important feature—is the ineffectiveness of military force and the constraints that this implies on fungibility of power across issue-areas. Sensitizing ourselves to the role of information and information-provision, at the international level brings another aspect of complex interdependence—the presence of multiple channels of contact among societies—back into the picture. Actors behave differently in information-rich environments than in information-poor ones where uncertainty prevails.

This is not a subject that can be explored in depth here.[29] I raise it, however, to clarify the nature of the multi-dimensional network of theories and research programs that I advocate for the study of world politics. We need both spare, logically tight theories, such as Structural Realism, and rich interpretations, such as those of the historically-oriented students of domestic structure and foreign policy. But we also need something in-between: systemic theories that retain some of the parsimony of Structural Realism, but that are able to deal better with differentiations between issue-areas, with institutions, and with change. Such theories could be developed on the basis of variations in power (as in Structural Realism), but they could also focus on variations in other systemic characteristics, such as levels and quality of information.

Conclusion: World Politics and Peaceful Change

As Gilpin points out, the problem of peaceful change is fundamental to world politics. Thermonuclear weapons have made it even more urgent than it was in the past. Realism demonstrates that peaceful change is more difficult to achieve in international politics than within well-ordered domestic societies, but it does not offer a theory of peaceful change.[30] Nor is such a theory available from other research traditions. The question remains for us to grapple with: Under what conditions will adaptations to shifts in power, in available technologies, or in fundamental economic relationships take place without severe economic disruption or warfare?

Recent work on "international regimes" has been addressed to this question, which is part of the broader issue of order in world politics (*International Organization*, Spring, 1982). Structural Realist approaches to understanding the origins and maintenance of international regimes are useful (Krasner, 1982), but since they ignore cognitive issues and questions of information, they comprise only part of the story (Haas, 1982).

Realism, furthermore, is better at telling us why we are in such trouble than how to get out of it. It argues that order can be created from anarchy by the exercise of superordinate power: periods of peace follow establishment of dominance in Gilpin's "hegemonic wars." Realism sometimes seems to imply, pessimistically, that order can *only* be created by hegemony. If the latter conclusion were correct, not only would the world economy soon become chaotic (barring a sudden resurgence of American power), but at some time in the foreseeable future, global nuclear war would ensue.

Complacency in the face of this prospect is morally unacceptable. No serious thinker could, therefore, be satisfied with Realism as the correct theory of world politics, even if the scientific status of the theory were stronger than it is. Our concern for humanity requires us to do what Gilpin does in the epilogue to *War and Change* (1981), where he holds out the hope of a "new and more stable international order" in the final decades of the twentieth century, despite his theory's contention that such a benign outcome is highly unlikely. Although Gilpin could be criticized for inconsistency, this would be beside the

point: the conditions of terror under which we live compel us to search for a way out of the trap.

The need to find a way out of the trap means that international relations must be a policy science as well as a theoretical activity.[31] We should be seeking to link theory with practice, bringing insights from Structural Realism, modified structural theories, other systemic approaches, and actor-level analyses to bear on contemporary issues in a sophisticated way. This does not mean that the social scientist should adopt the policy-maker's framework, much less his normative values or blinders about the range of available alternatives. On the contrary, independent observers often do their most valuable work when they reject the normative or analytic framework of those in power, and the best theorists may be those who maintain their distance from those at the center of events. Nevertheless, foreign policy and world politics are too important to be left to bureaucrats, generals, and lawyers—or even to journalists and clergymen.

Realism helps us determine the strength of the trap, but does not give us much assistance in seeking to escape. If we are to promote peaceful change, we need to focus not only on basic long-term forces that determine the shape of world politics independently of the actions of particular decision-makers, but also on variables that to some extent can be manipulated by human action. Since international institutions, rules, and patterns of cooperation can affect calculations of interest, and can also be affected incrementally by contemporary political action, they provide a natural focus for scholarly attention as well as policy concern.[32] Unlike Realism, theories that attempt to explain rules, norms, and institutions help us to understand how to create patterns of cooperation that could be essential to our survival. We need to respond to the questions that Realism poses but fails to answer: How can order be created out of anarchy *without* superordinate power; how can peaceful change occur?

To be reminded of the significance of inter-national relations as policy analysis, and the pressing problem of order, is to recall the tradition of Classical Realism. Classical Realism, as epitomized by the work of John Herz (1981), has recognized that no matter how deterministic our theoretical aspirations may be, there remains a human interest in autonomy and self-reflection. As Ashley puts it, the Realism of a thinker such as Herz is committed to an "emancipatory cognitive interest—an interest in securing freedom from unacknowledged constraints, relations of domination, and conditions of distorted communication and understanding that deny humans the capacity to make their future with full will and consciousness" (1981, p. 227).[33] We think about world politics not because it is aesthetically beautiful, because we believe that it is governed by simple, knowable laws, or because it provides rich, easily accessible data for the testing of empirical hypotheses. Were those concerns paramount, we would look elsewhere. We study world politics because we think it will determine the fate of the earth (Schell, 1982). Realism makes us aware of the odds against us. What we need to do now is to understand peaceful change by combining multi-dimensional scholarly analysis with more visionary ways of seeing the future.

Notes

1. An unfortunate limitation of this chapter is that its scope is restricted to work published in English, principally in the United States. I recognize that this reflects the Americanocentrism of scholarship in the United States, and I regret it. But I am not sufficiently well-read in works published elsewhere to comment intelligently on them. For recent discussions of the distinctively American stamp that has been placed on the international relations field see Hoffmann (1977) and Lyons (1982).

2. Nye and I, in effect, conceded this in our later work, which was more cautious about the drawbacks of conventional "state-centric" theory. (See Keohane and Nye, 1977.)

3. For a discussion of "theory as a set of questions," see Hoffmann (1960, pp. 1–12).

4. Bruce Russett has written a parallel essay on "International Interactions and Processes: The Internal vs. External Debate Revisited." Professor Russett discusses the extensive literature on arms control and on dependency, neither of which I consider here.

5. Stanley J. Michalak, Jr. pointed out correctly that our characterization of Realism in *Power and Interdependence* was unfair when taken literally, although he also seems to me to have missed the Realist basis of our structural models. (See Michalak, 1979.)

6. It has often been noted that Kuhn's definition of a paradigm was vague: one sympathetic critic identified 21 distinct meanings of the term in Kuhn's relatively brief book (Masterman, 1970). But Lakatos particularly objected to what he regarded as Kuhn's relativism, which in his view interpreted major changes in science as the result of essentially irrational forces. (See Lakatos, 1970, p. 178.)

7. Lakatos' comments on Marxism and psychology were biting, and a colleague of his reports that he doubted the applicability of the methodology of scientific research programs to the social sciences. (See Latsis, 1976, p. 2.)

8. Robert Jervis and Ann Tickner have both reminded me that Morgenthau and John H. Herz, another major proponent of Realist views in the 1960s, later severely qualified their adherence to what has generally been taken as Realist doctrine. (See Herz, 1981, and Boyle, 1980, p. 218.) I am particularly grateful to Dr. Tickner for obtaining a copy of the relevant pages of the latter article for me.

9. For commentary on this assumption, see Keohane and Nye (1972), and Mansbach, Ferguson, and Lampert (1976). In *Power and Interdependence*, Nye and I were less critical than we had been earlier of the state-centric assumption. In view of the continued importance of governments in world affairs, for many purposes it seems justified on grounds of parsimony. Waltz's rather acerbic critique of our earlier position seems to me essentially correct. (See Waltz, 1979, p. 7.)

10. Emphasis added. Thucydides also follows this "positive heuristic" of looking for underlying power realities in discussions of the Athenian–Corcyrean alliance (Chapter II), the decision of the Lacedemonians to vote that Athens had broken the treaty between them (Chapter III), and Pericles' Funeral Oration (Chapter IV). In the Modern Library edition, the passages in questions are on pp. 28, 49–50, and 83.

11. Bruce Bueno de Mesquita (1981, pp. 29–33) has an excellent discussion of the rationality assumption as used in the study of world politics.

12. As Waltz points out, Morgenthau's writings reflect the "first-image" Realist view that the evil inherent in man is at the root of war and conflict.

13. In an illuminating recent review essay, John Gerard Ruggie has criticized Waltz's assumption that the second dimension of structure, referring to the degree of differentiation of units, can be regarded as a constant (undifferentiated units with similar functions) in world politics. Ruggie argues that "when the concept differentiation is properly defined, the second structural level of Waltz's model . . . serves to depict the kind of institutional transformation illustrated by the shift from the medieval to the modern international system." See Ruggie (1983, p. 279).

14. Waltz denies that he relies on the rationality assumptions; but I argue in Section II that he requires it for his theory of the balance of power to hold.

15. Sustained earlier critiques of the fungibility assumption can be found in Keohane and Nye (1977, pp. 49–52) and in Baldwin (1979).

16. For a brilliant discussion of this theoretical strategy in micro-economics, see Latsis (1976, especially pp. 16–23).

17. Since the principal purpose of Realist analysis in the hands of Waltz and others is to develop an explanation of international political reality, rather than to offer specific advice to those in power, the label, "technical realism," seems too narrow. It also carries a pejorative intent that I do not share. "Structural Realism" captures the focus on explanation through an examination of the structure of the international system. Capitalization is used to indicate that Realism is a specific school, and that it would be possible to be a Realist—in the sense of examining reality as it really is—without subscribing to Realist assumptions. For a good discussion, see Krasner (1982).

18. This is the commonsense view of power, as discussed, for example, by Arnold Wolfers (1962, p. 103). As indicated in Section III, any such definition conceals a large number of conceptual problems.

19. My reading of Gilpin's argument on pp. 29–34 led me originally to believe that he also accepted the notion that power is fungible, since he argues that hegemonic war creates a hierarchy of prestige in an international system, which is based on the hegemon's "demonstrated ability to enforce its will on other states" (p. 34), and which in turn determines governance of the international system (p. 33). This appears to imply that a single structure of power resources exists, usable for a wide variety of issues. But in letters sent to the author commenting on an earlier draft of this paper, both Gilpin and Waltz explicitly disavowed the assumption that power resources are necessarily fungible. In *War and Change*, Gilpin is very careful to disclaim the notion,

which he ascribes to Political Realists but which I have not included in the hard core of Realism, that states seek to maximize their power: "Acquisition of power entails an opportunity cost to a society; some other desired good must be abandoned" (p. 51).

20. A similar issue is posed in Chapter 3 of Part II of *Lineages of the Absolutist State* (1974). Its author, Perry Anderson, addresses the puzzle of why it was Prussia, rather than Bavaria or Saxony, that eventually gained predominance in Germany. Despite his inclinations, Anderson has to rely on a variety of conjunctural, if not accidental, factors to account for the observed result.

21. For a lucid discussion of the security dilemma, see Jervis (1978).

22. The fact that sensitive Realists are aware of the limitations of Realism makes me less worried than Ashley about the policy consequences of Realist analysis.

23. Waltz does not accept Baldwin's (and Dahl's) definition of power in terms of causality, arguing that "power is one cause among others, from which it cannot be isolated." But this makes it impossible to falsify any power theory; one can always claim that other factors (not specified a priori) were at work. Waltz's discussion of power (1979, pp. 191–192) does not separate power-as-outcome properly from power-as-resources; it does not distinguish between resources that the observer can assess a priori from those only assessable post hoc; it does not relate probabilistic thinking properly to power theory; and it takes refuge in a notion of power as "affecting others more than they affect him," which would result (if taken literally) in the absurdity of attributing maximum power to the person or government that is least responsive to outside stimuli, regardless of its ability to achieve its purposes.

24. Jervis (1976, Chapter 1) has an excellent discussion of levels of analysis and the relationship between perceptual theories and other theories of international relations. Snyder and Diesing discuss similar issues in Chapter VI on "Crises and International Systems" (1977).

25. Waltz commented perceptively in *Man, the State and War* that contributions of behavioral scientists had often been "rendered ineffective by a failure to comprehend the significance of the political framework of international action" (1959, p. 78).

26. Thorough description—what Alexander George has called "process-tracing"—may be necessary to evaluate a structural explanation, since correlations are not reliable where only a small number of comparable cases is involved. (See George, 1979.)

27. I am indebted for this point to a conversation with Hayward Alker.

28. Latsis (1976) discusses the difference between "single-exit" and "multiple-exit" situations in his critique of

oligopoly theory. What he calls the research program of "situational determinism"—structural theory, in my terms—works well for single-exit situations, where only one sensible course of action is possible. (The building is burning down and there is only one way out: regardless of my personal characteristics, one can expect that I will leave through that exit.) It does not apply to multiple-exit situations, where more than one plausible choice can be made. (The building is burning, but I have to choose between trying the smoky stairs or jumping into a fireman's net: my choice may depend on deep-seated personal fears.) In foreign policy, the prevalence of multiple-exit situations reinforces the importance of decision-making analysis at the national level.

29. For a more detailed discussion of some aspects of this notion, and for citations to some of the literature in economics on which my thinking is based, see Keohane (1982). Discussions with Vinod Aggarwal have been important in formulating some of the points in the previous two paragraphs.

30. Morgenthau devotes a chapter of *Politics Among Nations* to peaceful change, but after a review of the reasons why legalistic approaches will not succeed, he eschews general statements for descriptions of a number of United Nations actions affecting peace and security. No theory of peaceful change is put forward. In *Politics Among Nations* Morgenthau put whatever faith he had in diplomacy. The chapter on peaceful change is Chapter 26 of the fourth edition (1966).

31. For a suggestive discussion of international relations as policy science, see George and Smoke (1974), Appendix, "Theory for Policy in International Relations," pp. 616–642.

32. Recall Weber's aphorism in "Politics as a Vocation": "Politics is the strong and slow boring of hard boards." Although much of Weber's work analyzed broad historical forces beyond the control of single individuals or groups, he remained acutely aware of "the truth that man would not have attained the possible unless time and again he had reached out for the impossible" (Gerth & Mills, 1958, p. 128). For a visionary, value-laden discourse on future international politics by a scholar "reaching out for the impossible," see North (1976, Chapter 7).

33. Ernst B. Haas, who has studied how political actors learn throughout his distinguished career, makes a similar point in a recent essay, where he espouses a "cognitive-evolutionary view" of change and argues that such a view "cannot settle for a concept of hegemony imposed by the analyst. . . . It makes fewer claims about basic directions, purposes, laws and trends than do other lines of thought. It is agnostic about the finality of social laws" (1982, pp. 242–243). The difference between Haas and me is that he seems to reject structural analysis in favor of an emphasis on cognitive evolution and learning, whereas I believe that modified structural analysis (more modest in its claims than Structural Realism) can provide a context within which analysis of cognition is politically more meaningful.

References

Aggarwal, Vinod, *Hanging by a thread: International regime change in the textile apparel system, 1950–1979.* Unpublished doctoral dissertation, Stanford University, 1981.

Anderson, Perry. *Lineages of the Absolutist State.* London: New Left Books, 1974.

Art, Robert J. Bureaucratic Politics and American Foreign Policy: A Critique. *Policy Sciences* 4, 1973, 467–490.

Ashley, Richard K. Political Realism and Human Interest. *International Studies Quarterly* 25, 1981, 204–236.

Ashley, Richard K. Realistic dialectics: Toward a critical theory of world politics. Paper presented at the Annual Meeting of the American Political Science Association, Denver, September 1982.

Axelrod, Robert (Ed.). *The Structure of Decision: The Cognitive Maps of Political Elites.* Princeton, N.J.: Princeton University Press, 1976.

Axelrod, Robert. The Emergence of Cooperation Among Egoists. *American Political Science Review* 25, 1981, 306–318.

Baldwin, David A. Power Analysis and World Politics: New Trends versus Old Tendencies. *World Politics* 31, 161–194.

Boyle, Francis A. The Irrelevance of International Law: The Schism Between International Law and International Politics. *California Western International Law Journal* 10, 1980.

Brecher, Michael, with Geist, Benjamin. *Decisions in Crisis: Israel 1967–1973.* Berkeley: University of California Press, 1980.

Bueno de Mesquita, Bruce. *The War Trap.* New Haven: Yale University Press, 1981.

Carr, E. H. *The Twenty Years' Crisis, 1919–1939,* 1st ed. London: Macmillan, 1946. (Originally published 1939.)

Choucri, Nazli and North, Robert C. *Nations in Conflict: National Growth and International Violence.* San Francisco: W. H. Freeman & Co., 1975.

Cipolla, Carlo. *The Economic Decline of Empires.* London: Methuen, 1970.

Dahl, Robert A. *Who Governs? Democracy and Power in an American City.* New Haven: Yale University Press, 1961.

Eckstein, Harry. Case Study and Theory in Political Science. In Fred I. Greenstein and Nelson W. Polsby (Eds.), *Handbook of Political Science* (Vol. 7) *Strategies of Inquiry*. Reading, MA: Addison-Wesley, 1975.

Geertz, Clifford. *The Interpretation of Cultures*. New York: Basic Books, 1973.

George, Alexander L. Case Studies and Theory Development: The Method of Structured, Focused Comparison. In Paul Gordon Lauren (Ed.), *Diplomacy: New Approaches in History, Theory and Policy*. New York: Free Press, 1979.

George, Alexander L. *Presidential Decision Making in Foreign Policy: The Effective Use of Information and Advice*. Boulder: Westview, 1980.

George, Alexander L. and George, Juliette. *Woodrow Wilson and Colonel House*. New York: Dover, 1964.

George, Alexander L., Hall, D. K. & Simons, W. E. *The Limits of Coercive Diplomacy*. Boston: Little, Brown, 1971.

George, Alexander L. and Smoke, Richard. *Deterrence in American Foreign Policy*. New York: Columbia University Press, 1974.

Gerschenkron, Alexander. *Economic Backwardness in Historical Perspective*. Cambridge: The Belknap Press of Harvard University Press, 1962.

Gerth, H. H., and Mills, G. Wright. *From Max Weber: Essays in Sociology*. New York: Oxford University Press, 1958.

Gilpin, Robert. *U.S. Power and the Multinational Corporation*. New York: Basic Books, 1975.

Gilpin, Robert. *War and Change in World Politics*. Cambridge: Cambridge University Press, 1981.

Gourevitch, Peter A. The Second Image Reversed: The International Sources of Domestic Politics. *International Organization* 32, 1978, 881–913.

Haas, Ernst B. Why Collaborate? Issue-linkage and International Regimes. *World Politics* 32, 1980, 357–405.

Haas, Ernst B. Words Can Hurt You: Or Who Said What to Whom About Regimes. *International Organization* 36, 1982, 207–244.

Harsanyi, John. Measurement of Social Power, Opportunity Costs, and the Theory of Two-Person Bargaining Games. *Behavioral Sciences* 7, 1962, 67–80.

Herz, John H. Political Realism Revisited. *International Studies Quarterly* 25, 1981, 182–197.

Hoffmann, Stanley. *Contemporary Theory in International Relations*. Englewood Cliffs, N.J.: Prentice Hall, 1960.

Hoffmann, Stanley. An American Social Science: International Relations. *Daedalus*, Summer 1977, 41–60.

Holsti, Ole. Foreign Policy Viewed Cognitively. In Robert Axelrod (Ed.), *The Structure of Decision: The Cognitive Maps of Political Elites*. Princeton, N.J.: Princeton University Press, 1976.

International Organization 36, 1982. Special issue on international regimes edited by Stephen D. Krasner.

Jervis, Robert. *Perception and Misperception in International Politics*. Princeton, N.J.: Princeton University Press, 1976.

Jervis, Robert. Cooperation Under the Security Dilemma. *World Politics* 30, 1978, 167–214.

Katzenstein, Peter J. *Between Power and Plenty: Foreign Economic Policies of Advanced Industrial States*. Madison: University of Wisconsin Press, 1978.

Keohane, Robert O. The Demand for International Regimes. *International Organization* 36, 1982, 325–356.

Keohane, Robert O., and Nye, Joseph (Eds.). *Transnational Relations and World Politics*. Cambridge, MA: Harvard University Press, 1972.

Keohane, Robert O., and Nye, Joseph. *Power and Interdependence: World Politics in Transition*. Boston: Little, Brown, 1977.

Krasner, Stephen D. *Defending the National Interest: Raw Materials Investments and U.S. Foreign Policy*. Princeton: Princeton University Press, 1978.

Krasner, Stephen D. Structural Causes and Regime Consequences: Regimes as Intervening Variables. *International Organization* 36, 1982, 185–206.

Kuhn, Thomas S. *The Structure of Scientific Revolutions*. Chicago: University of Chicago Press, 1962.

Kurth, James R. The Political Consequences of the Product Cycle: Industrial History and Political Outcomes. *International Organization* 33, 1979, 1–34.

Lakatos, Imre. Falsification and the methodology of scientific research programmes. In Imre Lakatos and Alan Musgrave (eds.), *Criticism and the Growth of Knowledge*, Cambridge: Cambridge University Press, 1970.

Latsis, Spiro J. A Research Programme in Economics. In Latsis, ed., *Method and Approval in Economics*. Cambridge: Cambridge University Press, 1976.

Lebow, Richard Ned. *Between Peace and War. The Nature of International Crisis*. Baltimore: Johns Hopkins University Press, 1981.

Lenin, V. I. *Imperialism: The Highest Stage of Capitalism*. New York: International Publishers, 1939. (Originally written 1916.)

Luttwak, Edward. *The Grand Strategy of the Roman Empire—From the First Century A.D. to the Third*. Baltimore: Johns Hopkins University Press, 1976.

Lyons, Gene M. Expanding the Study of International Relations: The French Connection. *World Politics* 35, 1982, 135–149.

Mansbach, Richard, Ferguson, Yale H. and Lampert, Donald E. *The Web of World Politics*. Englewood Cliffs, N.J.: Prentice Hall, 1976.

Mansbach, Richard and Vasquez, John A. *In Search of Theory: A New Paradigm for Global Politics*. New York: Columbia University Press, 1981.

March, James G. The Power of Power. In David Easton (ed.), *Varieties of Political Theory*. Englewood Cliffs, N.J.: Prentice Hall, 1966.

Masterman, Margaret. The Nature of a Paradigm. In Lakatos and Musgrave, eds., *Criticism and the Growth of Knowledge*. Cambridge: Cambridge University Press, 1970.

Michalak, Stanley J., Jr. Theoretical Perspectives for Understanding International Interdependence. *World Politics* 32, 1979, 136–150.

Moore, Barrington, Jr. *Social Origins of Dictatorship and Democracy: Lord and Peasant in the Making of the Modern World*. Boston: Beacon Press, 1966.

Morgenthau, Hans J. *Scientific Man Versus Power Politics*. Chicago: University of Chicago Press, 1946.

Morgenthau, Hans J. *Politics Among Nations*, 4th ed. New York: Knopf, 1966. (Originally published, 1948.)

North, Douglass C. *Structure and Change in Economic History*. New York: Norton, 1981.

North, Robert C. *The World That Could Be*. (The Portable Stanford: Stanford Alumni Association.) Palo Alto, CA: Stanford University, 1976.

Organski, A. F. K., and Kugler, Jacek. *The War Ledger*. Chicago: University of Chicago Press, 1980.

Oye, Kenneth A. The Domain of Choice. In Kenneth A. Oye, Donald Rothchild and Robert J. Lieber (eds.), *Eagle Entangled: U.S. Foreign Policy in a Complex World*. New York: Longman, 1979, pp. 3–33.

Oye, Kenneth A. *Belief Systems, Bargaining and Breakdown: International Political Economy 1929–1934*. Unpublished doctoral dissertation. Harvard University, 1983.

Rosenau, James N. Pre-theories and theories of foreign policy. In R. Barry Farrell (ed.), *Approaches to Comparative and International Politics*. Evanston, IL: Northwestern University Press, 1966.

Ruggie, John Gerard. Continuity and Transformation in the World Polity: Toward a Neo-Realist Synthesis. *World Politics* 35, 1983, 261–285.

Russett, Bruce M. The Calculus of Deterrence. *Journal of Conflict Resolution*, 1963, 97–109.

Schell, Jonathan. *The Fate of the Earth*. New York: Knopf, 1982.

Schelling, Thomas. *The Strategy of Conflict*. New York: Oxford University Press, 1960.

Simon, Herbert A. The Architecture of Complexity. In Simon, ed., *The Sciences of the Artificial*. Cambridge: MIT Press, 1969.

Snidal, Duncan. *Interdependence, Regimes, and International Cooperation*. Unpublished manuscript, University of Chicago, 1981.

Snyder, Glenn H. and Diesing, Paul. *Conflict Among Nations: Bargaining, Decision-Making and System Structure in International Crises*. Princeton, N.J.: Princeton University Press, 1977.

Sprout, Harold and Margaret. *Toward a Politics of the Planet Earth*. New York: Van Nostrand Reinhold, 1971.

Stein, Arthur. The Politics of Linkage. *World Politics* 33, 1980, 62–81.

Stein, Arthur. Coordination and Collaboration: Regimes in an Anarchic World. *International Organization* 36, 1982, 299–324.

Thucydides. *The Peloponnesian War* (John H. Finley, Jr., trans). New York: Modern Library, 1951. (Originally written c. 400 B.C.)

Tollison, Robert D. and Willett, Thomas D. An Economic Theory of Mutually Advantageous Issue Linkage in International Negotiations. *International Organization* 33, 1979, 425–450.

Toulmin, Stephen. *Foresight and Understanding: An Enquiry into the Aims of Science*. New York: Harper Torchbooks, 1963.

Wallerstein, Immanuel. The Rise and Future Demise of the World Capitalist System: Concepts for Comparative Analysis. In Wallerstein, *The Capitalist World Economy*. Cambridge: Cambridge University Press, 1979. (This essay was originally printed in *Comparative Studies in Society and History* 16, 1974.)

Wallerstein, Immanuel. *The Modern World-System II: Mercantilism and the Consolidation of the European World-Economy, 1600–1750*. New York: Academic Press, 1980.

Waltz, Kenneth N. *Man, the State and War*. New York: Columbia University Press, 1959.

Waltz, Kenneth N. *Foreign Policy and Democratic Politics: The American and British Experience*. Boston: Little, Brown, 1967.

Waltz, Kenneth N. *Theory of International Politics*. Reading, MA: Addison-Wesley, 1979, p. 7.

Wolfers, Arnold. *Discord and Collaboration: Essays on International Politics*. Baltimore: Johns Hopkins University Press, 1962.

The Accomplishments of International Political Economy

STEPHEN KRASNER

In this article, Professor Krasner reviews realist and liberal (i.e., pluralist) views of international political economy. He concludes with critical comments on postmodern epistemology.

Introduction

International political economy (IPE) is concerned with the political determinants of international economic relations. It tries to answer questions such as: How have changes in the international distribution of power among states affected the degree of openness in the international trading system? Do the domestic political structures and values of some states allow them to compete more effectively? Is the relative poverty of the Third World better explained by indigenous politics and economic conditions in individual countries or by the workings of the international political economy? When can international economic ties among states be used for political leverage?

International political economy can be contrasted with conventional economics and with security studies. Conventional economists ask many of the same questions as do students of IPE but their answers are related to economic factors such as savings rates, labour markets, or technical knowledge rather than political factors like the international distribution of power or the relationship between the state and the private sector. Students of international security ask different questions like: what are the causes of war? or when are alliances likely to be stable? but offer explanations that are similar to those deployed by scholars who work on international political economy.

The study of international political economy has been guided almost exclusively by the canons of what John Searle has labelled the Western Rationalistic Tradition which is characterized by the assumption that reality exists independently of the way in which it is represented by humans and that the truth of a statement depends on how well it conforms with this independent reality (Searle, 1993, p. 57). The "truth or falsity of the claims made is totally independent of the motives, the morality, or even the gender, the race, or the ethnicity of the maker" (Searle, 1993, p. 66). International political economy is deeply embedded in the standard epistemological methodology of the social sciences which, stripped to its bare bones, simply means stating a proposition and testing it against external evidence. Students of IPE have implicitly rejected the sceptical or antifoundational postmodernist position which claims that there is no there there; that "each society has its own regime of truth, its general politics of truth" (M. Foucault quoted in Rengger, 1992, p. 563).

Reprinted with permission of Cambridge University Press. From *International Theory: Positivism and Beyond*, 1996, edited by Steve Smith, Ken Booth, and Marysia Zalewski.

Some History

During the 1950s and 1960s international relations was concerned primarily with security. The Cold War dominated the interest of scholars and the attention of policy makers. International economic issues were a secondary concern. Between the East and the West, economic transactions were highly politicised and tightly controlled while within the West economic disputes were muted. Setting the rules of the game and achieving the optimal configuration of international economic transactions were seen as technical issues. There were only a few isolated scholars working on questions related to the political determinants of international economic relations. Before the mid-1970s there were no courses, at least not in the United States, called international political economy.

The attention devoted to international political economy increased dramatically after 1970 for several reasons, some intellectual and academic, others related to political events. OPEC and the rise of oil prices in 1973–4, the collapse of the Bretton Woods monetary system in 1971, and the demands of the Third World for a New International Economic Order in the mid-1970s made it clear that the major issues related to international economic relations could not be explained solely by strictly economic considerations.

Attention to international political economy was further reinforced by developments within the academy. The old agenda of international politics had become exhausted. The most interesting arguments about nuclear strategy as a rational strategic enterprise had been made by the early 1960s (Schelling, 1960, 1966). The study of international organisations had not moved beyond an arid formality expounded by specialists in international law. Economics, as an academic discipline, came increasingly to reward its members for expertise in the development of formal models and to discount institutional analysis. Hence, in the early 1970s there was an absence of systematic investigations of increasingly troublesome global economic developments. The field of international political economy developed to fill this gap.

IPE has been dominated by four major perspectives—liberalism, realism, domestic politics and Marxism. Only the first three will be discussed in this essay.

The central debate in IPE has been between liberal and realist analysts. Liberal analysis has focused on the incentives and opportunities for cooperation. Realists have focused on the way in which power has influenced both the character of international regimes and conflicts among specific states.

Explanations which emphasise the interaction between domestic and international politics, the way in which domestic structures, values and groups influence international interactions and vice versa have, in some specific cases, been deeply illuminating, but no one has presented a coherent general theory.

Liberalism

Liberalism makes the following *assumptions:*

1. There are many different kinds of actors including state-owned enterprises, multinational corporations, public international organisations, nongovernmental organisations, private foundations, and terrorists, as well as states.
2. These actors are all rational and calculating but they pursue different objectives: corporate executives want profits or sales; the rulers of states want security and higher levels of well-being for their populations; environmental groups want to preserve the ecosphere. Furthermore, different actors have different power capabilities in different areas; specific actors can influence outcomes in some arenas but not others.
3. International relations and especially international political economy offer opportunities for everyone to gain at the same time. Actors are more concerned with their absolute well-being than with their relative position *vis-à-vis* others.

The *explanatory variable* for liberalism is the configuration of interests and capabilities associated with a given issue area; that is, outcomes, including the creating of institutions designed to secure Pareto optimal outcomes (situations in which no actor can be made better off without making some other actor worse off), are a function of the preferences and capabilities of a variety of different actors concerned with maximising their own individual utility.

The *evidence* that is needed for a liberal analysis involves specifying the relevant actors (states, multinationals, etc.), assessing their resources and signifying their objectives (including not only their interests but also the constraints and incentives that are presented by existing institutional structures and other actors).

Every theoretical perspective works with an *exemplary problem* which is assumed to be the most important kind of issue in the international system and which can be analysed using the theoretical tools (assumptions, evidence and causal arguments) of that approach. The exemplary problem for contemporary liberal analysis is market failure; that is, situations in which the purely individual calculations of interest do not lead to Pareto optimal outcomes.

Liberalism offers a basically benign image of the global economy. There are many different actors. They have different interests. There are opportunities for cutting deals. Everyone can be better off at the same time. Human ingenuity and intelligence can create new institutions that encourage behaviour that leads to Pareto optimal outcomes.

The most important empirical development for all variants of the liberal perspective is the growth of global interactions. Transportation and communications costs have dramatically declined because of changes in technology. These changes have opened many new opportunities for mutual gain. Automobiles or computers can be assembled from parts that are produced in many different countries. Billions of pounds or dollars can be moved around the globe with a flick of a computer switch. Individuals with e-mail can sit in Bombay, Athens and Silicon Valley and work on the same software program. The benefits of an open world economy have increased. More and more actors have a stake in a stable international economic order.

Liberalism, like all of the major theoretical approaches to IPE, has several different variants: three of the most prominent are functionalism, transnationalism and cooperation theory. Functionalist and neofunctionalist theories were developed in the 1950s and 1960s primarily to explain the European Community. Functionalism was both an analysis and a prescription. As originally laid out by David Mitrany and others, the idea was to create institutions in Europe that would focus the interests and ultimately the loyalties of individual actors. Corporations, foundations, lawyers and individuals would see their economic interest and their self-identity increasingly tied up with European institutions rather than those of their national states. Neofunctionalist arguments put more emphasis on the role of the state arguing that integration would take place as a result of domestic political pressures to enhance regional institutions (political spillover), the inherent links between issue areas so that integration in one necessitated integration in another (functional spillover), and upgrading common interests by relying on integrative institutions to work out mutually beneficial issue linkages (Burley and Mattli, 1993, pp. 53–7).

The fate of functionalist arguments has waxed and waned with the degree of progress towards integration in Europe. The spillover effects that functional and neofunctional arguments expected were not obvious during the 1960s and early 1970s. Recently, however, functionalist arguments have been revived to explain the Single European Act, Maastricht and other manifestations of regional integration in Europe (Burley and Mattli, 1993).

Transnationalism is a second line of liberal analysis. Writing in 1971 Robert Keohane and

Joseph Nye defined transnational interactions as "the movement of tangible or intangible items across state boundaries when at least one actor is not an agent of a government or an intergovernmental organization" (Nye and Keohane, 1971, p. 5). While recognising that transnational relations had always existed Keohane and Nye went on to argue that governmental control had been restricted by changes in technology which facilitated interaction among societal actors in different countries (most notably, the subsidiaries of transnational corporations), by the increasing agendas of governments which impinged on more and more groups in civil society, and by the flow of information from the mass media. Effective management of this increasingly transnationalised world would require higher levels of cooperation (Nye and Keohane, 1971, pp. 725–9; and Keohane and Nye, 1977).

Transnational relations is the most immediately obvious liberal perspective because it resonates with the everyday experiences of many individuals. Examples of transnational flows include international air flights; ATM machines that can supply pounds in London, or yen in Tokyo from a bank account in Des Moines; international phone, fax and e-mail; the live global coverage by CNN and other networks of news events; and the movement of undocumented workers across territorial borders. As a research programme, however, transnational relations failed because in most cases it could not clearly specify *ex ante* actors, their interests, or their capabilities. If all actors are relevant, and actors can have many different interests, and the ability of actors to pursue these interests is not well defined, then any outcome in international politics would be consistent with the theory; that is, after the fact it would be possible to find some group of transnational actors that supported public policy that was ultimately selected. But if a theory can be made consistent with every possible outcome then it explains nothing.

One major exception to this generalisation about the inability of transnational relations the-

ory to generate an ongoing research effort is global finance. Richard Cooper, writing in 1968, argued that the size and mobility of international capital flows had severely constrained the ability of states to carry out an independent monetary policy. Efforts to raise interest rates, for instance, would only encourage the inflow of international capital, increasing the money supply, and driving interest rates down (Cooper, 1968; Krause, 1971, pp. 523–7). The advanced industrialised countries all abandoned efforts to permanently control short-term capital flows during the 1980s because the level of such flows had increased so dramatically (at an annual rate of 21.4 per cent from 1970 to 1985, compared with growth of 12.7 per cent for world trade), the ability of private multinationals to evade controls had increased as their operations had become ever more globalised, and because of the pressure from these same firms on their own governments to abandon regulations lest they be placed at a competitive disadvantage with their competitors who could more easily access international markets (Goodman and Pauly, 1993, pp. 51–2, 57–9).

The third, and now the most important line of liberal research is cooperation theory. Cooperation theory analyses market failure problems. States may fail to maximise their own utility because individual self-interested behaviour results, in some circumstances such as a prisoner's dilemma payoff structure or the provision of collective goods, in a Pareto suboptimal outcome. These failures can often be resolved by the creation of institutional arrangements that provide information, monitoring and salient solutions (Keohane, 1984; Stein, 1990). Cooperation theory is based upon analytic techniques, especially game theory and rational choice, that have exploded in the discipline of economics over the last decade. These techniques are heuristically very powerful; that is, they provide a set of analytic tools that can be used to examine many different issues.

Cooperation theory has been applied to issues related to trade, finance, the environment and economic sanctions. For instance, in the absence of international institutions states could fail to engage in free trade, despite the fact that such a policy would (at least according to standard, neoclassical trade theory) make all of them better off. The best policy for each individual state is to impose an optimal tariff. If, however, all countries attempt to impose such tariffs, then they would all be worse off. If one country refrains from imposing a tariff while others do so, it could be worse off. This potential market failure, in which every country imposes a tariff, can be overcome by establishing an international institution, such as GATT or now the World Trade Organisation, which can define standards for what constitutes cheating, provide rules that act as salient solutions, engage in some modest level of monitoring, and provide dispute settlement mechanisms.

A second example of the use of cooperation theory is international banking and finance. An individual country can maximise the business opportunities for its own financial institutions by having low capital requirements making it possible for their banks to loan more money. If all countries have low requirements, however, then there is a greater danger of an international financial collapse because the failure of one undercapitalised institution could lead to other failures. To overcome this potential problem of competitive undercapitalisation, central bankers from the major industrialised countries signed the Basle Agreement in 1988 which defines a common set of capital standards to which all signatories must adhere (Kapstein, 1989; Martin, 1992a, pp. 765–92 and Martin, 1992b).

In sum, liberal analysis in its various forms has provided explanations for a number of developments in the world political economy. Cooperation is manifest in many different areas despite the fact that the international system remains anarchical. Transnational flows have increased dramatically. The number of international institutions has exploded.

Liberal analysis is, however, much less adequate for addressing other questions. It has little to say about war. For military conflict, as opposed to international political economy, the basic liberal contention has been that the world is changing: the opportunities for mutual gain through exchange have increased and the cost of war has spiralled. It makes more sense to trade than to fight (Rosecrance, 1986; Doyle, 1983). This change in incentive structures does not, however, seem to have altered the behaviour of leaders in Iran, Iraq, Serbia, Bosnia, Croatia, Rwanda, Aden, Somalia and elsewhere. Liberal perspectives cannot explain the basic division of the global economy that existed during the Cold War with the United States and its allies working under one regime and the Soviet bloc under another. If changes in technology and the opportunities for mutual gain are driving national behaviour why not more integration between the East and the West? Realism, which focuses on power, security and distributional conflict offers answers to these questions as well as others.

Realism

Realism makes the following *assumptions*:

1. The constitutive actors in the international system are sovereign states. Other actors such as multinational corporations, or nongovernmental organisations are subordinate to states in that they must operate within governing structures established by states and they can be ruined by states, albeit sometimes at considerable cost.

2. The international system is in a state of anarchy: there is no accepted political authority. States engage in self-help; they determine their own national policies although their options may be severely constrained by the power of other states.

3. States must be concerned with their own security. At a minimum, a state must act to protect its territorial and political integrity. States cannot be oblivious to relative gains because in some situations changes in power capabilities can put their security at risk (Powell, 1991).

4. States are rational unified actors. Domestic politics, individual irrationality, or organisational failures have only a marginal impact on outcomes.

The *explanatory variable* for realism is the distribution of power among states. The basic claim of realism is that given a particular distribution of power among states it is possible to explain both the characteristics of the system and the behaviour of individual states. For instance, in a bipolar world the two poles are bound to be adversaries. Realism makes no effort to probe the domestic determinants of foreign policy; what counts is state power and external constraints.

The *evidence* that realists utilise requires operationalising the power of states by, for instance, looking at the size of armies, aggregate economic output, or the ability to make credible threats.

For realism the *exemplary problem* is to explain how either zero sum or distributional conflicts are resolved given the power and interests of states (Waltz, 1979). The world remains a dangerous place. Economic transactions among specific states can, in some circumstances, be used for political leverage. States struggle to define international regimes because different regimes have different distributional consequences (Krasner, 1991).

Realist analyses of international political economy have addressed two kinds of issues: first, how national power has influenced relations among specific countries; and, second, how the distribution of power in the system as a whole has determined international regimes.

In 1945 Albert Hirschman published *National Power and the Structure of Foreign Trade* which remains one of the most illuminat-ing discussions of the way in which power affects international economic relations among specific countries. He argued that there were two ways in which trading relations could be used to alter the capabilities or policies of another state: first, states could limit the availability of critical products or technology in an effort to weaken the resource base of their opponents; second, one state could attempt to change the foreign policy behaviour of another by threatening to change the rules of the game governing their economic transactions.

The policies of the Western alliance towards the Communist bloc during the Cold War are an example of an effort to limit the power capabilities of an enemy by restricting the flow of goods, loans and information. The Eastern bloc was almost completely excluded from international economic organisations—the international financial institutions (the World Bank, IMF, and the various regional banks), and the GATT (General Agreement on Tariffs and Trade). The Western alliance (including Japan and Europe) established the Coordinating Committee or COCOM whose members assembled a list of products whose sale to the Communist bloc was prohibited (Mastanduno, 1992; National Academy of Sciences, 1987, pp. 106–7).

Economic relations can also be used to change the foreign policy of a target state. If one state can credibly threaten to alter the existing pattern of exchange, the second state will acquiesce if the cost of the sanctions would be greater than the cost of compliance: better to go along with the preferences of the strong than to suffer economic harm. The critical question then is: what makes a threat credible? Hirschman provided a brilliant answer. A threat is only credible if the relative opportunity costs of change are asymmetrical. If the initiator can change its economic policies at little cost (cutting off trade for instance), but the cost of such a change would be high for the target, then the threat is credible.

If, in contrast, the opportunity costs of change, or altering the present state of affairs, is symmetrical, then the threat is not credible: the cost of implementing the threat would be as high for the initiator as for the target. Opportunity costs provide a way of operationalising power, a problem that has plagued realist analysis. Hirschman demonstrated that Nazi Germany had used asymmetrical costs to make credible threats against the smaller countries of Eastern and Central Europe in the 1930s and had successfully constrained their foreign policy options (Hirschman, 1945, part II).

One basic expectation of realist analysis is that there will be tension, although not necessarily war, among the major states in the international system regardless of their domestic political structures. Economic interactions, for instance, between the Soviet Union and the United States were limited. With the end of the Cold War Japan has emerged as the major challenger to the United States and tension between the two countries has increased. In some issue areas American policy makers have become more concerned with relative gains, more attentive, for instance, to the ways in which different kinds of arrangements between the two countries would affect the transfer of technology and potentially even military capability. American trade policy has increasingly differentiated Japan from other countries. American officials have pressured Japan to open specific markets including government procurement, medical equipment, automobile parts, cellular telephones, and rice. The success of these efforts remains in doubt at least in part because the relative opportunity costs of change are not highly asymmetrical; the actual imposition of trade sanctions by the United States against Japan would be costly for both countries (Mastanduno, 1991). Hence, examining the relationship among specific countries with regard to the interaction between power, security and economic transactions has been one major focus of realist analysis.

The second major focus of realism has been the relationship between the distribution of power among states in the international system and the nature of international economic regimes. The most prominent argument along these lines is the realist version of hegemonic stability theory which asserts that a stable open international economic system is most likely when there is a hegemonic distribution of power; that is, when there is one state that is much larger than any of the others. (There is also a liberal version of hegemonic stability which focuses not on imposition, power and distributional gains but on the need for a hegemon to provide collective goods, especially acting as a leader of last resort in the financial sector (Kindleberger, 1973).)

Robert Gilpin argued in *US Power and the Multinational Corporation* that first Britain in the nineteenth century and then the United States in the latter part of the twentieth century strongly supported open regimes for international investment. As the most advanced economic powers with the largest amount of capital they would be the major beneficiaries of such rules. Other countries, with more limited resources, might have preferred a more restrictive regime, one that would provide their own corporate actors with a greater competitive advantage.

The realist version of hegemonic stability theory also argues that if there is a hegemonic distribution of power there is likely to be an open regime for trade. The dominant power favours such a regime because it increases its economic well-being and economic growth, and provides it with more political leverage. A hegemon would also have the resources to entice or coerce other states into participating in an open regime, and to provide the system with collective goods. International openness has been associated with two periods when there has been an economic hegemon—Britain during the last part of the nineteenth century and the United States (for the non-Communist world) during the second half of the twentieth century. There is, however, far from a perfect fit between changes in the international distribution of power and changes in international regimes. Openness continued into the first decade of the twentieth century even though British power had declined and was not restored until after the Second World War even though the United States became a hegemon after the First World War (Krasner, 1976).

Another realist explanation for trade policy examines the links between alliances, security and economic transactions. By exploring comparative advantage states can increase their economic resources. With more resources they can increase their military power. In an anarchic world states must be alert to developments that could jeopardise their security. Hence, states are more likely to engage in open regimes with their allies than with their enemies, not only because openness provides economic benefits but also because it can strengthen the military capabilities of the alliance as a whole (Gowa, 1994, ch. 3).

More specific aspects of the trading regime can also be influenced by distributional (and even relative gains) conflicts. The Tokyo Round of trade negotiations, which was completed in 1979, included a number of codes dealing with non-tariff barriers such as subsidies, government procurement, customs valuation, import licensing procedures and dumping. Some of these codes were implemented in more effective ways than others. The variation, Joseph Grieco has argued, was the result of differences in American and European expectations about relative and absolute gains. For instance, the code on customs valuation was very effective while that covering government procurement had a much more limited impact. In the first case Europe and the United States expected balanced gains; in the second case Europe expected to lose. States acting as what Grieco has termed defensive positionalists were loath to cede greater benefits to a potential rival (Grieco, 1990).

Realist arguments can be applied in areas other than trade and capital flows. In the estab-

lishment of the International Monetary Fund, for instance, Britain wanted a large fund with liberal provisions for borrowing. The United States wanted a smaller fund with more restrictions on borrowing. Britain was a debtor; the United States was a creditor. The USA had more power because while Britain wanted to borrow, the United States was not compelled to lend. The Articles of Agreement of the IMF reflected American not British preferences.

In the area of telecommunications the development of satellites, a new technology initially controlled by the United States, led to the creation of new institutions. INTELSAT was established in 1964 to regulate communications satellites. It assumed activities that would otherwise have been under the purview of the International Telecommunications Union (ITU), the oldest established international organisation. The ITU was a one nation, one vote, organisation. Votes in INTELSAT were distributed in proportion to usage which meant that the United States got the largest share.

For realism this particular episode illustrates that changes in the distribution of power (in this case the development of a new technology by the United States) leads to changes in the international rules of the game. The United States wanted a new institution, INTELSAT rather than the ITU, because this would provide it with more control and a higher level of benefits. In this particular case relative gains were irrelevant; it was the distribution of absolute gains that counted (Krasner, 1991).

Realism and liberalism have defined the basic lines of debate in international political economy. Liberals see a rosy future. Technology is shrinking distance. The opportunities for mutual gain through international interaction are huge and growing.

Realism is pessimistic. While the United States remains the only global power, its capabilities in many important issue areas have deteriorated, suggesting that it will adopt a more narrowly self-interested policy. It will be less concerned about upholding international economic rules that are not optimal for itself, even if such rules would provide greater benefits for the system as a whole.

Liberalism predicts an increasingly integrated global economy. Realism predicts movement towards regional blocs, or greater differentiation across countries and sectors. Liberalism predicts the consolidation of universal international rules of the game which facilitate mutual interaction. Realism predicts specific rather than diffuse reciprocity with states focusing more on immediate than long-term benefits.

Domestic Politics

The final theoretical focus of international political economy has been the relationship between domestic politics and the international system. One of the successes of international political economy as an area of study is that it has integrated international relations and comparative politics, fields that were much more distinct before 1970. There have been two general lines of inquiry. The first examines the impact of the international system on domestic political structures and groups. The second investigates how variations in domestic political structures, group interests, and values and ideas affect foreign economic policies and outcomes.

There is no dominant argument about the influence of the international system on domestic political structures. The works of Peter Katzenstein, Ronald Rogowski, and Jeffry Frieden are illustrative. In *Small States in the World Economy*, Katzenstein argues that the development of what he calls democratic corporatism in the small European countries (Austria, Sweden, Switzerland, Denmark, the Netherlands, Norway and Belgium) reflects their heavy involvement in the international economy. Democratic corporatist structures are functionally efficient modes of organisations for such states. In democratic corporatist polities distinctions between state and society are blurred and

all important groups are incorporated into political decision making. Such inclusive political institutions are needed to lessen the risk of internecine quarrels that would be economically disastrous because they would preclude swift adaptation to rapidly changing external conditions. The small states of Europe cannot isolate themselves from external interactions nor (unlike more powerful states) can they control the external environment. They must be able to adjust.

Ronald Rogowski in *Commerce and Coalitions* shows how changes in the international opportunity for trade can impact on the power of domestic groups within a given political system. Countries export those products that use factors with which they are comparatively well endowed: countries with relatively large amounts of capital export capital-intensive goods; countries with large amounts of labour export labour-intensive goods. If trade becomes more open the position of abundant factors of production will be strengthened and that of scarce factors weakened. For instance, in advanced industrialised countries, which are generally capital abundant, open trading regimes have weakened the position of labour. Membership in labour unions has declined in many countries. Assuming that public policies reflect the preferences of groups in the society, the political influence of labour will also erode.

Jeffry Frieden has used a similar line of argument but emphasised sector specific factors. The more open the environment the more relative strength is gained by labour and capital in internationally competitive sectors. In an increasingly open global economy it is the holders of mobile international assets that have benefited the most (Frieden, 1991). The second line of inquiry relating domestic political factors and the international economic system examines the ways in which different domestic structures, values and ideas affect foreign economic policies. The most obvious argument points to the influence of domestic interest groups. International economic policy, like other policy, can be explained by the configuration of domestic pressures. Internationally competitive industries and factors will favour openness; import competing industries will favour closure. Large multinational firms want to be able to freely transfer capital, goods and labour. In contrast, labour-intensive sectors in industrialised countries want protection from goods produced with lower cost foreign labour (Milner, 1988).

Other analysts have focused not on the simple configuration of interests but also on how domestic institutional structures affect foreign economic policy. One prominent example of this kind of approach distinguishes between weak and strong states, where the term *state* refers to central decision-making institutions not to the polity as a whole. In weak states political power is fragmented among many institutions—the legislature, public bureaucracies, private pressure groups. It is difficult to formulate a coherent foreign economic policy. The United States is the most obvious example. Power is divided between the executive and a bicameral legislature. Political parties are weak. The judiciary and the central bank are relatively independent of direct political control. Specific bureaucracies have close ties with societal sectors (Krasner, 1978; Evans *et al.*, 1985).

In polities with strong states power is concentrated in the hands of a small number of actors in the executive branch who can set policy and secure, through coercion or incentives, the support of major groups in civil society. Japan is, arguably, the illustrative case. In Japan the Ministry of Finance and the Ministry of International Trade and Industry (MITI) have played a critical role in orchestrating and defining state policy. Since the conclusion of the Second World War Japan has focused on industrial development, a focus that can be attributed to a desire to reduce Japan's international vulnerability. The Liberal Democratic Party (LDP) governed from the early 1950s until the early 1990s. The central ministries had a more or less free hand in organising, albeit not dictating, the activities of the major internationally competitive Japanese industries on which economic growth depended. The LDP secured votes and political support from other sectors such as agriculture and construction (Johnson, 1982; Okimoto, 1989).

Aside from domestic political structures another line of argument has examined the impact of ideas. International political economy, like the rest of political science, has been primarily concerned with material interests and power even if the definitions of interest and power have been intensely debated. The influence of norms and ideas has received much less attention. The analytic problem in discussing the impact of ideas and values is that they often covary with other factors such as economic interests. When there is such covariance, it is impossible to make a compelling argument that ideas really matter, that they are anything more than rationalisations for more conventional concerns.

Recently, however, a number of scholars have demonstrated that ideas can be consequential; they have been able to isolate the independent impact of ideas. Peter Haas has developed the concept of epistemic communities. Epistemic communities are groups of individuals who share the same scientific understandings and the same policy agenda. Haas and his colleagues have been able to show that the presence of such a community within the policy-making apparatus of a country has altered public policy. For instance, donor countries stopped giving away international food aid because agricultural economists demonstrated that this destroyed the incentives for local production. The policies of north African governments towards pollution control in the Mediterranean changed when they established environmental ministries that were staffed by individuals with scientific knowledge (Haas, 1992).

Ideas can also be consequential because they become embedded in institutions, often for haphazard reasons, which then constrain the options available to policy makers. For instance, in the 1930s the United States opted for interventionist state policies for agriculture which included a high level of protection. At the same time, state intervention in the manufacturing sector failed in part because of rulings from the Supreme Court. These differences became embedded in American domestic legislation and were reflected in American foreign economic policy after the Second World War. Agriculture was excluded from GATT, largely as a result of initiatives taken by the United States despite the fact that America had the world's most competitive agrarian sector. Hence, decisions taken at one point in time that were associated with a specific set of ideas and interests persisted even though material circumstances had changed (Goldstein, 1989; Goldstein and Keohane, 1993).

Conclusion

The achievements of international political economy have been generated by an epistemology that conforms with the Western Rationalistic Tradition, not with those versions of postmodernism that reject any separation between the student and the object of study. The success of different approaches to IPE has been determined primarily by their ability to generate a progressive research programme. Theories have fallen from favour either because they did not conform with empirical evidence or because they could not be formulated in ways that were, in principle, testable.

Some arguments that were prominent in the literature twenty years ago have collapsed. The viability of dependency theory, for instance, which explained the poverty of the Third World in terms of the interactions between rich and poor countries, has been undermined by increasing variation in the economic performance of peripheral countries. Some, especially the east Asian newly industrialising countries

(Taiwan, Korea, Hong Kong, Singapore, and now Thailand and others as well), have been spectacularly successful, growing at faster rates than any other group of states. At the same time other countries, most of the states of Africa, have become mired in poverty. If the most important explanation for the economic prospects of a state is its peripheral position in the world capitalist system, it is impossible to explain this variation.

The central debate between liberal and realist analysis has not, however, been resolved even though the research programmes of both of these paradigms has changed. For liberalism, cooperation theory, which focuses on the way in which institutions can overcome market failure, has supplanted functionalism, neofunctionalism, and transnationalism as the dominant mode of analysis because these earlier liberal formulations either failed to confirm with empirical evidence (functionalism) or could not generate testable hypotheses (transnationalism). For realism hegemonic stability theory has been superseded by theoretical arguments that have demonstrated that different distributions of power can also lead to open international regimes (Lake, 1988) and that security concerns may drive foreign economic policies (Gowa, 1994; Mansfield, 1994).

To a large extent the enduring debate between realism and liberalism is about the nature of the exemplary problem in the contemporary international economic system. Is market failure the basic issue that states must address? In this case it is possible to make everyone better off at the same time by creating new institutions or cutting new deals. Or, are distributional conflicts or relative gains the basic questions that confront states? In this case outcomes will be determined by power; new institutions or strategies of issue linkage will reflect the preferences of the strong.

Issues related to the international environment, for instance, seem to cry out for liberal analysis since it appears that everyone can be made better off if institutions can be developed to deal with externalities including mechanisms for side payments. For example agreements banning the production of CFCs were reached quite quickly in the later 1980s when the scientific evidence for ozone depletion became unassailable and when, one must add, the major chemical companies, especially Dupont, were able to produce substitutes. Distributional conflicts were resolved by providing technical and material aid to tropical Third World states which stood to lose the most from the ban (Haas, 1992; Benedick, 1991). In contrast, the economic relationship between the Soviet bloc and the West during the Cold War was about distributional gains and relative power. Here, realism offers much better analytic tools.

If liberal and realist analyses, and the various approaches that attempt to integrate domestic and international politics, have not provided definitive answers, they have offered systematic frameworks within which issues can be addressed. They have made statements about causal variables (power, security, group interests, ideas, values) and they have suggested the kind of evidence that would be relevant for testing these alternative arguments.

What defines social science is a methodology based on argument and evidence. Even if the argument is not fully worked out and the evidence is muddy, social science is the best approach that we have to understanding social, political and economic phenomena. For IPE this conventional epistemology cannot be defended by arguing that some kind of breakthrough has been achieved which has provided answers that are so obvious that any reasonable observer must accept them. There has been no such breakthrough. The debates between liberalism and realism still rage as strongly as they did a decade ago albeit in somewhat different guises. The theories are rarely good enough to provide concrete guidance for policy makers. Conventional arguments have, however, demonstrated that some positions do not hold up in the face of

empirical evidence: dependency theories are wrong; hegemony is not the only path to economic openness; private interests do not, as functionalism suggests, necessarily generate political integration; domestic political structures are not insulated from external economic interactions.

The conventional epistemology that has informed the study of international political economy stands in sharp contrast with those variants of post-modernism that reject the Western Rationalistic Tradition. For these post-modernists there are many analytic categories each of which contains its own truth. Testing can never be definitive and is often entirely irrelevant.

Given the weakness of the findings in international political economy, the failure to clearly demonstrate the superiority of one paradigm over another, why not throw it all up? Adopt a postmodern stance. It would be more fun if it were not necessary to muck through all that messy and ambiguous data.

Despite the failings of IPE and other literatures informed by conventional methodology, to embrace postmodernism would be to strip social science of the most important contribution that it can make to the betterment of human society: that contribution is to discipline power with truth. In some rare instances it is possible to show decisionmakers what their best course of action is. Economics, for instance, has improved the well-being of the world's peoples by elaborating the relationship between government policy and macroeconomic performance; a replay of the Great Depression is unlikely because economists, and the policymakers they advise, have a much better understanding of how monetary policy works. In most cases, however, including the work in international political economy, social science can hardly claim to provide a right answer which is supported by definitive empirical evidence. Nevertheless, conventional social science can show that some arguments that policymakers use to justify their actions are wrong because their assertions do not conform with empirical evidence. The Western Rationalistic Tradition can contest claims by testing them against empirical data. This check on the assertions of the mighty is one of the bulwarks that modern society has constructed against the ravages of political extremism. None of the evil regimes of the twentieth century—Hitler's Germany, Stalin's Soviet Union, Mao's China—has supported the Western Rationalistic Tradition.

Postmodernism provides no methodology for adjudicating among competing claims. There is no reason to think that postmodern pronouncements will exercise any constraint over those with power. If Lysenko's theory supported Stalin's beliefs, then Lysenko was right. Darwinian biology simply disappeared in the Soviet Union. If each society has its own truth— apartheid in South Africa, nazism in Germany—what is the basis for arguing that they are wrong? The Western Rationalistic Tradition, the stipulation that theories be tested against empirical data, is no panacea for the prevention of evil. Nevertheless it does offer the best hope for academicians to make a positive contribution to the larger society because it can in some instances suggest a wise course for public policy and in others demonstrate that a policy is wrong. Postmodernism, in contrast, in its more extreme versions provides no such check. On the contrary, it leads directly to nihilism which can produce an intense and burning flame but which hardly moves society towards peace and justice.

References

Benedick, Richard (1991), *Ozone Diplomacy* (Cambridge: Harvard University Press).

Burley, Ann-Marie and Mattli, Walter (1993), 'Europe Before the Court: A Political Theory of Legal Integration', *International Organization*, 47, pp. 41–76.

Cooper, Richard (1968), *The Economics of Interdependence: Economic Policy in the Atlantic Community* (New York: McGraw-Hill).

Doyle, Michael (1983), 'Kant, Liberal Legacies, and Foreign Affairs', *Philosophy and Public Affairs*, 12, pp. 204–325.

Evans, Peter *et al.* (1985), *Bringing the State Back In* (New York: Cambridge University Press).

Frieden, Jeffry (1991), 'Invested Interests: The Politics of National Economic Policies in a World of Global Finance', *International Organization*, 45, pp. 425–51.

Gilpin, Robert (1975), *US Power and the Multinational Corporation* (New York: Basic Books).

Goldstein, Judith (1989), 'The Impact of Ideas on Trade Policy: The Origins of US Agriculture and Manufacturing Policies', *International Organization*, 43, pp. 31–71.

Goldstein, Judith and Keohane, Robert O. (eds.) (1993), *Ideas and Foreign Policy* (Ithaca: Cornell University Press).

Goodman, John B. and Pauly, Louis W. (1993), 'The Obsolescence of Capital Controls?: Economic Management in an Age of Global Markets', *World Politics*, 46, pp. 50–83.

Gowa, Joanne (1994), *Allies, Adversaries and International Trade* (Princeton: Princeton University Press).

Grieco, Joseph M. (1990), *Cooperation Among Nations: Europe, America, and Non-Tariff Barriers to Trade* (Ithaca: Cornell University Press).

Haas, Peter (1992), 'Banning Chlorofluorocarbons: Epistemic Community Efforts to Protect Stratospheric Ozone', in Haas (ed.), 'Knowledge, Power and International Policy', special issue of *International Organization*, 46, pp. 187–224.

Hirschman, Albert (1945), *National Power and the Structure of Foreign Trade* (Berkeley: University of California Press).

Johnson, Chalmers (1982), *MITI and the Japanese Miracle: The Growth of Industrial Policy 1925–75* (Stanford: Stanford University Press).

Kapstein, Ethan (1989), 'Resolving the Regulator's Dilemma: International Coordination of Banking Regulations', *International Organization*, 43, pp. 323–47.

Katzenstein, Peter J. (1985), *Small States in the World Economy* (Ithaca: Cornell University Press).

Keohane, Robert O. (1984), *After Hegemony* (Princeton: Princeton University Press).

Keohane, Robert and Nye, Joseph (1977), *Power and Interdependence* (Boston: Little Brown).

Kindleberger, Charles P. (1973), *The World in Depression: 1929–39* (Berkeley: University of California Press).

Krasner, Stephen (1976), 'National Power and the Structure of Foreign Trade', *World Politics*, 28, pp. 317–47.

(1978), *Defending the National Interest: Raw Materials Investment and American Foreign Policy* (Princeton: Princeton University Press).

(1991), 'Global Communications and National Power: Life on the Pareto Frontier', *World Politics*, 43, pp. 336–67.

Krause, Lawrence (1971), 'Private International Finance', *International Organization*, 25, pp. 523–40.

Lake, David (1988), *Power, Protection and Free Trade: International Sources of US Commercial Strategy, 1887–1939* (Ithaca: Cornell University Press).

Mansfield, Edward D. (1994), *Power, Trade, and War* (Princeton: Princeton University Press).

Martin, Lisa L. (1992a), 'Interests, Power and Multilateralism', *International Organization*, 46, pp. 765–92.

(1992b), *Coercive Cooperation: Explaining Multilateral Economic Sanctions* (Princeton: Princeton University Press).

Mastanduno, Michael (1991), 'Do Relative Gains Matter? America's Response to Japanese Industrial Policy', *International Security*, 16 (1), pp. 73–113.

(1992) *Economic Containment: Cocom and the Politics of East—West Trade* (Ithaca: Cornell UniversityPress).

Milner, Helen (1988), *Resisting Protectionism* (Princeton: Princeton University Press).

National Academy of Sciences (1987), *Balancing the National Interest: US National Security Export Controls and Global Economic Competition* (Washington: National Academy Press).

Nye, Joseph S. Jr. and Keohane, Robert O. (1971), 'Transnational Relations and World Politics: An Introduction', *International Organization*, 25, pp. 326–50.

Okimoto, Daniel (1989), *Between MITI and the Market: Japanese Industrial Policy for High Technology* (Stanford: Stanford University Press).

Powell, Robert (1991), 'Absolute and Relative Gains in International Relations Theory', *American Political Science Review*, 85, pp. 1303–21.

Rengger, N. J. (1992), 'No Time like the Present? Postmodernism and Political Theory', *Political Studies*, 40, pp. 561–70.

Rogowski, Ronald (1989), *Commerce and Coalitions* (Princeton: Princeton University Press).

Rosecrance, Richard (1986), *The Rise of the Trading State: Commerce and Conquest in the Modern World* (New York: Basic Books).

Schelling, Thomas (1960), *Strategy of Conflict* (Cambridge: Harvard University Press).

(1966), *Arms and Influence* (New Haven: Yale University Press).

Searle, John R. (1993), 'Rationality and Realism: What is at Stake?', *Daedalus*, 122, pp. 55–83.

Stein, Arthur (1990), *Why Nations Cooperate: Circumstance and Choice in International Relations* (Ithaca: Cornell University Press).

Waltz, Kenneth (1979), *Theory of International Politics* (Reading, MA: Addison Wesley).

Pluralism: Decision Making, Transnationalism, and Interdependence

MAJOR ACTORS AND ASSUMPTIONS: A SUMMARY

The pluralist image of international relations (also referred to by many in the field as *liberalism*) is based on four key assumptions. First, *nonstate actors* are important entities in world politics. International organizations, for example, may on certain issues be independent actors in their own right. They are more than simply forums within which states compete and cooperate with one another. The staff of a particular international organization may have a great deal of power in terms of agenda setting as well as in providing information which may influence how states define their interests. International organizations may also have an important role in implementing, monitoring, and adjudicating disputes arising from decisions made by constituent states of the organization. Over time, such functions may make the international organization indispensable to member states. Similarly, other nongovernmental, **transnational** organizations such as multinational corporations (MNCs) and human rights and environmental groups play important roles in world politics. The growth of transnational networks oriented around common strategies and goals epitomizes the rapid expansion of "sovereignty-free" actors and the coining of the term *global civil society*.

Second, for the pluralist, *the state is not a unitary actor*. It is composed of competing individuals, interest groups, and bureaucracies. Although it may be convenient for newspapers and governmental representatives to refer to "decisions taken by the United States," it is generally more accurate to speak of a decision made by a particular governmental coalition, bureaucracy, or even perhaps a single individual. The decision is not made by some abstract entity called "the United States" but by some combination of actors within the foreign policy establishment.

Different organizations, for example, may have different perspectives on a particular foreign policy issue. Competition, coalition building, and compromise will often result in a decision that is then announced in the name of the United States. Furthermore, this state decision may be the result of lobbying carried out by such nongovernmental actors as multinational corporations or interest groups or it may even be influenced by something as amorphous as public opinion. To the pluralist, the state cannot therefore be viewed as a unitary actor because to do so misses the multiplicity of actors composing the entity termed *the state*, the interactions occurring among these actors, and the role of influences emanating from beyond the territorial boundaries of the state as well as from domestic sources—ideas and values, international and transnational organizations, interest groups, and public opinion.

Third, pluralists *challenge the realist assumption of the state as rational actor*. Given their fragmented view of the state, it is assumed that the clash of interests, bargaining, and need for compromise do not always make for a rational decision-making process. Misperception or bureaucratic politics may dominate decision making, leading to poor decisions that are often *suboptimal*, or less than the best in terms of objectives sought. Instead of leading their country, statesmen may be tempted to take their cue from public opinion polls, evincing more concern for their personal standing or power position than for the good of the country as a whole. Pressure resulting from a crisis situation may also make a mockery of the notion of a cool and calculating decision-making process.

Finally, for pluralists, the *agenda of international politics is extensive*. Although national security concerns are important, the pluralist is also concerned with a number of economic, social, and ecological issues arising from the growth of **interdependence** among states and societies in the twentieth century. Certain pluralists, for example, emphasize trade, monetary, and energy issues and how these issues have come to be placed high on the international agenda. Other pluralists examine international attempts to deal with the world population problem and famine in parts of the **Third World.** Still others have studied the politics of international pollution and the degradation of the environment. The foreign affairs agendas of states are not exclusively preoccupied with national security issues, narrowly defined in terms of military matters. Economic and social issues can often have a direct bearing on the security and welfare of a particular regime or country. Because this is so, pluralists tend to reject the high versus low politics dichotomy accepted by most realists. Socioeconomic issues are often as important as military concerns. State preferences, in other words, are not fixed. Hence, pluralists are concerned with such general questions as: How and why do states cooperate? How do international norms of behavior develop, evolve, and influence state preferences and actions?

INTELLECTUAL PRECURSORS AND INFLUENCES

In the case of realism, it was relatively easy to identify its intellectual precursors. At least two of these, Grotius and E. H. Carr, have also had significant impact on scholars associated with the pluralist image. In the case of pluralism, however, the impact of particular theorists has tended to be more indirect. This is because many of these writers have not been observers of international relations per se but have been economists, social scientists, theologians, or political scientists interested in domestic politics. Their one common denominator, however, has been an interest in the individual or group as the unit of analysis, as opposed to the unified state that is the focus of realist writings. Therefore, we have organized the discussion of the intellectual precursors of pluralism around two themes within which individual theorists are mentioned: **liberalism** as a political philosophy and **interest group liberalism** as an approach to the study of domestic politics.

Although some aspects of liberal thought have also influenced realist scholars, we focus here on those aspects of liberalism that lead to rejection of a view of the state as unitary and rational actor. That the state is (or should be) disaggregated into component parts or becomes the battleground for competing interests is a view found in liberalism as well as interest group liberalism. Within the international relations discipline, works on **decision making** and transnationalism best reflect this view of the disaggregated state and the importance of nonstate actors.

Liberalism

Liberalism is a tradition of political thought composed of a set of practical goals and ideals. As noted above, many use the term *liberalism* interchangeably with what we call a *pluralist image* of world politics. For classical liberal theorists, the individual is the most important unit of analysis and the claimant of rights. The state is to play a minimal role in a liberal society, principally acting as arbiter in disputes between individuals and ensuring the maintenance of conditions under which individuals can enjoy their rights to the fullest. There are important differences among liberal theorists, but they do agree on the primacy of the individual in political life and on the role of the state as being limited to maintaining a stable political, social, and economic environment within which individuals can interact and pursue their chosen ends. This emphasis on the individual and the limited state is perhaps best exemplified in John Locke's *Second Treatise on Government,* published in England in 1689.[1]

Liberalism as an ideology came to dominate much of the political and economic thought in the eighteenth and nineteenth centuries, particularly in Great Britain and the United States. Liberal concerns for the individual were reinforced by Adam Smith's and David Ricardo's works in economics. They emphasized the important role of the individual entrepreneur, who should be relatively unconstrained by a minimalist state—a major theme in early capitalist writings. David Hume's contribution to logic and the philosophy of science similarly stressed the importance of the individual as the unit of analysis. The nineteenth-century essays of such **utilitarians** as Jeremy Bentham viewed people as rational, calculating individuals capable of deciding what was best for themselves without much government interference. Liberalism reigned supreme, virtually unchallenged in the United States and Great Britain until the turn of the century. The spirit of liberalism and its emphasis on the individual pervaded all spheres of life and thought—scientific, political, economic, social, and religious.[2] The industrial revolution, however, eventually resulted in modifications of liberal doctrine, which, although retaining an emphasis on the individual, now allowed the state to be given a somewhat more activist role in order to mitigate the most harmful effects of unrestrained economic competition.

For liberals, the minimal state was a possibility (and necessity) because it was assumed that there was an underlying harmony of interests among individuals. Just as the competition of the marketplace would produce the best goods, so too would the marketplace of ideas produce sound political sense. It followed that liberals emphasized the positive role played by public opinion in providing guidance to state officials and producing good public policy, including foreign policy. The state, therefore, was not some unitary, solitary actor pursuing its own course independently of the public. To the contrary, it was composed of numerous persons representing a multitude of interests. Nor were decisions the sole province of those individuals acting in the name of the state. Decisions were supposed to be informed by the public opinion and political consensus arising out of the clash of ideas and interests.

This view of the domestic polity was carried over into the international realm. Liberals recognized that war was a defining characteristic of international politics. They also agreed with realists that the state of anarchy that characterized world (as opposed to domestic) politics contributed to suspicion and distrust among states, posing an obstacle to cooperation and peace. But just as it was assumed that there could be a harmony of interests among individuals within a given state, so too did liberal theorists argue that a harmony of interests among states was possible.

It was recognized that war had existed down through the centuries. What, then, had changed to allow for this more optimistic view of interstate relations? Liberals made at least four arguments. First, advocates of what could be termed *commercial liberalism* argued that the expansion of the international economy made it more costly for states to go to war. As economic interdependence increased, there would be a disinclination to cut profitable economic ties.[3] Second, advocates of *democratic liberalism* claimed that the spread of democratic (or, more precisely, republican or representative) political systems meant that questions of war and peace were no longer confined to a small group of political and military elites, as in the past. Instead, leaders would have to be concerned with domestic public opinion that could act as a brake on any moves toward international confrontation and the outbreak of hostilities. Third, *regulatory liberalism* claims that the benefits of international law, accepted "rules of the game," and international organizations would contribute to the peaceful settlement of disputes among states and enhance global cooperation.[4] Finally, it was argued that western civilization had suffered enough from war and that leaders and citizens had learned how costly it was to wage it.

Undoubtedly the most important empirical expression of attempts to test the above propositions is to be found in the vast and growing literature on the *democratic peace*. Particularly with the end of the Cold War, scholars have asked the simple but important question: Are democracies more peaceful in their foreign relations? Academic studies conclude that while democracies certainly go to war, they rarely, if ever, go to war against each other. The virtual absence of war among democracies has led one scholar to conclude that this is "as close to anything we have to an empirical law in international relations." Such a claim is not without its realist critics. The answer to the question—are democracies more peaceful?—is obviously not merely of academic interest; it has major policy implications. On the one hand, state support of democratic movements around the world can be justified on the grounds of enhancing the prospects of peaceful relations among states. On the other hand, however, the literature on the democratic peace could be used (or misused) to justify interventions in the domestic affairs of other states or as a means to dismiss past acts of aggression by democracies.[5]

The German, or more precisely East Prussian, philosopher Immanuel Kant (1724–1804) observed that, over the years, it had become increasingly likely that *reason* would be a substitute for the use of force in world politics. Kant's emphasis on learning seems to have influenced modern works on regional integration and pluralist conceptions of international regimes.[6] Since World War I, liberal thinking has particularly stressed the positive role international law can play in promoting peace and harmony in world politics. Collaborative action by international organizations that represents the consensus of their constituent states works to mitigate the worst aspects of anarchy and to encourage cooperation.[7]

In sum, this brief overview of liberal thought highlights a number of concepts, arguments, and perspectives that directly or indirectly influence the pluralist image of international politics: the importance of the individual and societal **levels of analysis,** the disaggregated and nonunified state broken into its component parts, the intimate connection between international economics and politics, the role of public opinion, the importance of international law and organizations, and the ability of leaders to learn from past historical mistakes and disasters. The latter point is particularly important, injecting a voluntarist or social constructivist strand into thinking about international politics by holding out the prospect of some control over our fate. Current scholars whom we would term pluralist have not been equally influenced by all strands of liberal thought as it has developed over the years. Some have been particularly influenced by the liberal view of the disaggregated state with an emphasis on the *individual* as the unit of analysis. Others have been less influenced by such methodological questions, but more by the optimistic elements of liberalism concerning the possibilities for learning, peaceful change, and potential harmony in the international system.

Interest Group Liberalism

The roots of the pluralist image of international politics also lie in the view held by many scholars of the domestic political order. This is particularly true of American academics who are prone to see international politics through domestic political lenses. Indeed, the pluralist image of international politics held by many American international relations scholars can be understood as a projection of American political processes onto the entire globe. International political processes are not all that different from, and may even be considered an extension of, those conducted within the boundaries of a given state. As a result, pluralists tend to reject the realist distinction between "international" and "domestic" politics. For the pluralist, one is an extension of the other. This perspective is quite evident in much of the literature on decision making and transnationalism that disaggregates the state-as-actor.

The majority (but certainly not all) of authors we would term pluralist are American. Each has either directly or indirectly been influenced by political scientists who are students of the American political system. We use the term *interest group liberalism* to describe the perspective of these latter individuals.

The connection to the discussion of eighteenth- and nineteenth-century liberal thought is apparent. One critic of interest group liberalism, for example, makes the following observations. First, interest group liberalism assumes the "role of government is one of assuring access to the most effectively organized, and of ratifying the agreements and adjustments worked out among competing leaders and their claims."[8] Second, there is a "belief in a natural harmony of group competition." Finally, interest group liberalism defines both "the policy agenda and the public interest . . . in terms of the organized interests in society."[9] All three observations are consistent with the liberal notions of (1) the state as neutral arbiter, (2) the potential for a natural harmony of interest (in this case groups instead of individuals), and (3) public concern for, and participation in, a policy process not restricted to elites.

In the image of politics held by adherents of interest group liberalism, conflict and competition among interest groups play an important role. There is a proliferation of interest groups. Individuals form interest groups in attempts to outmaneuver, end-run, or overwhelm opposing groups or coalitions. Viewed in this way, politics is a game, but a game with very real stakes to be won or lost. Authoritative choices (or decisions) are made by government decisionmakers as the outcome of this process.

David Truman, whose writings are in the school of interest group liberalism, acknowledges his intellectual debt to Arthur F. Bentley, whose 1908 volume *The Process of Government* served as "the principal bench mark for my thinking." Truman observes that "the outstanding characteristic of American politics" is the "multiplicity of co-ordinate or nearly co-ordinate points of access to governmental decisions." He proceeds to describe the conflictual nature of American politics, but comments that "overlapping membership among organized interest groups" provides "the principal balancing force in the politics of a multi-group society such as the United States."[10]

The writings of Harold Lasswell and Robert Dahl are also illustrative of this image of American politics. Dahl describes American politics as a "system in which all the active and legitimate groups in the population can make themselves heard at some crucial stage in the process of decision."[11] Noting that it is a decentralized system, he observes that "decisions are made by endless bargaining." Groups are central to the process. Rather than either majority rule or minority rule, Dahl argues that the term *minorities rule* is the more accurate.[12] Politically active groups—minorities—are the most influential.

Thus, the image of politics that interest group liberals hold is of a fragmented political system, one in which multiple actors compete. The image is shared by most American political scientists even though their views may differ greatly on other conceptual and normative matters. The scholars mentioned are not, of course, creators of this image of American politics. Certainly *The Federalist Papers,* especially the writings of James Madison and later those of the Frenchman Alexis de Tocqueville, expose one to a good dose of this view of American domestic politics.[13]

In sum, what the group is to the interest group liberal, the individual is to the liberal philosopher. What they have in common is agreement on the fragmented nature of the state and society and the potential for harmony to develop out of competition and conflict. The state is not an independent, coherent, autonomous actor separated or aloof from society. Its primary function is as arbiter of conflicting demands and claims, or as an arena for the expression of such interests. Furthermore, the focus of analysis is less on the state and more on the competition among individuals and groups.

DECISION MAKING

If states were the only important actors and all states simply responded to their environment according to the same rational logic, there would be no need to disaggregate the state-as-actor or to consider a multiplicity of domestic and international influences. Although it is possible to chart relations among states (as realists sometimes do) without ever looking "inside" the states, pluralists argue that a complete understanding of the *reasons* for these relations requires analysis of the decision-making process. In this section, we first examine some early work on foreign policy decision making, and then we focus on scholarly literature that examines the role of individuals and bureaucracies in the formulation of foreign policy.

One of the first major attempts to develop a systematic decision-making approach to the study of international politics was made in the early 1950s by Richard C. Snyder and his colleagues.[14] Snyder stated that the focus of international relations research should be on the actions, reactions, and interactions of states. For him, the state is specifically its decisionmakers, and state action "is the action taken by those acting in the name of the state."[15] So far, realists would have little with which to disagree.

Snyder, however, emphasized that his analytical objective was to recreate the world as actual decisionmakers view it in order to explain behavior. This led him to discuss (1) subjective factors from the standpoint of decisionmakers—how they define the situation—not from the perspective of the analyst, and (2) potential sources of state action found in the decisionmakers' setting. The framework hence draws attention to numerous factors at different levels of analysis. Under the heading "internal setting," for example, domestic politics and public opinion are listed as potentially important elements in the formulation and execution of foreign policy. Nongovernmental factors and relations between countries (trade, family ties, shared values, mass media, migration, cultural exchanges) may also be important. Snyder therefore developed a decision-making framework consisting of numerous factors. It was up to the scholar to test them **empirically** by means of case studies. The relative importance of any one factor would vary from case to case.

This work is considered a pioneering effort, particularly given Snyder's claim that the foreign policy process could be studied scientifically. From the standpoint of the current state of the international relations discipline, such a perspective on decision making may seem passé, little more than an inventory of potentially relevant factors. For our purposes, it is important to point out that Snyder argued for the systematic consideration of a number of factors that may influence the decisions of flesh-and-blood policymakers. The framework explicitly emphasizes **perception** on the part of decisionmakers and the role of nongovernmental influences on the foreign policy process. These factors are part of the domestic, international, and decision-making settings within which policymakers operate. Hence, a plurality of factors is given prominence. Despite its innovative nature, Snyder's framework failed to generate more than one major empirical case study.[16] What it did do, however, was to encourage a shift in analytic focus away from the **reified,** abstract state.

The 1960s witnessed a proliferation of studies that identified an almost unending inventory of factors that may influence the foreign policy process. But as James N. Rosenau, a long-time student of foreign policy, stated in 1966:

> the dynamics of the processes which culminate in the external behavior of societies remain obscure. To identify factors is not to trace their influence. To uncover processes that affect external behavior is not to explain how and why they are operative under certain circumstances and not under others. To recognize that foreign policy is shaped by internal as well as external factors is not to comprehend how the two intermix or to indicate the conditions under which one predominates the other.[17]

What was missing were attempts to develop general theories of foreign policy—theories that contained testable hypotheses aimed at explaining the external behavior of more than one country. Single case studies were the norm.

Comparative studies—examining the similarities and differences of various decision-making systems—were rare until the late 1960s. Spurred by the comparative analysis of political systems, students of international relations began to generate and test hypotheses concerning the foreign policy behavior of states. Although different levels of analysis and different **variables** were used, what these studies had in common was a commitment to discovering common patterns or processes in the foreign (and defense) policies of states.[18] (Recent work that involves theorizing across levels of analysis will be discussed later.)

The Individual and Small Groups

Scholars engaged in studying decision-making processes from a pluralist perspective emphasize, as we have noted, that entities known as the "United States" or "Canada" do not make decisions; decisions are made by individuals. Similarly, a particular bureaucratic entity termed the "State Department" or "Foreign Office" is composed of individuals. It is, therefore, not surprising that the study of individuals and small groups has been a primary focus of analysis for a number of scholars.

The study of individuals and their role in international relations or foreign policy has drawn heavily on the disciplines of **psychology** and **social psychology.** Some of the work can be termed **psychohistory** and has focused on how life experiences influence an individual's foreign policy behavior and orientation. Other work by such scholars as Alexander George and Ole Holsti has attempted to discern an individual's belief system or **operational code.**[19]

A number of research efforts have drawn on the psychology literature in an attempt to generalize about the circumstances under which certain psychological processes occur. What these approaches have in common is an emphasis on how **cognitive** distortions undermine the realist view of decision making as a rational process. But unlike much of the earlier work, many of these scholars have also studied political science and history in addition to psychology and social psychology. As a result, their insights into the role that perception plays in the foreign policy process or during crisis situations is deserving of further comment.

The work of Robert Jervis, to take one example, starts with some realist assumptions, but then it focuses on individuals and individual perceptions, a more pluralist view.[20] Jervis is concerned less with how emotions affect foreign policy decision making and more with how cognitive factors and a confusing international environment can result in a poor decision even if the individual is relatively unemotional and as intelligent as he or she can be in evaluating alternatives. Furthermore, Jervis takes into account how the **anarchic** nature of international politics contributes to this confusing environment by encouraging cognitive processes that make decision making more difficult. Jervis accepts the realist argument that the anarchic **structure** of the international system breeds suspicion and distrust. The lack of a single **sovereign** or authority makes it a self-help system, and it is not necessarily irrational or a sign of paranoia to be preoccupied with real, potential, or imagined threats.

Jervis devotes a great deal of time to applying psychological concepts to historical events. According to him, his propositions are

> generalizations about how decision-makers perceive others' behavior and form judgments about their intentions. These patterns are explained by the general ways in which people draw inferences from ambiguous evidence and, in turn, help explain seemingly incomprehensible policies. They show how, why, and when highly intelligent and conscientious statesmen misperceive their environments in specified ways and reach inappropriate decisions.[21]

Jervis is interested in discerning how a decisionmaker comprehends a complex world filled with uncertainty. Each decisionmaker has a particular image of the world that has been shaped by his or her interpretations of historical events. Very often, these events (such as wars and revolutions) occurred when the individual was young and impressionable. Lessons learned from history, when combined with personal experiences, contribute to the development of particular expectations and beliefs concerning how the world operates that will have a major impact on the decisions made by policymakers. Once formed, these images of reality are difficult to change. Cognitive consistency is the norm. Information that conflicts with the decisionmaker's image tends either to be dismissed, ignored, or interpreted in such a manner as to buttress a particular policy preference or course of action.

Jervis emphasizes how the striving for cognitive consistency can have a negative effect on decision-making processes, and other scholars focus on how psychological stress arising out of difficult, emotion-laden situations affects rational calculations. One example of this perspective is the work of Irving L. Janis.

Janis has examined the tendency for social pressure to enforce conformity and consensus in cohesive decision-making groups. He calls this tendency **groupthink,** a "mode of thinking that people engage in when they are deeply involved in a cohesive in-group, when the members' strivings for unanimity override their motivation to realistically appraise alternative courses of action."[22] Indicators of groupthink include limiting discussions to only a few alternative courses of action, failing to reexamine initial decisions and possible courses of action initially rejected, and making little attempt to seek information from outside experts who may challenge a preferred policy. To make his case for the persuasiveness of concurrence seeking within a group and the resultant impact, Janis examines several foreign policy fiascos, such as the Bay of Pigs invasion in 1961, the military unpreparedness of the United States at Pearl Harbor in 1941, and the American decisions to escalate the Korean and Vietnam wars. He argues that in each case the pressure to conform to group norms interfered with critical, rational thinking.

A number of international relations scholars have been particularly interested in how psychological processes influence decision making during times of crisis—a situation between peace and war. The tendency for individuals to strive for cognitive consistency and for groups to enforce consensus among their members is particularly evident in crisis situations characterized by high stress, surprise, exhausting around-the-clock work schedules, and complex and ambiguous environments. As a result, there is a general erosion of cognitive capabilities. Tolerance for ambiguity is reduced, policy options are restricted, opposing actors and their motives are stereotyped. Compared to noncrisis situations, decisions are based even more on policymakers' predispositions, expectations, biases, and emotional states.[23]

In sum, scholarly work suggests that misperception can play a major role in crisis situations, perhaps contributing to the outbreak of war. Furthermore, it has been argued that not all decisionmakers operate with the same kind of rationality, making it difficult for leaders to judge what actions may deter an enemy.[24] The cumulative effect of such studies is to undermine the image of decision making as an essentially rational process. Nevertheless, scholars tend at the same time to exhort decisionmakers "to be more rational."[25]

By the mid-1980s, there was an evident decline in the amount of literature devoted to the role of cognition in international relations. Indeed, it was not fashionable to study the broader role of ideas in international relations. From the realist perspective, ideas were little more than ideological rationalizations of interests. The causative importance of ideas as independent variables was deemed virtually nil—material interests are a given and logically prior to any beliefs held by actors. The end of the decade, however, witnessed a revival of interest in the role of ideas. Although we will withhold discussion of *social constructivism* until later, we would note that substantial work exists that makes a case for the importance of ideas on policy. Judith Goldstein, for example, argues that in order to understand U.S. trade policies over the years, a reliance on international structural or domestic economic interests is insufficient. Rather, one must also take into account actors' causal beliefs as to which economic policies can best achieve preferred interests.[26] (A broader and more detailed discussion on the role of ideas is provided in the article by Goldstein and Keohane at the end of this chapter.)

No one would deny that the study of individuals is important if we wish to improve our understanding of international relations. The important question, however, is how much emphasis should be placed on the individual level of analysis as opposed to other levels. Recall Hans Morgenthau's observation in the previous chapter that in order to understand how a statesman reached a particular decision, we speculate how we would respond in similar circumstances. In other words, by keeping the decision-making environment constant, we could hypothesize that any rational individual would have acted in the same manner. Despite a diversity of backgrounds or temperaments, the structure of the situation encourages decisionmakers to respond in a similar fashion. What if, however, beliefs and perceptions *do* make a difference and individuals respond to common stimuli or the environment in divergent ways? If so, the individual as a focus of analysis *is* important.

This debate over the relative importance of the individual as opposed to the environment in explaining behavior is common to all the social sciences. It also touches on the matter of **determinism** versus **voluntarism.** If the international system is the key to understanding international relations, then other levels of analysis—individual, organizational, societal, or state—are by definition of less importance. If one accepts a more pluralistic view of international relations, however, then greater consideration and weight are given to the constructivist role of the individual. Individuals matter (as do groups and institutions) simply because their choices significantly affect the functioning of world politics.

Organizational Process and Bureaucratic Politics

Both the unitary and rational assumptions associated with realism are relaxed from the **organizational process** and **bureaucratic politics** perspectives. Graham Allison's organizational process model of foreign policy decision making, a view of bureaucracy that owes an intellectual debt to the German scholar Max Weber, sees organizational routines and procedures as determining at least some, and influencing other, foreign policy decisions and outcomes.[27] Organizational ethos and world view are also relevant considerations. In an often cited statement, Allison notes that where a given bureaucratic actor "stands" on a given issue is often determined by where he or she "sits"; one's view of alternative courses of action is highly colored by the perspective of the organization to which one belongs. Perceptions of what is the **optimal** or best course of action often vary from one bureaucratic actor to another, reflecting organizational biases that raise serious doubts concerning the rationality of the process as a whole. What assurance is there that optimal choices for the state as a whole will be made? Or is optimality, when achieved, purely accidental?

Allison's bureaucratic politics model of foreign policy decision making involves forming coalitions and countercoalitions among diverse bureaucratic actors in a competitive environment. The focus is on specific individuals in positions at the top of organizations and on the pulling and hauling among them. This is in contrast to the more routine, preprogrammed activity of the organizational process model. Hence, foreign policy decisions at times may be the result of which individual, or which coalition of individuals, can muster the most political power. What may be best for an individual or his bureaucracy in terms of increased prestige and relative standing within the government may lead to less than the best foreign policy for the state as a whole. Parochial personal and bureaucratic interests may reign over any expressed concern for the national interest.

Allison's work does not pose as direct a challenge to the unitary assumption about state behavior as does some of the other literature on decision making. Although multiple actors influenced by diverse organizational and individual interests compete to influence policy choices, in the final analysis, these decisions are still made by certain authoritative individuals. Notwithstanding all the competition and airing of alternative views, the state still speaks ultimately with one voice.[28] At the same time, however, the Allison study did at least raise some questions concerning the unitary character of the state in *implementation* of policy. Decisions made were not always carried out as quickly as anticipated or in precisely the same fashion as intended. After all, policy involves both **decisions** and **actions.** Even if the decisions are unitary and the state speaks with one voice (which may not always be the case), if consequent actions are fragmented or otherwise inconsistent, then how unitary is the state after all?

Robert Keohane, Joseph Nye, and others took the pluralist image a major step forward when they argued in their earlier work that the state may not be able to confine these bureaucratic actors.[29] Organizations, whether private or governmental, may well transcend the boundaries of states, forming coalitions with their foreign counterparts. Such transnational actors may even be working at cross-purposes with governmental leaders in their home states who possess the formal authority to make binding decisions. For example, the British Foreign Office may see a given issue similarly to its American State Department counterpart. On the other hand, the British Defence Ministry and the U.S. Defense Department may share a common view contrary to that of both diplomatic organizations. Moreover, nongovernmental interest groups in both countries may also form coalitions supportive of one or another **transgovernmental** coalition.

To what extent, then, do coalitions of bureaucratic actors, multinational corporations, and other transnational actors circumvent the authoritative decisionmakers of states through formation of such coalitions? An interesting example of a transgovernmental coalition that had a significant, though unpublicized, impact during the October 1962 Cuban missile crisis involved redeployment of Canadian naval units for an "exercise" in the North Atlantic. This decision effectively relieved the U.S. Navy of at least a part of its patrolling responsibilities there, allowing American ships to be redeployed to the Caribbean as part of the naval blockade of Cuba. All of this was apparently established between American and Canadian military officers while the Diefenbaker government was still debating the question of Canadian policy in the crisis. Was this circumvention by the Canadian navy an exception, or is it commonplace for bureaucratic actors to form coalitions across national borders that in effect make policy? Pluralists would argue that it is more commonplace than most realists would suppose.

If it *is* typically the way foreign policy is made, then focus by realists on the state as principal actor would seem to be misdirected. More attention should be given to the entire range of transnational actors and their interactions. On the other hand, if the example used here is indeed an exception, then it is an exception that makes the rule. The state in most cases retains its hard shell, precluding circumvention by transnational bureaucratic actors.

TRANSNATIONALISM

We have referred to transnational actors in the context of foreign policy decision making. We now turn to a lengthier discussion of transnationalism, a phenomenon closely associated with the pluralist image of international relations. Whereas the literature on decision making has generally emphasized political processes within states, the literature on transnationalism emphasizes ties between societies that include much more than state-to-state relations. As such, transnationalism in world politics can be understood as an extension of pluralist politics beyond the borders of any one state. James Rosenau has offered a useful definition of transnationalism, viewing it as "the processes whereby international relations conducted by governments have been supplemented by relations among private individuals, groups, and societies that can and do have important consequences for the course of events."[30] We begin with the question of what accounts for the increase in transnational ties and actors in the twentieth century.

Modernization

Realists stress the timeless quality of international relations. The insights of Thucydides, for example, are deemed relevant to the modern age of nuclear weapons. The same basic forces are at work, constraining and disposing actors to respond to similar situations in similar fashion. A certain continuity in international affairs is assumed.

Although they do not reject the foregoing assumption, pluralists believe it to be overstated. For them, the nature of international relations has indeed changed over the years. There is a qualitative difference between the world of seventeenth-century diplomacy and its Europe-oriented system and the twentieth-century international system characterized by more than 180 states. Modernization describes and explains this fundamental transformation of the international system. **Modernization** can be defined as the social, political, and economic prerequisites for, and consequences of, industrialization and technological development.[31] Proponents of this perspective point to the growth of scientific technology that allows for greater control over nature, the dramatic improvements in transportation and communication, the rise of mass consumption made possible by the industrial revolution, the growth of global ties as a legacy of colonialism, and the extension of European diplomatic and political ideologies throughout the world. National autonomy, the traditional goal of statecraft, has become increasingly difficult as economic activities spill over borders.

The distinction between domestic and foreign policy becomes blurred as domestic policy becomes foreign policy and economic and foreign policies become politicized. For example, protectionist tariff barriers to save jobs and rescue ailing industries are weighed against international consequences to include retaliatory trade or financial measures taken by states adversely affected. Borders become porous as ideas, capital, people, technology, goods, and services move from one geographic point to another.[32] For selfish reasons, states find it in their best interest to cooperate with one another, creating modest yet important international organizations designed to facilitate the flow of mail or more ambitious endeavors aimed at ensuring international peace.

If the invoking image for the realist is that of states as billiard balls colliding with one another, for the pluralist it is a latticework or cobweb image. Instead of visualizing international relations as states and their interactions in an anarchic environment, some scholars argue that a cobweb image depicts a much more complex system composed not simply of states with geographic and political boundaries.[33] Also included would be the interactions and behavior of nonstate actors such as multinational corporations, terrorist groups, international banks, and international organizations such as the European Union (EU), the Organization of African Unity (OAU), the United Nations, and the North Atlantic Treaty Organization (NATO). The cobweb image would also depict such transactions as migration, tourism, communications, and trade flows. For pluralists, a cobweb image is much more apt in depicting the world than is the billiard ball image with its almost exclusive attention to the interactions of sovereign states. The state-centric model may perhaps have been appropriate in seventeenth- or eighteenth-century Europe, but the modernization process has so transformed societies that pluralists believe an alternative image of the world is required if one is to grasp the nature of world affairs in the present century. An image of the world, as we have noted, is not a theory. How has the growth of transnationalism been dealt with theoretically? We turn now to examples of pluralist theorizing.

Integration

The impact of modernization on world politics, particularly the use of modern technology in the creation of weapons of mass destruction, is a phenomenon that drew the attention of certain international relations scholars in the period before and after World War II. One such scholar was David Mitrany.[34]

Mitrany was interested in investigating the possibility of how transnational ties might lead to international **integration,** the reduction of extreme nationalism, and hence increase the chances for a stable international peace. How might this come about?

Mitrany argued that, by definition, modern society has created a myriad of technical problems that can best be resolved by experts as opposed to politicians. This is true within states as well as between states. He believed that the proliferation of common problems logically requires collaborative responses from states. Hence, these essentially nonpolitical problems (economic, social, scientific) should be assigned to nonpolitical experts from the affected countries for resolution.

Mitrany reasoned that successful collaboration in one particular technical field or functional area would lead to further collaboration in other related fields. This process is what he termed **ramification.** Governments would recognize the common benefits to be gained by such cooperative endeavors and so would encourage or allow for a further expansion of collaborative tasks. In effect, Mitrany saw a way to sneak up on the authority of the sovereign state. As states and societies became increasingly integrated due to the expansion of collaboration in technical areas in which all parties gained, the cost of breaking these functional ties would be great and hence give leaders reason to pause before doing so. In particular, Mitrany emphasized how economic unification would contribute to the development of political integration. Hence, as opposed to a tendency among some realists to view international interactions as basically a **zero-sum game** (what one side wins the other loses), Mitrany instead argued that international interactions could be turned into a **variable-** or **positive-sum game** in which all the players could benefit. For Mitrany, this was not an idealistic dream far removed from reality. Rather, he grounded his analysis in what he believed to be a realistic assessment of the likelihood of the need for international cooperation to deal with common problems deriving from a complex and modern world. As international integration based on cooperation in functional, nonpolitical areas developed, the chances for international peace would be enhanced, he felt.

The interest in Mitrany's **functionalist** theory—and integration in general—was spurred by the successful creation of the European Coal and Steel Community (ECSC) in 1952 and the European Economic Community (EEC) or Common Market, in the 1956 Treaty of Rome. The EEC seemed to hold out promise for the eventual political integration of Western Europe. Furthermore, the EEC's initial successes in the realm of economic integration increased interest in the more general question: Under what conditions is integration among states possible? Scholars noted that what was occurring in Western Europe did not match the Hobbesian image of states constantly prepared to go to war, an image that included little faith in the possibility of collaborative behavior among sovereign states. Hence, alternative perspectives were devised to explain international cooperation.

One of the best-known theorists of regional integration, Ernst Haas, defined integration as a *process* "whereby political actors in several distinct national settings are persuaded to shift their loyalties, expectations and political activities toward a new centre, whose institutions possess or demand jurisdiction over the preexisting national states."[35] Haas's conceptual approach to the study of political integration soon acquired the label **neofunctionalism**—an acknowledgment of the intellectual debt owed to Mitrany, but with significant differences. Where Haas parted company with Mitrany was in his rejection of the notion that one could separate technical tasks from politics or welfare from power. For integration to occur, Haas argued that it must be perceived by political elites to be in their self-interest. The assigning of tasks to an international organization—even if this involves a seemingly technical function such as supervising an international mail system—will be attained and sustained only if actors believe their own interests are best served by making a political commitment to an international organization.

What Haas attempted to do, therefore, was to stipulate the conditions and processes whereby individuals find it in their own rational self-interest to collaborate for mutual gain, which results in the potential for a peaceful transformation of international politics. To put it another way, Haas directed his efforts *not* toward understanding conflict among states faced with a security dilemma but toward understanding how states achieve collaborative behavior. In terms of Rousseau's stag hunt fable discussed in Chapter Two, Haas focused on ways to encourage the group to pursue the stag as opposed to assuming individuals will always defect in pursuit of the hare.

Early predictions of progress in regional integration did not occur, at least not to the extent anticipated. That strong nationally oriented leaders would emerge (such as Charles DeGaulle in France) to block transfer of too much authority to regional institutions had not been anticipated. Beyond this strong-leader explanation for the slowing down of regional integration, however, a more fundamental evaluation of integration theory was offered by Haas himself.

Haas described the contemporary period as a "turbulent" one in which there are "confused and clashing perceptions of organizational actors which find themselves in a setting of great social complexity." Moreover, the number of actors is very large. Each pursues a variety of objectives which are mutually incompatible; but each is also unsure of the trade-offs between the objectives. Each actor is tied into a network of interdependencies with other actors that are as confused as the first. Yet some of the objectives sought by each cannot be obtained without cooperation from others.[36]

There is also uncertainty or outright confusion on means–ends relations—what the causes of international problems are or what their solutions might be in areas such as the environment, energy, industrial policy, research and development, and technology transfer. Indeed, the approach for dealing with a problem in one area may have negative implications in another. For example, in substituting coal or nuclear power for petroleum as principal sources of energy, there may be a trade-off in terms of an adverse impact on the environment.

Haas argued, therefore, that gaining control over such complexity is emerging as the major political task during the last part of the twentieth century. Significantly, states may be led to seek nonregional solutions to these problems, whatever may be the effect of such solutions on the objectives of regional integration. Haas concluded that his earlier "theory of regional integration ought to be subordinated to a general theory of interdependence."[37]

Moves toward greater integration in Europe have not caused Haas to change his position. Indeed, decisions to establish a single, open market among European Union members and to create by the end of the 1990s a European central banking system with a common currency were not so much the result of the neofunctional logic of **spillover.** Rather, these decisions resulted from the recognition by European leaders, prodded by the EU Commission, that European global competitiveness depended upon taking such steps. In short, integration has increased more as a response to external stimuli than to internal processes at work within the EU.[38]

Despite its predictive shortcomings, the literature on integration has provided important insights on the nature of world politics and has contributed to the development of the pluralist image of international relations.

First, the literature on regional integration downplays the state as the unit of analysis. Transactions—economic, social, and technical—have also been the focus of attention, as have interest groups, transnational nonstate actors, and public opinion.

Second, the neofunctionalist literature in particular has disaggregated the nation-state, examining such component parts as bureaucracies and elites. The latter are viewed as flesh-and-blood individuals having conflicting perspectives, opinions subject to change, and decision-making power.

Third, integration theorists pose the question of what other forms of political organization—aside from the territorially based nation-state—are possible. How can they be attained?

Finally, integration theorists have analyzed the conditions under which international cooperation is facilitated. The realist emphasis on state competition and international anarchy, it has been argued, provided few clues on this matter, but cooperation is just as much a defining characteristic of international relations as is conflict. Military and security affairs do not monopolize the agenda of international politics. Economic, social, and welfare issues also deserve attention, and integration theorists have addressed these topics.

Interdependence, Regimes, Multilateralism

The concept of interdependence is discussed by proponents of all three images of international relations, but the pluralists take it to heart because it captures much of the essence of their view of world politics. Interdependence is to many pluralists what **balance of power** is to realists and what **dependency** is to many globalists. The idea of international interdependence is certainly not new, and its basic notion—that two or more units are dependent on one another—is easy to grasp. In recent years, however, the term has been developed to give it some analytical utility and conceptual content useful for the development of international relations theory. Pluralists have argued that the term provides a more accurate grasp of the current nature of world politics than does the concept of balance of power.

Interdependence means different things to different people. As discussed in Chapter 2, realists tend to see it as the **vulnerability** of one state to another, a view that suggests that interdependence is to be avoided or at least minimized. A common view among pluralists, by contrast, is that interdependence involves "reciprocal effects among countries or among actors in different countries."[39] There is sensitivity in Country *B* to what is going on in or emanating from Country *A*. Although there are costs associated with interdependence, defined as **sensitivity,** benefits to either or both parties may outweigh these costs.[40] Thus, interdependence is not necessarily only a matter of country *B*'s vulnerability to Country *A*. Pluralists do not exclude consideration of interdependence as vulnerability but instead focus on the multiple channels that connect societies, including interstate, transgovernmental, and transnational relations. There is a decided absence of hierarchy among issues such that socioeconomic issues may be as or more important than security issues. Moreover, when such complex interdependence exists, military force tends to have less utility in the resolution of conflicts.[41]

To the pluralist, interdependence may have benign implications and may be worth seeking; this is the influence of the liberal view of international relations. Whether the issues are trade, finance, communications, environmental pollution, or transfer of technology, the pluralist sees at least the opportunity for building good relations among the interdependent units. Managing interdependent relations may even involve construction of sets of rules, procedures, and associated institutions or international organizations to govern interactions in these issue areas—so-called **international regimes.** The term *regime* is borrowed from domestic politics, where it refers typically to an existing governmental order (democratic, authoritarian, or otherwise) or to a set of rules and institutions established to govern relations among individuals, groups, or classes within a state. In its international context, given the absence of a superordinate or overarching central authority, these rules are voluntarily established by states to provide some degree of order in international relations. Thus, there is a strong Grotian strain in pluralist thought, particularly when talk turns to managing interdependence through the construction of regimes.[42]

Regimes are sets of rules, which may have international and nongovernmental organizations associated with them. Consistent with this understanding, Stephen Krasner defines regimes as "implicit or explicit principles, norms, rules, and decision-making procedures around which actors' expectations converge in a given area of international relations."[43] Hence, international regimes are not the same as international organizations—they do not have a mailing address. They are constructs defined by observers—an analytical concept. Regimes may accompany an organization, but the former do not have the capacity to act. Furthermore, an international organization associated with a particular regime may concern itself with more than one regime or issue area—the United Nations, for example.

The regime literature is concerned with such basic questions as: How and why are international regimes formed? How do regimes affect state behavior and collective outcomes in particular issue areas? How and why do regimes evolve or dissolve? There are at least three schools of thought.[44] *Power-based realist theories* emphasize, not surprisingly, the role of anarchy and the impact of the relative distribution of capabilities. The best-known realist regime theory, hegemonic stability, was mentioned in Chapter 2. The basic argument is that regimes are established and maintained when a state holds a preponderance of power resources, as did the United States after World War II. Once this hegemonic power declines and power is spread more equally among states, regimes are expected to decline as well. While a few realists are completely dismissive of international regimes and organizations, most would accept Stephen Krasner's view that regimes help states avoid uncoordinated action and in some cases can actually be a source of power for weaker states.[45]

Interest-based (or neoliberal) theories of regimes make a much stronger claim for the role that international regimes can play in helping states realize common interests. States are included along with non-state actors in these neoliberal formulations. The best example of such theories is termed **neoliberal institutionalism,** developed by Robert Keohane and others. Long associated with pluralism due to his writings on transnationalism and interdependence, Keohane's *After Hegemony* (1984) actually adopted several realist assumptions (e.g., the key role of power and the state) in order to explain why even self-interested, rational egoists would pursue multilateral cooperative behavior. A starting point for this extensive literature is the proposition that "state actions depend to a considerable degree on prevailing institutional arrangements."[46] It has been argued that neorealism and neoliberalism have enough in common or compatible that perhaps a theoretical synthesis could be achieved. Neorealists, however, argue that institutions and regimes matter only to the extent that they cause states to behave in ways they otherwise *would not* behave. Neoliberals, on the other hand, claim that institutions and regimes matter because they enable states to do things they otherwise *could not* do. Hence, neorealists view regimes as constraints on state behavior, and neoliberals view regimes more positively as actually enabling states to achieve mutually beneficial outcomes.

Joseph Grieco defends realism against a pluralist, "liberal-institutionalist" critique. Both realism and liberal institutionalism accept anarchy or the absence of central authority as the defining condition of international relations, but they differ substantially on the behavior that they see occurring within this anarchic milieu. Grieco takes issue with the optimistic view of liberal institutionalists that states will be satisfied with the absolute gains they achieve from cooperative endeavors. He counters that "states in anarchy must fear for their survival and their independence" and, as a result, they are concerned lest "others may achieve relatively greater gains"—concerns that are a significant obstacle to achieving cooperation under anarchy.[47]

Finally, *knowledge-based cognitive* theories have been critical of both of the first two perspectives due to their reliance on key realist assumptions. Cognition theorists argue that state interests are not given, but created. This leads them to examine the role of normative and causative beliefs of decisionmakers in explaining preferences and interest formation. If there is a change in beliefs and this, in turn, influences behavior, then a learning process has occurred. Cognition theorists attempt to demonstrate that states can redefine their interests without any shift in the overall systemic distribution of power and use regimes and institutions to "lock in" the learning that has occurred.

One way knowledge might come to be shared by decisionmakers is through the influence of transnational, *epistemic communities,* defined as "network[s] of professionals with recognized expertise and competence in a particular domain and an authoritative claim to policy-relevant knowledge within that domain."[48] Epistemic communities (for example, environmentalists, scientists, international economists, and other specialists), it is argued, can influence the creation and maintenance of international regimes in a number of ways. International regimes are embedded in the broader normative structures of international society and, as a result, states typically are not free to ignore institutional commitments without paying a price. A focus on self-interest alone will not explain regime maintenance. As Friedrich Kratochwil and John Ruggie argue, regimes have more than a regulative function that requires states to behave in accordance with certain norms and rules. They also create a common social world that interprets the meaning of international behavior. In other words, regimes have what is called a "constitutive" dimension. Kratochwil and Ruggie advocate opening "the positivist epistemology to more interpretive strains, more closely attuned to the reality of regimes."[49]

This view of regimes can be placed in a broader theoretical approach to international relations termed *social constructivism.* As the term implies, the focus is on the social construction of world politics and identities in particular. It is argued that actors in international politics make decisions based upon what the world appears to be and how they conceive their roles in it. These conceptions derive from what could be termed systemic, intersubjective "shared understandings, expectations, and social knowledge embedded in international institutions."[50] Norms are constitutive, meaning such concepts as "sovereignty" and "equality" are social constructions that help shape the identities and interests of international actors. Hence, social constructivists argue that the realist assumption of egoistic identities and treating state interests as givens is questionable; these factors should be treated instead as dependent variables—that which one is trying to explain.

Social constructivists argue that rule-governed cooperation can, over time, lead actors to change their beliefs about who they are and how they relate to the rest of the international system. As cooperation becomes habituated, states and other nonstate actors may develop more collective identities. These, in turn, further strengthen the readiness of international actors to cooperate. Through such a process, the structural transformation of the international system can gradually occur and states can escape the worst aspects of international anarchy. Constructivism, therefore, occupies the middle ground between positivist, rationalist (realist or neoliberal institutionalist), and critical theory approaches. Constructivists not only highlight the noncoercive, constraining effects of norms but also point to the important role played by nonstate actors and international organizations in the creation and evolution of these norms.

It should be noted that international regimes tend to be associated with particular issue areas. In recent years, an attempt has been made to understand international cooperation in a broader framework utilizing the concept of *multilateralism*. As noted by John Ruggie (see his article in the section following this chapter), multilateral norms and institutions helped to stabilize international politics during the collapse of the Soviet Union and its empire, and such norms and institutions continue to play "a significant role in the management of a broad array of regional and global changes in the world system today." Viewed as an organizing principle of international life, multilateralism is an institutional form that coordinates relations among states on the basis of generalized principles of conduct: (1) indivisibility (e.g., collective security arrangements whereby an attack on one is an attack against all); (2) nondiscrimination (all parties are treated equally, as in most-favored nation (MFN) trade agreements, which forbid discrimination among countries producing the same product); (3) diffuse reciprocity (states do not expect quid pro quo in exchange but rely on longer-term assurances that things will balance out over time). The specific institutional expressions of multilateralism will vary. As Ruggie notes in his article, multilateralism is not a theory of international relations, but rather a concept whose explication and application to empirical case studies may lead to theory building.

In sum, multilateralism in general (and regimes in particular) may be the vehicles for accommodating differences and upgrading the common interest. Consistent with Rousseau's stag hunt fable discussed in Chapter 2, the actors agree to collaborate in hunting the stag rather than serve only narrowly defined, short-term self-interest. Differences arise among actors, but at least a possibility for their peaceful resolution remains.

This is anything but determinist thinking. Voluntarism is central in this mode of thought. Individual statesmen can, if they are willing, shape the world order. They have to deal with power and they understand that political choices have to be made among competing alternatives if international regimes for the management of interdependence are to be maintained in such fields as money, trade, postal service, telecommunication, fishing, and environmental protection. Critical to pluralist work on integration, interdependence, international regimes, and multilateralism, therefore, is the assumption that statesmen and bureaucratic officials can *learn*. While realists tend to take the existence of state interests for granted, pluralists are concerned with how those interests are defined and redefined. In the words of Ernst Haas: "There is no fixed 'national interest' and no 'optimal regime.' "[51] This requires examining not only the interactions among states but also the manner in which domestic factors, perception, and international norms and organizations influence the formulation and reformulation of those interests.

In keeping with the pluralist interest of theorizing across the levels of analysis, recent years have witnessed work on the role of the structure of domestic politics in explaining international cooperation and the strength of regimes. The focus is not simply on interest groups or bureaucratic politics, but on other factors such as the type of electoral system, the division of governmental powers, links between state and society, and state strength.[52] The challenge is to develop theories that account simultaneously for the interaction of domestic and international factors—more easily said than done.

One approach to this challenge has been Robert Putnam's concept of "two-level games." Unlike state-centric theories, the two-level approach assumes that domestic conflict over what constitutes the "national interest" is inevitable. Hence, decision-makers have to reconcile domestic and international imperatives simultaneously.

Finally, it should be noted that efforts have been made to reinvigorate the concept of transnationalism. As mentioned earlier, the idea was a popular topic of discussion and investigation in the 1970s, but by the 1980s, the term remained theoretically underdeveloped. More recent work has linked the concept of transnationalism to domestic structures and international institutions. The argument is that the impact of transnational actors and coalitions on state policies in particular issue areas will vary in accordance with differences in domestic structures and degrees of international institutionalization (e.g., multilateral regimes and both international and nongovernmental organizations).[53]

SYSTEM

Pluralists do not always employ the concept of **system,** although it is common currency in the literature. To the extent that pluralists use the terminology, systems tend to be open.[54] This means that the system is open to both external influences and effective choice by actors within the system. The actors, or component units, of the system can have some effect on outcomes. It is not the system that determines what the actors will do as if the actors were automatons. Or, to put it another way, statesmen impose themselves on events, not the reverse.

There is a good deal of indeterminancy in most pluralist formulations. Outcomes depend on combinations of domestic and transnational actors that outmaneuver or overwhelm opposing coalitions. The result is authoritative decisions and actions or, in a word, **policy.** Of course, all this freedom, or indeterminacy, also has its costs. Pluralist theories of politics tend to have less predictive power. One can have a fairly clear understanding of the complexity associated with political processes seen through pluralist lenses without having too much insight as to the outcome that will ultimately be achieved. On the other hand, predictions offered by balance of power theorists in the realist school often are at a very high level of generality that is somewhat removed from day-to-day events.

Pluralists use the term *system* in at least four different ways. First, for some pluralists, the international system is merely the sum of the foreign policies of all states. Governmental actions are the principal focus. This is the view accepted by some realists as well. As we have seen, however, pluralists also tend to emphasize the role of specific bureaucracies and pressure groups in the formulation of foreign policy. They have direct impact on the final decision.

Second, other pluralists view the system as the sum of foreign policies plus the activities of nonstate actors. Nonstate actors include multinational corporations, terrorist groups, international banks, and transnational interest groups such as Amnesty International, the Red Cross, and Greenpeace.

Third, certain pluralists include all the foregoing elements in their definition of a system but add all other types of transactions such as ideas, values, communications, trade patterns, and financial flows. This most fully approximates the cobweb image mentioned earlier.[55]

For some, the combination of transnational actors and international transactions allows one to speak of a "global civil society" or "world civic politics" paralleling the interstate system. From this perspective, some transnational organizations are not merely interest groups attempting to influence the preferences and policies of states. Rather, they directly shape widespread behavior throughout the world. Environmental organizations, for example, work to shift public standards of good conduct, change corporate practices, and empower local communities.[56]

Fourth, despite the fact that many pluralists reject the concept of anarchy, a number of prominent pluralists (neoliberal institutionalists are a good example) accept the concept and the assumption that anarchy makes international cooperation difficult. Nevertheless, they are much more optimistic as to the ability of institutional multilateralism to achieve cooperation under anarchy.

What all these views have in common, however, is a belief in the difficulty (if not impossibility) of insulating the foreign policy process from domestic and international forces. Not only is foreign policy influenced by such factors as public opinion, lobbying, and the policies and performances of allies and foes; it is also influenced by the individual and bureaucratic infighting that occurs within and among most governmental institutions. Government and society in general are penetrated in innumerable ways, making the notion of the impermeable nation-state a myth.[57]

The focus for the pluralist thus tends to be on various parts of the political process and on particular issues. Islands of theory—rather than such general theory as realist proponents of balance of power theory offer—are constructed. As we have seen, a number of pluralists focus on perception and decision-making processes of small groups. Others have studied regional integration, the impact of domestic and bureaucratic politics on foreign policy, and the roles played by transnational actors in world politics.

Unfortunately for the pluralist, however, these theoretical parts have tended to be nonadditive. To attempt merely to combine islands of theory (referred to by some theorists as **microtheories**) does not necessarily result in a **general theory.** A pluralist does not start with the system and work down to assess its impact on component units, as many realists do. Instead, one creeps up on the system by trying to put its parts together in some coherent fashion, which is not an easy task.

On the other hand, interdependence has been a key concept entertained by theorists seeking to integrate pluralist thought by establishing some common denominator. There have been a number of attempts to measure interdependence as a systemic property or attribute.[58] As one might expect, findings on whether interdependence is rising, declining, or holding relatively constant depend heavily on the analyst's definition of the concept and on its **operationalization**—how it is measured through quantification or even by the use of nonquantitative indicators. Even if agreement were reached on these definitional and measurement problems, there remains considerable disagreement on such questions as whether increasing interdependence is more or less conducive to peace and world prosperity.[59]

Perhaps not surprisingly, the most fruitful issues for the pluralist approach have been the nonsecurity ones—those dealing with social, cultural, economic, technological, and related subjects. This has certainly been the case in **systemic** studies of inter-dependence and the construction and maintenance of international regimes.

CHANGE

It should be apparent by now that, compared to realists, pluralists place much greater emphasis on the possibilities of change, particularly peaceful change. This is quite evident, as we have noted, in the literature on integration and regimes in which policy-makers learn from their experiences in international collaboration. There is also a possibility, but by no means an inevitability, that sovereign state members of international organizations may choose to transfer some authority to these institutions. To the extent that a given state cannot address adequately problems that confront a larger number of states, it may be in the state's interest to effect such transfers of authority. Whether such transfers would be permanent or whether such international institutions would acquire supranational authority that could be exercised over states is not clear. Were either to occur, it would be a fundamental **transformation** of world politics as we now understand it. States, assuming they would continue to exist, would no longer perform the large number of functions they now do. Again, such an outcome is not understood by pluralists as being inevitable or necessarily even desirable. Indeed, the question of alternative futures or alternative world orders continues to be addressed by pluralists of different persuasions.[60] There is, in any event, no single vision of the future that has currency among contemporary pluralists. Where pluralists differ from most realists, however, is that their image of world politics allows for a greater possibility of change. Their states and statesmen are not so constrained by the existing international system and balances of power within that system.

Similarly, much of the work on decision making emphasizes **feedback** processes —actors monitoring responses to actions they have taken so that future policies can be adjusted if necessary. The emphasis on choice in much of the pluralist work reveals a philosophical commitment to voluntarism, a belief that people can control or at least have some impact on their individual and collective destinies. Hence, the international system is viewed as being open and subject to directed change. For pluralists interested in transnational ties and interdependence, understanding the dynamics of system change is one of the most important tasks of scholars. It is not enough to describe particular types of systems (bipolar or multipolar, for example). Instead, efforts need to be directed toward understanding why and how the international system is changing and what this means in terms of war, peace, and stability.

The separate efforts of Ernst Haas and James Rosenau are representative examples of pluralist views of the changing world order (see the subsequent articles in this book). The world is a turbulent one, not just due to the complexity produced by a proliferation of state and nonstate actors, but also due to the different mentalities individuals bring to the issues of the day. Haas focuses on cognitive variables, given the issue complexity he observes in which there is uncertainty and disagreement over both desirable ends to be sought and on the effective means to these ends in public policy deliberations within and across national borders. For his part, Rosenau also looks to the "micro" level, noting, for example, the effect on global processes of an expansion of analytical skills among individuals everywhere. Individual loyalties are also in flux, directed not just toward the traditional state authorities. One cannot understand changes in the "macro" structure of world politics without taking microlevel variables into account. Indeed, bifurcation between "multicentric" and "state-centric" forms or structures in competition with each other now characterizes world politics in an ever more complex, turbulent period.[61]

PLURALISTS AND THEIR CRITICS: AN OVERVIEW

The comments in this section are relatively brief but not because works based on the pluralist image lack their critics. Much of the criticism has already been discussed in Chapter 2 and earlier in this chapter.

Anarchy

As noted, pluralists generally tend to downplay the role of **anarchy** and the **security dilemma** in explaining international relations. It has been argued by realists, however, that no analysis of world politics is complete unless the anarchical structure of the system is taken into account. How is it possible to assess realistically the possibilities for cooperation and peace between states unless the role of anarchy in creating suspicion and distrust is considered? The realist would contend that if one ignores or reduces the importance of such considerations, thinking can quickly become **utopian** with little relation to reality. In addition, by emphasizing misperception and the role of bureaucratic politics, there is a danger in thinking that all conflicts result from essentially nonrational forces and that somehow better communication would reduce the amount of conflict in the international system. By contrast, realists argue that states often have fundamentally different interests that conflict, and the notions of "slipping into war" and "the war nobody wanted" are overused and misleading.[62]

A pluralist response is that placing so much emphasis on the security dilemma loads the dice against any change from the status quo. To see the world as nothing more than competition and conflict born of mistrust among states is itself a distortion of reality, or even a self-fulfilling prophecy. One's acts, if born of suspicion and distrust, will tend to produce similar responses in others, thus confirming one's initial suspicions.

Furthermore, the history of world politics is a history not only of conflict but also of collaboration. To study instances of when the security dilemma has been overcome is just as important as studying instances when it has contributed to the onset of war. Finally, to argue that misperception, bureaucratic politics, or domestic pressures may contribute to the onset of war is not to argue that states do not have conflicting national interests as well. Historical studies have shown time and again, however, that such factors as misperception are often critical in explaining the outbreak of wars.

Theory Building

Realists have argued that by describing the world in greater and greater detail, descriptive accuracy increases at the expense of developing a **parsimonious** theory of international relations. In other words, theories should be as simple as possible. Understanding increases by moving *away* from the real world, not by moving closer to it. At first, this statement might seem counterintuitive or different from what one might expect. But ambitious theories aim at producing valid generalizations by viewing the forest as a whole, not individual trees. By faithfully cataloguing the complexity of the world, pluralists, according to critics, are in danger of remaining in the realm of merely describing things as opposed to explaining why things happen the way they do.

In response, pluralists claim that before theories of international relations can be constructed, we need an accurate image of international relations. The pluralist image, it is argued, more accurately captures the nature of world politics. Yes, it is admitted, the pluralist image is not as neat and streamlined as the realist image. It consists of a number of different actors and influences that make for complexity, but theories of international relations should aspire to deal with such complexity and not pretend that it doesn't exist. How adequate are theories that fail to deal with and explain many of the changes that have occurred in the nature of world politics over the past century?

Voluntarism

If realists have been criticized for being excessively pessimistic concerning the human condition and the ability of individuals to control international events and forces, pluralists can be criticized for their heavy reliance on the assumption of voluntarism, or effective free will. Some pluralist writings leave one with the impression that international harmony can be achieved if only leaders *really* wanted it—that it is a simple matter of human volition, a mere matter of desiring cooperation as opposed to competition. Hence, the transformation of the nature of world politics is seen to be desirable as well as attainable. Either "bad leaders" or "bad governments" stand in the way; if they could be changed or removed, the world would be a better place. Once again, the influence of the liberal philosophy is evident, and once again, the realist evaluation would be that this view of international change and how it can be achieved ignores constraints placed on *all* leaders and states by the anarchical nature of the international system and the balance of power. Moreover, some realists would argue that people are indeed aggressive with a proclivity toward warlike behavior; it is part of human nature to behave so.

The emphasis on voluntarism is not always acknowledged by pluralist writings. Nor is it necessarily a function of a philosophical commitment to a belief in free will that can influence outcomes. It could also derive from the fact that the focus of analysis for many pluralists happens to be government bureaucracies or individual actors. By studying real individuals within real organizations, world politics takes on a human face.

Pluralists would claim that they are well aware of constraints imposed on the actions of individuals or groups. For example, studies of individual leaders may *not* emphasize voluntarism but, rather, psychological constraints resulting from life experiences. There remains, however, an array of possible options available to decision-makers and the ability to make real choices among these competing alternatives. After all, to the pluralist, both opportunities and constraints are associated with foreign policy choice. Too often, history is interpreted as if certain events were inevitable, that a particular war was the result of a number of trends inexorably coming together.

The often self-critical scholarly work of Ernst Haas stands as an exemplar of this voluntarist theoretical understanding. The politics of human choice—the importance of interests tied to ideas and carried by politically connected elites and other players—was evident in his earliest studies of the European Communities in the 1950s and 1960s, which spawned a research program in neofunctional integration in both regional and global institutional contexts. Individuals and groups of individuals, their interests, and their ideas mattered.

Following in this line were his subsequent studies of scientists and other technical elites as carriers of global cooperative and collaborative enterprises. The importance of social and organizational learning and the relation of knowledge to power are underscored in his view that "change in human aspirations and human institutions over long periods is caused mostly by the way knowledge about nature and about society is married to political interests and objectives."[63] His efforts are a foundation stone for many present-day efforts in cognition theory applied to international institutions.

For Haas, there is really no *new* institutionalism in the field—only, perhaps, a new emphasis on it. Indeed, it has long been the focus of his work that has also influenced the efforts of many others. What we now refer to as cognition theory and social constructivism reflect the *voluntarist* assumptions that have long been at the core of his work.

In his continuing theoretical and research efforts, Haas underscores the emphasis he places "on the role of ideas in the heads of actors."[64] Consistent with Max Weber, he sees interests filtered by ideas as central "the world views, which were created by ideas, have very often acted as the switches and channeled the dynamics of the interests."[65]

This understanding leads Haas to focus on cognitive progress that comes from learning as opposed merely to adapting to changing circumstances. His portrayal of nationalism as an "instrumental social construction" and often a very effective means for accomplishing human purposes challenges the view some have held on the obsolescence of nation-states. In comparative case studies of Great Britain, the United States, France, Germany, and Japan, he observes the constructive aspects of nationalist sentiment, ideology and myth, rationalization, and collective learning in producing "health, wealth, and peace" and thus advancing the human condition. Reason (science) informs collective decisions that produce the progress we experience.[66]

Far from giving a ringing endorsement for the nation-state as the only viable social construction for achieving progress, however, Haas brings the argument full circle in his reference to one of the fathers of European integration, Robert Schuman.[67] In Schuman's view, in a continuing human quest to achieve progress, we need not seek the elimination of states; it is enough to deemphasize them. In going beyond the nation-state, the state may still have a constructive role to play, albeit, perhaps, a lesser one than in the past. In any event, social constructions and human institutions are ultimately what we voluntarily choose to make of them.

Ethnocentrism

A final criticism of the pluralist image is that many scholars tend to view the world through the lenses of the American political system. If American government and processes are understood to conform to a pluralist image, then the same image is imposed on the rest of the world, where it may bear little relation to reality.

Acknowledging cultural, societal, and other differences, the pluralist who argues that bureaucracies, interest groups, and transnational actors are important to understanding international relations would deny that this image is merely American ethnocentrism imposed on the globe. It is, instead, a fairly accurate description of world politics. The actors and processes studied by pluralists are not confined to the states of the West but are found in and among political systems around the globe.

NOTES

1. John Locke, "An Essay Concerning the True, Original, Extent and End of Civil Government: Second Treatise on Government," in *Social Contract,* introduction by Sir Ernest Barker (London: Oxford University Press, 1962).
2. William Ebenstein, *Great Political Thinkers: Plato to the Present,* 4th ed. (New York: Holt, Rinehart & Winston, 1969), p. 63. Realists have also been influenced by liberalism, particularly by the emphasis on the rational individual pursuing his or her self-interest.
3. A recent work in this tradition is Richard Rosecrance, *The Rise of the Trading State* (New York: Basic Books, 1986).
4. Robert O. Keohane, "International Liberalism Reconsidered," in *The Economic Limits to Modern Politics,* ed. John Dunn (Cambridge, England: Cambridge University Press, 1990), pp. 165–94.
5. The quote is from Jack Levy, "The Causes of War: A Review of Theories and Evidence," in *Behavior, Society, and Nuclear War,* Vol. 1, ed. Philip E. Tetlock, et al. (New York: Oxford University Press), p. 270. For an excellent overview of the democratic peace literature, see Steve Chan, "In Search of Democratic Peace: Problems and Promise," *Mershon International Studies Review* 41 (May 1997): 59–91.
6. Immanuel Kant, *Idea of a Universal History of a Cosmological Plan* (Hanover, NH: The Sociological Press, 1972), and *Perpetual Peace,* trans. Lewis W. Beck (Indianapolis, IN: Bobbs-Merrill, 1957).
7. On the liberal view of international relations, see Kenneth N. Waltz, *Man, the State and War* (New York: Columbia University Press, 1959), pp. 95–123. See also Michael Howard, *War and the Liberal Conscience* (Oxford: Oxford University Press, 1957).
8. Theodore J. Lowi, *The End of Liberalism: Ideology, Policy, and the Crisis of Public Authority* (New York: Norton, 1969), p. 71.
9. Ibid., pp. 48, 71.
10. See David Truman, *The Governmental Process* (New York: Knopf, 1959), p. ix, 519–20.
11. Robert A. Dahl, *A Preface to Democratic Theory* (Chicago: University of Chicago Press, 1963), p. 173. Also see Harold D. Lasswell, *Politics: Who Gets What, When, How* (New York: McGraw-Hill, 1936), pp. 233–50. Reprinted in Dwaine Marvick, ed., *Harold D. Lasswell on Political Sociology* (Chicago: University of Chicago Press, 1977), pp. 108–13.
12. Dahl, *A Preface to Democratic Theory,* p. 128.
13. Alexis de Tocqueville, *Democracy in America,* ed. Phillips Bradley (New York: Vintage Books, 1954).
14. Richard C. Snyder, H. W. Bruck, and Burton Sapin, *Foreign Policy Decision Making: An Approach to the Study of International Politics* (New York: Free Press, 1962). The work was originally published in 1954. Other important early works include: Joseph Frankel, "Towards a Decision-Making Model in Foreign Policy," *Political Studies* 7 (1959): 1–11, and Karl W. Deutsch, "Mass Communications and the Loss of Freedom in National Decision-Making: A Possible Research Approach to Interstate Conflicts," *Journal of Conflict Resolution* 1 (1957): 200–11.
15. Snyder, Bruck, and Sapin, p. 65.
16. Glen D. Paige, *The Korean Decision* (New York: Free Press, 1968).
17. James N. Rosenau, "Pre-Theories and Theories of Foreign Policy," in *The Scientific Study of Foreign Policy,* 2d ed., rev. and enl., by James N. Rosenau (New York: Nichols, 1980), p. 118.
18. Maurice A. East, Stephen A. Salmone, and Charles F. Hermann, eds., *Why Nations Act: Theoretical Perspectives for Comparative Foreign Policy Studies* (Beverly Hills, CA: Sage Publications, 1978); Patrick J. McGowan and Howard B. Shapiro, *The Comparative Study of Foreign Policy* (Beverly

Hills, CA: Sage Publications, 1973); Jonathan Wilkenfeld, Gerald W. Hopple, Paul J. Rossa, and Stephen J. Andriole, *Foreign Policy Behavior: The Interstate Behavior Analysis Model* (Beverly Hills, CA: Sage Publications, 1980); Wolfram F. Hanrieder, ed., *Comparative Foreign Policy: Theoretical Essays* (New York: David McKay, 1971); James N. Rosenau, ed., *Comparing Foreign Policies: Theories, Findings, and Methods* (Beverly Hills, CA: Sage Publications, 1974); and Douglas J. Murray and Paul R. Viotti, eds., *The Defense Policies of Nations: A Comparative Study* (Baltimore, MD: Johns Hopkins University Press, 1982, 1993).

19. H. N. Hirsch, "Clio on the Couch," *World Politics* 32, no. 3 (April 1980): 406–24; Alexander George, "The Operational Code: A Neglected Approach to the Study of Political Leaders and Decision-Making," *International Studies Quarterly* 13, no. 2 (June 1969): 190–220; Robert Axelrod, ed., *The Structure of Decision* (Princeton, NJ: Princeton University Press, 1976); Harvey Starr, "The Kissinger Years: Studying Individuals and Foreign Policy," *International Studies Quarterly* 24, no. 4 (December 1980): 465–96; and Ole Holsti, "The Operational Code Approach to the Study of Political Leaders," *Canadian Journal of Political Science* 3, no. 1 (March 1970): 123–57.

20. Robert Jervis, *Perception and Misperception in International Politics* (Princeton, NJ: Princeton University Press, 1976), p. 29. See also Jervis, *The Logic of Images in International Relations* (Princeton, NJ: Princeton University Press, 1970); "Cooperation Under the Security Dilemma," *World Politics* 30, no. 2 (January 1978): 167–214; "Deterrence Theory Revisited," *World Politics* 31, no. 2 (January 1979): 289–324.

21. Jervis, *Perception and Misperception*, p. 9.

22. Irving L. Janis, *Victims of Groupthink* (Boston: Houghton Mifflin, 1972), p. 9. See also Janis and Leon Mann, *Decision Making: A Psychological Analysis of Conflict, Choice, and Commitment* (New York: Free Press, 1977).

23. On crises, see Ole Holsti, *Crisis, Escalation, War* (Montreal and London: McGill-Queen's University Press, 1972); Ole Holsti, "Historians, Social Scientists, and Crisis Management," *Journal of Conflict Resolution* 24, no. 4 (December 1980): 665–82; Richard Ned Lebow, *Between Peace and War: The Nature of International Crisis* (Baltimore: Johns Hopkins University Press, 1981). See also Alexander L. George, "Adaptation to Stress in Political Decision Making," in *Coping and Adaptation*, ed. G. Coelho, D. Hamburg, and J. Adams (New York: Basic Books, 1974).

24. Alexander L. George and Richard Smoke, *Deterrence in American Foreign Policy: Theory and Practice* (New York: Columbia University Press, 1974), p. 505.

25. Miriam Steiner, "The Search for Order in a Disorderly World: Worldviews and Prescriptive Decision Paradigms," *International Organization* 37, no. 3 (Summer 1983): 373–413.

26. Judith Goldstein, *Ideas, Interests, and American Trade Policy* (Ithaca: Cornell University Press, 1994). See also Peter Hall, ed., *The Political Power of Economic Ideas: Keynesianism across Nations* (Princeton: Princeton University Press, 1989).

27. See Graham Allison, "Conceptual Models and the Cuban Missile Crisis," *American Political Science Review* 63 (September 1969): 689–718. See also Allison, *Essence of Decision* (Boston, MA: Little, Brown, 1971); Graham Allison and Morton H. Halperin, "Bureaucratic Politics: A Paradigm and Some Policy Implications," in *Theory and Policy in International Relations*, ed. Raymond Tanter and Richard H. Ullman (Princeton, NJ: Princeton University Press, 1972), pp. 40–79; Halperin with Priscilla Clapp and Arnold Kanter, *Bureaucratic Politics and Foreign Policy* (Washington, DC: The Brookings Institution, 1974). See Weber's classic "Parliament and Government in a Reconstructed Germany," in *Economy and Society*, vol. 2, Appendix 2, ed. Guenther Roth and Claus Wittich (New York: Bedminster Press, 1968), pp. 1381–1469.

28. For realist critiques of Allison's work, see Stephen D. Krasner, "Are Bureaucracies Important? (or Allison's Wonderland)," *Foreign Policy* 7 (Summer 1972): 159–79; and Robert J. Art, "Bureaucratic Politics and American Foreign Policy: A Critique," *Policy Sciences* 4, no. 4 (December 1973): 467–90.

29. See Robert Keohane and Joseph Nye, eds., *Transnational Relations and World Politics* (Cambridge, MA: Harvard University Press, 1972) and their later *Power and Interdependence: World Politics in Transition* (Boston: Little, Brown, 1977). In the latter work an attempt is made to blend pluralist and realist approaches.

30. James N. Rosenau, *The Study of Global Interdependence: Essays on the Transnationalisation of World Affairs* (New York: Nichols, 1980), p. 1.

31. For a detailed treatment of the impact of modernization on international relations that resulted from the global spread of the effect of the industrial revolution, see Edward L. Morse, *Modernization and the Transformation of International Relations* (New York: Free Press, 1976). See also John H. Kautsky, *The Political Consequences of Modernization* (New York: Wiley, 1972); and C. E. Black, *The Dynamics of Modernization* (New York: Harper & Row, 1966).

32. For a defense of the concept of the "hard shell" of the state, see Stanley Hoffmann's realist perspective in his "Obstinate or Obsolete? The Fate of the Nation-State and the Case of Western Europe," *Daedalus* 3 (Summer 1966): 862–915. See also Samuel P. Huntington's argument that the state retains control over access to its territory by transnational actors in his "Transnational Organizations in World Politics," *World Politics* 26, no. 3 (April 1973): 333–68.

33. See Ernst B. Haas for the latticework metaphor in his "The Study of Regional Integration: Reflections on the Joy and Anguish of Pretheorizing," in *Regional Integration: Theory and Research,* ed. Leon N. Lindberg and Stuart A. Scheingold (Cambridge, MA: Harvard University Press, 1971) pp. 30–31. For the cobweb image, see Ernst Haas, *Tangle of Hopes: American Commitments and World Order* (Englewood Cliffs, NJ: Prentice-Hall, 1969), Chapter 1; and John W. Burton, *World Society* (Cambridge, England: Cambridge University Press, 1972).

34. See David Mitrany, *A Working Peace System* (Chicago: Quadrangle Books, 1966). See also Mitrany, "The Functional Approach to World Organization," *International Affairs* 24, no. 3 (July 1948): 350–63, and the discussion in Ernst B. Haas, *Beyond the Nation-State* (Stanford, CA: Stanford University Press, 1964), Chapter 1.

35. Ernst B. Haas, *The Uniting of Europe* (Stanford, CA: Stanford University Press, 1958), p. 16. See also the influential work by Karl W. Deutsch and associates, *Political Community and the North Atlantic Area* (Princeton, NJ: Princeton University Press, 1957), p. 5.

36. See Ernst B. Haas, "Turbulent Fields and the Theory of Regional Integration," *International Organization* 30, no. 2 (Spring 1976): 179. This article is a summary of a much more detailed treatment in a monograph by Haas, *The Obsolescence of Regional Integration Theory* (Berkeley: University of California Institute of International Studies, 1975). For antecedents of this argument, see his earlier "Study of Regional Integration."

37. Haas, "Turbulent Fields and Regional Integration," p. 199.

38. Conversation with Ernst Haas, September 1990.

39. Keohane and Nye, *Power and Interdependence,* p. 8.

40. Ibid., p. 9. Alex Inkeles differentiates between "inter-connectedness" or the effect of international transaction flows and "interdependence," which involves some degree of cost for the parties. Alex Inkeles, "The Emerging Social Structure of the World," *World Politics* 27, no. 4 (July 1975): 467–95.

41. See Keohane and Nye, *Power and Interdependence,* pp. 24–29.

42. See Stephen Krasner, ed., *International Regimes* (Ithaca, NY: Cornell University Press, 1983), p. 57. Oran R. Young, "International Regimes: Problems of Concept Formation," *World Politics* 32, no. 3 (April 1980): 331–56; Ernst Haas, Mary Pat Williams, and Don Babai, *Scientists and World Order: The Uses of Technical Knowledge in International Organizations* (Berkeley: University of California Press, 1977); Anthony J. Dolman, *Resources, Regimes, and World Order* (New York: Pergamon Press, 1981); John Gerard Ruggie, "International Organization: A State of the Art on an Art of the State." (Paper presented at the 1985 Annual Meeting of the American Political Science Association, New Orleans, August 29–September 1, 1985).

43. Stephen D. Krasner, "Structural Causes and Regime Consequences: Regimes as Intervening Variables," in *International Regimes,* ed. Stephen D. Krasner (Ithaca: Cornell University Press, 1983), p. 2.

44. Andreas Hansenclever, Peter Mayer, and Volker Rittberger, "Interests, Power, Knowledge: The Study of International Regimes," *Mershon International Studies Review* 40, no. 2 (October 1996): 177–228.

45. Stephen D. Krasner, "Global Communications and National Power: Life on the Pareto Frontier," *World Politics* 43 (1991): 363.

46. Robert O. Keohane, "Neoliberal Institutionalism: A Perspective on World Politics," in *International Institutions and State Power: Essays in International Relations Theory,* ed. Robert O. Keohane (Boulder, CO: Westview Press, 1989), p. 2.

47. See Joseph Grieco, *Cooperation among Nations* (Ithaca, NY: Cornell University Press, 1990), especially pp. 27–50.

48. Peter M. Haas, "Introduction: Epistemic Communities and International Policy Coordination," *International Organization* 46 (1992): 3.

49. Friedrich V. Kratochwil and John Gerard Ruggie, "International Organization: A State of the Art on an Art of the State," *International Organization* 40 (1986): 764, 766.

50. Alexander Wendt, "Collective Identity Formation and the International State," *American Political Science Review* 88 (1994): 389.

51. Ernst B. Haas, "Words Can Hurt You: Or Who Said What to Whom About Regimes," in *International Regimes,* ed. Stephen Krasner, p. 57. See also George Modelski's linking of learning and his long cycles theory in "Is World Politics Evolutionary Learning?" *International Organization* 44, no. 1 (Winter 1990): 1–24.

52. Peter Alexis Gourevitch, "Squaring the Circle: The Domestic Sources of International Cooperation," *International Organization* 50, no. 2 (Spring 1996): 349–73; Peter J. Katzenstein, ed., *Between Power and Plenty: Foreign Economic Policies of Advanced Industrial States* (Madison: University of Wisconsin Press, 1978); Peter F. Cowhey, "Domestic Institutions and the Credibility of International Commitments: Japan and the United States," *International Organization* 47, no. 2 (Spring 1993): 299–326.

53. Thomas Risse-Kappen, *Bringing Transnational Relations Back In* (Cambridge, England: Cambridge University Press, 1995).

54. See Ernst B. Haas, "On Systems and International Regimes," *World Politics* 27, no. 2 (January 1975): 152–53.

55. One approach to understanding transaction and communications flows in the international system is through the construction of cybernetic models. For example, see Karl W. Deutsch, *The Nerves of Government* (New York: Free Press, 1964).

56. Ronnie D. Lipschutz, "Reconstructing World Politics: The Emergence of Global Civil Society," *Millennium* 21, no. 3 (1992): 389–420; Paul Wapner, "Politics beyond the State: Environmental Activism and World Civic Politics," *World Politics* 47 (April 1995): 311–40.

57. See James N. Rosenau, ed., *Linkage Politics: Essays on the Convergence of National and International Systems* (New York: Free Press, 1969) and an earlier piece by Fred A. Sondermann, "The Linkage between Foreign Policy and International Politics," in *International Politics and Foreign Policy,* ed. James N. Rosenau (New York, Free Press, 1961), pp. 8–17.

58. See Richard Rosecrance and associates, "Whither Interdependence?" *International Organization* 31, no. 3 (Summer 1977): 425–71; Mary Ann Tetreault, "Measuring Interdependence," *International Organization* 34, no. 3 (Summer 1980): 429–43; and rejoinder by Rosecrance and William Gutowitz, followed by Tetreault's response in *International Organization,* 35, no. 3 (Summer 1981): 553–60.

59. For an antidote to the conventional wisdom that the effects of increased interdependence are benign and therefore desirable, see the realist critique of interdependence in Kenneth N. Waltz, "The Myth of National Interdependence," *The International Corporation,* ed. Charles P. Kindleberger (Cambridge, MA: MIT Press, 1970), pp. 205–23.

60. For an example, see Richard A. Falk, *A Study of Future Worlds* (New York: Free Press, 1975).

61. See Ernst B. Haas, *When Knowledge Is Power* (Berkeley: University of California Press, 1990) and James N. Rosenau, *Turbulence in World Politics* (Princeton, NJ: Princeton University Press, 1990).

62. See Christopher Layne, "1914 Revisited: A Reply to Miles Kahler," *Orbis* 14, no. 4 (Winter 1981): 719–50.

63. Ernst B. Haas, *When Knowledge Is Power* (Berkeley: University of California Press, 1990), p. 11. See the article drawn from this book and reprinted here as "Multilaterlism, Knowledge, and Power."

64. Ernst B. Haas, *Nationalism, Liberalism, and Progress* (Ithaca, NY: Cornell University Press, 1997), p. 3.

65. *Ibid.*, p. 2, citing Wolfgang Schluchter, *The Rise of Western Rationalism: Max Weber's Developmental History* (Berkeley: University of California Press, 1981), p. 25.
66. *Ibid.*, especially, pp. 322–23.
67. *Ibid.*, p. 322.

SELECTIONS FOR FURTHER READING AND REFERENCE

General

Burton, John W. *World Society*. New York: Cambridge University Press, 1972.

North, Robert C. *War, Peace, Survival: Global Politics and Conceptual Synthesis*. Boulder, CO: Westview, 1990.

Rosenau, James N. *Along the Domestic–Foreign Frontier: Exploring Governance in a Turbulent World*. New York: Cambridge University Press, 1997.

———. *Turbulence and World Politics: A Theory of Change and Continuity*. Princeton, NJ: Princeton University Press, 1990.

Rosenau, James N., and Ernst-Otto Czempiel, eds. *Governance without Government: Order and Change in World Politics*. New York: Cambridge University Press, 1992.

Rosenau, James N., and W. Michael Fagen. "A New Dynamism in World Politics: Increasingly Skillful Individuals?" *International Studies Quarterly* 41, 4 (December 1997): 655–86.

Ruggie, John G. *International Transformations: Essays in Continuity and Change*. London: Routledge, 1998.

Snyder, Jack, and Robert Jervis, eds. *Coping with Complexity in the International System*. Boulder, CO: Westview, 1993.

On the Relation between Democracy and Peace

Chan, Steve. "In Search of Democratic Peace: Problems and Promise." *Mershon International Studies Review* 41 (1997): 59–91.

Doyle, Michael W. *Ways of War and Peace*. New York: W. W. Norton, 1997. [Part Two addresses Liberalism.]

Mansfield, Edward D., and Jack Snyder. "Democratization and the Danger of War." *International Security* 20, 1 (1995): 5–38.

Maoz, Zeev, and Bruce Russett. "Normative and Structural Causes of Democratic Peace, 1946–86." *American Political Science Review* 87 (1993): 624–38.

Owen, John. "How Liberalism Produces Democratic Peace." *International Security* 19, 2 (1994): 87–125.

Russett, Bruce M. *Grasping the Democratic Peace*. Princeton, NJ: Princeton University Press, 1993.

Institutions, Cognition, and Social Constructivism

Adler, Emanuel and Beverly Crawford, eds. *Progress in Postwar International Relations*. New York: Columbia University Press, 1991.

Berger, Peter L., and Thomas Luckmann. *The Social Construction of Reality: A Treatise in the Sociology of Knowledge*. New York: Doubleday, 1966.

Finnemore, Martha. "Sociology's Institutionalism." *International Organization* 50, 2 (Spring 1996): 325–47.

Goldstein, Judith, and Robert O. Keohane. *Ideas and Foreign Policy: Beliefs, Institutions, and Political Change*. Ithaca, NY: Cornell University Press, 1993.

Haas, Ernst B. *Nationalism, Liberalism, and Progress*. Ithaca, NY: Cornell University Press, 1997.

———. *When Knowledge Is Power: Three Models of Change in International Organizations*. Berkeley: University of California Press, 1990.

Haas, Ernst B., Mary Pat Williams, and Don Babai. *Scientists and World Order: The Uses of Technical Knowledge in International Organizations*. Berkeley: University of California Press, 1977.

Haas, Peter M. *Knowledge, Power, and International Policy Coordination*. Columbia: University of South Carolina Press, 1997.

————. Special Issue on Epistemic Communities. *International Organization* 46 (Winter 1992).

Haas, Peter M., Robert Keohane, and Marc A. Levy, eds. *Institutions for the Earth*. Cambridge, MA: MIT Press, 1993.

Hawdon, James. *Emerging Organizational Forms: The Proliferation of Regional Intergovernmental Organizations in the Modern World System*. Westport, CT: Greenwood Press, 1996.

Kahler, Miles. *International Institutions and the Political Economy of Integration*. Washington, DC: Brookings Institution, 1995.

Katzenstein, Peter J., and Alexander Wendt, eds. *The Culture of National Security: Norms and Identity in World Politics*. New York: Columbia University Press, 1996.

Keohane, Robert O. "International Institutions: Two Approaches." *International Studies Quarterly* 32, 4 (December 1988): 379–96.

Keohane, Robert, and Stanley Hoffmann, eds. *The New European Community: Decisionmaking and Institutional Change*. Boulder, CO: Westview, 1991.

Lapid, Yosef, and Friedrich Kratochwil. *The Return of Culture and Identity in International Relations Theory*. Boulder, CO: Lynne Rienner, 1996.

Lipschutz, Ronnie D. "Reconstructing World Politics: The Emergence of Global Civil Society." *Millennium* 21, 3 (1992): 389–420.

Mearsheimer, John J. "The False Promise of International Institutions." *International Security* 19, 3 (Winter 1994): 5–49. [A realist critique of a pluralist enterprise.]

Risse-Kappen, Thomas. *Bringing Transnational Relations Back In: Non-State Actors, Domestic Structures and International Institutions*. New York: Cambridge University Press, 1995.

Ruggie, John G. *Multilateralism Matters: The Theory and Praxis of an Institutional Form*. New York: Columbia University Press, 1993.

————. *Winning the Peace*. New York: Columbia University Press, 1996.

Wendt, Alexander. "The Agent–Structure Problem in International Relations Theory." *International Organization* 41 (1987): 335–70.

————. "Collective Identity Formation and the International State." *American Political Science Review* 88, No. 2 (June 1994): 384–96.

————. "Constructing International Politics." *International Security* 20 (1995): 71–81.

————. *Social Theory of International Politics*. New York: Cambridge University Press, 1998.

Wendt, Alexander, and Michael Barnett. "Dependent State Formation and Third World Militarization." *Review of International Studies* 19 (1993): 321–47.

On the Construction of Regimes

Adler, Emanuel and Beverly Crawford, eds. *Progress in Postwar International Relations*. New York: Columbia University Press, 1991.

Donnelly, Jack. "International Human Rights: A Regime Analysis." *International Organization* 40, 3 (Summer 1986): 599–642.

Haas, Ernst B. "Is There a Hole in the Whole? Knowledge, Technology, Interdependence, and the Construction of International Regimes." *International Organization* 29, 3 (Summer 1975): 827–76.

————. "Why Collaborate? Issue-Linkage and International Regimes." *World Politics* 32, 3 (April 1980): 357–405.

Haas, Peter M. "Do Regimes Matter? Epistemic Communities and Mediterranean Pollution Control." *International Organization* 43, 3 (Summer 1989): 377–403.

Hasenclever, Andreas, Peter Mayer, and Volker Rittberger. "Interests, Power, Knowledge: The Study of International Regimes." *Mershon Studies International Review* 40, 2 (October 1996): 177–228.

Krasner, Stephen D., ed. *International Regimes*. Ithaca, NY: Cornell University Press, 1983.

Rittberger, Volker, ed. *Regime Theory and International Relations*. Oxford: Clarendon Press, 1993.

Young, Oran R. "The Politics of International Regime Formation." *International Organization* 43, 3 (Summer 1989): 349–75.

Young, Oran R., and Gail Osherenko, eds. *Polar Politics: Creating International Environmental Regimes*. Ithaca, NY: Cornell University Press, 1993.

Earlier Work on Transnationalism, Interdependence, and Integration

Deutsch, Karl, et al. *Political Community and the North Atlantic Area*. Princeton, NJ: Princeton University Press, 1957.

Etzioni, Amitai. *Political Unification*. New York: Holt, Rinehart & Winston, 1965.

Galtung, Johan. "A Structural Theory of Integration." *Journal of Peace Research* 5 (1968): 375–95.

Haas, Ernst B. *Beyond the Nation-State*. Stanford, CA: Stanford University Press, 1964.

———. "Turbulent Fields and the Theory of Regional Integration." *International Organization* 30, 2 (Spring 1976): 173–212.

Keohane, Robert O., and Joseph S. Nye, Jr. "International Interdependence and Integration." In *Handbook of Political Science,* Vol. 8, ed. Fred I. Greenstein and Nelson W. Polsby. Reading, MA: Addison-Wesley, 1975: 363–414.

———. *Power and Interdependence*. Boston: Little, Brown, 1977.

———. "Power and Interdependence Revisited." *International Organization* 41, 4 (Autumn 1987): 725–53.

———. "Transgovernmental Relations and International Organization." *World Politics* 27, 1 (October 1974): 39–62.

———, eds. *Transnational Relations and World Politics*. Cambridge, MA: Harvard University Press, 1971.

Lindberg, Leon N., and Stuart A. Scheingold, eds. *Regional Integration: Theory and Research*. Cambridge, MA: Harvard University Press, 1971.

Mitrany, David. *A Working Peace System*. Chicago: Quadrangle Books, 1966.

Modelski, George, ed. *Transnational Corporations and World Order*. San Francisco: W. H. Freeman and Co., 1979.

Morse, Edward L. *Modernization and the Transformation of International Relations*. New York: Free Press, 1976.

Nye, Joseph S. *Peace in Parts: Integration and Conflict in Regional Organization*. Boston, MA: Little, Brown, 1971.

Ruggie, John Gerard, ed. *The Antinomies of Interdependence*. New York: Columbia University Press, 1983.

Tsoukalis, Loukas. *The New European Economy: The Politics and Economics of Integration*. New York: Oxford University Press, 1991.

Vernon, Raymond. *Sovereignty at Bay: The Multinational Spread of U.S. Enterprises*. New York: Basic Books, 1971.

Earlier Work on Bureaucracies and Decision Making in Foreign Policy

Allison, Graham. *Essence of Decision*. Boston: Little, Brown, 1971.

Bendor, Jonathan. "Rethinking Allison's Models." *American Political Science Review* 86, 2 (June 1992): 301–22.

George, Alexander. "The Operational Code: A Neglected Approach to the Study of Political Leaders and Decision-Making." *International Studies Quarterly* 13, 2 (June 1969): 190–222.

Hermann, Margaret G., and Charles F. Hermann. "Who Makes Foreign Policy Decisions and How: An Empirical Inquiry." *International Studies Quarterly* 33, 4 (December 1989): 361–87.

Holsti, Ole R., and James N. Rosenau. "The Foreign Policy Beliefs of American Leaders: Some Further Thoughts on Theory and Method." *International Studies Quarterly* 30, 4 (December 1986): 375–409 and 473–84.

Janis, Irving L. *Victims of Groupthink*. Boston: Houghton Mifflin, 1972.

Jervis, Robert. *Perception and Misperception in International Politics*. Princeton, NJ: Princeton University Press, 1976.

Jervis, Robert, Richard Ned Lebow, and Janice Gross Stein. *Psychology and Deterrence*. Baltimore: Johns Hopkins University Press, 1985.

Levy, Jack F. "Misperception and the Causes of War." *World Politics* 36, 1 (October 1983): 76–99.

———. "Organization Routines and the Causes of War." *International Studies Quarterly* 30, 2 (June 1986): 193–222.

Neustadt, Richard E., and Ernest R. May. *Thinking in Time: The Uses of History for Decision Makers.* New York: Free Press, 1986.

Putnam, Robert D. "Diplomacy and Domestic Politics: The Logic of Two-Level Games." *International Organization* 42, 3 (Summer 1988): 427–60.

Snyder, Richard C., H. W. Bruck, and Burton Sapin. *Decisionmaking as an Approach to the Study of International Politics.* Princeton, NJ: Princeton University Press, 1954.

Steinbruner, John D. *The Cybernetic Theory of Decision.* Princeton, NJ: Princeton University Press, 1974.

Pluralist and Neoliberal Critiques of Realism and Neorealism

Baldwin, David A., ed. *Neorealism and Neoliberalism: The Contemporary Debate.* New York: Columbia University Press, 1993.

Grieco, Joseph M. "Anarchy and the Limits of Cooperation." *International Organization* 42, 3 (Summer 1988): 485–506.

Haas, Ernst B. "The Balance of Power: Prescription, Concept or Propaganda?" *World Politics* 5, 4 (July 1953): 442–77.

Kegley, Charles W., ed. *Controversies in International Relations Theory: Realism and the Neoliberal Challenge.* New York: St. Martin's, 1995.

Keohane, Robert O. *After Hegemony: Cooperation and Discord in the World Political Economy.* Princeton, NJ: Princeton University Press, 1984.

———. *International Institutions and State Power.* Boulder, CO: Westview, 1989.

———. ed. *Neorealism and Its Critics.* New York: Columbia University Press, 1986.

Keohane, Robert O., and Joseph S. Nye. *Power and Interdependence.* Boston: Little, Brown, 1977.

Mercer, Jonathan. *Reputation and International Politics.* Ithaca, NY: Cornell University Press, 1996.

Nye, Joseph. "Neorealism and Neoliberalism." *World Politics.* 40, 2 (January 1988): 235–51.

Sagan, Scott, and Kenneth N. Waltz. *The Spread of Nuclear Weapons: A Debate.* New York: W. W. Norton, 1995. [With his focus on organization theory, Sagan represents more of a pluralist understanding in contrast to Waltz's realism.]

Vasquez, John A. "The Realist Paradigm and Degenerative versus Progressive Research Programs." *American Political Science Review* 91, 4 (December 1997): 899–912.

———. *The War Puzzle.* Cambridge, England: Cambridge University Press, 1993.

Wendt, Alexander E. "The Agent–Structure Problem in International Relations Theory." *International Organization* 41, 3 (Summer 1987): 335–70.

Liberalism and World Politics

MICHAEL W. DOYLE

Building on a growing literature in international political science, the author reexamines the traditional liberal claim that governments founded on a respect for individual liberty exercise "restraint" and "peaceful intentions" in their foreign policy. He looks at three distinct theoretical traditions of liberalism, attributable to three theorists: Schumpeter, a democratic capitalist whose explanation of liberal pacifism we often invoke; Machiavelli, a classical republican whose glory is an imperialism we often practice; and Kant, a liberal republican whose theory of internationalism best accounts for what we aspire to be. Despite the contradictions of liberal pacifism and liberal imperialism, Professor Doyle finds, with Kant and other democratic republicans, that liberalism does leave a coherent legacy on foreign affairs. Liberal states are different and indeed peaceful, yet they are also prone at times to make war. Building upon Doyle's work and the theorists he cites, scholars in recent years have conceptually developed and empirically tested some of the arguments presented in this article, which is an excellent introduction to an extensive "democratic peace" literature.

I look at three distinct theoretical traditions of liberalism, attributable to three theorists: Schumpeter, a brilliant explicator of . . . liberal pacifism . . . ; Machiavelli, a classical republican whose glory is an imperialism we often practice; and Kant.

Despite the contradictions of liberal pacifism and liberal imperialism, I find, with Kant and other liberal republicans, that liberalism does leave a coherent legacy on foreign affairs. Liberal states are different. They are indeed peaceful, yet they are also prone to make war. . . . Liberal states have created a separate peace, as Kant argued they would, and have also discovered liberal reasons for aggression, as he feared they might. I conclude by arguing that the differences among liberal pacifism, liberal imperi-

alism, and Kant's liberal internationalism are not arbitrary but rooted in differing conceptions of the citizen and the state.

Liberal Pacifism

There is no canonical description of liberalism. What we tend to call *liberal* resembles a family portrait of principles and institutions, recognizable by certain characteristics—for example, individual freedom, political participation, private property, and equality of opportunity—that most liberal states share, although none has perfected them all. Joseph Schumpeter clearly fits within this family when he considers the international effects of capitalism and democracy.

Schumpeter's "Sociology of Imperialisms," published in 1919, made a coherent and sustained argument concerning the pacifying (in the sense of nonaggressive) effects of liberal institutions and principles (Schumpeter, 1955; see also Doyle, 1986, pp. 155–59). Unlike some of the earlier liberal theorists who focused on a single feature such as trade or failed to examine critically the arguments they were advancing, Schumpeter saw the interaction of capitalism and democracy as the foundation of liberal pacifism, and he tested his arguments in a sociology of historical imperialisms.

He defines *imperialism* as "an objectless disposition on the part of a state to unlimited forcible expansion" (Schumpeter, 1955, p. 6). Excluding imperialisms that were mere "catchwords" and those that were "objectful" (e.g., defensive imperialism), he traces the roots of objectless imperialism to three sources, each an atavism. Modern imperialism, according to Schumpeter, resulted from the combined impact of a "war machine," warlike instincts, and export monopolism.

Once necessary, the war machine later developed a life of its own and took control of a state's foreign policy: "Created by the wars that required it, the machine now created the wars it required" (Schumpeter, 1995, p. 25). Thus, Schumpeter tells us that the army of ancient Egypt, created to drive the Hyksos out of Egypt, took over the state and pursued militaristic imperialism. Like the later armies of the courts of absolutist Europe, it fought wars for the sake of glory and booty, for the sake of warriors and monarchs—wars *gratia* warriors.

A warlike disposition, elsewhere called "instinctual elements of bloody primitivism," is the natural ideology of a war machine. It also exists independently; the Persians, says Schumpeter (1955, pp. 25–32), were a warrior nation from the outset.

Under modern capitalism, export monopolists, the third source of modern imperialism, push for imperialist expansion as a way to expand their closed markets. The absolute monarchies were the last clear-cut imperialisms. Nineteenth-century imperialisms merely represent the vestiges of the imperialisms created by Louis XIV and Catherine the Great. Thus, the export monopolists are an atavism of the absolute monarchies, for they depend completely on the tariffs imposed by the monarchs and their militaristic successors for revenue (Schumpeter, 1955, pp. 82–83). Without tariffs, monopolies would be eliminated by foreign competition.

Modern (nineteenth century) imperialism, therefore, rests on an atavistic war machine, militaristic attitudes left over from the days of monarchical wars, and export monopolism, which is nothing more than the economic residue of monarchical finance. In the modern era, imperialists gratify their private interests. From the national perspective, their imperialistic wars are objectless.

Schumpeter's theme now emerges. Capitalism and democracy are forces for peace. Indeed, they are antithetical to imperialism. For Schumpeter, the further development of capitalism and democracy means that imperialism will inevitably disappear. He maintains that capitalism produces an unwarlike disposition; its populace is "democratized, individualized, rationalized" (Schumpeter, 1955, p. 68). The people's energies are daily absorbed in production. The disciplines of industry and the market train people in "economic rationalism"; the instability of industrial life necessitates calculation. Capitalism also "individualizes"; "subjective opportunities" replace the "immutable factors" of traditional, hierarchical society. Rational individuals demand democratic governance.

Democratic capitalism leads to peace. As evidence, Schumpeter claims that throughout the capitalist world an opposition has arisen to "war, expansion, cabinet diplomacy"; that contemporary capitalism is associated with peace parties; and that the industrial worker of capitalism is "vigorously anti-imperialist." In addition, he points out that the capitalist world has developed means of preventing war, such as the Hague Court and that the least feudal, most capitalist society—the United States—has demonstrated the least imperialistic tendencies (Schumpeter, 1955, pp. 95–96). An example of the lack of imperialistic tendencies in the U.S., Schumpeter thought, was our leaving over half of Mexico unconquered in the war of 1846–48.

Schumpeter's explanation for liberal pacifism is quite simple: Only war profiteers and military aristocrats gain from wars. No democracy would pursue a minority interest and tolerate the high costs of imperialism. When free trade prevails, "no class" gains from forcible expansion because

> raw materials and food stuffs are as accessible to each nation as though they were in its own territory. Where the cultural backwardness of a region makes normal economic intercourse dependent on colonization it does not matter, assuming free trade, which of the "civilized" nations undertakes the task of colonization. (Schumpeter, 1955, pp. 75–76)

Schumpeter's arguments are difficult to evaluate. In partial tests of quasi-Schumpeterian propositions, Michael Haas (1974, pp. 464–65) discovered a cluster that associates democracy, development, and sustained modernization with peaceful conditions. However, M. Small and J. D. Singer (1976) have discovered that there is no clearly negative correlation between democracy and war in the period 1816–1965—the period that would be central to Schumpeter's argument.

Later in his career, in *Capitalism, Socialism, and Democracy*, Schumpeter (1950, pp. 127–28) acknowledged that "almost purely bourgeois commonwealths were often aggressive when it seemed to pay—like the Athenian or the Venetian commonwealths." Yet he stuck to his pacifistic guns, restating the view that capitalist democracy "steadily tells . . . against the use of military force and for peaceful arrangements, even when the balance of pecuniary advantage is clearly on the side of war which, under modern circumstances, is not in general very likely" (Schumpeter, 1950, p. 128). A . . . study by R. J. Rummel (1983) of "libertarianism" and international violence is the closest test Schumpeterian pacifism has received. "Free" states (those enjoying political and economic freedom) were shown to have considerably less conflict at or above the level of economic sanctions than "nonfree" states. The free states, the partly free states (including the democratic socialist countries such as Sweden), and the nonfree states accounted for 24%, 26%, and 61%, respectively, of the international violence during the period examined.

These effects are impressive but not conclusive for the Schumpeterian thesis. The data are limited, in this test, to the period 1976 to 1980. It includes, for example, the Russo-Afghan War, the Vietnamese invasion of Cambodia, China's invasion of Vietnam, and Tanzania's invasion of Uganda but just misses the U.S., quasi-covert intervention in Angola (1975) and our not so covert war against Nicaragua. More importantly, it excludes the cold war period, with its numerous interventions, and the long history of colonial wars (the Boer War, the Spanish-American War, the Mexican Intervention, etc.) that marked the history of liberal, including democratic capitalist, states.

The discrepancy between the warlike history of liberal states and Schumpeter's pacifistic expectations highlights three extreme assumptions. First, his "materialistic monism" leaves little room for noneconomic objectives, whether espoused by states or individuals. Neither glory, nor prestige, nor ideological justification, nor the pure power of ruling shapes policy. These nonmaterial goals leave little room for positive-sum gains, such as the comparative advantages of trade. Second, and relatedly, the same is true for his states. The political life of individuals seems to have been homogenized at the same time as the individuals were "rationalized, individualized, and democratized." Citizens—capitalists and workers, rural and urban—seek material welfare. Schumpeter seems to presume that ruling makes no difference. He also presumes that no one is prepared to take those measures (such as stirring up foreign quarrels to preserve a domestic ruling coalition) that enhance one's political power, despite detrimental effects on mass welfare. Third, like domestic politics, world politics are homogenized. Materially monistic and democratically capitalist, all states evolve toward free trade and liberty together. Countries differently constituted seem to disappear from Schumpeter's analysis. "Civilized" nations govern "culturally backward" *regions*. These assumptions are not shared by Machiavelli's theory of liberalism.

Liberal Imperialism

Machiavelli argues, not only that republics are not pacifistic, but that they are the best form of state for imperial expansion. Establishing a republic fit for imperial expansion is, moreover, the best way to guarantee the survival of a state.

Machiavelli's republic is a classical mixed republic. It is not a democracy—which he thought would quickly degenerate into a tyranny—but is characterized by social equality, popular liberty, and political participation (Machiavelli, 1950, bk. 1, chap. 2, p. 112). The consuls serve as "kings," the senate as an aristocracy managing the state, and the people in the assembly as the source of strength.

Liberty results from "disunion"—the competition and necessity for compromise required by the division of powers among senate, consuls, and tribunes (the last representing the common people). Liberty also results from the popular veto. The powerful few threaten the rest with tyranny Machiavelli says because they seek to dominate. The mass demands not to be dominated, and their veto thus preserves the liberties of the state (Machiavelli, 1950, bk. 1, chap. 5, p. 122). However, since the people and the rulers

have different social characters, the people need to be "managed" by the few to avoid having their recklessness overturn or their fecklessness undermine the ability of the state to expand (Machiavelli, 1950, bk. 1, chap. 53, pp. 249–50). Thus the senate and the consuls plan expansion, consult oracles, and employ religion to manage the resources that the energy of the people supplies.

Strength, and then imperial expansion, results from the way liberty encourages increased population and property, which grow when the citizens know their lives and goods are secure from arbitrary seizure. Free citizens equip large armies and provide soldiers who fight for public glory and the common good because these are, in fact, their own (Machiavelli, 1950, bk. 2, chap. 2, pp. 287–90). If you seek the honor of having your state expand, Machiavelli advises, you should organize it as a free and popular republic like Rome, rather than as an aristocratic republic like Sparta or Venice. Expansion thus calls for a free republic.

"Necessity"—political survival—calls for expansion. If a stable aristocratic republic is forced by foreign conflict "to extend her territory, in such a case we shall see her foundations give way and herself quickly brought to ruin"; if, on the other hand, domestic security prevails, "the continued tranquility would enervate her, or provoke internal dissensions, which together, or either of them separately, will apt to prove her ruin" (Machiavelli, 1950, bk. 1, chap. 6, p. 129). Machiavelli therefore believes it is necessary to take the constitution of Rome, rather than that of Sparta or Venice, as our model.

Hence, this belief leads to liberal imperialism. We are lovers of glory, Machiavelli announces. We seek to rule or, at least, to avoid being oppressed. In either case, we want more for ourselves and our states than just material welfare (materialistic monism). Because other states with similar aims thereby threaten us, we prepare ourselves for expansion. Because our fellow citizens threaten us if we do not allow them either to satisfy their ambition or to release their political energies through imperial expansion, we expand.

There is considerable historical evidence for liberal imperialism. Machiavelli's (Polybius's) Rome and Thucydides' Athens both were imperial republics in the Machiavellian sense (Thucydides, 1954, bk. 6). The historical record of numerous U.S. interventions in the postwar period supports Machiavelli's argument, but the current record of liberal pacifism, weak as it is, calls some of his insights into question. To the extent that the modern populace actually controls (and thus unbalances) the mixed republic, its diffidence may outweigh elite ("senatorial") aggressiveness.

We can conclude either that (1) liberal pacifism has at least taken over with the further development of capitalist democracy, as Schumpeter predicted it would or that (2) the mixed record of liberalism—pacifism and imperialism—indicates that some liberal states are Schumpeterian democracies while others are Machiavellian republics. Before we accept either conclusion, however, we must consider a third apparent regularity of modern world politics.

Liberal Internationalism

Modern liberalism carries with it two legacies. They do not affect liberal states separately, according to whether they are pacifistic or imperialistic, but simultaneously.

The first of these legacies is the pacification of foreign relations among liberal states.[1] During the nineteenth century, the United States and Great Britain engaged in nearly continual strife; however, after the Reform Act of 1832 defined actual representation as the formal source of the sovereignty of the British parliament, Britain and the United States negotiated their disputes. They negotiated despite, for example, British grievances during the Civil War against the North's blockade of the South, with which Britain had close economic ties. Despite

severe Anglo-French colonial rivalry, liberal France and liberal Britain formed an entente against illiberal Germany before World War I. And from 1914 to 1915, Italy, the liberal member of the Triple Alliance with Germany and Austria, chose not to fulfill its obligations under that treaty to support its allies. Instead, Italy joined in an alliance with Britain and France, which prevented it from having to fight other liberal states and then declared war on Germany and Austria. Despite generations of Anglo-American tension and Britain's wartime restrictions on American trade with Germany, the United States leaned toward Britain and France from 1914 to 1917 before entering World War I on their side.

Beginning in the eighteenth century and slowly growing since then, a zone of peace, which Kant called the "pacific federation" or "pacific union," has begun to be established among liberal societies. More than 40 liberal states currently make up the union. Most are in Europe and North America, but they can be found on every continent.

Here the predictions of liberal pacifists (and President Reagan) are borne out: liberal states do exercise peaceful restraint, and a separate peace exists among them. This separate peace provides a solid foundation for the United States' crucial alliances with the liberal powers, e.g., the North Atlantic Treaty Organization and our Japanese alliance. This foundation appears to be impervious to the quarrels with our allies that bedeviled the Carter and Reagan administrations. It also offers the promise of a continuing peace among liberal states, and as the number of liberal states increases, it announces the possibility of global peace this side of the grave or world conquest.

Of course, the probability of the outbreak of war in any given year between any two given states is low. The occurrence of a war between any two adjacent states, considered over a long period of time, would be more probable. The apparent absence of war between liberal states, whether adjacent or not, for almost 200 years thus may have significance. Similar claims cannot be made for feudal, fascist, communist, authoritarian, or totalitarian forms of rule (Doyle, 1983a, pp. 222), nor for pluralistic or merely similar societies. More significant perhaps is that when states are forced to decide on which side of an impending world war they will fight, liberal states all wind up on the same side despite the complexity of the paths that take them there. These characteristics do not prove that the peace among liberals is statistically significant nor that liberalism is the sole valid explanation for the peace.[2] They do suggest that we consider the possibility that liberals have indeed established a separate peace—but only among themselves.

Liberalism also carries with it a second legacy: international "imprudence" (Hume, 1963, pp. 346–47). Peaceful restraint only seems to work in liberals' relations with other liberals. Liberal states have fought numerous wars with non-liberal states.

Many of these wars have been defensive and thus prudent by necessity. Liberal states have been attacked and threatened by nonliberal states that do not exercise any special restraint in their dealings with the liberal states. Authoritarian rulers both stimulate and respond to an international political environment in which conflicts of prestige, interest, and pure fear of what other states might do all lead states toward war. War and conquest have thus characterized the careers of many authoritarian rulers and ruling parties, from Louis XIV and Napoleon to Mussolini's fascists, Hitler's Nazis, and Stalin's communists.

Yet we cannot simply blame warfare on the authoritarians or totalitarians, as many of our more enthusiastic politicians would have us do. Most wars arise out of calculations and miscalculations of interest, misunderstandings, and mutual suspicions, such as those that characterized the origins of World War I. However, aggression by the liberal state has also character-

ized a large number of wars. Both France and Britain fought expansionist colonial wars throughout the nineteenth century. The United States fought a similar war with Mexico from 1846 to 1848, waged a war of annihilation against the American Indians, and intervened militarily against sovereign states many times before and after World War II. Liberal states invade weak nonliberal states and display striking distrust in dealings with powerful nonliberal states (Doyle, 1983b).

Neither realist (statist) nor Marxist theory accounts well for these two legacies. While they can account for aspects of certain periods of international stability, neither the logic of the balance of power nor the logic of international hegemony explains the separate peace maintained for more than 150 years among states sharing one particular form of governance—liberal principles and institutions. Balance-of-power theory expects—indeed is premised upon—flexible arrangements of geostrategic rivalry that include preventive war. Hegemonies wax and wane, but the liberal peace holds. Marxist "ultra-imperialists" expect a form of peaceful rivalry among capitalists, but only liberal capitalists maintain peace. Leninists expect liberal capitalists to be aggressive toward nonliberal states, but they also (and especially) expect them to be imperialistic toward fellow liberal capitalists.

Kant's theory of liberal internationalism helps us understand these two legacies. The importance of Immanuel Kant as a theorist of international ethics has been well appreciated, but Kant also has an important analytical theory of international politics. *Perpetual Peace,* written in 1795 (Kant, 1970, pp. 93–130), helps us understand the interactive nature of international relations. Kant tries to teach us methodologically that we can study neither the systemic relations of states nor the varieties of state behavior in isolation from each other. Substantively, he anticipates for use the ever-widening pacification of a liberal pacific union, explains this pacification, and at the same time suggests why liberal states are not pacific in their relations with nonliberal states. Kant argues that perpetual peace will be guaranteed by the ever-widening acceptance of three "definitive articles" of peace. When all nations have accepted the definitive articles in a metaphorical "treaty" of perpetual peace he asks them to sign, perpetual peace will have been established.

The First Definitive Article requires the civil constitution of the state to be republican. By *republican* Kant means a political society that has solved the problem of combining moral autonomy, individualism, and social order. A private property and market-oriented economy partially addressed that dilemma in the private sphere. The public, or political, sphere was more troubling. His answer was a republic that preserved juridical freedom—the legal equality of citizens as subjects—on the basis of a representative government with a separation of powers. Juridical freedom is preserved because the morally autonomous individual is by means of representation a self-legislator making laws that apply to all citizens equally, including himself or herself. Tyranny is avoided because the individual is subject to laws he or she does not also administer (Kant, *PP*, pp. 99–102).[3]

Liberal republics will progressively establish peace among themselves by means of the pacific federation, or union (*foedus pacificum*), described in Kant's Second Definitive Article. The pacific union will establish peace within a federation of free states and securely maintain the rights of each state. The world will not have achieved the "perpetual peace" that provides the ultimate guarantor of republican freedom until "a late stage and after many unsuccessful attempts" (Kant, *UH*, p. 47). At that time, all nations will have learned the lessons of peace through right conceptions of the appropriate constitution, great and sad experience, and good will. Only then will individuals enjoy perfect republican rights or the full guarantee of a global and just peace. In the meantime, the "pacific

federation" of liberal republics—"an enduring and gradually expanding federation likely to prevent war"—brings within it more and more republics—despite republican collapses, backsliding, and disastrous wars—creating an ever-expanding separate peace (Kant, *PP*, p. 105).[4] Kant emphasizes that

> it can be shown that this idea of federalism, extending gradually to encompass all states and thus leading to perpetual peace, is practicable and has objective reality. For if by good fortune one powerful and enlightened nation can form a republic (which is by nature inclined to seek peace), this will provide a focal point for federal association among other states. These will join up with the first one, thus securing the freedom of each state in accordance with the idea of international right, and the whole will gradually spread further and further by a series of alliances of this kind. (Kant, *PP*, p. 104)

The pacific union is not a single peace treaty ending one war, a world state, nor a state of nations. Kant finds the first insufficient. The second and third are impossible or potentially tyrannical. National sovereignty precludes reliable subservience to a state of nations; a world state destroys the civic freedom on which the development of human capacities rests (Kant, *UH*, p. 50). Although Kant obliquely refers to various classical interstate confederations and modern diplomatic congresses, he develops no systematic organizational embodiment of this treaty and presumably does not find institutionalization necessary. He appears to have in mind a mutual non-aggression pact, perhaps a collective security agreement, and the cosmopolitan law set forth in the Third Definitive Article.[5]

The Third Definitive Article establishes a cosmopolitan law to operate in conjunction with the pacific union. The cosmopolitan law "shall be limited to conditions of universal hospitality." In this Kant calls for the recognition of the "right of a foreigner not to be treated with hostility when he arrives on someone else's territory." This "does not extend beyond those conditions which make it possible for them [foreigners] to attempt to enter into relations [commerce] with the native inhabitants" (Kant, *PP*, p. 106). Hospitality does not require extending to foreigners either the right to citizenship or the right to settlement, unless the foreign visitors would perish if they were expelled. Foreign conquest and plunder also find no justification under this right. Hospitality does appear to include the right of access and the obligation of maintaining the opportunity for citizens to exchange goods and ideas without imposing the obligation to trade (a voluntary act in all cases under liberal constitutions).

Perpetual peace, for Kant, is an epistemology, a condition for ethical action, and, most importantly, an explanation of how the "mechanical process of nature visibly exhibits the purposive plan of producing concord among men, even against their will and indeed by means of their very discord" (Kant, *PP*, p. 108; *UH*, pp. 44–45). Understanding history requires an epistemological foundation, for without a teleology, such as the promise of perpetual peace, the complexity of history would overwhelm human understanding (Kant, *UH*, pp. 51–53). Perpetual peace, however, is not merely a heuristic device with which to interpret history. It is guaranteed, Kant explains in the "First Addition" to *Perpetual Peace* ("On the Guarantee of Perpetual Peace"), to result from men fulfilling their ethical duty or, failing that, from a hidden plan.[6] Peace is an ethical duty because it is only under conditions of peace that all men can treat each other as ends, rather than means to an end (Kant, *UH*, p. 50). In order for this duty to be practical, Kant needs, of course, to show that peace is in fact possible. The widespread sentiment of approbation that he saw aroused by the early success of the French revolutionaries showed him that we can indeed be moved by ethical sentiments with a cosmopolitan reach (Kant, *CF*, pp. 181–82). This does not mean, however, that perpetual peace is certain

("prophesiable"). Even the scientifically regular course of the planets could be changed by a wayward comet striking them out of orbit. Human freedom requires that we allow for much greater reversals in the course of history. We must, in fact, anticipate the possibility of backsliding and destructive wars—though these will serve to educate nations to the importance of peace (Kant, *UH*, pp. 47–48).

In the end, however, our guarantee of perpetual peace does not rest on ethical conduct. As Kant emphasizes,

> we now come to the essential question regarding the prospect of perpetual peace. What does nature do in relation to the end which man's own reason prescribes to him as a duty, i.e., how does nature help to promote his *moral purpose*? And how does nature guarantee that what man ought to do by the laws of his freedom (but does not do) will in fact be done through nature's compulsion, without prejudice to the free agency of man? . . . This does not mean that nature imposes on us a *duty* to do it, for duties can only be imposed by practical reason. On the contrary, nature does it herself, whether we are willing or not: *facta volentem ducunt, nolentem tradunt.* (*PP*, p. 112)

The guarantee thus rests, Kant argues, not on the probable behavior of moral angels, but on that of "devils, so long as they possess understanding" (*PP*, p. 112). In explaining the sources of each of the three definitive articles of the perpetual peace, Kant then tells us how we (as free and intelligent devils) could be motivated by fear, force, and calculated advantage to undertake a course of action whose outcome we could reasonably anticipate to be perpetual peace. Yet while it is possible to conceive of the Kantian road to peace in these terms, Kant himself recognizes and argues that social evolution also makes the conditions of moral behavior less onerous and hence more likely (*CF*, pp. 187–89). In tracing the effects of both political and moral development, he builds an account of why liberal states do maintain peace among themselves and of how it will (by implication, has) come about that the pacific union will expand. He also explains how these republics would engage in wars with nonrepublics and therefore suffer the "sad experience" of wars that an ethical policy might have avoided.

The first source of the three definitive articles derives from a political evolution—from a constitutional law. Nature (providence) has seen to it that human beings can live in all the regions where they have been driven to settle by wars. (Kant, who once taught geography, reports on the Lapps, the Samoyeds, the Pescheras.) "Asocial sociability" draws men together to fulfill needs for security and material welfare as it drives them into conflicts over the distribution and control of social products (Kant, *UH*, pp. 44–45; *PP*, pp. 110–11). This violent natural evolution tends towards the liberal peace because "asocial sociability" inevitably leads toward republican governments, and republican governments are a source of the liberal peace.

Republican representation and separation of powers are produced because they are the means by which the state is "organized well" to prepare for and meet foreign threats (by unity) and to tame the ambitions of selfish and aggressive individuals (by authority derived from representation, by general laws, and by nondespotic administration) (Kant, *PP*, pp. 112–13). States that are not organized in this fashion fail. Monarchs thus encourage commerce and private property in order to increase national wealth. They cede rights of representation to their subjects in order to strengthen their political support or to obtain willing grants of tax revenue.

Kant shows how republics, once established, lead to peaceful relations. He argues that once the aggressive interests of absolutist monarchies are tamed and the habit of respect for individual rights engrained by republican government, wars would appear as the disaster to the people's welfare that he and the other liberals thought them to be. The fundamental reason is this:

> If, as is inevitably the case under this constitution, the consent of the citizens is required to decide whether or not war should be declared, it is very natural that they will have a great hesitation in embarking on so dangerous an enterprise. For this would mean calling down on themselves all the miseries of war, such as doing the fighting themselves, supplying the costs of the war from their own resources, painfully making good the ensuing devastation, and, as the crowning evil, having to take upon themselves a burden of debts which will embitter peace itself and which can never be paid off on account of the constant threat of new wars. But under a constitution where the subject is not a citizen, and which is therefore not republican, it is the simplest thing in the world to go to war. For the head of state is not a fellow citizen, but the owner of the state, and war will not force him to make the slightest sacrifice so far as his banquets, hunts, pleasure palaces and court festivals are concerned. He can thus decide on war, without any significant reason, as a kind of amusement, and unconcernedly leave it to the diplomatic corps (who are always ready for such purposes) to justify the war for the sake of propriety. (Kant, *PP*, p. 100)

Yet these domestic republican restraints do not end war. If they did, liberal states would not be warlike, which is far from the case. They do introduce republican caution—Kant's "hesitation"—in place of monarchical caprice. Liberal wars are only fought for popular, liberal purposes. The historical liberal legacy is laden with popular wars fought to promote freedom, to protect private property, or to support liberal allies against nonliberal enemies. Kant's position is ambiguous. He regards these wars as unjust and warns liberals of their susceptibility to them (Kant, *PP*, p. 106). At the same time, Kant argues that each nation "can and ought to" demand that its neighboring nations enter into the pacific union of liberal states (*PP*, p. 102). Thus to see how the pacific union removes the occasion of wars among liberal states and not wars between liberal and nonliberal states, we need to shift our attention from constitutional law to international law, Kant's second source.

Complementing the constitutional guarantee of caution, international law adds a second source for the definitive articles: a guarantee of respect. The separation of nations that asocial sociability encourages is reinforced by the development of separate languages and religions. These further guarantee a world of separate states—an essential condition needed to avoid a "global, soul-less despotism." Yet, at the same time, they also morally integrate liberal states: "as culture grows and men gradually move towards greater agreement over their principles, they lead to mutual understanding and peace" (Kant, *PP*, p. 114). As republics emerge (the first source) and as culture progresses, an understanding of the legitimate rights of all citizens and of all republics comes into play; and this, now that caution characterizes policy, sets up the moral foundations for the liberal peace. Correspondingly, international law highlights the importance of Kantian publicity. Domestically, publicity helps ensure that the officials of republics act according to the principles they profess to hold just and according to the interests of the electors they claim to represent. Internationally, free speech and the effective communication of accurate conceptions of the political life of foreign peoples is essential to establishing and preserving the understanding on which the guarantee of respect depends. Domestically just republics, which rest on consent, then presume foreign republics also to be consensual, just, and therefore deserving of accommodation. The experience of cooperation helps engender further cooperative behavior when the consequences of state policy are unclear but (potentially) mutually beneficial. At the same time, liberal states assume that nonliberal states, which do not rest on free consent, are not just. Because nonliberal governments are in

a state of aggression with their own people, their foreign relations become for liberal governments deeply suspect. In short, fellow liberals benefit from a presumption of amity; nonliberals suffer from a presumption of enmity. Both presumptions may be accurate; each, however, may also be self-confirming.

Lastly, cosmopolitan law adds material incentives to moral commitments. The cosmopolitan right to hospitality permits the "spirit of commerce" sooner or later to take hold of every nation, thus impelling states to promote peace and to try to avert war. Liberal economic theory holds that these cosmopolitan ties derive from a cooperative international division of labor and free trade according to comparative advantage. Each economy is said to be better off than it would have been under autarky; each thus acquires an incentive to avoid policies that would lead the other to break these economic ties. Because keeping open markets rests upon the assumption that the next set of transactions will also be determined by prices rather than coercion, a sense of mutual security is vital to avoid security-motivated searches for economic autarky. Thus, avoiding a challenge to another liberal state's security or even enhancing each others' security by means of alliance naturally follows economic interdependence.

A further cosmopolitan source of liberal peace is the international market's removal of difficult decisions of production and distribution from the direct sphere of state policy. A foreign state thus does not appear directly responsible for these outcomes, and states can stand aside from, and to some degree above, these contentious market rivalries and be ready to step in to resolve crises. The interdependence of commerce and the international contacts of state officials help create crosscutting transnational ties that serve as lobbies for mutual accommodation. According to modern liberal scholars, international financiers and transnational and transgovernmental organizations create interests in favor of accommodation. Moreover, their variety has ensured that no single conflict sours an entire relationship by setting off a spiral of reciprocated retaliation (Brzezinski and Huntington, 1963, chap. 9; Keohane and Nye, 1977, chap. 7; Neustadt, 1970; Polanyi, 1944, chaps. 1–2). Conversely, a sense of suspicion, such as that characterizing relations between liberal and nonliberal governments, can lead to restrictions on the range of contacts between societies, and this can increase the prospect that a single conflict will determine an entire relationship.

No single constitutional, international, or cosmopolitan source is alone sufficient, but together (and only together) they plausibly connect the characteristics of liberal polities and economies with sustained liberal peace. Alliances founded on mutual strategic interest among liberal and nonliberal states have been broken; economic ties between liberal and nonliberal states have proven fragile; but the political bonds of liberal rights and interests have proven a remarkably firm foundation for mutual nonaggression. A separate peace exists among liberal states.

In their relations with nonliberal states, however, liberal states have not escaped from the insecurity caused by anarchy in the world political system considered as a whole. Moreover, the very constitutional restraint, international respect for individual rights, and shared commercial interests that establish grounds for peace among liberal states establish grounds for additional conflict in relations between liberal and nonliberal societies.

Conclusion

Kant's liberal internationalism, Machiavelli's liberal imperialism, and Schumpeter's liberal pacifism rest on fundamentally different views of the nature of the human being, the state, and international relations.[7] Schumpeter's humans are rationalized, individualized, and democratized. They are also homogenized, pursuing material interests "monistically." Because their material interests lie in peaceful trade, they and the democratic state that these fellow citizens

control are pacifistic. Machiavelli's citizens are splendidly diverse in their goals but fundamentally unequal in them as well, seeking to rule or fearing being dominated. Extending the rule of the dominant elite or avoiding the political collapse of their state, each calls for imperial expansion.

Kant's citizens, too, are diverse in their goals and individualized and rationalized, but most importantly, they are capable of appreciating the moral equality of all individuals and of treating other individuals as ends rather than as means. The Kantian state thus is governed publicly according to law, as a republic. Kant's is the state that solves the problem of governing individualized equals, whether they are the "rational devils" he says we often find ourselves to be or the ethical agents we can and should become. Republics tell us that

> in order to organize a group of rational beings who together require universal laws for their survival, but of whom each separate individual is secretly inclined to exempt himself from them, the constitution must be so designed so that, although the citizens are opposed to one another in their private attitudes, these opposing views may inhibit one another in such a way that the public conduct of the citizens will be the same as if they did not have such evil attitudes. (Kant, *PP*, p. 113)

Unlike Machiavelli's republics, Kant's republics are capable of achieving peace among themselves because they exercise democratic caution and are capable of appreciating the international rights of foreign republics. These international rights of republics derive from the representation of foreign individuals who are our moral equals. Unlike Schumpeter's capitalist democracies, Kant's republics—including our own—remain in a state of war with nonrepublics. Liberal republics see themselves as threatened by aggression from nonrepublics that are not constrained by representation. Even though wars often cost more than the economic return they generate, liberal republics also are prepared to protect and promote—sometimes forcibly—democracy, private property, and the rights of individuals overseas against nonrepublics, which, because they do not authentically represent the rights of individuals, have no rights to noninterference. These wars may liberate oppressed individuals overseas; they also can generate enormous suffering.

Preserving the legacy of the liberal peace without succumbing to the legacy of liberal imprudence is both a moral and a strategic challenge. The bipolar stability of the international system, and the near certainty of mutual devastation resulting from a nuclear war between the superpowers, have created a "crystal ball effect" that has helped to constrain the tendency toward miscalculation present at the outbreak of so many wars in the past (Carnesale, Doty, Hoffmann, Huntington, Nye, and Sagan, 1983, p. 44; Waltz, 1964). However, this "nuclear peace" appears to be limited to the super-powers. It has not curbed military interventions in the Third World. Moreover, it is subject to a desperate technological race designed to overcome its constraints and to crises that have pushed even the super-powers to the brink of war. We must still reckon with the war fevers and moods of appeasement that have almost alternately swept liberal democracies.

Yet restraining liberal imprudence, whether aggressive or passive, may not be possible without threatening, liberal pacification. Improving the strategic acumen of our foreign policy calls for introducing steadier strategic calculations of the national interest in the long run and more flexible responses to changes in the international political environment. Constraining the indiscriminate meddling of our foreign interventions calls for a deeper appreciation of the "particularism of history, culture, and membership" (Walzer, 1983, p. 5), but both the improvement in strategy and the constraint on intervention seem, in turn, to require an executive freed from the restraints of a representative legislature in the management of foreign policy and a political culture indifferent to the universal rights of individuals. These conditions, in their turn, could break the chain of constitutional guarantees, the respect for representative government, and the web of transnational contact that have sustained the pacific union of liberal states.

Perpetual peace, Kant says, is the end point of the hard journey his republics will take. The promise of perpetual peace, the violent lessons of war, and the experience of a partial peace are proof of the need for and the possibility of world peace. They are also the grounds for moral citizens and statesmen to assume the duty of striving for peace.

Notes

1. Clarence Streit (1938, pp. 88, 90–92) seems to have been the first to point out (in contemporary foreign relations) the empirical tendency of democracies to maintain peace among themselves, and he made this the foundation of his proposal for a (non-Kantian) federal union of the 15 leading democracies of the 1930s. . . . I use the term *liberal* in a . . . Kantian sense. . . . (Doyle, 1983a). In that essay, I survey the period from 1790 to the present and find no war among liberal states.

2. Babst (1972) did make a preliminary test of the significance of the distribution of alliance partners in World War I. He found that the possibility that the actual distribution of alliance partners could have occurred by chance was less than 1% (Babst, 1972, p. 56). However, this assumes that there was an equal possibility that any two nations could have gone to war with each other, and this is a strong assumption. Rummel (1983) has a further discussion of the issue of statistical significance as it applies to his libertarian thesis.

3. All citations from Kant are from *Kant's Political Writings* (Kant, 1970), the H. B. Nisbet translation edited by Hans Reiss. The works discussed and the abbreviations by which they are identified in the text are as follows:

PP   *Perpetual Peace* (1795)
UH   *The Idea for a Universal History with a Cosmopolitan Purpose* (1784)
CF   *The Contest of Faculties* (1798)
MM *The Metaphysics of Morals* (1797)

4. I think Kant meant that the peace would be established among liberal regimes and would expand by ordinary political and legal means as new liberal regimes appeared. By a process of gradual extension the peace would become global and then perpetual; the occasion for wars with nonliberals would disappear as nonliberal regimes disappeared.

5. Kant's *foedus pacificum* is thus neither a *pactum pacis* (a single peace treaty) nor a *civitas gentium* (a world state). He appears to have anticipated something like a less formally institutionalized League of Nations or United Nations. One could argue that in practice, these two institutions worked for liberal states and only for liberal states, but no specifically liberal "pacific union" was institutionalized. Instead, liberal states have behaved for the past 180 years as if such a Kantian pacific union and treaty of perpetual peace had been signed.

6. In the *Metaphysics of Morals* (the *Rechtslehre*) Kant seems to write as if perpetual peace is only an epistemological device and, while an ethical duty, is empirically merely a "pious hope" (*MM*, pp. 164–75)—though even here he finds that the pacific union is not "impracticable" (*MM*, p. 171). In the *Universal History* (*UH*), Kant writes as if the brute force of physical nature drives men toward inevitable peace. . . .

7. For a comparative discussion of the political foundations of Kant's ideas, see Shklar (1984, pp. 232–38).

References

Babst, Dean V. 1972. A Force for Peace. *Industrial Research*. 14 (April): 55–58.

Brzezinski, Zbigniew, and Samuel Huntington. 1963. *Political Power: USA/USSR*. New York: Viking Press.

Carnesale, Albert, Paul Doty, Stanley Hoffmann, Samuel Huntington, Joseph Nye, and Scott Sagan. 1983. *Living With Nuclear Weapons*. New York: Bantam.

Doyle, Michael W. 1983a. Kant, Liberal Legacies, and Foreign Affairs: Part 1. *Philosophy and Public Affairs* 12: 205–35.

Doyle, Michael W. 1983b. Kant, Liberal Legacies, and Foreign Affairs: Part 2. *Philosophy and Public Affairs* 12: 323–53.

Hume, David. 1963. Of the Balance of Power. *Essays: Moral, Political, and Literary*. Oxford: Oxford University Press.

Kant, Immanuel. 1970. *Kant's Political Writings*. Hans Reiss, ed. H. B. Nisbet, trans. Cambridge: Cambridge University Press.

Keohane, Robert, and Joseph Nye. 1977. *Power and Interdependence*. Boston: Little Brown.

Neustadt, Richard. 1970. *Alliance Politics*. New York: Columbia University Press.

Polanyi, Karl. 1944. *The Great Transformation*. Boston: Beacon Press.

Rummel, Rudolph J. 1983. Libertarianism and International Violence. *Journal of Conflict Resolution, 27*: 27–71.

Schumpeter, Joseph. 1950. *Capitalism, Socialism, and Democracy*. New York: Harper Torchbooks.

Schumpeter, Joseph. 1955. The Sociology of Imperialism. In *Imperialism and Social Classes*. Cleveland: World Publishing Co. (Essay originally published in 1919.)

Shklar, Judith. 1984. *Ordinary Vices*. Cambridge, MA: Harvard University Press.

Streit, Clarence. 1938. *Union Now: A Proposal for a Federal Union of the Leading Democracies*. New York: Harpers.

Thucydides. 1954. *The Peloponnesian War*. Rex Warner, ed. and trans. Baltimore: Penguin.

Waltz, Kenneth. 1964. The Stability of a Bipolar World. *Daedalus*, 93: 881–909.

Walzer, Michael. 1983. *Spheres of Justice*. New York: Basic Books.

Taking Preferences Seriously: A Liberal Theory of International Politics

ANDREW MORAVCSIK

In this article, the author reformulates basic elements of liberalism to create a paradigmatic alternative to realism and neoliberal institutionalism. In this extract, Moravcsik argues that the basic liberal insight about the centrality of state–society relations to world politics can be restated in terms of three positive assumptions concerning the primacy of societal actors, that states represent some subset of domestic society, and that the configuration of interdependent state preferences determines state behavior.

This article reformulates liberal international relations (IR) theory in a nonideological and nonutopian form appropriate to empirical social science. Liberal IR theory elaborates the insight that state–society relations—the relationship of states to the domestic and transnational social context in which they are embedded—have a fundamental impact on state behavior in world politics. Societal ideas, interests, and institutions influence state behavior by shaping state preferences, that is, the fundamental social purposes underlying the strategic calculations of governments. For liberals, the configuration of state preferences matters most in world politics—not, as realists argue, the configuration of capabilities and not, as institutionalists (that is, functional regime theorists) maintain, the configuration of information and institutions. This article codifies this basic liberal insight in the form of three core theoretical assumptions, derives from them three variants of liberal theory, and demonstrates that the existence of a coherent liberal theory has significant theoretical, methodological, and empirical implications. Restated in this

way, liberal theory deserves to be treated as a paradigmatic alternative empirically coequal with and analytically more fundamental than the two dominant theories in contemporary IR scholarship: realism and institutionalism.

Grounding liberal theory in a set of core social scientific assumptions helps overcome a disjuncture between contemporary empirical research on world politics and the language employed by scholars to describe IR as a field. Liberal hypotheses stressing variation in state preferences play an increasingly central role in IR scholarship. These include explanations stressing the causal importance of state–society relations as shaped by domestic institutions (for example, the "democratic peace"), by economic interdependence (for example, endogenous tariff theory), and by ideas about national, political, and socioeconomic public goods provision (for example, theories about the relationship between nationalism and conflict). Liberal hypotheses do not include, for reasons clarified later, functional regime theory. Yet the conceptual language of IR theory has not caught up with contemporary research. IR theorists con-

Excerpted from Andrew Moravcsik, "Taking Preferences Seriously: A Positive Liberal Theory of International Politics." *International Organization*, 51: 4 (Autumn 1997), pp. 513–553. © 1997 by the IO Foundation and the Massachusetts Institute of Technology.

tinue to speak as if the dominant theoretical cleavage in the field were the dichotomy between realism and ("neoliberal") institutionalism. The result: liberal IR theory of the kind outlined earlier is generally ignored as a major paradigmatic alternative.

Worse, its lack of paradigmatic status has permitted critics to caricature liberal theory as a normative, even utopian, ideology. Postwar realist critics such as Hans Morgenthau and E. H. Carr took rhetorical advantage of liberalism's historical role as an ideology to contrast its purported altruism ("idealism," "legalism," "moralism," or "utopianism") with realism's "theoretical concern with human nature as it actually is [and] historical processes as they actually take place."[1] Forty years later, little has changed. Robert Gilpin's influential typology in international political economy juxtaposes a positive mercantilist view ("politics determines economics") against a narrower and conspicuously normative liberal one ("economics *should* determine politics"). Kenneth Waltz, a realist critic, asserts that "if the aims . . . of states become matters of . . . central concern, then we are forced back to the descriptive level; and from simple descriptions no valid generalizations can be drawn."[2]

Liberals have responded to such criticisms not by proposing a unified set of positive social scientific assumptions on which a nonideological and nonutopian liberal theory can be based, as has been done with considerable success for realism and institutionalism, but by conceding its theoretical incoherence and turning instead to intellectual history. It is widely accepted that any nontautological social scientific theory must be grounded in a set of positive assumptions from which arguments, explanations, and predictions can be derived.[3] Yet surveys of liberal IR theory either collect disparate views held by "classical" liberal publicists or define liberal theory teleologically, that is, according to its purported optimism concerning the potential for peace, cooperation, and international institutions in world history. Such studies offer an indispensable source of theoretical and normative inspiration. Judged by the more narrowly social scientific criteria adopted here, however, they do not justify reference to a distinct "liberal" IR theory.

Leading liberal IR theorists freely concede the absence of coherent microfoundational assumptions but conclude therefrom that a liberal IR theory in the social scientific sense *cannot* exist. Robert Keohane, an institutionalist sympathetic to liberalism, maintains that "in contrast to Marxism and Realism, Liberalism is not committed to ambitious and parsimonious structural theory." Michael Doyle, a pioneer in analyzing the "democratic peace," observes that liberal IR theory, unlike others, lacks "canonical" foundations. Mark Zacher and Richard Matthew, sympathetic liberals, assert that liberalism should be considered an "approach," not a theory, since "its propositions cannot be . . . deduced from its assumptions."[4] Accurate though this may be as a characterization of intellectual history and current theory, it is second-best social science.

I seek to move beyond this unsatisfactory situation by proposing a set of core assumptions on which a general restatement of positive liberal IR theory can be grounded. I argue that the basic liberal insight about the centrality of state–society relations to world politics can be restated in terms of three positive assumptions, concerning, respectively, the nature of fundamental social actors, the state, and the international system.

Drawing on these assumptions, I then elaborate three major variants of liberal theory—each grounded in a distinctive causal mechanism linking social preferences and state behavior. Ideational liberalism stresses the impact on state behavior of conflict and compatibility among collective social values or identities concerning the scope and nature of public goods provision. Commercial liberalism stresses the impact on state behavior of gains and losses to individuals and groups in society from transnational economic interchange. Republican liberalism stresses the impact on state behavior of varying forms of domestic representation and the resulting incentives for social groups to engage in rent seeking.[5]

Finally, I demonstrate that the identification of coherent theoretical assumptions is not simply an abstract and semantic matter. It has significant methodological, theoretical, and empirical implications. The utility of a paradigmatic restatement should be evaluated on the basis of four criteria, each relevant to the empirical researcher: superior parsimony, coherence, empirical accuracy, and multicausal consistency.

First, a theoretical restatement should be *general and parsimonious,* demonstrating that a limited number of microfoundational assumptions can link a broad range of previously unconnected theories and hypotheses. This restatement does so by showing how *liberalism provides a general theory of IR linking apparently unrelated areas of inquiry.* The theory outlined here applies equally to liberal and nonliberal states, economic and national security affairs, conflictual and nonconflictual situations, and the behavior both of individual states ("foreign policy") and of aggregations of states ("international relations"). Liberal theory, moreover, explains important phenomena overlooked by alternative theories, including the substantive content of foreign policy, historical change, and the distinctiveness of interstate relations among modern Western states.

Second, a theoretical restatement should be *rigorous and coherent,* offering a clear definition of its own boundaries. This restatement does so by demonstrating that *institutionalist theories of regimes—commonly treated as liberal due to ideological and historical connotations—are in fact based on assumptions closer to realism than to liberalism.* This helps to explain why IR theorists have found it difficult to distill a set of coherent microfoundational assumptions for liberal theory.

Third, a theoretical restatement should *demonstrate empirical accuracy vis-à-vis other theories;* it should expose anomalies in existing

work, forcing reconsideration of empirical findings and theoretical positions. This restatement of liberal theory meets this criterion by *revealing significant methodological biases in empirical evaluations of realist theories of "relative gains-seeking" and constructivist analyses of ideas and IR due to the omission of liberal alternatives.* If these biases were corrected, liberal accounts might well supplant many widely accepted realist and institutionalist, as well as constructivist, explanations of particular phenomena in world politics.

Fourth, a theoretical restatement should *demonstrate multicausal consistency.* By specifying the antecedent conditions under which it is valid and the precise causal links to policy outcomes, a theory should specify rigorously how it can be synthesized with other theories into a multicausal explanation consistent with tenets of fundamental social theory. This restatement does so by reversing the nearly universal presumption among contemporary IR theorists that "systemic" theories like realism and institutionalism should be employed as an analytical "first cut," with theories of "domestic" preference formation brought in only to explain anomalies—a prescription that is both methodologically biased and theoretically incoherent. In its place, this restatement dictates the reverse: *Liberal theory is analytically prior to both realism and institutionalism because it defines the conditions under which their assumptions hold.*

If this proposed reformulation of liberal IR theory meets these four criteria, as I argue it does, there is good reason to accord it a paradigmatic position empirically coequal with and analytically prior to realism and institutionalism, as well as constructivism, in theory and research on world politics.

Core Assumptions of Liberal IR Theory

Liberal IR theory's fundamental premise—that the relationship between states and the surrounding domestic and transnational society in which they are embedded critically shapes state behavior by influencing the social purposes underlying state preferences—can be restated in terms of three core assumptions. These assumptions are appropriate foundations of any social theory of IR: they specify the nature of societal actors, the state, and the international system.

Assumption 1: *The Primacy of Societal Actors*

The fundamental actors in international politics are individuals and private groups, who are on the average rational and risk-averse and who organize exchange and collective action to promote differentiated interests under constraints imposed by material scarcity, conflicting values, and variations in societal influence.

Liberal theory rests on a "bottom-up" view of politics in which the demands of individuals and societal groups are treated as analytically prior to politics. Political action is embedded in domestic and transnational civil society, understood as an aggregation of boundedly rational individuals with differentiated tastes, social commitments, and resource endowments. Socially differentiated individuals define their material and ideational interests independently of politics and then advance those interests through political exchange and collective action.[6] Individuals and groups are assumed to act rationally in pursuit of material and ideal welfare.[7]

For liberals, the definition of the interests of societal actors is theoretically central. Liberal theory rejects the utopian notion that an *automatic* harmony of interest exists among individuals and groups in society; scarcity and differentiation introduce an inevitable measure of competition. Where social incentives for exchange and collective action are perceived to exist, individuals and groups exploit them: the greater the expected benefits, the stronger the incentive to act. In pursuing these goals, individuals are on the average risk-averse; that is, they strongly defend existing investments but remain more cautious about assuming cost and risk in pursuit of new gains. What is true about people on the average, however, is not necessarily true in every case: some individuals in any given society may be risk-acceptant or irrational.

Liberal theory seeks to generalize about the social conditions under which the behavior of self-interested actors converges toward cooperation or conflict. Conflictual societal demands and the willingness to employ coercion in pursuit of them are associated with a number of factors, three of which are relevant to this discussion: divergent fundamental beliefs, conflict over scarce material good, and inequalities in political power. Deep, irreconcilable differences in beliefs about the provision of public goods, such as borders, culture, fundamental political institutions, and local social practices, promote conflict, whereas complementary beliefs promote harmony and cooperation. Extreme scarcity tends to exacerbate conflict over resources by increasing the willingness of social actors to assume cost and risk to obtain them. Relative abundance, by contrast, lowers the propensity for conflict by providing the opportunity to satisfy wants without inevitable conflict and giving certain individuals and groups more to defend. Finally, where inequalities in societal influence are large, conflict is more likely. Where social power is equitably distributed, the costs and benefits of actions are more likely to be internalized to individuals—for example, through the existence of complex, cross-cutting patterns of mutually beneficial interaction or strong and legitimate domestic political institutions—and the incentive for selective or arbitrary coercion is dampened. By contrast, where power asymmetries permit groups to evade the costs of redistributing goods, incentives arise for exploitative, rent-seeking behavior, even if the result is inefficient for society as a whole.[8]

Assumption 2: *Representation and State Preferences*

States (or other political institutions) represent some subset of domestic society, on the basis of whose interests state officials define state preferences and act purposively in world politics.

In the liberal conception of domestic politics, the state is not an actor but a representative institution constantly subject to capture and recapture, construction and reconstruction by coalitions of social actors. Representative institutions and practices constitute the critical "transmission belt" by which the preferences and social power of individuals and groups are translated into state policy. Individuals turn to the state to achieve goals that private behavior is unable to achieve efficiently.[9] Government policy is therefore constrained by the underlying identities, interests, and power of individuals and groups (inside and outside the state apparatus) who constantly pressure the central decision makers to pursue policies consistent with their preferences.

This is not to adopt a narrowly pluralist view of domestic politics in which all individuals and groups have equal influence on state policy, nor one in which the structure of state institutions is irrelevant. No government rests on universal or unbiased political representation; every government represents some individuals and groups more fully than others. In an extreme hypothetical case, representation might empower a narrow bureaucratic class or even a single tyrannical individual, such as an ideal-typical Pol Pot or Josef Stalin. Between theoretical extremes of tyranny and democracy, many representative institutions and practices exist, each of which privileges particular demands; hence the nature of state institutions, alongside societal interests themselves, is a key determinant of what states do internationally.

Representation, in the liberal view, is not simply a formal attribute of state institutions but includes other stable characteristics of the political process, formal or informal, that privilege particular societal interests. Clientelistic authoritarian regimes may distinguish those with familial, bureaucratic, or economic ties to the governing elite from those without. Even where government institutions are formally fair and open, a relatively inegalitarian distribution of property, risk, information, or organizational capabilities may create social or economic monopolies able to dominate policy. Similarly, the way in which a state recognizes individual rights may shape opportunities for voice.[10] Certain domestic representational processes may tend to select as leaders individuals, groups, and bureaucracies socialized with particular attitudes toward information, risk, and loss. Finally, cost-effective exit options, such as emigration, noncompliance, or the transfer of assets to new jurisdictions or uses, insofar as they constrain governments, may be thought of as substitutes for formal representation.[11]

Societal pressures transmitted by representative institutions and practices alter "state preferences." This term designates an ordering among underlying substantive outcomes that may result from international political interaction. Here it is essential—particularly given the inconsistency of common usage—to avoid conceptual confusion by keeping state "preferences" distinct from national "strategies," "tactics," and "policies," that is, the particular transient bargaining positions, negotiating demands, or policy goals that constitute the everyday currency of foreign policy. State preferences, as the concept is employed here, comprise a set of fundamental interests defined across "states of the world." Preferences are by definition causally independent of the strategies of other actors and, therefore, prior to specific interstate political interactions, including external threats, incentives, manipulation of information, or other tactics. By contrast, strategies and tactics—sometimes also termed "preferences" in game-theoretical analyses—are policy options defined across intermediate political aims, as when governments declare an "interest" in "maintaining the balance of power," "containing" or "appeasing" an adversary, or exercising "global leadership."[12] Liberal theory focuses on the consequences for state behavior of shifts in fundamental preferences, not shifts in the strategic circumstances under which states pursue them.

Representative institutions and practices determine not merely which social coalitions are represented in foreign policy, but how they are represented. Two distinctions are critical. First, states may act in either a unitary or "disaggregated" way. In many traditional areas of foreign policy, "politics stops at the water's edge," and there is strong coordination among national officials and politicians. In other areas, the state may be "disaggregated," with different elements—executives, courts, central banks, regulatory bureaucracies, and ruling parties, for example—conducting semiautonomous foreign policies in the service of disparate societal interests.[13] Second, domestic decision making may be structured so as to generate state preferences that satisfy a strong rationality condition, such as transitivity or strict expected utility maximization, or so as to satisfy only the weaker rationality criterion of seeking efficient means. Recently, formal theorists have derived specific conditions under which nonunitary state behavior can be analyzed "as if" it were unitary and rational, implying that much superficially "nonrational" or "nonunitary" behavior should actually be understood in terms of shifting state preferences.[14]

Taken together, assumptions 1 and 2 imply that states do not automatically maximize fixed, homogeneous conceptions of security, sovereignty, or wealth per se, as realists and institutionalists tend to assume. Instead they are, in Waltzian terms, "functionally differentiated"; that is, they pursue particular interpretations and combinations of security, welfare, and sovereignty preferred by powerful domestic groups enfranchised by representative institutions and practices.[15] As Arnold Wolfers, John Ruggie, and others have observed, the nature and intensity of national support for any state purpose—even apparently fundamental concerns like the defense of political and legal sovereignty, territorial integrity, national security, or economic welfare—varies decisively with the social context.[16] It is not uncommon for states knowingly to surrender sovereignty, compromise security,

or reduce aggregate economic welfare. In the liberal view, trade-offs among such goals, as well as cross-national differences in their definition, are inevitable, highly varied, and causally consequential.[17]

Assumption 3: Interdependence and the International System

The configuration of interdependent state preferences determines state behavior.

For liberals, state behavior reflects varying patterns of state preferences. States require a "purpose," a perceived underlying stake in the matter at hand, in order to provoke conflict, propose cooperation, or take any other significant foreign policy action. The precise nature of these stakes drives policy. This is not to assert that each state simply pursues its ideal policy, oblivious of others; instead, each state seeks to realize *its* distinctive preferences under varying constraints imposed by the preferences of *other* states. Thus liberal theory rejects not just the realist assumption that state preferences must be treated as if naturally conflictual, but equally the institutionalist assumption that they should be treated as if they were partially convergent, comprising a collective action problem.[18] To the contrary, liberals causally privilege variation in the configuration of state preferences, while treating configurations of capabilities and information as if they were either fixed constraints or endogenous to state preferences.

The critical theoretical link between state preferences, on the one hand, and the behavior of one or more states, on the other, is provided by the concept of policy interdependence. Policy interdependence is defined here as the set of costs and benefits created for foreign societies when dominant social groups in a society seek to realize their preferences, that is, the pattern of transnational externalities resulting from attempts to pursue national distinctive purposes. Liberal theory assumes that the pattern of interdependent state preferences imposes a binding constraint on state behavior.

Patterns of interdependence or externalities induced by efforts to realize state preferences can be divided into three broad categories, corresponding to the strategic situation (the pattern of policy externalities) that results.[19] Where preferences are naturally compatible or harmonious, that is, where the externalities of unilateral policies are optimal for others (or insignificant), there are strong incentives for coexistence with low conflict.

Where, by contrast, underlying state preferences are zero-sum or deadlocked, that is, where an attempt by dominant social groups in one country to realize their preferences through state action *necessarily* imposes costs (negative externalities) on dominant social groups in other countries, governments face a bargaining game with few mutual gains and a high potential for interstate tension and conflict. The decisive precondition for costly attempts at coercion, for example, is neither a particular configuration of power, as realists assert, nor of uncertainty, as institutionalists maintain, but a configuration of preferences conflictual enough to motivate willingness to accept high cost and risk.[20] In other words, intense conflict requires that an aggressor or revisionist state advance demands to which other states are unwilling to submit. Revisionist preferences—underlying, socially grounded interests in revising the status quo—are distinct from revisionist "strategies," that is, a need to alter the status quo to protect enduring interests under new strategic circumstances. Liberals focus on the former, realists (and institutionalists) on the latter. Hence while both theories predict security conflict, they do so under different circumstances. For example, increased military spending in response to an adversary's arms buildup is a change in strategy with fixed preferences consistent with realism; increased spending initiated by a new ruling elite ideologically committed to territorial aggrandizement is a

preference-induced change in strategy consistent with liberalism.[21]

Where, finally, motives are mixed such that an exchange of policy concessions through coordination or precommitment can improve the welfare of both parties relative to unilateral policy adjustment (i.e., a collective action problem), states have an incentive to negotiate policy coordination. Games like coordination, assurance, prisoner's dilemma, and suasion have distinctive dynamics, as well as impose precise costs, benefits, and risks on the parties. Within each qualitative category, incentives vary further according to the intensity of preferences.

For liberals, the form, substance, and depth of cooperation depends directly on the nature of these patterns of preferences. Hence where "Pareto-inefficient" outcomes are observed— trade protection is a commonly cited example —liberals turn first to countervailing social preferences and unresolved domestic and transnational distributional conflicts, whereas institutionalists and realists, respectively, turn to uncertainty and particular configurations of interstate power.[22]

Liberal Theory as Systemic Theory

These liberal assumptions, in particular the third—in essence, "what states want is the primary determinant of what they do"—may seem commonsensical, even tautological. Yet mainstream IR theory has uniformly rejected such claims for the past half-century. At the heart of the two leading contemporary IR theories, realism and institutionalism, is the belief that state behavior has *ironic* consequences.[23] Power politics and informational uncertainty constrain states to pursue second- and third-best strategies strikingly at variance with their underlying preferences.[24] Thus varying state preferences should be treated as if they were irrelevant, secondary, or endogenous. In his classic definition of realism Morgenthau contrasts it to "two popular fallacies: the concern with motives and the concern with ideological preferences."[25] Neorealist Waltz's central objection to previous, "reductionist" theories is that in world politics "results achieved seldom correspond to the intentions of actors"; hence "no valid generalizations can logically be drawn" from an examination of intentions.[26] Though the interests it assumes are different, Keohane's institutionalism relies on a similar as if assumption: it "takes the existence of mutual interests as given and examines the conditions under which they will lead to cooperation."[27] In short, Powell observes that "structural theories . . . lack a theory of preferences over outcomes."[28] What states do is primarily determined by strategic considerations—what they can get or what they know—which in turn reflect their international political environment. In short, variation in means, not ends, matters most.[29]

Liberal theory reverses this assumption: *Variation in ends, not means, matters most.* Realists and institutionalists, as well as formal theorists who seek to integrate the two, criticize this core liberal assumption because it appears at first glance to rest on what Waltz terms a "reductionist" rather than a "systemic" understanding of IR. In other words, liberalism appears to be a purely "domestic" or "unit-level" theory that ignores the international environment. In particular, realists are skeptical of this view because it appears at first glance to be grounded in the utopian expectation that every state can do as it pleases. This commonplace criticism is erroneous for two important reasons.

First, state preferences may reflect patterns of transnational *societal* interaction. While state preferences are (by definition) invariant in response to changing interstate political and strategic circumstances, they may well vary in response to a changing transnational *social* context. In the political economy for foreign economic policy, for example, social demands are derived not simply from "domestic" economic assets and endowments, but from the relative position of those assets and endowments in global markets. Similarly, the position of partic-

ular values in a transnational cultural discourse may help define their meaning in each society. In this regard, liberalism does not draw a strict line between domestic and transnational levels of analysis.[30]

A second and more Waltzian reason why the charge of "reductionism" is erroneous is that according to liberal theory the expected behavior of any single state—the strategies it selects and the systemic constraints to which it adjusts—reflect not simply its own preferences, but the configuration of preferences of *all* states linked by patterns of significant policy interdependence. National leaders must always think systemically about their position within a structure composed of the preferences of other states. Since the pattern of and interdependence among state preferences, like the distribution of capabilities and the distribution of information and ideas, lies outside the control of any single state, it conforms to Waltz's own definition of systemic theory, whereby interstate interactions are explained by reference to "how [states] stand in relation to one another."[31] Hence the causal preeminence of state preferences does not imply that states always get what they want.

One implication of liberalism's systemic, structural quality is that, contra Waltz, it can explain not only the "foreign policy" goals of individual states but the "systemic" outcomes of interstate interactions. That systemic predictions can follow from domestic theories of preferences should be obvious simply by inspecting the literature on the democratic peace.[32] In addition, by linking social purpose to the symmetry and relative intensity of state preferences, liberalism offers *a distinctive conception of political power* in world politics—something traditionally considered unique to realist theory.

The liberal concept of power is based on an assumption *more* consistent with basic theories of bargaining and negotiation than those underlying realism: namely that the willingness of states to expend resources or make concessions is itself primarily a function of preferences, not capabilities. In this view—the foundation of [this] bargaining analysis, which has been extended to IR by Albert Hirshman, Keohane, Joseph Nye, and others—bargaining outcomes reflect the nature and relative intensity of actor preferences.[33] The "win-set," the "best alternative to negotiated agreement," the pattern of "asymmetrical interdependence," the relative opportunity cost of forgoing an agreement—all these core terms in negotiation analysis refer to different aspects of the relationship of bargaining outcomes on the preference functions of the actors. The capability-based power to threaten central to realism enters the equation in specific circumstances and only through linkage to threats and side-payments. Even where capability-based threats and promises are employed, preference-based determinants of the tolerance for bearing bargaining costs, including differential temporal discount rates, risk-acceptance, and willingness to accept punishment, remain central.[34]

The liberal claim that the pattern of interdependence among state preferences is a primary determinant not just of individual foreign policies, but of systemic outcomes, is commonsensical. Nations are rarely prepared to expend their entire economic or defense capabilities, or to mortgage their entire domestic sovereignty, in pursuit of any single foreign policy goal. Few wars are total, few peaces Carthaginian. Treating the willingness of states to expend resources in pursuit of foreign policy goals as a strict function of existing capabilities thus seems unrealistic. On the margin, the binding constraint is instead generally "resolve" or "determination"—the *willingness* of governments to mobilize and expend social resources for foreign policy purposes.

Extensive empirical evidence supports this assumption. Even in "least likely" cases, where political independence and territorial integrity are at stake and military means are deployed, relative capabilities do not necessarily determine outcomes. A "strong preference for the issue at stake can compensate for a deficiency in capabilities," as demonstrated by examples like the Boer War, Hitler's remilitarization of the Rhineland, Vietnam, Afghanistan, and Chechnya. In each case the relative intensity of state preferences reshaped the outcome to the advantage of the "weak." Such examples suggest that the liberal view of power politics, properly understood, generates plausible explanations not just of harmony and cooperation among nations, but of the full range of phenomena central to the study of world politics, from peaceful economic exchange to brutal guerrilla warfare.

Notes

1. See Morgenthau 1960, 4; Keohane 1989, 68, n. 17; and Howard 1978, 134.
2. See Waltz 1979, 65, 27; Gilpin 1975, 27 (emphasis in original); and Gilpin 1987.
3. See Bueno de Mesquita 1996, 64–65; and Keohane 1986.
4. See Keohane 1990, 166, 172–73; Doyle 1986, 1152; Zacher and Matthew 1992, 2; Matthew and Zacher 1995, 107–11, 117–20; Hoffmann 1987, 1995; and Nye 1988.
5. For other such distinctions, see Keohane 1990; and Doyle 1983.
6. This does not imply a "pre-social" conception of the individual unencumbered by nation, community, family, or other collective identities but only that these identities enter the political realm when individuals and groups engage in political exchange on the basis of them; see, for example, Coleman 1990.
7. Kant 1991, 44.
8. Milgrom and Roberts 1990, 86–87.
9. Representative political institutions and practices result from prior contracts and can generally be taken for granted in explaining foreign policy; but where the primary interests and allegiances of individuals and private groups are transferred to subnational or supranational institutions empowered to represent them effectively, a liberal analysis would naturally shift to these levels.
10. Doyle 1997, 251–300.
11. North and Thomas 1973, 87.
12. The phrase "country *A* changed its preferences in response to an action by country *B*" is thus a misuse of the term as defined here, implying less than consistently rational behavior; see Sebenius 1991, 207.
13. See Slaughter 1995; and Keohane and Nye 1989.
14. Achen 1995.
15. Ruggie 1983, 265.

16. Ruggie 1982, 1983.

17. On the contradictions within Waltz's effort to avoid these ambiguities, see Baldwin 1997, 21–22.

18. Keohane 1984; 10; 1986, 193. Note that these are all "as if" assumptions. The world must be consistent with them, but need not fulfill them precisely.

19. See Stein 1982; Snidal 1985; and Martin 1992.

20. Note that some rationalist analyses dismiss such risk-acceptant preferences as "irrational"; see Fearon 1995.

21. For example, Van Evera 1990–91, 32.

22. Grieco 1990.

23. What about Marxism? Marxism provides distinctive normative insights (Doyle 1997), but its nonteleological positive assumptions—the centrality of domestic economic interests, the importance of transnational interdependence, the state as a representative of dominant social forces—are quite compatible with this restatement of liberalism. For examples, see the contribution by Frieden and Rogowski in Keohane and Milner 1996.

24. Waltz 1979, 60–67, 93–97.

25. The resulting "autonomy of the political" in geopolitics gives realism its "distinctive intellectual and moral attitude"; see Morgenthau 1960, 5–7. The fact that Morgenthau distinguished nonrealist elements of his own thought illustrates a further danger of defining realism not in terms of social scientific assumptions, but in terms of its intellectual history, that is, assuming that everything a "realist" wrote constitutes a coherent realist theory; see Morgenthau 1960, 5, 227.

26. Waltz follows Morgenthau almost verbatim: "Neo-realism establishes the autonomy of international politics and thus makes a theory about it possible"; see Waltz 1979, 29, and also 65–66, 79, 90, 108–12, 196–98, 271.

27. See Keohane 1984, 6; and Hellmann and Wolf 1993.

28. Powell 1994, 318.

29. Ruggie 1983, 107–10.

30. For example, see Gourevitch 1978.

31. Ruggie 1983, 90–91.

32. For a more general argument, see Elman 1996, especially 58–59.

33. See Harsanyi 1977; Hirshman 1945.

34. See Raiffa 1982; Sebenius 1991; Evans, Jacobson, and Putnam 1993.

References

Achen, Christopher. 1995. How Can We Tell a Unitary Rational Actor When We See One? Paper presented at the Midwest Political Science Association Convention, April.

Baldwin, David. 1997. The Concept of Security. *Review of International Studies* 23 (1): 5–26.

Bueno de Mesquita, Bruce. 1996. The Benefits of a Social Scientific Approach to Studying International Relations. In *Explaining International Relations Since 1945*, edited by Ngaire Woods. Oxford: Oxford University Press.

Coleman, James S. 1990. *Foundations of Social Theory.* Cambridge, Mass.: Harvard University Press.

Doyle, Michael. 1983. Kant, Liberal Legacies, and Foreign Affairs: Parts One and Two. *Philosophy and Public Affairs* 12 (summer–fall): 205–35, 325–53.

———. 1986. Liberalism and World Politics. *American Political Science Review* 80 (December): 1151–69.

———. 1997. *Ways of War and Peace.* New York: Norton.

Elman, Colin. 1996. Horses for Courses: Why Not Neorealist Theories of Foreign Policy? *Security Studies* 6 (autumn): 45–90.

Ekelund, Robert B., and Robert B. Tollison. 1981. *Mercantilism in a Rent-Seeking Society: Economic Regulation in Historical Perspective.* College Station, Tex.: Texas A&M Press.

Evans, Peter B., Harold K. Jacobson, and Robert D. Putnam, eds. 1993. *Double-Edged Diplomacy: International Bargaining and Domestic Politics.* Berkeley: University of California Press.

Fearon, James D. 1995. Rationalist Explanations of War. *International Organization* 49 (summer): 379–414.

Gilpin, Robert. 1975. *U.S. Power and the Multinational Corporation: The Political Economy of Direct Foreign Investment.* New York: Basic Books.

———. 1989. *The Political Economy of International Relations.* Princeton, N.J.: Princeton University Press.

Grieco, Joseph M. 1988. Anarchy and the Limits of Cooperation: A Realist Critique of the Newest Liberal Institutionalism. *International Organization* 42 (summer): 485–508.

———. 1990. *Cooperation Among Nations: Europe, America, and Non-Tariff Barriers to Trade.* Ithaca, N.Y.: Cornell University Press.

Gourevitch, Peter. 1978. The Second Image Reversed: The International Sources of Domestic Politics. *International Organization* 32 (autumn): 881–912.

Harsanyi, John. 1977. *Rational Behavior and Bargaining Equilibrium in Games and Social Situations.* Cambridge: Cambridge University Press.

Hellmann, Gunther, and Reinhard Wolf. 1993. Neorealism, Neoliberal Institutionalism, and the Future of NATO. *Security Studies* 3 (autumn): 3–43.

Hirschleifer, Jack. 1987. On the Emotions as Guarantors of Threats and Promises. In *The Latest on the Best: Essays on Evolution and Optimality*, edited by John Dupre, 307–26. Cambridge, Mass.: MIT Press.

Hirschman, Albert. 1945. *National Power and the Structure of Foreign Trade.* Berkeley: University of California Press.

Hoffmann, Stanley. 1987. Liberalism and International Affairs. In *Essays in the Theory and Practice of International Politics,* edited by Janus and Minerva Hoffmann, 394–417. Boulder, Colo.: Westview Press.

———. 1995. The Crisis of Liberal Internationalism. *Foreign Policy* 98 (spring): 159–79.

Howard, Michael. 1978. *War and the Liberal Conscience.* New Brunswick, N.J.: Rutgers University Press.

Kant, Immanuel, 1991. *Kant: Political Writings.* 2d ed. Edited by Hans Reiss, 41–53, 61–92, 93–130. Cambridge: Cambridge University Press.

Keohane, Robert O. 1984. *After Hegemony: Cooperation and Discord in the World Political Economy.* Princeton, N.J.: Princeton University Press.

———. 1986. Theory of World Politics: Structural Realism and Beyond. In *Neo-Realism and its Critics,* edited by Robert O. Keohane, 158–203. New York: Columbia University Press.

———. 1989. *International Institutions and State Power: Essays in International Relations Theory.* Boulder, Colo.: Westview Press.

———. 1990. International Liberalism Reconsidered. In *The Economic Limits to Modern Politics,* edited by John Dunn. Cambridge: Cambridge University Press.

Keohane, Robert O., and Helen V. Milner, eds. 1996. *Internationalization and Domestic Politics.* Cambridge: Cambridge University Press.

Keohane, Robert O., and Joseph S. Nye. 1989. *Power and Interdependence: World Politics in Transition.* 2d ed. Boston: Little, Brown.

Martin, Lisa. 1992. *Coercive Cooperation: Explaining Multilateral Economic Sanctions.* Princeton, N.J.: Princeton University Press.

Matthew, Richard A., and Mark W. Zacher. 1995. Liberal International Theory: Common Threads, Divergent Strands. In *Controversies in International Relations Theory: Realism and the Neo-Liberal Challenge,* edited by Charles Kegley, 107–50. New York: St. Martin's Press.

Milgrom, Paul, and John Roberts. 1990. Bargaining, Influence Costs, and Organization. In *Perspectives on Positive Political Economy,* edited by James E. Alt and Kenneth A. Schepsle, 57–89. Cambridge: Cambridge University Press.

Morgenthau, Hans J. 1960. *Politics Among Nations: The Struggle for Power and Peace.* 3d ed. New York: Alfred Knopf.

North, Douglass C., and Robert Paul Thomas. 1973. *The Rise of the Western World: A New Economic History.* Cambridge: Cambridge University Press.

Nye, Joseph S. 1988. Neorealism and Neoliberalism. *World Politics* 40 (January): 235–51.

Powell, Robert. 1994. Anarchy in International Relations Theory: The Neorealist-Neoliberal Debate. *International Organization* 48 (spring): 313–44.

Raiffa, Howard. 1982. *The Art and Science of Negotiation.* Cambridge, Mass.: Harvard University Press.

Ruggie, John Gerard. 1982. International Regimes, Transactions, and Change: Embedded Liberalism in the Postwar Economic Order. *International Organization* 36 (spring): 195–231.

———. 1983. Continuity and Transformation in the World Polity: Toward a Neorealist Synthesis. *World Politics* 35 (January): 261–85.

Sebenius, James K. 1991. Negotiation Analysis. In *International Negotiations: Analysis, Approaches, Issues,* edited by Victor A. Kremenyuk, 65–77. San Francisco: Jossey-Bass.

Slaughter Anne-Marie. 1995. Law in a World of Liberal States. *European Journal of International Law* 6 (December): 503–38.

Snidal, Duncan. 1985. Coordination Versus Prisoner's Dilemma: Implications for International Cooperation and Regimes. *American Political Science Review* 79 (December): 923–42.

Stein, Arthur A. 1982. Coordination and Collaboration: Regimes in an Anarchic World. *International Organization* 36 (spring): 299–324.

Van Evera, Stephen. 1990. Primed for Peace: Europe After the Cold War. *International Security* 15 (Winter): 5–57.

Walt, Stephen. 1987. *The Origins of Alliances.* Ithaca, N.Y.: Cornell University Press.

Waltz, Kenneth N. 1979. *Theory of International Politics.* Reading, Mass.: Addison-Wesley.

Perception and Misperception
in International Politics

ROBERT JERVIS

In a presentation based on psychology and social psychology, Professor Jervis discusses the relations among different levels of analysis used by students of international relations. He also makes a case for the importance of understanding individual perception (and misperception) in the study of foreign policy and world politics. In a "two-step" model, actor images and perceptions are related to the actor's understanding of reality based on available information.

Do Perceptions Matter?

Before discussing the causes and consequences of the ways in which decision-makers draw inferences from the world, we must ask a preliminary question: do the decision-makers' perceptions matter? This is an empirical question. Logic permits us to distinguish between the "psychological milieu" (the world as the actor sees it) and the "operational milieu" (the world in which the policy will be carried out) and to argue that policies and decisions must be mediated by statesmen's goals, calculations, and perceptions.[1] But it does not follow from this that we must deal with these intervening variables in order to understand and predict behavior. This is not an uncommon claim:

> One may describe particular events, conditions, and interactions between states without necessarily probing the nature and outcome of the processes through which state action evolves. However, and the qualification is crucial, if one wishes to probe the "why" questions underlying the events, conditions, and interaction patterns which rest upon state action, then decision-making analysis is certainly necessary. We would

go so far as to say *that the "why" questions cannot be answered without analysis of decision-making.*[2]

But theory and explanation need not fill in all the links between cause and effect. Indeed, this is impossible. One can always ask for the links between the links. High density theories have no privileged status; they are not automatically illuminating or fruitful.[3] It is true that re-creating a decision-maker's goals, calculations, and perceptions is a satisfying method of explaining his behavior because the scholar, sharing as he does the decision-maker's characteristics of being a thinking, goal-seeking person, can easily say: "If that is the way the statesman saw the situation, it is no wonder that he acted as he did." But the comfort we feel with this form of explanation should not blind us to the fact that, unless there are significant variations in the ways people see the world that affect how they act, we need not explore decision-making in order to explain foreign policy. Most case studies assume that the details presented significantly affected the outcomes. This may not be true, however. "Pleikus are streetcars," McGeorge Bundy said in explaining that the Viet Cong attack on the American installation in February 1965 had affected only the timing of the American bombing of North Vietnam.[4] If you are waiting for one, it will come along. The specifics of the triggering event cannot explain the outcome because so many probable events could have substituted for it. To understand the American policy of bombing the North we should not examine the attack on Pleiku. Had it not occurred, something else would have happened that would have permitted the same response. Logic alone cannot tell us that a similar claim about the decision-making process is invalid: the way people perceive others and make decisions only marginally influences outcomes. So we must seek empirical evidence on the question: do the important explanatory variables in international relations involve decision-making? In terms of perceptions this can be separated into two subsidiary questions: "are important differences in policy preferences traceable to differences in decision-makers' perceptions of their environments?" and "are there important differences between reality and shared or common perceptions?"[5]

These questions raise the familiar level of analysis problem. Although it has been much debated, agreement is lacking not only on the substantive dispute but even on the number of levels. Arnold Wolfers proposes two, Kenneth Waltz three, and James Rosenau five.[6] To fill in the sequence, we will discuss four. One is the level of decision-making, the second is the level of the bureaucracy, the third is that of the nature of the state and the workings of domestic politics, and the fourth focuses on the international environment.[7] Which level one focuses on is not arbitrary and is not a matter of taste—it is the product of beliefs (or often hunches) about the nature of the variables that influence the phenomena that concern one. To restate the first question in terms of the level of analysis problem, we need not adopt a decision-making approach if all states behave the same way in the same objective situation, if all states of the same kind (i.e., with the same internal

characteristics and politics) behave the same way in the same objective situation, or if state behavior is determined by bureaucratic routines and interests.

Although the empirical questions are central here, we should also note that the level of analysis problem has important moral implications. When all people would respond the same way to a given situation, it is hard to praise or blame the decision-maker. Thus, those accused of war crimes will argue that their behavior did not differ from others who found themselves in the same circumstances. And the prosecution will charge, as it did against Tojo and his colleagues, that, "These defendants were not automatons; they were not replaceable cogs in a machine. . . . It was theirs to choose whether their nation would lead an honored life . . . or . . . would become a symbol of evil throughout the world. They made their choice. For this choice they must bear the guilt." Similarly, if all nations follow similar courses of action, one cannot argue that some deserve to be branded as immorally aggressive. Thus in 1918 Bethmann-Hollweg rebutted those who blamed Germany for the war by pointing to the "general disposition towards war in the world . . . how else explain the senseless and impassioned zeal which allowed countries like Italy, Rumania and even America, not originally involved in the war, no rest until they too had immersed themselves in the bloodbath?"[8]

The three non-decision-making levels assert the importance of various aspects of the objective situation or the actor's role.[9] They say that if we know enough about the setting—international, national, or bureaucratic—we can explain and predict the actor's behavior. An interesting sidelight is that if other actors believed that the setting is crucial they would not need to scrutinize the details of the state's recent behavior or try to understand the goals and beliefs held by the state's decision-makers. It would be fruitless and pointless to ask what the state's intentions are if its behavior is determined by the situation in which it finds itself. Instead, observers would try to predict how the context will change because this will tell them what the state's response will be. Decision-makers could then freely employ their powers of vicarious identification and simply ask themselves how they would act if they were in the other's shoes. They would not have to worry about the possibility that the other might have values and beliefs that differed from theirs. It is interesting, although not decisive, to note that decision-makers rarely feel confident about using this method. They usually believe both that others may not behave as they would and that the decision-makers within the other state differ among themselves. So they generally seek a great deal of information about the views of each significant person in the other country.

Of course it is unlikely that there is a single answer to the question of which level is most important. Rather than one level containing the variables that are most significant for all problems, the importance of each level may vary from one issue area to another. Furthermore, which level of analysis is the most important may be determined by how rich and detailed an answer we are seeking. The environment may influence the general outline of the state's policy but not its specific responses. Thus it can be argued that, while decision-making analysis is needed to explain why World War I broke out in August 1914, the external situation would have led the states to fight sooner or later. Or the importance of variables at each level may vary with the stages of a decision. For example, domestic politics may dictate that a given event be made the occasion for a change in policy; bargaining within the bureaucracy may explain what options are presented to the national leaders; the decision-maker's predisposition could account for the choice that was made; and the interests and routines of the bureaucracies could explain the way the decision was implemented. And the same variable may have different effects at different stages of the decision-making process—for example, conflicts among subordinates may increase the variety of information and the number of opportunities for decision that the top decision-maker gets, but may simultaneously decrease his ability to see that his decisions are faithfully implemented.

The importance of variables at one level can also vary with the state of variables at other levels. Rosenau suggests that the international environment is more important in determining the policy of small states than it is of large ones and Stanley Hoffmann argues that nuclear weapons and bipolarity have reversed this relationship.[10] More generally, the importance of the other levels decreases if the variables in one level are in extreme states. Thus, maneuvering within the bureaucracy may be more important when the top decision-makers are inexperienced or preoccupied with other matters. And Wolfers argues that states tend to behave the same way when they are faced with extreme danger or extreme opportunity, but that when environmental constraints are less severe there will be differences in behavior that must be explained at the decision-making level. More complex interactions among the levels are also possible. For example, the effect of internal instability on expansionism could vary with the opportunities for success in war. Unstable states may be more prone to aggression than stable ones when the chances of victory are high but might be more cautious than others when their leaders perceive a significant probability of defeat or even of temporary setback. Or the stability of the regime might influence its propensity for aggression, but the nature of the regime (e.g., whether it is democratic or dictatorial) might be more important in explaining how it makes peace.

To deal with all these questions would require another book. Here all I will try to do is to outline the kinds of evidence necessary to establish the validity of simple propositions about the importance of the various levels. In doing so, I will sketch the most extreme arguments for the importance of each level. It is obvious that the questions and arguments could be rephrased in more subtle terms but since I am concerned with the kinds of evidence that the propositions call for the gain in analytical clarity is worth the sacrifice involved in ignoring more complete explanations that combine a multitude of variables at many levels.

The International Environment

To argue that the international environment determines a state's behavior is to assert that all states react similarly to the same objective external situation. Changes in a state's domestic regime, its bureaucratic structure, and the personalities and opinions of its leaders do not lead to changes of policies. Changes in the external situation, however, do alter behavior, even when variables on the other levels remain constant. To test these claims, we would need good measures of all the variables, especially the nature of the objective situation and the state's policies. Even if we had such indicators, we would have to cope with the paucity of the most desired kinds of comparisons. This is easily understood by glancing at the similar issue in the study of individual behavior—the debate over the relative importance of situation and role versus idiosyncratic variables in determining individual behavior. Because so many people of widely differing backgrounds, personalities, and opinions fill the same role and because the same person fills many different roles, we can try to determine the relative impact of situational and idiosyncratic variables by examining how a person's behavior varies as his role changes and how people of widely differing characteristics perform in similar situations.

It is much harder to make the analogous comparisons in international relations. In only a few international systems do we find many cases in which states play, either simultaneously or consecutively, several roles and in which each role is filled by states that are otherwise quite

different. This would occur in a long-lasting system where there were frequent changes in the relations among the actors. Thus each state might at one time be a neutral, a "holder of the balance," a state with aggressive designs, a defender faced by a state whose intentions are difficult to determine, and so on. To a limited degree this test is possible in a balance-of-power system. But it is not available for most other systems, for example the one prevailing since World War II. Most nations have not changed roles, and indeed cannot do so because of such permanent factors as size and geography. The United States can never play the role of a second-ranking state caught between two blocs of greater powers. France can never be the leader of one of two dominant blocs. And while the United States and France may have played roles similar to these in the past, the extensive differences in the situation mean that any differences in response that might be found would not show that roles are unimportant.

Compulsion in Extreme Circumstances. It is worthwhile to look at cases of the kind that are supposed to show most strongly the influence of external conditions. If there are differences of behavior here, the argument for not ignoring the other levels of analysis will apply a fortiori to a wider domain of cases. Arnold Wolfers argues that, the greater the external compulsion, the greater the homogeneity of behavior and therefore the less the need to study decision-making. In a well-known passage he says: "Imagine a number of individuals, varying widely in their predispositions, who find themselves inside a house on fire. It would be perfectly realistic to expect that these individuals, with rare exceptions, would feel compelled to run toward the exits. . . . Surely, therefore, for an explanation of the rush for the exits, there is no need to analyze the individual decisions that produced it."[11]

But the case is not as clear as this analogy suggests. If a situation were so compelling that all people would act alike, decision-makers would not hesitate nor feel torn among several alternative policies, nor would there be significant debates within the decision-making elite. In fact, key decisions that are easily reached, such as those involving the Truman Doctrine and Marshall Plan, stand out because they are so rare. For despite the implication of Wolfer's proposition that we know when we are faced by extreme danger, just as we can tell when the house is on fire, in fact this question is often bitterly contested. (To say that once decision-makers perceive the fire they will head for the exits leads us back to decision-making analysis.) For Churchill, the house was burning soon after Hitler took power in Germany; for Chamberlain, this was the case only after March 1939; and for others there never was a fire at all. To some decision-makers, the Soviet Union is a threat to which the United States is compelled to respond. To others the threat passed years ago. Again, to a growing number of scholars it never existed. Similarly, American statesmen saw a much greater threat from communism in both Europe and Southeast Asia than did the leaders of our allies. Decision-makers may even agree that their state's existence is threatened but disagree about the source of the threat. This was true, for example, in the United States around the turn of the nineteenth century, when the Federalists believed France so much a menace that they favored war with her. At the same time, the Republicans believed England an equal menace. (It should be noted that this disagreement was rooted as much in differences in values and interests as in divergent empirical analyses of the situation.)

In extreme cases we can specify with some certainty an indicator of the "fire" that all decision-makers will recognize—for example a large armed attack—and we can be relatively certain that the state will react. But even then the objective situation will not determine all aspects of the state's response. There are apt to be several exits from the burning house. Will the state limit the extent of its involvement? What will its war

aims be? While the United States may have had no choice but to declare war on Japan after Pearl Harbor, the major decisions that followed were less compelled and require further explanation. For example: the United States decided not to concentrate its energies on the country that had attacked it but to fight Germany first; the war was to be fought with few considerations for the shape of the postwar world; and no compromise with the enemies would be accepted (had the Japanese realized this would be the case, they almost certainly would not have attacked).

Even if all states and all statesmen responded similarly to similar high threats, we have to explain how the threat arose—i.e., why the adversary was so aggressive. In some cases we may be able to do this by reference to the other's objective situation, for example by focusing on the anarchic nature of the international system and the resulting security dilemma. . . . But when this analysis is insufficient, the state (and later scholars) must examine variables at other levels of analysis to establish some of the most important facts about the objective situation that the state faces.

Finally, one cannot prove that the external environment determines the response by simply showing that the decision-makers believed this to be the cause. It is not enough to say with Kecskemeti that "In tense war situations, the decision-maker is likely to feel that he is acting from necessity rather than from deliberate choice." Nor is it sufficient to cite Holsti's finding that the decision-makers on both sides in July 1914 felt that they had no choice but to make the decision they did, or to show that when "Mr. Acheson was advised not to favor the production of the first thermonuclear bomb, he is reported to have declared that its production was a matter of necessity and not of choice: in other words, that he was experiencing 'compulsion.' "[12] The subjective feeling of determinancy is interesting and may lead decision-makers unnecessarily to restrict their search for alternatives, but it does not show that other decision-makers in the same situation would have felt the same compulsion and acted in the same way. Indeed the theory of cognitive dissonance . . . and other theories of irrational cognitive consistency . . . lead us to expect that decision-makers may avoid psychological conflict by thinking that they had no choice but to act as they did. This also means that, when scholars claim that a situation permitted no policy other than the one that was adopted, it may be that at least part of the reason why the circumstances appear overwhelming in retrospect is that they were claimed to be so by the decision-makers.

These arguments are, of course, far from conclusive. The necessary comparisons have merely been mentioned, not made. But, as we have seen, there are many points at which people can disagree about what the objective situation is or what policies will best cope with it, and there is little evidence for the existence of the homogeneity of behavior that would allow us to ignore everything except the international setting.

Domestic Determinants

Even if all states do not behave similarly in similar situations, the details of decision-making and images may not be significant. Instead, the state may be the appropriate level of analysis—i.e., variations in decision-makers' policies may be accounted for by variations in social and economic structure and domestic politics of the states they are serving. Wilsonian and Marxist theories are examples of this position. Other theories at this level of analysis argue for the importance of a state's geographical position, its traditions, its national style, or the consequences, often unintended, of domestic conflicts. Extreme formulations hold that the state's internal system determines its foreign policy, while weaker versions claim that foreign policies are a product of both domestic politics and international circumstances.

The forms of the assertions correspond to those discussed in the previous section. States with the same critical internal attributes behave the same way in similar situations—and often

behave the same way in the face of significant variations in the environment—and this behavior is different from that displayed by other states with different attributes even when the setting is the same. The latter claim denies the overriding importance of the international environment. Thus while Cold War revisionists stress the importance of America's domestic political and economic needs, others reply that American actions were heavily influenced by external constraints and that her behavior was not peculiarly American or peculiarly capitalist but rather was typical of any great power in such a situation. Because we are concerned with examining the importance of decision-making, we will not treat this part of the argument that deals with conflicts between claims for two other levels of analysis.

If states of the same type behave in the same way, then changes in a state's leadership will not produce significant changes in foreign policy, and we need not examine the images, values, and calculations of individual decision-makers. Unfortunately, claims about continuity in a state's foreign policy are notoriously difficult to judge. We might try to see whether we could deduce changes in the identities of the state's decision-makers from the course of its foreign policy. Could we tell when Democrats replaced Republicans or Conservatives replaced Labour governments? Scholars used to agree that Stalin's death led to major foreign policy changes, but now even this is in doubt.[13] Before taking office, decision-makers often claim they will introduce new policies. But these promises are often neglected. Eisenhower's foreign policy more closely resembled that of his predecessor than it did his campaign rhetoric. Gladstone pledged himself to avoid immoral and wasteful imperialism, and, although he successfully extricated Britain from some entanglements, he was eventually drawn into commitments similar to those made by Disraeli. And while in 1937 Clement Atlee said that "the foreign policy of a Government is the reflection of its internal policy," when his party took power the foreign secretary declared that "Revolutions do not change geography, and revolutions do not change geographical needs."[14]

Many arguments about the wisdom of policies can be understood in terms of claims about the autonomy of the decision-making level. Those who praise Bismarck's diplomacy claim that, had he continued in office, he would have been able to maintain German security by avoiding the errors of severing Germany's ties to Russia, being forced to rely on Austria, and recklessly antagonizing several powerful countries. The rejoinder is that the dynamics of German domestic society and of the international system would have destroyed Bismarck's handiwork no matter who was in power. The glittering skill of Bismarck's diplomacy could not alter the underlying forces at work. Debates about the origins of the Cold War must deal with the similar question of whether Roosevelt's death changed American policy. Most traditional accounts argue that F. D. R. was coming to an anti-Soviet position and would have acted much as Truman did. This view is shared by those revisionists who look to the American political and economic system for the roots of foreign policy but is disputed by those who see the Cold War as avoidable. Similarly, those who defend President Kennedy but opposed the war in Vietnam argue that he would not have acted as Johnson did. Those who either favored the war or opposed not only it but also most recent American foreign policies argue that the policies of these—and other—presidents were consistent. While those who supported the war see the determinants as international and those who criticize the general lines of America's postwar policy see the causes as domestic, both argue that few significant differences can be traced to the identity of the president.

These questions are so difficult to resolve partly because the situation facing the new government always differs from that which confronted the old. Kennedy was never forced to choose between defeat in Vietnam and fighting a major war. F. D. R. did not live to see Russia consolidate her hold over East Europe. The questions must then be hypothetical, and the comparisons that underlie our judgments are often strained. This problem can be avoided by using alternative comparisons—by examining the views of members of the elite to see whether they favor the policy that was adopted. Of course disagreement with a policy does not prove that a person would have acted on his views were he in office. His opposition might be rooted in his role in the government, lack of information, freedom from the pressures that accompany holding power, or the belief that opposition is politically expedient. But when these explanations are not satisfactory, internal elite disagreement reveals the limits of the impact of both domestic politics and the international situation.

The Bureaucracy

Even if state behavior cannot be explained by the state's internal politics and external environment, we still may not need to examine the perceptions and calculations of the top decision-makers. The workings of the bureaucracy may determine policy. It is not enough for proponents of this position to show that the state's course of action appears inconsistent and lacks value integration. Such inadequacies can be the product of individual decision-making. As we will show later, normal human behavior often does not fit even a loose definition of rationality. Individuals as well as organizations fail to coordinate their actions and to develop carefully designed strategies. The fact that people must reach decisions in the face of the burdens of multiple goals and highly ambiguous information means that policies are often contradictory, incoherent, and badly suited to the information at hand. Unless we understand this, puzzling state behavior will automatically be seen as the product of either internal bargaining or the autonomous operation of different parts of the government. Thus if we did not know better it would be tempting to argue that the contradictory and erratic behavior displayed by Richard Nixon on Watergate and related matters shows that "Nixon" is not a single individual at all, but rather a title for the set of behaviors that are produced by the interaction of conflicting entities, each pursuing its own narrow interests in ignorance of or indifference to any wider goal of the "general Nixon interest." Similarly, if we were to insist that theories of individual behavior apply only when the actor is following a coherent path guided by his self-interest, we would have to say that Spiro Agnew was an uncoordinated bureaucracy rather than a person because he simultaneously accepted kickbacks and sought the presidency.

Because incoherent policy is insufficient evidence for the importance of bureaucracies, the "pure" theories of this type must make two basic assertions. First, bureaucrats' policy preferences are determined by their positions in the government: "Where you stand is determined by where you sit." The external environment and the nature of the state and domestic politics have only limited and indirect impact on these preferences. Of course if the concept of bureaucratic interest is to be more useful than the concept of national interest, we must be able to specify in advance what the bureaucratic position will be. Even if we cannot do this, it would still be significant if everyone in each unit of the government had the same position on a given issue. If, on the other hand, there is a good deal of disagreement within the organization about the goals to be sought or the means that are appropriate, then we would have to apply decision-making analysis to the bureaucratic level, and so this approach would lose much of its distinctiveness. More importantly, if people in different units share the same policy preferences or if preferences are distributed at random throughout the government, then the first assertion would be undermined.

The second basic claim of theories on this level of analysis is that the state's policies are formed by bureaucratic bargains and routines. Bureaucratic actions either determine the statesman's decision or else implement it in a way that renders the decision largely irrelevant to what is actually done. This point is vital because, even if bureaucrats' policy preferences were linked to their positions within the government, this would be relatively unimportant unless these preferences explain policy outcomes. But we should note at the start that even if this were true we would have to explore the sources of power of parts of the bureaucracy. If we find, for example, that the military often prevails in conflicts with the organization in charge of arms control, this may be because over a period of years the state's leaders have supported the former more than the latter. Sometimes we can go back some years to find a decisive action that set the guidelines for both the policy and the distribution of power within the bureaucracy. In less dramatic cases the relative strengths of interests represent the standing decision of the decision-makers—and often of wider publics—and their choices among competing policies and values. To the extent that this distribution of power is both important and accounted for by factors outside the bureaucracy, an explanation of specific outcomes in terms of bureaucratic maneuvering will be superficial at best.

Are policy preferences determined by one's role within the government? With the important exception of questions of military hardware and doctrine, the evidence is limited and ambiguous. It is not hard to find examples of units taking consistent and unified stands and political appointees adopting their units' views and thus expressing different opinions depending upon their positions in the government. "General Marshall, while Chief of Staff, opposed the State Department's idea of using aid to promote reforms in the Chinese government. Then, when he became Secretary of State, he defended this very idea against challenges voiced by the new chiefs of Staff." In "1910, Winston Churchill, as Home Secretary, led the attack upon the demand of McKenna, First Lord of the Admiralty, for more ships; by 1913 they had exchanged offices and each, with equal conviction, maintained the opposite view." When Samuel Hoare was secretary of state for air, he strongly fought against naval control of the Fleet Air Arm; when he later served as first lord of the Admiralty he took the opposite position. When Théophile Delcassé was the minister of colonies in France before the turn of the century, he supported an expedition to the Nile that would give France a lever to use against Britain. As foreign secretary, he sought to recall the adventure.

But not all policy disagreements are traceable to roles. Organizational perspectives and loyalties are less important when issues are unusual rather than routine, necessitate relatively quick decisions, and involve important and generally shared values. Beliefs about the most important issues of foreign policy—those involving war and peace—are usually unrelated to roles. When we look at the major decisions of American foreign policy—those that set the terms for future debates and established the general framework within which policy was then conducted—it does not seem to be true, at least for the top decision-makers, that "where you sit determines where you stand."

In several important cases what is most striking is the degree of unanimity. In the spring of 1947 there was general agreement within the government that massive aid for Europe was needed. Three years later most officials felt that foreign policy considerations argued for large-scale rearmament, although there was a disagreement—which was not tightly connected with bureaucratic interests—over whether domestic political and economic constraints made such a policy feasible. Once the Korean War removed this opposition, government officials were again in general agreement. In other important cases there are basic disputes, but the key to them is not divergent bureaucratic interests. Doves and hawks on Vietnam were to be found in all parts of the American government. Views on whether to take a hard line toward Japan before World War II, and specifically on the crucial issue of embargoing oil and other vital raw materials, were only loosely related to organizational affiliations. The advice that Truman received at the start of the Berlin blockade and the Korean War and most of the differences that emerged in the discussions during the Cuban missile crisis were not predictable by the participants' roles.

In the missile crisis none of the leading officials espoused views that were linked to his position within the government. The Republican secretary of the treasury was concerned about the effects of a "soft" response on the fortunes of the Democratic party in the coming elections; the secretary of defense at first argued that the missiles did not present a major military threat; the secretary of state did not take a strong position and did not pay special attention to the political consequences of various moves; and the attorney general opposed an air strike. (It should also be noted that his view carried great weight not because of his governmental position or independent political resources, but because he was thought to speak for the president.)

The other claim—that policies can be explained by bureaucratic maneuvering—could be supported in either of two ways. First, it could be shown that different parts of the government carry out, or fail to carry out, policies in ways that are consistent with their preferences and routines rather than with the decisions of the national leaders. But the other possible linkage in the second point—the argument that authoritative decisions can be explained by the interaction of bureaucratic stands—raises difficulties that go deeper than the temporary absence of evidence. To verify this claim we must be able to specify the expected relationship between the variety of bureaucratic positions on the one hand and policy outcomes on the other. It is not enough to show that the outcome can be seen as a compromise among views that have been advocated by various parts of the government. Almost any decision could fit this description. The theory must provide generalizations that tell us more exactly what the outcome will be. If the goals of different parts of the bureaucracy are complementary, then presumably each agency will give up its position on the part of the program it cares least about in order to gain a larger voice on those issues that are more important to it. Presumably the success of an organization in conflicts with others is related to its strength (determined independently of outcomes), although as we noted this raises further questions. Still another likely pattern is that the symbols will be given to one side in a bureaucratic conflict and the substance to the other. But much more detail is needed. Furthermore, these generalizations must not involve the values and beliefs that vary with the identity of the top decision-makers, and they must be able to explain how policies change. The latter task poses great problems since bureaucratic structures and interests often remain constant over periods in which policies shift.

Although the paucity of research on this level makes conclusions especially tentative, it is hard to see how any of the major decisions of American foreign policy in recent years could meet this test. The Marshall Plan, the establishment of NATO, the crucial decisions in Korea, the rearmament that followed, the decision to integrate West Germany into West Europe, the New Look in defense, American policy in the Suez crisis, Kennedy's attempt to increase conventional forces in Europe, the major decisions to fight and later withdraw from Vietnam, and crucial choices in the Cuban missile crisis cannot be explained as the outcome of intrabureaucratic conflict. That these decisions combined major elements of positions held within the bureaucracy is hardly surprising because different parts of the bureaucracy serve and represent divergent values that the president seeks to further. Thus what seems to be a clash of bureaucratic interests and stands can often be more fruitfully viewed as a clash among values that are widely held in both the society and the decision-makers' own minds. What embarrasses the theories under consideration here is that, while the decisions listed above did embody some of the

preferences that had been articulated by parts of the bureaucracy, they did not combine them in a way that can be predicted by rules of bureaucratic politics. Or, to put the argument more exactly, until we have a theory that specifies how policy is formed out of conflicting bureaucratic perspectives and preferences, we cannot tell whether any given outcome can be explained by this level of analysis. As things stand now, there is no way to explore the extent to which bureaucratic factors cause the outcome because we have no ground for claiming that a different constellation of bureaucratic interests and forces would have produced a different result or that the outcome would have been different were there no bureaucracies at all.

Perceptions, Reality, and a Two-Step Model

Our discussion thus far leads to the conclusion that it is often impossible to explain crucial decisions and policies without reference to the decision-makers' beliefs about the world and their images of others. That is to say, these cognitions are part of the proximate cause of the relevant behavior and other levels of analysis cannot immediately tell us what they will be. And even if we found that people in the same situation— be it international, domestic, or bureaucratic— behave in the same way, it is useful to examine decision-making if there are constant differences between the decision-makers' perceptions and reality. In this case all people might react in the same way to the same situation, but this behavior would puzzle an observer because it was self-defeating, based on incorrect beliefs about the world, or generally lacking in a high degree of rationality. Many of the propositions advanced in here fit in this category: they are generalizations about how decision-makers perceive others' behavior and form judgments about their intentions. These patterns are explained by the general ways in which people draw inferences from ambiguous evidence and, in turn, help explain many seemingly incomprehensible policies. They show how, why, and when highly intelligent and conscientious statesmen misperceive their environments in specified ways and reach inappropriate decisions.

Other propositions deal with cases in which an analysis of decision-making is necessary because people in the same situations behave differently. This is often the case because people differ in their perceptions of the world in general and of other actors in particular. Sometimes it will be useful to ask who, if anyone, was right; but often it will be more fruitful to ask why people differed and how they came to see the world as they did.

The exploration of the images actors hold and the development of the two kinds of propositions discussed above should be seen in the context of a mediated or two-step model.[15] Rather than trying to explain foreign policies as the direct consequence of variables at the three levels of analysis previously discussed, we will examine the actor's perceptions as one of the immediate causes of his behavior. Thus Britain and France felt that their security was endangered by Germany before both world wars. They may have been mistaken in the first case and correct in the second, but both cases can be grouped together in discussing the immediate causes of their responses.

Our understanding of the actor's images and beliefs affects the further question that we ask about that event and the behavior that we expect of the actor in other cases. For example, when it was believed that most American decision-makers had thought that escalation would bring a quick victory in Vietnam, the interesting questions concerned the reasons for the error and the ways by which successive small steps increased the stakes of the conflict. If the decision-makers believed that victory was cheap, it is not surprising that they acted as they did. But by revealing that the decision-makers had a relatively accurate view of the chances of success, the Pentagon Papers and related commentaries have shown that the crucial question is why saving Vietnam was considered important enough to justify the high expected price. This then leads us to look at

this and other American actions in terms of beliefs about "domino effects" rather than directing our attention to commitments that develop inadvertently and "quagmires" that trap unwary statesmen. Similarly, the question about Russian behavior raised by the Cuban missile crisis probably is not "What Soviet calculus and risk-taking propensity could explain this bold and dangerous step?" but rather "How could they have so badly misestimated the probable American response?"[16] And previous Soviet behavior can be re-examined to see if it could be explained by similar misperceptions. . . . Actors as well as scholars must engage in these kinds of analyses.

Of course perceptions, and more specifically perceptions of other actors, are not the only decision-making variables that are important. That two actors have the same perceptions does not guarantee that they will adopt the same response. But their responses will often be the same and, when they are not, it is usually relatively easy to find the causes of the differences. Although people with different images of an adversary may agree on the appropriate response, just as people may favor the same policy for different reasons, this agreement is apt to be short-lived. . . . The roots of many important disputes about policies lie in differing perceptions. And in the frequent cases when the actors do not realize this, they will misunderstand their disagreement and engage in a debate that is unenlightening.

Images, however, are not first causes, and so we will try to find the causes both of common misperceptions and of differences in perceptions. Thus the second step in the model involves relating the images held, if not to reality, then at least to the information available to the actor. How, for example, do statesmen come to develop their images of other actors? What evidence do they pay most attention to? What makes them perceive threat? Under what conditions do they think that the other, although hostile, has only limited objectives? What differentiates legitimate inducements from bribes? What kinds of behavior are most apt to change an established image?

This is not to claim that we will be able to explain nearly all state behavior. Propositions about both the causes and the effects of images can only be probabilistic. There are too many variables at work to claim more. In the cases in which we are interested, decision-makers are faced with a large number of competing values, highly complex situations, and very ambiguous information. The possibilities and reasons for misperceptions and disagreements are legion. For these reasons, generalizations in this area are difficult to develop, exceptions are common, and in many instances the outcomes will be influenced by factors that, from the standpoint of most theories, must be considered accidental. Important perceptual predispositions can be discovered, but often they will not be controlling.

Notes

1. See especially the following works by Harold and Margaret Sprout: *Man–Milieu Relationship Hypotheses in the Context of International Politics* (Princeton: Center of International Studies, 1956); *The Ecological Perspective on Human Affairs* (Princeton: Princeton University Press, 1965); and *An Ecological Paradigm for the Study of International Politics* (Princeton: Center of International Studies, Princeton University, Research Monograph No. 30, March, 1968).

2. "Decision-Making As an Approach to the Study of International Politics," in Richard Snyder, H. W. Bruck, and Burton Sapin, eds., *Foreign Policy Decision-Making* (New York: Free Press, 1962), p. 33. . . .

3. Hirschi and Selvin, *Delinquency Research,* p. 38. . . .

4. Quoted in Townsend Hoopes, *The Limits of Intervention* (New York: McKay, 1969), p. 30.

5. The question of the existence and nature of reality need not be treated here in its profound sense. For our purposes the consensus of later observers usually provides an adequate operational definition of reality.

6. Arnold Wolfers, "The Actors in International Politics," in *Discord and Collaboration* (Baltimore, Md: Johns Hopkins Press, 1962), pp. 3–24; Kenneth Waltz, *Man, the State and War* (New York: Columbia Univer-

sity Press, 1959); James Rosenau, "Pre-Theories and Theories of Foreign Policy," in R. Barry Farrell, ed., *Approaches to Comparative and International Politics* (Evanston, IL: Northwestern University Press, 1966), pp. 29–92.

7. We refer to the international environment rather than the international system because we are not dealing with systems theories. Our concern is with explaining specific foreign policies rather than finding general patterns of interaction.

8. Quoted in Robert Butow, *Tojo and the Coming of the War* (Princeton: Princeton University Press, 1961), p. 506; quoted in Egmont Zechlin, "Cabinet versus Economic Warfare in Germany," in H. W. Koch, ed., *The Origins of the First World War* (London: Macmillan & Co., 1972), p. 165.

9. See K. Holsti, "National Role Conceptions in the Study of Foreign Policy," *International Studies Quarterly* 14 (September 1970), 233–309.

10. James Rosenau, "Pre-Theories and Theories of Foreign Policy," pp. 47–48; Stanley Hoffmann, "Restraints and Choices in American Foreign Policy," *Daedalus* (Fall 1962), 692–94.

11. Wolfers, *Discord and Collaboration,* p. 13.

12. Paul Kecskemeti, *Strategic Surrender* (New York: Atheneum, 1964), pp. 19–20; Ole Holsti, "The 1914 Case," *The American Political Science Review* 59 (June 1965), 365–78; Wolfers, *Discord and Collaboration,* p. 14.

13. Marshall Shulman, *Stalin's Foreign Policy Reappraised* (Cambridge, MA: Harvard University Press, 1963).

14. Michael Gordon, *Conflict and Consensus in Labour's Foreign Policy, 1914–1965* (Stanford, CA: Stanford University Press, 1969), p. 6; M. A. Fitzsimons, *The Foreign Policy of the British Labour Government, 1945–1951* (Notre Dame, IN: University of Notre Dame Press, 1953), p. 26.

15. See Charles Osgood, "Behavior Theory and the Social Sciences," in Roland Young, ed., *Approaches to the Study of Politics* (Evanston, IL: Northwestern University Press, 1958), pp. 217–44. . . .

16. Daniel Ellsberg, "The Quagmire Myth and the Stalemate Machine," in *Papers on the War* (New York: Simon and Schuster, 1972), pp. 42–135; Leslie Gelb, "Vietnam: The System Worked," *Foreign Policy* No. 3 (Summer 1971), 140–67; Klaus Knorr, "Failures in National Intelligence Estimates: The Case of the Cuban Missiles," *World Politics* 16 (April 1967), 455–67. . . .

Crisis Decision Making

O L E   R.   H O L S T I

The author reviews theoretical work done on crisis decision making, especially the World War I (1914) and the Cuban missile crisis (1962) cases. Cognitive rigidity, time pressures, and stress are among the factors that challenge the rationality of decisionmakers in crises.

One of the more interesting bodies of theory on crisis behavior is that concentrating upon individual stress. This approach, as indicated previously, focuses upon the impact of crisis-induced stress on certain aspects of cognitive performance that are critical in decision making. In assessing the potential impact of crisis on cognitive performance, it is important to do so against realistic standards. Cognitive limits on rationality include, as suggested by evidence from psychology, limits on the individual's capacity to receive, process, and assimilate information about the situation; an inability to generate the entire set of policy alternatives; fragmentary knowledge about the consequences of each option; and an inability to order preferences for all possible consequences on a single utility scale.[1] Because these constraints exist in all but the most trivial decision-making situations, it is not instructive to assess the impact on crises against a standard of synoptic rationality. A more modest and useful set of criteria might include an individual's ability to do the following:

Identify adequately the objectives to be fulfilled;

Survey the major alternative courses of action;

Estimate the probable costs and risks, as well as the positive consequences, of various al-

ternatives (and, as a corollary, distinguish the possible from the probable);

Search for new information relevant to assessment of the options;

Maintain an open mind to new information, even that which calls into question the validity of preferred courses of action (and as corollaries, discriminate between relevant and irrelevant information, resist premature cognitive closure, and tolerate ambiguity);

Assess the situation from the perspective of other parties;

Resist both defensive procrastination and premature decision;

Make adjustments to meet real changes in the situation (and, as a corollary, distinguish real from apparent changes).

A vast body of theory and evidence suggests that intense and protracted crises tend to erode rather than enhance these cognitive abilities. Figure 1—a series of hypotheses linking the defining attributes of crisis,[2] first to stress and then to selected aspects of cognitive and decision-making performance—is a variant of the individual stress model. . . . These propositions are presented not as iron laws but as an alternative to the view that crisis heightens propensities toward rational and calculated decision processes. The remainder of this section sum-

From Paul Gordon Lauren. *Diplomacy: New Approaches in History, Theory and Policy* (New York: 1979), reprinted by permission.

marizes briefly some of the relevant psychological evidence.

An important aspect of crises is that they are characterized by high stress for the individuals and organizations involved. That a severe threat to important values is stress inducing requires little elaboration. The element of surprise is also a contributing factor; there is evidence that unanticipated and novel situations are generally viewed as more threatening. Finally, crises are often marked by almost around-the-clock work schedules, owing to the severity of the situation (high threat), the absence of established routines for dealing with them (surprise), and the absence of extended decision time. Lack of rest and diversion, combined with excessively long working hours, are likely to magnify the stresses in the situation. Moreover, crisis decisions are rarely if ever analogous to the familiar multiple-choice question, in which the full range of options is neatly outlined. The theoretical universe of choices usually exceeds by a substantial margin the number that can or will be considered. Especially in unanticipated situations for which there are no established SOPs (standard operating procedures) or decision rules, it is necessary to search out and perhaps create alternatives. Thus, the decision process itself may be a significant source of stress, arising, for example, from efforts to cope with cognitive constraints on rationality, role factors, small group dynamics, and bureaucratic politics.

Some degree of stress is an integral and necessary precondition for individual or organizational problem solving; in its absence there is no motivation to act. Low levels of stress alert us to the existence of a situation requiring our attention, increase our vigilance and our preparedness to cope with it. Increasing stress to moderate levels may heighten our propensity and ability to find a satisfactory solution to the problem. Indeed, for some elementary tasks a rather high degree of stress may enhance performance, at least for limited periods of time. If the problem is qualitatively simple and performance is measured by quantitative criteria, stress can increase output. Our primary concern, however, is not with the effects of crisis on persons engaged in manual or routine tasks, but with its consequences on the performance of officials in leadership positions during major international crises. These are nearly always marked by complexity and ambiguity, and they usually demand responses which are judged by qualitative rather than quantitative criteria. It is precisely these qualitative aspects of performance that are most likely to suffer under high stress.

Experimental findings generally indicate a curvilinear relationship, most easily described as an "inverted U," between stress and the performance of individuals and groups. A moderate level of anxiety can be beneficial, but at higher levels it disrupts decision processes. Observational evidence from related field research (e.g., studies of natural disasters, or performance in combat and other dangerous circumstances) also suggests that intense and protracted stress often erodes rather than enhances the ability of individuals to cope with complex problems. To summarize, in situations of high stress, "there is a narrowing of the cognitive organization at the moment; the individual loses broader perspective, he is no longer able to 'see' essential aspects of the situation and his behavior becomes, consequently, less adaptive."[3]

At this point we shall consider in more detail some potential consequences of stress for cognitive rigidity, span of attention, and time perspectives.

Cognitive Rigidity. Charles Lindblom suggests that "a serious emergency or crisis often transforms a policy analyst's perceptions (and sometimes galvanizes his energies) with the result that he gets a new grasp on his problem."[4] But there is also evidence that the effects of stress on cognitive performance are often less benign. Persons experiencing intense stress tend to suffer increased cognitive rigidity, and erosion of general cognitive abilities, including creativity

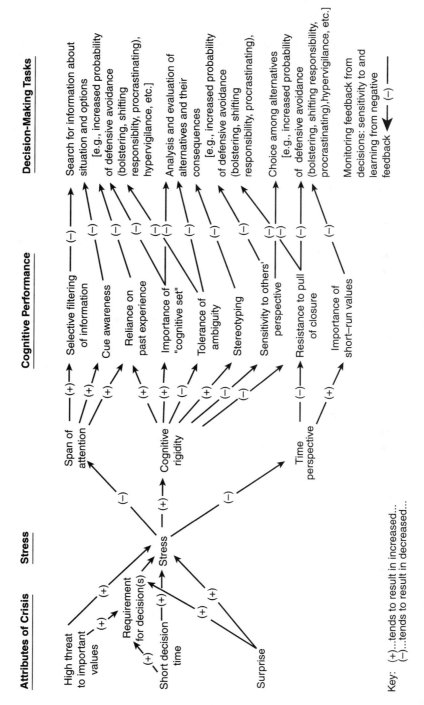

FIGURE 3.1 Individual Decision Making in Crisis: Some Hypotheses

and the ability to cope with complexity. As a consequence, the range of perceived policy options may be narrow. The decision maker is likely to establish a dominant percept through which to interpret information, and to maintain it tenaciously in the face of information that might seem to call for a reappraisal. Often this percept is a familiar one transferred from previous situations (e.g., "lessons of history"), even though it may be inappropriate for the circumstances at hand, and it is more likely to be characterized by stereotypes than by subtlety as the complexity of the psychological field is reduced. To change one's beliefs and theories each time some discrepant information is received is neither possible nor wise, but it is at least useful to be aware that evidence about an unfolding situation may be consistent with more than a single explanation. A finding of special relevance for crisis decision making is that tolerance for ambiguity is reduced when there is high stress. Under these conditions individuals made decisions before adequate information was available, with the result that they performed much less capably than persons working under normal conditions. The combination of stress and uncertainty leads some persons to feel that "the worst would be better than this."[5] Finally, caricatures of motivational structures may develop: the anxious become more anxious, the energetic become more energetic, the repressors become more repressive, and so on. The effects of stress on perception have been summarized as follows:

> Perceptual behavior is disrupted, becomes less well controlled than under normal conditions, and hence is less adaptive. The major dimensions of perceptual function are affected: selection of percepts from a complex field becomes less adequate and sense is less well differentiated from nonsense; there is maladaptive accentuation in the direction of aggression and escape; untested hypotheses are fixated recklessly.[6]

As a result of these effects of stress, search for information and policy options may be adversely affected in several ways. Other actors and their motives are likely to be stereotyped, for example, and the situation itself may be defined in overly simple, one-dimensional terms—such as, that it is a zero-sum situation, or that everything is related to everything else. The ability to invent nonobvious solutions to complex problems may also be impaired. Finally, complex problems are more likely to be defined by "what is already in" (the decision maker's beliefs, expectations, cognitive and emotional predispositions), and less by the "objective" attributes of the situation.[7]

The inception of a crisis usually results in a sharply increased pace of individual and bureaucratic activity and, concomitantly, an increasing volume of communication. Conversely, information overload in a decision-making situation may itself be a source of serious stress. One way of coping with this phenomenon is to *narrow one's span of attention* to a few aspects of the decision-making task. This may be a functional strategy if it permits the executive to eliminate trivial distractions, filter out irrelevant information, and develop an agenda of priorities. However, a number of costs may offset or even outweigh these benefits.

An experimental study of complex situations revealed that increased information loads resulted in fewer strategic integrated decisions and more unintegrated and simple retaliatory decisions. As the volume of information directed at policy makers rises, the search for information within the communication system will tend to become less thorough, and selectivity in what is read, believed, and retained takes on increasing importance. In ambiguous situations or in circumstances of information overload, one may also be more likely to screen information and to respond in terms of personal predispositions. Unpleasant information and that which does not support preferences and expectations may fall by the wayside, unless it is of such an unambiguous nature that it cannot be disregarded. "All Presidents, at least in modern times," writes Sorensen, "have complained about their reading pile, and few have been able to cope with it. There is a temptation, consequently, to cut out all that is unpleasant."[8] Thus, more communication may in fact result in less useful and valid information being available to policymakers.

Time perspectives are also likely to be affected by high stress. For example, the ability to judge time is impaired in situations which increase anxiety. Thus, there appears to be a two-way relationship between time and stress. On the one hand, short decision time, a defining characteristic of crisis, is likely to increase the stress under which the executive must operate. On the other hand, increasing levels of stress tend to heighten the salience of time and to distort judgements about it. It has been found in "real life" crisis situations, as well as experimentally, that as danger increases there is a significant overestimation of how fast time is passing.

Perceived time pressure may affect decision making in several ways. A number of studies indicate that some time pressure can enhance creativity as well as the rate of performance, but most of the evidence suggests that beyond a moderate level it has adverse effects. Because complex tasks requiring feats of memory and inference suffer more from time pressure, its effects on the most important decisions—which are usually marked by complexity—are likely to be particularly harmful. In such situations there is a tendency to fix upon a single approach, to continue using it whether or not it proves effective, and to hang on to familiar solutions, applying them even to problems that may be substantially different.

Experimental research has often shown a curvilinear relationship between time pressure and performance. Under severe time pressure, normal subjects produce errors similar to those committed by schizophrenics. Another study revealed that, although a moderate increase in time pressure can increase the productivity of groups, an increase from low to high pressure

has an adverse effect. Increasing the number of decisions required in a given period of time by a factor of five led to a fifteenfold rise in decision errors. There is, in addition, evidence that time pressure increases the propensity to rely upon stereotypes, disrupts both individual and group problem solving, narrows the focus of attention, and impedes the use of available information. Finally, both experimental and historical evidence indicates that high stress tends to result in a shorter time perspective and, as consequence, reduced resistance to premature closure.

When decision time is short, the ability to estimate the range of possible consequences arising from a particular policy choice is likely to be impaired. Both experimental and field research indicate that severe stress is likely to give rise to a single-minded concern for the present and immediate future at the sacrifice of attention to longer range considerations. The uncertainties attending severe crisis make it exceptionally difficult to follow outcomes from a sequence of actions and responses very far into the future. Increasing stress also tends to narrow the focus of attention, thereby further limiting perceptions of time to the more immediate future. During the Korean War, for instance, it was observed that combat troops "cannot exercise complex functions involving the scanning of a large number of factors or long-term foresight because the stress is too massive and time too short for anything but the immediately relevant."[9]

This brief overview of evidence is suggestive rather than exhaustive. Moreover, the emphasis has been on processes rather than on decision outputs and, just as we cannot assume that "good" processes will ensure high-quality decisions, we cannot assume that erratic processes will always result in low-quality decisions. But even if Figure 1 describes only some potential tendencies rather than unvarying responses to crisis, there is sufficient evidence to call into question the universal validity of the premise that we always rise to the occasion in crisis, drawing if necessary upon hidden reservoirs of strength. The evidence cited here suggests that among the more probable casualties of crises and the accompanying high stress are the very abilities that distinguish men from other species: to establish logical links between present actions and future goals; to search effectively for relevant policy options; to create appropriate responses to unexpected events; to communicate complex ideas; to deal effectively with abstractions; to perceive not only blacks and whites, but also to distinguish them from the many subtle shades of gray that fall in between; to distinguish valid analogies from false ones, and sense from nonsense; and, perhaps most important of all, to enter into the frame of references of others. With respect to these precious cognitive abilities, the law of supply and demand seems to operate in a perverse manner; as crisis increases the need for them, it also appears to diminish the supply. . . .

Decision Making in the 1914 Crisis

The assassination of Archduke Franz Ferdinand on June 28, 1914, set off a chain of events that, within six weeks, brought all of the major powers of Europe into war. Soon after Prince von Bülow asked German Chancellor Bethmann Hollweg how the war had come about. "At least I said to him: 'Well, tell me, at least, how it all happened,' He raised his long, thin arms to heaven and answered in a dull exhausted voice: 'Oh—if I only knew.' " Another colleague wrote that "since the Russian mobilization the Chancellor gave one the impression of a drowning man."[10] Are these merely the self-serving recollections of war criminals or of fools whose incompetence visited upon the world a war of unparalleled devastation? If the answer is an affirmative one, the 1914 case is of little interest to the student of crisis, and the prescription is relatively simple—keep war criminals and fools out of high office.

But perhaps the answer to "how it all happened" is not quite so simple. . . . The individual stress model may help to explain the disastrous events of 1914. . . . Unless we adopt a deterministic view—as is implied, for example, by the popular metaphor of the assassination as a lighted match thrown into a keg of powder—it is appropriate to consider not only the European context in 1914, but also the decision processes. The focus here is on two aspects of Figure 1—perceptions of time pressure and of policy options.

Perceptions of Time Pressure

To examine the effects of deepening crisis on perceptions of time pressure, techniques of content analysis were employed. All documents written by high-ranking foreign policy officials were coded for evidence of time pressure as a factor in policy decisions. The resulting 167 statements are classified according to date and nation and specific issue discussed. Statements of concern about decision time increased steadily (except in the case of Austria–Hungary), not only in absolute frequency, but even in relation to the total number of policy themes. Perceptions of time pressure were also associated with increasing stress. . . .

This inquiry into time pressures associated with the 1914 crisis supports the hypothesis that one reaction to decisional stress is hypervigilance. Concern for time increased as the crisis deepened, and it is also clear that time pressures were related to the central rather than peripheral issues in the crisis. When there was a conflict between the need to delay action in order to seek nonmilitary means of resolving the crisis and the perceived needs of military preparedness, the latter consideration prevailed, in large part because so many officials throughout Europe felt that the costs of falling behind the adversary's timetable would be catastrophic. Many decisions during the crisis were undertaken in great haste, and the processes by which they were made were at times highly erratic. For example, the initial Russian decision for a general mobilization was followed shortly by an order for only a partial callup of forces, and then by another reversal to the original decision. In the meanwhile, when it became clear that the conflict between Serbia and Austria–Hungary might lead to a general European war, a series of highly contradictory messages was dispatched from Berlin to Vienna. Demands for restraint in some of them were offset by a telegram from Moltke stating that Austria–Hungary should immediately mobilize against Russia, and that Germany would soon follow suit.

Policy Options

One way of coping with decision stress is a form of bolstering, attributing to the adversary sole responsibility for choices and outcomes, while absolving oneself, owing to the absence of real alternatives. Data from the 1914 crisis provide some striking support for the proposition that, in a crisis situation, decision makers will tend to perceive the range of their own alternatives to be more restricted than those of their opponents. That is, they will perceive their own decision making to be characterized by *necessity* and *closed* options, whereas those of the adversary are characterized by *open* choices. . . .

The 1914 documents are filled with such words as "must," "compelled," "obliged," "unable," "driven," "impossible," and "helpless," but these rarely occur except when the author is referring to the policies of his own nation. To students of strategy the assertions of the Kaiser, the Czar, and others that they were helpless once they had set their military machines into motion may appear to be a "real life" application of the tactics of *commitment,* "a device to leave the last clear chance to decide the outcome with the other party, in a manner that he fully appreciates; it is to relinquish further initiative, having rigged the incentives so that the other party must choose in one's favor."[11] This explanation may be valid for messages that were intended for wide circulation among officials in allied or enemy countries. On the other hand, the most "private" documents—those

intended only for circulation within the various foreign offices—do not differ materially from the entire set of documents in respect to the findings reported here. The clearest evidence in support of this assertion is to be found in the Kaiser's marginal notations and in the various minutes of Eyre Crowe, Assistant Under-Secretary of State, in the British Foreign Office.

Even a cursory survey of the diplomatic documents reveals that, with exception of Austria–Hungary European leaders consistently perceived fewer options open to themselves than to their adversaries. . . .

Just as European leaders tended to perceive fewer alternatives open to themselves than to their adversaries, so they regarded their allies to be in a similar position vis-à-vis their enemies. . . .

The few attempts made to restrain the militant members of each alliance were either halfhearted or too late. . . .

Decision Making during the Missile Crisis

A single U–2 American surveillance plane took off on October 14, 1962 for a reconnaissance flight over Cuba. Immediately upon returning, its high-altitude cameras were unloaded. After intensive study of the developed films, intelligence analysts uncovered unmistakable evidence of two medium-range ballistic missile (MRBM) sites in areas previously photographed and found to be empty. Overflights three days later confirmed these reports and revealed nine sites—36 launch positions—six for the 1,100-mile MRBM and three for 2,200-mile intermediate-range ballistic missiles (IRBM) in various states of readiness. Thus began the most serious international crisis of the nuclear era, a confrontation during which President Kennedy estimated that the chances of a nuclear war between the United States and the Soviet Union were one in three.

The 1914 and Cuban situations were similar in a number of respects and differed in many others. The similarity of present interest is that both episodes conform to the definition of crisis used here. Despite widespread rumors of Soviet missile installations in Cuba, photographic evidence of their presence was a surprise to virtually all officials in Washington, including the President; the rate of construction on the missile sites made it evident that any decision to prevent their completion could not long be delayed; and, with the exception of Secretary of Defense Robert McNamara, all who joined the American decision group interpreted the Soviet move as a serious threat to national security. As one participant in these discussions put it: "Everyone round the table recognized that we were in a major crisis. We didn't know, that day, if the country would come through it with Washington intact."[12]

The most significant difference between these two events is that the 1914 crisis led to a world war, whereas the Cuban confrontation was resolved without recourse to violence. Thus, the situation that confronted national leaders in the two crises shared a number of attributes (surprise, high threat, short decision time), but the decisions they made led to significantly different results: peaceful settlement versus a world war. In an attempt to explain the different outcomes, the remainder of this section examines several aspects of the decision-making process in 1962, again with special attention to time pressure and the search for and appraisal of alternatives.

Perceptions of Time Pressure

Several sources of time pressure impinged on the President and his advisers during the missile crisis. Initially, there was the need to formulate a policy before the Soviets were alerted by the stepped-up U–2 flights to the fact that their launching installations had been discovered. Conversely, once developments in Cuba became public knowledge, there would be no further time for deliberation and debate on the proper response.

An overriding concern throughout the period was the knowledge that construction on the missile sites was continuing at a rapid pace. The first photographic evidence of construction activities in Cuba indicated that they would be operational within a week to ten days. American officials perceived that their task would become immeasurably more difficult once construction on the launching sites was completed: "For all of us know that, once the missile sites under construction became operational, and capable of responding to any apparent threat or command with a nuclear volley, the President's options would be dramatically changed."[13] Thus, the situation did not compel a reflex-like response—at least, as it was defined by the President. But in relation to the task at hand decision time was indeed short, and all firsthand accounts of decision making during the Cuban crisis, especially that of Robert Kennedy, are replete with indications of time pressure.

Despite the sense of urgency created by these deadlines, the President and his advisers sought to reduce the probability that either side would respond by a "spasm reaction." Efforts were made to delay taking overt actions as long as the situation permitted. Equally important, discussions in Washington revealed a sensitivity for the time pressures under which the adversary was operating. There was a concern that Premier Khrushchev not be rushed into an irrevocable decision; it was agreed among members of the decision group that "we should slow down the escalation of the crisis to give Khrushchev time to consider his next move."[14] Measures designed to increase Soviet decision time included the President's management of the naval quarantine. He ordered American ships to delay intercepting Soviet vessels until the last possible moment, *and had the order transmitted in the clear.* The Soviets, who were certain to intercept the message, would thus learn that they had additional time in which to formulate a response to the blockade. This play also revealed a sophisticated understanding of the social psychology of communication; information from a distrusted source is more likely to be believed if it is obtained through the recipient's own efforts. The Soviet decision on October 25 to slow down the westward progress of their ships in mid-Atlantic can also be interpreted as an effort to lengthen decision time.

A comparison of the 1914 and 1962 crises points to the importance of a subjective rather than an objective definition of decision time. Owing to vast differences in military capabilities, time was objectively of far greater importance in 1962 than in 1914. Hence, Soviet and American leaders were no less aware of time pressures and of the potential costs of delaying action than were their counterparts in 1914. But they also perceived the dangers of acting in haste, and they were successful in mitigating the most severe dangers attending such pressures. They resisted the pressures for premature decisions and took a number of actions which avoided putting their adversaries in a position of having to respond in haste. President Kennedy later acknowledged that the ability to delay a decision after receipt of the photographic evidence of missile sites was crucial to the *content* of American policy: "If we had had to act on Wednesday [October 17], in the first 24 hours, I don't think probably we would have chosen as prudently as we finally did the quarantine against the use of offensive weapons.[15]

Policy Options

During the missile crisis, the search for alternatives was intimately related to time pressures; in the words of Arthur Schlesinger, "The deadline defined the strategy."[16] Pressures of time notwithstanding, American policy makers made efforts to prevent premature foreclosure of options. McGeorge Bundy noted that upon receiving the first news of the photographic evidence, "his [Kennedy's] first reaction was that we must make sure, and were we making sure, and would there be evidence on which he could decide that this was in fact really the case." As late as October 18, a series of alternatives was being considered pending more accurate information, and while the decision to institute a blockade was being hammered out, open discussion of the alternatives was encouraged. The President recalled that "though at the beginning there was a much sharper division . . . this was very valuable, because the people involved had particular responsibilities of their own."[17] Another participant in the crisis decision group asserted that President Kennedy, aware that discussion of alternatives in the National Security Council would be more frank in his absence, encouraged the group to hold preliminary meetings without him. Thus, the eventual decision was reached by relatively open and frank discussion.

Six alternative responses emerged from the initial discussions between the President's advisers. Ultimately, the choice narrowed down to the blockade and the air strike. Initially, the option of a sudden air strike against the missile sites had strong support among most of the conferees, including that of the President. An informal vote is reported to have revealed an 11–6 majority in favor of the blockade. The United States Air Force could not guarantee, however, that an air strike would be 100 percent effective. The blockade did not necessarily guarantee success; on the other hand, it did not rule out further measures. After much shifting of positions, the blockade option was selected, partly on the reasoning that "the course we finally adopted had the advantage of permitting other steps, if this one was unsuccessful. In other words, we were starting, in a sense, at a minimum place."[18]

The desire to avoid killing Soviet troops also weighed heavily against the air strike option. The blockade shifted the immediate burden of decision concerning the use of violence to Premier Khrushchev and, should the blockade have proved unsuccessful, it did not preclude later employment of a "much more massive action."[19] By adopting the strategy, no irrevocable decisions on the use of violence had been made and multiple options remained for possible future actions by the United States. At the same time, Soviet leaders were given the time and the opportunity to assess their own choices. Thus, unlike several of the key foreign policy officials in the 1914 crisis, those in October 1962 seemed to perceive a close relationship between their own actions and the options of their adversaries. According to Theodore Sorensen, "We discussed what the Soviet reaction would be to any possible move by the United States, what our reaction with them would have to be to that Soviet reaction, and so on, trying to follow each of those roads to their ultimate conclusion."[20]

American decision makers also displayed a sensitivity for the position and perspective of the adversary, trying to insure that a number of options other than total war or total surrender were available to Soviet leaders. An important advantage of the blockade over other strategies was that it appeared to avoid placing Soviet leaders in that situation. An air strike on the missile bases or invasion of the island would have left Soviet leaders only the alternatives of capitulating to the United States or of counterattacking. In that case, the latter might have seemed the less distasteful course. In disagreeing with General Curtis LeMay's optimistic assessment of the likely Soviet response to air raids on the missile installations, the President asserted, "They, no more than we, can let these things go by without doing something."[21] A blockade, on the other hand, gave the Soviet government a choice between turning back the weapons-bearing ships or running the blockade.

By October 26 it seemed clear that, Khrushchev's earlier threats to the contrary notwithstanding, Soviet ships would not challenge the blockade. Despite the advent of negotiations, however, it was far from certain that the Soviet missiles would be removed from Cuba; indeed, there was ample evidence of an accelerated pace of construction on the launching sites in Cuba that, it was then believed, would be completed by October 30. Thus, the question of further steps to be taken in case the blockade proved insufficient to force withdrawal of all

offensive missiles again confronted American leaders. Among the options considered were: tightening the blockade to include all commodities other than food and medicine, increased low-level flights over Cuba for purposes of reconnaissance and harassment, action within Cuba, an air strike, and an invasion. In the meanwhile, the President's brother delivered an ultimatum to the Soviet ambassador, and both direct and indirect bargaining resulted in a settlement. Just before "the most serious meeting ever to take place at the White House"[22] was to have started, Premier Khrushchev agreed to withdraw all offensive missiles from Cuba in exchange for President Kennedy's pledge not to invade Cuba.

Time pressure and the search for alternatives are key elements in crisis decision making. Data from 1914 indicates that these factors did in fact vary as crisis-induced stress increased, and these changes apparently had serious consequences for critical policy decisions. A more impressionistic analysis of the Cuban confrontation suggests that the ability of American decision makers to mitigate some of the adverse consequences of crisis contributed to its eventual peaceful resolution. In many respects, President Kennedy's behavior during the Cuban crisis appeared consciously designed to avert repetition of the 1914 disaster. Indeed, he frequently referred to the decision processes leading up to World War I as a source of negative lessons. Having read Barbara Tuchman's *The Guns of August,* for example, the President said: "I am not going to follow a course which will allow anyone to write a comparable book about this time, *The Missiles of October.* If anybody is around to write after this, they are going to understand that we made every effort to find peace and every effort to give our adversary room to move. I am not going to push the Russians an inch beyond what is necessary."[23] Even when discussing the Cuban missile crisis some weeks after its conclusion, he asserted, "Well now, if you look at the history of this century where World War I really came through a series of misjudgments of the intentions of others . . . it's very difficult to always make judgments here about what the effect will be of our decisions on other countries."[24] Yet the ability of American and Soviet leaders to avoid a nuclear Armageddon in October 1962, is not assurance that even great skill in crisis management will always yield a peaceful solution. As President Kennedy said some months later, referring to the missile crisis, "You can't have too many of those."[25]

Conclusion. . . .

During crises advisory groups may be vulnerable to such malfunctions as "groupthink."[26] For various reasons, including perceived needs for secrecy, easier coordination, and the like, decision-making groups tend to become smaller during crises. There may be, moreover, a tendency to consult others less as the pressure of time increases, as well as to rely more heavily upon those who support the prevailing "wisdom."[27] Finally, leaders differ not only in their "executive styles" (note, for example, the strikingly different problem-solving styles exhibited by presidents Coolidge, Franklin Roosevelt, and Nixon), but also in their abilities to employ advisory groups effectively—that is, in ways that may help them to counteract some of the potentially adverse consequences of crisis. Even the same executive may demonstrate great skill during one crisis and equal ineptitude in another instance. John F. Kennedy's use of advisers during the missile crisis and the Bay of Pigs fiasco are illustrative in this respect. . . .

Certainly, the two cases are not representative of all crises in any statistical sense. Thus, the results described here should be viewed as illustrative rather than definitive. Moreover, the analysis focused on very limited aspects of crises, to the exclusion of many other potentially fruitful comparisons. The results suggest that the individual stress model identifies some important elements of crises decision making. . . .

The rather different findings for the 1914 and 1962 crises raise a series of additional questions—about the necessary and sufficient conditions for avoiding decision-making malfunctions—that have barely been touched upon here. The individual stress model focuses on a few aspects of crisis and consciously excludes others. By posing some questions and not others, we have limited the range of answers. Every model or theoretical perspective does so, with some inevitable losses and, it is to be hoped, at least some commensurate gains. The proper question to ask, then, is not whether this approach serves as a complete model for all crises—the answer is unquestionably negative—but whether it directs our attention to important phenomena that might otherwise remain beyond our purview. . . .

Sustained interest in the effects of crisis-induced stress does not depend on finding that *every* crisis from the historical past resulted in substandard decision-making performance, any more than concern for the consequences of smoking must await evidence that all smokers develop lung cancer. The much more interesting and important questions emerge precisely at the point of recognizing that the dangers and opportunities inherent in crises can give rise to various patterns of coping. At that point our attention is directed to a series of further questions—for example, what are the decision-making structures, personal attributes of leaders, strategies of crisis management, and other variables that are associated with more or less successful coping. . . .

Notes

1. Herbert Simon, *Organizations* (New York: Wiley, 1958), p. 138.

2. Figure 1 is an expanded version of a diagram that initially appeared in Ole R. Holsti and Alexander L. George, "The Effects of Stress on the Performance of Foreign Policy-Makers," in Cornelius P. Cotter (ed.), *Political Science Annual* (Indianapolis: Bobbs-Merrill, 1975), VI: 284.

3. Sheldon J. Korchin, "Anxiety and Cognition," in Constance Sheerer (ed.), *Cognition: Theory, Research, Promise* (New York: Harper & Row, 1964), p. 63.

4. Charles E. Lindblom, *The Policy-Making Process* (Englewood Cliffs, NJ: Prentice Hall, 1968), p. 22.

5. C. D. Smock, "The Influence of Psychological Stress on the 'Intolerance of Ambiguity,' " *Journal of Abnormal and Social Psychology* 50 (March 1955): 177–182.

6. Leo Postman and Jerome S. Bruner, "Perception under Stress," *Psychological Review* 55 (1948): 322.

7. Jerome Bruner, cited in Louis C. Gawthrop, *Bureaucratic Behavior in the Executive Branch* (New York: Free Press, 1969), p. 113.

8. Theodore C. Sorensen, *Decision-Making in the White House* (New York: Columbia University Press, 1964), p. 38.

9. Korchin, "Anxiety and Cognition," p. 63.

10. Prince Bernhard von Bülow, *Memoirs of Prince von Bülow*, 3 vols. (Boston: Little, Brown, 1932), III: 166; and Alfred von Tirpitz, *My Memoirs* (London: Hurst and Blackett, 1919), p. 280.

11. Schelling, *The Strategy of Conflict* (New York: Oxford University Press, 1963), pp. 137–138.

12. Douglas Dillon, quoted in Elie Abel, *The Missile Crisis* (Philadelphia: Lippincott, 1966), p. 48.

13. Theodore Sorensen, *Decision-Making in the White House* (New York: Columbia University Press, 1963), p. 31.

14. National Broadcasting Company, "Cuba: The Missile Crisis" (mimeo. transcript, February 9, 1964), p. 12.

15. Columbia Broadcasting System, "Conversation with President Kennedy" (mimeo. transcript, December 17, 1963), pp. 2–3.

16. Arthur M. Schlesinger, Jr., *A Thousand Days* (New York: Houghton Mifflin, 1965), p. 804.

17. *Ibid.*, p. 808.

18. CBS, "Conversation with President Kennedy," p. 4.

19. Ibid.

20. NBC, "Cuba," p. 17.

21. Quoted in Snyder and Diesing, *Conflict Among Nations,* p. 301.

22. NBC, "Cuba," p. 42.

23. Robert F. Kennedy, *Thirteen Days* (New York: Norton, 1969), p. 127.

24. CBS, "Conversation with President Kennedy," p. 3.

25. Theodore Sorensen, *Kennedy* (New York: Harper & Row, 1965), p. 726.

26. Janis, *Victims of Groupthink;* and Roland L. Frye and Thomas M. Stritch, "Effects of Timed vs. Non-timed Discussion Upon Measures of Influence and Change in Small Groups," *Journal of Social Psychology* 63 (June 1964); 139–143.

27. Dean G. Pruitt, "Problem Solving in the Department of State" (unpublished paper, Northwestern University, 1961).

Conceptual Models and the Cuban Missile Crisis

G R A H A M   T .   A L L I S O N

The author presents three models of the foreign policy decision-making process. The first (the rational actor model) tends to dominate the realist perspective. The organizational process and bureaucratic politics models, reflecting what we call a pluralist perspective, raise questions concerning the appropriateness of relying exclusively on the rational actor model to explain foreign policy choices. The focus in this now classic article on institutional ethos, procedures, and processes is consistent with present-day approaches that place renewed emphasis on institutions.

Reprinted by permission of the American Political Science Association from *American Political Science Review* 63 (September 1969): 689–718.

The Cuban missile crisis is a seminal event. For thirteen days of October 1962, there was a higher probability that more human lives would end suddenly than ever before in history. Had the worst occurred, the death of 100 million Americans, over 100 million Russians, and millions of Europeans as well would make previous natural calamities and inhumanities appear insignificant. Given the probability of disaster—which President Kennedy estimated as "between 1 out of 3 and even"—our escape seems awesome.[1] This event symbolizes a central, if only partially thinkable, fact about our existence. That such consequences could follow from the choices and actions of national governments obliges students of government as well as participants in governance to think hard about these problems. . . .

The general argument can be summarized in three propositions:

1. Analysts think about problems of foreign and military policy in terms of largely implicit conceptual models that have significant consequences for the content of their thought.[2]

Though the present product of foreign policy analysis is neither systematic nor powerful, if one carefully examines explanations produced by analysts, a number of fundamental similarities emerge. Explanations produced by particular analysts display quite regular, predictable features. This predictability suggests a substructure. These regularities reflect an analyst's assumptions about the character of puzzles, the categories in which problems should be considered, the types of evidence that are relevant, and the determinants of occurrences. The first proposition is that clusters of such related assumptions constitute basic frames of reference or conceptual models in terms of which analysts both ask and answer the question: What happened? Why did the event happen? What will happen?[3] Such assumptions are central to the activities of explanation and prediction, for in attempting to explain a particular event, the analyst cannot simply describe the full state of the world leading up to that event. The logic of explanation requires that he single out the relevant, important determinants of the occurrence. Moreover, as the logic of prediction underscores, the analyst must summarize the various determinants as they bear on the event in question. Conceptual models both fix the mesh of the nets that the analyst drags through the material in order to explain a particular action or decision and direct him to cast his net in select ponds, at certain depths, in order to catch the fish he is after.

2. Most analysts explain (and predict) the behavior of national governments in terms of various forms of one basic conceptual model, here entitled the Rational Policy Model (Model 1).[4]

In terms of this conceptual model, analysts attempt to understand happenings as the more or less purposive acts of unified national governments. For these analysts, the point of an explanation is to show how the nation or government could have chosen the action in question, given the strategic problem that it faced. For example, in confronting the problem posed by the Soviet installation of missiles in Cuba, rational policy model analysts attempt to show how this was a reasonable act from the point of view of the Soviet Union, given Soviet strategic objectives.

3. Two "alternative" conceptual models, here labeled an Organizational Process Model (Model II) and a Bureaucratic Politics Model (Model III) provide a base for improved explanation and prediction.

Although the standard frame of reference has proved useful for many purposes, there is powerful evidence that it must be supplemented, if not supplanted, by frames of reference which focus upon the large organizations and political actors involved in the policy process. Model I's implication that important events have important causes, i.e., that monoliths perform large actions for big reasons, must be balanced by an appreciation of the facts (a) that monoliths are black boxes covering various gears and levers in a highly differentiated decision-making structure, and (b) that large acts are the consequences of innumerable and often conflicting smaller actions by individuals at various levels of bureaucratic organizations in the service of a variety of only partially compatible conceptions of national goals, organizational goals, and political objectives. Recent developments in the field of organization theory provide the foundation for the second model. According to this organizational process model, what Model I categorizes as "acts" and "choices" are instead *outputs* of large organizations functioning according to certain regular patterns of behavior. Faced with the problem of Soviet missiles in Cuba, a Model II analyst identifies the relevant organizations and displays the patterns of organizational behavior from which this action emerged. The third model focuses on the internal politics of a government. Happenings in foreign affairs are understood, according to the bureaucratic politics model, neither as choices nor as outputs. Instead, what happens is categorized as *outcomes* of various overlapping bargaining games among players arranged hierarchically in the national government. In confronting the problem posed by Soviet missiles in Cuba, a Model III analyst displays the perceptions, motivations, positions, power, and maneuvers of principal players from which the outcome emerged.[5]

A central metaphor illuminates differences among these models. Foreign policy has often been compared to moves, sequences of moves, and games of chess. If one were limited to observations on a screen upon which moves in the chess game were projected without information as to how the pieces came to be moved, he would assume—as Model I does—that an individual chess player was moving the pieces with references to plans and maneuvers toward the

goal of winning the game. But a pattern of moves can be imagined that would lead the serious observer, after watching several games, to consider the hypothesis that the chess player was not a single individual but rather a loose alliance of semi-independent organizations, each of which moved its set of pieces according to standard operating procedures. For example, movement of separate sets of pieces might proceed in turn, each according to a routine, the king's rook, bishop, and their pawns repeatedly attacking the opponent according to a fixed plan. Furthermore, it is conceivable that the pattern of play would suggest to an observer that a number of distinct players, with distinct objectives but shared power over the pieces, were determining the moves as the resultant of collegial bargaining. For example, the black rook's move might contribute to the loss of a black knight with no comparable gain for the black team, but with the black rook becoming the principal guardian of the "palace" on that side of the board. . . .

Model I: Rational Policy. . . .

The U.S. Blockade of Cuba: A First Cut[6]

The U.S. response to the Soviet Union's emplacement of missiles in Cuba must be understood in strategic terms as simple value-maximizing escalation. American nuclear superiority could be counted on to paralyze Soviet nuclear power; Soviet transgression of the nuclear threshold in response to an American use of lower levels of violence would be wildly irrational since it would mean virtual destruction of the Soviet Communist system and Russian nation. American local superiority was overwhelming: it could be initiated at a low level while threatening with high credibility an ascending sequence of steps short of the nuclear threshold. All that was required was for the United States to bring to bear its strategic and local superiority in such a way that American determination to see the missiles removed would be demonstrated, while at the same time allowing Moscow time and room to retreat without humiliation. The naval blockade— euphemistically named a "quarantine" in order to circumvent the niceties of international law— did just that.

The U.S. government's selection of the blockade followed this logic. Apprised of the presence of Soviet missiles in Cuba, the President assembled an Executive Committee (ExCom) of the National Security Council and directed them to "set aside all other tasks to make a prompt and intense survey of the dangers and all possible courses of action."[7] This group functioned as "fifteen individuals on our own, representing the President and not different departments."[8] As one of the participants recalls, "The remarkable aspect of those meetings was a sense of complete equality."[9] Most of the time during the week that followed was spent canvassing all the possible tracks and weighing the arguments for and against each. Six major categories of action were considered.

1. Do nothing. U.S. vulnerability to Soviet missiles was no new thing. Since the U.S. already lived under the gun of missiles based in Russia, a Soviet capability to strike from Cuba too made little real difference. The real danger stemmed from the possibility of U.S. over-reaction. The U.S. should announce the Soviet action in a calm, casual manner thereby deflating whatever political capital Khrushchev hoped to make of the missiles.

This argument fails on two counts. First, it grossly underestimates the military importance of the Soviet move. Not only would the Soviet Union's missile capability be doubled and the U.S. early warning system outflanked. The Soviet Union would have an opportunity to reverse the strategic balance by further installations, and indeed, in the longer run, to invest in cheaper, shorter-range rather than more expensive longer-range missiles. Second, the political importance of this move was undeniable. The Soviet Union's

act challenged the American President's most solemn warning. If the U.S. failed to respond, no American commitment would be credible.

2. Diplomatic pressures. Several forms were considered: an appeal to the U.N. or O.A.S. for an inspection team, a secret approach to Khrushchev, and a direct approach to Khrushchev, perhaps at a summit meeting. The United States would demand that the missiles be removed, but the final settlement might include neutralization of Cuba, U.S. withdrawal from the Guantanamo base, and withdrawal of U.S. Jupiter missiles from Turkey or Italy.

Each form of the diplomatic approach had its own drawbacks. To arraign the Soviet Union before the U.N. Security Council held little promise since the Russians could veto any proposed action. While the diplomats argued, the missiles would become operational. To send a secret emissary to Khrushchev demanding that the missiles be withdrawn would be to pose untenable alternatives. On the one hand, this would invite Khrushchev to seize the diplomatic initiative, perhaps committing himself to strategic retaliation in response to an attack on Cuba. On the other hand, this would tender an ultimatum that no great power could accept. To confront Khrushchev at a summit would guarantee demands for U.S. concessions, and the analogy between U.S. missiles in Turkey and Russian missiles in Cuba could not be erased.

But why not trade U.S. Jupiters in Turkey and Italy, which the President had previously ordered withdrawn, for the missiles in Cuba? The U.S. had chosen to withdraw these missiles in order to replace them with superior, less vulnerable Mediterranean Polaris submarines. But the middle of the crisis was no time for concessions. The offer of such a deal might suggest to the Soviets that the West would yield and thus tempt them to demand more. It would certainly confirm European suspicions about American willingness to sacrifice European interests when the chips were down. Finally, the basic issue should be kept clear. As the President stated in reply to Bertrand Russell, "I think your attention might well be directed to the burglars rather than to those who have caught the burglars."[10]

3. A secret approach to Castro. The crisis provided an opportunity to separate Cuba and Soviet Communism by offering Castro the alternatives, "split or fall." But Soviet troops transported, constructed, guarded, and controlled the missiles. Their removal would thus depend on a Soviet decision.

4. Invasion. The United States could take this occasion not only to remove the missiles but also to rid itself of Castro. A Navy exercise had long been scheduled in which Marines, ferried from Florida in naval vessels, would liberate the imaginary island of Vieques.[11] Why not simply shift the point of disembarkment? (The Pentagon's foresight in planning this operation would be an appropriate antidote to the CIA's Bay of Pigs!)

Preparations were made for an invasion, but as a last resort, American troops would be forced to confront 20,000 Soviets in the first Cold War case of direct contact between the troops of the super powers. Such brinksmanship courted nuclear disaster, practically guaranteeing an equivalent Soviet move against Berlin.

5. Surgical air strike. The missile sites should be removed by a clean, swift conventional attack. This was the effective counter-action which the attempted deception deserved. A surgical strike would remove the missiles and thus eliminate both the danger that the missiles might become operational and the fear that the Soviets would discover the American discovery and act first.

The initial attractiveness of this alternative was dulled by several difficulties. First, could the strike really be "surgical"? The Air Force could

not guarantee destruction of all the missiles.[12] Some might be fired during the attack; some might not have been identified. In order to assure destruction of Soviet and Cuban means of retaliating, what was required was not a surgical but rather a massive attack—of at least 500 sorties. Second, a surprise air attack would of course kill Russians at the missile sites. Pressures on the Soviet Union to retaliate would be so strong that an attack on Berlin or Turkey was highly probable. Third, the key problem with this program was that of advance warning. Could the President of the United States, with his memory of Pearl Harbor and his vision of future U.S. responsibility, order a "Pearl Harbor in reverse"? For 175 years, unannounced Sunday morning attacks had been an anathema to our tradition.[13]

6. Blockade. Indirect military action in the form of a blockade became more attractive as the ExCom dissected the other alternatives. An embargo on military shipments to Cuba enforced by a naval blockade was not without flaws, however. Could the U.S. blockade Cuba without inviting Soviet reprisal in Berlin? The likely solution to joint blockades would be the lifting of both blockades, restoring the new *status quo,* and allowing the Soviets additional time to complete the missiles. Second, the possible consequences of the blockade resembled the drawbacks which disqualified the air strike. If Soviet ships did not stop, the United States would be forced to fire the first shot, inviting retaliation. Third, a blockade would deny the traditional freedom of the seas demanded by several of our close allies and might be held illegal, in violation of the U.N. Charter and international law, unless the United States could obtain a two-thirds vote in the O.A.S. Finally, how could a blockade be related to the problem, namely, some 75 missiles on the island of Cuba, approaching operational readiness daily? A blockade offered the Soviets a spectrum of delaying tactics with which to buy time to complete the missile installations. Was a *fait accompli* not required?

In spite of these enormous difficulties the blockade had comparative advantages: (1) It was a middle course between inaction and attack, aggressive enough to communicate firmness of intention, but nevertheless not so precipitous as a strike. (2) It placed on Khrushchev the burden of choice concerning the next step. He could avoid a direct military clash by keeping his ships away. His was the last clear chance. (3) No possible military confrontation could be more acceptable to the U.S. than a naval engagement in the Caribbean. (4) This move permitted the U.S., by flexing its conventional muscle, to exploit the threat of subsequent nonnuclear steps in each of which the U.S. would have significant superiority.

Particular arguments about advantages and disadvantages were powerful. The explanation of the American choice of the blockade lies in a more general principle, however. As President Kennedy stated in drawing the moral of the crisis:

> Above all, while defending our own vital interests, nuclear powers must avert those confrontations which bring an adversary to a choice of either a humiliating retreat or a nuclear war. To adopt that kind of course in the nuclear age would be evidence only of the bankruptcy of our policy—of a collective death wish for the world.[14]

The blockade was the United States' only real option.

Model II: Organizational Process

For some purposes, governmental behavior can be usefully summarized as action chosen by a unitary, rational decisionmaker: centrally controlled, completely informed, and value maximizing. But this simplification must not be allowed to conceal the fact that a "government" consists of a conglomerate of semi-feudal, loosely allied organizations, each with a sub-

stantial life of its own. Government leaders do sit formally, and to some extent in fact, on top of this conglomerate. But governments perceive problems through organizational sensors. Governments define alternatives and estimate consequences as organizations process information. Governments act as these organizations enact routines. Government behavior can therefore be understood according to a second conceptual model, less as deliberate choice of leaders and more as *outputs* of large organizations functioning according to standard patterns of behavior.

To be responsive to a broad spectrum of problems, governments consist of large organizations among which primary responsibility for particular areas is divided. Each organization attends to a special set of problems and acts in quasi-independence on these problems. But few important problems fall exclusively within the domain of a single organization. Thus government behavior relevant to any important problem reflects the independent output of several organizations, partially coordinated by government leaders. Government leaders can substantially disturb, but not substantially control, the behavior of these organizations.

To perform complex routines, the behavior of large numbers of individuals must be coordinated. Coordination requires standard operating procedures: rules according to which things are done. Assured capability for reliable performance of action that depends upon the behavior of hundreds of persons requires established "programs." Indeed, if the eleven members of a football team are to perform adequately on any particular down, each player must not "do what he thinks needs to be done" or "do what the quarterback tells him to do." Rather, each player must perform the maneuvers specified by a previously established play which the quarterback has simply called in this situation.

At any given time, a government consists of *existing* organizations, each with a *fixed* set of standard operating procedures and programs. The behavior of these organizations—and consequently of the government—relevant to an issue in any particular instance is, therefore, determined primarily by routines established in these organizations prior to that instance. But organizations do change. Learning occurs gradually, over time. Dramatic organizational change occurs in response to major crises. Both learning and change are influenced by existing organizational capabilities.

Borrowed from studies of organizations, these loosely formulated propositions amount simply to *tendencies*. Each must be hedged by modifiers like "other things being equal" and "under certain conditions." In particular instances, tendencies hold—more or less. In specific situations, the relevant question is: more or less? But this is as it should be. For, on the one hand, "organizations" are no more homogeneous a class than "solids." When scientists tried to generalize about "solids," they achieved similar results. Solids tend to expand when heated, but some do and some don't. More adequate categorization of the various elements now lumped under the rubric "organizations" is thus required. On the other hand, the behavior of particular organizations seems considerably more complex than the behavior of solids. Additional information about a particular organization is required for further specification of the tendency statements. In spite of these two caveats, the characterization of government action as organizational output differs distinctly from Model I. Attempts to understand problems of foreign affairs in terms of this frame of reference should produce quite different explanations. . . .[15]

The U.S. Blockade of Cuba: A Second Cut

Organizational Intelligence.   At 7:00 P.M. on October 22, 1962, President Kennedy disclosed the American discovery of the presence of Soviet strategic missiles in Cuba, declared a "strict quarantine on all offensive military equipment under shipment to Cuba," and demanded that

"Chairman Khrushchev halt and eliminate this clandestine, reckless, and provocative threat to world peace."[16] This decision was reached at the pinnacle of the U.S. Government after a critical week of deliberation. What initiated that precious week were photographs of Soviet missile sites in Cuba taken on October 14. These pictures might not have been taken until a week later. In that case, the President speculated, "I don't think probably we would have chosen as prudently as we finally did."[17] U.S. leaders might have received this information three weeks earlier—if a U–2 had flown over San Cristobal in the last week of September. What determined the context in which American leaders came to choose the blockade was the discovery of missiles on October 14.

There has been considerable debate over alleged American "intelligence failures" in the Cuban missile crisis.[18] But what both critics and defenders have neglected is the fact that the discovery took place on October 14, rather than three weeks earlier or a week later, as a consequence of the established routines and procedures of the organizations which constitute the U.S. intelligence community. These organizations were neither more nor less successful than they had been the previous month or were to be in the months to follow.

The notorious "September estimate," approved by the United States Intelligence Board (USIB) on September 19, concluded that the Soviet Union would not introduce offensive missiles into Cuba.[19] No U–2 flight was directed over the western end of Cuba (after September 5) before October 4. No U–2 flew over the western end of Cuba until the flight that discovered the Soviet missiles on October 14. Can these "failures" be accounted for in organizational terms?

On September 19 when USIB met to consider the question of Cuba, the "system" contained the following information: (1) shipping intelligence had noted the arrival in Cuba of two large-hatch Soviet lumber ships, which were riding high in the water; (2) refugee reports of countless sightings of missiles, but also a report that Castro's private pilot, after a night of drinking in Havana, had boasted: "We will fight to the death and perhaps we can win because we have everything, including atomic weapons"; (3) a sighting by a CIA agent of the rear profile of a strategic missile; (4) U–2 photos produced by flights of August 29, September 5 and 17 showing the construction of a number of SAM sites and other defensive missiles. Not all of this information was on the desk of the estimators, however. Shipping intelligence experts noted the fact that large-hatch ships were riding high in the water and spelled out the inference: the ships must be carrying "space consuming" cargo. These facts were carefully included in the catalogue of intelligence concerning shipping. For experts sensitive to the Soviets' shortage of ships, however, these facts carried no special signal. The refugee report of Castro's private pilot's remark had been received at Opa Locka, Florida, along with vast reams of inaccurate reports generated by the refugee community. This report and a thousand others had to be checked and compared before being sent to Washington. The two weeks required for initial processing could have been shortened by a large increase in resources, but the yield of this source was already quite marginal. The CIA agent's sighting of the rear profile of a strategic missile had occurred on September 12: transmission time from agent sighting to arrival in Washington typically took 9 to 12 days. Shortening this transmission time would impose severe cost in terms of danger to sub-agents, agents, and communication networks.

On the information available, the intelligence chiefs who predicted that the Soviet Union would not introduce offensive missiles into Cuba made a reasonable and defensible judgment. Moreover, in the light of the fact that these organizations were gathering intelligence not only about Cuba but about potential occurrences in all parts of the world, the informa-

tional base available to the estimators involved nothing out of the ordinary. Nor, from an organizational perspective, is there anything startling about the gradual accumulation of evidence that led to the formulation of the hypothesis that the Soviets were installing missiles in Cuba and the decision on October 4 to direct a special flight over western Cuba.

The ten-day delay between that decision and the flight is another organizational story. At the October 4 meeting, the Defense Department took the opportunity to raise an issue important to its concerns. Given the increased danger that a U–2 would be downed, it would be better if the pilot were an officer in uniform rather than a CIA agent. Thus the Air Force should assume responsibility for U–2 flights over Cuba. To the contrary, the CIA argued that this was an intelligence operation and thus within the CIA's jurisdiction. Moreover, CIA U–2's had been modified in certain ways which gave them advantages over Air Force U–2's in averting Soviet SAM's. Five days passed while the State Department pressed for less risky alternatives such as drones and the Air Force (in Department of Defense guise) and CIA engaged in territorial disputes. On October 9 a flight plan over San Cristobal was approved by COMOR, but to the CIA's dismay, Air Force pilots rather than CIA agents would take charge of the mission. At this point details become sketchy, but several members of the intelligence community have speculated that an Air Force pilot in an Air Force U–2 attempted a high altitude overflight on October 9 that "flamed out", i.e., lost power, and thus had to descend in order to restart its engine. A second round between Air Force and CIA followed, as a result of which Air Force pilots were trained to fly CIA U–2's. A successful overflight took place on October 14.

This ten-day delay constitutes some form of "failure." In the face of well-founded suspicions concerning offensive Soviet missiles in Cuba that posed a critical threat to the United States' most vital interest, squabbling between organizations whose job it is to produce this information seems entirely inappropriate. But for each of these organizations, the question involved the issue: "*Whose job was it to be?*" Moreover, the issue was not simply, which organization would control U–2 flights over Cuba, but rather the broader issue of ownership of U–2 intelligence activities—a very long standing territorial dispute. Thus though this delay was in one sense a "failure," it was also a nearly inevitable consequence of two facts: many jobs do not fall neatly into precisely defined organizational jurisdictions; and vigorous organizations are imperialistic.

Organizational Options. Deliberations of leaders in ExCom meetings produced broad outlines of alternatives. Details of these alternatives and blueprints for their implementation had to be specified by the organizations that would perform these tasks. These organizational outputs answered the question: What, specifically, *could* be done?

Discussion in the ExCom quickly narrowed the live options to two: an air strike and a blockade. The choice of the blockade instead of the air strike turned on two points: (1) the argument from morality and tradition that the United States could not perpetrate a "Pearl Harbor in reverse"; (2) the belief that a "surgical" air strike was impossible. Whether the United States *might* strike first was a question not of capability but of morality. Whether the United States *could* perform the surgical strike was a factual question concerning capabilities. The majority of the members of the ExCom, including the President, initially preferred the air strike. What effectively foreclosed this option, however, was the fact that the air strike they wanted could not be chosen with high confidence of success. After having tentatively chosen the course of prudence—given that the surgical air strike was not an option—Kennedy reconsidered. On Sunday morning, October 21, he called the Air Force experts to a special meeting in his living quarters where he probed once more for the option of a

"*surgical*" air strike. General Walter C. Sweeny, Commander of Tactical Air Forces, asserted again that the Air Force could guarantee no higher than ninety percent effectiveness in a surgical air strike. That "fact" was false.

The air strike alternative provides a classic case of military estimates. One of the alternatives outlined in the ExCom was named "air strike." Specification of the details of this alternative was delegated to the Air Force. Starting from an existing plan for massive U.S. military action against Cuba (prepared for contingencies like a response to a Soviet Berlin grab), Air Force estimators produced an attack to guarantee success. This plan called for extensive bombardment of all missile sites, storage depots, airports, and in deference to the Navy, the artillery batteries opposite the naval base at Guantanamo. Members of the ExCom repeatedly expressed bewilderment at military estimates of the number of sorties required, likely casualties, and collateral damage. But the "surgical" air strike that the political leaders had in mind was never carefully examined during the first week of the crisis. Rather, this option was simply excluded on the grounds that since the Soviet MRBM's in Cuba were classified "mobile" in U.S. manuals, extensive bombing was required. During the second week of the crisis, careful examination revealed that the missiles were mobile, in the sense that small houses are mobile: that is, they could be moved and reassembled in 6 days. After the missiles were reclassified "movable" and detailed plans for surgical air strikes specified, this action was added to the list of live options for the end of the second week.

Organizational Implementation. ExCom members separated several types of blockade: offensive weapons only, all armaments, and all strategic goods including POL (petroleum, oil and lubricants). But the "details" of the operation were left to the Navy. Before the President announced the blockade on Monday evening, the first stage of the Navy's blueprint was in motion, and a problem loomed on the horizon. The Navy had a detailed plan for the blockade. The President had several less precise but equally determined notions concerning what should be done, when and how. For the Navy the issue was one of effective implementation of the Navy's blockade—without the meddling and interference of political leaders. For the President, the problem was to pace and manage events in such a way that the Soviet leaders would have time to see, think, and blink.

A careful reading of available sources uncovers an instructive incident. On Tuesday, the British Ambassador, Ormsby–Gore, after having attended a briefing on the details of the blockade, suggested to the President that the plan for intercepting Soviet ships far out of reach of Cuban jets did not facilitate Khrushchev's hard decision. Why not make the interception much closer to Cuba and thus give the Russian leader more time? According to the public account and the recollection of a number of individuals involved, Kennedy "agreed immediately, called McNamara and over emotional Navy protest, issued the appropriate instructions."[20] As Sorensen records, "in a sharp clash with the Navy, he made certain his will prevailed."[21] The Navy's plan for the blockade was thus changed by drawing the blockade much closer to Cuba.

A serious organizational orientation makes one suspicious of this account. More careful examination of the available evidence confirms these suspicions, though alternative accounts must be somewhat speculative. According to the public chronology, a quarantine drawn close to Cuba became effective on Wednesday morning, the first Soviet ship was contacted on Thursday morning, and the first boarding of a ship occurred on Friday. According to the statement by the Department of Defense, boarding of the *Marcula* by a party from the *John R. Pierce* "took place at 7:50 A.M., E.D.T., 180 miles northeast of Nassau." The *Marcula* had been trailed since about 10:30 the previous evening. Simple calculations suggest that the *Pierce* must have been

stationed along the Navy's original arc which extended 500 miles out to sea from Cape Magsi, Cuba's eastern most tip. The blockade line was *not* moved as the President ordered, and the accounts report.

What happened is not entirely clear. One can be certain, however, that Soviet ships passed through the line along which American destroyers had posted themselves before the official "first contact" with the Soviet ship. On October 26 a Soviet tanker arrived in Havana and was honored by a dockside rally for "running the blockade." Photographs of this vessel show the name *Vinnitsa* on the side of the vessel in Cyrillic letters. But according to the official U.S. position, the first tanker to pass through the blockade was the *Bucharest,* which was hailed by the Navy on the morning of October 25. Again simple mathematical calculation excludes the possibility that the *Bucharest* and the *Vinnitsa* were the same ship. It seems probable that the Navy's resistance to the President's order that the blockade be drawn in closer to Cuba forced him to allow one or several Soviet ships to pass through the blockade after it was officially operative.

This attempt to leash the Navy's blockade had a price. On Wednesday morning, October 24, what the President had been awaiting occurred. The 18 dry cargo ships heading toward the quarantine stopped dead in the water. This was the occasion of Dean Rusk's remark, "We are eyeball to eyeball and I think the other fellow just blinked." But the Navy had another interpretation. The ships had simply stopped to pick up Soviet submarine escorts. The President became quite concerned lest the Navy—already riled because of Presidential meddling in its affairs—blunder into an incident. Sensing the President's fears, McNamara became suspicious of the Navy's procedures and routines for making the first interception. Calling on the Chief of Naval Operations in the Navy's inner sanctum, the Navy Flag Plot, McNamara put his questions harshly. Who would make the first interception?

Were Russian-speaking officers on board? How would submarines be dealt with? At one point McNamara asked Anderson what he would do if a Soviet ship's captain refused to answer questions about his cargo. Picking up the Manual of Navy Regulations the Navy man waved it in McNamara's face and shouted, "It's all in there." To which McNamara replied, "I don't give a damn what John Paul Jones would have done; I want to know what you are going to do now." The encounter ended on Anderson's remark: "Now, Mr. Secretary, if you and your Deputy will go back to your office the Navy will run the blockade."

Model III: Bureaucratic Politics

The leaders who sit on top of organizations are not a monolithic group. Rather, each is, in his own right, a player in a central, competitive game. The name of the game is bureaucratic politics: bargaining along regularized channels among players positioned hierarchically within the government. Government behavior can thus be understood according to the third conceptual model not as organizational outputs, but as outcomes of bargaining games. In contrast with Model I, the bureaucratic politics model sees no unitary actor but rather many actors as players, who focus not on a single strategic issue but on many diverse intra-national problems as well, in terms of no consistent set of strategic objectives but rather according to various conceptions of national, organizational, and personal goals, making government decisions not by rational choice but by the pulling and hauling that is politics.

The apparatus of each national government constitutes a complex arena for the intra-national game. Political leaders at the top of this apparatus plus the men who occupy positions on top of the critical organizations form the circle of central players. Ascendancy to this circle assures some independent standing. The necessary decentralization of decisions required for action on the broad range of foreign policy problems guarantees that each player has considerable discretion. Thus power is shared.

The nature of problems of foreign policy permits fundamental disagreement among reasonable men concerning what ought to be done. Analyses yield conflicting recommendations. Separate responsibilities laid on the shoulders of individual personalities encourage differences in perceptions and priorities. But the issues are of first order importance. What the nation does really matters. A wrong choice could mean irreparable damage. Thus responsible men are obliged to fight for what they are convinced is right.

Men share power. Men differ concerning what must be done. The differences matter. This milieu necessitates that policy be resolved by politics. What the nation does is sometimes the result of the triumph of one group over others. More often, however, different groups pulling in different directions yield a resultant distinct from what anyone intended. What moves the chess pieces is not simply the reasons which support a course of action, nor the routines of organizations which enact an alternative, but the power and skill of proponents and opponents of the action in question.

This characterization captures the thrust of the bureaucratic politics orientation. If problems of foreign policy arose as discreet issues, and decisions were determined one game at a time, this account would suffice. But most "issues," e.g., Vietnam or the proliferation of nuclear weapons, emerge piecemeal, over time, one lump in one context, a second in another. Hundreds of issues compete for players' attention every day. Each player is forced to fix upon his issues for that day, fight them on their own terms, and rush on to the next. Thus the character of emerging issues and the pace at which the game is played converge to yield government "decisions" and "actions" as collages. Choices by one player, outcomes of minor games, outcomes of central games, and "foul-ups"—these pieces, when stuck to the same canvas, constitute government behavior relevant to an issue.

The concept of national security policy as political outcome contradicts both public imagery and academic orthodoxy. Issues vital to national security, it is said, are too important to be settled by political games. They must be "above" politics. To accuse someone of "playing politics with national security" is a most serious charge. What public conviction demands, the academic penchant for intellectual elegance reinforces. Internal politics is messy; moreover, according to prevailing doctrine, politicking lacks intellectual content. As such, it constitutes gossip for journalists rather than a subject for serious investigation. Occasional memoirs, anecdotes in historical accounts, and several detailed case studies to the contrary, most of the literature of foreign policy avoids bureaucratic politics. The gap between academic literature and the experience of participants in government is nowhere wider than at this point. . . .

The U.S. Blockade of Cuba: A Third Cut

The Politics of Discovery.   A series of overlapping bargaining games determined both the *date* of discovery of the Soviet missiles and the *impact* on this discovery on the Administration. An explanation of the politics of the discovery is consequently a considerable piece of the explanation of the U.S. blockade.

Cuba was the Kennedy Administration's "political Achilles' heel."[22] The months preceding the crisis were also months before the Congressional elections, and the Republican Senatorial and Congressional Campaign Committee had announced that Cuba would be "the dominant issue of the 1962 campaign."[23] What the administration billed as a "more positive and indirect approach of isolating Castro from developing, democratic Latin America," Senators Keating, Goldwater, Capehart, Thurmond, and others attacked as a "do-nothing" policy.[24] In statements on the floor of the House and Sen-

ate, campaign speeches across the country, and interviews and articles carried by national news media, Cuba—particularly the Soviet program of increased arms aid—served as a stick for stirring the domestic political scene.

These attacks drew blood. Prudence demanded a vigorous reaction. The President decided to meet the issue head-on. The Administration mounted a forceful campaign of denial designed to discredit critics' claims. The President himself manned the front line of this offensive, though almost all Administration officials participated. In his news conference on August 19, President Kennedy attacked as "irresponsible" calls for an invasion of Cuba, stressing rather "the totality of our obligations" and promising to "watch what happens in Cuba with the closest attention." On September 4, he issued a strong statement denying any provocative Soviet action in Cuba. On September 13 he lashed out at "loose talk" calling for an invasion of Cuba. The day before the flight of the U–2 which discovered the missiles, he campaigned in Capehart's Indiana against those "self-appointed generals and admirals who want to send someone else's sons to war."

On Sunday, October 14, just as a U–2 was taking the first pictures of Soviet missiles, McGeorge Bundy was asserting:

> I *know* that there is no present evidence, and I think that there is no present likelihood that the Cuban government and the Soviet government would, in combination, attempt to install a major offensive capability.[25]

In this campaign to puncture the critics' charges, the Administration discovered that the public needed positive slogans. Thus, Kennedy fell into a tenuous semantic distinction between "offensive" and "defensive" weapons. This distinction originated in his September 4 statement that there was no evidence of "offensive ground to ground missiles" and warned "were it to be otherwise, the gravest issues would arise." His September 13 statement turned on this distinction between "defensive" and "offensive" weapons and announced a firm commitment to action if the Soviet Union attempted to introduce the latter into Cuba. Congressional committees elicited from administration officials testimony which read this distinction and the President's commitment into the *Congressional Record*.[26]

What the President least wanted to hear, the CIA was most hesitant to say plainly. On August 22 John McCone met privately with the President and voiced suspicions that the Soviets were preparing to introduce offensive missiles into Cuba. Kennedy heard this as what it was: the suspicion of a hawk. McCone left Washington for a month's honeymoon on the Riviera. Fretting at Cap Ferrat, he bombarded his deputy, General Marshall Carter, with telegrams, but Carter, knowing that McCone had informed the President of his suspicions and received a cold reception, was reluctant to distribute these telegrams outside the CIA. On September 9 a U–2 "on loan" to the Chinese Nationalists was downed over mainland China. The Committee on Overhead Reconnaissance (COMOR) convened on September 10 with a sense of urgency. Loss of another U–2 might incite world opinion to demand cancellation of U–2 flights. The President's campaign against those who asserted that the Soviets were acting provocatively in Cuba had begun. To risk downing a U–2 over Cuba was to risk chopping off the limb on which the President was sitting. That meeting decided to shy away from the western end of Cuba (where SAMs were becoming operational) and modify the flight pattern of the U–2s in order to reduce the probability that a U–2 would be lost. USIB's unanimous approval of the September estimate reflects similar sensitivities. On September 13 the President had asserted that there were no Soviet offensive missiles in Cuba and committed his Administration to act if offensive missiles were discovered. Before Congressional committees, Administration officials were denying that there was any evidence whatever of offensive missiles in Cuba. The implications of a National

Intelligence estimate which concluded that the Soviets were introducing offensive missiles into Cuba were not lost on the men who constituted America's highest intelligence assembly.

The October 4 COMOR decision to direct a flight over the western end of Cuba in effect "overturned" the September estimate, but without officially raising that issue. The decision represented McCone's victory for which he had lobbied with the President before the September 10 decision, in telegrams before the September 19 estimate, and in person after his return to Washington. Though the politics of the intelligence community is closely guarded, several pieces of the story can be told. By September 27, Colonel Wright and others in DIA believed that the Soviet Union was placing missiles in the San Cristobal area. This area was marked suspicious by the CIA on September 29 and certified top priority on October 3. By October 4 McCone had the evidence required to raise the issue officially. The members of COMOR heard McCone's argument, but were reluctant to make the hard decision he demanded. The significant probability that a U–2 would be downed made overflight of western Cuba a matter of real concern.

The Politics of Issues.   The U–2 photographs presented incontrovertible evidence of Soviet offensive missiles in Cuba. This revelation fell upon politicized players in a complex context. As one high official recalled, Khrushchev had caught us "with out pants down." What each of the central participants saw, and what each did to cover both his own and the Administration's nakedness, created the spectrum of issues and answers.

At approximately 9:00 A.M., Tuesday morning, October 16, McGeorge Bundy went to the President's living quarters with the message: "Mr. President, there is now hard photographic evidence that the Russians have offensive missiles in Cuba." Much has been made of Kennedy's "expression of surprise."[27] but "surprise" fails to capture the character of his initial reaction. Rather, it was one of startled anger, most adequately conveyed by the exclamation: "He can't do that to *me!*" In terms of the President's attention and priorities at that moment, Khrushchev had chosen the most unhelpful act of all. Kennedy had staked his full Presidential authority on the assertion that the Soviets would not place offensive weapons in Cuba. Moreover, Khrushchev had assured the President through the most direct and personal channels that he was aware of the President's domestic political problem and that nothing would be done to exacerbate this problem. The Chairman had *lied* to the President. Kennedy's initial reaction entailed action. The missiles must be removed. The alternatives of "doing nothing" or "taking a diplomatic approach" could not have been less relevant to *his* problem.

These two tracks—doing nothing and taking a diplomatic approach—were the solutions advocated by two of his principal advisors. For Secretary of Defense McNamara, the missiles raised the spectre of nuclear war. He first framed the issue as a straightforward strategic problem. To understand the issue, one had to grasp two obvious but difficult points. First, the missiles represented an inevitable occurrence: narrowing of the missile gap. It simply happened sooner rather than later. Second, the United States could accept this occurrence since its consequences were minor: "seven-to-one missile 'superiority,' one-to-one missile 'equality,' one-to-seven missile 'inferiority'—the three postures are identical." McNamara's statement of this argument at the first meeting of the ExCom was summed up in the phrase, "a missile is a missile. It makes no great difference," he maintained, "whether you are killed by a missile from the Soviet Union or Cuba." The implication was clear. The United States should not initiate a crisis with the Soviet Union, risking a significant probability of nuclear war over an occurrence which had such small strategic implications.

The perceptions of McGeorge Bundy, the President's Assistant for National Security Affairs, are the most difficult of all to reconstruct. There is no question that he initially argued for a diplomatic track. But was Bundy laboring under his acknowledged burden of responsibility in Cuba I? Or was he playing the role of devil's advocate in order to make the President probe his own initial reaction and consider other options?

The President's brother, Robert Kennedy, saw most clearly the political wall against which Khrushchev had backed the President. But he, like McNamara, saw the prospect of nuclear doom. Was Khrushchev going to force the President to an insane act? At the first meeting of the ExCom, he scribbled a note, "Now I know how Tojo felt when he was planning Pearl Harbor." From the outset he searched for an alternative that would prevent the air strike.

The initial reaction of Theodore Sorensen, the President's Special Counsel and "alter ego," fell somewhere between that of the President and his brother. Like the President, Sorensen felt the poignancy of betrayal. If the President had been the architect of the policy which the missiles punctured, Sorensen was the draftsman. Khrushchev's deceitful move demanded a strong counter-move. But like Robert Kennedy, Sorensen feared lest the shock and disgrace lead to disaster.

To the Joint Chiefs of Staff the issue was clear. *Now* was the time to do the job for which they had prepared contingency plans. Cuba I had been badly done; Cuba II would not be. The missiles provided the *occasion* to deal with the issue: cleansing the Western Hemisphere of Castro's Communism. As the President recalled on the day the crisis ended, "An invasion would have been a mistake—a wrong use of our power. But the military are mad. They wanted to do this. It's lucky for us that we have McNamara over there."

McCone's perceptions flowed from his confirmed prediction. As the Cassandra of the incident, he argued forcefully that the Soviets had installed the missiles in a daring political probe which the United States must meet with force. The time for an air strike was now.

The Politics of Choice.   The process by which the blockade emerged is a story of the most subtle and intricate probing, pulling, and hauling; leading, guiding, and spurring. Reconstruction of this process can only be tentative. Initially the President and most of his advisers wanted the clean, surgical air strike. On the first day of the crisis, when informing Stevenson of the missiles, the President mentioned only two alternatives: "I suppose the alternatives are to go in by air and wipe them out, or to take other steps to render them inoperable." At the end of the week a sizeable minority still favored an air strike. As Robert Kennedy recalled: "The fourteen people involved were very significant. . . . If six of them had been President of the U.S., I think that the world might have been blown up." What prevented the air strike was a fortuitous coincidence of a number of factors—the absence of any one of which might have permitted that option to prevail.

First, McNamara's vision of holocaust set him firmly against the air strike. His initial attempt to frame the issue in strategic terms struck Kennedy as particularly inappropriate. Once McNamara realized that the name of the game was a strong response, however, he and his deputy Gilpatric chose the blockade as a fallback. When the Secretary of Defense—whose department had the action, whose reputation in the Cabinet was unequaled, in whom the President demonstrated full confidence—marshalled the arguments for the blockade and refused to be moved, the blockade became a formidable alternative.

Second, Robert Kennedy—the President's closest confidant—was unwilling to see his brother become a "Tojo." His arguments against the air strike on moral grounds struck a chord in the President. Moreover, once his brother had stated these arguments so forcefully, the President could not have chosen his initially preferred course without, in effect, agreeing to become what RFK had condemned.

The President learned of the missiles on Tuesday morning. On Wednesday morning, in order to mask our discovery from the Russians, the President flew to Connecticut to keep a campaign commitment, leaving RFK as the unofficial chairman of the group. By the time the President returned on Wednesday evening, a critical third piece had been added to the picture. McNamara had presented his argument for the blockade. Robert Kennedy and Sorensen had joined McNamara. A powerful coalition of the advisors in whom the President had the greatest confidence, and with whom his style was most compatible, had emerged.

Fourth, the coalition that had formed behind the President's initial preference gave him reason to pause. *Who* supported the air strike—the Chiefs, McCone, Rusk, Nitze, and Acheson—as much as *how* they supported it, counted. Fifth, a piece of inaccurate information, which no one probed, permitted the blockade advocates to fuel (potential) uncertainties in the President's mind. When the President returned to Washington Wednesday evening, RFK and Sorensen met him at the airport. Sorensen gave the President a four-page memorandum outlining the areas of agreement and disagreement. The strongest argument was that the air strike simply could not be surgical. After a day of prodding and questioning, the Air Force had asserted that it could not guarantee the success of a surgical air strike limited to the missiles alone.

Thursday evening, the President convened the ExCom at the White House. He declared his tentative choice of the blockade and directed that preparations be made to put it into effect by Monday morning. Though he raised a question about the possibility of a surgical air strike subsequently, he seems to have accepted the experts' opinion that this was no live option.

(Acceptance of this estimate suggests that he may have learned the lesson of the Bay of Pigs—"Never rely on experts"—less well than he supposed.)[28] But this information was incorrect. That no one probed this estimate during the first week of the crisis poses an interesting question for further investigation.

A coalition, including the President, thus emerged from the President's initial decision that something had to be done; McNamara, Robert Kennedy, and Sorensen's resistance to the air strike; incompatibility between the President and the air strike advocates; and an inaccurate piece of information.

Conclusion. . . .

The preliminary, partial paradigms presented here provide a basis for serious reexamination of many problems of foreign and military policy. Model II and Model III cuts at problems typically treated in Model I terms can permit significant improvements in explanation and prediction. Full Model II and III analyses require large amounts of information. . . .

The present formulation of paradigms is simply an initial step. As such it leaves a long list of critical questions unanswered. Given any action, an imaginative analyst should always be able to construct some rationale for the government's choice. By imposing, and relaxing, constraints on the parameters of rational choice (as in variants of Model I) analysts can construct a large number of accounts of any act as a rational choice. But does a statement of reasons why a rational actor would choose an action constitute an explanation of the *occurrence* of that action? How can Model I analysis be forced to make more systematic contributions to the question of the determinants of occurrences? . . . The world is contiguous. But governments sometimes make sharp departures. Can an organizational process model be modified to suggest where change is likely? Attention to organiza-

tional change should afford greater understanding of why particular problems and SOPs are maintained by identifiable types of organizations and also how a manager can improve organizational performance. Model III tells a fascinating "story." But its complexity is enormous, the information requirements are often overwhelming, and many of the details of the bargaining may be superfluous. How can such a model be made parsimonious? The three models are obviously not exclusive alternatives. Indeed, the paradigms highlight the partial emphasis of the framework—what each emphasizes and what it leaves out. Each concentrates on one class of variables, in effect, relegating other important factors to a *ceteris paribus* clause. Model I concentrates on "market factors": pressures and incentives created by the "international strategic marketplace." Models II and III focus on the internal mechanism of the government that chooses in this environment. But can these relations be more fully specified? Adequate synthesis would require a typology of decision and actions, some of which are more amenable to treatment in terms of one model and some to another. . . .

Notes

1. Theodore Sorensen, *Kennedy* (New York, 1965), p. 705.

2. In attempting to understand problems of foreign affairs, analysts engage in a number of related, but logically separable enterprises: (a) description, (b) explanation, (c) prediction, (d) evaluation, and (e) recommendation. This essay focuses primarily on explanation (and by implication, prediction).

3. In arguing that explanations proceed in terms of implicit conceptual models, this essay makes no claim that foreign policy analysts have developed any satisfactory, empirically tested theory. In this essay, the use of the term "model" without qualifiers should be read "conceptual scheme."

4. Earlier drafts of this argument have aroused heated arguments concerning proper names for these models. To choose names for ordinary language is to court confusion, as well as familiarity. Perhaps it is best to think of these models as I, II, and III.

5. In strict terms, the "outcomes" which these three models attempt to explain are essentially actions of national governments, i.e., the sum of activities of all individuals employed by a government relevant to an issue. These models focus not on a state of affairs, i.e., a full description of the world, but upon national decision and implementation. This distinction is stated clearly by Harold and Margaret Sprout, "Environmental Factors on the Study of International Politics," in James Rosenau (ed.), *International Politics and Foreign Policy* (Glencoe, Illinois, 1961), p. 116. . . .

6. As stated in the introduction, this "case snapshot" presents, without editorial commentary, a Model I analyst's explanation of the U.S. blockade. The purpose is to illustrate a strong, characteristic rational policy model account. This account is (roughly) consistent with prevailing explanations of these events.

7. Theodore Sorensen, *op. cit.*, p. 675.

8. Ibid., p. 679.

9. Ibid., p. 679.

10. Elie Abel, *The Missile Crisis* (New York, 1966), p. 144.

11. Ibid., p. 102.

12. Sorensen, *op. cit.*, p. 684.

13. Ibid., p. 685. Though this was the formulation of the argument, the facts are not strictly accurate. Our tradition against surprise attack was rather younger than 175 years. For example, President Theodore Roosevelt applauded Japan's attack on Russia in 1904.

14. *New York Times,* June, 1963.

15. The influence of organizational studies upon the present literature of foreign affairs is minimal. Specialists in international politics are not students of organization theory. Organization theory has only recently begun to study organizations as decisionmakers and has not yet produced behavioral studies of national security organizations from a decision-making perspective. It seems unlikely, however, that these gaps will remain unfilled much longer. . . . The "decisionmaking" approach represented by Richard Snyder, R. Bruck, and B. Sapin, *Foreign Policy Decision-Making* (Glencoe, Illinois, 1962), incorporates a number of insights from organization theory.

16. U.S. Department of State, *Bulletin,* XLVII, pp. 715–720.

17. Arthur Schlesinger, *A Thousand Days* (Boston: 1965), p. 803.

18. See U.S. Congress, Senate, Committee on Armed Services, Preparedness Investigation Subcommittee, *Interim Report on Cuban Military Build-up,* 88th Congress, 1st Session, 1963, p. 2; Hanson Baldwin, "Growing Risks of Bureaucratic Intelligence," *The Reporter* (August 15, 1963), 48–50; Roberta Wohlstetter, "Cuba and Pearl Harbor," *Foreign Affairs* (July, 1965), 706.

19. R. Hilsman, *To Move a Nation* (New York, 1967), pp. 172–173.

20. Schlesinger, *op. cit.*, p. 818.

21. Sorensen, *Kennedy,* p. 710.

22. Sorensen, *Kennedy,* p. 670.

23. Ibid.

24. Ibid., pp. 670ff.

25. Cited by Abel, *op. cit.*, p. 13.

26. Senate Foreign Relations Committee; Senate Armed Services Committee; House Committee on Appropriations; House Select Committee on Export Control.

27. Abel, *op. cit.*, pp. 44f.

28. Schlesinger, *op. cit.*, p. 296.

Ideas and Foreign Policy

JUDITH GOLDSTEIN AND ROBERT O. KEOHANE

The authors identify ideas *as a significant independent variable in explanations of foreign policy. World views, principled beliefs, and causal beliefs are ideas that become embedded in institutions and impact the making of policy by acting as cognitive road maps.*

This [article] is about how ideas, which we define as beliefs held by individuals, help to explain political outcomes, particularly those related to foreign policy. As social scientists we are interested in using empirical evidence to evaluate the hypothesis that ideas are often important determinants of government policy. Our argument is that ideas influence policy when the principled or causal beliefs they embody provide road maps that increase actors' clarity about goals or ends-means relationships, when they affect outcomes of strategic situations in which there is no unique equilibrium, and when they become embedded in political institutions.

For millennia philosophers and historians have wrestled with the issue of the role of ideas in social and political life, and for as long as social science has existed its practitioners have debated these questions. In many ways this [article] is an extension of the approach first enunciated by Max Weber. Like Weber, we do not argue that ideas *rather than* interests (as interpreted by human beings) move the world. Instead, we suggest that ideas *as well as* interests have causal weight in explanations of human action.

If the study of the impact of ideas on policy is so old, why revive it now? Simply because in modern political economy and in international relations, the impressive elaboration of rationalist explanations of behavior has called into question old assumptions about whether the substantive content of people's ideas really matters for policy. To many economists, and to political scientists captivated by their modes of thinking, ideas are unimportant or epiphenomenal either because agents correctly anticipate the results of their actions or because some selective process ensures that only agents who behave as if they were rational succeed. In such functional arguments, effects explain causes through rational anticipation or natural selection.[1] The extreme version of this argument is that ideas are just hooks: competing elites seize on popular ideas to propagate and to legitimize their interests, but the ideas themselves do not play a causal role.[2] These interests may be strictly material—in many economic models, individuals are wealth-maximizers—but they also may encompass broader utility functions, in which such values as status and power are included. Whatever the details, in this rationalist view interests are given and logically prior to any beliefs held by the actors.

The most widely accepted systematic approaches to the study of international relations, realism and liberal institutionalism, take rationalist models as their starting points. Both realism and institutionalism assume that self-interested actors maximize their utility, subject to constraints. In such models, actors' preferences and causal beliefs are given, and attention focused on the variation in the constraints faced by actors.[3] Most analysts who rely on such approaches have relegated ideas to a minor role.[4]

[W]e seek to show that ideas matter for policy, even when human beings behave rationally to achieve their ends. Indeed, rationalist analysts of international politics have often recognized that the assumption of rationality, like that of egoism, "is a theoretically useful simplification of reality rather than a true reflection of it."[5] But even if we accept the rationality premise, actions taken by human beings depend on the substantive quality of available ideas, since such ideas help to clarify principles and conceptions of causal relationships, and to coordinate individual behavior. Once institutionalized, furthermore, ideas continue to guide action in the absence of costly innovation.[6] Hence [we] criticize approaches that deny the significance of ideas, but do not challenge the premise that people behave in self-interested and broadly rational ways.

More far-reaching criticisms of rationalistic models have become common in the literature on international relations. According to this "reflectivist" view, beliefs are a central element of all research because, in the words of Alexander Wendt, analysis turns on how "knowledgeable practices constitute subjects." Reflectivists "share a cognitive, intersubjective conception of process in which identities and interests are endogenous to interaction, rather than a rationalist-behavioral one in which they are exogenous."[7] This reflectivist critique is irrefutable in the abstract and reminds researchers to investigate not just what strategies are devised to attain interests but how preferences are formed and how identities are shaped. The key issue, however, is not whether identities matter but *how* they matter, and how their effects can be systematically studied by social scientists. Unfortunately, reflectivist scholars have been slow to articulate or test hypotheses. Without either a well-defined set of propositions about behavior or a rich empirical analysis, the reflectivist critique remains more an expression of understandable frustration than a working research program.

[We have] written as a challenge to both rationalist and reflectivist approaches. Although we concede that the rationalist approach is often a valuable starting point for analysis, we challenge its explanatory power by suggesting the existence of empirical anomalies that can be resolved only when ideas are taken into account. We demonstrate this need to go beyond pure rationalist analysis by using its own premise to generate our null hypothesis: that variation in policy across countries, or over time, is entirely accounted for by changes in factors *other than* ideas. Like reflectivists, we explore the impact of ideas, or beliefs, on policy. But [we] also pose an explicit challenge to the antiempiricist bias of much work in the reflectivist tradition, for we believe that the role played by ideas can and should be examined empirically with the tools of social science.

Our line of argument should also be distinguished from that suggested by psychological approaches. Cognitive psychology has shown convincingly that people frame information in ways that depart significantly from ideal-typical rationality.[8] Political scientists have used psychological insights and social-psychological work on group decision making to build a substantial literature stressing how cognitive processing affects foreign policy choices.[9] Work on foreign policy has emphasized how collective myths that affect conceptions of self-interest can be created and then perpetuated through propaganda and socialization of children in schools.[10] On issues such as deterrence, a vigorous debate has ensued about the relative adequacy of rationalist theories versus interpretations based on cognitive psychology.[11]

Cognitive psychology certainly concerns ideas, since it investigates beliefs of individuals about social reality that identify possibilities for action, reflect moral principles, and specify causal relationships. [Our concern is] not with the implications of cognitive psychology for interpretation of reality but with another facet of the role of ideas. We focus on the impact of particular beliefs—shared by large numbers of people—about the nature of their worlds that have implications for human action. Such beliefs range from general moral principles to agreement on a specific application of scientific knowledge. When we refer to ideas we refer to such beliefs. Since all of these beliefs were processed through human brains, it seems safe to assume that cognitive psychology played a role in their emergence; but we are interested in the impact of particular beliefs, not on the relation between beliefs and objective reality (however defined and determined). We do not seek to explain the sources of these ideas; we focus on their effects.

In our critique of both rationalist and reflective approaches to the study of foreign policy, we conceive of beliefs in a manner consistent with the logic of these two schools of thought and not that suggested by cognitive analyses. A sophisticated rationalist view could agree that interests are always interpreted through psychological processes, yet hold that knowledge of these interests, thus interpreted, enables the observer to understand behavior. Similarly, a reflectivist approach would not dispute that psychological forces are at work on the human brain. But like their rationalistic colleagues, reflectivists are far more interested in shared behavioral regularities attributable to linguistic constraints, for example, than in error attributable to deficiencies in human processing.[12] Reflectivist research focuses not on misinterpretations of human environments but on the constraints imposed by language, culture, and history on all aspects of individuals' abilities to define and act on "objective" interests. . . .

Three Types of Beliefs

At the most fundamental level, ideas define the universe of possibilities for action. As John Ruggie has pointed out, "fundamental modernist concepts such as market rationality, sovereignty, and personal privacy would not have been comprehensible before the development of appropriate terms of social discourse."[13] These conceptions of possibility, or *world views*, are embedded in the symbolism of a culture and deeply affect modes of thought and discourse. They are not purely normative, since they include views about cosmology and ontology as well as about ethics. Nevertheless, world views are entwined with people's conceptions of their identities, evoking deep emotions and loyalties. The world's great religions provide world views; but so does the scientific rationality that is emblematic of modernity.

Ideas have their broadest impact on human action when they take the form of world views. The world's major religions, for instance, have deeply affected human social life in a variety of ways and across millennia.[14] Similarly, it has often been argued that new conceptions of sovereignty led, at the Peace of Westphalia in 1648, to a new international order, dominated by independent states.[15] Still, the connections between world views and shifts in material power and interests are complex and need investigation. They do not all run in one direction. . . . notions of magic or fate. . . . Human beings are assumed [here] to be active agents in the construction of their own destinies. For traditionalist or religious fundamentalist societies even today, the individualistic and secular scientific premises of this world view remain intellectually and morally alien. . . . Understanding the impact of world views on general politics or foreign policy would require a broader comparative study of cultures, such as that on which Hedley Bull was engaged at the end of his too-brief career.[16]

Our second category of ideas, *principled beliefs*, consists of normative ideas that specify criteria for distinguishing right from wrong and just from unjust. The views that "slavery is wrong," that "abortion is murder," and that human beings have the "right of free speech" are principled beliefs. Principled beliefs are often justified in terms of larger world views, but those world views are frequently expansive enough to encompass opposing principled beliefs as well. For instance, although many opponents of slavery justified their arguments with references to Christianity, Christianity had tolerated slavery for almost two millennia. Principled beliefs mediate between world views and particular policy conclusions; they translate fundamental doctrines into guidance for contemporary human action. Millions of people have died on behalf of their principled beliefs; many people now alive are willing to do so. The revolutions of 1989 in Eastern Europe attest to the continuing vibrancy of principled beliefs in politics: people risked their lives in mass demonstrations, although material self-interest alone would have led them to be "free riders."

Changes in principled beliefs, as well as changes in world views, have a profound impact on political action. . . . For example, Kathryn Sikkink argues that the killing, torture, and maltreatment of millions of innocent people during World War II led both Europeans and Americans to believe that human rights should properly be a matter for international agreement and regulation, not shielded from international surveillance by the doctrine of sovereignty. The effects on policy were profound, since new ideas on human rights conditioned the definition of nations' interests. "The adoption of human rights policies," she suggests, "represented not

the neglect of national interests but a fundamental shift in the perception of long-term national interests." [See ch. 6 of *Ideas and Foreign Policy.*—Ed.]

The ideas in a third category, *causal beliefs*, are beliefs about cause-effect relationships which derive authority from the shared consensus of recognized elites, whether they be village elders or scientists at elite institutions. Such causal beliefs provide guides for individuals on how to achieve their objectives. Scientific knowledge may reveal how to eliminate smallpox, for instance, or how to slow down the greenhouse effect in the earth's atmosphere. Similarly, the Hungarian and Polish revolutions in the fall of 1989 showed people in East Germany and Czechoslovakia that unarmed mass protests could bring down long-standing repressive governments. Under such conditions, the efficacy of individual action depends on support from many other people, and therefore on the existence of a set of shared beliefs. Causal beliefs imply strategies for the attainment of goals, themselves valued because of shared principled beliefs, and understandable only within the context of broader world views.

Changes in the conceptualization of cause-effect relationships take place more frequently and more quickly than do changes in either world views or principled beliefs. Thus specific policy shifts can often be traced to such changes, particularly when technical knowledge is expanding. The foreign policies of the United States and many other countries with respect to regulation of the production of chlorofluorocarbons (CFCs), for example, changed dramatically between 1985 and 1990, largely in response to new scientific evidence about the hole in the atmospheric ozone layer over Antarctica. Policy shifted because scientific models linked ozone loss to cancer and climate change, and attributed much of it to increased levels of CFCs in the atmosphere. . . .[17]

Our categorization of beliefs is clearest in the abstract; in social life all three aspects of ideas may be linked. Doctrines and movements often weave conceptions of possibilities and principled and causal ideas together into what may seem to be a seamless web. The "epistemic communities" studied by Peter Haas and other scholars, for example, are constituted by knowledge-based experts who share both cause-effect conceptions and sets of normative and principled beliefs.[18] Nevertheless, it is worthwhile for purposes of causal analysis to distinguish ideas that develop or justify value commitments from those that simply provide guidance as to how to achieve preferred objectives.[19]

The Impact of Ideas on Policy

The central issue . . . concerns causality: Do ideas have an impact on political outcomes, and if so, under what conditions? The most egregious error that proponents of the role of ideas have made is to assume a causal connection between the ideas held by policy makers and policy choices. Ideas are always present in policy discussions, since they are a condition for reasoned discourse. But if many ideas are available for use, analysts should not assume that some intrinsic property of an idea explains its choice by policy makers. Choices of specific ideas may simply reflect the interests of actors. It is crucial for anyone working on ideas and policy to recognize that the delineation of the existence of particular beliefs is no substitute for the establishment of their effects on policy. Advocates of an ideational approach to political analysis must begin by identifying the ideas being described and the policy outcomes or institutional changes to be explained. We must also provide evidence about the conditions under which causal connections exist between ideas and policy outcomes.

In general, we see ideas in politics playing a role akin to that enunciated by Max Weber early in this century: "Not ideas, but material and ideal interests, directly govern men's conduct. Yet very frequently the 'world images' that have

been created by ideas have, like switchmen, determined the tracks along which action has been pushed by the dynamic of interest."[20] Ideas help to order the world. By ordering the world, ideas may shape agendas, which can profoundly shape outcomes. Insofar as ideas put blinders on people, reducing the number of conceivable alternatives, they serve as invisible switchmen, not only by turning action onto certain tracks rather than others, as in Weber's metaphor, but also by obscuring the other tracks from the agent's view.[21]

We do not suggest a theory for the creation of these switches, or even a fully worked-out model to explain the process by which ideas are selected. Rather, we suggest three causal pathways through which ideas hold the potential of influencing policy outcomes.[22] The first pathway derives from the need of individuals to determine their own preferences or to understand the causal relationship between their goals and alternative political strategies by which to reach those goals. On this pathway, ideas become important when actors believe in the causal links they identify or the normative principles that they reflect. Thus *ideas serve as road maps.* Analysis of this pathway does not account for which ideas are available and persuasive, but once an idea is selected, this pathway limits choice because it logically excludes other interpretations of reality or at least suggests that such interpretations are not worthy of sustained exploration.

On our second pathway, ideas affect strategic interactions, helping or hindering joint efforts to attain "more efficient" outcomes—outcomes that are at least as good as the status quo for all participants. Here *ideas contribute to outcomes in the absence of a unique equilibrium.* They may serve as focal points that define cooperative solutions or act as coalitional glue to facilitate the cohesion of particular groups—which may even prevent agreement on a wider basis. In any case, policy varies because of the choice of some ideas rather than others.

Whatever the reason for the enactment of a policy idea, the choice itself has long-lasting implications. Once ideas become embedded in rules and norms—that is, once they become institutionalized—they constrain public policy. Policies are influenced by earlier road maps, by past agreement to some policy focal point, or by the existence of some coalitional pattern rather than another. In short, *ideas embedded in institutions specify policy in the absence of innovation*. Analysis of this institutional path says nothing about why ideas were originally adopted; in fact, ideas may become important solely because of the interests and power of their progenitors. But once a policy choice leads to the creation of reinforcing organizational and normative structures, that policy idea can affect the incentives of political entrepreneurs long after the interests of its initial proponents have changed.

The way ideas influence policy outcomes varies with the paths. Still, on all three paths, ideas matter: policy would have been different in the absence of the idea in question. . . . Although we hold neither that a theory of ideas can stand alone nor that we can understand politics without understanding interests and power, we suggest that policy outcomes can be explained only when interests and power are combined with a rich understanding of human beliefs.

Ideas as Road Maps

Rationalistic analysis typically stipulates, but does not explain, individuals' preferences for some outcome. Yet people's preferences for particular policy outcomes are not given but acquired. World views and principled beliefs structure people's views about the fundamental nature of human life and the morality of practices and choices. They reflect beliefs about the nature of the universe, and about right and wrong. To understand the formation of preferences, we need to understand what ideas are available and how people choose among them.

Furthermore, even the most rationalistic analysts agree that people have incomplete information when they select strategies by which to pursue their preferred outcomes. The ideas individuals hold therefore become important elements in the explanation of policy choice, even if preferences are clear and actors are motivated purely by self-interest. If actors do not know with certainty the consequences of their actions, it is the *expected* effects of actions that explain them. And under conditions of uncertainty, expectations depend on causal beliefs as well as on institutional arrangements for authoritative decision making. Causal ideas help determine which of many means will be used to reach desired goals and therefore help to provide actors with strategies with which to further their objectives; embodied in institutions, they shape the solutions to problems. . . .[23]

In sum, when we view politics as an arena in which actors face continual uncertainties about their interests and how to maximize them, the need for ideas to act as road maps becomes apparent. Ideas serve the purpose of guiding behavior under conditions of uncertainty by stipulating causal patterns or by providing compelling ethical or moral motivations for action. Ideas can be broad or narrow; they can stipulate what is right and wrong, provide new social visions, or merely suggest what economic policy will steer a nation toward increased wealth. New ideas may even lead—even if not immediately—to a significant change in the very constitution of interests. This change may come about when an existing set of ideas is discredited by events or when a new idea is simply so compelling that it captures the attention of a wide array of actors. There is a difference, of course, between the ways in which causal and principled ideas relate to uncertainty. Causal ideas respond directly to uncertainty by reducing it, whereas principled ideas enable people to behave decisively despite causal uncertainty. Principled ideas can shift the focus of attention to moral issues and away from purely instrumental ones focused on material interests and power.[24]

Depression, wars, the decline of a political party, and the overthrow of a government may all cause ideas to become important because all constitute exogenous shocks that undermine the existing order. At such moments radical shifts in the political agenda may occur because of the common acceptance of some new normative or causal set of beliefs. The logic here is the opposite of that suggested by a functional model. Ideas are important even though actions based on their premises may lead to no gain in efficiency. Whereas a functional approach leads analysts to look to the purposes to which ideas are put, this first path suggests that the uncertainties that confront political actors can lead to reliance on beliefs as guides to action *even if* those ideas do not lead to benefits for society at large.

Coordination: Ideas as Focal Points and Glue

The folk theorem of repeated games emphasizes that players' rational strategies often fail to result in a unique equilibrium outcome: "In a very wide class of situations of strategic interaction—indeed, in virtually any game that takes place over time or in which there is a nontrivial informational structure—almost any outcome can occur in some game theoretic equilibrium."[25] Thus, from a game-theoretic perspective, ideas may be important precisely because unique predictions cannot be generated solely through an examination of interests and strategic interactions (utility functions and payoff matrices). Because almost all games with repeated play have multiple equilibria, the ideas held by players are often the key to a game's outcome.[26] It is not only the set of objective constraints and opportunities that guides action; individuals rely on beliefs and expectations when they select from a range of viable outcomes.

On this pathway, the key role played by ideas is to alleviate coordination problems arising from the absence of unique equilibrium

solutions.[27] Ideas can serve as focal points, as solutions to problems associated with incomplete contracting, or as the means to counteract problems of collective action. When political actors must choose between sets of outcomes that would represent Pareto improvements for all, and when there are no "objective" criteria on which to base choice, ideas focus expectations and strategies.[28] Political elites may settle upon courses of action on the basis of shared cultural, normative, religious, ethnic, or causal beliefs. Other policies may be ignored. As Geoffrey Garrett and Barry Weingast state the issue, "to assert that institutions help assure adherence to the rules of the game is to overlook a prior and critical issue. If the members of a community cannot agree to one set of rules, the fact that institutions might facilitate adherence to them would be irrelevant. . . ."[29]

Institutionalization

Ideas can matter in a third sense. Regardless of how a particular set of beliefs come to influence politics, use of those ideas over time implies changes in existing rules and norms. Ideas have a lasting influence on politics through their incorporation into the terms of political debate; but the impact of some set of ideas may be mediated by the operation of institutions in which the ideas are embedded. Once ideas have influenced organizational design, their influence will be reflected in the incentives of those in the organization and those whose interests are served by it. In general, when institutions intervene, the impact of ideas may be prolonged for decades or even generations. In this sense ideas can have an impact even when no one genuinely believes in them as principled or causal statements. One of the best examples of this process is seen in the case of legal doctrines—socially constructed sets of ideas that constrain contemporary policy making.[30]

Our third causal path focuses on how political institutions—administrative agencies, laws, norms, and operating procedures—mediate between ideas and policy outcomes.[31] In this model, ideas become institutionalized at some point in time. Although this institutionalization may reflect the power of some idea, its existence may also reflect the interests of the powerful.[32] But even in this case, the interests that promoted some statute may fade over time while the ideas encased in that statute nevertheless continue to influence politics. Thus at a later time, these institutionalized ideas continue to exert an effect: it is no longer possible to understand policy outcomes on the basis of contemporary configurations of interest and power alone.[33]

When ideas are powerfully institutionalized, we must both analyze the contemporary importance of old rules and socially embedded norms and undertake an archaeology of ideas in order to understand how one set of ideas rather than another came to be institutionalized. Consider, for instance, Judith Goldstein's work on United States trade policy. Contemporary variations in the treatment of industries in U.S. trade policy are not fully explained by variations in their economic positions or political resources. Different laws apply to antidumping and escape-clause issues, and we can understand these laws only by exploring the circumstances under which they were first enacted including the ideas about trade policy then held by the powerful. . . .[34]

In sum, ideas that become institutionalized play a role in generalizing rules and linking issue areas. When collective action requires persuasion rather than mere coercion, and when consistency of policy is demanded on the basis of principles institutionalized in the form of rulers, reasons must be given for proposed courses of action; when reasons are required, ideas become important. The significance of law in the European Community, and therefore of beliefs incorporated in legal doctrines, demonstrates how the demand for reasons can enhance the impact of ideas on policy, spreading it beyond areas originally contemplated by policy makers. Indeed, one consequence of international institutions is that they provide settings in which governments must provide reasons (whether genuine or not) for their positions. The existence of international institutions gives states greater incentives to make their policies more consistent with one another and with prevailing norms, so that they can be more successfully defended in international forums. . . .

Reflectivist students of the impact of ideas on policy often argue that interests cannot be conceptualized apart from the ideas that constitute them, and that it is therefore futile to try to distinguish interests and ideas analytically, as we seek to do. Adoption of such a view, however, would foreclose the possibility of evaluating the hypothesis that ideas are hooks against our argument that they often exert a major impact on policy. Reflectivists who assert that interests cannot be evaluated apart from the ideas that constitute them set aside materialist and rationalistic arguments without subjecting them to serious empirical evaluation. Thus a potentially rich debate is consigned to the purgatory of incompatible epistemologies.

We recognize that ideas and interests are not phenomenologically separate and that all interests involve beliefs, and therefore ideas as we conceive them. Yet, for us the important question is the extent to which *variation* in beliefs, or the manner in which ideas are institutionalized in societies, affect political action under circumstances that are otherwise similar. . . .

Notes

1. See Kenneth Shepsle, "Institutional Arrangement and Equilibrium in Multidimensional Voting Models," *American Journal of Political Science* 23 (1979): 27–60. For a sophisticated discussion, see Paul Milgrom, Douglass North, and Barry Weingast, "The Role of Institutions in the Revival of Trade: The Law Merchant, Private Judges, and the Champagne Fairs," *Economics and Politics* 2 (1990): 1–23.

2. Kenneth A. Shepsle, "Comment," in *Regulatory Policy and the Social Sciences*, ed. Roger Noll, pp. 231–37 (Berkeley: University of California Press, 1985).

3. A striking contrast can be found in the work of Henry R. Nau, who emphasizes purposes and ideas in *The Myth of America's Decline: Leading the World Economy into the 1990s* (New York: Oxford University Press, 1990), esp. chap. 1. Classical liberal arguments have also emphasized the role of domestic politics and society in shaping preferences. See Andrew Moravcsik, "Liberalism and International Relations Theory," Working Paper no. 92–6, Center for International Affairs, Harvard University (October 1992).

4. Ideas, like political culture, have traditionally been granted the status of "unexplained variance." For such a treatment of ideas in realist analysis, see Stephen Krasner, *Defending the National Interest* (Princeton: Princeton University Press, 1978). Among rationalistic works that seek to explain cooperation in a nonrealist way but do not focus on ideas are Robert O. Keohane, *After Hegemony: Cooperation and Discord in the World Political Economy* (Princeton: Princeton University Press, 1984), and Kenneth A. Oye, ed., *Cooperation under Anarchy* (Princeton: Princeton University Press, 1986).

5. Keohane, *After Hegemony*, p. 108.

6. A notable study of the role of ideas on policy is Peter A. Hall, ed., *The Political Power of Economic Ideas: Keynesianism across Nations* (Princeton: Princeton University Press, 1989). The research design of that study, however, differs from ours. Hall controls for knowledge of Keynesian ideas of macroeconomic management in a variety of countries, and accounts for the variety of outcomes on the basis of other variables, such as the orientation of the governing party, the structure of the state and state-society relations, the structure of political discourse, and the impact of World War II. We explore a variety of issue areas, with each author seeking to show how variations in the ideas available affected policy outcomes.

7. Alexander Wendt, "Anarchy Is What States Make of It: The Social Construction of Power Politics," *International Organization* 46 (Spring 1992): 392. For a discussion of reflective vs. rationalistic views, see Robert O. Keohane, "International Institutions: Two Approaches," *International Studies Quarterly* 32 (December 1988): 379–96, reprinted in Keohane, *International Institutions and State Power: Essays in International Relations Theory* (Boulder, Colo.: Westview, 1989), pp. 158–79. For examples of the reflectivist critique not otherwise cited, see Richard Ashley and R. B. J. Walker, "Speaking the Language of Exile: Dissident Thought in International Studies," *International Studies Quarterly* 34 (September 1990): 259–68; Thomas J. Biersteker, "Critical Reflections on Post-positivism in International Relations," *International Studies Quarterly* 33 (September 1989): 263–67; Robert Cox, *Production, Power, and World Order* (New York: Columbia University Press, 1987);

Yosef Lapid, "The Third Debate: On the Prospects of International Theory in a Post-positivist Era," *International Studies Quarterly* 33 (September 1989): 235–54; Alexander Wendt, "The Agent-Structure Problem in International Relations Theory," *International Organization* 41 (Summer 1987): 335–70.

8. Daniel Kahneman and Amos Tversky, "Choices, Values, and Frames," *American Psychologist* 39 (1984): 341–50; Amos Tversky and Daniel Kahneman, "The Framing of Decisions and the Psychology of Choice," *Science* 211 (1981): 453–58.

9. See, inter alia, Robert Jervis, *Perception and Misperception in International Politics* (Princeton: Princeton University Press, 1976); Deborah Welch Larson, *Origins of Containment: A Psychological Explanation* (Princeton: Princeton University Press, 1985); Richard Ned Lebow, *Between Peace and War: The Nature of International Crisis* (Baltimore: Johns Hopkins University Press, 1981); Robert Jervis, Richard Ned Lebow, and Janice Gross Stein, *Psychology and Deterrence* (Baltimore: Johns Hopkins University Press, 1985).

10. Stephen Van Evera, "The Cult of the Offensive and the Origins of the First World War," *International Security* 9 (Summer 1984): 58–107; Jack Snyder, *Myths of Empire: Domestic Politics and International Ambition* (Ithaca: Cornell University Press, 1991).

11. See "The Rational Deterrence Debate: A Symposium," *World Politics* 41 (January 1989).

12. See, e.g., Friedrich Kratochwil, "The Force of Prescriptions, *International Organization* 38 (Autumn 1984): 685–708.

13. Memo prepared for the SSRC-sponsored conference on ideas and foreign policy, Stanford, California, January 18–20, 1990.

14. Max Weber, *The Protestant Ethic and the Spirit of Capitalism* (1994–5; rpt. New York: Scribner's, 1958), and "The Social Psychology of the World Religions" (1913), in *From Max Weber: Essays in Sociology*, ed. H. H. Gerth and C. Wright Mills (New York: Oxford University Press, 1958).

15. Leo Gross, "The Peace of Westphalia, 1648–1948," *American Journal of International Law* 42 (1948): 20–41; John Gerard Ruggie, "Continuity and Transformation in the World Polity: Toward a Neorealist Synthesis," *World Politics* 35, no. 2 (1983): 261–85.

16. Hedley Bull and Adam Watson, eds., *The Expansion of International Society* (Oxford: Clarendon, 1984).

17. Richard Elliot Benedick, *Ozone Diplomacy: New Directions in Safeguarding the Planet* (Cambridge: Harvard University Press, 1991); Edward A. Parson, "Protecting the Ozone Layer," in *Institutions for The Earth: Sources of Effective International Environmental Protection*, ed. Peter M. Haas, Robert O. Keohane, and Marc A. Levy (Cambridge: MIT Press, 1993), pp. 27–74.

18. Peter M. Haas, "Introduction: Epistemic Communities and International Policy Coordination," *International Organization* 46 (Winter 1992): 1–35. Our interest in ideas extends beyond epistemic communities, but the recent work on epistemic communities provides substantial support, within particular institutional contexts, for the thesis that ideas matter. Peter Haas contributed significantly to our thinking on these issues through his participation in our meetings.

19. This distinction parallels Weber's between "substantive rationality," which applied "criteria of ultimate ends," and "formal rationality," which denotes that "action is based on 'goal-oriented' rational calculation with the technically most adequate available methods." See Max Weber, *Economy and Society*, ed. Guenther Roth and Claus Wittich (Berkeley: University of California Press, 1968), p. 85. It is also similar to the distinction in rational choice analysis between preferences and strategies.

20. Max Weber, "Social Psychology of the World's Religions," p. 280.

21. For instance, the hegemony of utilitarian, market-oriented language and modes of thinking in contemporary capitalist democracies rules out certain community-based and value-laden policies as irrational, excluding them from serious consideration as public policy.

22. We borrow the idea of causal pathways from a working paper by David Dessler, "The Architecture of Causal Analysis," Center for International Affairs, Harvard University, April 1992.

23. Ideas, embodied in institutions, may shape the stream of solutions, to be matched conjuncturally with a separate stream of problems. See M. D. Cohen and J. G. March, "A Garbage Can Model of Organizational Choice," *Administrative Science Quarterly* 17 (1972): 1–25.

24. For an excellent discussion of morality and foreign policy, see Robert McElroy, *Morality and American Foreign Policy* (Princeton: Princeton University Press, 1992).

25. Memo by John Ferejohn, written for our January 18–20, 1990, conference, pp. 8–9.

26. This is the insight of the folk theorem. See Drew Fudenberg and Eric Maskin, "The Folk Theorem in Repeated Games with Discounting or with Incomplete Information," *Econometrica* 54 (1986): 533–54. This is true even in the more restrictive situation in which players have both complete and perfect information; that is, they know the strategies selected by players in the past and they are completely aware of the payoff structure.

27. For an interesting related discussion, see Lisa Martin, "The Rational State Choice of Multilateralism," in *Multilateralism Matters*, ed. John Gerard Ruggie, pp. 91–121 (New York: Columbia University Press, 1993).

28. For the generalized argument, see David Kreps, "Corporate Culture and Economic Theory," in *Perspectives on Positive Political Economy*, ed. James Alt and Kenneth Shepsle (Cambridge: Cambridge University Press, 1990).

29. Geoffrey Garrett and Barry Weingast, "National Autonomy, European Law, and the Internal Market: Norms, Institutions, and European Integration," paper prepared for our April 1991 conference, p. 18.

30. We are indebted to John Ferejohn for this example.

31. We define norms as implicit prescriptions accepted as valid by a particular society to govern relationships within it or by more than one society to govern their relations with one another. The concept of norms, however, is contested, and we have not imposed this definition on all of the authors in this volume.

32. In this model, therefore, whether ideas shaped institutions at their creation is less important than the effects of the institution that embodies the ideas.

33. The importance of the institutionalization of ideas was particularly brought home to us by James E. Alt, "Crude Politics: Oil and the Political Economy of Unemployment in Britain and Norway, 1970–85." *British Journal of Political Science* 17 (April 1987): 149–99. Alt shows how Norway's institutionalization of sectoral ideas about the economy, in the form of a disaggregated model used by the Norwegian Ministry of Finance, enabled it to react effectively to increases in the price of crude oil; Britain's treasury relied on models that had institutionalized aggregate conceptions of the economy, using a single equation for all exported manufactures. For this as well as for larger political reasons, Britain was less able than Norway to limit the unemployment-creating effects of oil price increases. See ibid., pp. 161–63.

34. Judith Goldstein, *Ideas, Interests, and American Trade Policy* (Ithaca: Cornell University Press, 1993).

Realism and Complex Interdependence

ROBERT O. KEOHANE AND JOSEPH S. NYE, JR.

The authors contrast the realistic perspective on international relations with the complex interdependence perspective on world politics associated with the pluralist image. Complex interdependence includes the multiple channels that connect societies; a diverse set of issues on policy agendas, the priority of which is not always clear or consistent; and the utility of military force is highly variable.

Interdependence in World Politics

We live in an era of interdependence. This vague phrase expresses a poorly understood but widespread feeling that the very nature of world politics is changing. The power of nations—that age-old touchstone of analysts and statesmen—has become more elusive: "calculations of power are even more delicate and deceptive than in previous ages."[1] Henry Kissinger, though deeply rooted in the classical tradition, has stated that "the traditional agenda of international affairs—the balance among major powers, the security of nations—no longer defines our perils or our possibilities. . . . Now we are entering a new era. Old international patterns are crumbling: old slogans are uninstructive; old solutions are unavailing. The world has become interdependent in economics, in communications, in human aspirations."[2]

How profound are the changes? A modernist school sees telecommunications and jet travel as creating a "global village" and believes that burgeoning social and economic transactions are creating a "world without borders."[3] To greater or lesser extent, a number of scholars see our era as one in which the territorial state, which has been dominant in world politics for the four centuries since feudal times ended, is being eclipsed by nonterritorial actors such as multinational corporations, transnational social movements, and international organizations. As one economist put it, "the state is about through as an economic unit."[4]

Traditionalists call these assertions unfounded "globaloney." They point to the continuity in world politics. Military interdependence has always existed, and military power is still important in world politics—witness nuclear deterrence; the Vietnam, Middle East, and India-Pakistan wars, and Soviet influence in Eastern Europe or American influence in the Caribbean. Moreover, as the Soviet Union has shown, authoritarian states can, to a considerable extent, control telecommunications and social transactions that they consider disruptive. Even poor and weak countries have been able to nationalize multinational corporations, and the prevalence of nationalism casts doubt on the proposition that the nation-state is fading away.

Neither the modernists nor the traditionalists have an adequate framework for understanding the politics of global interdependence.[5] Modernists point correctly to the fundamental changes now taking place, but they often assume without sufficient analysis that advances in technology and increases in social and economic transactions will lead to a new world in which

From Robert O. Keohane and Joseph S. Nye, Jr., *Power and Interdependence: World Politics in Transition* (Boston: Little, Brown, 1977), pp. 3–5, 8–11, 23–37. Reprinted by permission.

states, and their control of force, will no longer be important.[6] Traditionalists are adept at showing flaws in the modernist vision by pointing out how military interdependence continues, but find it very difficult accurately to interpret today's multidimensional economic, social, and ecological interdependence.

Our task . . . is not to argue either the modernist or traditionalist position. Because our era is marked by both continuity and change, this would be fruitless. Rather, our task is to provide a means of distilling and blending the wisdom in both positions by developing a coherent theoretical framework for the political analysis of interdependence. We shall develop several different but potentially complementary models, or intellectual tools, for grasping the reality of interdependence in contemporary world politics. Equally important, we shall attempt to explore the *conditions* under which each model will be most likely to produce accurate predictions and satisfactory explanations. Contemporary world politics is not a seamless web; it is a tapestry of diverse relationships. In such a world, one model cannot explain all situations. The secret of understanding lies in knowing which approach or combination of approaches to use in analyzing a situation. There will never be a substitute for careful analysis of actual situations.

Yet theory is inescapable; all empirical or practical analysis rests on it. Pragmatic policymakers might think that they need pay no more heed to theoretical disputes over the nature of world politics than they pay to medieval scholastic disputes over how many angels can dance on the head of a pin. Academic pens, however, leave marks in the minds of statesmen with profound results for policy. Not only are "practical men who believe themselves to be quite exempt from any intellectual influences" unconscious captives of conceptions created by "some academic scribbler of a few years back," but increasingly the scribblers have been playing a direct role in forming foreign policy.[7] Inappropriate images and ill-conceived perceptions of world politics can lead directly to inappropriate or even disastrous national policies.

Rationale and rationalization, systematic presentation and symbolism, become so intertwined that it is difficult, even for policymakers themselves, to disentangle reality from rhetoric. Traditionally, classical theories of world politics have portrayed a potential "state of war" in which states' behavior was dominated by the constant danger of military conflict. During the Cold War, especially the first decade after World War II, this conception, labeled "political realism" by its proponents, became widely accepted by students and practitioners of international relations in Europe and the United States.[8] During the 1960s, many otherwise keen observers who accepted realist approaches were slow to perceive the development of new issues that did not center on military-security concerns.[9] The same dominant image in the late 1970s or 1980s would be likely to lead to even more unrealistic expectations. Yet to exchange it for an equally simple view—for instance, that military force is obsolete and economic interdependence benign—would condemn one to equally grave, though different, errors. . . .

Interdependence as an Analytic Concept

In common parlance, *dependence* means a state of being determined or significantly affected by external forces. *Interdependence*, most simply defined, means *mutual* dependence. Interdependence in world politics refers to situations characterized by reciprocal effects among countries or among actors in different countries.

These effects often result from international transactions—flows of money, goods, people, and messages across international boundaries. Such transactions have increased dramatically since World War II: "Recent decades reveal a general tendency for many forms of human interconnectedness across national boundaries to be doubling every ten years."[10] Yet this interconnectedness is not the same as interdependence. The effects of transactions on interdependence will depend on the constraints, or costs, associated with them. A country that imports all of its oil is likely to be more dependent on a continual flow of petroleum than a country importing furs, jewelry, and perfume (even of equivalent monetary value) will be on uninterrupted access to these luxury goods. Where there are reciprocal (although not necessarily symmetrical) costly effects of transactions, there is interdependence. Where interactions do not have significant costly effects, there is simply interconnectedness. The distinction is vital if we are to understand the *politics* of interdependence.

Costly effects may be imposed directly and intentionally by another actor—as in Soviet-American strategic interdependence, which derives from the mutual threat of nuclear destruction. But some costly effects do not come directly or intentionally from other actors. For example, collective action may be necessary to prevent disaster for an alliance (the members of which are interdependent), for an international economic system (which may face chaos because of the absence of coordination, rather than through the malevolence of any actor), or for an ecological system threatened by a gradual increase of industrial effluents.

We do not limit the term *interdependence* to situations of mutual benefit. Such a definition would assume that the concept is only useful analytically where the modernist view of the world prevails: where threats of military force are few and levels of conflict are low. It would exclude from interdependence cases of mutual dependence, such as the strategic interdependence between the United States and the Soviet Union. Furthermore, it would make it very ambiguous whether relations between industrialized countries and less developed countries should be considered interdependent or not. Their inclusion would depend on an inherently subjective judgment about whether the relationships were "mutually beneficial."

Because we wish to avoid sterile arguments about whether a given set of relationships is characterized by interdependence or not, and

because we seek to use the concept of interdependence to integrate rather than further to divide modernist and traditional approaches, we choose a broader definition. Our perspective implies that interdependent relationships will always involve costs, since interdependence restricts autonomy; but it is impossible to specify *a priori* whether the benefits of a relationship will exceed the costs. This will depend on the values of the actors as well as on the nature of the relationship. Nothing guarantees that relationships that we designate as "interdependent" will be characterized by mutual benefit.

Two different perspectives can be adopted for analyzing the costs and benefits of an interdependent relationship. The first focuses on the joint gains or joint losses to the parties involved. The other stresses *relative* gains and distributional issues. Classical economists adopted the first approach in formulating their powerful insight about comparative advantage: that undistorted international trade will provide overall net benefits. Unfortunately, an exclusive focus on joint gain may obscure the second key issue: how those gains are divided. Many of the crucial political issues of interdependence revolve around the old question of politics, "who gets what?"

It is important to guard against the assumption that measures that increase joint gain from a relationship will somehow be free of distributional conflict. Governments and nongovernmental organizations will strive to increase their shares of gains from transactions, even when they both profit enormously from the relationship. Oil-exporting governments and multinational oil companies, for instance, share an interest in high prices for petroleum; but they have also been in conflict over shares of the profits involved.

We must therefore be cautious about the prospect that rising interdependence is creating a brave new world of cooperation to replace the bad old world of international conflict. As every parent of small children knows, baking a larger pie does not stop disputes over the size of the slices. An optimistic approach would overlook the uses of economic and even ecological interdependence in competitive international politics.

The difference between traditional international politics and the politics of economic and ecological interdependence is *not* the difference between a world of "zero-sum" (where one side's gain is the other side's loss) and "nonzero-sum" games. Military interdependence need not be zero-sum. Indeed, military allies actively seek interdependence to provide enhanced security for all. Even balance of power situations need not be zero-sum. If one side seeks to upset the status quo, then its gain is at the expense of the other. But if most or all participants want a stable status quo, they can jointly gain by preserving the balance of power among them. Conversely, the politics of economic and ecological interdependence involve competition even when large net benefits can be expected from cooperation. There are important continuities, as well as marked differences, between the traditional politics of military security and the politics of economic and ecological interdependence.

We must also be careful not to define interdependence entirely in terms of situations of *evenly balanced* mutual dependence. It is *asymmetries* in dependence that are most likely to provide sources of influence for actors in their dealings with one another. Less dependent actors can often use the interdependent relationship as a source of power in bargaining over an issue and perhaps to affect other issues. At the other extreme from pure symmetry is pure dependence (sometimes disguised by calling the situation interdependence); but it too is rare. Most cases lie between these two extremes. And that is where the heart of the political bargaining process of interdependence lies. . . .

Realism and Complex Interdependence

One's assumptions about world politics profoundly affect what one sees and how one constructs theories to explain events. We believe that the assumptions of political realists, whose theories dominated the postwar period, are often an inadequate basis for analyzing the politics of interdependence. The realist assumptions about world politics can be seen as defining an extreme set of conditions or *ideal type*. One could also imagine very different conditions. In this article, we shall construct another ideal type, the opposite of realism. We call it *complex interdependence*. After establishing the differences between realism and complex interdependence, we shall argue that complex interdependence sometimes comes closer to reality than does realism. When it does, traditional explanations of change in international regimes become questionable and the search for new explanatory models becomes more urgent.

For political realists, international politics, like all other politics, is a struggle for power but, unlike domestic politics, a struggle dominated by organized violence. In the words of the most influential postwar textbook, "All history shows that nations active in international politics are continuously preparing for, actively involved in, or recovering from organized violence in the form of war."[11] Three assumptions are integral to the realist vision. First, states as coherent units are the dominant actors in world politics. This is a double assumption: states are predominant; and they act as coherent units. Second, realists assume that force is a usable and effective instrument of policy. Other instruments may also be employed, but using or threatening force is the most effective means of wielding power. Third, partly because of their second assumption, realists assume a hierarchy of issues in world politics, headed by questions of military security: the "high politics" of military security dominates the "low politics" of economic and social affairs.

These realist assumptions define an ideal type of world politics. They allow us to imagine a world in which politics is continually characterized by active or potential conflict among states, with the use of force possible at any time. Each state attempts to defend its territory and interests from real or perceived threats. Political integration among states is slight and lasts only as long as it serves the national interests of the most powerful states. Transnational actors either do not exist or are politically unimportant. Only the adept exercise of force or the threat of force permits states to survive, and only while statesmen succeed in adjusting their interests, as in a well-functioning balance of power, is the system stable.

Each of the realist assumptions can be challenged. If we challenge them all simultaneously, we can imagine a world in which actors other than states participate directly in world politics, in which a clear hierarchy of issues does not exist, and in which force is an ineffective instrument of policy. Under these conditions—which we call the characteristics of complex interdependence—one would expect world politics to be very different than under realist conditions.

We will explore these differences in the next section of this chapter. We do not argue, however, that complex interdependence faithfully reflects world political reality. Quite the contrary: both it and the realist portrait are ideal types. Most situations will fall somewhere between these two extremes. Sometimes, realist assumptions will be accurate, or largely accurate, but frequently complex interdependence will provide a better portrayal of reality. Before one decides what explanatory model to apply to a situation or problem, one will need to understand the degree to which realist or complex interdependence assumptions correspond to the situation.

The Characteristics of Complex Interdependence

Complex interdependence has three main characteristics:

1. *Multiple channels* connect societies, including informal ties between governmental elites as well as formal foreign office arrangements; informal ties among nongovernmental elites (face-to-face and through telecommunications); and transnational organizations (such as multi-national banks or corporations). These channels can be summarized as interstate, transgovernmental, and transnational relations. *Interstate* relations are the normal channels assumed by realists. *Transgovernmental* applies when we relax the realist assumption that states act coherently as units; *transnational* applies when we relax the assumption that states are the only units.

2. The agenda of interstate relationships consists of multiple issues that are not arranged in a clear or consistent hierarchy. This *absence of hierarchy among issues* means, among other things, that military security does not consistently dominate the agenda. Many issues arise from what used to be considered domestic policy, and the distinction between domestic and foreign issues becomes blurred. These issues are considered in several government departments (not just foreign offices), and at several levels. Inadequate policy coordination on these issues involves significant costs. Different issues generate different coalitions, both within governments and across them, and involve different degrees of conflict. Politics does not stop at the waters' edge.

3. Military force is not used by governments toward other governments within the region, or on the issues, when complex interdependence prevails. It may, however, be important in these governments' relations with governments outside that region, or on other issues. Military force could, for instance, be irrelevant to resolving disagreements on economic issues among members of an alliance, yet at the same time be very important for that alliance's political and military relations with a rival bloc. For the former relationships this condition of complex interdependence would be met; for the latter, it would not.

Traditional theories of international politics implicitly or explicitly deny the accuracy of these three assumptions. Traditionalists are therefore tempted also to deny the relevance of criticisms based on the complex interdependence ideal type. We believe, however, that our three conditions are fairly well approximated on some global issues of economic and ecological interdependence and that they come close to characterizing the entire relationship between some countries. One of our purposes here is to prove that contention. . . .

The Political Processes of Complex Interdependence

The three main characteristics of complex interdependence give rise to distinctive political processes, which translate power resources into power as control of outcomes. As we argued earlier, something is usually lost or added in the translation. Under conditions of complex interdependence the translation will be different than under realist conditions, and our predictions about outcomes will need to be adjusted accordingly.

In the realist world, military security will be the dominant goal of states. It will even affect issues that are not directly involved with military power, or territorial defense. Nonmilitary problems will not only be subordinated to military ones; they will be studied for their politico-military implications. Balance of payments issues, for instance, will be considered at least as much in the light of their implications for world power generally as for their purely financial ramifications. McGeorge Bundy conformed to realist expectations when he argued in 1964 that devaluation of the dollar should be seriously considered if necessary to fight the war in Vietnam.[12] To some extent, so did former Treasury Secretary Henry Fowler when he contended in 1971 that the United States needed a trade surplus of $4 billion to $6 billion in order to lead in Western defense.[13]

In a world of complex interdependence, however, one expects some officials, particularly at lower levels, to emphasize the *variety* of state goals that must be pursued. In the absence of a clear hierarchy of issues, goals will vary by issue, and may not be closely related. Each bureaucracy will pursue its own concerns; and although several agencies may reach compromises on issues that affect them all, they will find that a consistent pattern of policy is difficult to maintain. Moreover, transnational actors will introduce different goals into various groups of issues.

Linkage Strategies

Goals will therefore vary by issue area under complex interdependence, but so will the distribution of power and the typical political processes. Traditional analysis focuses on *the* international system, and leads us to anticipate similar political processes on a variety of issues. Militarily and economically strong states will dominate a variety of organizations and a variety of issues, by linking their own policies on some issues to other states' policies on other issues. By using their overall dominance to prevail on their weak issues, the strongest states will, in the traditional model, ensure a congruence between the overall structure of military and economic power and the pattern of outcomes on any one issue area. Thus world politics can be treated as a seamless web.

Under complex interdependence, such congruence is less likely to occur. As military force is devalued, militarily strong states will find it more difficult to use their overall dominance to control outcomes on issues in which they are weak. And since the distribution of power resources in trade, shipping, or oil, for example, may be quite different, patterns of outcomes and distinctive political processes are likely to vary from one set of issues to another. If force were readily applicable, and military security were the highest foreign policy goal, these variations in the issue structures of power would not matter very much. The linkages drawn from them to military issues would ensure consistent dominance by the overall strongest states. But when military force is largely immobilized, strong states will find that linkage is less effective. They may still attempt such links, but in the absence of a hierarchy of issues, their success will be problematic.

Dominant states may try to secure much the same result by using overall economic power to affect results on other issues. If only economic objectives are at stake, they may succeed: money, after all, is fungible. But economic objectives have political implications, and economic linkage by the strong is limited by domestic, transnational, and transgovernmental actors who resist having their interests traded off. Furthermore, the international actors may be different on different issues, and the international organizations in which negotiations take place are often quite separate. Thus it is difficult, for example, to imagine a militarily or economically strong state linking concessions on monetary policy to reciprocal concessions in oceans policy. On the other hand, poor weak states are not similarly inhibited from linking unrelated issues, partly because their domestic interests are less complex. Linkage of unrelated issues is often a means of extracting concessions or side payments from rich and powerful states. And unlike powerful states whose instrument for linkage (military force) is often too costly to use, the linkage instrument used by poor, weak states—international organization—is available and inexpensive.

Thus as the utility of force declines, and as issues become more equal in importance, the distribution of power within each issue will become more important. If linkages become less effective on the whole, outcomes of political bargaining will increasingly vary by issue area.

The differentiation among issue areas in complex interdependence means that linkages among issues will become more problematic and will tend to reduce rather than reinforce international hierarchy. Linkage strategies, and defense against them, will pose critical strategic choices for states. Should issues be considered separately or as a package? If linkages are to be drawn, which issues should be linked, and on which of the linked issues should concessions be made? How far can one push a linkage before it becomes counterproductive? For instance,

should one seek formal agreements or informal, but less politically sensitive, understandings? The fact that world politics under complex interdependence is not a seamless web leads us to expect that efforts to stitch seams together advantageously, as reflected in linkage strategies, will, very often, determine the shape of the fabric.

The negligible role of force leads us to expect states to rely more on other instruments in order to wield power. For the reasons we have already discussed, less vulnerable states will try to use asymmetrical interdependence in particular groups of issues as a source of power; they will also try to use international organizations and transnational actors and flows. States will approach economic interdependence in terms of power as well as its effects on citizens' welfare, although welfare considerations will limit their attempts to maximize power. Most economic and ecological interdependence involves the possibility of joint gains, or joint losses. Mutual awareness of potential gains and losses and the danger of worsening each actor's position through overly rigorous struggles over the distribution of the gains can limit the use of asymmetrical interdependence.

Agenda Setting

Our second assumption of complex interdependence, the lack of clear hierarchy among multiple issues, leads us to expect that the politics of agenda formation and control will become more important. Traditional analyses lead statesmen to focus on politico-military issues and to pay little attention to the broader politics of agenda formation. Statesmen assume that the agenda will be set by shifts in the balance of power, actual or anticipated, and by perceived threats to the security of states. Other issues will only be very important when they seem to affect security and military power. In these cases, agendas will be influenced strongly by considerations of the overall balance of power.

Yet, today, some nonmilitary issues are emphasized in interstate relations at one time, whereas others of seemingly equal importance are neglected or quietly handled at a technical level. International monetary politics, problems of commodity terms of trade, oil, food, and multinational corporations have all been important during the last decade; but not all have been high on interstate agendas throughout that period.

Traditional analysts of international politics have paid little attention to agenda formation: to how issues come to receive sustained attention by high officials. The traditional orientation toward military and security affairs implies that the crucial problems of foreign policy are imposed on states by the actions or threats of other states. These are high politics as opposed to the low politics of economic affairs. Yet, as the complexity of actors and issues in world politics increases, the utility of force declines and the line between domestic policy and foreign policy becomes blurred; as the conditions of complex interdependence are more closely approximated, the politics of agenda formation becomes more subtle and differentiated.

Under complex interdependence we can expect the agenda to be affected by the international and domestic problems created by economic growth and increasing sensitivity interdependence. Discontented domestic groups will politicize issues and force more issues once considered domestic onto the interstate agenda. Shifts in the distribution of power resources within sets of issues will also affect agendas. During the early 1970s the increased power of oil-producing governments over the transnational corporations and the consumer countries dramatically altered the policy agenda. Moreover, agendas for one group of issues may change as a result of linkages from other groups in which power resources are changing; for example, the broader agenda of North-South trade issues changed after the OPEC price rises and the oil embargo of 1973–74. Even if capabilities among states do not change, agendas may

be affected by shifts in the importance of transnational actors. The publicity surrounding multinational corporations in the early 1970s, coupled with their rapid growth over the past twenty years, put the regulation of such corporations higher on both the United Nations agenda and national agendas.

Politicization—agitation and controversy over an issue that tend to raise it to the top of the agenda—can have many sources, as we have seen. Governments whose strength is increasing may politicize issues, by linking them to other issues. An international regime that is becoming ineffective or is not serving important issues may cause increasing politicization, as dissatisfied governments press for change. Politicization, however, can also come from below. Domestic groups may become upset enough to raise a dormant issue, or to interfere with interstate bargaining at high levels. In 1974 the American secretary of state's tacit linkage of a Soviet-American trade pact with progress in détente was upset by the success of domestic American groups working through Congress to link a trade agreement with Soviet policies on emigration.

The technical characteristics and institutional setting in which issues are raised will strongly affect politicization patterns. In the United States, congressional attention is an effective instrument of politicization. Generally, we expect transnational economic organizations and transgovernmental networks of bureaucrats to seek to avoid politicization. Domestically based groups (such as trade unions) and domestically oriented bureaucracies will tend to use politicization (particularly congressional attention) against their transnationally mobile competitors. At the international level, we expect states and actors to "shop among forums" and struggle to get issues raised in international organizations that will maximize their advantage by broadening or narrowing the agenda.

Transnational and Transgovernmental Relations

Our third condition of complex interdependence, multiple channels of contact among societies, further blurs the distinction between domestic and international politics. The availability of partners in political coalitions is not necessarily limited by national boundaries as traditional analysis assumes. The nearer a situation is to complex interdependence, the more we expect the outcomes of political bargaining to be affected by transnational relations. Multinational corporations may be significant both as independent actors and as instruments manipulated by governments. The attitudes and policy stands of domestic groups are likely to be affected by communications, organized or not, between them and their counterparts abroad.

Thus the existence of multiple channels of contact leads us to expect limits, beyond those normally found in domestic politics, on the ability of statesmen to calculate the manipulation of interdependence or follow a consistent strategy of linkage. Statesmen must consider differential as well as aggregate effects of interdependence strategies and their likely implications for politicization and agenda control. Transactions among societies—economic and social transactions more than security ones—affect groups differently. Opportunities and costs from increased transnational ties may be greater for certain groups—for instance, American workers in the textile or shoe industries—than for others. Some organizations or groups may interact directly with actors in other societies or with other governments to increase their benefits from a network of interaction. Some actors may therefore be less vulnerable as well as less sensitive to changes elsewhere in the network than are others, and this will affect patterns of political action.

The multiple channels of contact found in complex interdependence are not limited to nongovernmental actors. Contacts between governmental bureaucracies charged with similar tasks may not only alter their perspectives but lead to transgovernmental coalitions on particular policy questions. To improve their chances of success, government agencies attempt to bring actors from other governments into their own decision-making processes as allies. Agencies of powerful states such as the United States have used such coalitions to penetrate weaker governments in such countries as Turkey and Chile. They have also been used to help agencies of other governments penetrate the United States bureaucracy.[14] Transgovernmental politics frequently characterizes Canadian-American relations, often to the advantage of Canadian interests.

The existence of transgovernmental policy networks leads to a different interpretation of one of the standard propositions about international politics—that states act in their own interest. Under complex interdependence, this conventional wisdom begs two important questions: which self and which interest? A government agency may pursue its own interests under the guise of the national interest; and recurrent interactions can change official perceptions of their interests. As a careful study of the politics of United States trade policy has documented, concentrating only on pressures of various interests for decisions leads to an overly mechanistic view of a continuous process and neglects the important role of communications in slowly changing perceptions of self-interest.[15]

The ambiguity of the national interest raises serious problems for the top political leaders of governments. As bureaucracies contact each other directly across national borders (without going through foreign offices), centralized control becomes more difficult. There is less assurance that the state will be united when dealing with foreign governments or that its components will interpret national interests similarly when negotiating with foreigners. The state may prove to be multifaceted, even schizophrenic.

National interests will be defined differently on different issues, at different times and by different governmental units. States that are better placed to maintain their coherence (because of a centralized political tradition such as France's) will be better able to manipulate uneven interdependence than fragmented states that at first glance seem to have more resources in an issue area.

Role of International Organizations

Finally, the existence of multiple channels leads one to predict a different and significant role for international organizations in world politics. Realists in the tradition of Hans J. Morgenthau have portrayed a world in which states, acting from self-interest, struggle for "power and peace." Security issues are dominant; war threatens. In such a world, one may assume that international institutions will have a minor role, limited by the rare congruence of such interests. International organizations are then clearly peripheral to world politics. But in a world of multiple issues imperfectly linked, in which coalitions are formed transnationally and transgovernmentally, the potential role of international institutions in political bargaining is greatly increased. In particular, they help set the international agenda, and act as catalysts for coalition-formation and as arenas for political initiatives and linkage by weak states.

Governments must organize themselves to cope with the flow of business generated by international organizations. By defining the salient issues, and deciding which issues can be grouped together, organizations may help to determine governmental priorities and the nature of interdepartmental committees and other arrangements within governments. The 1972 Stockholm Environment Conference strengthened the position of environmental agencies in various governments. The 1974 World Food Conference focused the attention of important parts of the United States government on prevention of food shortages. The September 1975 United Nations special session on proposals for a New International Economic Order generated an intragovernmental debate about policies toward the Third World in general. The International Monetary Fund and the General Agreement on Tariffs and Trade have focused governmental activity on money and trade instead of on private direct investment, which has no comparable international organization.

By bringing officials together, international organizations help to activate potential coalitions in world politics. It is quite obvious that international organizations have been very important in bringing together representatives of less developed countries, most of which do not maintain embassies in one another's capitals. Third World strategies of solidarity among poor countries have been developed in and for a series of international conferences, mostly under the auspices of the United Nations.[16] International organizations also allow agencies of governments, which might not otherwise come into contact, to turn potential or tacit coalitions into explicit transgovernmental coalitions characterized by direct communications. In some cases, international secretariats deliberately promote this process by forming coalitions with groups of governments, or with units of governments, as well as with nongovernmental organizations having similar interests.[17]

International organizations are frequently congenial institutions for weak states. The one-state–one-vote norm of the United Nations system favors coalitions of the small and powerless. Secretariats are often responsive to Third World demands. Furthermore, the substantive norms of most international organizations, as they have developed over the years, stress social and economic equity as well as the equality of states. Past resolutions expressing Third World positions, sometimes agreed to with reservations by industrialized countries, are used to legitimize other demands. These agreements are rarely binding, but up to a point the norms of the institution make opposition look more harshly self-interested and less defensible.

International organizations also allow small and weak states to pursue linkage strategies. In the discussion on a New International Economic Order, Third World states insisted on linking oil price and availability to other questions on which they had traditionally been unable to achieve their objectives. Small and weak states have also followed a strategy of linkage in the series of Law of the Sea conferences sponsored by the United Nations.

Complex interdependence therefore yields different political patterns than does the realist conception of the world. (Table 1 summarizes these differences.) Thus, one would expect traditional theories to fail to explain international regime change in situations of complex interdependence. But, for a situation that approximates realist conditions, traditional theories should be appropriate.

TABLE 1   Political Processes under Conditions of Realism and Complex Interdependence

	Realism	Complex Interdependence
Goals of Actors	Military security will be the dominant goal.	Goals of states will vary by issue area. Transgovernmental politics will make goals difficult to define. Transnational actors will pursue their own goals.
Instruments of State Policy	Military force will be most effective, although economic and other instruments will also be used.	Power resources specific to issue areas will be most relevant. Manipulation of interdependence, international organizations, and transnational actors will be major instruments.
Agenda Formation	Potential shifts in the balance of power and security threats will set the agenda in high politics and will strongly influence other agendas.	Agenda will be affected by changes in the distribution of power resources within issue areas; the status of international regimes; changes in the importance of transnational actors; linkages from other issues and politicization as a result of rising sensitivity interdependence.
Linkages of Issues	Linkages will reduce differences in outcomes among issue areas and reinforce international hierarchy.	Linkages by strong states will be more difficult to make since force will be ineffective. Linkages by weak states through international organizations will erode rather than reinforce hierarchy.
Roles of International Organizations	Roles are minor, limited by state power and the importance of military force.	Organizations will set agendas, induce coalition-formation, and act as arenas for political action by weak states. Ability to choose the organizational forum for an issue and to mobilize votes will be an important political resource.

Notes

1. Stanley Hoffmann, "Notes on the Elusiveness of Modern Power." *International Journal* 30: (Spring 1975): 184.

2. "A New National Partnership," speech by Secretary of State Henry A. Kissinger at Los Angeles, January 24, 1975. News release, Department of State, Bureau of Public Affairs, Office of Media Services, p. 1.

3. See, for example, Lester R. Brown, *World Without Borders: The Interdependence of Nations* (New York: Foreign Policy Association, Headline Series, 1972).

4. Charles Kindleberger, *American Business Abroad* (New Haven, CT: Yale University Press, 1969), p. 207.

5. The terms are derived from Stanley Hoffmann, "Choices," *Foreign Policy* 12 (Fall 1973): 6.

6. For instance, see Robert Angell, *Peace on the March: Transnational Participation* (New York: Van Nostrand, 1969).

7. John Maynard Keynes, *The General Theory of Employment, Interest and Money* (London: Macmillan, 1957), p. 383.

8. For the classic contemporary formulation of political realism, see the works of Hans J. Morgenthau, particularly *Politics Among Nations: The Struggle for Power and Peace* (New York: Knopf, 1948 and subsequent editions). See also Morgenthau, "Another 'Great Debate': The National Interest of the United States," *American Political Science Review* 46 (December 1952): 961–88; and Morgenthau, *Scientific Man Versus Power Politics* (Chicago: University of Chicago Press, 1946). A different but equally impressive statement of a "realist" position can be found in E. H. Carr, *The Twenty Years' Crisis, 1919–1939,* 2nd ed. (London: Macmillan, 1946). Carr, however, emphasizes economic sources of power more strongly.

9. In *The Troubled Partnership* (New York: McGraw-Hill for the Council on Foreign Relations, 1965). Henry A. Kissinger discussed alliance problems with hardly a reference to economic issues, although economic issues were beginning seriously to divide the NATO allies.

10. Alex Inkeles, "The Emerging Social Structure of the World," *World Politics* 27 (July 1975): 479.

11. Hans J. Morgenthau, *Politics Among Nations: The Struggle for Power and Peace,* 4th ed. (New York: Knopf, 1967), p. 36.

12. Henry Brandon. *The Retreat of American Power* (New York: Doubleday, 1974), p. 218.

13. *International Implications of the New Economic Policy,* U.S. Congress, House of Representatives, Committee on Foreign Affairs, Subcommittee on Foreign Economic Policy, Hearings, September 16, 1971.

14. For a more detailed discussion, see Robert O. Keohane and Joseph S. Nye, Jr., "Transgovernmental Relations and International Organizations," *World Politics* 27, no. 1 (October 1974): 39–62.

15. Raymond Bauer, Ithiel de Sola Pool, and Lewis Dexter, *American Business and Foreign Policy* (New York: Atherton, 1963), chap. 35, esp. pp. 472–75.

16. Branislav Gosovic and John Gerard Ruggie, "On the Creation of a New International Economic Order: Issue Linkage and the Seventh Special Session of the UN General Assembly," *International Organization* 30, no. 2 (Spring 1976): 309–46.

17. Robert W. Cox, "The Executive Head," *International Organization* 23, no. 2 (Spring 1969): 205–30.

Multilateralism, Knowledge, and Power

ERNST B. HAAS

Individuals are not the captives of system structure, but can influence the course of events. Changing knowledge can lead to redefining interests; organizations can adapt and learn.

Imagine historians in the twenty-third century busily interpreting the events and documents of international relations in the second half of the twentieth century. They would note, of course, that the world was organized into separate sovereign states and that their number had tripled over the previous half-century. But they would note another curious phenomenon: even though the people who ruled these states seemed to treasure their mutual independence as much as ever, they also built an imposing network of organizations that had the task of managing problems that these states experienced in common. Sometimes these international organizations had the task of transferring wealth from the richer to the poorer states. At other times they were asked to make and monitor rules by which all the states had agreed to live. At still other times the task of these organizations was the prevention of conflict among states. In short, rulers seemed to concede that without institutionalized cooperation among these states, life would be more difficult, dreary, and dangerous. Proof lies in the number and kind of such organizations, which increased at a stupendous rate after 1945.

Our historians would also note a second phenomenon, which gathered force around 1980. Everybody seemed to be disappointed with these organizations. Some of the most powerful states sought to disengage from them. Others demanded more benefits but received fewer. The very idea of moderating the logic of the cohabitation of 160 sovereign units on the same planet with institutionalized cooperation lost its appeal. Did international organizations disappear to give rise to alternative modes of collaboration? Did states examine the reasons for their disappointment and reform the network of international organizations? Did rulers question the very principle of a world order based on sovereign and competing states? Our historians know the eventual outcome. We do not. We can only speculate about the future of international cooperation and wonder whether it will make use of international organizations. I wish to construct concepts that might advance the enterprise of systematic speculation.

The Argument Summarized

Since the speculation is to be systematic, my underlying assumptions require specification. They are as follows: All international organizations are deliberately designed by their founders to "solve problems" that require collaborative action for a solution. No collaboration is conceivable except on the basis of explicit articulated interests. What are the interests? Contrary to lay usage, interests are *not* the opposite of ideals or values. An actor's sense of self-interest includes the desire to hedge against uncertainty, to minimize risk. One cannot have a notion of risk without some experience with choices that turned out to be less than optimal; one's interests are shaped by one's experiences. But one's satisfaction with an experience is a function of what is ideally desired, a function of one's values. Interests cannot be articulated without values. Far from (ideal) values being pitted against (material) interests, interests are unintelligible without a sense of values-to-be-realized. The interests to be realized by collaborative action are an expression of the actors' values.

My speculations concern the future of international organizations, but my assumptions force me to consider the future as a function of the history of collaboration as that history is experienced in the minds of collective actors: national and international bureaucracies. That history is the way "the problem to be solved" was seen at various times by the actors. What . . . [I seek] to explain, then, is *the change in the definition of the problem to be solved by a given organization.* Let us take an example. In 1945 the problem the World Bank was to solve was how most speedily to rebuild war-ravaged Europe. By 1955 the problem the bank was to solve was how most effectively to spur industrial growth in the developing countries. By 1975 the problem to be solved had become the elimination of poverty in the Third World. The task . . . is to explain the change in problem definition, to make clear whether and how the implicit theories held by actors changed.

I shall argue that problems are redefined through one of two complicated processes that I call "adaptation" and "learning." These processes differ in their dependence on new knowledge that may be introduced into decision making.

Adaptation

1. Behavior changes as actors add new activities (or drop old ones) without examining the implicit theories underlying their programs. Underlying values are not questioned.

2. The ultimate purpose of the organization is not questioned. The emphasis is on altering means of action, not ends. Technical rationality triumphs.

3. New ends (purposes) are added without worrying about their coherence with existing ends. Change is incremental without any attempt at nesting purposes logically.

Learning

1. Behavior changes as actors question original implicit theories underlying programs and examine their original values.

2. The ultimate purpose is redefined, as means as well as ends are questioned. Substantive rationality triumphs.

3. New nested problem sets are constructed because new ends are devised on the basis of consensual knowledge that has become available, as provided by epistemic communities.

I return to the example of the World Bank. Suppose the bank had been asked to solve problems by simply adding new tasks to old ones, without seeking to justify industrialization as a means toward the eradication of poverty, without explaining infrastructure development projects as a means toward industrial growth, which in turn was eventually seen as a means for eliminating poverty. There was no new theory of economic development, and no cohesive group of experts that "sold" that theory to the bank's management. I call this sequence "change by adaptation." If, conversely, these successive new purposes came about as the result of a systematic pattern of subsuming new means under new ends, legitimated by a new theory of economic development advocated by an epistemic community, then the pattern conforms to what I call "learning."

I argue that adaptation can take place in two different settings, each a distinct model of organizational development. One, labeled "incremental growth," features the successive augmentation of an organization's program as actors add new tasks to older ones without any change in the organization's decision-making dynamics or mode of choosing. The other, labeled "turbulent nongrowth," involves major changes in organizational decision making: ends no longer cohere; internal consensus on both ends and means disintegrates. In contrast, learning is associated with a model of organizational change I call "managed interdependence," in which the reexamination of purposes is brought about by knowledge-mediated decision-making dynamics.

The point . . . is to suggest when and where each model prevails, how a given organization can change from resembling one model to resembling one of the others, and how adaptation can give way to learning and learning to adaptation. Therefore, a set of descriptive variables is introduced to make possible the delineation of key conditions and attributes that vary from model to model. These descriptive variables include the setting in which international organizations operate, the power they have at their disposal, and the modes of behavior typical in their operations.

Description, however, is not enough to permit us to make the judgments we seek. A second set of variables is provided to make possible an evaluation of the variation disclosed by studying the descriptive variables. These evaluative concepts stress the types of knowledge used by the actors in making choices, their political objectives, and the manner in which issues being negotiated are linked into packages. Further evaluations are made about the type of bargaining produced by issue linkage, whether these bargains result in agreement on new ways of conceptualizing the problems to be solved, and whether new problem sets imply institutional changes leading to gains (or losses) in the legitimacy and authority enjoyed by the organization.

I foreshadow some conclusions that will be demonstrated in greater detail later. The World Bank began life in conformity with the incremen-

tal-growth model and later developed into the managed-interdependence model. The United Nations' (U.N.) collective-security practices degenerated from incremental growth into the turbulent nongrowth pattern; the U.N. Educational, Scientific, and Cultural Organization (UNESCO) always functioned in conformity with the turbulent nongrowth model. In the World Bank no decline in organizational power occurred. In fact, the president's autonomous ability to lead has increased over the years; merit remains the principle for selecting staff; outside consultants always serve in their personal capacity. Over the years, issue linkage was increasingly informed by technical knowledge and by political objectives of a progressively more complex and interconnected type. As new and more elaborate institutional practices developed, these also became more authoritative in the eyes of the membership, even if they did not become more legitimate as well. The innovations summarized as "peacekeeping" and associated with the special crisis management leadership style of Dag Hammarskjöld suggest that in 1956 U.N. activity relating to collective security conformed to the incremental-growth model, too. But unlike the bank, the United Nations thirty years later has become the victim of turbulent nongrowth. Earlier institutionalization and increases in authority were dissipated, no improvements in technical knowledge informed decision making, political goals became simpler and more immediacy oriented, and the leadership of the secretary-general was all but invisible. Possibly, however, the successes scored by Javier Pérez de Cuéllar in 1988 will reverse this trend. UNESCO, finally, never enjoyed a coherent program informed by consensual knowledge and agreed political objectives; it suffered no decline in institutionalization and power because it had very little of these in the first place. Both authority and legitimacy declined to a nadir in 1986 after decades of internal controversy over the organization's basic mission.

So what? How does the mapping of movement from one model to another help us with the future of international organizations? I want to answer a question that not only incorporates my own uncertainty about that future but also seeks to generalize from the uncertainties against which political actors try to protect themselves. We assume that their attempts are informed by interests that are shaped by implicit theories. States acting on their perceived interests, not scholars writing books, are the architects that will design the international organizations of the future. These interests are informed by the values political leaders seek to defend, not by the ideals of observers. Actors carry in their heads the values that shape the issues contained in their briefing papers. My effort to conceptualize the process of coping with uncertainty is based on this given. Scholarly concern with the question of how we might approach the international organizations of the future relies on understanding how self-conscious actors can learn to design organizations that will give them more satisfaction than the generation of international organizations with which we are familiar. If my demonstration . . . is persuasive, it will give us the tools for saying, "If an organization of type A regularly produces certain outcomes, then this type will (or will not) serve the perceived needs of its members; therefore they will seek to design an organization of type B if they are dissatisfied or will retain type A if they are happy."

Only idealists would presume to prescribe for the future by using their personal values as the definer of suggestions. I am not an idealist. The suggestions for a particular type of organizational learning developed in the final chapter [of my book *When Knowledge Is Power*] are consistent with the nonidealistic line of analysis pursued in the body of the book even though they also project my views as to what ought to be learned.

A Typology Is Not a Theory

To avoid even the appearance of inflated claims, I maintain that the typological argument I offer

falls short of constituting a theory. The demonstrations just made about the World Bank, UNESCO, and the United Nations are not full explanations of what happened to these organizations; nor do they display all the causes for these events. No pretense is made that these partial post hoc explanations provide all the ingredients needed for an informed prediction. Why then offer a typology of models of change?

I want to inquire into only one aspect of organizational life: why and how actors change their explicit or implicit views about what they see as a problem requiring collaborative measures for a solution. The "problem" can be any item on the international agenda. My dependent variable is change in the explicit or implicit view of actors in international organizations about the nature of a "problem." My inquiry, however, depends on my being able (1) to specify the interests and values held by actors and (2) to show how actors redefine interests and perhaps values in response to earlier disappointments. Moreover, I want to determine whether the processes that take place inside international organizations can be credited with the redefinition of interests and values. The idealist takes for granted that such redefining is likely to occur; scholars who stress the predominance of bureaucracies and political forces at the national capitals place the locus of change elsewhere. Granting that important changes in perception are unlikely to occur primarily in Geneva and New York, we must nevertheless hold open the possibility that some of the influences experienced there have a role in the national decision-making process that produces the changes we seek to explore. If that is true, then it also makes sense to observe international organizations in their possible role as innovators. And if international organizations can innovate, then we can inquire whether and when governments look to them as mechanisms for delivering newly desired goods and services. If governments think of international organizations as innovators, finally, we are entitled to ask how they go about redesigning international organizations to improve the solution of a newly redefined set of problems.

In what follows, then, I shall not be testing a theory. I merely experiment with the explanatory power of ideal types of organizations that reflect my conviction that the knowledge actors carry in their heads and project in their international encounters significantly shapes their behavior and expectations. My perspective is more permissive of the workings of volition, of a kind of free will, than is allowed by many popular theories of international politics. If my stance is not "idealist," it is not "structural" either.

The structuralist argues that international collaboration of the multilateral kind is intended to provide a collective good for the parties that bilateral relations could not provide. The provision of that good, in turn, may result in a more harmonious world—though the harmony is likely to be confined to expectations related solely to the good in question. It probably cannot be generalized into the utopia associated with idealism. As for international organizations, they are important in this causal chain only if they are necessary for providing the collective good. International organizations, therefore, are not given a privileged place in the causal chain of the structuralist.

I disagree with this stance because it tends to overstate the constraints on choice and to understate decision makers' continuing enmeshment in past experiences with collaboration mediated by international organizations. Structuralism seeks to discover various deep-seated constraints on the freedom of actors to choose. Although organizations, like any other institutions, can act as constraints, I want to look at them as fora for choosing innovations. Structural constraints may be implicit in the logic of situations, such as the condition of strategic interdependence in anarchic international systems. Belief in the power of such constraints depends on the assumption that actors respond only to *present* incentives and disincentives, that they never try

to "climb out" of the system to reshape opportunities for gain. Strategic interdependence as a permanent constraint is compelling only as long as there is no evidence that somebody works actively toward changing the rules of the game. Modern international life is replete with such efforts. However, it is equally true that the kinds of constraints on choice that structuralists stress provide the most telling explanation as to why new international organizations are created in the first place. But if we stop our inquiry with this explanation, we never proceed to ask the questions that interest me, questions about the role of changing knowledge in the redefinition of interest.[1]

Unlike structuralists, neorealists, game theorists, and theorists of regimes, I am not offering a theory; at best I am offering a probe that might lead to a theory. I am not testing my approach against rival explanations because other approaches are not rivals. Game theory or structural explanations do not "fit better" than explanations of change derived from the interplay of knowledge and political objectives, from cognitive and perceptual observations; they "fit differently." Nor is it my purpose to subsume or colonize other theories, or to assert my hegemony over them. Other explanations, given the questions other scholars raise, may be as valid as mine. My effort should be understood as complementary to theirs, not as an approach with unique power. Cognitive explanations coexist, epistemologically speaking, with other approaches to the study of international organizations; they do not supplant them. If I persuade the reader that the history of an organization can be viewed in the context of cognitive variables, then the reader will interpret that history in a novel form, without rendering all other interpretations obsolete. But the success of my claim to novelty still falls short of a real theory.[2]

Nor do the three models around which my interpretations are built constitute a true theory. They remain Weberian ideal types; together they constitute a typology for conceptualizing organizational change, for summing up whether and how adaptation or learning occurs. Yet the models are not just heuristic; they are intended to be "real," albeit not exhaustive, representations of what took place. They seek to abstract selectively (but not arbitrarily) from a historical series of events. The crucial point is this: the notion of causation implicit in these models is as elusive and as nonlinear as in all of Weber's typologies. My approach differs sharply from the more direct ideas of causation embedded in behavioral and in rational-choice approaches to the phenomena studied here because it rejects simple notions of causality.

Basically, I anchor my approach on this bet: the knowledge available about "the problem" at issue influences the way decision makers define the interest at stake in the solution to the problem; political objectives and technical knowledge are combined to arrive at the conception of what constitutes one's interest. But since decision makers are sentient and self-reflective beings, the conceptualization cannot stop here because decision makers take available knowledge into account, including the memory of past efforts to define and solve "the problem." They know that their knowledge is approximate and incomplete. Being aware of the limits of one's knowledge also influences one's choices. Being critical about one's knowledge implies a readiness to reconsider the finality of what one knows and therefore to be willing to redefine the problem.

This point distinguishes my approach from that of theorists of rational choice who are inspired by microeconomics. In the logic of game theory, for instance, what matters is not the history of a perceived preference or the way a utility (interest?) came into being, but the mere fact that at the crucial "choice points," interests are what they are because preferences are as they are stipulated in game theory. It makes sense to speak of shared interests if, at the choice point, the separate interests of the bargainers happen to be sufficiently similar to permit an agreement. In my approach the decision

makers are thought to be concerned with causation, with the reasons why a particular definition of their interests matter, as compared with other possible definitions. My analysis must be concerned, therefore, with the question of *why* particular demands are linked into packages, *why* problems are conceived in relatively simple or in very complex ways. Implicit or explicit theories of causation in the actors' minds imply degrees of knowledge, not merely momentarily shared interests. My theory of causation must reflect and accommodate the notions of causation assumed to be in the minds of the decision makers, notions that are true to the insight that there is always another turn of the cognitive screw to be considered.

I reiterate: the typologies that result from this mode of analysis are not truly representative of all of reality. They capture types of behavior, clusters of traits, bundles of results from antecedent regularities in bureaucratic perception that are logically possible, but not necessarily encountered frequently. Many of Weber's typologies, although exhaustive in the sociological and cultural dimensions he wished to represent, nevertheless produced sparsely populated cells. We will find that the managed-interdependence model is rarely encountered in the real world and that learning is far less common than adaptation. But then so is charismatic leadership and the routinization of charisma into bureaucratic practice.

Therefore, we will not follow the mode of demonstration preferred by those who work in the behavioral tradition. We will not seek to cull from our large list of descriptive variables those clusters of traits that most frequently "predict" (or are associated with) either successful adaptation or successful learning. Many of the descriptive variables will be shown to be weakly associated with any pattern, any regularities; some will not vary from type to type. Nevertheless, such variables will not be permitted to "drop out" even though they explain nothing behavioral. They are real because they describe international organizations. They matter in pinpointing what is unique about international organizations, and they may turn up as more powerful in some later analysis or some new set of historical circumstances. Remaining true to a typological commitment demands that the traditional canons of causal theorizing be sacrificed to a less economical procedure that forgoes the search for clusters or straight paths as unique explanations. I am, after all, using systematic speculation and historical reconstruction to anticipate events that have yet to occur.

Knowledge, Power, and Interest

My typological approach is anchored on an additional bet, similar to the first one but less moderate: change in human aspirations and human institutions over long periods is caused mostly by the way knowledge about nature and about society is married to political interests and objectives. I am not merely asserting that changes in scientific understanding trigger technological innovations, which are then seized upon by political actors, though this much is certainly true. I am also asserting that as scientific knowledge becomes common knowledge and as technological innovation is linked to institutional tinkering, the very mode of scientific inquiry infects the way political actors think. Science, in short, influences the way politics is done. Science becomes a component of politics because the scientific way of grasping reality is used to define the interests that political actors articulate and defend. The doings of actors can then be described by observers as an exercise of defining and realizing interests informed by changing scientific knowledge about man and nature.

Therefore, it is as unnecessary as it is misleading to juxtapose as rival explanations the following: science to politics, knowledge to power or interest, consensual knowledge to common interests. We do ourselves no good by pretending that scientists have the key for giving us peace and plenty; but we do no better in

holding that politicians and capitalists, in defending their immediate interests with superior power, stop creative innovation dead in its tracks. We overestimate the resistance to innovation on the part of politicians and the commitment to change on the part of the purveyors of knowledge if we associate science and knowledge with good, with reform, with disinterested behavior, while saddling political actors with the defense of vested interests. When knowledge becomes consensual, we ought to expect politicians to use it in helping them to define their interests; we should not suppose that knowledge is opposed to interest. Once this juxtaposition is abandoned, it becomes clear that a desire to defend some interests by invoking superior power by no means prevents the defense of others by means of institutional innovations. Superior power is even used to force innovations legitimized by new knowledge, while knowledge-legitimated interest can equally well be used to argue against innovation.

Economists prefer to explain events by stressing the *interests* that motivate actors: coalitions of actors are thought capable of action only if they succeed in defining their *common interests*. Political scientists like to explain events in terms of the *power* to impose preferences on allies and antagonists. Sociologists tend to put the emphasis on *structured* or *institutionalized norms* and to find the origin of such norms in the *power* of some group or class. My claim is that these formulations are consistent with the use of knowledge in decision making. My argument is that we need not pit these divergent formulations against each other as explanations of human choice. We are entitled to hold that interests can be (but need not be) informed by available knowledge, and that power is normally used to translate knowledge-informed interests into policy and programs. My concern is to analyze those situations in which interests are so informed and the exercise of power is so motivated, not to deal with instances of interests, norms, and power as triggers of choice.

I return to the case of the World Bank to illustrate the possible convergence of explanations combining knowledge with interest and power. In the late 1960s the bank changed its basic philosophy of development lending from supporting infrastructure projects that were relatively remote from the direct experiences of poor people—hence the reliance on the theory of trickle-down—to the policy of supporting the advancement of basic human needs, with its implication of much more direct and intrusive intervention in the borrowers' domestic affairs in order to gain access to their poor citizens. Was new knowledge used in motivating the shift? The shift occurred because economists and other development specialists had serious doubts about the adequacy of trickle-down policies and claimed that new techniques were becoming available to help the poor more directly. Was this knowledge generally accepted? This knowledge was generally accepted only by the coalition of donors that dominates the bank; the borrowers frequently opposed the shift and argued that the basic-human needs approach was not in their interest. Was the shift consistent with the interests of the dominant coalition? Indeed it was, because the coalition's common interest in supporting economic development appeared to be implemented more effectively by virtue of the new knowledge.

My account shows how interest informed by knowledge reinforces the explanation of what occurred. What about power? Let us keep in mind that there are at least three different ways of thinking about power in these situations. If the hegemonial power of the capitalist class—as expressed in the instructions issued to the delegates of the donor countries—is considered, then the decision of the bank is an expression of the persuasiveness and influence of that class in foisting a realistic conception of the common interest on the dominant coalition, even though it may also be an instance of false consciousness. Suppose we ignore Gramsci and think of power as the straightforward imposition of the view of

the strongest. Even though the United States is the single most powerful member of the bank, its position is not strong enough to enable it to dictate bank policy (in part because the U.S. presidents of the bank often entertained views at variance with opinions within the U.S. government). Power as direct imposition does not explain anything.[3] That leaves a conception of power as the ability of a stable coalition to impose its will simply by virtue of its superior voting strength or as a result of its Gramscian ability to socialize and persuade its opponents into the position the coalition prefers. The new policy, then, is the common interest of the coalition, arrived at by negotiations utilizing knowledge and imposed by threat or verbal guile on the unwilling borrowers. Far from being a rival explanation of what occurred to explanations that rely on interest informed by knowledge, power simply enables us to give a more complete account without having to offer sacrifices at the jealous conceptual altars of any single social science profession.

Why International Organizations Are Important as Innovators

I am arguing that some, not all, innovations in international life result from the experience of decision makers in international organizations. I am suggesting that we study multilateral processes as agents of change, not that they are the only, or even the most important, such agents. Multilateral processes provide one avenue for the transideological sharing of meanings in human discourse, not the only one. Much more may be going on in bilateral encounters and in informal contacts outside the organizational forum. But since my task is the study of international organizations, I need to stress the role of these entities in mounting innovations without denying the importance of other channels.

Experiences such as the World Bank's permit us to use the history of key international organizations as diagnostic devices for testing when and where knowledge infects multilateral decision making. I want to explore whether international organizations can provide, or have provided, a boundedly rational forum for the mounting of innovations, not a forum for furnishing a collective good determined on the basis of optimization. If we identify the manner of attaining the collective good with pure rational choice, we forget that the choice to be made is not "pure" because it is constrained by what the choosers have already experienced.[4] The game, for them, started some time ago. They are still enmeshed in its consequences and may seek to change the rules if they are unhappy with them. The fact is that the disappointments were, for the most part, associated with policies that were filtered through, and derived much of their legitimacy from, their place on a multilateral agenda. This is true even though such policies usually originated in the politics, the bureaucrats, and the think tanks of the member states. International organizations are part of everybody's experience because they are mediators of policies. They are a part of the international repertory of fora that talk about and authorize innovation. Hence we can study them as agents of innovation.

We can do more. We can also make observations about relative effectiveness in the performance of these organizations and offer suggestions on how to improve effectiveness. In other words, we can contribute to effective innovation on the basis of critical typological study.

My treatment takes for granted that the goals valued by the states that set up organizations are the single most important determinant of later events. Nevertheless, such things as the task environment in which the organization must operate, its choice of core technology to carry out its tasks, and the institutional structure imposed on the staff must influence and probably constrain the attainment of these goals. A concern with institutional innovation must therefore consider environment, structure,

and technology along with changing or constant goals.[5]

Must organizations remain the tools their creators have in mind when they set them up—means toward the attainment of some end valued by the creators? Or, alternatively, can international organizations become ends in their own right, become valued as institutions quite apart from the services they were initially expected to perform? If so, what kinds of innovations can or should be designed to bring about such a transition? One might also ask whether effectiveness is good for the survival and prospects of the organization as opposed to the welfare of the world in general; the two outcomes need not be mutually supportive. If they turn out to be contradictory, we might then think of design suggestions to mitigate the contradiction.

Some organizations are hierarchically structured; others are flat. Possibly, each form is optimal for the performance of some task, but not all tasks. Possibly, structure and effective performance are not well matched. If so, our comparative typological study may enable us to offer suggestions on how to adapt structure to effective performance. All organizations select a "core technology" to do their job, and the character of that technology interacts with institutional structure and task environment. It is possible, however, that the technology is not optimal for good performance, or not well integrated with the task environment or the structure. Innovations in design made apparent by historical study may then become appropriate. So can rearrangements in institutional structure, especially when it becomes apparent that better performance requires a different coordinate arrangement among several organizations active in the field. Our first step, then, is the application of organization theory to our study. . . .

In the incremental-growth model, the knowledge available to policymakers does not become more consensual, though it may be growing in scope, and no single epistemic community dominates the flow of knowledge. Politicians in the dominant coalition entertain static and narrowly focused goals; politicians associated with member states outside the dominant coalition, however, are advancing dynamic and expanding goals. Prevalent decision-making styles pit eclectics and/or skeptics against each other. They will link issues tactically for the most part, though some pressure for engaging in fragmented linkages will be in evidence. The modesty of the goals and the relative irrelevance of novel bodies of knowledge result in bargains that are "similar" at the intragovernmental and intracoalitional levels, and only "slightly dissimilar" at the level of intercoalitional encounters. The resulting problem definition is most likely to be a fully decomposable set; we have no reason to expect much intellectual coherence among the constituents of the organization's program, as each item can flourish or founder on its merits without being aided or hindered by other items.

Things work quite differently in the turbulent nongrowth model. Knowledge *among* coalitions is not becoming more consensual; however, *within* some coalitions knowledge applicable to the organization's mandate does command more and more agreement. Some politicians defend static and specific objectives while others advocate dynamic and interconnected ones; the two sets of politicians (and their associated experts) confront each other for control of the dominant coalition. The decision-making style pits skeptics and/or pragmatists against each other. They are able to link issues only in tactical terms, resulting in a bargaining pattern dominated by "dissimilar" styles at all levels. This of course results in a program that is so decomposable as not to merit the label "set" at all. While under conditions of incremental growth, the decomposable program items lack coherence without interfering with each other, under conditions of turbulent nongrowth, the lack of coherence may actually hinder the successful implementation of program items.

Both models of organizational adaptation, then, operate in such a fashion as to give us fully decomposable problem sets, looser and more fragmented than the actors' conceptualization that preceded the change we code. We cannot tell whether the new and more disaggregated set will lead to member-state dissatisfaction: demands for still another reconceptualization of problem sets would depend on whether satisfaction of the members, or its lack, takes the form of an ideologically unified critique.

The managed-interdependence model is the only one capable of inspiring a redefinition of the organization's mandate, giving us nondecomposable, or nearly nondecomposable, sets; but a fully decomposable set may also be produced if the learning pattern suggests this solution as superior to its alternatives. Consensual knowledge, depending on its substantive content, could in principle lead to any of these outcomes.

Our cases of learning to manage interdependence, however, fail to confirm this variety of theoretical possibilities. Mainly, they show that reconceptualization leads to the articulation of nearly nondecomposable sets. The typical sequence of events is as follows. The knowledge being purveyed by experts as relevant to improved organizational performance is becoming more consensual; the objectives of politicians are at the same time expanding and are seen as more tightly interconnected as well. The decision-making style of policymakers will be pragmatic and/or analytic; issue linkage is fragmented, shading into substantive connections among items. Bargaining among members of the same government is likely to become "dissimilar," while intracoalitional negotiations are showing "similar" issue-linkage patterns. Intercoalitional negotiations are becoming "almost similar." This combination of features must result in a problem set that is nested so as to make the disaggregation of the constituent parts very difficult, if not impossible.

True, the increasingly consensual knowledge could also suggest the wisdom of disaggregating issues; the fact that the objectives of politicians are expanding in scope need not imply a tight interconnection among objectives. Decision making would then be consistently pragmatic, and issue linkage would remain fragmented without accretions of substantive linkage. Intercoalitional bargaining would be "dissimilar," or, if "similar" in the sense that only the fragmented style prevails, the substantive differences in positions that the negotiators profess would still militate in favor of decomposability among problems. . . .

None of this amounts to serious advice about deliberately designing organizations that engage in permanent cognitive evolution. In the last analysis, observers and well-wishers of international organizations have very little to offer. There are powerful reasons for the sway of routine, just as there are good reasons for questioning habit. The people responsible for the flawed ways that we call the "crisis of multilateralism" are far from being either fools or knaves. We must admit this, or any attempt to prescribe novel ways of coordinating activities to usher in a more benign world is an act of ultimate hubris. Instead, we ought to look to a master of science fiction for a more playful and permissive view of evolution.

In his novel—set on the planet Solaris, which is dominated by a huge, sentient ocean—Stanislaw Lem describes an imperfect but evolving god. The ocean of Solaris evinces curiosity, cruelty, creativity, and detachment—qualities that baffle the scientists from Earth. The ocean appears to be a god still in his infancy, who plays at being creative and curious without quite knowing why. He is "an evolving god, who develops in the course of time, grows, and keeps increasing in power while remaining aware of his powerlessness." "For this god," says one scientist to another, "the divine condition is a situation without a goal. And understanding that, he despairs. . . . Solaris could be the first phase of the despairing god. Perhaps its intelligence will grow enormously. All the contents of our Solarist libraries could be just a record of his teething troubles . . . and we will have been the baby's toys for a while."[6]

One can think about human progress in similar terms, as an open-ended groping for self-improvement, without a final goal, without a transcendent faith, but with frequent reverses and sporadic self-questioning about the trajectory of change. The very meaning of self-improvement will not stand still. Its content means one utopia for one generation, country, or group; it means quite another one for later generations. Progress is a childlike, groping god, not a purposeful master of the universe. It is difficult to have faith in such a deity. But the lack of faith should not prevent us from asking what makes progress happen.

Progress is a secular god who tolerates the things people, nations, and other large human collectivities do to themselves and to one another. Progress manifests itself more directly and forcefully when such collectivities pause to think about what they do, when they consider doing things differently in the future. Then they engage in what we usually call "learning."

Notes

1. I call attention to the discovery on the part of Snyder and Diesing that even the situations of crisis they investigated under structuralist assumptions showed a wide variety of actual features with too much variation in behavior and outcome to permit the positing of a small number of structural constraints as determinants. See Glenn Snyder and Paul Diesing, *Conflict Among Nations* (Princeton, NJ: Princeton University Press, 1977), chap. 7. Robert O. Keohane, in *After Hegemony* (Princeton, NJ: Princeton University Press, 1984), concludes that even under microeconomic-structural assumptions the behavior of states in regimes is highly variable and not reliably determined by structuralist assumptions. The case for institutional constraints on behavior is explored and duly qualified by James G. March and Johan P. Olsen in "The New Institutionalism: Organizational Factors in Political

Life," *American Political Science Review* 78 (1984): 734–49. My nonstructural epistemological stance is spelled out in greater detail in "Why Collaborate?" *World Politics* 32 (April 1980), and "Words Can Hurt You," *International Organization* 36 (Spring 1982). The present essay is an effort to extend and apply this view to the future of international organizations.

Theorists and metatheorists customarily differ on how a given writer is to be classified in a field of contending approaches. Even though I reject the labels "idealist" and "liberal" for my theoretical position because of the characteristics I associate with the schools of thought properly so described, I am quite comfortable with being called a "neoidealist," if we follow the description of that stance offered by Charles W. Kegley, Jr., in "Neo-Idealism," *Ethics and International Affairs* 2 (1988): 173–98, although I would be most uncomfortable being identified as a "neoliberal" as defined by Joseph S. Nye, Jr., in "Neorealism and Neoliberalism," *World Politics* 40 (January 1988): 235–51. I am most content, however, to be classed with the nonrationalistic (as he defines them) "reflective" writers elaborated in Robert O. Keohane, "International Institutions: Two Approaches," *International Studies Quarterly* 32 (December 1988).

2. A complete theory would have to offer an explanation of what occurred in an international organization even if the emphasis on changes in the mixture of knowledge and political objective fails. An explanation that stresses changes in available knowledge ought to be able to offer an account of the origin of that knowledge. A claim that issue linkages and bargains that represent different mixtures of knowledge and political goals explain different modes of organizational development ought to be able to specify the kinds of knowledge and goals most prominent in that history. I am able to specify only *that* a certain mixture was or was not present, not *why* it was present. I am in a position to show only that knowledge was or was not available, not how or why the actors required it.

3. The same lesson emerges from another episode in the history of the World Bank. During the 1980s the U.S. Congress sought to link the authorization of the United States' financial contribution to instructions that no loans should be made to governments that violated a number of congressional preferences in the field of economic policy and the status of human rights. U.S. representatives duly voted against such loans, but in most instances the bank's decision was made in disregard of congressional directives and U.S. votes because the other members of the bank's dominant coalition disagreed with the U.S. definition of interests; the United States' preference did not become the common interest of the coalition. Moreover, the European countries and Japan disputed the U.S. effort to "politicize" the bank's lending policy, arguing that a knowledge of economic development needs makes such efforts illegitimate. The United States' efforts to change the knowledge-informed interests failed.

4. James G. March, one of the theorists of decisions in organizations on whom I rely heavily, clearly explained why this approach is not considered to be in the tradition of pure rational-choice theories. Such theories "portray decision-making as intentional, consequential, and optimizing. That is, they assume that decisions are based on preferences (e.g., wants, needs, values, goals, interests, subjective utilities) and expectations about outcomes associated with different alternative actions. And they assume that the best possible alternative (in terms of its consequences for a decision maker's preferences) is chosen." [James G. March, *Decisions and Organizations* (London: Basil Blackwell, 1988), 1–2]. The decision-making theory of direct concern to me is that which covers decision making "under ambiguity," the opposite of the conditions associated with rational-choice theories derived from microeconomics. The "correctness" of such decisions is always a matter of debate and can never be ascertained in the absence of considerable historical distance from the events. For a telling illustration of the kind of social rationality associated with decisions made in and by organizations, see Ronald Dore's discussion of "relational contracting" in "Goodwill and the Spirit of Market Capitalism," *British Journal of Sociology* 34 (December 1983): 459–82.

5. Gayl D. Ness and Steven Brechin, "Bridging the Gap: International Organizations as Organizations," *International Organization* 42 (Winter 1988), offer a detailed list of suggestions along these lines, on which my treatment draws.

It is useful to think about the theoretical literature on organizations as being concerned primarily either with decision making or with seeking to explain the persistence of structural forms. The literature on which I rely is essentially the literature on decision making constrained by organizational forms and practices. I am only incidentally interested in the persistence of organizational forms and make no consistent use of the literature in that area, though this theme will make a rather prominent appearance in the final chapter.

6. Stanislaw Lem, *Solaris* (1961; New York: Basic Books, 1971), 205–6.

Multilateralism: The Anatomy of an Institution

J O H N   G E R A R D   R U G G I E

The author examines the role of normative constraints and institutions in international relations. In arguing that norms and institutions do, in fact, matter, he clarifies the meanings of the term multilateralism *and discusses its conceptual utility.*

Seen through the lenses of conventional theories of international relations, which attribute outcomes to the underlying distribution of political or economic power, the roles played by normative constraints and institutions in the current international transformation must seem paradoxical. Norms and institutions do not matter much in that literature to begin with; they are viewed as byproducts of, if not epiphenomenal adjuncts to, the relations of force or the relations of production. What is more, insofar as the conventional literature has any explanation at all of extensive institutionalization in the international system, the so-called theory of hegemonic stability is it. But in addition to all the other historical and logical problems from which that theory suffers, merely finding the hegemony to which the current array of regional and global institutional roles could be ascribed is a daunting, if not insurmountable, challenge.

The fact that norms and institutions matter comes as no surprise to the "new institutionalists" in international relations; after all, that has long been their message.[1] But, curiously, little explicit and detailed analytical attention has been paid in this literature to a core feature of current international institutional arrangements: their multilateral form. A literature search keyed on the concept of multilateralism turns up relatively few entries, and only a tiny number of these are of any interest to the international relations theorist. The focus of the new institutionalists has been on "cooperation" and "institutions" in a generic sense, with international regimes and formal organizations sometimes conceived as specific institutional subsets.[2] For example, no scholar has contributed more to the new institutionalism in international relations than Robert Keohane. Yet the concept of multilateralism is used sparingly in his work, even in a literature survey on that subject. And the definition of multilateralism that he employs is purely nominal: "the practice of coordinating national policies in groups of three or more states."[3]

The nominal definition of multilateralism may be useful for some purposes. But it poses the problem of subsuming institutional forms that traditionally have been viewed as being expressions of bilateralism, not multilateralism—instances of the Bismarckian alliance system, for example, such as the League of the *Three* Emperors. In short, the nominal definition of multilateralism misses the *qualitative* dimension of the phenomenon that makes it distinct.[4]

In a superb discussion of this issue, attempting to sort out the enormous variety of trade relations in the world today, William Diebold insists for starters on the need to distinguish between "formal" and "substantive" multilateralism—by which he means roughly what I mean by nominal vs. qualitative. "But that is far from the end of the matter. The bilateral agreements of Cordell Hull were basically different from those of Hjalmar Schacht."[5] That is to say, the issue is not the number of parties so much, Diebold suggests, as the *kind of relations* that are instituted among them. It is this substantive or qualitative characteristic of multilateralism that concerns me in the present essay, not only for trade, but also for the institutional dimension of international relations in general.

Nor is the missing qualitative dimension captured entirely by the concepts of international regimes or intergovernmental organizations. Instances of international regimes exist that were not multilateral in form, such as the Nazi trade and monetary regimes, to which we will return momentarily. As for multilateral formal organizations, although they entail no analytical mystery, all practitioners of the new institutionalism agree that these organizations constitute only one small part of a broader universe of international institutional forms that interest them.

The missing qualitative dimension of multilateralism immediately comes into focus, however, if we return to an older institutionalist discourse, one informed by the postwar aims of the United States to restructure that international order. When we speak here of multilateralism in international trade we know immediately that it refers to trade organized on the basis of certain principles of state conduct, above all, nondiscrimination. Similarly, when we speak here of multilateralism in security relations we know that it refers to some expression or other of collective security or collective self-defense. And when President George Bush [enunciated] a "new world order" for the Middle East and elsewhere—universal aspirations, cooperative deterrence, joint action against aggression—whether it constitutes vision or rhetoric, the notion evokes and is entirely consistent with the American postwar multilateralist agenda, as we shall see below. In sum, what is distinctive about multilateralism is not merely that it coordinates national policies in groups of three or more states, which is something that other organizational forms also do, but additionally that it does so on the basis of certain principles of ordering relations among those states.

Thus, a compound anomaly exists in the world of international relations theory today. An institutional phenomenon of which conventional theories barely take note is both widespread and significant, but at the same time, the particular features that make it so are glossed over by most students of international institutions themselves. This essay is intended to help resolve both parts of the anomaly.

The premise of the present paper is that we can better understand the role of multilateral norms and institutions in the current international transformation by recovering the principled meanings of multilateralism from actual historical practice, by showing how and why those principled meanings have come to be institutionalized throughout the history of the modern interstate system, and by exploring how and why they may perpetuate themselves today even as the conditions that initially gave rise to them have changed.

My "grounded" analysis of the concept suggests a series of working hypotheses, which require more extensive testing before strong validity claims can be made for them. Nevertheless, we believe that they are sufficiently interesting, and that the case we make for them is sufficiently plausible, to warrant such further study, and we present them here in that spirit. The argument, in brief, goes something like this. Multilateralism is a generic institutional form of modern international life, and as such it has been present from the start. The generic institutional form of multilateralism must not be confused with formal multilateral organizations, a relatively recent arrival and still of only relatively modest importance. Historically, the generic form of multilateralism can be found in institutional arrangements to define and stabilize the international property rights of states, to manage coordination problems, and to resolve collaboration problems. The last of these uses of the multilateral form historically is the least frequent. In the literature, that fact traditionally has been explained by the rise and fall of hegemonies and, more recently, by various functional considerations. Our analysis suggests that a permissive domestic environment in the leading powers of the day is at least as important. Looking more closely at the post-World War II situation, for example, it was less the fact of American *hegemony* that accounts for the explosion of multilateral arrangements than of *American* hegemony. Finally, we suggest that institutional arrangements of the multilateral form have adaptive and even reproductive capacities which other institutional forms may lack and which may, therefore, help explain the roles that multilateral arrangements play in stabilizing the current international transformation.

The Meanings of Multilateralism

At its core, multilateralism refers to coordinating relations among three or more states in accordance with certain principles. But what, precisely, are those principles? And to what, precisely, do those principles pertain? To facilitate the construction of a more formal definition, let us begin by examining a historical instance of something that everyone agrees multilateralism is not: bilateralism.

Earlier in this century, Nazi Germany succeeded in finely honing a pure form of bilateralism into a systemic organizing principle. Now, as Diebold notes, the everyday term *bilateral* is

entirely neutral with regard to the qualitative relationship that is instituted among countries.[6] So as to give expression to its qualitative nature, the Nazi system therefore typically has been referred to as bilatera*list* in character, or as embodying bilatera*lism* as its organizing principle. In any case, once the New Plan of the Nazi government took effect in 1934, Hjalmar Schacht devised a scheme of bilateralist trade agreements and clearing arrangements.[7] The essence of the German international trade regime was that the state negotiated "reciprocal" agreements with its foreign trading partners. These negotiations determined which goods and services were to be exchanged, their quantities, and their price. Often, Germany deliberately imported more from its partners than it exported to them. But it required that its trading partners liquidate their claims on Germany through reinvestment there or by purchasing deliberately over-priced German goods. Thus, its trading partners were doubly dependent on Germany.

This trade regime in turn was linked to bilateralist monetary clearing arrangements. Under these arrangements, a German importer would, for example, pay marks to the German Reichsbank for its imports rather than to the foreign source of the goods or services, while the foreign counterpart of the transaction would receive payment in home country currency from its central bank—and vice versa for German exports. No foreign exchange changed hands, the foreign exchange markets were bypassed, and artificial exchange rates prevailed. The permissible total amounts to be cleared in this manner were negotiated by the two states.

German bilateralism typically but not exclusively focused on smaller and weaker states in East-Central Europe, the Balkans, and Latin America, exchanging primary commodity imports for manufactured exports. But the scheme had no inherent limit; it could have been geographically universalized to cover the entire globe, with an enormous spiderweb of bilateralist agreements radiating out from Germany.[8]

The nominal definition of multilateralism would not exclude the Schachtian bilateralist device: it coordinated economic relations among more than three states. Nor is the fact decisive that negotiations took place bilaterally: after all, many tariff reductions in the General Agreement on Tariffs and Trade (GATT) are also negotiated bilaterally. The difference is, of course, that within GATT bilaterally negotiated tariff reductions are extended to all other parties on the basis of most-favored nation (MFN) treatment, whereas the Schachtian scheme was inherently and fundamentally discriminatory, so that bilateral deals held only on a case-by-case and product-by-product basis *even if* they covered the entire globe in doing so.

Let us examine next an institutional arrangement that is generally acknowledged to embody multilateralist principles: a collective security system. None has ever existed in pure form, but in principle the scheme is quite simple. It rests on the premise that peace is indivisible, so that a war against one ipso facto is considered a war against all. The community of states is therefore obliged to respond to threatened or actual aggression, first by diplomatic means, then through economic sanctions, and finally by the collective use of force if necessary. Facing the prospect of such a community-wide response, any rational potential aggressor would be deterred and would desist. Thus, the incidence of war would gradually decline.

A collective-security scheme certainly coordinates security relations among three or more states. But so too, as noted above, did the League of the Three Emperors, which was nothing more than a set of traditional alliances.[9] What is distinct about a collective-security scheme is that it comprises, as Sir Arthur Salter put it a half-century ago, a permanent potential alliance "against the *unknown* enemy"[10] and, he should have added, in behalf of the *unknown* victim. The in-

stitutional difference between a bilateral alliance and a collective-security scheme can be simply put: in both instances, state *A* is pledged to come to the aid of *B* if *B* is attacked by *C*. In a collective-security scheme, however, *A* is *also* pledged to come to the aid of *C* if *C* is attacked by *B*. Thus,

> A cannot regard itself as the ally of B more than of C, because theoretically it is an open question whether, if an act of war should occur, B or C would be the aggressor. In the same way B has indeterminate obligations towards A and C, and C towards A and B, and so on with a vast number of variants as the system is extended to more and more states.[11]

It was precisely this difference between a collective-security system and alliances that ultimately doomed the fate of the League of Nations in the U.S. Senate.[12]

The United States frequently invoked the collective-security model in leading the anti-Iraq coalition in the Persian Gulf crisis and then war, though what if any permanent institutional consequences will follow from that effort remains to be seen. NATO reflects a truncated version of the model, in which a subset of states organized a collective self-defense scheme of indefinite duration, de jure against any potential aggressor though de facto against one. Nevertheless, internally the scheme was predicated on the indivisibility of threats to the collectivity— that is, it did not matter whether Germany or Great Britain, or the Netherlands, or Norway was attacked, nor in theory by whom—together with the requirement of an unconditional collective response.

We are now in a position to be more precise about the core meaning of multilateralism. Keohane has defined institutions, generically, as "persistent and connected sets of rules, formal and informal, that prescribe behavioural roles, constrain activity, and shape expectations."[13] Very simply, the term *multilateral* is an adjective that modifies the noun *institution*. Thus, multilateralism depicts a *generic institutional form* in international relations. How does multilateral modify institution? [We] suggest that multilateralism is an institutional form that coordinates relations among three or more states on the basis of generalized principles of conduct: that is, principles which specify appropriate conduct for a class of actions, without regard to the particularistic interests of the parties or the strategic exigencies that may exist in any specific occurrence. MFN treatment is a classic example in the economic realm: it forbids discrimination among countries producing the same product—full stop. Its counterpart in security relations is the requirement that states respond to aggression whenever and wherever it occurs—whether or not any specific instance suits their individual likes and dislikes. In contrast, the bilateral form, such as the Schachtian device and traditional alliances, differentiates relations case-by-case based precisely on a priori particularistic grounds or situational exigencies.

Bilateralism and multilateralism do not exhaust the institutional repertoire of states. Imperialism can be considered a third generic institutional form. Imperialism is also an institution that coordinates relations among three or more states, though, unlike bilateralism and multilateralism, it does so by denying the sovereignty of the subject states.[14]

Two corollaries follow from our definition of multilateralism. First, generalized organizing principles logically entail an indivisibility among the members of a collectivity with respect to the range of behavior in question. Depending on circumstances, that indivisibility can take very different forms, ranging from the physical ties of railway lines that the collectivity chooses to standardize across frontiers, all the way to the adoption by states of the premise that peace is indivisible. But note that indivisibility here is a *social construction*, not a technical condition: in a collective-security scheme, states *behave as though* peace were indivisible, and thereby make it so. Similarly, in the case of trade, *adherence to* the MFN norm makes the system of trade an indivisible whole among the member collectivity, not some inherent attribute of trade itself.[15] Bilateralism, in contrast, segments relations into multiples of dyads and compartmentalizes them. Second, as we shall see below, successful cases of multilateralism in practice appear to generate among their members what Keohane has called expectations of "diffuse reciprocity."[16] That is to say, the arrangement is expected by its members to yield a rough equivalence of benefits in the aggregate and over time. Bilateralism, in contrast, is premised on specific reciprocity, the simultaneous balancing of specific quids pro quos by each party with every other at all times.[17]

What follows from this definition and its corollaries is that multilateralism is a highly demanding institutional form. Its historical incidence is, therefore, likely to be less frequent than that of its alternatives, and if its relative incidence at any time were to be high, that fact would pose an interesting puzzle to be explained.

The obvious next issue to address is the fact that, as Keohane points out, the generic concept of international institution applies in practice to many different types of institutionalized relations among states.[18] So too, therefore, does the adjective *multilateral*: the generic attribute of multilateralism, that it coordinates relations among three or more states in accordance with generalized principles of conduct, will have different specific expressions depending on the type of institutionalized relations to which it pertains. Let us examine some instances. Common usage in the literature distinguishes among three institutional domains of interstate relations: international orders, international regimes, and international organizations. Each type can be, but need not be, multilateral in form.

The literature frequently refers to international economic orders, international security orders, international maritime orders, and so on. An "open" or "liberal" international economic order is multilateral in form, as is a maritime order based on the principle of *mare liberum*. The New Economic Order of the Nazis was not multilateral in form, for reasons I have already suggested, and neither was the European security order crafted by Bismarck. The concept of multilateralism here refers to the constitutive rules that order relations in given domains of international life—their architectural dimension, so to speak. Thus, the quality of "openness" in an international economic order refers to such characteristics as the prohibition of exclusive blocs, spheres, or similar barriers to the conduct of international economic relations. The corresponding quality in an international security order—which would cause it to be described as "collective"—is the condition of equal access to a common security umbrella. To the extent that these conditions are met, the order in question may be said to be multilateral in form. In short, multilateralism here depicts the character of an overall order of relations among states; definitionally it says nothing about *how* that order is achieved.

Regimes are more concrete than orders: typically, the term refers to functional or sectoral components of orders. Moreover, the concept of regime encompasses more of the "how" question than does the concept of order in that, broadly speaking, the term "regime" is used to refer to common, deliberative, though often highly asymmetrical means of conducting interstate relations. That much is clear from common usage. But while there is a widespread assumption in the literature that all regimes are, ipso facto, multilateral in character, this assumption is egregiously erroneous. For example, there is no reason not to call the Schachtian schemes for organizing monetary and trade relations international regimes; they fully meet the standard criteria specified by Stephen Krasner

and his colleagues.[19] Moreover, it is entirely possible to imagine the emergence of regimes between *two* states—superpower security regimes, for example, were a topic of some discussion in the 1980s[20]—but such regimes by definition would not be multilateral either. In sum, what makes a regime a *regime* is that it satisfies the definitional criterion of encompassing principles, norms, rules, and decision-making procedures around which actor expectations converge. But in and of themselves, those terms are empty of substance. What makes a regime *multilateral* in form, beyond involving three or more states, is that the substantive meanings of those terms roughly reflect the appropriate generalized principles of conduct. By way of illustration, in the case of a multilateral trade regime, these would include the norm of MFN treatment, corresponding rules about reciprocal tariff reductions and the application of safeguards, and collectively sanctioned procedures for implementing the rules. In the case of a collective-security regime, they would include the norm of nonaggression, uniform rules for use of sanctions to deter or punish aggression, and, again, collectively sanctioned procedures for implementing them.

Finally, formal international organizations are palpable entities with headquarters and letterheads, voting procedures, and generous pension plans. They require no conceptual elaboration. But, again, their relationship to the concept of multilateralism is less self-evident than is sometimes assumed. Two issues deserve brief mention. The first, though it may be moot at the moment, is that there have been international organizations that were not multilateral in form. The Comintern and later Cominform come to mind; they were based explicitly on Leninist principles of organization, which were quite different from their multilateral counterparts. Along the same lines, the . . . collapsed Soviet-East European system of organizations differed from multilateral forms in ways that students of international organization never fully came to grips with. The second issue is more problematic even today. A common tendency exists in the world of actual international organizations, and sometimes in the academic community, to equate the very phenomenon of multilateralism with the universe of multilateral organizations or diplomacy. The preceding discussion makes clear why that view is in error. It may be the case empirically that decisions concerning aspects of international orders or, more likely, international regimes are in fact made in multilateral forums. The European [Union] exhibits this empirical pattern most extensively; the failed quest by developing countries for a New International Economic Order in the 1970s exhibits the desire to achieve it; and decisions on most international trade and monetary matters fall somewhere in between. But definitionally, multilateral organization is a separate and distinct type of institutionalized behavior, defined by such generalized decision-making rules as voting or consensus procedures.

In sum, the term *multilateral* is an adjective that modifies the noun *institution*. What distinguishes the multilateral form from others is that it coordinates behavior among three or more states on the basis of generalized principles of conduct. Accordingly, any theory of international institutions that does not include this qualitative dimension of multilateralism is bound to be a fairly abstract theory and one that is silent about one of the most crucial distinctions within the repertoire of international institutional forms. Moreover, for analytic purposes it is important not to (con)fuse the very meaning of multilateralism with any one particular institutional expression of it, be it an international order, regime, or organization. Each can be, but need not be, multilateral in form. In addition, the multilateral form should not be equated with universal geographical scope; the attributes of multilateralism characterize relations within specific collectivities that may and often do fall short of the whole universe of nations. Finally, it should be kept in mind that

these are formal definitions, not empirical descriptions of actual cases, and we would not expect actual cases to conform fully to the formal definitions. . . .

Conclusion

This essay was written with two sets of protagonists in mind. The first are those theorists of international relations for whom institutions matter little. It may be true, as these theorists insist, that they do not purport to explain everything but that what they do explain is important.[21] It does not follow, however, that what they leave unexplained is unimportant. And institutions, clearly, are not unimportant.

The second set of protagonists are those of my fellow institutionalists for whom the form that institutions take is left unexplored. Their focus is on institutions in a generic sense or on cooperation even more generally. Much can be learned about international relations from that perspective. But at the same time, too much is left unsaid. And what is left unsaid—the form that institutions assume—affects vitally the role which institutions play on the world stage today. Above all else, policymakers groping for alternatives amid rapid change, hoping to grasp the flow of events and channel it in desirable directions, do not deal in generic choices; theirs are palpably concrete.

A core and concrete feature of current international institutional arrangements is in their multilateral form. Why both the conventional literature on international relations and the literature on institutions should remain relatively silent on it may well have something to do with the atomistic ontology of the one and the instrumental-rationalist epistemology of the other, as James Caporaso and Friedrich Kratochwil, in different ways, suggest. . . . Or, as Martin counters, the limitations may be, not inherent to those approaches, but simply the product of past neglect that future practice can and will rectify. Be that as it may, I hope I have established, at minimum, that the effort is worthwhile: form matters.

No theory has been advanced in the present essay; no theory was vindicated or even tested. We cannot explain what we have not first described. And conceptual explication is a requisite for theoretically informed description, leading ultimately to theory building itself. My main objective here has been to explicate the concept of multilateralism . . . and to offer some preliminary guiding hypotheses about what may and may not explain its incidence and correlates, about how and why it matters.

Notes

1. I mean to include here both strands of theorizing identified by Robert O. Keohane: the rationalist and the reflectivist. "International Institutions: Two Approaches," *International Studies Quarterly* (December 1988), vol. 32.

2. Stephen D. Krasner, ed., *International Regimes* (Ithaca, N.Y.: Cornell University Press, 1983); Kenneth A. Oye, ed., *Cooperation Under Anarchy* (Princeton: Princeton University Press, 1986); and Robert O. Keohane, *After Hegemony* (Princeton: Princeton University Press, 1984).

3. Robert O. Keohane, "Multilateralism: An Agenda for Research," *International Journal* (Autumn 1990), 45:731. After introducing the concept and defining it in this manner, Keohane essentially goes on to discuss international institutions in the generic sense. See also Keohane, *After Hegemony*, in which there are but two fleeting references to multilateralism, both to specific agreements in trade; and Keohane, *International Institutions and State Power* (Boulder, Colo.: Westview Press, 1989), which contains no entry under multilateralism in its index. I must admit that this is equally true of my own writings on the subject of institutions. Keohane has kindly referred to a 1975 paper of mine as having "foreshadowed much of the conceptual work of the next decade." Alas, it also foreshadowed this blind spot, my having been concerned primarily with differentiating the study of international organization from the study of formal international organizations—hence the introduction of the concept of "regimes." Keohane, "Multilateralism," p. 755, fn. 44, referring to Ruggie, "International Responses to Technology: Concepts and Trends," *International Organization* (Summer 1975), vol. 29.

4. In the United Nations context, what Keohane defines as multilateral is called multi*national*—for example, the multinational (non-U.N.) observer team in the Sinai. In the United Nations, only that is considered multilateral which is duly authorized by a multilateral forum. But if Keohane's definition is analytically too loose, the U.N. conception is too limiting, as will be discussed below.

5. William Diebold, Jr., "The History and the Issues," in Diebold, ed., *Bilateralism, Multilateralism and Canada in U.S. Trade Policy* (Cambridge, Mass.: Ballinger, for the Council on Foreign Relations, 1988), p. 1. Diebold seeks to formulate some principled basis for distinguishing what kind of recent trade measures—unilateral, bilateral, and what he calls plurilateral—are consistent with, and what kind undermine, the principles of multilateralism on which the GATT regime is based.

6. William Diebold, "The History and the Issues."

7. The classic, and appropriately titled, study of the Nazi system is Albert O. Hirschman, *National Power and the Structure of Foreign Trade* (Berkeley and Los Angeles: University of California Press, 1945; 1980); see also Leland B. Yeager, *International Monetary Relations: Theory, History, and Policy* (New York: Harper & Row, 1976), ch. 18.

8. Several major states, including Great Britain and the United States, had limited *Sondermark* agreements with Germany—marks that foreigners could earn through the sale of specified products to Germany but that Germany in turn restricted to particular purchases from Germany.

9. A. J. P. Taylor, *The Struggle for Mastery of Europe: 1848–1918* (New York: Oxford University Press, 1971), ch. 12.

10. Sir Arthur Salter, *Security* (London: Macmillan, 1939), p. 155, emphasis in original.

11. G. F. Hudson, "Collective Security and Military Alliances," in Herbert Butterfield and Martin Wight, eds, *Diplomatic Investigations* (Cambridge, Mass.: Harvard University Press, 1968), pp. 176–177. See also Charles A. Kupchan and Clifford A. Kupchan, "Concerts, Collective Security, and the Future of Europe," *International Security* (Summer 1991), vol. 16.

12. Contrary to folklore, Woodrow Wilson was not prepared to commit the United States to specific and automatic military obligations under the League of Nations; his collective-security scheme would have relied on public opinion, arms limitations, and arbitration more than on enforcement mechanisms. Senator Henry Cabot Lodge's fundamental objection to the League was its permanence and universalism and the limitless entanglements he saw that entailing for the United States, as well as his fear that it would violate the Monroe Doctrine and allow European meddling even in U.S. internal

affairs. Lloyd E. Ambrosius, *Woodrow Wilson and the American Diplomatic Tradition* (New York: Cambridge University Press, 1987).

13. Keohane, "Multilateralism," p. 732.

14. Michael Doyle, *Empires* (Ithaca, N.Y.: Cornell University Press, 1986), ch. 1. Some of the more predatory expressions of the Nazi arrangements came very close to, if they did not actually constitute, the imperial form.

15. Obviously, such technical factors as the existence of nuclear weapons or economic interdependence and externalities can and probably do affect the social constructions states choose. I am not imputing causality here but simply clarifying a concept.

16. Robert O. Keohane, "Reciprocity in International Relations," *International Organization* (Winter 1985), vol. 40.

17. Bilateral balancing need not imply equality; it simply means establishing a mutually acceptable balance between the parties, however that is determined in prac-

tice. For an extended discussion of this difference, see Karl Polanyi, "The Economy as Instituted Process," in Karl Polanyi, Conrad M. Arensberg, and Harry W. Pearson, *Trade & Market in the Early Empires* (Glencoe, Ill.: Free Press, 1957).

18. Keohane, "International Institutions."

19. Krasner, *International Regimes.*

20. Steve Weber predicted the emergence of a superpower security regime in "Realism, Detente, and Nuclear Weapons," *International Organization* (Winter 1990), vol. 44; Robert Jervis discussed the possibility in "Security Regimes," in Krasner, ed., *International Regimes*, and Jervis, "From Balance to Concert: A Study of International Security Cooperation," *World Politics* (October 1985), vol. 38.

21. This has been Waltz's standard refrain; see, for example, "Reflections on Theory of International Politics: A Response to My Critics," in Robert O. Keohane, ed., *Neorealism and Its Critics* (New York: Columbia University Press, 1986).

4 Globalism: Dependency and the Capitalist World-System

MAJOR ACTORS AND ASSUMPTIONS: A SUMMARY

We have seen that realists organize their work around the basic question: How can stability be maintained in an anarchic world? Many pluralists ask how peaceful change can be promoted in a world that is increasingly interdependent politically, militarily, socially, and economically. Our third and final image of international relations, globalism, tends to concentrate on the broad question of why so many **Third World** states in Latin America, Africa, and Asia have been unable to develop. For some globalists, this question is part of a larger effort to develop a theory of world capitalist development.

We have avoided the label **Marxism** because there are both Marxists and non-Marxists who work within what we have chosen to call the globalist image. Indeed, some globalists decidedly avoid Marxian modes of analysis. We acknowledge that in adopting the term *globalism* we have appropriated a word sometimes used by pluralists or realists to describe their images of the world. One could, perhaps, find another word as yet unclaimed. But we think *globalism* is particularly apt for those who see the **capitalist world-system** as their starting point or who focus on **dependency** relations within a global political economy. As already noted in Chapter One, we are not alone in using the term *globalism* in this context.

Globalists are guided by four key assumptions. First, it is necessary to understand the *global context within which states and other entities interact*. Globalists argue that to explain behavior at any and all **levels of analysis**—the individual, bureaucratic, societal, and between states or between societies—one must first understand the overall structure of the global system within which such behavior takes place. As with some realists, globalists believe that the starting point of analysis should be the international system. To a large extent, the behavior of individual actors is explained by a system that provides constraints and opportunities.

Second, globalists stress the importance of *historical analysis* in comprehending the international system. Only by tracing the historical evolution of the system is it possible to understand its current structure. The key historical factor and defining characteristic of the system as a whole is **capitalism.** This particular economic system works to the benefit of some individuals, states, and societies but at the expense of others. Even socialist states must operate within a capitalist world economy that significantly constrains their options. Hence, for globalists, the East-West division—even during the height of the Cold War—was not nearly as important as the **North-South** divide and competition among such advanced capitalist states as Germany, Japan, and the United States.

Third, globalists assume that particular *mechanisms of domination* exist that keep Third World states from developing and that contribute to worldwide **uneven development.** To understand these mechanisms requires an examination of dependency relations between the northern industrialized states (Europe and North America) and their poorer neighbors in the southern hemisphere (Africa, Latin America, Asia).

Finally, globalists assume that *economic factors* are absolutely critical in explaining the evolution and functioning of the world capitalist system and the relegation of Third World states to a subordinate position.

The globalist approach would seem to share certain commonalities with the other two perspectives. As noted, globalists and realists both place greater emphasis on the importance of the systems level, or world as a whole, in affecting actors' behavior than do the pluralists. But they differ as to how they characterize the systems level components. Globalists tend to focus on the capitalist mode of production and realists on the distribution of aggregate power. Furthermore, globalists are much more likely than realists to emphasize the intimate connection between the international system and domestic politics—state and society are never viewed as being encapsulated by a metaphorical hard shell.

Globalists and pluralists share at least three commonalities that can be viewed as criticisms of the realist perspective. First, both stress an approach to international relations grounded in **political economy.** The distinction of high politics versus low politics is rejected—if not totally reversed for certain globalists—in terms of the relative importance of economic as compared to political-military factors. For the globalist, various manifestations of political and military power generally reflect the driving force of underlying economic factors. Politics depends on economics; it is not an autonomous realm.

Secondly, both the globalists and pluralists are much more attuned to events, processes, institutions, and actors operating both within and between states; the impermeable billiard ball (the unitary rational actor) is broken down into its component parts. Both approaches tend to range up and down the levels of analysis and focus on a greater variety of actors, but the globalists place a much greater emphasis on the context (i.e., the capitalist nature of the international system) within which these actors operate than do the pluralists.

Third, both the globalists and those pluralists who write in the **transnationalist** tradition emphasize socioeconomic or welfare issues. A number of pluralists have a normative commitment to peaceful change. International relations do not have to be viewed and played as a **zero-sum game** with winners and losers but can be seen as a **positive-sum game** in which the restructuring of interstate relations is achieved through bargaining and compromise, allowing all parties to gain. Although the globalists are also concerned with the welfare of **less developed countries (LDCs),** they are not so optimistic about the possibility of peaceful change. The hierarchical nature of world politics with South subordinated to North and the economic dictates of the world capitalist system make it unlikely that the northern industrialized states will make any meaningful concessions to the Third World. Change, peaceful or revolutionary, is problematic. In sum, there are major differences between globalists and pluralists.

Although the globalists are primarily concerned with the question of why LDCs cannot develop, answering such a query is difficult. How and why did capitalism develop in Western Europe? How did it expand outward to other continents? As an international phenomenon, how has capitalism changed over the centuries? What are the specific mechanisms of dependency that allow for the maintenance of exploitative relations? What is the relationship between the elites of the wealthy **center** countries (the **First World**) and the elites of the poorer **periphery?** Is it possible for an LDC to break out of a dependent situation? Answers to such questions are addressed in this chapter.

INTELLECTUAL PRECURSORS AND INFLUENCES

Karl Marx

All globalists have been influenced either directly or indirectly by the works of Karl Marx (1818–1883). This is certainly not to suggest that all globalists are Marxists any more than that all Marxists accept without qualification the sum total of Marx's efforts. It is simply to acknowledge that they owe an intellectual debt to him in terms of their methods of analysis and certain critical insights into the functioning, development, and expansion of the capitalist mode of production. To appreciate Marx as scholar, one does not have to ascribe to the views of Marx as revolutionary.

Karl Marx's work concerns mankind's historical growth process and movement toward final self-realization and fulfillment in a society he called *communist*. For Marx, history was not so much the story of the rise and fall of particular city-states, empires, and nation-states as it was the story of **class conflict** generated by economic modernization. Having evolved out of a **feudal** system, capitalism reigned supreme in nineteenth-century Europe. Marx argued that capitalism—which involves market exchanges, labor as a commodity, and the **means of production** held in private hands—produced particular political, social, and cultural effects. Marx's discussion and analysis of capitalism have influenced globalists in at least three ways.

First, Marx was concerned with exploitation of the many by the few. He may have recognized the historically progressive role played by capitalists (the **proletarian revolution** would not be possible until after the establishment of a capitalist system), but his personal sympathies were with the downtrodden.

Second, according to Marx, capitalism exhibited certain law-like qualities in terms of its development and expansion. He viewed capitalism as part of a world historical process unfolding **dialectically,** an economic system riddled with clashing contradictions or internal tensions that could be resolved only by transformation into a socialist mode of production.

Finally, Marx insisted that a society must be studied in its totality, not piecemeal. An analyst must be aware of how various parts of society were interrelated, including those aspects not so apparent to the casual observer.[1]

This perspective has deeply influenced the globalists, some of whom earlier in their careers had little use for history and were preoccupied almost exclusively with such **units of analysis** as states or individuals. As two leading globalists have argued: "If there is one thing which distinguishes a world-system perspective from any other, it is its insistence that the unit of analysis is a *world*-system defined in terms of *economic* processes and links, and not any units defined in terms of juridical, political, cultural, geographical, or other criteria."[2] Although such units of analysis are not ignored by the globalists, they take on connotations different from those of the realist or pluralist. The state, for example, is not viewed in terms of its being a **sovereign** entity preoccupied with security concerns. Rather, it derives its significance from the role it plays in actively aiding or hindering the capitalist accumulation process. Any one particular state is not viewed in isolation but in terms of how it fits into the overall global capitalist system.

In sum, Marx has influenced contemporary scholars working within the globalist image by virtue of his emphasis on exploitation, discernible historical patterns of capitalist development and expansion, and the importance of understanding the "big picture" and then asking how individual parts fit into the whole.

Hobson and Imperialism

Marx's observations on capitalism in the nineteenth century have since been modified and generalized to cover the entire globe under various theories of **imperialism.** Imperialism assumes an international, hierarchical division of labor between rich and poor regions of the world, but the relation is not one of mutually beneficial **comparative advantage.** Rather, it is one of exploitation.

Ironically, perhaps one of the most significant theories of imperialism was devised by a non-Marxist, the English economist John A. Hobson (1858–1940). Near the turn of the century, Hobson noted that capitalist societies were faced with three basic interrelated problems: overproduction, underconsumption by workers and other classes, and oversavings on the part of capitalists. As the capitalist owners of industry continued to exploit workers and pay the lowest possible wages, profits mounted and goods began to pile up. But who was to purchase the excess goods? Given the low wages, not the mass of the working class, because members of this class did not have sufficient purchasing power. The efficiency of the capitalist mode of production resulted, however, in the relentless production of more and more goods the society was unable to consume.

What could capitalists have done with excess goods and profits, and how could they have resolved the problem of underconsumption? Redistribute wealth? Highly unlikely. Because capitalist European and North American powers were experiencing overproduction and domestic underconsumption, investment opportunities in other developed countries remained limited.

The solution reached by capitalists was to invest in what are now known as Third World countries. The result was imperialism: "the endeavor of the great controllers of industry to broaden the channel for the flow of their surplus wealth by seeking foreign markets and foreign investments to take off the goods and capital they cannot sell or use at home." Hobson argued against "the supposed inevitability of imperial expansion." He stated that it is "not inherent in the nature of things that we should spend our natural resources on militarism, war, and risky, unscrupulous diplomacy, in order to find markets for our goods and surplus capital."[3] Hobson hence rejected the **determinism** so often found in the work of Marxist scholars who write on imperialism.

For Hobson, imperialism did not benefit the home country as a whole. Instead, selected groups such as industrialists, financiers, and the individuals who staffed the colonial empires profited. Furthermore, because the flag followed trade, large military expenditures were required to protect the imperialist system. The drive for capitalist profits by securing overseas territories led to competition and rivalry among European powers. Hence, imperialism was to Hobson a major cause of war, and Hobson suggested that capitalists might indeed profit from such conflicts.

Lenin

V. I. Lenin's (1870–1924) *Imperialism: The Highest Stage of Capitalism* is his most important theoretical work of interest to globalists. Writing in the midst of World War I (1916), Lenin was interested in developing a theory that explained the necessity for capitalist exploitation of lesser developed countries and the causes of war among advanced capitalist states. He drew heavily upon the works of Hobson and the German Social Democrat, Rudolph Hilferding (1877–1941).

From Hobson, Lenin accepted the key argument that underconsumption and overproduction caused capitalists to scramble for foreign markets beyond Europe and to engage in colonialism. From Hilferding, Lenin took the notion that imperialist policies reflected the existence of monopoly and finance capital, or the highest stage of capitalism. In other words, capitalism had developed such that oligopolies and monopolies controlled the key sectors of the economy, squeezing out or taking over smaller firms and milking domestic markets dry. The result was a need to look elsewhere for investment opportunities. This logically entailed the creation of overseas markets. As markets expanded, they required more economic inputs such as raw materials, which encouraged the further spread of imperialism to secure such resources.

Marx had seen that rates of profits would decline because of overproduction and underconsumption and that greater misery for the working class would result because more and more people would be out of jobs or receive even less in wages. **Proletarian,** or working-class, consciousness would grow, leading ultimately to revolution in all capitalist countries. For Lenin, imperialism explained why Marx's prediction of proletarian revolution in Europe had failed to come about. Economic contradictions inherent in the capitalist mode of production still existed, but imperialism allowed capitalists a breathing space. Imperialism provided the European working class a taste or small portion of the spoils derived from the exploitation of overseas territories—new markets, cheap labor, and natural resources. By buying off the European working class in the short term, imperialism delayed the inevitable revolution. But an important trade-off was involved. Domestic stability was achieved at the cost of wars among the capitalist powers that resulted from the continual struggle for overseas markets. Once the globe had been effectively divided up, further expansion could come about only at the expense of a capitalist rival.

For Lenin, imperialism was therefore driven by *economic forces,* and it was inevitable that such exploitation and eventual conflict would occur. Hence, he disagreed with Hobson and later theorists (e.g., Joseph Schumpeter) who argued that other factors such as primitive or irrational instincts or an enjoyment of struggle and conquest also played a role in explaining imperialist policies. He also disagreed with writers who argued that imperialism was simply the chosen policy of capitalists and hence was subject to change. Lenin rejected this line of thinking. For him, imperialism was not a matter of choice but of inevitability. The capitalists could not save themselves. Imperialism was the direct result of the attainment of monopoly capital. The resulting competition among states, reflecting the domination of capitalist class interests and the differential growth rates of capitalist economies (i.e., **uneven development**), unavoidably led to world wars such as the one being experienced at the time of Lenin's writing.

Although Lenin's theory of imperialism has been subject to a great deal of **empirical** and **conceptual** criticism over the years, Lenin was writing not just as a theorist but also as a revolutionary whose writings were designed to mobilize support for a socialist revolution. He is a prime example of a writer blending theory and practice. In combination with his works on the importance of revolutionary organization, Lenin's *Imperialism* has had a great deal of influence on revolutionaries throughout the Third World.

Strictly as a theorist, Lenin has particularly influenced the globalist literature with his emphasis on the global nature of capitalism and its inherent exploitativeness that primarily benefits the **bourgeoisie** in advanced capitalist states at the expense of poorer countries. Although there is arguably a good deal of determinism in his theory of imperialism, his work as a revolutionary (like that of Marx) reflected considerable voluntarism in practice.[4] The actions of revolutionaries were at the very least to serve as catalysts to the worldwide proletarian revolution whenever the objective conditions of working class exploitation were ripe or had reached their revolutionary stage.[5]

Luxemburg and Revolution vs. Reform

Not to be seduced by the appeal of peaceful, gradual change or reformism, Rosa Luxemburg (1870–1919) expressed deep commitment to revolution as the only effective means of transforming society. She wrote as a critic of Eduard Bernstein's late nineteenth-century German Social Democratic Party politics of **reformism.** She saw reformism as an abandonment of Marxist principles, however helpful such policies might appear to be for the workers in the short run. Luxemburg argued vociferously the necessity for revolution to effect "removal of obstacles that a privileged minority places in the path of social progress."[6] By contrast, she believed that reformism involves compromise with the bourgeoisie, strengthening the hand of the capitalist class: "Only the hammer blow of revolution, that is to say, the conquest of political power by the proletariat," or working class, "can break down this wall" of opposition posed by capitalists to "socialist society."[7] She also described the negative impact of imperialism on colonies.[8]

The issue of whether the kinds of changes anticipated by many globalists can be achieved by reformist tactics or whether they can be achieved only through revolutionary violence remains a matter for dispute. Many globalists are reform-minded, non-Marxists. Globalists who claim to be Marxists are divided. There are reform-minded Marxists in the tradition of Eduard Bernstein who are opposed by those who see revolution as the only effective means to change the existing world order. Even the latter disagree: When will the revolution occur, or when should it occur? Does one wait until objective conditions are ripe, or does one take some affirmative action to move the process along? Are revolutions inevitable, or must they be made? How much is the result of voluntary action, and how much is determined by "historical inevitabilities"? The one point on which these theorists tend to agree is the desirability of change from the present unjust order.[9]

Antonio Gramsci

The Italian Marxist, Antonio Gramsci (1891–1937), departed from more hard-line, Marxist-Leninist formulations and offered a constructivist, or volitional, approach to both theory and practice. Writing in prison during the fascist period, his *Prison Notebooks* are a rich source of his views. Gramsci's emphasis on political voluntarism clearly has roots in his study of Machiavelli, who understood the importance of practical action.[10] A key concept in his work that influences some present-day globalist scholarship is the historical and ideological *bloc*,[11] which may well be a *block* or obstacle to social change, thus maintaining a pattern of dominance in society or even on a global scale. For example, Craig Murphy sees a Gramsci-style, North–South historical *bloc* as, perhaps, composed of an "Atlantic" or "Trilateral" ruling class, some of the subordinate classes within advanced industrial states, and a rising governing class, or "organizational bourgeoisie," in dependent Third World states that maintain a collective position of dominance over those subordinate to them. To be sure, the bloc has many interrelated or interconnected, reinforcing faces—economic, political, and cultural—that facilitate maintenance of this dominance.[12]

DEPENDENCY THEORISTS

ECLA and UNCTAD Arguments

Some of the more provocative work in the globalist tradition has been produced by Latin Americanists representing various branches of the social sciences. They have come to be known collectively as dependency theorists, and they now include North

American and European scholars as well as Latin Americans. Several of these writers were associated in the 1960s with the Economic Commission on Latin America (ECLA) and the United Nations Conference on Trade and Development (UNCTAD). They were concerned with the important problem of explaining why Latin America and other Third World regions were not developing as anticipated. North American social science models had predicted an economic takeoff for LDCs.[13] What had gone wrong? What explained economic stagnation, **balance of payments** difficulties, and deteriorating **terms of trade?** Why wasn't the North American–Western European experience being repeated?

One response came from mainstream **modernization** writers. This modernization literature attempted to answer these questions by exploring the difficulties of LDCs in moving from "traditional" to "modern" societies. The tradition–modernity dichotomy has been used in one form or another by social scientists as a tool of analysis since the mid-nineteenth century. The ethos and organization of a traditional society, it is argued, are both a cause and an expression of underdevelopment. The cultural values of a traditional society are postulated to be a hindrance to modernization. The LDCs are wedded to their pasts, reflecting a lack of entrepreneurial spirit that was found in European society during the rise of capitalism in the sixteenth century.[14]

This view of development and underdevelopment as the outcomes of internal processes has been criticized on a number of grounds. Two important criticisms are, first, that the modernization writers assume that the tradition–modernity dichotomy is universally applicable. But is the Latin American experience really so similar to the European experience? Are there really no significant historical differences between Africa and the West? Second, the modernization literature usually neglects a state's or society's external environment, particularly international political and economic factors. Instead, modernization writers have tended to focus on state or society, generally ignoring the state's or society's place in the world capitalist order. Is there any society, even in the European historical experience, that is immune to outside influences? Very unlikely, respond the dependency theorists, who place particular emphasis on Latin America's colonial heritage and a historical legacy of exploitation.

The focus of the ECLA and UNCTAD economists was initially quite narrow. They examined the unequal terms of trade between LDCs that exported raw materials and northern industrialized countries that exported finished manufactured goods. They questioned the supposed benefits of free trade. The ECLA at one point favored the diversification of exports, advising that LDCs produce goods instead of importing them. This policy did not result in the anticipated amount of success and in fact increased the influence of foreign multinational corporations brought in to facilitate domestic production.

Did all countries fail to experience economic growth? No, some economies did grow, but growth tended to occur in an LDC only when the developed countries had a need for a particular raw material or agricultural product. Because many LDCs are dependent on only a few of these commodities for their foreign exchange earnings, a drastic decline in the demand for one of them (perhaps caused by a recession in North America) would have a calamitous impact on an LDC's economy. Or, alternatively, a bumper crop in several LDCs heavily dependent on one particular export (such as coffee or sugar) would also cause prices to fall.

The volatility of prices for minerals and agricultural products and the generally downward tendency of those prices contrast sharply with more stable and gradually increasing prices for manufactured items produced by industrial countries. Thus, the terms of trade are thought to be stacked against those Third World states that export farm products or natural resources.

Radical Critiques

Writers in ECLA and UNCTAD (e.g., Argentine economist Raul Prebisch), although critical of the more conservative views of development, nevertheless tended to restrict their analyses to economic dimensions and to cast their arguments in terms of nationalism and the need for state-guided capitalism.[15] Other writers, however, more boldly emphasized political and social factors within the context of a capitalist economic system that bind Latin America to North America. Development, it was argued, is not autonomous. If it occurs at all, it is reflexive—subject to the vagaries and ups and downs of the world's advanced economies. Choices for Latin American countries are restricted or constrained as a result of the dictates of capitalism but also due to supporting political, social, and cultural relations. The result is a structure of domination. This multifaceted web of dependency reinforces unequal exchange between the northern and southern parts of the hemisphere. Opportunities for LDCs are few and far between because LDCs are allocated a subordinate role in world capitalism.

That various states and societies produce those things of which they are relatively the most efficient producers or sell those items in which they have a comparative advantage is seen by dependency theorists as a "one-way advantage." Economic exploitation of LDCs by the industrialized states is not an accident or simply an additional means by which these states enrich themselves. Rather, economic exploitation is an integral part of the capitalist system and is required to keep it functioning.

The result is a situation of dependency, succinctly defined as a "situation in which a certain number of countries have their economy conditioned by the development and expansion of another . . . , placing the dependent countries in a backward position exploited by the dominant countries."[16] The modernization experience of a particular society should not be seen in isolation, "but as part of the development of an internationalist capitalist system, whose dynamic has a determining influence on the local processes." As a result, underdevelopment is not "a moment in the evolution of a society which has been economically, politically and culturally autonomous and isolated."[17] Instead, Latin American and other Third World countries are attempting to develop under historical conditions quite different from those of the northern industrialized states.

Some globalists use Marxist terminology and Leninist insights to explain this situation of dependency. More important than relations between states are transnational class coalitions linking elites in industrially developed countries (the center) with their counterparts in the South (or periphery). This version of class analysis emphasizes how transnational ties within the global bourgeois or capitalist class work to the disadvantage of workers and peasants in the periphery. The multinational corporation (MNC) and international banks, therefore, are viewed from a much different perspective than that of the realist or pluralist. To the pluralist, MNCs and international banks appear merely as other, potentially benign, actors. To the realist, they tend to be of secondary importance because of the emphasis on the state-as-actor. To the globalist, however, they are central players in establishing and maintaining dependency relations. To globalists of Marxist persuasion, MNCs and banks are agents *par excellence* of the international bourgeoisie. They represent two of the critical means by which Third World states are maintained in their subordinate position within the world capitalist economy.

Domestic Forces

Dependency theorists deal not only with external factors (such as foreign states, multinational corporations, international banks, multilateral lending institutions, foreign control of technology, and an international bourgeoisie). They also deal increasingly with internal constraints on development (such as patterns of land tenure, social structures, class alliances, and the role of the state). These internal factors tend to reinforce instruments of foreign domination. It is argued, for example, that the inability to break out of a dependent situation is often strengthened by citizens of a Latin American country who accrue selfish benefits at the expense of the country as a whole. This so-called **comprador class,** or national bourgeoisie, aids in the exploitation of its own society. Allied with foreign capitalists, its self-serving policies encourage the expansion of social and economic inequality, which may take the form of an ever-widening rural–urban gap. Although limited development may occur in a few urban centers, the countryside stagnates and is viewed only as a provider of cheap labor and raw materials. These exploiters, therefore, have more in common with the elites of the center countries than they do with their fellow citizens of the periphery.

Such arguments are rather sweeping in scope. The importance of internal dimensions, however, will vary depending on the particular country under examination. Class coalitions, for example, will differ and may relate to external actors in a variety of ways. As two noted dependency theorists have stated:

> We conceive the relationship between external and internal forces as forming a complex whole whose structural links are not based on mere external forms of exploitation and coercion, but are rooted in coincidence of interests between local dominant classes and international ones.[18]

In some cases, this "coincidence of interests" might even involve portions of the working class.

As a result of the interplay of external and internal factors, the nature of the development or underdevelopment of a society will vary. Changes in the international economy will affect LDCs in different ways. Dependency theorists, therefore, do not claim that economic stagnation in LDCs is always and inevitably the norm. They argue, however, that development benefits some at the expense of others, increases social inequalities, and leads to greater foreign control over Third World economies.

THE CAPITALIST WORLD-SYSTEM

The dependency theorists pointed the way for scholars who write from what is known as the capitalist world-system perspective. This perspective is truly globalist and differs from dependency in two ways.

First, advocates of the capitalist world-system perspective not only are concerned with the lack of Third World development but also wish to understand the economic, political, and social development of regions throughout the *entire* world. Developed and underdeveloped states, winners and losers, are all examined in attempts to explain the global existence of uneven development.

Second, the goal is to understand the fate of various parts of the world at various times in history within the larger context of a developing world political economy. Latin America, for example, is not unique. Its experience is an integral part of the capitalist world-system. Third World underdevelopment and exploitation are central to maintaining the present structure of dominance in the capitalist world-system. The first priority, therefore, is to understand this global system from a historical perspective. Only then can the fates of particular societies or regions of the globe be understood.

The writings of Immanuel Wallerstein represent the most ambitious of the globalist work and have been the catalyst for an extensive amount of subsequent research. In attempting to understand the origins and dynamics of the modern world economy and the existence of worldwide uneven development, he aspires to no less than a historically based theory of global development, which he terms *world-system theory*.[19]

Wallerstein begins by analyzing the emergence of capitalism in Europe, tracing its development into a capitalist world-system that contains a **core,** a **periphery,** and a **semi-periphery.** The core areas historically have engaged in the most advanced economic activities: banking, manufacturing, technologically advanced agriculture, and ship building. The periphery has provided raw materials such as minerals and timber to fuel the core's economic expansion. Unskilled labor is repressed, and the peripheral countries are denied advanced technology in those areas that might make them more competitive with core states. The semi-periphery is involved in a mix of production activities, some associated with core areas and others with peripheral areas. The semi-periphery also serves a number of other functions such as being an outlet for investment when wages in core economies become too high. Over time, particular regions of the world may gravitate between core, peripheral, and semi-peripheral status.

Class structure varies in each zone depending on how the dominant class relates to the world economy. Contrary to the liberal economic notion of specialization based on comparative advantage, this division of labor *requires* as well as *increases* inequality between regions. States in the periphery are weak in that they are unable to control their fates, whereas states in the core are economically, politically, and militarily dominant.

The basic function of the state is to ensure the continuation of the capitalist mode of production.

Wallerstein's explanatory goals are breathtaking in scope, and his debt to Marx and other globalist intellectual precursors is evident. He deals with such topics as the cause of war among states and factors leading to the rise and fall of core powers. These issues are discussed in the context of the creation and expansion of capitalism as a historical world system. The focus is first and foremost on economic processes and how they in turn influence political and security considerations.

System

Wallerstein and other globalists insist that in order to understand the development of global economic, political, and social processes, we must keep our eye on the development of capitalism. Capitalism is a system-wide, or global, phenomenon. We should not concentrate on individual states and national economies and then extrapolate from their experiences. Instead, we should examine capitalism as an integrated, historically expanding system that transcends any particular political or geographic boundaries. By first understanding capitalism as a truly integrated world-system, we then can better understand the fate of particular countries. This emphasis on the system as the key to understanding may sound familiar. It should; some realists also claim that to develop a true theory of international relations, one must give precedence to the system as opposed to focusing on individual states. Do globalists operating from the world-system perspective in fact share the realist view as to what constitutes the international system? There are some interesting parallels, particularly if one closely examines Wallerstein's work.

First, some realists acknowledge that Wallerstein is attempting to develop a systems-level theory, although he emphasizes economic factors over political variables.[20]

Second, Wallerstein explicitly recognizes the importance of **anarchy,** a concept of critical importance to many realist writers. Recall that anarchy simply refers to the absence of a superordinate or central political authority. Wallerstein notes that "the absence of a single political authority makes it impossible for anyone to legislate the general will of the world-system and hence to curtail the capitalist mode of production."[21] Anarchy, therefore, is defined in political terms for both Wallerstein, who notes the absence of a single world empire, and those realists who discuss the importance of the absence of any central authority in the world.

The implications of anarchy for the realist and globalist are quite different, however, as evidenced by the latter part of the quotations: "to curtail the capitalist mode of production." For the realist, anarchy leads one to examine international political stability, war, and balance-of-power politics involving major states. For the globalist, the economic ramifications of political anarchy are paramount. The political anarchy of the interstate system facilitates the development and expansion of world capitalism because no single state can control the *entire* world economy. The result is an economic division of labor involving a core, a periphery, and a semi-periphery that is the focal point of globalist analysis. Political anarchy becomes a backdrop for an extensive analysis of capitalist dynamics.

Finally, Wallerstein addresses the issue of the international distribution of capabilities or power. Once again, it would appear that Wallerstein has much in common with the realists. The following quotation is illustrative:

> Of course, we shall find on closer inspection that there are periods where one state is relatively quite powerful and other periods where power is more diffuse and contested, permitting weaker states broader ranges of action. We can talk then of the relative tightness or looseness of the world-system as an important variable and seek to analyze why this dimension tends to be cyclical in nature, as it seems to have been for several hundred years.[22]

There is, however, a major difference in how realists and Wallerstein use this notion of a distribution of capabilities.

For Wallerstein, *the very existence* of a particular distribution of power or capabilities cannot be explained without reference to the underlying *economic* order. In other words, he would argue that realists spend a great deal of time talking about the balance of power but that they fail to appreciate that there are important economic processes at work that are critical in accounting for the particular distribution of capabilities or balance of power in the first place!

In sum, despite sharing a similar systems vocabulary, the use and relative importance of these concepts is quite different. For a globalist such as Wallerstein, merely focusing on the distribution of capabilities among states is insufficient if one wishes to comprehend fully the nature of the world-system. The international system has always been composed of weak and strong political units. Differential power alone is not the defining characteristic of the system. Once again, what is critical for the Wallersteinian globalist is the fact that the key aspect of the system is its capitalist nature, the existence of global class relations, and the various functions states and societies perform in the world economy. Capitalism has been the defining attribute of the international system since the sixteenth century. It is capitalism that helps to account for a core, a periphery, and a semi-periphery. It is capitalism that provides the critical environment in which states and classes operate by constraining, shaping, and channeling behavior. Some states and classes are rewarded. Others are doomed to play subordinate roles in a worldwide division of labor determined by the dictates of capitalism. So, although states and politics are certainly important to the globalist, they must be analyzed in the context of the capitalist world-system.

In a post–Cold War volume, Wallerstein puts the events of 1989 in historical perspective, taking a long, multicentury view of global capitalism. Liberalism—an ideology he identifies as associated with the capitalist world-system, has served as a "legitimating geoculture." On North–South relations, he depicts the North's wealth as largely "the result of a transfer of surplus value from the South." Vulnerability in a capitalist world economy comes from "ceaseless accumulation of capital" that approaches its limit "to the point where none of the mechanisms for restoring the normal functioning of the system can work effectively any longer." Grossly unequal distribution of material gains contributes to "multiple strains on the system" and undermines "state structures," notably "their ability to maintain order in a world of widespread civil warfare, both global and state level."[23]

Political, Economic, and Social Factors

As noted in Chapter 1, realists understand the importance of economic factors, but they focus on power, the balance of power, and political explanations of international relations. Pluralists interested in transnationalism emphasize political, economic, and social factors, depending on the issue. And globalists tend to stress economic factors as underlying or driving politics.

These are generalizations, and as with all generalizations, they are subject to qualification. All globalists emphasize economic factors in their conceptions of the world-system, but the degree of their emphasis varies. There even has been recent debate as to whether the capitalist mode of production has been overemphasized. At one extreme, there is Wallerstein, who is claimed by critics to have reduced the derivation and operation of the state system to economics. Other globalists, although accepting the logic of the capitalist world-system approach, stress the interdependence of political and economic **variables.** Christopher Chase-Dunn, for example, argues that "the capitalist mode of production exhibits a single logic in which both political-military power" and exploitative economic processes "play an integrated role."[24] Patrick McGowan states that "distinctions between economic and political processes represent false dichotomies. . . . Accumulation, imperialism, and conflict can be considered part of a single dynamic whereby a hegemonic core state in an increasingly competitive world-system attempts to ensure its own stability, prosperity, and primacy."[25] Political processes, however, are still basically derivative of the world capitalist mode of production, or they are placed in the context of economic structures and processes. Chase-Dunn, for example, develops the argument that "both the attempts and the failures of imperium can be understood as responses to the pressures of uneven development in the world-economy. . . . The interstate system is dependent on the institutions and opportunities presented by the world market for its survival."[26]

Johan Galtung goes one step further in his perspective on imperialism, which has had a major impact on globalists.[27] In examining the mechanisms of imperialism that cause and perpetuate the tremendous inequality within and among nations, Galtung parts company with Marx and Lenin in that for him, imperialism is not simply an economic relation arising out of capitalism. Imperialism is a structural relation of dominance defined in political, economic, military, cultural, and communication terms. These types of imperialism have to be seen in their totality. It is not enough for international relations scholars to be preoccupied with only political and military factors, or economists to restrict their focus to economic factors. The entire structure of dominance has to be comprehended.

Equally important, Galtung argues that one must look *inside* societies to understand the effects of interactions *among* them. Imperialism means, for example, that elites in center nations dominate and collaborate with elites in periphery nations to the disadvantage of the majority of people in the latter. This would be a political effect of imperialism. Economic effects would include the production of only a few commodities by a periphery state, and trade being concentrated with a particular center state. Equal emphasis, however, is given to other forms of imperialism.

CHANGE

Many international relations scholars are interested in understanding system change. A common distinction is between changes *of* the system and lesser changes *within* an existing system that retains its basic characteristics. For globalists, changes within the world-system appear to fall into three categories. First, there are changes in the actors' positions within the world capitalist economy. As Wallerstein states: "There is constant and patterned movement between groups of economic actors as to who shall occupy various positions in the hierarchy of production, profit, and consumption."[28] The Dutch empire of the seventeenth century, for example, gave way to British domination, and eventually the United States rose to prominence in the twentieth century. Despite different core powers, however, the hierarchical nature of the system remains the same.

Second, some scholars identify phases or cycles of capitalist growth and contraction that affect all societies. A period of relative social stability and economic stagnation precedes twenty or thirty years of rapid economic growth. This is then followed by another two or three decades of economic decline, followed again by expansion. Overproduction, a key factor discussed by Hobson, is central to the interplay of economic, social, and political forces.[29]

Third, there is what has been termed a *structural transformation* of the system. This term refers to the historical and geographical expansion of the capitalist world-system, incorporating new areas of the globe and nonintegrated sectors of the world economy.[30] Although the term *transformation* is used, these changes could still be viewed as changes within the system because the capitalist mode of production, although perhaps changing its character, is still capitalist. In sum, the globalist view of the capitalist world-system is hardly static. The world-system is dynamic, reflecting a myriad of activities and changes.[31]

But what about changes *of* the capitalist system? World-system theorists point to one major historical occurrence: the transformation of feudalism into capitalism in sixteenth-century Europe. What are the chances of going beyond capitalism? Globalists are ambivalent on this point. Wallerstein may entitle one article "The Rise and Future Demise of the World Capitalist System," but he also refers to "The Limited Possibilities of Transformation within the Capitalist World Order." Similarly, in the early 1980s, a number of theorists discussed how Eastern European and socialist states might succumb to the powerful forces of the capitalist world-system. Their analysis proved accurate.[32]

Other globalists point to possible transformational processes that might make significant system change possible. Such non-Marxist scholars as Hayward Alker and Johan Galtung, for example, downplay the notion of constraints that supposedly limit the evolution of alternative world orders. Alker sees change occurring through the dialectical clash of world forces and different visions of world futures. These contradictory world-order contenders (capitalist power balancing, socialism, collective self-reliance, and corporatist authoritarianism) make system transformation possible. For his part, Galtung sees the international system as open and subject to change. He even speculates on the decline not only of the nation-state but also of multinational corporations and even any world government that may be constructed in the distant future.[33]

What role does human volition play in system change? At one extreme, there are scholars who apparently see large-scale historical processes as relatively immune from the actions of human beings. A strong dose of determinism seems to be reflected in their work. They are challenged by critics who downplay constraints. Some of these critics call for revolutions to end capitalist exploitation. They argue that despite the "particularity" of Latin America or other Third World regions that is emphasized by dependency theorists, these areas remain consistent with the patterns of capitalist development discussed by Marx. The "subordinated classes," they claim, have been neglected by some globalists in favor of a focus on exchange relations among societies. Such critics state that class contradictions and the intensification of class conflict still make possible the type of worker revolution discussed by Marx. Hence, these authors have taken the more voluntarist position in a long-standing Marxist debate on the potential for revolution in the Third World—that revolutionaries can help produce world-system change.[34] With the collapse of the Soviet Union, however, less has been heard from these writers in recent years.

Some world-system theorists take an intermediate position. Powerful "structures of domination" are acknowledged, but so also is the permanent struggle among classes. As Henrique Cardoso states of dependency theory: "Instead of accepting the existence of a determined course in history, there is a return to conceiving of it as an open-ended process. Thus, if structures delimit the range of oscillation, the actions of humans, as well as their imagination, revive and transfigure these structures and may even replace them with others that are not predetermined."[35] Similarly, Terence Hopkins and Immanuel Wallerstein argue that the study of the capitalist world economy is the "theoretical side of the practical work of transforming the modern world-system into the socialist world-order that modern social change has made at once politically necessary and historically possible."[36] In this formulation, there is room for human political will to effect transformation. Thus, if one accepts globalists at their word (and some critics do not), globalist theory is not determinist. It allows for (and even requires) political action.

In recent years, a good deal of interesting work has been done under the heading of *neostructuralism*. In keeping with the globalist emphasis, these authors are critical of the realist reliance on the unitary, rational, state-as-actor. While they recognize the importance of earlier dependency and world-system work, their influences also include Fernand Braudel, Karl Polanyi, and Antonio Gramsci. Neostructuralism is interested in understanding how global processes interact with other processes of state/social transformation occurring at many other levels of the world-system. The study of international relations, therefore, is not limited to foreign policy or patterns of distributions of capabilities, nor confined to reducing international relations to economic variables. Given the fact that the focus of analysis is on transformative processes, states as well as economic and social forces have to be taken into account. A web of relations and forces are intricately linked, transcending all levels of analysis. Nevertheless, neostructuralists are consistent with the globalist tradition in that governments play a secondary role to socioeconomic structures and forces when it comes to explaining world politics.

GLOBALISTS AND THEIR CRITICS: AN OVERVIEW

The globalist literature has been subject to a great deal of criticism by specialists in international relations and comparative politics. Much of the criticism is harsh, particularly of dependency theorists and Immanuel Wallerstein's ambitious work. Much of this criticism also perhaps reflects ideological biases. We first discuss some of the more telling critiques and then present rebuttals from globalists.

The Question of Causality

Some critics question whether dependency creates economic and social backwardness (as globalists claim), or whether it is economic and social backwardness that leads to a situation of dependency. In short, there is no agreement on causality—whether dependency is the *cause* of backwardness or whether it is the *effect* of this condition.

Reliance on Economics

Critics have argued that some globalists have reduced the operation of the international system down to the process of capital accumulation and related dynamics. What of other, noneconomic explanations of imperialism and relations among states? Are not political and strategic motives equally or even more important? For example, how can one account for nineteenth-century European states scrambling for economically low-value pieces of terrain such as present-day Chad or lifeless Pacific atolls? What was the economic motive? If the competitive interstate system is derived from the capitalist mode of production, how does one explain similar competitive behavior among political units in precapitalist eras before the fifteenth century? For example, recall Thucydides' discussion of the Peloponnesian War that lends support to the validity of such notions as anarchy and the security dilemma. This suggests the autonomy of the political realm and a distinctly political dynamic involving competition among sovereign units well before the emergence of a capitalist world-system.

The economic variable, critics claim, cannot carry the very great explanatory weight assigned to it. Insights generated from the contemplation of international relations over the centuries should not be ignored. Realists, for example, would argue that if anything, it is the international political-security system that largely determines the international economic system, not the other way around.

System Dominance

Despite globalist references to internal factors, critics claim that there is an excessive globalist reliance on international factors in explaining poverty and dependence in the periphery and that domestic variables are downplayed. The cruder dependency work, it is argued, is too sweeping in its claims, blaming virtually every Third World political, economic, and social problem on the northern industrialized states. Lack of economic growth, social unrest, and repressive governments are all laid at the doorstep of the richer capitalist countries.

Theoretical Rigidity

The criticism of economics and system dominance as bases for causality logically leads to the following: It is claimed that individual cases are examined solely in terms of general theoretical constructs such as "dependency" or "capitalist world-system." A society's experiences are reduced to or explained in terms of one or two concepts. Major political, economic, and social changes all supposedly fall under the general explanatory logic of a term such as *dependency*. Furthermore, rather than modifying the theories or concepts in light of empirical evidence (often supposedly lacking) or questions raised by case studies, it is claimed that case studies are used by globalists only when they appear to provide evidence to support the line of argument. There is no tension between theory and findings, little questioning of the framework, and an unwillingness to consider alternative hypotheses. Such criticisms, however, could just as easily be leveled at work associated with both the realist and pluralist images.

Accounting for Anomalies

It is also argued that the globalists are unable to account for Third World countries that have been relatively successful economically: Venezuela, Brazil, Singapore, South Korea. In addition, there is the greatest success story of any non-European, non-North American country: Japan. What is it about these countries that has allowed them to escape abject poverty? Nor are they examples of autonomous development. In fact, they seem to have benefited greatly from international ties.

In response, it should be noted that no theory can be expected to explain everything. The virtue of good theorizing is that it points out and accounts for commonalities, what particular cases have in common. Anomalies are expected and do not detract from the utility of the theory if it can be adequately explained why a unique case does not fit the general pattern.

Critics comment, however, that globalists such as Wallerstein and the dependency theorists simply group all anomalies under the concept of the semi-periphery, a theoretically and empirically poorly defined concept. Furthermore, what of the insights of authors who argue that there are certain advantages to backwardness when a state is trying to catch up economically with more advanced states? What of the work by scholars who emphasize the importance of different types of state structures, political and social coalitions, and shifting alliances in accounting for the differential modernization success of various countries? Such literature is ignored, it is argued, because the globalist perspective refuses to give due consideration to domestic factors that are not the result of capitalist dynamics.

Defining Alternatives and Science as Ideology

It is argued that some globalists have done a poor job in defining reasonable alternative world futures, let alone strategies, for LDCs to pursue. What is meant, for example, by the call for autonomous development? Is such as goal feasible? How is it to be achieved? What would a world socialist system entail? Would redistributive policies of a world government be combined with political repression and the abuse of power?

Critics also charge that value preferences infuse the globalist work. Globalists, however, are not apologetic for their normative commitment to fundamental changes in the relations between the North and the South. As one noted writer has stated, in analyses of dependency relations "there is no presumption of scientific neutrality." Such works are considered to be "more true because they assume that, by discerning which are the historical agents capable of propelling a process of transformation . . . , these analyses thus grasp the meaning of historical movement and help to negate a given order of domination."[38]

Critics of the dependency literature in particular believe that much of the work seeks less to explain underdevelopment than to unite Third World nationalists and socialists against the West by providing a politically attractive doctrine packaged in social science terms that blames all LDC problems on outside powers. By diverting attention from domestic sources of underdevelopment that have little to do with external factors, the dependency theorists, it is claimed, actually help to perpetuate the very problem they seek to resolve.

Responses

Why has the globalist literature—when it has not been totally ignored—received such a great deal of criticism? Is it simply because it is deserving of such critical scrutiny? Three comments are in order.

First, it is not surprising that most of the criticism comes from scholars working within mainstream North American social science. The vocabulary of the globalist literature is alien to many of these scholars. Analyses based on Marxian insights and categories are generally viewed with distrust in North American universities and often dismissed out of hand. And although some of the globalist work is characterized as being ideological, globalists have similarly surmised that the attacks on them are based less on dispassionate critiques and more on the value preferences of the reviewer. Ideological biases are wrapped in the cloak of supposedly objective criticisms.

Second, it was pointed out that a number of critics charge that the dependency literature in particular has been insufficiently empirical, failing to marshal evidence based on the dictates of scientific behavioralism. Where's the data, they ask? In fact, it is claimed that the empirical testing of selective hypotheses from the dependency literature indicates that these hypotheses do not hold up.

Dependency theorists respond that such a charge is based on the assumption that the behavioralist methods are the only means to comprehend reality. In point of fact, critics argue, there are alternative **epistemological** premises or assumptions from which one can start that question the value of formal hypothesis testing with its often exclusive focus on what can be measured, counted, and added. As one dependency theorist notes:

> The divergence is not merely methodological-formal. It is, rather, at the very heart of studies of dependency. If these studies do in fact have any power of attraction at all, it is not merely because they propose a methodology to substitute for a previously existing paradigm or because they open up a new set of themes. It is principally because they do this from a *radically critical* viewpoint.[39]

Furthermore, many of these supposed empirical tests of dependency hypotheses completely ignore location and timing—the spatial and temporal context in which development occurs. They are, in other words, nonhistorical empirical tests of globalist hypotheses. Empirical tests cognizant of the historical context, by contrast, are said to support dependency propositions.[40] In addition, much of the world-system literature has actually been conspicuously empirical in a number of cross-national studies.[41]

Finally, some of the more insightful criticisms of the globalist literature are not based on antipathy toward the work but are meant to strengthen it by pointing out its weaknesses.[42]

To conclude, judging by the international relations textbooks currently on the market, it is apparent that the globalist perspective is not considered mainstream. Realist and pluralist writers dominate the literature, but this certainly does not mean that the globalist image of international relations is unimportant or undeserving of attention. Its contribution to increased understanding of the world around us should not be seen only as a function of its degree of popularity with professors and textbook publishers. By providing a very different, challenging, and provocative perspective on world politics, it is worthy of attention. After all, as Thomas Kuhn has noted, dominant scientific paradigms of one particular period have a tendency to decay. What is at one time considered to be heretical or at the fringes of "normal science" may one day itself become the prevailing orthodoxy.[43] At a minimum, the globalist perspective should encourage the student of international relations to analyze critically the realist and pluralist images and the assumptions on which they are based. At the maximum, globalist writers have provided challenging hypotheses concerning the dynamics and development of the international system.

NOTES

1. As Robert L. Heilbroner states, "The entire contribution of Marxism to social thought rests ultimately on its effort to penetrate the veil of appearances to discover the hidden essence of things, the web of relations that is the real ground of reality and not the surface manifestations that are its facade." *Marxism: For and Against* (New York: Norton, 1980), p. 49.
2. Terence K. Hopkins, Immanuel Wallerstein, and associates, "Patterns of Development of the Modern World-System," in *World-System Analysis: Theory and Methodology,* ed. Hopkins, Wallerstein, and associates (Beverly Hills, CA: Sage Publications, 1982), p. 72.
3. John A. Hobson, *Imperialism: A Study* (Ann Arbor: University of Michigan Press, 1965), pp. 85–86.
4. For example, see Lenin's "What Is to Be Done?" in *The Lenin Anthology,* ed. Robert C. Tucker (New York: Norton, 1975), pp. 12–114.
5. Others who would later write in this tradition would argue that revolutionaries play more of a role than mere catalysts. They can actually create the conditions for revolution; the "subjective" can create the "objective." This is most explicit in the writings, for example, of Che Guevara, although one also finds shades of it in Mao Zedong's writings on guerrilla warfare. As Karl Marx argued, "Men make their own history, but they do not make it just as they please; they do not make it under circumstances chosen by themselves, but under circumstances directly found, given, and transmitted from the past. The tradition of all dead generations weighs heavily like a nightmare on the brain of the living." "The Eighteenth Brumaire of Louis Bonaparte" in *The Marx-Engels Reader,* ed. Robert C. Tucker (New York: Norton, 1972), p. 436.

6. Rosa Luxemburg, *Reform or Revolution* (New York: Pathfinder Press, 1970, 1973), p. 72. The original publication was in German in 1898 and 1899.

7. Ibid., p. 29.

8. Rosa Luxemburg, *The Accumulation of Capital* (New Haven, CT: Yale University Press, 1951).

9. For important early discussions, see Leon Trotsky, *The Russian Revolution* (New York: Doubleday, 1959); N. I. Bukharin, *Imperialism and World Economy* (New York: International Publishers, 1929); and Eduard Bernstein, *Evolutionary Socialism* (New York: B. W. Huebsch, 1911).

10. See Quintin Hoare, and Geoffrey Nowell Smith, eds. *Selections from the Prison Notebooks.* (New York: International Publishers, 1971), especially Part II, ch. 1 on the Modern Prince, Machiavelli, Marx, voluntarism, and Social Masses, pp. 123–205.

11. *Ibid.*, in the *ideological field*, pp. 60–61, 72, 105, 328, 332–33; in the *social and political field*, pp. 74, 76, 94–96, 100, 157–58, 202–05, 223; and in the *historic field*, pp. 137, 168, 360, 366, 377, 418.

12. See Craig Murphy. "Freezing the North–South Bloc(k) After the East–West Thaw." *Socialist Review* 20, 3 (July–September 1990): 25–46 and reprinted in the second edition of this book (1993), pp. 513–31.

13. W. W. Rostow, *The Process of Economic Growth*, 2d ed. (New York: Norton, 1962).

14. The classic statement is found in Max Weber, *The Protestant Ethic and the Spirit of Capitalism* (New York: Scribner's, 1958).

15. Raul Prebisch, *Towards a Dynamic Development Policy for Latin America* (New York: United Nations, 1963).

16. Theotonio dos Santos, "La crisis del desarrollo, las relaciones de dependencia en America Latina," in *La Dependencia politico-economica de America Latina*, ed. H. Jaguaribe et al. (Mexico, 1970), p. 180, as cited in J. Samuel Valenzuela and Arturo Valenzuela, "Modernization and Dependency: Alternative Perspectives in the Study of Latin American Underdevelopment," *Comparative Politics* 10, no. 4 (July 1978): 544.

17. Osvaldo Sunkel, "Big Business and Dependencia: A Latin American View," *Foreign Affairs* 50, no. 3 (1972): 519–20.

18. Fernando Henrique Cardoso and Enzo Faletto, *Dependency and Development in Latin America* (Berkeley: University of California Press, 1979), p. xvi. See also three works by Samir Amin, *Imperialism and Unequal Development* (New York: Monthly Review Press, 1977); *Neo-Colonialism in West Africa* (New York: Monthly Review Press, 1974); and *Accumulation on a World Scale: A Critique of the Theory of Underdevelopment* (New York: Monthly Review Press, 1974). See also Walter Rodney, *How Europe Underdeveloped Africa* (London: Bogle-l'Ouverture, 1973); Arghiri Emmanuel, *Unequal Exchange* (New York: Monthly Review Press, 1972); A. G. Frank, *World Accumulation, 1492–1789* (New York: Monthly Review Press, 1978).

19. Immanuel Wallerstein, *The Modern World-System I: Capitalist Agriculture and the Origins of the European World-Economy in the Sixteenth Century* (New York: Academic Press, 1974); and *The Modern World-System II: Mercantilism and the Consolidation of the European World-Economy, 1600–1750* (New York: Academic Press, 1980). For a discussion of the non-Marxist elements upon which Wallerstein's work is based, see Robert Brenner, "The Origins of Capitalist Development: A Critique of Neo-Smithian Marxism," *New Left Review* 104 (July–August 1977): 25–92.

20. Kenneth N. Waltz, *Theory of International Politics* (Reading, MA: Addison-Wesley, 1979), p. 38.

21. Immanuel Wallerstein, *The Capitalist World-Economy* (Cambridge, England: Cambridge University Press, 1979), p. 69.

22. Ibid., p. 25.

23. Immanuel Wallerstein, *After Liberalism* (New York: New Press, 1995).

24. Christopher Chase-Dunn, "Interstate System and Capitalist World-Economy: One Logic or Two?" in *World System Structure: Continuity and Change*, ed. W. Ladd Hollist and James N. Rosenau (Beverly Hills, CA: Sage Publications, 1981), p. 31.

25. Patrick J. McGowan with Bohdan Kordan, "Imperialism in World-System Perspective: Britain 1870–1914," in *World System Structure*, ed. Hollist and Rosenau, p. 78.

26. Chase-Dunn, "Interstate System and Capitalist World-Economy," pp. 50–51.

27. Johan Galtung, "A Structural Theory of Imperialism," *Journal of Peace Research* 2 (1971): 81–98.

28. Wallerstein, *Capitalist World-Economy,* p. 67.

29. Hopkins and Wallerstein, "Structural Transformations of the World-Economy," in *World-System Analysis,* pp. 121–122. For a discussion of cycles, see also Wallerstein, *Modern World-System II,* Chapter 1.

30. Ibid., p. 123.

31. For the argument that a new version of capitalism is emerging, see Robert J. S. Ross and Kent Trachte, "The Theory of Global Capitalism and Change in the World System: The New Leviathan." Paper presented at the annual meeting of the International Studies Association, March 1985, Washington, DC.

32. Immanuel Wallerstein, "The Rise and Future Demise of the World Capitalist System," *Comparative Studies in Society and History* 16, no. 4 (September 1974): 387–415, and his "Dependence in an Interdependent World: The Limited Possibilities of Transformation Within the Capitalist World Economy," *African Studies Review* 18, no. 1 (April 1974): 1–26. Christopher Chase-Dunn, ed., *Socialist States in the World-System* (Beverly Hills, CA: Sage Publications, 1982).

33. Hayward R. Alker, Jr., "Dialectical Foundations of Global Disparities," in *World System Structure,* ed. Hollist and Rosenau, pp. 80–109; Johan Galtung, "Global Processes and the World in the 1980s," in *World System Structure,* ed. Hollist and Rosenau, pp. 110–138. Chase-Dunn (also in Hollist and Rosenau, p. 43) states that transformation might involve the dissolution of states, the elimination of economic exchanges between national territories, or the creation of a world state.

34. Augustin Cueva, "A Summary of Problems and Perspectives of Dependency Theory," *Latin American Perspectives* 3, no. 4 (Fall 1976): 12–16. On the need to build a revolutionary party, see Raul A. Fernandez and Jose F. Ocampo, "The Latin American Revolution: A Theory of Imperialism, Not Dependence," *Latin American Perspectives* 1 (Spring 1974): 30–61.

35. Fernando Henrique Cardoso, "The Consumption of Dependency Theory in the United States," *Latin American Research Review* 12, no. 3 (1977): 10–11.

36. Hopkins and Wallerstein, *World-System Analysis,* p. 8.

37. See, for example, Alexander Gerschenkron, *Economic Backwardness in Historical Perspective* (New York: Praeger, 1965); Barrington Moore, *Social Origins of Dictatorship and Democracy* (Boston: Beacon Press, 1966); Theda Skocpol, *States and Social Revolutions* (New York: Cambridge University Press, 1979).

38. Henrique Cardoso, "The Consumption of Dependency Theory," p. 16. See also the comments by James A. Caporaso, "Introduction," *International Organization* 32, no. 1 (Winter 1978): 2–3. A special issue on dependence and dependency.

39. Ibid.

40. David Sylvan and associates, "The Peripheral Economies: Penetration and Economic Distortion," in *Contending Approaches to World System Analysis,* ed. William R. Thompson (Beverly Hills, CA: Sage Publications, 1983), pp. 79–111. See also Raymond Duvall, et al., "A Formal Model of Dependencia Theory: Structure and Measurement," in *From National Development to Global Community,* ed. Richard Merritt and Bruce Russett (London: George Allen & Unwin, 1981), pp. 312–50.

41. See John W. Meyer and Michael T. Hannan, eds., *National Development and the World System: Educational, Economic, and Political Change, 1950–1970* (Chicago: University of Chicago Press, 1979); Albert Bergesen, ed., *Studies of the Modern World-System* (New York: Academic Press, 1980); Richard Rubinson, "The World Economy and the Distribution of Income Within States: A Cross-National Study," *American Sociological Review* 41 (1976): 638–59; and Christopher Chase-Dunn, "The Effects of International Economic Dependence on Development and Inequality: A Cross-National Study," *American Sociological Review* 40 (1975):720–38.

42. See, for example, Theda Skocpol, "Wallerstein's World Capitalist System: A Theoretical and Historical Critique," *American Journal of Sociology* 82, no. 5 (March 1977): 1075–91.

43. Thomas S. Kuhn, *The Structure of Scientific Revolutions* (Chicago: University of Chicago Press, 1970).

SELECTIONS FOR FURTHER READING AND REFERENCE

General

Boggs, Carl. *Gramsci's Marxism*. London: Pluto Press, 1976.

Doyle, Michael W. *Ways of War and Peace*. New York: W. W. Norton, 1997. [Part Three addresses Marxism, Leninism, and Socialism.]

Gramsci, Antonio. *Selections from the Prison Notebooks*, ed. Quentin Hoare and Geoffrey Nowell Smith. New York: International Publishers, 1971.

Heilbroner, Robert. *The Nature and Logic of Capitalism*. New York: W. W. Norton, 1985.

———. *21st Century Capitalism*. New York: W. W. Norton, 1993.

Holm, Hans-Henrik, and Georg Sorensen. *Whose World Order? Uneven Globalization and the End of the Cold War*. Boulder: Westview, 1995.

Jowitt, Kenneth. "After Leninism: The New World Disorder." *Journal of Democracy* 2, 1 (Winter 1991): 11–20.

Murphy, Craig N. *International Organization and Industrial Change*. New York: Oxford University Press, 1994.

Murphy, Craig N., and Roger Tooze, eds. *The New International Political Economy*. Boulder: Lynne Rienner, 1991.

Pala, Ronen P., and Barry Gills, eds. *Transcending the State-Global Divide: A Neostructuralist Agenda in International Relations*. Boulder, CO: Lynne Rienner, 1994.

On Capitalism and the Capitalist World-System

Boswell, Terry, and Immanuel Wallerstein, eds. *Revolution in the World System*. Westport, CT: Greenwood, 1989.

Chase-Dunn, Christopher. *Global Formation: Structures of the World Economy*. Oxford, England: Blackwell, 1989.

Chase-Dunn, Christopher, and Thomas D. Hall, eds. *Core-Periphery Relations in Pre-Capitalist Worlds*. Boulder, CO: Westview, 1991.

Cox, Robert W. *Power, Production, and World Order*. New York: Columbia University Press, 1987.

Frank, Andre Gunder. "A Plea for World System History." *Journal of World History* 2, 1 (Winter 1991).

Galtung, Johan. "A Structural Theory of Imperialism." *Journal of Peace Research*, 2 (1971): 81–98.

Klink, Frank F. "Rationalizing Core-Periphery Relations." *International Studies Quarterly* 34, 2 (June 1990): 183–209.

Murphy, Craig N. "Freezing the North–South Bloc(k) After the East–West Thaw." *Socialist Review* 20, 3 (July–September 1990): 25–46.

Schaeffer, Robert K., and Immanuel Wallerstein, eds. *War in the World-System*. Westport, CT: Greenwood, 1989.

Shannon, Thomas Richard. *An Introduction to the World-System Perspective*. Boulder, CO: Westview 1989.

Skocpol, Theda. "Wallerstein's World Capitalist System: A Theoretical and Historical Critique." *American Journal of Sociology* 82, 5 (March 1977): 1075–90.

Wallerstein, Immanuel. *After Liberalism*. New York: New Press, 1995.

———. *The Capitalist World Economy*. Cambridge, England: Cambridge University Press, 1979.

———. *Geopolitics and Geoculture: Essays on the Changing World System*. New York: Cambridge University Press, 1991.

———. *Historical Capitalism*. London: Verso, 1983.

———. *The Modern World System* I. New York: Academic Press, 1974.

———. *The Modern World System* II. New York: Academic Press, 1980.

———. *The Politics of the World-Economy*. New York: Cambridge University Press, 1984.

———. "The Rise and Future Demise of the World Capitalist System." *Comparative Studies in Society and History* 16, 4 (September 1974): 387–415.

———. "Systeme Mondiale contre Systeme-Monde." *Sociologie et Societe* 22, 2 (October 1990).

On Dependency

Berger, Mark T. *Under Northern Eyes: Latin American Studies and U.S. Hegemony in the Americas, 1898–1990*. Bloomington: Indiana University Press, 1995.

Halebsky, Sandor, and Richard L. Harris. *Capital, Power and Inequality in Latin America*. Boulder, CO: Westview, 1995.

Packenham, Robert. *The Dependency Movement: Scholarship and Politics in Development Studies*. Cambridge, MA: Harvard University Press, 1992.

Tetreault, Mary Ann, and Charles Frederick Abel, eds. *Dependency Theory and the Return of High Politics*. Westport, CT: Greenwood, 1986.

Wendt, Alexander, and Michael Barnett. "Dependent State Formation and Third World Militarization." *Review of International Studies* 19 (1993): 321–47.

Earlier Work

Caporaso, James A. "Dependence, Dependency, and Power in the Global System." *International Organization* 32, 1 (Winter 1978): 13–44.

———. "Dependency Theory: Continuities and Discontinuities in Development Studies." *International Organization* 34, 4 (Autumn 1980): 605–28. [A review essay.]

Cardoso, Fernando Henrique. "Associated-Dependent Development." In *Authoritarian Brazil*, ed. Alfred Stepan. New Haven, CT: Yale University Press, 1973.

———. "The Consumption of Dependency Theory in the United States." *Latin American Research Review* 12, 3 (1977): 7–24.

———. "Dependency and Development in Latin America." *New Left Review* 74 (July–August 1972): 83–95.

———. "Imperialism and Dependency in Latin America." In *Structures of Dependency*, ed. Frank Bonilla and Robert Girling. Stanford, CA: Stanford Institute of Political Studies, 1973.

Cardoso, Fernando and Enzo Faletto. *Dependency and Development in Latin America*. Princeton, NJ: Princeton University Press, 1979.

dos Santos, Theotonio. "The Structure of Dependence." *American Economic Review* 60, 2 (May 1970): 231–36.

Evans, Peter. *Dependent Development*. Princeton, NJ: Princeton University Press, 1979.

Frank, Andre Gunder. *Capitalism and Underdevelopment in Latin America*. London: Penguin, 1971.

———. *Dependent Accumulation and Underdevelopment*. London: Macmillan, 1978.

Prebisch, Raul. *Towards a Dynamic Development Policy for Latin America*. New York: United Nations, 1963.

Smith, Tony. "The Underdevelopment of Development Literature: The Case of Dependency Theory." *World Politics* 31, 2 (January 1979): 247–88.

Sunkel, Osvaldo. "Big Business and Dependencia." *Foreign Affairs* (April 1972).

———. "National Development Policy and External Dependence in Latin America." *Journal of Development Studies* 61 (1969): 23–48.

Valenzuela, J. Samuel, and Arturo Valenzuela. "Modernization and Dependency." *Comparative Politics* 10 (July 1978): 535–57.

The Economic Taproot of Imperialism

J. A. HOBSON

John Hobson discusses the economic taproot, or driving force, of imperialism. A high rate of savings and the power of production outstrip consumption. Industrialists and manufacturers therefore seek foreign sources of investment and markets in Third World countries to solve these problems. Hobson's views had direct influence on Lenin and others who would be highly critical of imperialism as an advanced stage of capitalism.

No mere array of facts and figures adduced to illustrate the economic nature of the new imperialism will suffice to dispel the popular delusion that the use of national force to secure new markets by annexing fresh tracts of territory is a sound and a necessary policy for an advanced industrial country like Great Britain. It has indeed been proved that recent annexations of tropical countries, procured at great expense, have furnished poor and precarious markets, that our aggregate trade with our colonial possessions is virtually stationary, and that our most profitable and progressive trade is with rival industrial nations, whose territories we have no desire to annex, whose markets we cannot force, and whose active antagonism we are provoking by our expansive policy.

But these arguments are not conclusive. It is open to Imperialists to argue thus: "We must have markets for our growing manufactures, we must have new outlets for the investment of our surplus capital and for the energies of the adventurous surplus of our population: such expansion is a necessity of life to a nation with our great and growing powers of production. An ever larger share of our population is devoted to the manufactures and commerce of towns, and is thus dependent for life and work upon food and raw materials from foreign lands. In order to buy and pay for these things we must sell our goods abroad. During the first three-quarters of the nineteenth century we could do so without difficulty by a natural expansion of commerce with continental nations and our colonies, all of which were far behind us in the main arts of manufacture and the carrying trades. So long as England held a virtual monopoly of the world markets for certain important classes of manufactured goods, Imperialism was unnecessary. After 1870 this manufacturing and trading supremacy was greatly impaired: other nations, especially Germany, the United States, and Belgium, advanced with great rapidity, and while they have not crushed or even stayed the increase of our external trade, their competition made it more and more difficult to dispose of

From John A. Hobson, *Imperialism*. Reprinted by permission of George Allen & Unwin.

the full surplus of our manufactures at a profit. The encroachments made by these nations upon our old markets, even in our own possessions, made it most urgent that we should take energetic means to secure new markets. These new markets had to lie in hitherto undeveloped countries, chiefly in the tropics, where vast populations lived capable of growing economic needs which our manufacturers and merchants could supply. Our rivals were seizing and annexing territories for similar purposes, and when they had annexed them closed them to our trade. The diplomacy and the arms of Great Britain had to be used in order to compel the owners of the new markets to deal with us: and experience showed that the safest means of securing and developing such markets is by establishing 'protectorates' or by annexation. The value in 1905 of these markets must not be taken as a final test of the economy of such a policy; the process of educating civilized needs which we can supply is of necessity a gradual one, and the cost of such Imperialism must be regarded as a capital outlay, the fruits of which posterity would reap. The new markets might not be large, but they formed serviceable outlets for the overflow of our great textile and metal industries, and, when the vast Asiatic and African populations of the interior were reached, a rapid expansion of trade was expected to result.

"Far larger and more important is the pressure of capital for external fields of investment. Moreover, while the manufacturer and trader are well content to trade with foreign nations, the tendency for investors to work towards the political annexation of countries which contain their more speculative investments is very powerful. Of the fact of this pressure of capital there can be no question. Large savings are made which cannot find any profitable investment in this country; they must find employment elsewhere, and it is to the advantage of the nation that they should be employed as largely as pos-

sible in lands where they can be utilized in opening up markets for British trade and employment for British enterprise.

"However costly, however perilous, this process of imperial expansion may be, it is necessary to the continued existence and progress of our nation; if we abandoned it we must be content to leave the development of the world to other nations, who will everywhere cut into our trade, and even impair our means of securing the food and raw materials we require to support our population. Imperialism is thus seen to be, not a choice, but a necessity."

The practical force of this economic argument in politics is strikingly illustrated by the later history of the United States. Here is a country which suddenly broke through a conservative policy, strongly held by both political parties, bound up with every popular instinct and tradition, and flung itself into a rapid imperial career for which it possessed neither the material nor the moral equipment, risking the principles and practices of liberty and equality by the establishment of militarism and the forcible subjugation of peoples which it could not safely admit to the condition of American citizenship.

Was this a mere wild freak of spread-eaglism, a burst of political ambition on the part of a nation coming to a sudden realization of its destiny? Not at all. The spirit of adventure, the American "mission of civilization," were as forces making for Imperialism, clearly subordinate to the driving force of the economic factor. The dramatic character of the change is due to the unprecedented rapidity of the industrial revolution in the United States from the eighties onwards. During that period the United States, with her unrivalled natural resources, her immense resources of skilled and unskilled labour, and her genius for invention and organization, developed the best equipped and most productive manufacturing economy the world has yet seen. Fostered by rigid protective tariffs, her metal, textile, tool, clothing, furniture, and other manufactures shot up in a single generation from infancy to full maturity, and, having passed through a period of intense competition, attained, under the able control of great trust-makers, a power of production greater than has been attained in the most advanced industrial countries of Europe.

An era of cut-throat competition, followed by a rapid process of amalgamation, threw an enormous quantity of wealth into the hands of a small number of captains of industry. No luxury of living to which this class could attain kept pace with its rise of income, and a process of automatic saving set in upon an unprecedented scale. The investment of these savings in other industries helped to bring these under the same concentrative forces. Thus a great increase of savings seeking profitable investment is synchronous with a stricter economy of the use of existing capital. No doubt the rapid growth of a population, accustomed to a high and an always ascending standard of comfort, absorbs in the satisfaction of its wants a large quantity of new capital. But the actual rate of saving, conjoined with a more economical application of forms of existing capital, exceeded considerably the rise of the national consumption of manufactures. The power of production far outstripped the actual rate of consumption, and, contrary to the older economic theory, was unable to force a corresponding increase of consumption by lowering prices.

This is no mere theory. The history of any of the numerous trusts or combinations in the United States sets out the facts with complete distinctness. In the free competition of manufactures preceding combination the chronic condition is one of "over-production," in the sense that all the mills or factories can only be kept at work by cutting prices down towards a point where the weaker competitors are forced to close down, because they cannot sell their goods at a price which covers the true cost of production. The first result of the successful formation of a trust or combine is to close down the worse equipped or worse placed mills, and supply the entire market from the better equipped and better placed ones. This course may or may not be attended by a rise of price and some restriction of consumption: in some cases trusts take most of their profits by raising prices, in other cases by reducing the costs of production through employing only the best mills and stopping the waste of competition.

For the present argument it matters not which course is taken; the point is that this concentration of industry in "trusts," "combines," etc. at once limits the quantity of capital which can be effectively employed and increases the share of profits out of which fresh savings and fresh capital will spring. It is quite evident that a trust which is motivated by cut-throat competition, due to an excess of capital, cannot normally find inside the "trusted" industry employment for that portion of the profits which the trust-makers desire to save and to invest. New inventions and other economies of production or distribution within the trade may absorb some of the new capital, but there are rigid limits to this absorption. The trustmaker in oil or sugar must find other investments for his savings: if he is early in the application of the combination principles to his trade, he will naturally apply his surplus capital to establish similar combinations in other industries, economising capital still further, and rendering it ever harder for ordinary saving men to find investments for their savings.

Indeed, the conditions alike of cut-throat competition and of combination attest the congestion of capital in the manufacturing industries which have entered the machine economy. We are not here concerned with any theoretic question as to the possibility of producing by modern machine methods more goods than can find a market. It is sufficient to point out that the manufacturing power of a country like the

United States would grow so fast as to exceed the demands of the home market. No one acquainted with trade will deny a fact which all American economists assert, that this is the condition which the United States reached at the end of the century, so far, as the more developed industries are concerned. Her manufactures were saturated with capital and could absorb no more. One after another they sought refuge from the waste of competition in "combines" which secure a measure of profitable peace by restricting the quantity of operative capital. Industrial and financial princes in oil, steel, sugar, railroads, banking, etc. were faced with the dilemma of either spending more than they knew how to spend, or forcing markets outside the home area. Two economic courses were open to them, both leading towards an abandonment of the political isolation of the past and the adoption of imperialist methods in the future. Instead of shutting down inferior mills and rigidly restricting output to correspond with profitable sales in the home markets, they might employ their full productive power, applying their savings to increase their business capital, and, while still regulating output and prices for the home market, may "hustle" for foreign markets, dumping down their surplus goods at prices which would not be possible save for the profitable nature of their home market. So likewise they might employ their savings in seeking investments outside their country, first repaying the capital borrowed from Great Britain and other countries for the early development of their railroads, mines and manufactures, and afterwards becoming themselves a creditor class to foreign countries.

It was this sudden demand for foreign markets for manufactures and for investment which was avowedly responsible for the adoption of Imperialism as a political policy and practice by the Republican party to which the great industrial and financial chiefs belonged, and which belonged to them. The adventurous enthusiasm of President Theodore Roosevelt and his "manifest destiny" and "mission of civilization" party must not deceive us. It was Messrs. Rockefeller, Pierpont Morgan, and their associates who needed Imperialism and who fastened it upon the shoulders of the great Republic of the West. They needed Imperialism because they desired to use the public resources of their country to find profitable employment for their capital which otherwise would be superfluous. . . .

It is this economic condition of affairs that forms the taproot of Imperialism. If the consuming public in this country raised its standard of consumption to keep pace with every rise of productive powers, there could be no excess of goods or capital clamorous to use Imperialism in order to find markets: foreign trade would indeed exist, but there would be no difficulty in exchanging a small surplus of our manufactures for the food and raw material we annually absorbed, and all the savings that we made could find employment, if we chose, in home industries. . . .

Patterns and Perspectives of the Capitalist World-Economy

IMMANUEL WALLERSTEIN

Professor Wallerstein outlines key concepts and propositions associated with the capitalist world-system. A present-day Marxist scholar, Wallerstein sees capitalism as best understood as a global, system-wide phenomenon.

1. The Nature of the World-Economy

1.1. The concept world-economy (*économie-monde* in French) should be distinguished from that of world economy (*économie mondiale*) or international economy. The latter concept presumes there are a series of separate "economies" which are "national" in scope, and that under certain circumstances these "national economies" trade with each other, the sum of these (limited) contacts being called the international economy. Those who use this latter concept argue that the limited contacts have been expanding in the 20th century. It is thus asserted that the world has become "one world" in a sense it wasn't prior to the 20th century.

By contrast, the concept "world-economy" assumes that there exists an "economy" wherever (and if but only if) there is an ongoing extensive and relatively complete social division of labor with an integrated set of production processes which relate to each other through a "market" which has been "instituted" or "created" in some complex way. Using such a concept, the world-economy is not new in the 20th century, nor is it a coming together of "national economies," none of the latter constituting complete divisions of labor. Rather, a world-economy, capitalist in form, has been in existence in at least part of the globe since the 16th century. Today, the entire globe is operating within the framework of this singular social division of labor we are calling the capitalist world-economy.

1.2. The capitalist world-economy has, and has had since its coming into existence, boundaries far larger than that of any political unit. Indeed, it seems to be one of the basic defining features of a capitalist world-economy that there exists no political entity with ultimate authority in all its zones.

Rather, the political superstructure of the capitalist world-economy is an interstate system within which and through which political structures called "sovereign states" are legitimized and constrained. Far from meaning the total autonomy of decision-making, the term "sovereignty" in reality implies a formal autonomy combined with real limitations on this autonomy, which are implemented both via the explicit and implicit rules of the interstate system and via the power of other states in the interstate system. No state in the interstate system, even the single most powerful one at any

Reprinted with permission of Immanuel Wallerstein and *Contemporary Marxism,* No. 9 San Francisco: Synthesis Publications, 1984. Originally prepared for Seminar on Culture and Thought in the Transformation of the World (third international seminar of the United Nations University Project on Socio-Cultural Development Alternatives in a Changing World), held in Algiers, 13–17 December 1981.

given time, is totally autonomous—but obviously some enjoy far greater autonomy than others.

1.3. The world-economy is a complex of cultures—in the sense of languages, religions, ideologies—but this complex is not haphazard. There exists a *Weltanschauung* of imperium, albeit one with several variants, and there exist cultures of resistance to this imperium.

1.4. The major social institutions of the capitalist world-economy—the states, the classes, the "peoples," and the households—are all shaped (even created) by the ongoing workings of the world-economy. None of them are primordial, in the sense of permanent, pre-existing relatively fixed structures to which the working of the capitalist world economy are exogenous.

1.5. The capitalist world-economy is a *historical* social system. It came into existence, and its genesis must be explained. Its existence is defined by certain patterns—both cyclical rhythms and secular trends—which must be explicated. It is highly probable that it will one day go out of existence (become transformed into another type of historical social system), and we can therefore assess the historical alternatives that are before us.

2. The Patterns of the World-Economy

All historical structures constantly evolve. However, the use of any concept is a capturing in fixed form of some continuing pattern. We could not discern the world, interpret it, or consciously change it unless we used concepts, with all the limitations that any reification, however slight, implies.

2.1. The world-economy has a capitalist mode of production. This is an empirical statement. Although there have been other world-economies (as defined above) known in history, the modern one of which we are speaking is the only one which has survived over a long period of time without either disintegrating or being transformed into a world-empire (with a singu-

lar political structure). This modern one has had a capitalist mode of production—that is, its economy has been dominated by those who operate on the primacy of endless accumulation, such entrepreneurs (or controllers of production units) driving from the arena those who seek to operate on other premises. Since only one world-economy has survived over a long period of time, and since this one has been capitalist in form, we may suspect that the two phenomena are theoretically linked: that a world-economy to survive must have a capitalist mode of production, and inversely that capitalism cannot be the mode of production except in a system that has the form of a world-economy (a division of labor more extensive than any one political entity).

2.2. The capitalist world-economy has operated via a social relationship called capital/labor, in which the surplus created by direct producers has been appropriated by others either at the point of production or at the most immediate market place, in either case by virtue of the fact that the appropriators control the "capital" and that their "rights" to the surplus are legally guaranteed. The extractors of surplus-value may in many cases be individuals, but they have tended increasingly to be collective entities (private or state corporations).

2.3. Once surplus-value has been extracted, it has yet to be "distributed" among a network of beneficiaries. The exchange processes of the "market" are one mode through which this redistribution occurs, in particular, the structure of the world-economy permits an unequal exchange of goods and services (primarily transstate), such that much of the surplus-value extracted in the peripheral zones of the world-economy is transferred to the core zones.

2.4. The exchange of products containing unequal amount of social labor we may call the core/periphery relationship. This is pervasive, continuing, and constant. There tend to be geographical localizations of productive activities such that core-like production activities and periphery-like production activities tend each to be spatially grouped together. We can thus, for shorthand purposes, refer to some states as core states and others as peripheral states.

2.5. Insofar as some states function as loci of mixed kinds of production activities (some core-like, some periphery-like), we can speak of such states as semi-peripheral. There always exist semi-peripheral zones.

2.6. While the pattern of a spatial hierarchy of production processes within the capitalist world-economy is a constant, the position of any given state is not, since there have been regular partial relocations of core-like and periphery-like economic activities.

2.7. Since what makes a production process core-like or periphery-like is the degree to which it incorporates labor-value, is mechanized, and is highly profitable, and all these characteristics shift over time for any given product because of "product cycles," it follows that no product is inherently core-like or periphery-like, but has that characteristic for a given time. Nonetheless, there are always some products which are core-like and others which are periphery-like at any given time.

2.8. Because the imperatives of accumulation operate via the individual decisions of entrepreneurs, each seeking to maximize his profit—the so-called anarchy of production—there is an inherent tendency to the expansion of absolute volume of production in the world-economy. Profit can, however, only be realized if there is effective demand for the global product. World effective demand, however, is a function of the sum of political arrangements in the various states (the result of prior class struggles), which determine the real distribution of the global surplus. These arrangements are stable for intermediate periods of time. Consequently, world supply expands at a steady rate while world demand remains relatively fixed for intermediate periods. Such a system must result, and historically has resulted, in recurring bottlenecks for accumulation, which are translated into periods of economic stagnation. The A-phases of expansion and the B-phases of stagnation seem to have occurred historically in cycles of 40–55 years (sometimes called "Kondratieff cycles").

2.9. Each period of stagnation has created pressures to restructure the network of production processes and the social relations that underlie them in ways that would overcome bottlenecks to accumulation. Among the mechanisms that have operated to renew expansion are:

a. reduction of production costs of former core-like products by further mechanization and/or relocation of these activities in lower-wage zones;

b. creation of new core-like activities ("innovation"), which promise high initial rates of profit, thus encouraging new loci of investment;

c. an intensified class struggle both within the core states and between groups located in different states such that there may occur at the end of the process some political redistribution of world surplus to workers in core zones (often by means of fully proletarianizing hitherto semi-proletarian households) and to bourgeois in semi-peripheral and peripheral zones, thereby augmenting world effective demand;

d. expansion of the outer boundaries of the world-economy, thereby creating new pools of direct producers who can be involved in world production as semi-proletarianized workers receiving wages below the cost of reproduction.

2.10. States in which core-like activities occur develop relatively strong state apparatuses which can advance the interests of their bourgeoisies, less by protection (a mechanism of the medium-strong seeking to be stronger) than by preventing other states from erecting political barriers to the profitability of these activities. In general, states seek to shape the world market in ways that will advance the interests of some entrepreneurs against that of others.

2.11. There seem to be cycles as well, within the interstate system. On three separate occasions, one state has been able to achieve what may be called a hegemonic position in the world-economy: the United Provinces, 1620–1650; the United Kingdom, 1815–1873; the United States, 1945–1967. When producers located within a given state can undersell producers located in other core states in the latter's "home market," they can over time transform this production advantage into one in the commercial arena and then into one in the financial arena. The combined advantages may be said to constitute hegemony and are selected as well in a political-military advantage in the interstate system. Such hegemonies are relatively short-lived, since the production advantages cannot be sustained indefinitely and mechanisms of the balance of power intrude to reduce the political advantage of the single most powerful state.

2.12. The core states in general, and the hegemonic state when one exists in particular, seek to reinforce the advantages of their producers and to legitimize their role in the interstate system by imposing their cultural dominance on the world. To some extent, this occurs in the easily visible form of language, religion, and mores, but more importantly this occurs in the form of seeking to impose modes of thought and analysis, including in particular the paradigms that inform philosophy and the sciences/social sciences.

3. The Secular Trends of the World-Economy

The patterns of the world-economy may be at first glance cyclical in form, but they are not perfectly cyclical. The world-economy has a historical development which is structural and can be analyzed in terms of its secular trends.

3.1. The drive to accumulate leads to the constant deepening of the capitalist development. The search to reduce long-term costs of production leads to a steady increase in the degree to which production is mechanized. The search for the least expensive source of factors of production (including as an expense delays in time in acquiring access) leads to a steady increase in the degree to which these factors (land, labor, and goods) are commodified. The desire to reduce barriers to the process of accumulation leads to a steady increase in the degree to which economic transactions are contractualized. It is important to recognize two things about these processes of mechanization, commodification, and contractualization.

3.1.1. While there are regular increases in the world-economy taken as a whole of the degree of mechanization, commodification, and contractualization, the pattern is not linear but stepwise, each significant advance leading to overall expansion, and each overall stagnation leading to a restructuring of the world-economy such that there is further advance.

3.1.2. The capitalist development of the world-economy at the world level is far from complete in the 20th century. These processes are still in full operation.

3.2 The recurring stagnations of the world-economy, which have led to the regular restructuring of this world-economy, have involved as part of restructuring the expansion of the "outer" boundaries of the world-economy, a process which, however, has been nearly completed as of now. This expansion, which was central to world history of the past several hundred years, gradually eliminated from the globe other kinds of historical social systems, creating the historically unique situation of there being for all effects and purposes, a single social division of labor on the earth.

3.3 The steady but still incomplete commodification of labor, side by side with the now largely completed expansion of the outer boundaries of the world-economy, accounts for the shape of two of the major institutional structures of the capitalist world-economy: the classes and the households.

3.3.1. The commodification of labor ultimately means a structure in which direct producers have no access to the means of production except by selling their labor-power on a market; that is, they become proletarians. Although the percentage of direct producers who are full-lifetime proletarians has been growing worldwide over time, nonetheless, even today such proletarians are still probably no more than half of the world's work force.

3.3.2 The commodification of land and capital ultimately means a structure in which controllers of land or capital (including "human capital") have no access to the maintenance and reproduction of land and capital except by pursuing an active policy of maximizing the accumulation of capital; that is, they become bourgeois. In the 20th century, there are very few who control land or capital—directly (individually) or indirectly (collectively)—who are not bourgeois, that is, persons whose economic raison d'être is the accumulation of capital.

3.3.3. Hence, we have a situation in which a *part but not all* of the direct producers are (full-lifetime) proletarians (the other part we may designate as "semi-proletarians"), but *most* of the controllers of land and capital are bourgeois.

3.3.4. The creation of two large worldwide classes has led to the molding of appropriate household structures as the member-units of these classes. We mean by household the unit which, over a longish (30–50 year) period, pools the income of all its members, from whatever source and in whatever form is this income.

3.3.5. The "semi-proletarian" household, so extensive in peripheral zones in the world-economy, permits the wage-employment of some of its members for parts of their lives at wages below the proportionate cost of reproduction by pooling this wage-income with that received from subsistence, petty commodity, rental, and transfer income. This is what is meant by "super-exploitation" (since in this case the employer of the wage-laborer is receiving not merely the surplus-value created by the wage-

laborer, but that which other members of the household are creating).

3.3.6. The proletarian household, tending to receive wage-income approximating the real costs of reproduction (no less but also not much more) tends to move in the direction of more "nucleated" households, sloughing off *affines* and others not defined as pulling their full weight.

3.3.7. The bourgeois household, seeking to maximize the use of capital, the direct control of which tends to increase by age, and utilizing the family structure as the primary mechanism of avoiding social redistribution, tends to take the form of extended, multilocal households.

3.4 The steady (now largely completed) expansion of the outer boundaries of the world-economy, combined with the continuing competition among bourgeois for advantage in the capitalist world-economy, accounts for the shape of the other two major institutional structures of the capitalist world-economy: the states and the peoples.

3.4.1. The drive of bourgeois for competitive advantage has led to increasing definition ("power") of the states as political structures and increasing emphasis on their constraint by the interstate system. This push for a "strong" state (strong vis-à-vis both other internal loci of power and vis-à-vis other states and external nonstate forces) has been greatest and therefore most efficacious in those states with core-like production activities. The strong state has been the principal mechanism by which the bourgeois controlling these core-like production activities have been able a) to limit and moderate the economic demands of their national work forces, b) to shape the world market so as to compete effectively with bourgeoisies located in other states, and c) to incorporate new zones into the world-economy, thus constantly re-creating new centers of peripheral production activities.

3.4.2. The increasing definition of state structures has led to the shaping, reshaping, creation, destruction, and revival of "peoples." To the extent that these "peoples" are defined by themselves (and by others) as controlling or having the "moral" right to control state structures, these "peoples" become "nations." To the extent that they are not defined as having the right to control a state structure, these people become "minorities" or "ethnic groups." Defining given states as nation–states is an aid in strengthening the state. Such a definition requires emphasizing one "people" and de-emphasizing, even destroying (conceptually or literally), others. This is particularly important for semi-peripheral states seeking to transform their structural role in the world-economy. Various groups have interests supporting and opposing any particular nation–state definition. "Nationalism" is a mechanism both of imperium/integration and of resistance/liberation. The peoples are not haphazardly defined but neither are they simple and unfixed derivations from a historical past. They are solidarity groupings whose boundaries are a matter of constant social transmittal/redefinition.

3.5. As the classes come to be defined vis-à-vis the developing division of labor in the world-economy and the peoples come to be defined vis-à-vis the increasing rationalized interstate system, the locational concentration of various oppressed groups gives rise over time to anti-systemic movements. These movements have organized in two main forms around two main themes: the social movement around "class" and the national movement around "nation" or people.

3.5.1. The seriously anti-systemic (or revolutionary) forms of such movements first emerged in *organized* form in the 19th century. Their general objective, human equality, was by definition incompatible with the functioning of the capitalist world-economy, a hierarchical system based on uneven development, unequal exchange, and the appropriation of surplus-value. However, the political structure of the capitalist world-economy—the fact that it was

not a single unit but a series of sovereign states —pressed the movements to seek the transformation of the world-system via the achievement of political power within separate states. The organization of these anti-systemic movements at the state level had contradictory effects.

3.5.2. Organization at the state level for the social movement was ideologically confusing from the beginning, as it counterposed the logical and ideological necessity of worldwide struggle (proletarian internationalism) against the immediate political need of achieving power within one state. Either the social movement resisted "nationalism" and was rendered inefficacious or it utilized nationalism and then faced ambiguously the so-called "national question" —that is, the "nationalisms" of the "minorities" within the boundaries of the state. Whatever the tactic of a given social movement, the achievement of partial or total state power involved power in a structure constrained by the interstate system, hence unable by itself to transform the system entirely (that is, to withdraw totally from the capitalist world-economy).

3.5.3. Organization at the state level created dilemmas for the national movements as well. The smaller the zone within which the national movement defined itself, the easier the access to state power but the less consequential. Hence, all national movements have oscillated in terms of the unit of definition, and the various "pan-" movements have had limited success. But defeats of "pan-" movements have tended to dilute the anti-systemic thrust of particular national movements.

3.5.4. In general, both social and national movements have had a difficult time reconciling long-run anti-systemic objectives and short-run "developmentalist" or "catching-up" objectives, which tend to reinforce rather than undermine the world-system. Nonetheless, the collective momentum of the social and national movements over time has been anti-systemic in effect, despite the "reformism" or "revisionism" of the various movements taken separately. Furthermore, the collective momentum of these movements has been such as to confound increasingly the social and national movements, which has in fact been a source of additional strength.

3.6. The unfolding of the institutional structures of the world-system—the classes, the states, the peoples, the households—has been reflected in the cultural mosaic of the world-system, whose pattern has been increasingly that of the tension between imperium and resistance.

3.6.1. As the axial division of labor became more pronounced and more unequal, the need to facilitate its operation through the allocation of work forces and the justification of inequality led to an ideology of racism that became the central organizing cultural theme of the world bourgeoisie. The existence of superior groups (whether in particular instances these groups were defined as Caucasians or Anglosaxons or other variants on this theme) became a method of simple *triage* in job and income allocation.

3.6.2. Whereas racism has served as a mechanism of worldwide control of direct producers, the bourgeoisie of strong core states (and particularly of the hegemonic power) sought also to direct the activities of the bourgeois of other states and various middle strata worldwide into channels that would maximize the close integration of production processes and the smooth operation of the interstate system such that the accumulation of capital was facilitated. This required the creation of a world bourgeois cultural framework that could be grafted onto "national" variations. This was particularly important in terms of science and technology, but quite important too in the realm of political ideas and of the social sciences.

3.6.3. The concept of a neutral "universal" culture to which the cadres of the world division of labor would be "assimilated" (the passive tense being important here) hence came to serve as one of the pillars of the world-system as it historically evolved. The exaltation of progress, and later of "modernization," summarized this set of ideas, which served less as true norms of social action than as status-symbols of obeisance and of participation in the world's upper strata.

3.6.4. Resistance to this cultural assimilationism was to be found among competitive bourgeois in semi-peripheral and nonhegemonic core states and took the form of asserting the autonomy of "national" traditions and/or antipathy to structural generalizations in the domain of ideas. It also took the form of reinforcing alternative world linguistic groupings to the hegemonic one (in practice, of English).

3.6.5. More fundamental cultural resistance on the part of anti-systemic movements has come slowly to take the form of positing civilizational alternatives to dominant cultural forms. In particular, it has counterdistinguished civilizations (plural) to civilization (singular and imperial).

4. The System in Crisis

4.1. A system that has cyclical patterns has recurring downturns, whatever we wish to call them. We have argued the regularity of world economic stagnations as one of the patterns of the capitalist world-economy. But insofar as there are also mechanisms that regularly bring these stagnations to an end and relaunch world economic expansion, we cannot count these cyclical downturns as crises, however much they are perceived as such by the individuals living through them.

4.2. Rather, a "crisis" is a situation in which the restitutive mechanisms of the system are no longer functioning well, and therefore the system will either be transformed fundamentally or disintegrate. It is in this sense that we could talk for example of the "crisis of feudalism" in Europe in the period 1300–1450, a crisis whose resolution was the historical emergence of a capitalist world-economy located in that particular geographic arena. We may say that this capitalist world-economy in turn entered into a long "crisis" of a comparable nature in the 20th century, a crisis in the midst of which we are living.

4.3. The causes of the crisis are internal to the system, the result of the contradictions built into the process.

4.3.1. One of the mechanisms whereby the world-economy has overcome its downturn phases has been the expansion of the outer boundaries of the world-economy, but this is a process which has inbuilt limits which are nearly reached.

4.3.2. Another of the mechanisms whereby the world-economy has overcome its downturn phases has been the expansion of world effective demand, in part through proletarianization of the direct producers, in part by redistribution of the surplus among the world bourgeoisie.

4.3.2.1. Proletarianization is also a process that has inbuilt limits. While they have hardly yet been reached, the process has been speeding up, and one can foresee it reaching its asymptote within the coming century.

4.3.2.2. Redistribution of the surplus among the bourgeoisie is itself the result of bourgeoisification, which has entailed an increase of the total percentage of the world population who are bourgeois. If one distinguishes between the small group of bourgeois who control most of the fixed capital and the much larger group of bourgeois who control principally human capital, the growth and social concentration of the latter group have resulted in their acquisition of considerable political power in core states. They have been able, as the price of their political support for the world-system as a system, to ensure that an increasing proportion of the appropriated surplus will be redistributed to them, reducing over the long run the rate of profit to the holders of fixed capital.

4.4. Increasing proletarianization and the increasing constraint on individual mobility because of the degree to which definitions of peoples have been linked to position in the world-economy have led to the rise of the anti-systemic movements. These movements have a cumulative effect which may be said to draw a logarithmic curve. We have entered into the phase of acute escalation.

4.5. The fact that we are in a systemic crisis and have been in one at least since the Russian Revolution—which was its symbolic detonator and has always been seen as such—does not mean that the capitalist development of the world-economy has come to an end. Quite the contrary. It is as vigorous as ever, perhaps more so. This is indeed the prime cause of the crisis. The very vigor of capitalist development has been and will continue to be the main factor that exacerbates the contradictions of the system.

4.6. It is therefore not the case that the crisis will be imminently resolved. A crisis of a system is a long, slow, difficult process, and for it to play itself out over a 150-year period is scarcely surprising. We have little perspective on it as we are amidst it, and we therefore tend to exaggerate each minor fork in the road. There is some constructive value in being overly optimistic in a short run, but the negative side of such exaggeration is the disillusionments it breeds. A crisis is best navigated by a cool, long-run strategy. It cannot however be totally planned, as the crisis itself gives rise to new possibilities of human action. . . .

The Neostructuralist Agenda in International Relations

BARRY GILLS & RONEN P. PALAN

"Neostructuralists" focus on the "specific patterns of transformative processes" at work in the local, national, or global-level systems and try "to analyze and explain the social and structural forces" that are "arrayed in these transformative processes." States are not so much units as they "are disaggregated into classes, social forces, institutions, individuals, genders, races, peoples, regions, localities" and the like. The state is often presented as "an articulation of class interests."

For most of this century the discipline of International Relations was normally presumed to treat the relations *between* states, the latter viewed as cohesive social actors driven by their desire for power and prestige. The raison d'être of the discipline was originally to provide a social science explanation and solution for the pressing problems of war and peace plaguing the modern world order. As political acts of sovereign states, war and peace focused attention on the interaction state A had with state B, and with state C and so on, in terms of narrowly defined "political relations." International Relations theory was about understanding the patterning of these relations, conceived of at the level of high politics; usually diplomacy, alliances, and war behavior. In this burning concern with human destiny, given greater urgency with the advent of nuclear weapons, there seemed to be little place for scholastic squabbling over the finer aspects of state theory, let alone what appeared to be esoteric methodological debates. The internal workings of states, as policymaking units and actors in international relations, were often scrutinized, no doubt, but with a definite reluc-

tance to go beyond certain limits. The intricate nature of the domestic political process was therefore recognized from time to time, but recognition never extended to the essential theoretical framework. In practice International Relations appeared increasingly complex and multifaceted, but in "theory" it was still about the interactions of volitional unities seeking power and prestige.

With mounting evidence to the contrary, it was not simply the fantasy of an utterly cohesive state sharing human sensibilities—"sensitive and vulnerable" (according to Keohane and Nye); endowed with "survival instincts" (Waltz); "friendly," "distrustful" (Wolfers)—which began to be questioned (but seldom challenged). It was also the myth of the utility of the "billiard ball" model which had been exploded—and comprehensively so. In recent debates it has been more widely recognized that in order to adequately address these central questions, so defined, economic and socioeconomic relations are fundamental elements of any explanatory framework. For some, however, the critical question remains: What *is* the appropriate subject matter of the discipline of International Relations? Neorealism moved a step closer to addressing a wider set of economic and societal relations that are seen as partly determinant of the outcomes in high politics among state actors. But the neorealists addressed these wider issues, it seems, in order to neutralize them: already announcing that the "survival instinct (of states) rules the world," one has no recourse but to accept all other potential political concerns—profit, for instance—as secondary. But the neorealists never convincingly proved that "survival instincts" (*whose* instincts exactly is never clear) indeed rule the world.

To some, neorealists and regime theorists represent the state of the art of mainstream International Relations. However, the agenda of International Relations has been further broadened in recent years and its fundamental questions are posed entirely anew by an entirely different tradition. However, like the flickering transmission of stars from another galaxy, we hear only fragments of thoughts of this tradition: names such as Fernand Braudel, Karl Polanyi, Antonio Gramsci, and even Michael Mann and Nicos Poulantzas are mentioned. But there is no apparent logic or history to this tradition—nor is it entirely clear what its implications are for the discipline of International Relations. One sometimes hears of dependency theory and world-systems analysis: but much has happened since Frank published his seminal book on *Development and Underdevelopment in Latin America* (1967) and Wallerstein his *Modern World System* (1974).

In our view, some of the most exciting recent contributions to the study of globalization and the states system have originated in this theoretical space. It is the expressed design [here] . . . to bridge this gap by attempting to unite these scattered flickerings into something approaching a coherent agenda. In organizing this [effort] . . . , our purpose has been twofold: first, we wanted to bring together some of the more innovative thinkers on these issues. The reader will find that these are not necessarily names that will immediately be associated with International Relations—rather they are drawn from a variety of disciplines, each concerned with certain aspects of the international system. Second, and perhaps more importantly, by presenting them together in a single work, we hope to demonstrate that amongst apparently disparate studies a new consensus may be emerging around certain key concepts and methodological questions.

What, then, is the nature of this common agenda? In our view, the contributors [in this effort] seek to bridge several important gaps in the International Relations literature. First and foremost, the emerging new agenda entails a shift in focus from the interaction between supposedly discrete unities to the dynamics of social development within the international system as a whole. Formerly, the dominant theories of state transformation took each state to be an ontologically distinct and organic entity. The preponderance of theoretical work during the postwar period was unilinear and evolutionary, privileging endogenous factors of change over exogenous or "external" "international" stimuli of transformation. These dominant theories of state and societal transformation identified each state with a single society which, however, evolved according to the pattern preestablished by the most advanced states. What was in fact a theory derived from this specific world-historical time frame presented itself as universal and timeless. Both modernization theory and even much of what passed as orthodox "development" were examples of this tendency.

The structural approach represented by both dependency theory and world-system theory sought to counter these prevailing orthodoxies. They shifted the analytical focus away from the single nation or state-society and toward what were posited to be governing processes of state and societal transformation occurring globally. These world processes were largely determinant of processes at lower levels in the structural hierarchy of the world. Though this counterattack was welcomed by many, it still suffered from a tendency to focus too intently on the governing processes on the world scale without always sufficiently problematizing the domestic level of response and transformation. This gave rise to a positional preoccupation, which though often useful and explanatory in many ways, sometimes contributed to holding back further extension of the sociological agenda of inquiry into the state/society transformations occurring at other levels.

Partly as a result of the well-known criticism of structuralism, structuralist research is now moving into a new era that may be called neostructuralism. Neostructuralism, however, is not a compromise between past structuralist and neorealist positions. It is an attempt to redefine the very focus of inquiry within a new conceptualization of International Relations. Neostructuralism asks how global processes interact with other processes of state/societal transformation occurring at many other levels of the world system. It posits that the subject matter of International Relations is not only foreign policy or power patterns, as in realism and neorealism, nor only economically derived positional relations, as in much structuralist analysis. All of the above are constituent elements in larger state/societal transformative processes of the world as a whole. All states and societal forces in the modern world participate in these global governing processes and in the many levels of response to them. Therefore, the first-order questions of neostructuralist approaches to International Relations are on the order of how state/society transformation at level A is affected by and in turn affects the transformations at level B, and C, and so on. *It is the transformative processes themselves that are placed at the center of analysis.*

The neostructuralist approach suggests an entirely new conception of the real subject matter of International Relations. Rather than the mere relations among states—narrowly defined as governments—the subject matter is an overall transformative process wherein all states and societal forces are constantly being transformed through participation in the world system as a whole in terms of their fundamental characteristics and structure. Neostructuralism seeks to analyze and explain the social and structural forces, including the conjunctural, arrayed in these transformative processes.

In this sense International Relations in neostructuralist terms can be regarded as a *vast transmission mechanism* and stimulus for state and societal transformations: stimulated by and responded to at the global level as well as at many other definable levels, all of which are intricately interwoven. The "strong" as well as the "weak," and the "advanced" as well as the "backward" all mutually participate in this transmission of transformative pressures. The specific patterns of these transformative processes are therefore the proper empirical subject matter of International Relations. This is the main idea we wish to advance. . . . This approach transcends any strict dichotomies between levels of the world system and does not restrict the category "state" to discrete territorial "nation-states," nor does it restrict the category "society" or social forces to the single-state framework. Indeed, it does not adhere to any of the former sacrosanct discrete systems boundaries. Thereby it counteracts both the unilinearity of evolutionary theories bounded by the state and its endogenous factors on the one hand, and offers a new antidote to the dangers of oversystematizing the world processes identified by structural theories, without abandoning some of the useful aspects of either.

By refocusing on the transformative processes, the neostructuralists seek—and this is the second plank of neostructuralism—to *problem-*

atize the concept of the state. Indeed, the entire approach is rooted in, and enters into dialogue with, state theory. This contrasts sharply with both traditional International Relations and the structuralist approach, which have often tended to take the state for granted. But in placing the stress on the state and state theory, the neostructuralists distance themselves also from the more recent neo-Weberian approaches. This . . . may remind some readers of an earlier collection edited by Evans, Rueschmeyer, and Skoçpol titled *Bringing the State Back In* (1985). . . . Our aim is somewhat similar to theirs in that we wish to strengthen the link between sociological theories of the state and International Relations. Nonetheless, [this effort] differs from that of Evans et al. in three vital respects. First, whereas Evans et al. hold to a "Weberian" or "statist" theory of the state, the neostructuralists are, by and large, nearer to what Bob Jessop described as the "relational theory of the state" (1985).

The main difficulty we find with the neo-Weberians' perspective is that it shares the traditional realists' perception of the state as a cohesive actor, albeit this time the state is no longer equated with society at large, but with the bureaucratic machinery that is legally defined as the state. In doing so, the neo-Weberians are making a number of critical but unwarranted assumptions: they idealize the state-bureaucracy, its aims and functions, and yet possess at the same time an exaggerated perception of its powers. They appear to accept what Wallerstein called "the ideology of statism" at face value, namely, the self-glorification of the bureaucracy as a functionally neutral social body solely concerned with the pursuit of the common good and the "national interest." Krasner, for instance, argues that it can be demonstrated empirically that: "The objective sought by the state cannot be reduced to some summation of private desires. These objectives can be called appropriately the national interest" (1978, 5). Mann repeats the famous Weberian theme of

the enabling, socially (and implicitly class-) neutral state:

> The four most persistent types of state activities are:
>
>   1. The maintenance of internal order. . . .
>   2. Military defence/aggression, directed against foreign foes. . . .
>   3. The maintenance of communications infrastructures. . . .
>   4. Economic redistribution: the authoritative distribution of scarce material resources . . . different ecological niches, age-groups, sexes, regions, classes, etc. (1984, 120, 121).

This view idealizes, reifies, and mystifies the state: it is far too one-sided. Braudel's position, which may be regarded as broadly representative of the views taken [here] . . . , provides what we regard to be a more accurate picture of the role of the state: "The state was there to preserve inequality, the cornerstone of the social order. Culture and its spokesmen were generally on hand to preach resignation to one's lot" (1979, II, 515). Mann and Skoçpol do concede, as an afterthought, that the state plays a significant class role. Skoçpol, for instance, accepts that "states usually do function to preserve existing economic and class structures" (1979, 30). But their theoretical framework is not attentive enough to the subtleties of political power and process: of the nature of political power, its attainment and maintenance. The very assumption of the unity of function and purpose of the bureaucracy stands in the way of the more difficult task of understanding the intricate character of political power.

At the same time, the neo-Weberians credit the bureaucracy with a large measure of autonomy. Naturally, the greater the degree of autonomy and cohesiveness attained by the bureaucracy, the lesser the importance attached to the domestic political processes. Like traditional realists, neo-Weberians therefore often ignore or downplay the importance of the domestic political process. As a consequence, the relations between domestic processes and global processes are not explored properly.

In contrast to the neo-Weberians, the neostructuralists stress the secondary role of the government and regime in relation to socioeconomic structures. The state itself is no longer seen as a set of institutions or a cohesive actor but as a type of social relations, an articulation of class interests within a given territorial context. Several of the neostructuralists prefer to talk to the "social formation" rather than the state. We may say that the neostructuralists focus on state theory, not on the state. Consequently, as the focus is brought back to the state, the state as a *category* is likewise deprivileged and placed within a wider sociological context transcending discrete state boundaries. In the best tradition of sociological investigation of state and power, states are disaggregated into classes, social forces, institutions, individuals, genders, races, peoples, regions, localities, and so forth. It is then reassembled not as a unified consciousness, but as a complex play of forces that shapes and is in turn reshaped by socioeconomic forces, domestic and international culture, and ideologies.

It is important to bear in mind, therefore, that when [neostructuralists] speak of "the state," they do not have a political subject, let alone an object, in mind. To neostructuralists, the "state" cannot be a volitional subject: it has no needs, it does not pursue "power and prestige," it does not possess a unique agenda. It is not an "it." Indeed, the very question "What is the state?" although undoubtedly a legitimate one, may set us on the wrong course. For the question implicitly suggests that we are dealing with a unit, a phenomenon, whereas in reality, the only way of understanding the state as a working concern is to view it as "the heart of political power" (Poulantzas 1978, 81). It is, as [Alain] Lipietz . . . approvingly quotes Marx and Engels: "the apparatus by which society equips

itself in order that the different groups of which it is constituted do not exhaust themselves in a struggle without end."

State policies therefore cannot be explained in terms of a volitional being: the state does not pursue a "national interest," it possesses no distinct "reason of state." State policies must be explained therefore by other means. Central to the neostructuralist agenda is the concern with the interrelation between policies and the wider socioeconomic and ideological domestic and international setting.

Finally, the neostructuralists share a common perception of the notion of totality or the "international system." We have been accustomed in International Relations to view the entire globe as a single unidimensional framework of activities. The organizing concepts of such a globalized system range from the "international society" (Bull), the "system of states" (Morgenthau, Wight), the "world-system" (Wallerstein), and so on. Each of these organizing concepts suggests that the entire international system operates to the tune of one logic and uniform rhythm. The neostructuralists share a common concern to correct this one-dimensional theory of the international system. The essence of neostructuralism lies in the conviction that there are inherent limitations in the capacity of global or international patterns to create totalizing systems. The reason being that any one-dimensional global system negates, by its very nature, the myriad of transformative processes, be they at the local, national, or global level, which are at the heart of this analysis.

Since the neostructuralists reject the notion of one unifying transnational totality, they are naturally faced with the question of how the "separate" levels and instances relate to each other in any given situation. The neostructuralists respond to this problem by elevating the concept of the historical conjuncture. The "whole," or what the structuralists call the world-system, is thought by the neostructuralists to consist of a multiplicity of factors. Each of these factors needs to be understood at one and the same time in isolation, i.e., as a separate system—thus, [Susan] Strange, for instance, talks of four systems: security, finance, production, and knowledge—but at the same time, in relation to the wider picture. The conjuncture is the historical moment where these various factors meet and combine to produce specific outcomes. The conjuncture therefore suggests that any given historical event must ultimately be explained in its given historical context. There must be, in other words, a certain distance between theory and history.

Ultimately neostructuralism may be read as a call for more modesty on the part of theorists: theory can help explain so much but no more. What we therefore hope the reader will find . . . is less a new unified theory of International Relations and more a new spirit of dialogue among scholars from a variety of disciplines concerned with a similar set of issues. This spirit is animated by an underlying basic methodological and philosophical affinity as to their view of the underlying forces shaping the international system. It is this affinity that creates the basis for a common agenda. While the unsuspecting reader might be prone to see neostructuralism as just another approach to a discipline that already appears to be in general disarray, we feel, on the contrary, that [there is] . . . a more profound movement toward a set of issues different from those that have traditionally occupied the discipline of International Relations. In other words, neostructuralism is here to stay. For not only have the methodological and philosophical concerns of the neostructuralists been incorporated to varying degrees by existing approaches, but

now, with the end of the Cold War, these concerns at last have an opportunity to blossom into a consistent body of thought in its own right. But even more so, neostructuralism is bound to flourish because, paradoxically, although it may appear at first sight to make a sharp break from traditional International Relations theories, it draws its strength in fact from a renewal of the classical tradition of political economy. It was this very break with the classical tradition of political economy that severely impoverished the discipline of International Relations throughout the Cold War period. And as shown throughout history, it is often by way of a creative return to the classics that we come to gain a more profound understanding of the present.

Bibliography

Braudel, Fernand. *The Perspective of the World: Civilization and Capitalism, 15th–18th Century*. V. II. New York: Harper and Row, 1979.

Bull, Hedley. *The Anarchical Society*. New York: Columbia University Press, 1977.

Jessop, Bob. *State Theory: Putting Capitalist States in Their Place*. London: Polity, 1990.

Krasner, Stephen. *Defending the National Interest*. Princeton: Princeton University Press, 1978.

Mann, Michael. "The Autonomous Power of the State." *Archives europeenes de sociologie* V. 25 (1984): 185–213.

Morgenthau, Hans. *Politics Among Nations*. 4th ed. New York: Knopf, 1967.

Poulantzas, Nico. "The Capitalist State: A Reply to Miliband and Laclau." *New Left Review* 95 (January–February 1976): 65–83.

Skoçpol, Theda. *States and Social Revolutions*. Cambridge: Cambridge University Press, 1979.

Wallerstein, Immanuel. *The Modern World System*. V. 1. New York: Academic Press, 1974.

Wight, Martin. *Systems of States*. Leicester: Leicester University Press, 1974.

International Organization and Industrial Change

CRAIG N. MURPHY

In a nondeterminist (or voluntarist) formulation, the author relies conceptually on the Italian Marxist Antonio Gramsci's bloc concept, referring to ideas and values concretized as institutional or international organizations designed to serve identifiable interests in a capitalist, global economy. International organizations emerge from global capitalism and perform functions to maintain the global political economy.

Today's system of self-regarding territorial governments recognizing no higher authority can be traced back as far as Italy's early modern trading states, where some of today's oldest private fortunes also began. Dante's *Monarchia,* of around 1310, began the tradition of criticizing this modern—originally, strictly *European*—state system and advocating its replacement with a universal government (Hinsley 1963; Parkinson 1977: 143–54). The tradition continues. We still hear calls for a more universal government, now a *world* government, that would resolve the contradictions within the now globalized European state system and even humanize its fraternal twin, modern capitalism (Lens 1983; Chase-Dunn 1990).

While I, too, am critical of both the state system and the modern world economy, [mine] is not another call for world government. Nor is it a challenge to shape the nature of a world government that will "inevitably" develop in the near future, like the one issued by Saul Mendlovitz for the World Order Models Project in the early 1970s. Unlike Mendlovitz, I do not believe we are living at the beginning of the first century of world government, although, in some ways, we may be living at its end. I expect that the world government we will have at the end of this century will differ little from the world government that existed when the century began. It will be no more, or less, significant.

One of the best ways to explore *global governance,* what world government we actually have had, is to consider the history of *world organizations,* those intergovernmental and quasi-governmental global agencies that have (nominally) been open to any independent state (even though all states may not have joined). Such institutions have existed since the 1860s, the result of diplomatic efforts that began more than a decade before. Some world organizations have contributed to substantive regulation of world society. Others have pointed to the existence of governance exercised elsewhere, for example, through the widespread adoption of similar national regulations, the enforcement of formal international agreements by a few powerful states, and the global imposition of rules by private, transnational associations. Others, the smallest number, have just been reflections of utopian dreams. . . .

The greatest impact of the world organizations themselves has been on industrial change. They have helped create international markets in industrial goods by linking *communication and transportation infrastructure,* protecting *intellectual property,* and reducing legal and economic barriers to *trade.* As a result, world organizations have played a role in the periodic replacement of lead industries, a critical dynamic of the world economy since the Industrial Revolution: By the mid-1800s the early industrial economy of cotton mills yielded to that of railroads and steel and then to an economy dominated by the mass production of consumer products by the electrical, chemical, and food-processing industries of the turn-of-the-century "Second Industrial Revolution." The automobile and jet age of the twentieth century followed, and today many argue that we are entering another industrial era led by the information industries—computers and telecommunications—and the financial and leisure service sectors they have fostered.

The scale of capitalism has changed with each new set of lead industries. Firms grew. Their markets grew. And the industrial world expanded. World organizations facilitated these changes in scale. By helping secure ever larger market areas for industrial goods, the global agencies helped make it profitable for firms to invest in new technologies. At the same time the world organizations, and the other systems of governance to which they point, have helped mitigate conflicts that go along with the expansion of the industrial system: they privileged some workers in the industrialized nations, insured investment in previously less developed countries (LDCs), and strengthened the states of the less industrialized world. The agencies have also helped perfect the state system itself by extending it to all parts of the globe and mitigating some of the terror inherent in an anarchical system of states armed with the weapons of the industrial age. In strengthening the nation-state and the state system, the global intergovern-mental organizations (IGOs) of the UN era also helped encapsulate the major challengers to industrial capitalism, the Soviet and Chinese communist systems, for more than a generation. Today some of the same agencies have been charged with helping reincorporate the post-communist states into the capitalist world order.

While world organizations may have acted as part of the "super-structure" of the capitalist world economy, they have by no means simply been institutions "functional" to capitalism that somehow were "inevitable" results of the workings of capitalism itself. Their history is part of the dialectic between capitalism and the alternative ways of organizing economic and political life.

In helping encapsulate antagonistic social systems, the world organizations also helped them thrive, at least for a time. In helping to create privileged labor markets in the industrial capitalist world, global IGOs also helped secure the power of part of the industrial working class. And (in the long run, perhaps most significantly) in seeking the legitimacy needed to carry out their other activities, the global agencies have strengthened social movements that hope to replace today's national governments with universal institutions securing human rights, meeting basic human needs, and preserving the global environment.

Nonetheless, even while the global IGOs may sometimes contribute to forces undermining capitalist industrialism, a prima facie case can be made that they have become necessary for its success. Consider just the period since the early 1970s when both the network of world organizations and the global economy have been in trouble. First, conflict between industrialized capitalist nations and their poorer partners began to split the UN. Then price-fixing by Third World oil producers sent an already weak world economy into a tailspin. Liberal internationalist observers of the simultaneous crises began to argue that the crisis in the world economy would end only if the crisis in international institutions was overcome. Sociologist Daniel Bell contended that the nation-state had become "an ineffective instrument for dealing with the scale of major economic problems" (1977: 134). New, more global arrangements were needed. Business and government leaders in the Club of Rome (Tinbergen 1976) argued for a global kind of Keynesian liberalism under which world organizations would be given the task of boosting production and assuring ever higher standards of living. And the Independent Commission on International Development Issues under the leader of Germany's Social Democrats, Willy Brandt, proposed reforms of international institutions based on the same global Keynesian design (Brandt Commission 1980, 1983).

Yet the case that effective world organizations are needed before the world economy will revive is far from proven by the experience of [recent decades]. After all, by 1985 the major industrial economies had recovered from the deep recession of the early 1980s, while it took the Gulf War and the dissolution of the Soviet Union to revive the UN system, or at least to have a reinvigorated Security Council intervening in conflicts left over from the Cold War and in the new ones created by the collapse of Europe's communist states (while the International Monetary Fund (IMF) and World Bank tried to ease their transition back into the capitalist world). In the late 1980s even many Keynesian liberals were ready to concede that a reinvigorated world economy had been a matter of the "right" domestic economic policies, and that a reinvigorated system of international organizations was actually a consequence of this economic change, not its cause, a position championed by neoliberal fundamentalists of the Reagan and Thatcher governments.

Yet, despite the signs of a reinvigorated world economy in the late 1980s, most of us continued to experience the hardships of what the Keynesian Paul Krugman (1990a) has called an "age of diminished expectations" which began in the 1970s. The real wages of many industrial workers are no higher in the early 1990s than they were in the early 1960s, while people in the former communist states and most LDCs face even more dismal prospects. Throughout the world the high expectations of a generation raised in the boom years of the 1950s and 1960s have not been met.

Similarly, despite the optimistic image of today's UN forging consensus in hot spots around the world, or even that of the IMF calmly and professionally overseeing the recovery and transformation of dozens of former communist states, a much deeper incoherence remains. The chronically underfunded central organs of the UN can barely make ends meet, while even the better endowed IMF and World Bank do not have the money to complete all the new tasks they have been given. The argument that more fundamental changes in international institutions will be needed before the return of anything like the postwar boom years remains relevant.

[One can explore] that argument by looking at the history of today's world organizations and their predecessors[—]the ideas underlying these institutions, the intellectual and political leaders who established them, the tasks the agencies were given, how and to what extent they or other systems of governance carried out those jobs, and what effect these actions have had, especially on the world economy. The venerable liberal internationalist case that such institutions can create widespread and long-lasting prosperity plays a major role in the story because the argument has influenced every generation of world organizations, which is, in part, a consequence of its continuing plausibility.

Yet we can see the best evidence for the liberal argument only if we divide the history of world organizations a little differently than most liberal analysts do. Instead of treating the nineteenth-century "Public International Unions," the League of Nations system, and the postwar UN system as the three successive generations of world organizations, we need to link their history to that of industry by saying that each new generation begins when an agency regulating a revolutionary new communication technology appears. In 1865 the agency was the International Telegraph Union (ITU), the first major Public International Union. In 1906 it was the Radiotelegraph Union (RTU), designed to regulate the airwaves. In 1964 it was Intelsat, the International Telecommunications Satellite Organization, a new kind of world organization, a global public utility, outside the UN system, providing part of the world communications infrastructure instead of just regulating services provided by others.

Further experiments in international organization quickly followed each of these three beginnings. The Universal Postal Union and a half-dozen other organizations all appeared before 1890. Agencies serving some of the other new industries of the early twentieth century—the chemical, electrical, and automobile industries—succeeded the RTU, as did the peace organizations created at the 1907 Hague Conference and its successor of 1919, the League of Nations. Similarly, despite recent fears about the future of the UN system, new global agencies have been created in every year since 1965, most of them still inside the UN system, but most, like Intelsat, designed to promote the new industries of the late twentieth century.

Today's crises of international institutions and of the world economy also have their earlier analogues. Each generation of world organizations began in a period of crisis, and its key economic organizations appeared only at the end of the crisis, after years of war involving the great powers and after years of economic malaise. In the late nineteenth century the crisis began with the Austro-Prussian and Franco-Prussian wars and continued through the Long Depression. The Public International Unions that helped liberalize the world economy after the Long Depression were established only in its last five years. The League of Nations operated in an era of crisis which began with the First

World War, ended with the Second World War, and had the Great Depression in between. The economic agencies of the UN era were created as the crisis ended, the IMF and the World Bank at the 1944 Bretton Woods Conference and the General Agreement on Tariffs and Trade (GATT) within three years of the end of the war.

In both generations international transportation agreements immediately preceded the key economic pacts: the European Rail Union (the Central Office for International Rail Transport) in 1890 and the International Civil Aviation Organization (ICAO), the first of the UN specialized agencies, in 1943. Both agencies eventually worked with the earlier communication agency to provide the infrastructure for a larger market in which industrial goods could be traded. The ITU and the Rail Union allowed a Europe-wide market for industrial goods to emerge, while the radio and aviation agencies created a potentially global market.

The actual turn-of-the-century trading area that was partly regulated by the Public International Unions extended the continental market to the overseas dependencies of the European empires. In contrast, the actual trading area partly governed by the IGOs after the Second World War remained smaller than the world linked by radio and the airplane. It covered the Organization for Economic Cooperation and Development (OECD), the club of wealthy market countries (linking western Europe, Canada, the US, Japan, Australia, and New Zealand), and all their economic dependencies in Africa, Asia, the Caribbean, and the Pacific, but excluded China and the Soviet bloc.

Within these geographic limits appeared successive *world orders,* concrete historical political and economic systems, the turn-of-the-century *Interimperial Order* and the postwar *"Free World" Order.* These "interrelated trading area(s)" provide what W. W. Rostow's earliest work on economic development called "the optimum unit for the study of economic history . . . the frame within which many of the most important national, regional, or even international problems must be placed if they are to be fully understood" (1948: 12–23).

The limits of these trading areas were the result of economic agreements that followed the Rail Union and the ICAO. The Brussels-based International Union for the Publication of Customs Tariffs of 1890 signaled the beginning of a wave of European trade liberalization in the 1890s. The GATT marked the beginning of a similar wave throughout the postwar Free World.

Liberal internationalists, both Reagan-era fundamentalists and global Keynesians, argue that the wider markets created in Europe in the 1890s and throughout the capitalist world after the world wars were the keys to the subsequent eras of unprecedented economic growth: Europe's Second Industrial Revolution and the Free World's boom years. If we accept the liberal argument about the earlier eras, we should expect that a new wave of trade liberalization could assure another era of unprecedented prosperity within an even larger trading area that might include China and the postcommunist states.

The argument certainly has some validity[,] . . . global IGOs have played a role in the growth and development of industrial society for over a century. In periods of peace and prosperity they have acted as part of what some social theorists call the "social structures of accumulation" (Gordon 1980, 1988) or "modes of regulation" (Boyer 1990; Lipietz 1987, 1992) that have allowed capitalist industrialism to work as well as it sometimes has. They have also helped industrial societies move out of those times when the system has not worked well—times of economic and geopolitical crisis—by contributing to the rise of the new leading industries of the next era of political order and economic growth.

. . . [C]ontemporary neoliberal fundamentalists [may well] underestimate the roles that "world government" must play in the genesis

and maintenance of eras of peace and prosperity. Liberalizing trade was never enough. World organizations also encouraged investment in new industries, protected people who could be harmed by further extensions of the industrial system, increased the capabilities of states both within and outside the Interimperial Order and the Free World Order, and encouraged all states to be more open and responsive to their own societies. And now that the environmental consequences of industrialism are finally catching up with us, the agenda for a new generation of global IGOs will be even larger.

At the same time, the longer history of industry and international organization indicates that the task of creating the necessary global institutions may be easier than many of today's liberal commentators believe. They look back to the United States's role in creating the Free World and argue that significant reform of the present system will have to await the rise of another predominant power. Yet the Public International Unions of the Interimperial Order were created without the leadership of the dominant power of the day, Great Britain. Less powerful governments, well-placed citizens, and older global agencies have provided the necessary intellectual and political leadership to create world organizations that have helped fulfill the liberal internationalist vision in the past. They can do so again.

Nevertheless, even if they do, the same institutions may contribute to the forces that eventually end the new era of prosperity and peace. Both the Public International Unions and the UN system did. These institutions contributed to industrial growth but failed to cope with social conflict fostered by that growth. While supporters of the UN system are right when they argue that the men and women who designed it learned from the past and anticipated conflicts the designers of the Public International Unions had ignored, it is also true that their immediate predecessors, the designers of the League, first *forgot* much of what the designers of the Public

International Unions once knew. Like today's neoliberal fundamentalists, many of the League's designers overlooked the active role that governments have had to play in building the infrastructure of a liberal industrial economy, as well as in managing the social conflicts that it inevitably creates.

It is easier to remember those lessons if we look at the history of industry and international organization through a lens that is wider than the one provided by the liberals themselves. The social theory developed by the early twentieth-century Italian political strategist, Antonio Gramsci, offers such a lens. Gramsci created a Marxist synthesis of the liberal idealism of the celebrated historian and activist Benedetto Croce with the longer Italian tradition of political realism that goes back to Machiavelli. This synthesis can help us understand the many roles that world organizations have performed—those highlighted by the liberal tradition and those that some liberals discount. At the same time, Gramsci's theory lets us understand the greatest failures of what world government we have had: the eventual disintegration of the two eras of prosperity and peace into periods of war and economic stagnation. Gramsci's framework allows us to integrate the powerful realist and Marxist explanations of these crises, explanations that many liberals discount or ignore.

Gramsci's concept of a unified social order as a *historical bloc* linked by both coercive institutions of *the state proper* and consensual institutions of *civil society* can help us remember that the world organizations, as cooperative institutions of *international* civil society, have only been effective when they have worked alongside a coherent system of coercive power at the international level, a stable military order. And Gramsci's analysis of civil society reminds us to look beyond the regulatory roles played by juridically constituted public institutions to uncover the roles played by less formal domestic, international, and transnational institutions. We need to look for "what world government

we've had" outside the multilateral institutions created by sovereign states.

Consider just one key example: the system of mass production and mass consumption that Gramsci dubbed *Fordism* certainly played a central role in the cooperative regulation of the Free World Order. But Fordism began as a matter of industrial relations *within* firms and was later supported by the Keynesian welfare state. The postwar world organizations point to the significance of Fordism and the Keynesian welfare state through the promotion by the International Labor Organization (ILO) of collective bargaining and the IMF's system for encouraging cooperation in public finance, but we would surely misunderstand a critical part of the postwar world order, and of its eventual crisis, if we looked only at the activities of these formal intergovernmental agencies themselves.

Gramsci's ideas also help us understand how a new world order emerges from a crisis. His analysis of the role of *intellectual* and *political leadership* in establishing social orders can help us clear up questions about the mechanics of reform that recent liberal analysts have left in a muddle. When we distinguish between these two types of leadership we can see a wider range of options for effective reform of global IGOs than those recognized by most contemporary liberal internationalists, whether neoliberal fundamentalists or global Keynesians.

Gramsci's method of understanding the role of a particular set of institutions within a larger social order was first to establish the economic and political context in which the social order arose, and then to analyze why the institution was established: the designs of the intellectual leaders who envisioned it and the political process that realized the ideas, including the concrete relationships between intellectual leaders and political leaders, and between both and the larger social forces that they represented. He would then look at the institution's consequences, its contribution (if any) to cementing a new historical bloc, as well as its impact on social forces that might eventually challenge that social order. . . .

The utopia to which today's world organizations point remains the one first mapped by Adam Smith and Immanuel Kant and later only partially explored by the nineteenth-century public systems builders and the mid twentieth-century Keynesians. Despite the world order crisis of the last decade we still have reason to believe that the promise of liberal internationalism can again be fulfilled in a new world order more extensive, and with benefits more widespread, than the last.

Some of those who discount the continuing relevance of Smith's project argue that revolutions in the scale of production triggered by wider markets are things of the past. But today's suggestions along this line sound like those of the pundits of 1890 who argued that the movement toward large-scale production had run its course (Thorp 1924: 45), or the economist who claimed in 1948 that "long-term, general, and pervasive increase in plant size throughout most industry has come to an end" (Blair 1948: 151). There was, at the time, some truth in these statements, but in both cases fundamentally new economies of scale and scope would soon fuel decades of growth.

The connection between the scale of markets for industrial goods and new investment certainly still holds in the emerging world of "globalized" production where a "plant" has become a regular set of relationships of purchases among large and small companies, often separated by hundreds of miles, but all contributing to the same value-added chain. In this new world, the typical "plant" remains a connected set of physical processes achieving "scale" results—more output for the same input—and the resources needed to create such systems remain vast. So far, most of the "globalized plants" simply produce products of older industries at lower costs (usually by seeking lower-wage labor), but, as Adam Smith would have expected, we can identify a range of new prod-

ucts that would require larger, secure markets for industrial goods. These range from computers capable of recognizing voice commands and translating natural languages (Somerlatte 1982: 29), to a new generation of cost-efficient supersonic transports (Rosen and Williams 1993), to a host of new means to minimize pollution and restore the environment (M. Porter 1991; E. Smith 1992). All of these products have such high research and development costs that they could be recovered only if the resulting goods could be sold throughout today's major industrial markets: not only North America, western Europe, and Japan, but also the growing markets of China, India, eastern Europe, and the NICs.

The first wave of transportation and communication infrastructure that would be needed for such a huge market area has begun to be put in place. In fact, some of those who study "long waves" of industrial development (Grübler and Naki´cenovi´c 1991) suggest that the global diffusion of jet aircraft in the late twentieth century so closely matches that of railways in the European and North American continents a little over a century ago that we should simply expect the "third industrial revolution" to arrive in ten or 15 years. This new industrial revolution would be led by industries producing goods carried by planes, the way the Second Industrial Revolution was led by industries producing goods carried by trains.

However, no such inevitable connections exist among the various long-wave patterns that scholars can find in historical data. In the future, as in the past, any new period of relative prosperity and peace will require the creation of new institutions to end stagnation and conflict. We can look to the past only to help understand the purposes those institutions must serve.

The two long waves of industrial development . . . could each be summarized in the verbal formula: *build, thrive, clash, grab, hoard.*[1] A run of good years followed the building of both world orders, but faltered as unresolved conflicts came to the surface. After temporarily resolving these conflicts, capitalists and the most powerful states succumbed to the temptation of domination and grabbed for profits through the frenzied speculation of casino capitalism and through liberal fundamentalist public policies that benefited the rich at the expense of more vulnerable people both at home and abroad. In the 1930s, at least, the explosion of a few speculative bubbles led to an era of simple hoarding, when productive, future-oriented investment continued to be rare.

Ending those unproductive eras of clashing, grabbing, and hoarding required creative acts of intellectual and political leadership designed to extend international civil society in order to secure the wider market areas that new communication and transportation technologies allowed. The new potential markets, thus secured, encouraged the long-term, productive investment needed to begin and sustain the next industrial wave.

This, then, would appear to be the current agenda of global governance. We need to create international institutions that will assure the maximum diffusion of today's most advanced transportation technologies, define rules encouraging trade in the products of the new industries that are next on the horizon, and manage both the current conflicts between those who are more advantaged and less advantaged by the industrial system and the new conflicts that are likely to emerge in the next industrial era. . . .

Both the nature of the next industrial wave, and both the institutions needed to start it are current matters of dispute. Throughout the "age of diminished expectations" many liberal scholars have looked backward, to the era of the Public International Unions and before, to find models of limited international institutions with none of the perceived failings of the "overtly managerial" UN and the Bretton Woods agencies (Gallaroti 1991: 186; cf. Adelman 1988; Conybeare 1980). Such organizations would not only rely on the market as a political institution,

they would also forgo any attempt to overcome powerful market tendencies. . . .

For many years the United States government championed this hyperliberal vision of the institutions needed to end the world order crisis. . . . There are good reasons to expect that this attempt at building a hyperliberal world order might be more effective than the one that was tried 60 years earlier. The major incentives today's hyperliberals offer to long-term productive investment—an extended and stricter international regime covering intellectual property —are directed toward those industries that many analysts consider to be among the most likely leaders of the next industrial wave (Mass · and Senge 1981). A related US policy of trying to extend the GATT to cover "service" sectors— from advertising and insurance to the various "cultural" industries producing TV programs, music videos, and computer games—also taps into sectors that could continue to grow by leaps and bounds (Alleyne 1992; Alleyne and Sen 1992).

On the other hand, the similar American attempt to use GATT to establish free trade in agriculture and other older sectors has pushed Europe and North America apart, convincing leaders on both continents to emphasize new regional trade liberalization pacts—the North American Free Trade Area (NAFTA) and a newly broadened and deepened European Community—over a global order (Paarlberg 1991). Even so, a hyperliberal world order would not necessarily fail even if its most important trading areas were regional blocs—that is, a somewhat extended NAFTA including the Caribbean, South America, and perhaps even part of east Asia; the European Community with its own near peripheries to the east; and an Asian bloc centered on Japan and China but also including much of southeast Asia and perhaps even Asian Russia. Paul Krugman (1991) argues that, given current costs of transportation and other factors that correlate with geography, a world of three trading blocs might, in theory, provide only marginally fewer welfare benefits than those that could be achieved in the initial phase of any deepening integration across the entire industrial world.

However, by relying on the market to build the transportation infrastructure of global trade, this hyperliberal world would probably never see more efficient links built between the separate trading blocs, such as a new generation of efficient supersonic transports (Rosen and Williams 1993). In a sense, this social order would be less advantageous than an order designed with the lessons of the public system builders in mind. Similarly, relying on the market to establish industrial standards would probably prove to be less efficient than the current system of coordination through industrial committees (Farrell and Saloner 1987) and any move away from WIPO-style requirements to work patents will diminish the incentive to share intellectual property throughout the industrial world (Penrose 1951: 136, 233). Moreover, the entire range of conflicts related to the growth of industry could increase under a hyperliberal world order.

In fact, new forms of international labor resistance have been growing in many of the more populous newly industrializing countries where liberal fundamentalists hold out the greatest hope for finding relatively inexpensive and relatively skilled labor to staff the new "global" factories: places like Brazil, Mexico, Poland, and South Africa. These movements tend to see workers' interests as opposed both to capitalists and to the state, but not necessarily to the national society. Their international connections have been secured by alliances with global ecological, human rights, peace, and women's movements that have arisen in the political space created by the waning world order. Examples include the consumer boycotts organized by Greenpeace and the Interfaith Center on Corporate Responsibility of the World Council of Churches (Waterman 1988).

Given that the champions of a hyperliberal world do not promise the Fordist era's wide generalization of prosperity or relief from the burden of debt under which many of the low-wage industrialized countries suffer, we should not be surprised that the new labor internationalism already resists this fundamentalist vision. In some of the most populous nations (Brazil, Mexico, India, Indonesia) that resistance could push national governments to pull out of the liberal order and become centers of significant antagonistic alternative orders, the way China and the Soviet Union became centers of hostility toward the Free World (Murphy 1990).

Beyond increasing the conflicts that go along with capitalist industrialism, the hyperliberal order would do little to cope with the global environmental issues that have lately absorbed so much of the attention of the UN system and that will undoubtedly continue to be topics of global concern simply due to the rate at which human activity is changing the biosphere. Throughout the 1980s many global Keynesians began highlighting these issues as an argument for their alternative to a hyperliberal world order. Boston University economist Jonathan Harris put it this way: "The future world economic system will have to be based on kind of a global ecological Keynesianism, with significant social direction of capital flows, demand management, and technological choices, to promote ecological sustainability."

. . . The "technological choices" made by the US in establishing Intelsat, by European governments in mapping out a new continent-wide system of high-speed railways (Protzman 1992), and by the many industrial countries now funding designs for a new generation of supersonic civilian jets that would cause minimal environmental damage (Rosen and Williams 1993) all suggest that lessons of the public systems builders have been remembered. In fact, one of the newest communication infrastructures—the "Internet" of global pathways linking public and private computers (usually without cost to individual users)—was built following something very much like the short-distance system for financing railways that John Wright saw as the foundation of global governance over a century ago; institutions may connect to the network simply by agreeing to help others connect to the network through their node.

Moreover, despite the American push to de-emphasize intergovernmental work on industrial standards and to put intellectual property under the GATT, the older regimes encouraging the rapid diffusion of technology are still in place; governments have recently added new commitments, however vague, to encourage rapid sharing of any innovative, environmentally sound technologies that can replace older, polluting practices. These commitments would become increasingly significant if environmental concerns do come to drive the next generation of rapid economic growth. Whether they do or not depends, as Harris would say, on the "social direction of capital flows" and the particular form of "demand management" adopted by the wealthiest and most powerful states. . . .

[There] has been a shift in Third World blueprints for a new world order. In the early 1990s the global Keynesians who staffed UNCTAD argued that the Uruguay Round should be capped by the transformation of GATT into a full-fledged world trade organization. In 1992 they helped prepare the texts endorsed by UNCTAD's full membership that included references to a host of principles that earlier had been championed only by the OECD: an unambiguous preference for free markets, disregard of any notion of delinking from the world economy, an equation of democratization and the protection of human rights with development, and all the Reagan-era rhetoric about the need to decrease the corruption and increase the efficiency of governments in the South. Meanwhile, similar signs of convergence came from the "other side" as the IMF's managing director endorsed the idea of "sustainable development" and the argument that Michael Stewart (1984) had made a decade before about the similar logics of cascading

monetarism and of mounting problems of transborder pollution in a purely market-based order (Camdessus 1992).

This relatively new idea of "sustainable development," which had first appeared in the early 1970s as part of an antimaterialist critique of Fordism (Murphy 1992: 53–5), has become an important focus of the revised global Keynesian message. Unlike previous attempts to find a global Keynesian alternative to neoliberal fundamentalism, the call for "sustainable development" encouraged support from the kind of business and government interests that had helped create the international social structures of the European Second Industrial Revolution and the postwar Free World Order. These included major firms involved in leading, high-technology industrial sectors and, as was the case a century ago, some of the major industrial states only one tier removed from the leading economic power.

The 1987 report of the World Commission on the Environment and Development, under Norwegian Prime Minister Gro Brundtland (Brundtland Commission 1992), included Stewart's conclusions about the similarity of global environmental problems and the problem of cascading monetarism and added global Keynesian arguments about development in the Third World then being made by critics of the liberal fundamentalist prescriptions championed by the US and the Bretton Woods institutions. The Commission appealed to growth-oriented Keynesians in the North by arguing for agreement on international institutional structures of accumulation that would allow a return to the more egalitarian days of rapid economic growth in the 1960s and 1970s. It appealed to northern environmentalists as well as a growing ecological movement in the South by pointing out both the unsustainability of the North's growth patterns and the planetary responsibilities of Third World governments for maintaining the habitats and the biodiversity of their lands. And it appealed to southern exponents of the failed NIEO, and their northern allies who had supported the earlier Brandt Commission reports, by providing a new, potentially more convincing set of arguments for the North's responsibilities toward the South (Murphy 1992: 56).

Critics of the Brundtland Commission, including S. M. Lélé (1991: 616), admonished it for sneaking in the idea that free trade is almost always desirable. Yet by embracing the globalization of the market economy the advocates of "sustainable development" put themselves squarely in the tradition of liberal internationalism and improved their chances to mobilize powerful business interests to join the other social forces pushing for international responses to contemporary social problems.

The success of this tactic has been reflected in the work of the Business Council on Sustainable Development (BCSD), a new nongovernmental organization that brings together the leaders of a host of the world's largest firms, from the Dow Chemical Company, to Nippon Steel, to India's giant TATA, to Volkswagen. The only thing that all these companies clearly have in common is that all have learned from experience that it can pay to be a first mover on environmental issues. Generalizing from their individual experiences, they have convinced the International Organization for Standardization to establish a Strategic Advisory Group on the Environment to prepare international standards for the "eco-efficiency" of industrial products and services. The aim is to ensure that products have standard "eco-labeling" and that public entities purchasing goods and products look at life-cycle analyses and environmental audits (Schmidheiny 1992: 95).

The self-interest of the BCSD firms is transparent even if it is enlightened. They believe that in a global market of green consumers and of governments increasingly influenced by the environmental concerns of their publics, ISO standards labeling the environmental desirability of every product and service will benefit the BCSD firms, those that already have experience as environmental first movers. . . .

The problem of finding political sponsors and benefactors for the international institutions of the next world order will be at least as complex as it was a century ago. It has been compounded by what the nineteenth-century public system builders might recognize as the "lack of political efficiency" of many of the solutions proposed by intellectuals of the critical tradition to today's North–South conflicts.

Many involve the all-too-visible transfer of new northern resources to the South. This may seem justified given that net financial flows went from South to North throughout the 1980s, and that after 1985 even the World Bank and IMF became net recipients of funds from the countries that, in the Bank's case at least, they are mandated to aid. Nevertheless, most OECD legislatures are unlikely to tax their citizens to reverse such transfers, especially when some governments have to consider unprecedented accumulations of government debt and all face the other consequences of years of slow growth.

There really may be no way around this dilemma, especially as it relates to the funding of multilateral development programs. The costs of the operational development activities far exceed those of any of the other activities of the world organizations, even the maintenance of peacekeeping forces. This means that the traditional pattern of one or few states as the benefactors of new activities will not work very well in these fields. It is one thing to pick up many of the bills for a big global meeting, or even support a secretariat by seconding staff and making voluntary contributions; it is quite another thing to foot the bill for a host of development operations.

There is a lesson in the way the US actually played that benefactor role at the beginning of the Free World Order, but it is not the usual lesson of the Marshall Plan's generosity. Rather, it is the lesson of the Bretton Woods institutions. The initial deposits of gold and hard currencies by the US (and the very few other original members whose money was convertible) created a pool of loan money that could immediately be expanded enormously by the IMF and the World Bank both by fiat and by borrowing. The long-standing Keynesian proposal using increases in IMF reserves to create a pool for development assistance, the SDR-Link, has the same advantage of invisibility, the same political efficiency. Of course, that particular proposal has been unworkable ever since the floating exchange rate system appeared in the early 1970s. Nevertheless, rather than bemoaning either that fact or the inadequacy of today's funding for multilateral activities that comes through the increasingly used mechanism of voluntary contributions (Taylor 1991: 380), global Keynesians should recognize that this necessary voluntarism reflects the way that innovation in global governance usually takes place. Calls for new Marshall Plans for the environment, for Africa, or for the former communist countries will be less successful than other proposals that would establish regular (even if initially quite small) sources of development finance linked to a growing part of the world economy. . . .

Notes

1. Alain Noël (1993) would probably find even this open-ended formula much too mechanical. In his excellent critique of various regulation theories he says that the historical record teaches us that:

> regulation is more akin to the snowforts children build in winter. The participants erect a wall, add a motif—inspired by the neighbor's snowfort— open a loophole, break a side-wall in an unexpected battle, in short, they continuously build and renovate, without ever stopping, until the whole project is finally destroyed by a war, a celebration, or a heavy rainfall. An ongoing project, the snowfort is never finished until it is lost or abandoned. What matters for the participants is less the outcome than the process, less the snowfort itself than the always fragile agreement of all around a common vision, which organizes the games for a period.

I find Noël's image compelling, but more can be said about what happens as the game ends. When the visions that organized the Interimperial Order and the Free World Order stopped being held in common, similar conflicts (*clashes*) came to the fore. In both cases the response of both a significant group of cosmopolitan capitalists and the governments of leading states was to abandon the hegemonic project of liberal internationalism and to seek what Gramsci would call "domination" in the eras of "grabbing" and "hoarding." In both cases these periods (roughly, the 1920s and the 1980s) appeared at times when some of the earlier clashes had ended and a modified version of the older world order was restored. It was as if first some of the largest and most powerful children in the snowfort had worked with close friends to throw out of the game children who wanted to play by different rules (Imperial Germany and the OPEC-led Third World alliance); then the big kids themselves modified the rules in order to lord over the weaker children they had temporarily befriended.

Selected References

Adelman, Carol C. (ed.) 1988: *International Regulation: New Rules in a Changing World Order*. San Francisco.

Alleyne, Mark D. 1992: Liberalization in Nonregime Areas: The Twenty-Year Debate over Cultural Industries, from UNESCO's NWICO to the GATT's Uruguay Round. Paper presented at the annual meeting of the International Studies Association, Atlanta, April.

Alleyne, Mark D. and Shinjinee Sen 1992: Fact Sheet on International Trade in Cultural Products. International Communications Program, Department of Comparative and Regional Studies, American University, Washington, D.C.

Bell, Daniel 1977: The Future World Disorder: The Structural Context of Crisis. *Foreign Policy*, 13: 223–8.

Blair, John M. 1948: Technology and Size. *American Economic Review*, 38(2): 121–71.

Boyer, Robert A. 1990: *The Regulation School: A Critical Introduction*. New York.

Brandt Commission 1980: *North–South: A Program for Survival*. Cambridge, Mass.

——— 1983: *Common Crisis North–South: Cooperation for World Recovery*. Cambridge, Mass.

Brundtland Commission 1987: *Our Common Future*. New York.

Camdessus, Michel 1992: Remarks to the Annual Meeting of the Academic Council on the UN System at the International Monetary Fund. Washington, D.C., June.

Chase-Dunn, Christopher 1990: The Limits of Hegemony: Capitalism and Global State Formation. In

David P. Rapkin (ed.), *World Leadership and Hegemony*. Boulder, Colo.

Conybeare, John 1980: International Organization and the Theory of Property Rights. *International Organization,* 34(3): 307–34.

Cox, Robert W. 1977: Labor and Hegemony. *International Organization,* 31(3): 385–424.

—— 1979: Ideologies and the New International Economic Order: Reflections on Some Recent Literature. *International Organization,* 33(2): 257–302.

—— 1980a: The Crisis of World Order and the Problem of International Organization in the 1980s. *International Journal,* 35(2): 370–95.

—— 1980b: Labor and Hegemony: A Reply. *International Organization,* 31(1): 159–76.

—— 1987: *Production, Power, and World Order: Social Forces in the Making of History.* New York.

Cox, Robert W. and Harold K. Jacobson (eds.) 1974: *The Anatomy of Influence: Decision Making in International Organization.* New Haven.

——. 1977: Decision Making. *International Social Science Journal,* 29(1): 115–35.

Farrell, Joseph and Garth Saloner 1987: Coordination through Committees and Markets. Massachusetts Institute of Technology, Alfred P. Sloan School of Management.

Gallaroti, Giulio M. 1991: The Limits of International Organization: Systematic Failure in the Management of International Relations. *International Organization,* 45 (2): 181–220.

Galtung, Johan 1980: *The True Worlds.* New York.

Gordon, David M. 1980: Stages of Accumulation and Long Economic Cycles. In Terence K. Hopkins and Immanuel Wallerstein (eds.), *Processes of the World-System,* Beverly Hills, Ca.

—— 1988: The Global Economy: New Edifice or Crumbling Foundations? *New Left Review,* 169: 24–64.

Gramsci, Antonio 1971: *Selections from the Prison Notebooks* (1929–35), ed. and trans. Quintin Hoare and Geoffrey Nowell Smith. New York.

—— 1992. *Prison Notebooks, Volume I* (1929–35), trans. Joseph A. Buttigieg and Antonio Callan. New York.

Grübler, Arnulf and Nebojsa Naki´cenovi´c 1991: Long Waves, Technology Diffusion, and Substitution. *Review,* 14(2): 313–42.

Hinsley, F. H. 1963: *Power and the Pursuit of Peace: Theory and Practice in the History of the Relations between States.* Cambridge.

Krugman, Paul R. 1990a: *The Age of Diminished Expectations.* Cambridge, Mass.

—— 1990b: *Rethinking International Trade.* Cambridge, Mass.

—— 1991: The Move to Free Trade Zones. Paper presented at the symposium on policy implications of trade and currency zones, Jackson Hole, Wyo., August.

Lélé, S. M. 1991: Sustainable Development: A Critical Review. *World Development,* 19(6): 607–22.

Lens, Sidney 1983: World Government Reconsidered. *The Nation,* Sept. 17: 201 ff.

Lipietz, Alain 1987: *Mirages and Miracles: The Crisis of Global Fordism.* London.

—— 1992: *Towards a New Economic Order: Postfordism, Ecology, and Democracy.* Cambridge.

Murphy, Craig N. 1984: *The Emergence of the New International Economic Order Ideology.* Boulder, Colo.

—— 1988: Global Institutions and the Pursuit of Human Needs. In Roger A. Coate and Jerel A. Rosati (eds.), *The Power of Human Needs in World Society,* Boulder, Colo.

—— 1990: Freezing the North–South Bloc(k) after the East–West Thaw. *Socialist Review,* 90(3): 25–46.

—— 1992: The United Nations Capacity to Promote Sustainable Development: The Lessons of a Year that "Eludes all Facile Judgment." In Legault, Murphy and Ofuatey-Kodjoe.

Murphy, Craig N. and Enrico Augelli 1993: International Institutions, Decolonization, and Development. *International Political Science Review,* 14(1): 71–85.

Noël, Alain 1993: The Regulation Approach and International Political Economy: A Scientific Realist Assessment. Paper presented at the annual meeting of the International Studies Association, Acapulco, March.

Paarlberg, Robert L. 1991: Why Agriculture Has Blocked the Uruguay Round. Harvard University Center for International Affairs.

Parkinson, Fred 1977: *The Philosophy of International Relations: A Study in the History of Thought.* Beverly Hills, Ca.

Penrose, Edith T. 1951: *The Economics of the International Patent System.* Baltimore.

Porter, Michael 1991: Green Competitiveness. *New York Times,* June 5.

Protzman, Ferdinand 1992: To Track Unity in Europe, Watch its Fast Trains. *New York Times,* Oct. 25.

Rosen, Robert and Louis J. Williams 1993: The Rebirth of Supersonic Transport. *Technology Review* (Feb.–Mar.): 22–9.

Rostow, W. W. 1948: *The British Economy of the Nineteenth Century.* Oxford.

—— 1985: *Eisenhower, Kennedy, and Foreign Aid.* Austin, Tex.

Schmidheiny, Stephan 1992: *Changing Course: A Global Business Perspective on Development and the Environment*. Cambridge, Mass.

Smith, Emily T. 1992: Growth versus Environment. *Business Week*, no. 3265: 66–75.

Snow, Marcellus S. 1976: *International Commercial Satellite Communication*. New York.

Sommerlatte, Tom W. H. A. 1982: Strategic Approaches to Office Automation. In Kathleen Lancaster (ed.), *International Telecommunication: User Requirements and Supplier Strategies*, Lexington, Mass.

Stewart, Michael 1984: *The Age of Interdependence: Economic Policy in a Shrinking World*. Cambridge, Mass.

Taylor, Paul 1991: The United Nations System under Stress: Financial Pressures and their Consequences. *Review of International Studies*, 17(4): 365–82.

Taylor, Paul and A. J. R. Groom (eds.) 1988: *International Institutions at Work*. London.

——— (eds.) 1989: *Global Issues in the United Nations Framework*. Basingstoke.

Thorp, W. L. 1924: *The Integration of Industrial Operations*. Washington, D.C.

Tinbergen, Jan (coordinator) 1976: *Reshaping International Order: A Report to the Club of Rome*. New York.

Waterman, Peter 1988: The New Internationalisms; A More Real Thing than Big, Big Coke? *Review*, 11(3): 289–328.

Wright, Quincy 1930: *Mandates under the League of Nations*. Chicago.

——— 1942: *A Study of War*. Chicago.

CHAPTER 5

Normative Considerations and International Relations Theory

Until recent years, textbooks on international relations were conspicuous for the absence of much discussion of **normative** or value considerations.[1] This was a rather strange turn of events in that the intellectual traditions underlying realism, pluralism, and globalism are a blend of normative (what *should* be the case?) and **empirical** questions (what *is* the case?). For writers as divergent as Machiavelli, Kant, Carr, Madison, or Marx, it was inconceivable to discuss politics without at least some attention to the relation between facts and values. The two were thought by them to be inseparable.

In this chapter, we raise some of the issues and value considerations central to an understanding of normative international relations theory. When, if ever, is war just, and what is just conduct in war? Are there universally understood human rights? Is the global distribution of wealth equitable, and if not, what authoritative steps should be taken to alter the status quo? On what moral bases should statesmen make foreign policy choices? It is not our intention here to delve deeply into such complex questions, an enterprise well beyond the scope of this effort. Over the centuries, many international relations theorists have grappled with value questions, and we want to alert the readers to some of the most critical of these.

Second, we also want to recognize normative international relations theory building as a legitimate enterprise worthy of more scholarly efforts. As discussed in Chapter 1, normative theory differs fundamentally from empirical theory. Propositions in normative theory that deal with what *ought* to be are not subject to the formal empirical tests of hypotheses about what *is*, which is the realm of empirical theory. This fact does not make normative theory any less important, however. Choices among competing alternatives made by policymakers are informed not just by knowledge of what *is* or could be but also by a rationale for what *ought* to be. Developing the basis for such value choices is the domain of normative theory.

Finally, value orientations are present even among empirical theorists in all three international relations images we identify. *What* is studied and *how* it is studied are preferences that vary from theorist to theorist across all three images. True, empirical theorists try to minimize the effect of individual value bias through objective testing of hypotheses, but personal values cannot be filtered out completely. We have recognized these value preferences in previous chapters, but we find it useful to identify them explicitly in this chapter as well.

MORAL CHOICE: ALTERNATIVE CRITERIA

Various criteria exist for providing guidance as to what constitutes **moral** choice in international relations. The **relativist** position—that values are not universal in character but are specific to a particular culture, situation, or set of circumstances—holds that such universal criteria cannot be devised or discerned. This relativist view is rejected by those who hold to **Kantian, utilitarian**, and **social contract** bases for moral choice. If what is *right* is so variable as potentially to mean so many different things to the relativist, then does it really mean anything?

Relativist thinking is, therefore, a rejection of the universalist tradition in Western thought that has its roots in ancient Stoic and Roman writings. For example, the Roman orator Cicero (106–43 B.C.) states that "true law is right reason in agreement with nature; it is of universal application, unchanging and everlasting." He asserts: "Justice is one; it binds all society, and is based on one law." Indeed, he observes: "Justice does not exist at all if it does not exist in Nature."[2]

This universalism was the basis for the idea of a law common to the nations of the Roman empire. That values transcend a single community or state, thus having truly global reach *and* that they are revealed in scripture or can be discovered as part of natural law by use of right reason would be central to the thought of Augustine, Aquinas, and other religious writers of the Middle Ages. As discussed in Chapter 2, Grotius and others would provide a secular basis for international law—whether based on general principles, customary international practice, the writings of jurists, or treaties or conventions voluntarily undertaken by states. The important point, however, is that values exist that are applicable to all leaders and their states.

Immanuel Kant (1724–1804), whose work has already been mentioned in Chapter 3, is best known for his writings on ethics and reason, but he also addressed war and peace in international society. According to Kant, the individual has free will to choose the correct moral course, clearly a **voluntarist** position. Individual behavior is not predetermined, but the individual is obligated, nevertheless, to follow the moral law that is discoverable through the proper exercise of reason. What this means is that the individual is to treat other human beings as ends worthy in themselves, not just as means. Moreover, the correct prescription for a moral conduct is knowable by the individual and amounts to those precepts that have universally binding character.[3]

It is this universal dimension in Kantian ethics that is also the basis for his thinking on international relations. The Kantian ideal was a cosmopolitan international society of individuals, states, or other actors following ethical principles and aiming toward perfection. In other words, "right reason" is to be used to discern obligations stemming from a universal law that transcends the laws made by individual states. This was to be the path toward "perpetual peace"—a world free of war. A federation of peaceful states could (but would not necessarily) come to be established as a response to the very real security needs of states.

By contrast to Kantian ethics, the writings of Jeremy Bentham (1748–1832), John Stuart Mill (1806–1873), and others focus on attaining the greatest good for the greatest number as the principal criterion of utilitarian thought. A "society is rightly ordered," according to utilitarians, if "its major institutions are arranged so as to achieve the greatest net balance of satisfaction."[4] In principle, utilitarian and Kantian criteria may provide a philosophical basis for international law because the application of these criteria transcends the boundaries of any given state or society. In practice, however, given the present division of the world into separate, sovereign states with very different perspectives on global issues, it is not clear that either Kantian or utilitarian ethics *can*, as a practical matter, be the basis for constructing some radically new and just world order.

Yet another approach to finding a guide to right behavior is that of the social contract: that individuals may voluntarily agree to bind or obligate themselves to some set of principles. In Rousseau's stag hunt discussed in Chapter 2, the hunters in a state of nature can be understood as maximizing individual, short-term self-interest by going for the hare. In a Hobbesian world of no sovereign authority to compel collaboration or to force the honoring of contracts, no other outcome can be expected. On the other hand, by making assumptions different from Hobbes about human beings in a hypothetical state of nature, there is at least the possibility that the hunters may agree to upgrade their common interest by collaborating to hunt the stag. Such agreement is a social contract in its most primitive form. Binding obligations are made as a voluntary, positive act.

Building on this approach as a means to finding justice, for example, John Rawls asks what would be considered fair if individuals were in a state of nature and none knew in advance what one's place in society, class position, or social status would be. Behind this common "veil of ignorance" about outcomes, what principles of **distributive justice** would these hypothetically free agents choose?

One principle taken from Rawls' analysis is that "all social values—liberty and opportunity, income and wealth, and the bases of self-respect—are to be distributed equally unless an unequal distribution of any, or all, of these values is to everyone's advantage."[5] Beyond that, socioeconomic inequality is admissible only if it benefits everyone in society and if there is an equal opportunity for everyone to acquire those positions associated with unequal rewards. Whether one extends such propositions as the basis for global justice for individuals or for states as if they were individuals is not altogether clear. Rawls himself makes no such claim. Indeed, he formulates a "conception of justice for the basic structure of society" and observes that "the conditions for the law of nations may require different principles arrived at in a somewhat different way."[6] Nevertheless, Rawls' notion of justice could conceivably provide the philosophical basis for the demands of poor Third World countries for a new international economic order designed to reduce the gap between **North** and **South**. Moreover, the idea of constructing an international or global *society* calls for the application of universal norms.

If social contract theory cannot be applied to states as if they were persons, it cannot be a source of moral or legal obligations among states. If one allows it, however, to be applied to states (as if they were individual persons) social contract becomes a basis for a **positivist** interpretation of international law. Among positivists, international law and the obligation to follow other international rules or norms stem not from natural law or religious notions but from affirmative actions taken by states. Kantian, utilitarian, or other principles may be part of the calculus of deciding which rules are to be made binding, but it is the voluntary contract, or choice, made by states in the form of a treaty, convention, or customary practice (so routine in performance as to amount to an implicit contract) that creates the obligation. That there is no higher authority to enforce obligations undertaken by states makes them no less binding in principle.

Values, therefore, are not new to the study of international relations. They may be addressed in terms of "right reason" to discern obligations stemming from some natural law. Alternatively, they may conform more closely to a positivist approach to constructing international law—that treaties, for example, are binding (*pacta sunt servanda*) and that such obligations *ought* to be kept. The Kantian perspective in particular contrasts sharply with the views of Machiavelli and Hobbes described in Chapter 2. Although values and value choices certainly are present in classic realism, power and the balance of power have clearly been the more important considerations in this tradition. It is, however, incorrect to view power and values as if they were mutually exclusive approaches to international politics. As E. H. Carr noted:

> The utopian who dreams that it is possible to eliminate self-assertion from politics and to base a political system on morality alone is just as wide of the mark as the realist who believes that altruism is an illusion and that all political action is self-seeking.[7]

In short, international politics involves a blend of values and power, utopianism and realism. Such a perspective can be found in virtually all the intellectual precursors discussed in this book. There is disagreement, however, as to the relative importance of values and power, and which values should be pursued.[8]

THE PROBLEM OF JUSTICE AND WAR

One fairly well developed area that stands as an exception to our general observation of the paucity of normative international relations theory is that which deals with the morality of war itself (*jus ad bellum*) and the ethical constraints within any given war (*jus in bello*). Scholars have pondered the subject, building on a tradition in Western thought extending to the writings of St. Augustine (354–430 A.D.) and before. Contrary to the absolute pacifism of early Christians, Augustine drew from the work of Cicero and addressed war as something that was to be avoided but that was sometimes necessary: "It is the wrong-doing of the opposing party which compels the wise man to wage wars."[9] The corpus of just war theory grew with additions made by Aquinas, Suarez, Vitoria, and other political philosophers of the medieval period. That we can develop a theory of just war through the exercise of right reason and right conduct are philosophical assumptions underlying normative theory on armed conflict.

Perhaps not surprisingly, given their preoccupation with national security issues, much contemporary thinking on just war has occurred primarily among realists. Not all realists would accept the Machiavellian characterization of war as something useful for acquiring or maintaining rule and that, if postponed, might work only to the advantage of the enemy. A Machiavellian principle underscored by Clausewitz is that war is decidedly not a legitimate end in itself but is merely a means used to achieve essentially political purposes. That war should not be waged without "legitimate" purpose—that it should at least be subordinate to the political objective or serve some national interest—can be understood as a limited but nevertheless moral statement in itself.

Defense against provoked aggression is generally conceded (except by absolute pacifists) to be a legitimate political objective justifying war. Nevertheless, in just-war thinking, war is a last resort to be undertaken only if there appears to be some chance of success. The death and destruction wrought by war are to be minimized, consistent with achieving legitimate military purposes. Indeed, there can be no positive moral content in war unless legitimate political objectives and military purposes are served. Following conventional military logic, the purpose in any war is to destroy or substantially weaken an enemy's war-making capability. Military necessity, so defined, however, does not justify the use of means disproportionate to the ends sought or the use of weapons that are indiscriminate or that cause needless human suffering. Moreover, the lives of noncombatants are to be spared.[10]

Realists of Grotian persuasion identify rules or laws that constrain states, statesmen, and soldiers in the exercise of their war powers. Beginning with the Hague Conventions in the late nineteenth and early twentieth centuries, a large body of treaties and conventions based largely on earlier just-war thinking has come into force, providing the basis for the contemporary law of war. There are difficulties, however, beyond the usual problem of no international enforcement authority and the problems of defining aggression and dealing with insurgencies, in which the very legitimacy of the parties is in question. Quite apart from such concerns, however, the focus on limits in just-war theory and international law are seen by some theorists to be impractical in an age dominated by weapons of mass destruction. Moreover, some theorists question whether just war theory can be used to legitimate deterrence doctrines that argue that in order to maintain peace one must threaten devastation on a global scale.[11] These objections aside, to others the effort in just war theory remains to put practical limits on the use of force and thus to reduce, if not completely eliminate, the barbarity of warfare in a still emergent global civil society.

JUSTICE AND HUMAN RIGHTS

The quest for universal understanding of socioeconomic, political, and legal rights belonging to individuals, groups, classes, societies, and humanity as a whole has also proven to be an evolutionary and still ongoing process.[12] Although the concept of rights in western thought has roots in ancient Greek, Roman, and religious writings, it was the Enlightenment and the social contract theorists that collectively provided stronger philosophical ground for specifying human aspirations for liberty and equality, coupled with communitarian concerns and human obligations in society. The liberal spirit of the Enlightenment would, of course, be developed further in the nineteenth-century work of the utilitarians and Kantians.

Although Hobbes, Locke, Rousseau, and other classic social-contract theorists differed on the relative emphasis or importance each placed on liberty, equality, community, and order, a common theme was that human beings—the people—are the ultimate source of legitimate political authority in society. This democratic understanding is explicit in Locke and Rousseau. Even for Hobbes, the monarch (or "assembly" acting as legislature) rested legitimately not on divine right but rather on the people who vested the sovereign with authority and power to maintain societal order in the interest of their own security.

The thirteenth-century English Magna Carta and the late eighteenth-century U.S. Bill of Rights and French Declaration of the Rights of Man are documentary artifacts of aspirations to rights taking political or legal form. Content analysis of these documents, however, reveals greater focus on *individual* political and legal rights in the English and American documents, while the French declaration extends itself to the socioeconomic realm with applications not just to individuals, but also to larger aggregations at both communal and societal levels. In short, a people may have rights as a class, group, or society as a whole.

In the present-day global society, these differences in understandings across societies and cultures remain. Culture obviously matters in how we interpret or understand rights in different social contexts. There are differences in relative importance, for example, of liberty, equality, and order and whether rights or obligations are to be applied primarily at the individual level of analysis or at larger human aggregations. Thus, the United States tends to focus on human rights as individual political and legal rights and liberties, whereas many other states and societies accept these civil rights and liberties as part of a much larger package that also puts a higher premium on socioeconomic rights and communitarian understandings.

Notwithstanding different cultural understandings or interpretations of how human rights should be defined and implemented, human-rights advocates adopt a universalist rather than relativist view. Whether using a methodology of social contract, utilitarian, Kantian, or religious origin, advocates search for universal, underlying values that inform our understandings of human rights in practice. Thus, respect for life, human dignity, and justice or fairness are broadly understood and accepted even as there is disagreement on how these values are to be applied in particular human-rights contexts. Even so, because there is an understanding of such underlying, universal values as respect for life and human dignity, there is at least a basis for discourse aimed in the interest of justice and fairness at resolving differences in how these values are applied across societies.

Although politics clearly plays a role in these determinations, giving a relatively louder voice to the preferences of some states over others, at a more fundamental level is the continuing discourse that develops consensus across cultures and societies on the realization of these values in common practice. Thus, the Universal Declaration of Human Rights adopted by the U.N. General Assembly in 1948 emphasizes the political and legal, individual preferences of its sponsors. Nevertheless, six of the thirty articles— 20 percent of the declaration—did address socioeconomic and cultural rights, albeit in individual, rather than collective terms.[13]

Importantly, this 20 percent would serve as a foundation for later expansion in U.N. treaties or agreements not just on civil and political rights, but also on such matters as economic, social, and cultural rights; elimination of racial discrimination; elimination of discrimination against women; and providing for a children's bill of rights. Moreover, substantial progress in delineating rights has also been made in U.N. specialized agencies such as the International Labor Organization (ILO), the World Health Organization (WHO), and the United Nations Educational, Scientific, and Cultural

Organization (UNESCO) as well as in such regional organizations as the Council of Europe, the European Union, the Organization for Cooperation and Security in Europe (OSCE), the Organization of American States (OAS), and the Organization of African Unity (OAU). Thus, global consensus building toward construction of human-rights regimes takes place in many different institutional forums.[14]

A problem area, of course, is that human rights claims often collide with the prerogatives of sovereign states. After all, in international law the government of a sovereign state claims a right to exclusive jurisdiction over people within its territory. On the other hand, some human-rights advocates see both moral and legal bases for action when decisions or policies of governments violate human rights—particularly when these states have legally bound themselves in treaties specifying commitment to these same rights. From this perspective, when human-rights violations threaten international peace and security, there is also a legal basis for humanitarian intervention under U.N. auspices (namely under Articles 34, 41, and 42). By contrast, opponents of this view politically oppose what they see as an expansion of the U.N. agenda—seeing such efforts as meddling in the internal affairs of sovereign states that amounts to a violation of international law.

ALTERNATIVE IMAGES AND FOREIGN POLICY CHOICE

The relative emphasis placed on *order, justice, freedom*, and *change*—values that are part of foreign policymaking and that have a direct bearing on international politics—varies widely among realists, pluralists, and globalists. Realist concern with power and the balance of power is closely related to value commitments of statesmen who see order as essential to national security. If they are committed further to the avoidance of war, they may see their tasks as one of managing conflict and seeking to maximize accomplishment of state objectives, however constrained by states comprising the balance. Following Machiavelli, the realist sees national security or the national interest—at a minimum, survival in an anarchic world—as the *raison d'état* justifying state policy.

Justice and freedom may also be valued by realists, particularly those of Grotian persuasion, but even they must first confront the realities of power among states. Some states rise in power relative to others, and other states decline. Power and the balance of power persist, nevertheless. Changes in international politics occur within the international system or among states, but the anarchic nature of the international system (or of international politics) remains as a constant condition. Fundamental change of the international system that would alter the anarchy of sovereign states remains a possibility, but to most realists, this seems unlikely to occur any time soon. Moreover, consistent with liberal thought that, as discussed in Chapter 3, has also had major impact on the pluralist school, there is a preference among many realists for a world order in which states are "free"—that is, not constrained by any superior authority. There is, then, a conservative value bias among realists that leads most of them to view schemes for new world orders as so much wishful thinking, products of utopian thought and divorced from reality.

To some extent, the value bias among pluralists is also conservative, if not to the same degree. To pluralists, change tends to be evolutionary and incremental. If change is to be willed, then *reformist*, not *revolutionary*, measures are the appropriate ones. Pluralist theories, given the fragmentation of states and proliferation of actors that are their starting point, focus on the formation of coalitions and countercoalitions, whether within a state or across national borders. This is hardly the environment for radical changes that would require greater societal unity or at least a strong and unitary leadership. Faction against faction, governmental department against governmental department—the Madisonian formula underlying the American Constitution—is not the means to sweeping change. There are simply too many obstacles (or potential obstacles in the form of opposing groups or factions) to make change easy to come by.

Although for different theoretical reasons and to a different degree, pluralists therefore share with realists a conservative bias and a predisposition toward order as a desired value. Many pluralists, however, place greater emphasis on democratic notions of *human rights* and *justice* for individuals, groups, and societies than they do on order within and among states. Richard Falk, for example, identifies four values to be maximized as part of his World Order Models Project: "minimization of collective violence; maximization of economic well-being; maximization of social and political justice; and maximization of ecological quality."[15] To minimize collective violence, order remains important to Falk, but his focus quickly shifts to social and welfare issues that need to be addressed as part of the world order. The pluralism in Falk's approach is evident in his characterization of it as "a transnational social movement dedicated to global reform."[16]

Justice, especially *distributive* justice, is a central concern not only to a number of pluralists but also to many globalists. Rawls presents a non-Marxist formulation that supports the normative preferences of both pluralists like Falk and those globalists who focus on inequalities in the distribution of wealth between the industrial countries of the North and the less-developed countries of the South. Globalists of Marxist persuasion do not need Rawls, of course, given their own long-standing moral concern with exploitative class relations and associated prescriptions for overturning what they see as the existing, unjust world order.

To many globalists, reformism and incremental change are merely prescriptions for maintaining the status quo. If justice is to be served, what may be needed is revolutionary change that sweeps out an unjust world order and replaces it with one that allows for an equitable distribution of wealth and resources. Whether understood as exploitation of peasants and workers by an international **bourgeoisie** or as domination by highly industrial core states and societies over poor, industrially underdeveloped peripheral states, the answer is always the same: justice requires change. Order, peace, and individual freedom will only be established after fundamental (or revolutionary) change of the existing order has been effected.

RATIONALITY AND FOREIGN POLICY CHOICE

Foreign policy choice is the domain in which values apply directly. On the basis of some set of criteria, decisionmakers choose authoritatively among competing alternatives. The rational model, often a critical element in realist thinking, amounts to policymakers' ordering of alternatives, making decisions, and taking actions to achieve the most *efficient* outcome in terms of ends sought. This process is not value free. First, determining the objective or ends to be sought obviously involves value choices.[17] Second, the idea that the means chosen to achieve these goals should be the most efficient, the best, or even just "good enough" is itself a value underlying the decision-making calculus. Finally, even if statesmen can reach a consensus on what general values should be pursued internationally, there may be honest disagreement as to how these values are to be defined and implemented. A good example of this problem involves human rights.

Notwithstanding a Universal Declaration of Human Rights in 1948 and a number of human rights conventions since then, it often has been difficult to forge a consensus among governments on which criteria should apply in approaching questions of human rights: which rights are to be protected, the relative importance or weight of different values when they conflict, and whose rights—individuals, groups, classes, states—take precedence. As Ernst Haas comments: "Rights come in various hues and stripes."[18] Indeed, the Jeffersonian tradition in American politics predisposes U.S. decisionmakers to emphasize political and civil rights of individuals. As a consequence, economic, social, and cultural rights of groups and classes that receive greater emphasis in many other countries tend to be downgraded or ignored by makers of American foreign policy. Rights claimed by other states to be due them as *sovereign* entities also receive less American emphasis when prerogatives exercised by them are seen as infringing on individual rights.[19]

In sum, contrary to what one might first presume, the rational model of foreign policy decision making is by no means a value-free approach, particularly given the wide range of values pursued by statesmen and different views as to how a particular value should be defined and implemented. As has been discussed in chapters 1 and 3, many pluralists challenge whether foreign policy decision making can ever conform to a rational model when the actors involved are various organizations and small groups of individuals and when decisions are typically the outcome of bargaining, compromise, "end-running," or related tactics. Each separate actor may act rationally to achieve its own goals and values, but this is not the same thing as assuming that statesmen act rationally to achieve the goals or interests of the entire state and society. Similarly, some globalists may question the rationality of a decision-making or foreign policy process that, from their point of view, is dominated by narrow class interests. Whatever may be the rationality of individuals, institutions, or classes in maximizing or serving their own values or interests, the outcome for the whole may be suboptimal or less than the best.

VALUES, CHOICES, AND THEORY

Normative theory is relevant to each of the images and associated empirical theories we discuss in this book to the extent that one finds allowance for the exercise of human will within them. How much can statesmen affect the course of events? If those statesmen are driven internally, consistent with some psychological theories, or if they are severely constrained by their external environment, then normative theory plays a reduced, if any, role in their decision making. On the other hand, if human beings do have some degree of control over their affairs, including international relations, and if empirical theories take this effect of the will into account and exclude determinist "inevitabilities," then why has the normative part often been neglected in international relations theory?

A central argument made in this book is that the image and set of assumptions one holds concerning international relations do affect interpretations—the sense one makes of facts and the causal explanations or predictions one offers. Realists evaluate what they see in a manner that is different from those persons holding what we have labeled pluralist and globalist images of international relations. Nor are these three images necessarily the last word. Other competing images may emerge and in time supersede the three discussed in this volume.

Although it is important to come to an understanding of biases or perspectives associated with any particular image of international relations, we are by no means making the argument that knowledge of international relations is a function only of prior assumptions, preferences, or values. Reality will not so easily be subordinated to myth, however deeply held or sacred these myths may seem. When what we see as facts contradicts the image we hold, then it is the image that should be altered or even over-turned to accommodate new information.[20] Our knowledge of international relations is imperfect and various biases color our vision, but facts have a way of breaking down our preconceptions when these preconceptions are fallacious. Scientific skepticism about claims to truth forces testing of various propositions or hypotheses with histor-ical or other empirical data. Whether in the natural or social realms, scientific progress that enhances our knowledge of the world is painfully slow, but it is persistent.

NOTES

1. One can draw a distinction between normative and value considerations, perhaps seeing value as just one part of normative theory. Indeed, one can see that some normative considerations are nonmoral ones, as when an artist uses the terms *ought* and *right* in an esthetic context that does not have the moral content usually associated with these words. For our purposes, however, we use the terms *normative, moral,* and *value* interchangeably.
2. See, for example, Cicero, " 'The Republic' and 'The Laws' " in William Ebenstein, *Great Political Thinkers*, 4th ed. (New York: Holt, Rinehart and Winston, 1969), pp. 136–38.
3. According to Kant, one should exercise free will and act according to the "categorical imperative" whereby one acts "according to the maxim which you can at the same time will to be a universal law." Moreover, one should "treat humanity, in your own person, and in the person of everyone else as an end as well as a means, never merely as a means." The literature on Kant is vast, and no attempt is made to summarize it here. We are particularly drawn, however, to the late Hannah Arendt's *Lectures on Kant's Political Philosophy* (Chicago: University of Chicago Press, 1982). There are numerous translations of what is perhaps Kant's most important contribution to the international relations literature, his *Perpetual Peace*.
4. See John Rawls, *A Theory of Justice* (Cambridge, MA: Harvard University Press, 1971), p. 22.
5. Ibid., p. 62.
6. Ibid., p. 8.
7. E. H. Carr, *The Twenty Years' Crisis, 1919–1939* (New York: Harper & Row, 1964), p. 97.
8. Part of an effort to revive and develop normative international relations theory is a study by Charles R. Beitz. See his *Political Theory and International Relations* (Princeton, NJ: Princeton University Press, 1979). The selection for further reading at the end of this chapter indicates sub-stantial growth in the normative study of international relations.
9. See, for example, St. Augustine, "The City of God" in Ebenstein, *Great Political Thinkers*, pp. 181–84.
10. Noncombatancy, particularly if "innocents" are involved, may be construed as conveying an absolute immunity. As a practical matter, however, attacks in war on what are understood to be

legitimate military targets are usually accompanied by some collateral death and destruction. Following the logic of just war, however, such effects should always be minimized.

11. See, for example, Louis René Beres, *Mimicking Sisyphus: America's Countervailing Nuclear Strategy* (Lexington, MA: Lexington Books, 1983).

12. For an excellent treatment of human rights as a global issue, theories of human rights, and the politics of constructing human-rights regimes, see Jack Donnelly, *International Human Rights* (Boulder, CO: Westview, 1993). Cf. Donnelly, *Universal Human Rights in Theory and Practice* (Ithaca, NY: Cornell University Press, 1989). See also Philip Alston, ed., *The United Nations and Human Rights* (New York: Oxford University Press, 1992).

13. Geoffrey Best, "Human Rights as Universal and/or International Norms," paper presented to the London School of Economics, April 29, 1994. On law and the use of force, see also his *War and Law Since 1945* (New York: Oxford University Press, 1994).

14. For an excellent, single source for documents and selected writings on human rights, see Micheline R. Ishay, ed., *The Human Rights Reader* (New York: Routledge, 1997).

15. See Richard A. Falk, *A Study of Future Worlds* (New York: Free Press, 1975), pp. 11–30.

16. Richard A. Falk, *The End of World Order: Essays on Normative International Relations* (New York: Holmes and Meier, 1983), p. 53.

17. For an early summary of theories of rational choice, see Anthony Heath, *Rational Choice and Social Exchange: A Critique of Exchange Theory* (London: Cambridge University Press, 1976). See also Mancur Olson, *The Logic of Collective Action: Public Goods and the Theory of Groups* (Cambridge, MA: Harvard University Press, 1971), and William Riker, *The Theory of Political Coalitions* (New Haven, CT: Yale University Press, 1962).

18. See Ernst B. Haas, *Global Evangelism Rides Again: How to Protect Human Rights Without Really Trying* (Berkeley, CA: Institute of International Studies, 1978), pp. 1–23.

19. Thus, sovereign state jurisdiction exercised during the Cold War by the USSR over its citizens clashed with what was claimed by the U.S. government to be a fundamental human right of those Jews wishing to emigrate to the West.

20. Thomas Kuhn, for example, did not argue that one paradigm was as good as another. To the contrary, it was when anomalies accumulated to the point at which the empirical validity of a perspective was undermined that an alternative paradigm, one better able to account for such anomalies, would emerge. See Kuhn's *The Structure of Scientific Revolutions*, 2d ed. (Chicago: University of Chicago Press, 1970).

SELECTIONS FOR FURTHER READING AND REFERENCE

General

Arendt, Hannah. *Lectures on Kant's Political Philosophy*, ed. Ronald Beiner. Chicago: University of Chicago Press, 1982.

Beck, Robert J., Anthony Clark Arend, and Robert D. Vander Lugt, eds. *International Rules*. New York: Oxford University Press, 1996.

Beitz, Charles R. *Political Theory and International Relations*. Princeton, NJ: Princeton University Press, 1979.

Donelan, Michael. *Elements of International Political Theory*. New York: Oxford University Press, 1990.

Falk, Richard. *Explorations at the Edge of Time: The Prospects for World Order*. Philadelphia: Temple University Press, 1992.

———. *On Humane Governance: Toward a New Global Politics*. University Park: Pennsylvania State University Press, 1995.

Franck, Thomas M. *Fairness in International Law and Institutions*. New York: Oxford University Press, 1995.

Frost, Mervyn. *Ethics in International Relations: A Constitutive Theory*. Cambridge, England: Cambridge University Press, 1996.

———. *Towards a Normative Theory of International Relations*. Cambridge, England: Cambridge University Press, 1986.

Gilbert, Alan. *Democratic Individuality*. Cambridge, England: Cambridge University Press, 1990.

Hoffmann, Stanley. *Duties beyond Borders: On the Limits and Possibilities of Ethical International Politics*. Syracuse, NY: Syracuse University Press, 1981.

Nolan, Cathal J., ed. *Ethics and Statecraft: The Moral Dimension of International Affairs*. Westport, CT: Praeger, 1995.

Onuf, Nicholas. *World of Our Making: Rules and Rule in Social Theory and International Relations*. Columbia: University of South Carolina Press, 1989.

Raymond, Gregory A. "Problems and Prospects in the Study of International Norms." *Mershon International Studies Review* 4, Suppl. 2 (November 1997): 205–45.

Rosenthal, Joel H., ed. *Ethics and International Affairs*. Washington, DC: Georgetown University Press, 1995.

Thompson, Jana. *Justice and World Order: A Philosophical Inquiry*. New York: Routledge, Chapman & Hall, 1992.

On Human Rights

Barry, Brian, and Robert E. Goodin, eds. *Free Movement: Ethical Issues in the Transnational Migration of People and Money*. University Park: Pennsylvania State University Press, 1992.

Donnelly, Jack. *International Human Rights*. Boulder, CO: Westview Press, 1993.

———. *Universal Human Rights in Theory and Practice*. Ithaca, NY: Cornell University Press, 1989.

Haas, Ernst B. *Global Evangelism Rides Again: How to Protect Human Rights without Really Trying*. Berkeley: University of California Institute of International Studies, 1978.

———. *Human Rights and International Action: The Case of Freedom of Association*. Stanford, CA: Stanford University Press, 1970.

Ishay, Micheline R., ed. *The Human Rights Reader*. New York: Routledge, 1997.

Shute, Stephen, and Susan Hurley, eds. *On Human Rights: The Oxford Amnesty Lectures, 1993*. New York: Basic Books, 1993.

Walzer, Michael. *Thick and Thin: Moral Argument at Home and Abroad*. Notre Dame, IN: University of Notre Dame Press, 1994.

On War and Peace

Arendt, Hannah. *On Violence*. New York: Harcourt, Brace and World, 1970.

Bull, Hedley. "Recapturing the Just War for Political Theory." *World Politics* 31, 4 (July 1979): 588–99. [A review of Walzer, *Just and Unjust Wars*.]

Best, Geoffrey. *War and Law Since 1945*. New York: Oxford University Press, 1994.

Booth, Ken. *Law, Force and Diplomacy*. London: Allen & Unwin, 1985.

Doyle, Michael W. *Ways of War and Peace*. New York: W. W. Norton, 1997. [Part Four addresses conscience and power.]

Hoffmann, Stanley. *On War and Morality*. Princeton: Princeton University Press, 1989.

Howard, Michael, et al., eds. *The Laws of War: Constraints on Warfare in the Western World*. New Haven, CT: Yale University Press, 1994.

Johnson, James Turner. *Can Modern War Be Just?* New Haven, CT: Yale University Press, 1984.

———. *Just War Tradition and the Restraint of War*. Princeton, NJ: Princeton University Press, 1981.

O'Brien, William V. *The Conduct of Just and Limited War*. New York: Praeger, 1981.

Ramsey, Paul. *The Just War: Force and Political Responsibility*. New York: University Press of America, 1968, 1983.

Rapoport, Anatol. *The Origins of Violence*. New Brunswick, NJ: Transaction Publishers, 1989, 1995.

———. *Peace: An Idea Whose Time Has Come*. Ann Arbor: University of Michigan Press, 1992.

———. *Strategy and Conscience*. New York: Schocken Books, 1969.

Reisman, W. Michael, and Christ T. Antonious, eds. *The Laws of War: A Comprehensive Collection of Primary Documents on International Law Governing Armed Conflict*. New York: Vintage, 1994.

Thompson, Kenneth W., ed. *Ethics and International Relations*. New Brunswick, NJ: Transaction Books, 1985.

———. *Traditions and Values in Politics and Diplomacy*. Baton Rouge, LA: State University Press, 1992.

Walzer, Michael. *Just and Unjust Wars*. New York: Basic Books, 1977.
Welch, David A. *Justice and the Genesis of War*. New York: Cambridge University Press, 1993.

On Idealism and Realism—An Old Debate

Carr, E. H. *The Twenty Years' Crisis, 1919–1939*. New York: Harper & Row, 1964.
Herz, John H. *The Nation-State and the Crisis of World Politics*. New York: David McKay, 1976.
———. *Political Realism and Political Idealism*. Chicago: University of Chicago Press, 1951.
———. "Political Realism Revisited." *International Studies Quarterly* 25, 2 (June 1981): 182–97.
Kegley, Charles W. "Neo-Idealism: A Practical Matter." *Ethics and International Affairs* 2 (1988): 173–97.
Kennan, George F. "Morality and Foreign Policy." *Foreign Affairs* 64, 2 (Winter 1985–86): 205–18.
Morgenthau, Hans J. *In Defense of the National Interest*. New York: Alfred A. Knopf, 1960.
———. *Politics among Nations*, 5th ed. New York: Knopf, 1978.
———. *Truth and Power*. New York: Praeger, 1970.
Niebuhr, Reinhold. *Christian Realism and Political Problems*. New York, Scribners, 1953.
Osgood, Robert E. *Ideals and Self-Interest in American Foreign Relations*. Chicago: University of Chicago Press, 1953.
Wolfers, Arnold. "Statesmanship and Moral Choice." *World Politics* (1949): 175–95.

War, Peace, and the Law of Nations

HUGO GROTIUS

The "father of international law," focusing on the problem of war and peace, develops the idea of law among nations. The Grotian view of international relations is one of states constrained by mutually agreed-upon rules or law to govern their interactions with one another in both war and peace. That international relations ought to be governed by law is a classic statement in normative political theory. The Grotian perspective has been enormously influential on the English school's focus on international society.

The municipal law of Rome and of other states has been treated by many, who have undertaken to elucidate it by means of commentaries or to reduce it to a convenient digest. That body of law, however, which is concerned with the mutual relations among states or rulers of states, whether derived from nature, or established by divine ordinances, or having its origin in custom and tacit agreement, few have touched upon. Up to the present time no one has treated it in a comprehensive and systematic manner; yet the welfare of mankind demands that this task be accomplished.

Cicero justly characterized as of surpassing worth a knowledge of treaties of alliance, conventions, and understandings of peoples, kings and foreign nations—a knowledge, in short, of the whole law of war and peace. And to this knowledge Euripides gives the preference over an understanding of things divine and human, for he represents Theoclymenus as being thus addressed:

For you, who know the fate of men and gods
What is, what shall be, shameful world it be
To know not what is just.

Such a work is all the more necessary because in our day, as in former times, there is no lack of men who view this branch of law with contempt as having no reality outside of an empty name. On the lips of men quite generally is the saying of Euphemus, which Thucydides quotes, that in the case of a king or imperial city nothing is unjust which is expedient. Of like implication is the statement that for those whom fortune favors might makes right, and that the administration of a state cannot be carried on without injustice.

Furthermore, the controversies which arise between peoples or kings generally have Mars as their arbiter. That war is irreconcilable with all law is a view held not alone by the ignorant populace; expressions are often let slip by well-informed and thoughtful men which lend coun-

From Hugo Grotius, *Prolegomena to the Law of War and Peace*, trans. Francis W. Kelsey. (New York: Liberal Arts Press, 1957). Published with the permission of the Carnegie Endowment for International Peace.

tenance to such a view. Nothing is more common than the assertion of antagonism between law and arms. Thus Ennius says:

> Not on grounds of right is battle joined,
> But rather with the sword do men
> Seek to enforce their claims

Horace, too describes the savage temper of Achilles in this wise:

> Laws, he declares, were not for him ordained;
> By dint of arms he claims all for himself.

Another poet depicts another military leader as commencing war with the words:

> Here peace and violated laws I leave behind.

Antigonus when advanced in years ridiculed a man who brought to him a treatise on justice when he was engaged in besieging cities that did not belong to him. Marius declared that the din of arms made it impossible for him to hear the voice of the laws. Even Pompey, whose expression of countenance was so mild dared to say: "When I am in arms, am I to think of laws?"

Among Christian writers a similar thought finds frequent expression. A single quotation from Tertullian may serve in place of many: "Deception, harshness, and injustice are the regular business of battles." They who so think will no doubt wish to confront us with this passage in Comedy:

> These things uncertain should you, by reason's aid,
> Try to make certain, no more would you gain
> Than if you tried by reason to go mad.

Since our discussion concerning law will have been undertaken in vain if there is no law, in order to open the way for a favorable reception of our work and at the same time to fortify it against attacks, this very serious error must be briefly refuted. In order that we may not be obliged to deal with a crowd of opponents, let us assign to them a pleader. And whom should we choose in preference to Carneades?[1] For he had

attained to so perfect a mastery of the peculiar tenet of his Academy that he was able to devote the power of his eloquence to the service of falsehood not less readily than to that of truth.

Carneades, then, having undertaken to hold a brief against justice, in particular against that phase of justice with which we are concerned, was able to muster no argument stronger than this, that, for reasons of expediency, men imposed upon themselves laws, which vary according to customs, and among the same peoples often undergo changes as times change: moreover, that there is no law of nature, because all creatures, men as well as animals, are impelled by nature toward ends advantageous to themselves, that, consequently, there is no justice, or, if such there be, it is supreme folly, since one does violence to his own interests if he consults the advantage of others.

What the philosopher [Horace] here says, and the poet reaffirms in verse,

> And just from unjust Nature cannot know,

must not for one moment be admitted. Man is, to be sure, an animal, but an animal of a superior kind, much farther removed from all other animals than the different kinds of animals are from one another; evidence on this point may be found in the many traits peculiar to the human species. But among the traits characteristic of man is an impelling desire for society, that is, for the social life—not of any and every sort, but peaceful, and organized according to the measure of his intelligence, with those who are of his own kind; this social trend the Stoics called "sociableness." Stated as a universal truth, therefore, the assertion that every animal is impelled by nature to seek only its own good cannot be conceded. . . .

This maintenance of the social order, which we have roughly sketched, and which is consonant with human intelligence, is the source of law properly so called. To this sphere of law belong the abstaining from that which is another's, the restoration to another of anything of his which we may have, together with any gain which we may have received from it; the obligation to fulfill promises, the making good of a loss incurred through our fault, and the inflicting of penalties upon men according to their desserts.

From this signification of the word "law" there has flowed another and more extended meaning. Since over other animals man has the advantage of possessing not only a strong bent toward social life, of which we have spoken, but also a power of discrimination which enables him to decide what things are agreeable or harmful (as to both things present and things to come), and what can lead to either alternative, in such things it is meet for the nature of man, within the limitations of human intelligence, to follow the direction of a well-tempered judgment, being neither led astray by fear or the allurement of immediate pleasure, nor carried away by rash impulse. Whatever is clearly at variance with such judgment is understood to be contrary also to the law of nature, that is, to the nature of man. . . .

Herein, then, is another source of law besides the source in nature, that is, the free will of God, to which beyond all cavil our reason tells us we must render obedience. But the law of nature of which we have spoken, comprising alike that which relates to the social life of man and that which is so called in a larger sense, proceeding as it does from the essential traits implanted in man, can nevertheless rightly be attributed to God because of his having willed that such traits exist in us. In this sense, too, Chrysippus and the Stoics used to say that the origin of law should be sought in no other source than Jupiter himself; and from the name Jupiter the Latin word for law (*ius*) was probably derived. . . .

Again, since it is a rule of the law of nature to abide by pacts (for it was necessary that among men there be some method of obligating themselves one to another, and no other natural method can be imagined), out of this source the bodies of municipal law have arisen. For those who had associated themselves with some group, or had subjected themselves to a man or to men, had either expressly promised, or from

the nature of the transaction must be understood impliedly to have promised, that they would conform to that which should have been determined, in the one case by the majority, in the other by those upon whom authority had been conferred.

What is said, therefore, in accordance with the view not only of Carneades but also of others, that

> Expediency is, as it were, the mother
> Of what is just and fair

is not true, if we wish to speak accurately. For the very nature of man, which even if we had no lack of anything would lead us into the mutual relations of society, is the mother of the law of nature. But the mother of municipal law is that obligation which arises from mutual consent; and since this obligation derives its force from the law of nature, nature may be considered, so to say, the great-grandmother of municipal law.

The law of nature nevertheless has the reinforcement of expediency; for the author of nature willed that as individuals we should be weak, and should lack many things needed in order to live properly, to the end that we might be the more constrained to cultivate the social life. But expediency afforded an opportunity also for municipal law, since that kind of association of which we have spoken, and subjection to authority, have their roots in expediency. From this it follows that those who prescribe laws for others in so doing are accustomed to have or ought to have some advantage in view.

But just as the laws of each state have in view the advantage of that state, so by mutual consent it has become possible that certain laws should originate as between all states, or a great many states; and it is apparent that the laws thus originating had in view the advantage, not of particular states, but of the great society of states. And this is what is called the law of nations, whenever we distinguish that term from the law of nature.

This division of law Carneades passed over altogether. For he divided all law into the law of nature and the law of particular countries. Nevertheless if undertaking to treat of the body of law which is maintained between states—for he added a statement in regard to war and things acquired by means of war—he would surely have been obliged to make mention of this law. . . .

But, not to repeat what I have said, that law is not founded on expediency alone, there is no state so powerful that it may not at some time need the help of others outside itself, either for purposes of trade, or even to ward off the forces of many foreign nations united against it. In consequence we see that even the most powerful peoples and sovereigns seek alliances, which are quite devoid of significance according to the point of view of those who confine law within the boundaries of states. Most true is the saying that all things are uncertain the moment men depart from law.

If no association of men can be maintained without law, as Aristotle showed . . . also that association which binds together the human race, or binds many nations together, has need of law; this was perceived by him who said that shameful deeds ought not to be committed even for the sake of one's country. Aristotle takes sharply to task those who, while unwilling to allow anyone to exercise authority over themselves except in accordance with law, yet are quite indifferent as to whether foreigners are treated according to law or not. . . .

Least of all should that be admitted which some people imagine, that in war all laws are in abeyance. On the contrary war ought not to be undertaken except for the enforcement of rights; when once undertaken, it should be carried on only within the bounds of law and good faith. Demosthenes well said that war is directed against those who cannot be held in check by judicial processes. For judgments are efficacious against those who feel that they are too weak to resist; against those who are equally strong, or think that they are, wars are undertaken. But in order that wars may be justified, they must be carried on with not less scrupulousness than judicial processes are wont to be.

Let the laws be silent, then, in the midst of arms, but only the laws of the state, those that the courts are concerned with, that are adapted only to a state of peace; not those other laws, which are of perpetual validity and suited to all times. It was exceedingly well said by Dio of Prusa, that between enemies written laws, that is, laws of particular states, are not in force, but that unwritten laws are in force, that is, those which nature prescribes, or the agreement of nations has established. This is set forth by that ancient formula of the Romans: "I think that those things ought to be sought by means of a war that is blameless and righteous."

The ancient Romans, as Varro noted, were slow in undertaking war, and permitted themselves no license in that matter, because they held the view that a war ought not to be waged except when free from reproach. Camillus said that wars should be carried on justly no less than bravely; Scipio Africanus, that the Roman people commenced and ended wars justly. In another passage you may read: "War has its laws no less than peace." Still another writer admires Fabricius as a great man who maintained his probity in war—a thing most difficult—and believed that even in relation to an enemy there is such a thing as wrongdoing.

The histories in many a passage reveal how great in war is the influence of the consciousness that one has justice on his side; they often attribute victory chiefly to this cause. Hence the proverbs that a soldier's strength is broken or increased by his cause; that he who has taken up arms unjustly rarely comes back in safety; that hope is the comrade of a good cause; and others of the same purport.

No one ought to be disturbed, furthermore, by the successful outcome of unjust enterprises. For it is enough that the fairness of the cause exerts a certain influence, even a strong influence upon actions, although the effect of that influence, as happens in human affairs, is often nullified by the interference of other causes. Even for winning friendships, of which for many reasons nations as well as individuals have need, a reputation for having undertaken war not rashly nor unjustly, and of having waged it in a manner above reproach, is exceedingly efficacious. No one readily allies himself with those in whom he believes that there is only a slight regard for law, for the right, and for good faith.

Fully convinced, by the considerations which I have advanced, that there is a common law among nations, which is valid alike for war and in war, I have had many and weighty reasons for undertaking to write upon this subject. Throughout the Christian world I observed a lack of restraint in relation to war, such as even barbarous races should be ashamed of; I observed that men rush to arms for slight causes, or no cause at all, and that when arms have once been taken up there is no longer any respect for law, divine or human; it is as if, in accordance with a general decree, frenzy had openly been let loose for the committing of all crimes.

Confronted with such utter ruthlessness, many men who are the very furthest from being bad man, have come to the point of forbidding all use of arms to the Christian, whose rule of conduct above everything else comprises the duty of loving all men. To this opinion sometimes John Ferus and my fellow countryman Erasmus seem to incline, men who have the utmost devotion to peace in both Church and State; but their purpose, as I take it, is, when things have gone in one direction, to force them in the opposite direction, as we are accustomed to do, that they may come back to a true middle ground. But the very effort of pressing too hard in the opposite direction is often so far from being helpful that it does harm, because in such arguments the detection of what is extreme is easy, and results in weakening the influence of other statements which are well within the bounds of truth. For both extremes therefore a remedy must be found, that men may not believe either that nothing is allowable, or that everything is.

At the same time through devotion to study in private life I have wished—as the only course now open to me, undeservedly forced out from my native land, which had been graced by so many of my labors—to contribute somewhat to the philosophy of the law, which previously, in public service, I practiced with the utmost degree of probity of which I was capable. Many heretofore have purposed to give to this subject a well-ordered presentation; no one has succeeded. And in fact such a result cannot be accomplished unless—a point which until now has not been sufficiently kept in view—those elements which come from positive law are properly separated from those which arise from nature. For the principles of the law of nature, since they are always the same, can easily be brought into a systematic form; but the elements of positive law, since they often undergo change and are different in different places, are outside the domain of systematic treatment, just as other notions of particular things are. . . .

In order to prove the existence of this law of nature, I have, furthermore, availed myself to the testimony of philosophers, historians, poets; finally also of orators. Not that confidence is to be reposed in them without discrimination, for they were accustomed to serve the interests of their sect, their subject, or their cause. But when many at different times and in different places affirm the same thing as certain, that ought to be referred to a universal cause; and this cause, in the lines of inquiry which we are following, must be either a correct conclusion drawn from the principles of nature, or common consent. The former points to the law of nature, the latter to the law of nations.

The distinction between these kinds of law is not to be drawn from the testimonies themselves (for writers everywhere confuse the terms law of nature and law of nations), but from the character of the matter. For whatever cannot be deduced from certain principles by a sure process of reasoning, and yet is clearly observed everywhere, must have its origin in the free will of man.

These two kinds of law, therefore, I have always particularly sought to distinguish from each other and from municipal law. . . .

In my work as a whole I have, above all else, aimed at three things: to make the reasons for my conclusions as evident as possible; to set forth in a definite order the matters which needed to be treated; and to distinguish clearly between things which seemed to be the same and were not.

I have refrained from discussing topics which belong to another subject, such as those that teach what may be advantageous in practice. For such topics have their own special field, that of politics, which Aristotle rightly treats by itself, without introducing extraneous matter into it. Bodin, on the contrary, mixed up politics with the body of law with which we are concerned. In some places nevertheless I have made mention of that which is expedient, but only in passing, and in order to distinguish it more clearly from what is lawful.

If anyone thinks that I have had in view any controversies of our own times, either those that have arisen or those which can be foreseen as likely to arise, he will do me an injustice. With all truthfulness I aver that, just as mathematicians treat their figures as abstracted from bodies, so in treating law I have withdrawn my mind from every particular fact. . . .

I beg and adjure all those into whose hands this work shall come, that they assume toward me the same liberty which I have assumed in passing upon the opinions and writings of others. They who shall find me in error will not be more quick to advise me than I to avail myself of their advice.

And now if anything has here been said by me inconsistent with piety, with good morals, with Holy Writ, with the concord of the Christian Church, or with any aspect of truth, let it be as if unsaid.

Note

1. 214(?)–129 B.C., Greek skeptic philosopher and founder of the New or Third Academy in Athens.

Morality, Politics, and Perpetual Peace

IMMANUEL KANT

In this essay, Kant presents an argument for politics compatible with moral principle within a state and among states. He rejects classic notions that in politics might makes right or that one must compromise ethics for prudential reasons.

Taken objectively, morality is in itself practical, being the totality of unconditionally mandatory laws according to which we ought to act. It would obviously be absurd, after granting authority to the concept of duty, to pretend that we cannot do our duty, for in that case this concept would itself drop out of morality (*ultra posse nemo obligatur*). Consequently, there can be no conflict of politics, as a practical doctrine of right, with ethics, as a theoretical doctrine of right. That is to say, there is no conflict of practice with theory, unless by ethics we mean a general doctrine of prudence, which would be the same as a theory of the maxims for choosing the

From Immanuel Kant, *Perpetual Peace*, ed. Lewis White Beck (Indianapolis and New York: Bobbs-Merrill Company, 1957), pp. 35–46. Reprinted by permission.

most fitting means to accomplish the purposes of self-interest. But to give this meaning to ethics is equivalent to denying that there is any such thing at all.

Politics say, "Be ye wise as serpents"; morality adds, as a limiting condition, "and guileless as doves." If these two injunctions are incompatible in a single command, then politics and morality are really in conflict; but if these two qualities ought always to be united, the thought of contrariety is absurd, and the question as to how the conflict between morals and politics is to be resolved cannot even be posed as a problem. Although the propositions, "Honesty is the best policy," implies a theory which practice unfortunately often refutes, the equally theoretical "Honesty is better than any policy" is beyond refutation and is indeed the indispensable condition of policy.

The tutelary divinity of morality yields not to Jupiter, for this tutelary divinity of force still is subject to destiny. That is, reason is not yet sufficiently enlightened to survey the entire series of predetermining causes, and such vision would be necessary for one to be able to foresee with certainty the happy or unhappy effects which follow human actions by the mechanism of nature (though we know enough to have hope that they will accord with our wishes). But what we have to do in order to remain in the path of duty (according to rules of wisdom) reason instructs us by her rules, and her teaching suffices for attaining the ultimate end.

Now the practical man, to whom morality is mere theory even though he concedes that it can and should be followed, ruthlessly renounces our fond hope [that it will be followed]. He does so because he pretends to have seen in advance that man, by his nature, will never will what is required for realizing the goal of perpetual peace. Certainly the will of each individual to live under a juridical constitution according to principles of freedom (i.e., the distributive unity of the will of all) is not sufficient to this end. That all together should will this condition (i.e., the collective

unity of the united will)—the solution to this troublous problem—is also required. Thus a whole of civil society is formed. But since a uniting cause must supervene upon the variety of particular volitions in order to produce a common will from them, establishing this whole is something no one individual in the group can perform; hence in the practical execution of this idea we can count on nothing but force to establish the juridical condition, on the compulsion of which public law will later be established. We can scarcely hope to find in the legislator a moral intention sufficient to induce him to commit to the general will the establishment of a legal constitution after he has formed the nation from a horde of savages; therefore, we cannot but expect (in practice) to find in execution wide deviations from this idea (in theory).

It will then be said that he who once has power in his hands will not allow the people to prescribe laws for him; a state which once is able to stand under no external laws will not submit to the decision of other states how it should seek its rights against them; and one continent, which feels itself superior to another, even though the other does not interfere with it, will not neglect to increase its power by robbery or even conquest. Thus all theoretical plans of civil and international laws and laws of world citizenship vanish into empty and impractical ideas, while practice based on empirical principles of human nature, not blushing to draw its maxims from the usages of the world, can alone hope to find a sure ground for its political edifice.

If there is no freedom and no morality based on freedom, and everything which occurs or can occur happens by the mere mechanism of nature, certainly politics (which is the art of using this mechanism for ruling men) is the whole of practical wisdom, and the concept of right is an empty thought. But if we find it necessary to connect the latter with politics, and even to raise it to a limiting condition thereon, the possibility of their being united must be conceded. I can easily conceive of a moral politician, i.e., one who so chooses political principles that they are consistent with those of morality; but I cannot conceive of a political moralist, one who forges a morality in such a way that it conforms to the statesman's advantage.

When a remediable defect is found in the constitution of the state or in its relations to others, the principle of the moral politician will be that it is a duty, especially of the rulers of the state, to inquire how it can be remedied as soon as possible in a way conforming to natural law as a model presented by reason; this he will do even if it costs self-sacrifice. But it would be absurd to demand that every defect be immediately and impetuously changed, since the disruption of the bonds of a civil society or a union of world citizens before a better constitution is ready to take its place is against all politics agreeing with morality. But it can be demanded that at least the maxim of the necessity of such a change should be taken to heart by those in power, so that they may continuously approach the goal of the constitution that is best under laws of right. A state may exercise a republican rule, even though by its present constitution it has a despotic sovereignty, until gradually the people become susceptible to the influence simply of the idea of the authority of law (as if it possessed physical power) and thus is found fit to be its own legislator (as its own legislation is originally established on law). If a violent revolution, engendered by a bad constitution, introduces by illegal means a more legal constitution, to lead the people back to the earlier constitution would not be permitted; but, while the revolution lasted, each person who openly or covertly shared in it would have justly incurred the punishment due to those who rebel. As to the external relations of states, a state cannot be expected to renounce its constitution even though it is a despotic one (which has the advantage of being stronger in relation to foreign enemies) so long as it is exposed to the danger of being swallowed up by other states. Thus

even in the case of the intention to improve the constitution, postponement to a more propitious time may be permitted.[1]

It may be that despotizing moralists, in practice blundering, often violate rules of political prudence through measures they adopt or propose too precipitately; but experience will gradually retrieve them from their infringement of nature and lead them on to a better course. But the moralizing politician, by glossing over principles of politics which are opposed to the right with the pretext that human nature is not capable of the good as reason prescribes it, only makes reform impossible and perpetuates the violation of law.

Instead of possessing the *practical science* they boast of, these politicians have only *practices*; they flatter the power which is then ruling so as not to be remiss in their private advantage, and they sacrifice the nation and, possibly, the whole world. This is the way of all professional lawyers (not legislators) when they go into politics. Their task is not to reason too nicely about the legislation but to execute the momentary commands on the statute books; consequently, the legal constitution in force at any time is to them the best, but when it is amended from above, this amendment always seems best, too. Thus everything is preserved in its accustomed mechanical order. Their adroitness in fitting into all circumstances gives them the illusion of being able to judge constitutional principles according to concepts of right (not empirically, but a priori). They make a great show of understanding *men* (which is certainly something to be expected of them, since they have to deal with so many) without understanding *man* and what can be made of him, for they lack the higher point of view of anthropological observation which is needed for this. If with these ideas they go into civil and international law, as reason prescribes it, they take this step in a spirit of chicanery, for they still follow their accustomed mechanical routine of despotically imposed coercive laws in a field where only concepts of reason can establish a legal compulsion according to the principles of freedom, under which alone a just and durable constitution is possible. In this field the pretended practical man thinks he can solve the problem of establishing such a constitution without the rational idea but solely from the experience he has had with what was previously the most lasting constitution—a constitution which in many cases was opposed to the right.

The maxims which he makes use of (though he does not divulge them) are, roughly speaking, the following sophisms:

1. *Fac et excusa.* Seize every favourable opportunity for usurping the right of the state over its own people or over a neighboring people; the justification will be easier and more elegant *ex post facto*, and the power can be more easily glossed over, especially when the supreme power in the state is also the legislative authority which must be obeyed without argument. It is much more difficult to do the violence when one has first to wait upon the consideration of convincing arguments and to meet them with counterarguments. Boldness itself gives the appearance of inner conviction of the legitimacy of the deed, and the god of success is afterward the best advocate.

2. *Si fecisti, nega.* What you have committed, deny that it was your fault—for instance, that you have brought your people to despair and hence to rebellion. Rather assert that it was due to the obstinacy of your subjects; or, if you have conquered a neighboring nation, say that the fault lies in the nature of man, who, if not met by force, can be counted on to make use of it to conquer you.

3. *Divide et impera.* That is, if there are certain privileged persons in your nation who have chosen you as their chief (*primus inter pares*), set them at variance with one another and embroil them with the people. Show the latter visions of greater freedom, and all will soon depend on your untrammeled will. Or if it is foreign states that concern you, it is a pretty safe means to sow discord among them so that, by seeming to protect the weaker, you can conquer them one after another.

Certainly no one is now the dupe of these political maxims, for they are already universally known. Nor are they blushed at, as if their injustice were too glaring, for great powers blush only at the judgment of other great powers but not at that of the common masses. It is not that they are ashamed of revealing such principles (for all of them are in the same boat with respect to the morality of their maxims); they are ashamed only when these maxims fail, for they still have political honor which cannot be disputed—and this honor is the aggrandizement of their power by whatever means.[2]

All these twistings and turnings of an immoral doctrine of prudence in leading men from their natural state of war to a state of peace prove at least that men in both their private and their public relationships cannot reject the concept of right or trust themselves openly to establish politics merely on the artifices of prudence. Thus they do not refuse obedience to the concept of public law, which is especially manifest in international law; on the contrary, they give all due honor to it, even when they are inventing a hundred pretenses and subterfuges to escape from it in practice, imputing its authority as the source and union of all laws, to crafty force.

Let us put an end to this sophism, if not to the injustice it protects, and force the false representatives of power to confess that they do not plead in favor of the right but in favor of might. This is revealed in the imperious tone they assume as if they themselves could command the right. Let us remove the delusion by which they and others are duped, and discover the supreme principle from which the intention to perpetual peace stems. Let us show that everything evil which stands in its way derives from the fact that the political moralist begins where the moral politician would correctly leave off, and that, since he thus subordinates principles to the end (putting the cart before the horse), he vitiates his own purpose of bringing politics into agreement with morality.

To make practical philosophy self-consistent, it is necessary, first, to decide the question: In problems of practical reason, must we begin from its material principles, i.e., the end as the object of choice? Or should we begin from the formal principles of pure reason, i.e., from the principle which is concerned solely with freedom in outer relations and which reads, "So act that you can will that your maxim could become a universal law regardless of the end"?

Without doubt it is the latter which has precedence, for as a principle of law it has unconditional necessity. On the other hand, the former is obligatory only if we presuppose the empirical conditions of the proposed end, i.e., its practicability. Thus if this end (in this case, perpetual peace) is a duty, it must be derived from the formal principle of the maxims of external actions. The first principle, that of the political moralist, pertaining to civil and international law and the law of world citizenship, is merely a problem of technique (*problema technicum*); the second, as the problem of the moral politician to whom it is an ethical problem (*problema morale*), is far removed from the other in its method of leading toward perpetual peace, which is wished not merely as a material good but also as a condition issuing from an acknowledgment of duty.

For the solution of the former, the problem of political prudence, much knowledge of nature is required so that its mechanism may be employed toward the desired end; yet all this is uncertain in its results for perpetual peace, with whatever sphere of public law we are concerned. It is uncertain, for example, whether the people are better kept in obedience and maintained in prosperity by severity or by the charm of distinctions which flatter their vanity, by the power of one or the union of various chiefs, or perhaps merely by a serving nobility or by the power of the people. History furnishes us with contradictory examples from all governments (with the exception of the truly republican, which can alone appeal to the mind of a moral politician). Still more uncertain is an international law allegedly erected on the statutes of ministries. It is, in fact, a word without meaning, resting as it does on compacts which, in the very act of being concluded, contain secret reservations for their violation.

On the other hand, the solution of the second problem, that of political wisdom, presses itself upon us, as it were; it is clear to everyone and puts to shame all affectation. It leads directly to the end, but, remembering discretion, it does not precipitately hasten to do so by force; rather, it continuously approaches it under the conditions offered by favorable circumstances.

Then it may be said, "Seek ye first the kingdom of pure practical reason and its righteousness, and your end (the blessing of perpetual peace) will necessarily follow." For it is the peculiarity of morals, especially with respect to its principles of public law and hence in relation to a politics known a priori, that the less it makes conduct depend on the proposed end, i.e., the intended material or moral advantage, the more it agrees with it in general. This is because it is the universal will given a priori (in a nation or in the relations among different nations) which determines the law among men, and if practicing consistently follows it, this will can also, by the mechanism of nature, cause the desired result and make the concept of law effective. So, for instance, it is a principle of moral politics that a people should unite into a state according to juridical concepts of freedom and equality, and this principle is based not on prudence but on duty. Political moralists may argue as much as they wish about the natural mechanism of a mass of men forming a society, assuming a mechanism which would weaken those principles and vitiate their end; or they may seek to prove their assertions by examples of poorly organized constitutions of ancient and modern times (for instance, of democracies without representative systems). They deserve no hearing, particularly as such a pernicious theory may itself occasion the evil which it prophesies, throwing human beings into one class with all other living machines, differing from them only in their consciousness that they are not free, which makes them, in their own judgment, the most miserable of all beings in the world.

The true but somewhat boastful sentence which has become proverbial, *Fiat iustitia, pereat mundus* ("Let justice reign even if all the rascals in the world should perish from it"), is a stout principle of right which cuts asunder the whole tissue of artifice or force. But it should not be misunderstood as a permission to use one's own right with extreme rigor (which would conflict with ethical duty); it should be understood as the obligation of those in power not to limit or to extend anyone's right through sympathy or disfavor. This requires, first, an internal constitution of the state erected on pure principles of right, and, second, a convention of the state with other near or distant states (analogous to a universal state) for the legal settlement of their differences. This implies only that political maxims must not be derived from the welfare or happiness which a single state expects from obedience to them, and thus not from the end which one of them proposes for itself. That is, they must not be deduced from volition as the supreme yet empirical principle of political wisdom, but rather from the pure concept of the duty of right, from the *ought* whose principle is given a priori by pure reason, regardless of what the physical consequences may be. The world will by no means perish by a diminution in the number of evil men. Moral evil has the . . . property of being opposed to and destructive of

its own purposes (especially in the relationships between evil men); thus it gives place to the moral principle of the good, though only through a slow progress.

Thus objectively, or in theory, there is no conflict between morals and politics. Subjectively, however, in the selfish propensity of men (which should not be called "practice," as this would imply that it rested on rational maxims), this conflict will always remain. Indeed, it should remain, because it serves as a whetstone of virtue, whose true courage (by the principle, *tu ne cede malis, sed contra audentior ito*)[3] in the present case does not so much consist in defying with strong resolve evils and sacrifices which must be undertaken along with the conflict, but rather in detecting and conquering the crafty and far more dangerously deceitful and treasonable principle of evil in ourselves, which puts forward the weakness of human nature as justification for every transgression.

In fact, the political moralist may say: The ruler and people, or nation and nation, do each other no injustice when by violence or fraud they make war on each other, although they do commit injustice in general in that they refuse to respect the concept of right, which alone could establish perpetual peace. For since the one does transgress his duty against the other, who is likewise lawlessly disposed toward him, each gets what he deserves when they destroy each other. But enough of the race still remains to let this game continue into the remotest ages in order that posterity, some day, might take these perpetrators as a warning example. Hence providence is justified in the history of the world, for the moral principle in man is never extinguished, while with advancing civilization reason grows pragmatically in its capacity to realize ideas of law. But at the same time the culpability for the transgressions also grows. If we assume that humanity never will or can be improved, the only thing which a theodicy seems unable to justify is creation itself, the fact that a race of such corrupt beings ever was on earth. But the point of view necessary for such an assumption is far too high for us, and we cannot theoretically support our philosophical concepts of the supreme power which is inscrutable to us.

To such dubious consequences we are inevitably driven if we do not assume that pure principles of right have objective reality, i.e., that they may be applied, and that the people in a state and, further, states themselves in their mutual relations should act according to them, whatever objections empirical politics may raise. Thus true politics can never take a step without rendering homage to morality. Though politics by itself is a difficult art, its union with morality is no art at all, for this union cuts the knot which politics could not untie when they were in conflict. The rights of men must be held sacred, however much sacrifice it may cost the ruling power. One cannot compromise here and seek the middle course of a pragmatic conditional law between the morally right and the expedient. All politics must bend its knee before the right. But by this it can hope slowly to reach the stage where it will shine with an immortal glory.

Notes

1. These are permissive laws of reason. Public law laden with injustice must be allowed to stand, either until everything is of itself ripe for complete reform or until this maturity has been brought about by peaceable means; for a legal constitution, even though it be right to only a low degree, is better than none at all, the anarchic condition which would result from precipitate reform. Political wisdom, therefore, will make it a duty to introduce reforms which accord with the ideal of public law. But even when nature herself produces revolutions, political wisdom will not employ them to legitimize still greater oppression. On the contrary, it will use them as a call of nature for fundamental reforms to produce a lawful constitution founded upon principles of freedom, for only such a constitution is durable.

2. Even if we doubt a certain wickedness in the nature of men who live together in a state, and instead plausibly cite lack of civilization, which is not yet sufficiently advanced, i.e., regard barbarism as the cause of those antilawful manifestations of their character, this viciousness is clearly and incontestably shown in the foreign relations of states. Within each state it is veiled by the compulsion of civil laws, because the inclination to violence between the citizens is fettered by the stronger power of the government. This relationship not only gives a moral veneer (*causae non causae*) to the whole but actually facilitates the development of the moral disposition to a direct respect for the law by placing a barrier against the outbreak of unlawful inclinations. Each person believes that he himself would hold the concept of law sacred and faithfully follow it provided he were sure that he could expect the same from others, and the government does in part assure him of this. Thereby a great step (though not yet a moral step) is taken toward morality, which is attachment to this concept of duty for its own sake and without regard to hope of a similar response from others. But since each one with his own good opinion of himself presupposes a malicious disposition on the part of all the others, they all pronounce the judgment that they in fact are all worth very little. We shall not discuss how this comes about, though it cannot be blamed on the nature of man as a free being. But since even respect for the concept of right (which man cannot absolutely refuse to respect) solemnly sanctions the theory that he has the capacity of conforming to it, everyone sees that he, for his part, must act according to it, however others may act.

3. "Yield not to evils, but go against the stronger" (*Aeneid* VI. 95).

The Nature of Politics

E. H. CARR

The late English writer, E. H. Carr, argues that the practice and study of politics require an appreciation of realism as well as utopianism, power as well as morality. He explores the tension between realism and utopian thought.

Man has always lived in groups. The smallest kind of human group, the family, has clearly been necessary for the maintenance of the species. But so far as is known, men have always from the most primitive times formed semi-permanent groups larger than the single family; and one of the functions of such a group has been to regulate relations between its members. Politics deals with the behavior of men in such organised permanent or semi-permanent groups. All attempts to deduce the nature of society from the supposed behavior of man in isolation are purely theoretical, since there is no reason to assume that such a man ever existed. Aristotle laid the foundation of all sound thinking about politics when he declared that man was by nature a political animal.

Man in society reacts to his fellow men in two opposite ways. Sometimes he displays egoism, or the will to assert himself at the expense of others. At other times he displays sociability, or the desire to cooperate with others, to enter into reciprocal relations of good-will and friendship with them, and even to subordinate himself to them. In every society these two qualities can be seen at work. No society can exist unless a substantial proportion of its members exhibits in some degree the desire for cooperation and mutual good-will. But in every society some sanction is required to produce the measure of solidarity requisite for its maintenance; and this sanction is applied by a controlling group or individual acting in the name of the society. Membership of most societies is voluntary, and the only ultimate sanction which can be applied is expulsion. But the peculiarity of political society, which in the modern world takes the form of the state, is that membership is compulsory. The state, like other societies, must be based on some sense of common interests and obligations among its members. But coercion is regularly exercised by a governing group to enforce loyalty and obedience; and this coercion inevitably means that the governors control the governed and "exploit" them for their own purposes.[1]

The dual character of political society is therefore strongly marked. Professor Laski tells us that "every state is built upon the consciences of men."[2] On the other hand, anthropology, as well as much recent history, teaches that "war seems to be the main agency in producing the state"; and Professor Laski himself, in another passage, declares that "our civilisation is held together by fear rather than by good-will."[3] There is no contradiction between these apparently opposite views. When Tom Paine, in the *Rights of Man*, tries to confront Burke with the dilemma that "governments arise either *out* of the people or *over* the people," the answer is that they do both. Coercion and conscience, enmity and good-will, self-assertion and self-subordination, are present in every political society. The state is built up out of these two conflicting aspects of human nature. Utopia and reality, the ideal and the institution, morality and power, are from the outset inextricably blended in it. In the making of the United States, as a modern American writer has said, "Hamilton stood for strength, wealth, and power, Jefferson, for the American dream"; and both the power and the dream were necessary ingredients.[4]

If this be correct, we can draw one important conclusion. The utopian who dreams that it is possible to eliminate self-assertion from politics and to base a political system on morality alone is just as wide of the mark as the realist who believes that altruism is an illusion and that all political action is based on self-seeking. These errors have both left their mark on popular terminology. The phrase "power politics" is often used in an invidious sense, as if the element of power or self-assertion in politics were something abnormal and susceptible of elimination from a healthy political life. Conversely, there is a disposition, even among some writers who are not strictly speaking realists, to treat politics as the science of power and self-assertion and exclude from it by definition actions inspired by the moral consciousness. Professor Catlin describes the *homo politicus* as one who "seeks to bring into conformity with his own will the wills of others, so that he may the better attain his own ends."[5] Such terminological implications are misleading. Politics cannot be divorced from power. But the *homo politicus* who pursues nothing but power is as unreal a myth as the *homo economicus* who pursues nothing but gain. Political action must be based on a coordination of morality and power.

This truth is of practical as well as theoretical importance. It is as fatal in politics to ignore power as it is to ignore morality. The fate of China in the nineteenth century is an illustration of what happens to a country which is content to believe in the moral superiority of its own civilisation and to despise the ways of power. The Liberal Government of Great Britain

nearly came to grief in the spring of 1914 because it sought to pursue an Irish policy based on moral authority unsupported (or rather, directly opposed) by effective military power. In Germany, the Frankfort Assembly of 1848 is the classic example of the impotence of ideas divorced from power; and the Weimar Republic broke down because many of the policies it pursued—in fact, nearly all of them except its opposition to the communists—were unsupported, or actively opposed, by effective military power.[6] The utopian, who believes that democracy is not based on force, refuses to look these unwelcome facts in the face.

On the other hand, the realist, who believes that, if you look after the power, the moral authority will look after itself, is equally in error. The most recent form of this doctrine is embodied in the much-quoted phrase: "The function of force is to give moral ideas time to take root." Internationally, this argument was used in 1919 by those who, unable to defend the Versailles Treaty on moral grounds, maintained that this initial act of power would pave the way for subsequent moral appeasement. Experience has done little to confirm this comfortable belief. The same fallacy is implicit in the once popular view that the aim of British policy should be "to rebuild the League of Nations, to make it capable of holding a political aggressor in restraint by armed power, and thereafter to labour faithfully for the mitigation of just and real grievances."[7] Once the enemy has been crushed or the "aggressor" restrained by force, the "thereafter" fails to arrive. The illusion that priority can be given to power and that morality will follow, is just as dangerous as the illusion that priority can be given to moral authority and that power will follow.

Before proceeding, however, to consider the respective roles of power and morality in politics, we must take some note of the views of those who, though far from being realists, identify politics with power and believe that moral concepts must be altogether excluded from its scope. There is, according to this view, an essential antinomy between politics and morality; and the moral man as such will therefore have nothing to do with politics. This thesis has many attractions, and reappears at different periods of history and in different contexts. It takes at least three forms.

1. Its simplest form is the doctrine of non-resistance. The moral man recognises the existence of political power as an evil, but regards the use of power to resist power as a still greater evil. This is the basis of such doctrines of non-resistance as those of Jesus or of Gandhi, or of modern pacifism. It amounts, in brief, to a boycott of politics.

2. The second form of the antithesis between politics and morality is anarchism. The state, as the principal organ of political power, is "the most flagrant, most cynical and most complete negation of humanity."[8] The anarchist will use power to overthrow the state. This revolutionary power is, however, not thought of as political power, but as the spontaneous revolt of the outraged individual conscience. It does not seek to create a new political society to take the place of the old one, but a moral society from which power, and consequently politics, are completely eliminated. "The principles of the Sermon on the Mount," an English divine recently remarked, would mean "sudden death to civilised society."[9] The anarchist sets out to destroy "civilised society" in the name of the Sermon on the Mount.

3. A third school of thought starts from the same premise of the essential antithesis between morality and politics, but arrives at a totally different conclusion. The injunction of Jesus to "render unto Caesar the things that are Caesar's, and unto God the things that are God's," implies the coexistence of two separate spheres: the political and the moral. But the moral man is under an obligation to assist—or at any rate not to obstruct—the politician in the discharge of his non-moral functions. "Let every soul be subject to the higher powers. The powers that be are ordained of God." We thus recognise politics as necessary but non-moral. This tradition, which remained dormant throughout the Middle Ages, when the ecclesiastical and the secular authority was theoretically one, was revived by Luther in order to effect his compromise between reformed church and state. Luther "turned on the peasants of his day in holy horror when they attempted to transmute the 'spiritual' kingdom into an 'earthly' one by suggesting that the principles of the gospel had social significance."[10] The division of functions between Caesar and God is implicit in the very conception of an "established" church. But the tradition has been more persistent and more effective in Lutheran Germany than anywhere else. "We do not consult Jesus," wrote a German liberal nineteenth-century pastor, "when we are concerned with things which belong to the domain of the construction of the state and political economy"[11] and Bernhardi declared that "Christian morality is personal and social, and in its nature cannot be political."[12] The same attitude is inherent in the modern theology of Karl Barth, which insists that political and social evils are the necessary product of man's sinful nature and that human effort to eradicate them is therefore futile; and the doctrine that Christian morality has nothing to do with politics is vigorously upheld by the Nazi régime. This view is basically different from that of the realist who makes morality a function of politics. But in the field of politics it tends to become indistinguishable from realism.

The theory of the divorce between the spheres of politics and morality is superficially attractive, if only because it evades the insoluble problem of finding a moral justification for the use of force.[13] But it is not ultimately satisfying. Both non-resistance and anarchism are counsels of despair, which appear to find widespread acceptance only where men feel hopeless of achieving anything by political action; and the attempt to keep God and Caesar in watertight compartments runs too much athwart the deep-seated desire of the human mind to reduce its view of the world to some kind of moral order. We are not in the long run satisfied to believe that what is politically good is morally bad; and since we can neither moralise power nor expel power from politics, we are faced with a dilemma which cannot be completely resolved.[14] The planes of utopia and of reality never coincide. The ideal cannot be institutionalised, nor the institution idealised. "Politics," writes Dr. Niebuhr, "will, to the end of history, be an area where conscience and power meet, where the ethical and coercive factors of human life will interpenetrate and work out their tentative and uneasy compromises."[15] The compromises, like solutions of other human problems, will remain uneasy and tentative. But it is an essential part of any compromise that both factors shall be taken into account.

We have now therefore to analyse the part played in international politics by these two cardinal factors: power and morality.

Notes

1. "Everywhere do I perceive a certain conspiracy of the rich men seeking their own advantage under the name and pretext of the commonwealth" (More, *Utopia*). "The exploitation of one part of society by another is common to all past centuries." (*Communist Manifesto*)

2. *A Defence of Liberty against Tyrants (Vindiciae contra Tyrannos)*, ed. Laski, Introd. p. 55.

3. Linton, *The Study of Man*, p. 240; Laski, *A Grammar of Politics*, p. 20.

4. J. Truslow Adams, *The Epic of America*, p. 112. The idea that the state has a moral foundation in the consent of its citizens as well as a power foundation was propounded by Locke and Rousseau and popularised by the American and French revolutions. Two recent expressions of the idea may be quoted. The Czecho-Slovak declaration of independence of October 18, 1918, described Austria-Hungary as "a state which has no justification for its existence, and which, since it refuses to accept the fundamental basis of modern world-organisation [i.e. self-determination], is only an artificial and unmoral construction." In February 1938, Hitler told Schuschnigg, the then Austrian Chancellor, that "a régime lacking every kind of legality and which in reality ruled only by force, must in the long run come into continually increasing conflict with public opinion" (speech in the Reichstag of March 17, 1938). Hitler maintained that the two pillars of the state are "force" and "popularity." (*Mein Kampf*, p. 579)

5. Catlin, *The Science and Method of Politics*, p. 309.

6. It is significant that the word *Realpolitik* was coined in the once famous treatise of von Rochau, *Grundsätze der Realpolitik* published in 1853, which was largely inspired by the lessons of Frankfort. The inspiration which Hitler's *Realpolitik* has derived from the lessons of the Weimar Republic is obvious.

7. Winston Churchill, *Arms and the Covenant*, p. 368. The argument that power is a necessary motive force for the remedy of "just" grievances is further developed on pp. 209–216.

8. Bakunin, (*Œuvres*, i. p. 150; cf. vi. p. 17: "If there is a devil in all human history, it is this principle of command and authority."

9. The Dean of St. Paul's, quoted in a leading article in *The Times*, August 2, 1937.

10. R. Niebuhr, *Moral Men and Immoral Society*, p. 77.

11. Quoted in W. F. Bruck, *Social and Economic History of Germany*, p. 65.

12. Bernhardi, *Germany and the Next War* (Engl. transl.), p. 29.

13. "Force in the right place," as Mr. Maxton once said in the House of Commons, is a meaningless conception, "because the right place for me is exactly where I want to use it, and for him also, and for everyone else." (House of Commons, November 7, 1933: *Official Record*, col. 130). Force in politics is always the instrument of some kind of group interest.

14. Acton was fond of saying that "great men are almost always bad men," and quotes Walpole's dictum that "no great country was ever saved by good men" (*History of Freedom*, p. 219). Rosebery showed more acuteness when he remarked that "there is one question which English people ask about great men: Was he 'a good man'?" (*Napoleon: The Last Phase*, p. 364)

15. R. Niebuhr, *Moral Man and Immoral Society*, p. 4.

6

The Future of International Relations Theory: Toward a New Synthesis?

We conclude with several observations concerning the current state of scholarly thinking about international relations. A constant lament among scholars and students is that the field consists of a confusing array of competing perspectives and conceptual approaches. Professors have trouble deciding which theories from this intellectual smorgasbord to emphasize in a ten- to fifteen-week class, and students have to wrestle with the problem of coming to terms with vast amounts of material for upcoming exams. The basic question we pose is whether the field is becoming less fragmented—whether there are indications of movement toward a greater degree of consensus on how to approach the study of international phenomena. One could argue that this is not a burning issue, and in fact a multiplicity of interests, methods, paradigms, concepts, and value preferences is actually beneficial and should be applauded. Greater unity, it is feared, could result in uniformity and the intellectual tyranny of a dominant paradigm or school of thought. Hence, eclecticism is to be encouraged, and any signs of uniformity regarded with suspicion.

No one would argue against diversity per se—it is the lifeblood of scientific enquiry. Seemingly unrelated research may some day come together to help explain a significant aspect of international relations. The concern, however, is whether diversity might more appropriately be described as parochialism. Scholars at times engage in narrowly focused research programs that ignore alternative conceptual approaches, develop specialized jargon that unintentionally serves to confuse and mystify the uninitiated, and unduly restrict their course syllabus to literature that reinforces their own value and theoretical preferences. It is to overcome parochialism, encourage communication among scholars, and stimulate the growth of cumulative knowledge on such important issues as war and peace that have led scholars to search for common threads that may serve to bring a greater degree of unity to the field, not some desire to stifle alternative perspectives or create some sort of paradigmatic Leviathan. Are there any indications of increasing unity or coherence in the study of international relations? We will examine this question in three areas: underlying images, theory building, and normative concerns.

UNDERLYING IMAGES

By simply positing the existence of three basic images that influence theory building, we have in effect argued that a certain degree of coherence already exists in the study of international relations. A logical follow-up question is whether it is possible to combine elements of the three perspectives to provide a more comprehensive and integrated approach to the study of international politics that draws on the strengths of all three images. Simply combining all the actors and assumptions would result in a conceptual grab bag having contradictory elements. But what about a more careful selection of certain insights and assumptions? This could possibly result in creative and fruitful theory building.

To date, calls for such a synthesis have involved combining elements of realism and pluralism. Two scholars whose earlier work is associated with pluralism, Robert Keohane and John Ruggie, have indicated why such a synthesis is desirable and how it might be achieved.[1] Both argue that in attempting to construct a theory of international relations, one must begin with the realist emphasis on power and the state. Structural analyses of international politics that stress the importance of the system provide the critical context, they argue, in which pluralist insights and actors are to be analyzed. By itself, realism is inadequate in explaining recent patterns of interaction and changes in the world political economy. The same is true of pluralism. Realist systemic theory, however, provides a necessary "first cut," or context, within which international regimes, transnational actors, the political structure of states, bureaucratic politics, and the perceptions of decisionmakers are examined. Some of the best work in the pluralist image, it is noted, takes explicit account of the international system within which such actors and domestic institutions operate.

What of the globalists? Can their work also be combined with elements of the other two perspectives? There appears to be some common ground. First, as noted in Chapter 4, pluralists and globalists have a common interest in political economy, transnational actors and processes, and welfare issues. It was argued, however, that they deal with these topics in fundamentally different ways.

Second, and more important, globalists very often focus on hegemonic states or groups of states that reflect the distribution of power during a particular historical epoch. This is also characteristic of many realist analyses. Some globalists, however, might contend that this use of state-centered analysis is an exception and that a focus on broader patterns of social, economic, and political domination tends to be the norm. Nevertheless, a number of observers have noted an affinity between realist and globalist discussions of hegemony when it comes to explaining particular international events and outcomes.[2]

Third, it should be recalled that both the globalist and the realist images of world politics have proponents of structural, systemic analysis such as Immanuel Wallerstein and Kenneth Waltz. The former, however, emphasizes economic structures and processes, whereas the latter emphasizes political, military, and economic components of power and capabilities.

Finally, John Ruggie has made the interesting observation that modern political relations as exemplified by the nation-state (the realist preoccupation) as well as modern modes of capitalist production (a concern for many globalists) are both derived from the same historical factors: the redefinition of property rights toward the end of the medieval era, which occurred simultaneously with the emergence of the principle of sovereignty as a legitimation for the interstate order.[3] If realism (emphasizing political factors) and globalism (emphasizing economic factors) are both derived from similar roots, is it possible that they may be at least partially reconciled?

Our expectations should remain suitably modest. A problem that is difficult to overcome concerns the basic incommensurability of the three images.[4] First, the topics addressed are often incommensurable. Realists may examine balances of power, pluralists transnational processes, and globalists patterns of domination. Different topics may require not only the use of different levels of analysis but also conflicting assumptions. Second, meanings are often incommensurable, the same term being defined in different ways by different theorists. The concept of imperialism is a good example. Morgenthau defined it as "a reversal of the power relations between two or more nations," and Lenin defined it as "the highest stage of capitalism."[5] Finally, there is the problem of competing normative prescriptions often embedded in alternative images and theories. At the extreme, this might mean the adoption of a particular research program designed to produce results consistent with the expectations of a private or public funding agency. More commonly, the relative attractiveness of a realist or globalist explanation of imperialism, for example, may be based on one's personal value preferences rather than on critical scholarly scrutiny.

Notwithstanding the apparent incommensurability of the three images, earlier and recent work often defies easy categorization in just one of the three images. What about work being done in sociological institionalism on hypotheses concerning a common global culture which compete with those of realism and pluralism, yet share some common ground with English school theorists (both seek generalizations about historical change) and social constructivists (both view world culture as a social structure)?[6] Indeed, scholars often cross the images, operating on some assumptions and orientations of one image combined with certain assumptions and orientations of another. For example, one can place work of the English school under *realism;* however, some of these efforts are equally conversant with pluralist understandings of institutions and society.[7] For that matter, elements of *social constructivism* and *institutionalism* can be found not just in realist and pluralist (or neoliberal) but also in globalist scholarship.

Cognitive theory and constructivism inform much of the pluralist work of, for example, Ernst Haas, John Ruggie, Friedrich Kratochwil, and Martha Finnemore. Earlier pluralist (or liberal) theory had placed more emphasis on international organizations and other nonstate actors, tending to relegate the state as an actor of substantially diminishing importance. More recent pluralist (or neoliberal) scholarship, however, has, in some respects, made peace with the state, acknowledging that it continues and is likely to continue to play a substantial role alongside nonstate actors in the international milieu.

Lest this leave the impression that social constructivism is the exclusive domain of pluralist scholarship, we note that a leading constructivist, Alexander Wendt (whose article stating that anarchy is what states make of it is reprinted after this chapter), readily accepts many key realist assumptions and orientations—that states are key units that act rationally and that systemic factors in relation to states must be taken into account.[8] Certainly, even some classic realists put great stock in volitional aspects of international politics, seeing power balances not so much as systemic outcomes (as structural realists would have it), but rather as the social constructions of diplomats and statesmen.

There is also a voluntarist and constructivist element, we should note, in some globalist scholarship. For example, Craig Murphy (whose article drawn from his book on international organization and industrial change is reprinted following Chapter 4) adopts a nondeterminist perspective that sees international organizations emerging from global capitalism as human constructions designed to serve identifiable interests in maintenance of the global political economy. This constructivist influence is apparent in at least some globalist work based on Antonio Gramsci's earlier voluntarist formulations, which owe much to his reading of both Marx and Machiavelli.

Notwithstanding the problems we have noted here, the three images that are the backbone of this volume remain a durable guide to theoretical work in the field. Michael Doyle's book on *Ways of War and Peace*[9] continues the three-image construct we and others have adopted as a still-convenient taxonomy. In a very well developed treatment, Doyle explores the historical and philosophical underpinnings of what he refers to as Realism, Liberalism, and Socialism, as we have also done here and in our *Global Philosophers,* which searched for the intellectual roots of realism, pluralism and globalism.[10]

Having acknowledged the durability of the trichotomy of images we have adopted, important theoretical work remains ahead. Reconciling structural approaches in realist and globalist work with constructivist and voluntarist formulations advanced more recently in all three images will hardly be an easy task. Nevertheless, we applaud synthetic efforts in the field lest scholars continue ceaselessly to talk past one other in mutually exclusive terms.

THEORY BUILDING

In Chapter 1, we noted that we did not find the traditionalist–behavioralist debate of the late 1960s on the issue of appropriate methodology to be of overwhelming importance. In the 1990s, scholars still have not reached a consensus on the relative merits of quantitative versus nonquantitative research, in-depth single-case studies versus an examination of multiple cases, or inductive as opposed to deductive approaches to theory building. Each still has its advocates and practitioners. Furthermore, in recent years **critical theory** perspectives not only have challenged mainstream methodological approaches but also have raised basic issues concerning the **ontology** and **epistemology** underlying most of the international relations literature.[11] As a result, periodic reviews of the literature characterize the field using such terms as *disarray, chaotic,* and *fragmented.* It is therefore best to discuss recent trends in theory-building efforts as opposed to signs of any growing consensus.

First, pure empiricism in the form of mere correlation of variables is in general disrepute. Studies involving bivariate and multivariate relations flourished in the 1960s, and it was assumed that various patterns in and of themselves told us something significant about international relations. Such studies have been criticized for simply seeking out that which is easily quantifiable, ignoring the larger context within which states interact, and failing to relate the empirical efforts to more general theoretical constructs or research programs. This supposedly hampered the goal of cumulative research.

Second, there is a heightened awareness of the need to take into account the structure of the international system when engaged in theorizing. According to Kenneth Waltz's influential formulation, the existence of anarchy and various distributions of capabilities constrain and influence states and other actors to behave in certain ways. Simply examining state interactions is insufficient. In recent years, a number of scholars interested in alliance formation, theories of foreign policy, and military doctrine have worked to link the structure of the international system to state–societal variables.[12]

Third, and in part as a response to the influence of neorealist writings, there is a growing interest in understanding the historical development of such important concepts as "anarchy," "sovereignty," and "structure," particularly for those scholars working from a social-constructivist perspective. This is part of a larger trend: a renewed interest in the political thought of writers dating back to Thucydides, and the manner in which the works of these scholars have influenced contemporary international relations theorizing.[13]

Finally, there has been greater emphasis on theoretical rigor, which requires explicitly stating one's theoretical assumptions, delineating causal links, and noting the types of evidence to be used in testing propositions and hypotheses. This may all seem commonsensical and basic to any theoretical effort. In fact, very often work fails to meet such standards of theoretical rigor.[14]

NORMATIVE CONCERNS

Some scholars of international relations are quite explicit about their normative concerns. J. David Singer, for example, states, "Specialists in world affairs have a special responsibility to not only teach and conduct high-quality research, but to address the major problems confronting the global village. . . . The human condition is, on balance, morally unacceptable. Too many of our fellows continue to die prematurely from war, terrorism, assassination, poverty, starvation, disease, and even more of them suffer untold misery, pain, and degradation en route to the grave."[15] Few scholars would disagree that the ultimate goal of research should be to contribute to the storehouse of knowledge in an effort to ameliorate, if not eliminate, the scourge of war and poverty. The road may be difficult, the degree of commitment may vary, but few persons would probably care to admit even to themselves that they had no interest in furthering our understanding of the problems faced by the global community. The choice of a particular research topic may reflect a normative concern, but we believe that there is also a general consensus in the discipline that the final product should be the result of a good-faith effort to avoid allowing personal values to affect directly the construction of models, gathering of data, empirical testing of hypotheses and propositions, and interpretation of results. A normative commitment to improving our understanding of global problems does not sanction conducting biased research. Indeed, biased research could very well hinder the amelioration of the very problems of concern to a scholar.

Finally, as we noted in Chapter 5, some scholars are concerned with developing normative theories. Although both empirical and normative theorists may be motivated by such similar concerns as the devastation wrought by war, they operate in different domains. Normative theorists hope to provide the logical or philosophical bases for value choices facing decisionmakers and others by addressing such questions as "When is war justified?" or "Do wealthier states and societies have obligations to assist their less-fortunate counterparts in the third world?" We consider work in both domains to be important. In this regard, we applaud a recent upsurge in interest in normative international relations theory while, at the same time, we call for continued efforts to develop better empirical theory.

NOTES

1. See Keohane's "Theory of World Politics" in this volume and John Gerard Ruggie, "Continuity and Transformation in the World Polity: Toward a Neorealist Synthesis," *World Politics* 35, no. 2 (January 1983): 261–85. See also Robert O. Keohane, *After Hegemony: Cooperation and Discord in the World Political Economy* (Princeton, NJ: Princeton University Press, 1984); Joseph S. Nye, Jr., "Neorealism and Neoliberalism," *World Politics* 40, no. 2 (January 1988): 235–41.

2. See, for example, Robert Brenner, "The Origins of Capitalist Development: A Critique of Neo-Smithian Marxism," *New Left Review* 104 (July–August 1977): 25–92; David J. Sylvan, "The Newest Mercantilism," *International Organization* 35, no. 2 (Spring 1981): 375–93. As Keohane notes, the globalist Fred Block and the realist Robert Gilpin "both emphasize the role of U.S. hegemony in creating order after the Second World War and the disturbing effects of the erosion of American power." Keohane, *After Hegemony,* p. 42.

3. Ruggie, "Continuity and Transformation," p. 281. As he argues: "Despite its defects, Waltz's model is powerful and elegant. And, as I have suggested, its defects can be compensated for in a suitably amended and augmented neo-realist formulation. Such a formulation would also go some way toward subsuming the major competing systemic theories" (p. 285).

4. See Stephen D. Krasner, "Toward Understanding in International Relations," *International Studies Quarterly* 29, no. 2 (June 1985): 138–140.

5. Krasner uses the imperialism example to illustrate the problem of competing normative prescriptions, but it is just as relevant to the problem of incommensurability in meaning.

6. For an excellent review of this literature, see Martha Finnemore, "Norms, Culture, and World Politics: Insights from Sociology's Institutionalism," *International Organization* 50, no. 2 (Spring 1996): 325–47.

7. See Barry Buzan, "From International System to International Society: Structural Realism and Regime Theory Meet the English School," *International Organization* 47, no. 3 (Summer 1993): 327–52.

8. Alexander Wendt, "Constructing International Politics," *International Security* 20, no. 1 (Summer 1995): 71–72. See also Emanuel Adler, "Seizing the Middle Ground: Constructivism in World Politics," *European Journal of International Relations* 3, no. 3 (1997): 319–63.

9. See Michael W. Doyle, *Ways of War and Peace* (New York: W. W. Norton, 1997).

10. Mark V. Kauppi and Paul R. Viotti, *The Global Philosophers: World Politics in Western Thought* (New York and San Francisco: Lexington Books/Macmillan, now Jossey-Bass, 1992).

11. Jim George and David Campbell, "Patterns of Dissent and the Celebration of Difference: Critical Social Theory and International Relations," *International Studies Quarterly* 34, no. 3 (September 1990): 269–93. Cf. Smith, this volume, pp. 38–54.

12. Kenneth N. Waltz, *Theory of International Politics* (Reading, MA: Addison-Wesley, 1979). Waltz is repeatedly criticized for his explanatory emphasis on the structure of the international system. He, in turn, repeatedly states that he is interested in constructing a theory of international politics, not a theory of the foreign policy behavior of states. Waltz is all too aware of the importance

of the state–societal units and levels of analysis when it comes to the development of theories of foreign policy. As he stated in 1967 in his book on American and British foreign policy: "The principal purpose of the book remains . . . to determine the ways in which the internal politics of democracies affect their external policies." *Foreign Policy and Democratic Politics: The American and British Experience* (Boston: Little, Brown, 1967), p. 17.

In terms of linking levels of analysis, it is fair to ask "So what's new?" In 1969, James Rosenau called for "systematic conceptual exploration of the flow of influence across the changing boundaries of national and international systems." The difference between then and now, however, is the consideration of the concept of system structure. James N. Rosenau, "Introduction: Political Science in a Shrinking World" in *Linkage Politics: Essays on the Convergence of National and International Systems,* ed. James N. Rosenau (New York: Free Press, 1969), p. 3.

13. Helen Milner, "The Assumption of Anarchy in International Relations Theory: A Critique," *Review of International Studies* 17, no. 1 (January 1991): 67–85; R. B. J. Walker and Saul H. Mendlovitz, eds., *Contending Sovereignties: Redefining Political Community* (Boulder, CO.: Lynne Rienner, 1990); Nicholas Greenwood Onuf, "Sovereignty: Outline of a Conceptual History," *Alternatives* 16, no. 4 (Fall 1991): 425–46; John Gerard Ruggie, "International Structure and International Transformation: Space, Time, and Method," in *Global Changes and Theoretical Challenges: Approaches to World Politics for the 1990s,* eds. Ernst-Otto Czempiel and James N. Rosenau (Lexington, Mass.: Lexington Books, 1989), 21–35; Richard Ned Lebow and Barry S. Strauss, eds., *Hegemonic Rivalry: From Thucydides to the Nuclear Age* (Boulder, CO.: Westview Press, 1991); Mark V. Kauppi and Paul R. Viotti, *The Global Philosophers: World Politics in Western Thought* (New York: Macmillan/Lexington, 1992).

14. For a discussion covering these and other points, see the articles by Bruce Bueno de Mesquita, Robert Jervis, and Stephen Krasner in *International Studies Quarterly* 29, no. 2 (June 1985).

15. J. David Singer, "The Responsibilities of Competence in the Global Village," *International Studies Quarterly* 29, no. 3 (September 1985): 245, 259.

SELECTIONS FOR FURTHER READING AND REFERENCE

Buzan, Barry and Gerald Segal. *Anticipating the Future.* London: Simon and Schuster, 1998.

Checkel, Jeffrey T. "The Constructivist Turn in International Relations Theory." *World Politics* 50, 2 (January 1998): 324–81.

Doyle, Michael W. *Ways of War and Peace.* New York: W. W. Norton, 1997. [Part Five addresses the future of war and peace.]

Falk, Richard. *Explorations at the Edge of Time: The Prospects for World Order.* Philadelphia: Temple University Press, 1992.

———. *On Humane Governance: Toward a New Global Politics.* University Park: Pennsylvania State University Press, 1995.

Finnemore, Martha. *National Interests in International Society.* Ithaca: Cornell University Press, 1996.

Heilbroner, Robert. *21st Century Capitalism.* New York: W. W. Norton, 1993.

Hopf, Ted. "The Promise of Constructivism in International Relations Theory." *International Security* 23, 1 (Summer 1998): 171–200.

Katzenstein, Peter J., and Alexander Wendt, eds. *The Culture of National Security: Norms and Identity in World Politics.* New York: Columbia University Press, 1996.

Kratochwil, Friedrich. "Of Systems, Boundaries, and Territoriality: An Inquiry into the Formation of the State System." *World Politics* 39, 1 (October 1986): 27–52.

Lapid, Yosef and Friedrich V. Kratochwil, eds., *The Return of Culture and Identity in International Relations Theory.* Boulder, CO: Lynne Rienner, 1996.

Onuf, Nicholas. *World of Our Making: Rules and Rule in Social Theory and International Relations.* Columbia: University of South Carolina Press, 1989.

Anarchy Is What States Make of It:
The Social Construction of Power Politics

ALEXANDER WENDT

In a presentation that underscores voluntarism, the author constructs theories of international relations as grounded in interactive effects of agency, process, and social structure. Adopting a constructivist approach, he endorses the "liberal claim" that "international institutions can transform state identities and interests." In this regard, his critical examination of structural realism leads him to conclude that "self-help and power politics are socially constructed under anarchy"—not necessary or essential attributes of international politics. Thus, the neorealist construct of "self-help is an institution, one of various structures of identity and interest that may exist under anarchy." Indeed, "it is collective meanings that constitute the structures which organize our actions." Systems do not have an independent existence; they are what states make of them. Following this logic, states have the capacity to "transform a competitive security system into a cooperative one."

The debate between realists and liberals has reemerged as an axis of contention in international relations theory.[1] Revolving in the past around competing theories of human nature, the debate is more concerned today with the extent to which state action is influenced by "structure" (anarchy and the distribution of power) versus "process" (interaction and learning) and institutions. Does the absence of centralized political authority force states to play competitive power politics? Can international regimes overcome this logic, and under what conditions? What in anarchy is given and immutable, and what is amenable to change?

The debate between "neorealists" and "neoliberals" has been based on a shared commitment to "rationalism."[2] Like all social theories, rational choice directs us to ask some questions and not others, treating the identities and interests of agents as exogenously given and focusing on how the behavior of agents generates outcomes. As such, rationalism offers a fundamentally behavioral conception of both process and institutions: they change behavior but not identities and interests.[3] In addition to this way of framing research problems, neorealists and neoliberals share generally similar assumptions about agents: states are the dominant actors in

Alexander Wendt, "Anarchy Is What States Make of It: The Social Construction of Power Politics," *International Organization* 46, 2 (Spring 1992), pp. 391–425. © 1992 by the IO Foundation and the Massachusetts Institute of Technology.

the system, and they define security in "self-interested" terms. Neorealists and neoliberals may disagree about the extent to which states are motivated by relative versus absolute gains, but both groups take the self-interested state as the starting point for theory.

This starting point makes substantive sense for neorealists, since they believe anarchies are necessarily "self-help" systems, systems in which both central authority and collective security are absent. The self-help corollary to anarchy does enormous work in neorealism, generating the inherently competitive dynamics of the security dilemma and collective action problem. Self-help is not seen as an "institution" and as such occupies a privileged explanatory role vis-à-vis process, setting the terms for, and unaffected by, interaction. Since states failing to conform to the logic of self-help will be driven from the system, only simple learning or behavioral adaptation is possible; the complex learning involved in redefinitions of identity and interest is not.[4] Questions about identity- and interest-formation are therefore not important to students of international relations. A rationalist problématique, which reduces process to dynamics of behavioral interaction among exogenously constituted actors, defines the scope of systemic theory.

By adopting such reasoning, liberals concede to neorealists the causal powers of anarchic structure, but they gain the rhetorically powerful argument that process can generate cooperative behavior, even in an exogenously given, self-help system. Some liberals may believe that anarchy does, in fact, constitute states with self-interested identities exogenous to practice. Such "weak" liberals concede the causal powers of anarchy both rhetorically and substantively and accept rationalism's limited, behavioral conception of the causal powers of institutions. They are realists before liberals (we might call them "weak realists"), since only if international institutions can change powers and interests do they go beyond the "limits" of realism.[5]

Yet some liberals want more. When Joseph Nye speaks of "complex learning," or Robert Jervis of "changing conceptions of self and interest," or Robert Keohane of "sociological" conceptions of interest, each is asserting an important role for transformations of identity and interest in the liberal research program and, by extension, a potentially much stronger conception of process and institutions in world politics.[6] "Strong" liberals should be troubled by the dichotomous privileging of structure over process, since transformations of identity and interest through process are transformations of structure. Rationalism has little to offer such an argument, which is in part why, in an important article, Friedrich Kratochwil and John Ruggie argued that its individualist ontology contradicted the intersubjectivist epistemology necessary for regime theory to realize its full promise.[7] Regimes cannot change identities and interests if the latter are taken as given. Because of this rationalist legacy, despite increasingly numerous and rich studies of complex learning in foreign policy, neoliberals lack a systematic theory of how such changes occur and thus must privilege realist insights about structure while advancing their own insights about process.

The irony is that social theories which seek to explain identities and interests do exist. Keohane has called them "reflectivist";[8] because I want to emphasize their focus on the social construction of subjectivity and minimize their image problem, following Nicholas Onuf I will call them "constructivist."[9] Despite important differences, cognitivists, poststructuralists, standpoint and postmodern feminists, rule theorists, and structurationists share a concern with the basic "sociological" issue bracketed by rationalists—namely, the issue of identity- and interest-formation. Constructivism's potential contribution to a strong liberalism has been obscured, however, by recent epistemological debates between modernists and postmodernists. . . .[10] Real issues animate this debate, which also divides constructivists. With respect to the substance of international relations, however, both modern and postmodern constructivists are interested in how knowledgeable practices constitute subjects, which is not far from the strong liberal interest in how institutions transform interests. They share a cognitive, intersubjective conception of process in which identities and interests are endogenous to interaction, rather than a rationalist-behavioral one in which they are exogenous.

My objective in this article is to build a bridge between these two traditions (and, by extension, between the realist-liberal and rationalist-reflectivist debates) by developing a constructivist argument, drawn from structurationist and symbolic interactionist sociology, on behalf of the liberal claim that international institutions can transform state identities and interests.[11] In contrast to the "economic" theorizing that dominates mainstream systemic international relations scholarship, this involves a "sociological social psychological" form of systemic theory in which identities and interests are the dependent variable.[12] Whether a "communitarian liberalism" is still liberalism does not interest me here. What does is that constructivism might contribute significantly to the strong liberal interest in identity- and interest-formation and thereby perhaps itself be enriched with liberal insights about learning and cognition which it has neglected.

My strategy for building this bridge will be to argue against the neorealist claim that self-help is given by anarchic structure exogenously to process. Constructivists have not done a good job of taking the causal powers of anarchy seriously. This is unfortunate, since in the realist view anarchy justifies disinterest in the institutional transformation of identities and interests and thus building systemic theories in exclusively rationalist terms; its putative causal powers must be challenged if process and institutions are not to be subordinated to structure. I argue that self-help and power politics do not follow either logically or causally from anarchy and that if today we find ourselves in a self-help

world, this is due to process, not structure. There is no "logic" of anarchy apart from the practices that create and instantiate one structure of identities and interests rather than another; structure has no existence or causal powers apart from process. Self-help and power politics are institutions, not essential features of anarchy. *Anarchy is what states make of it.*

In the subsequent sections of this article, I critically examine the claims and assumptions of neorealism, develop a positive argument about how self-help and power politics are socially constructed under anarchy, and then explore three ways in which identities and interests are transformed under anarchy: by the institution of sovereignty, by an evolution of cooperation, and by intentional efforts to transform egoistic identities into collective identities.

Anarchy and Power Politics

Classical realists such as Thomas Hobbes, Reinhold Niebuhr, and Hans Morgenthau attributed egoism and power politics primarily to human nature, whereas structural realists or neorealists emphasize anarchy. The difference stems in part from different interpretations of anarchy's causal powers. Kenneth Waltz's work is important for both. In *Man, the State, and War,* he defines anarchy as a condition of possibility for or "permissive" cause of war, arguing that "wars occur because there is nothing to prevent them."[13] It is the human nature or domestic politics of predator states, however, that provide the initial impetus or "efficient" cause of conflict which forces other states to respond in kind.[14] Waltz is not entirely consistent about this, since he slips without justification from the permissive causal claim that in anarchy war is always possible to the active causal claim that "war may at any moment occur."[15] But despite Waltz's concluding call for third-image theory, the efficient causes that initialize anarchic systems are from the first and second images. This is reversed in Waltz's *Theory of International Politics,* in which first- and second-image theories are spurned as "reductionist," and the logic of anarchy seems by itself to constitute self-help and power politics as necessary features of world politics.[16]

This is unfortunate, since whatever one may think of first- and second-image theories, they have the virtue of implying that practices determine the character of anarchy. In the permissive view, only if human or domestic factors cause A to attack B will B have to defend itself. Anarchies may contain dynamics that lead to competitive power politics, but they also may not, and we can argue about when particular structures of identity and interest will emerge. In neorealism, however, the role of practice in shaping the character of anarchy is substantially reduced, and so there is less about which to argue: self-help and competitive power politics are simply given exogenously by the structure of the state system.

I will not here contest the neorealist description of the contemporary state system as a competitive, self-help world;[17] I will only dispute its explanation. I develop my argument in three stages. First, I disentangle the concepts of self-help and anarchy by showing that self-interested conceptions of security are not a constitutive property of anarchy. Second, I show how self-help and competitive power politics may be produced causally by processes of interaction between states in which anarchy plays only a permissive role. In both of these stages of my argument, I self-consciously bracket the first- and second-image determinants of state identity, not because they are unimportant (they are indeed important), but because like Waltz's objective, mine is to clarify the "logic" of anarchy. Third, I reintroduce first- and second-image determinants to assess their effects on identity-formation in different kinds of anarchies.

Anarchy, Self-Help, and Intersubjective Knowledge

Waltz defines political structure on three dimensions: ordering principles (in this case, anarchy), principles of differentiation (which here drop out), and the distribution of capabilities.[18] By itself, this definition predicts little about state behavior. It does not predict whether two states will be friends or foes, will recognize each other's sovereignty, will have dynastic ties, will be revisionist or status quo powers, and so on. These factors, which are fundamentally intersubjective, affect states' security interests and thus the character of their interaction under anarchy. In an important revision of Waltz's theory, Stephen Walt implies as much when he argues that the "balance of threats," rather than the balance of power, determines state action, threats being socially constructed.[19] Put more generally, without assumptions about the structure of identities and interests in the system, Waltz's definition of structure cannot predict the content or dynamics of anarchy. Self-help is one such intersubjective structure and, as such, does the decisive explanatory work in the theory. The question is whether self-help is a logical or contingent feature of anarchy. In this section, I develop the concept of a "structure of identity and interest" and show that no particular one follows logically from anarchy.

A fundamental principle of constructivist social theory is that people act toward objects, including other actors, on the basis of the meanings that the objects have for them.[20] States act differently toward enemies than they do toward friends because enemies are threatening and friends are not. Anarchy and the distribution of power are insufficient to tell us which is which. U.S. military power has a different significance for Canada than for Cuba, despite their similar "structural" positions, just as British missiles have a different significance for the United States than [did] Soviet missiles. The distribution of power may always affect states' calculations, but how it does so depends on the intersubjective understandings and expectations, on the "distribution of knowledge," that constitute their conceptions of self and other.[21] If society "forgets" what a university is, the powers and practices of professor and student cease to exist; if the United States and Soviet Union decide that they are no longer enemies, "the cold war is over." It is collective meanings that constitute the structures which organize our actions.

Actors acquire identities—relatively stable, role-specific understandings and expectations about self—by participating in such collective meanings.[22] Identities are inherently relational: "Identity, with its appropriate attachments of psychological reality, is always identity within a specific, socially constructed world," Peter Berger argues.[23] Each person has many identities linked to institutional roles, such as brother, son, teacher, and citizen. Similarly, a state may have multiple identities as "sovereign," "leader of the free world," "imperial power," and so on.[24] The commitment to and the salience of particular identities vary, but each identity is an inherently social definition of the actor grounded in the theories which actors collectively hold about themselves and one another and which constitute the structure of the social world.

Identities are the basis of interests. Actors do not have a "portfolio" of interests that they carry around independent of social context; instead, they define their interests in the process of defining situations.[25] As Nelson Foote puts it: "Motivation . . . refer[s] to the degree to which a human being, as a participant in the ongoing social process in which he necessarily finds himself, defines a problematic situation as calling for the performance of a particular act, with more or less anticipated consummations and consequences, and thereby his organism releases the energy appropriate to performing it."[26] Sometimes situations are unprecedented in our experience, and in these cases we have to construct their meaning, and thus our interests, by analogy or invent them de novo. More often they have routine qualities in which we assign meanings on the basis of institutionally defined roles. When we say that professors have an "interest" in teaching, research, or going on leave, we are saying that to function in the role identity of "professor," they have to define certain situations as calling for certain actions. This does not mean that they will necessarily do so (expectations and competence do not equal performance), but if they do not, they will not get tenure. The absence or failure of roles makes

defining situations and interests more difficult, and identity confusion may result. This seems to be happening today in the United States and the former Soviet Union: without the cold war's mutual attributions of threat and hostility to define their identities, these states seem unsure of what their "interests" should be.

An institution is a relatively stable set or "structure" of identities and interests. Such structures are often codified in formal rules and norms, but these have motivational force only in virtue of actors' socialization to and participation in collective knowledge. Institutions are fundamentally cognitive entities that do not exist apart from actors' ideas about how the world works.[27] This does not mean that institutions are not real or objective, that they are "nothing but" beliefs. As collective knowledge, they are experienced as having an existence "over and above the individuals who happen to embody them at the moment."[28] In this way, institutions come to confront individuals as more or less coercive social facts, but they are still a function of what actors collectively "know." Identities and such collective cognitions do not exist apart from each other; they are "mutually constitutive."[29] On this view, institutionalization is a process of internalizing new identities and interests, not something occurring outside them and affecting only behavior; socialization is a cognitive process, not just a behavioral one. Conceived in this way, institutions may be cooperative or conflictual, a point sometimes lost in scholarship on international regimes, which tends to equate institutions with cooperation. There are important differences between conflictual and cooperative institutions to be sure, but all relatively stable self-other relations—even those of "enemies"— are defined intersubjectively.

Self-help is an institution, one of various structures of identity and interest that may exist under anarchy. Processes of identity-formation under anarchy are concerned first and foremost with preservation or "security" of the self. Concepts of security therefore differ in the extent to which and the manner in which the self is identified cognitively with the other, and, I want to suggest, it is upon this cognitive variation that the meaning of anarchy and the distribution of power depends. Let me illustrate with a standard continuum of security systems.[30]

At one end is the "competitive" security system, in which states identify negatively with each other's security so that ego's gain is seen as alter's loss. Negative identification under anarchy constitutes systems of "realist" power politics: risk-averse actors that infer intentions from capabilities and worry about relative gains and losses. At the limit—in the Hobbesian war of all against all—collective action is nearly impossible in such a system because each actor must constantly fear being stabbed in the back.

In the middle is the "individualistic" security system, in which states are indifferent to the relationship between their own and others' security. This constitutes "neoliberal" systems: states are still self-regarding about their security but are concerned primarily with absolute gains rather than relative gains. One's position in the distribution of power is less important, and collective action is more possible (though still subject to free riding because states continue to be "egoists").

Competitive and individualistic systems are both "self-help" forms of anarchy in the sense that states do not positively identify the security of self with that of others but instead treat security as the individual responsibility of each. Given the lack of a positive cognitive identification on the basis of which to build security regimes, power politics within such systems will necessarily consist of efforts to manipulate others to satisfy self-regarding interests.

This contrasts with the "cooperative" security system, in which states identify positively with one another so that the security of each is perceived as the responsibility of all. This is not self-help in any interesting sense, since the "self" in terms of which interests are defined is the community; national interests are international interests.[31] In practice, of course, the extent to which states' identification with the community varies, from the limited form found in "concerts" to the full-blown form seen in "collective security" arrangements.[32] Depending on how well developed the collective self is, it will produce security practices that are in varying degrees altruistic or prosocial. This makes collective action less dependent on the presence of active threats and less prone to free riding. Moreover, it restructures efforts to advance one's objectives, or "power politics," in terms of shared norms rather than relative power.

On this view, the tendency in international relations scholarship to view power and institutions as two opposing explanations of foreign policy is therefore misleading, since anarchy and the distribution of power only have meaning for state action in virtue of the understandings and expectations that constitute institutional identities and interests. Self-help is one such institution, constituting one kind of anarchy but not the only kind. Waltz's three-part definition of structure therefore seems underspecified. In order to go from structure to action, we need to add a fourth: the intersubjectively constituted structure of identities and interests in the system.

This has an important implication for the way in which we conceive of states in the state of nature before their first encounter with each other. Because states do not have conceptions of self and other, and thus security interests, apart from or prior to interaction, we assume too much about the state of nature if we concur with Waltz that, in virtue of anarchy, "international political systems, like economic markets, are formed by the coaction of self-regarding units."[33] We also assume too much if we argue that, in virtue of anarchy, states in the state of nature necessarily face a "stag hunt" or "security dilemma."[34] These claims presuppose a history of interaction in which actors have acquired "selfish" identities and interests; before interaction (and still in abstraction from first- and second-image factors) they would have no experience upon which to base such definitions of self and other. To assume otherwise is to attribute to states in the state of nature qualities that they can only possess in society.[35] Self-help is an institution, not a constitutive feature of anarchy.

What, then, *is* a constitutive feature of the state of nature before interaction? Two things are left if we strip away those properties of the self which presuppose interaction with others. The first is the material substrate of agency, including its intrinsic capabilities. For human beings, this is the body; for states, it is an organizational apparatus of governance. In effect, I am suggesting for rhetorical purposes that the raw material out of which members of the state system are constituted is created by domestic society before states enter the constitutive process of international society, although this process implies neither stable territoriality nor sovereignty, which are internationally negotiated terms of individuality (as discussed further below). The second is a desire to preserve this material substrate, to survive. This does not entail "self-regardingness," however, since actors do not have a self prior to interaction with an other; how they view the meaning and requirements of this survival therefore depends on the processes by which conceptions of self evolve.

This may all seem very arcane, but there is an important issue at stake: are the foreign policy identities and interests of states exogenous or endogenous to the state system? The former is the answer of an individualistic or undersocialized systemic theory for which rationalism is appropriate; the latter is the answer of a fully socialized systemic theory. Waltz seems to offer the latter and proposes two mechanisms, competition and socialization, by which structure conditions state action.[36] The content of his argument about this conditioning, however, presupposes a self-help system that is not itself a constitutive feature of anarchy. As James Morrow points out, Waltz's two mechanisms condition behavior, not identity and interest.[37] This explains how Waltz can be accused of both "individualism" and "structuralism."[38] He is the former with respect to systemic constitutions of

identity and interest, the latter with respect to systemic determinations of behavior.

Anarchy and the Social Construction of Power Politics

If self-help is not a constitutive feature of anarchy, it must emerge causally from processes in which anarchy plays only a permissive role.[39] This reflects a second principle of constructivism: that the meanings in terms of which action is organized arise out of interaction.[40] This being said, however, the situation facing states as they encounter one another for the first time may be such that only self-regarding conceptions of identity can survive; if so, even if these conceptions are socially constructed, neorealists may be right in holding identities and interests constant and thus in privileging one particular meaning of anarchic structure over process. In this case, rationalists would be right to argue for a weak, behavioral conception of the difference that institutions make, and realists would be right to argue that any international institutions which are created will be inherently unstable, since without the power to transform identities and interests they will be "continuing objects of choice" by exogenously constituted actors constrained only by the transaction costs of behavioral change.[41] Even in a permissive causal role, in other words, anarchy may decisively restrict interaction and therefore restrict viable forms of systemic theory. I address these causal issues first by showing how self-regarding ideas about security might develop and then by examining the conditions under which a key efficient cause—predation—may dispose states in this direction rather than others.

Conceptions of self and interest tend to "mirror" the practices of significant others over time. This principle of identity-formation is captured by the symbolic interactionist notion of the "looking-glass self," which asserts that the self is a reflection of an actor's socialization.

Consider two actors—ego and alter—encountering each other for the first time. Each wants to survive and has certain material capabilities, but neither actor has biological or domestic imperatives for power, glory, or conquest (still bracketed), and there is no history of security or insecurity between the two. What should they do? Realists would probably argue that each should act on the basis of worst-case assumptions about the other's intentions, justifying such an attitude as prudent in view of the possibility of death from making a mistake. Such a possibility always exists, even in civil society; however, society would be impossible if people made decisions purely on the basis of worst-case possibilities. Instead, most decisions are and should be made on the basis of probabilities, and these are produced by interaction, by what actors *do*.

In the beginning is ego's gesture, which may consist, for example, of an advance, a retreat, a brandishing of arms, a laying down of arms, or an attack.[42] For ego, this gesture represents the basis on which it is prepared to respond to alter. This basis is unknown to alter, however, and so it must make an inference or "attribution" about ego's intentions and, in particular, given that this is anarchy, about whether ego is a threat.[43] The content of this inference will largely depend on two considerations. The first is the gesture's and ego's physical qualities, which are in part contrived by ego and which include the direction of movement, noise, numbers, and immediate consequences of the gesture. The second consideration concerns what alter would intend by such qualities were it to make such a gesture itself. Alter may make an attributional "error" in its inference about ego's intent, but there is also no reason for it to assume a priori—before the gesture—that ego is threatening, since it is only through a process of signaling and interpreting that the costs and probabilities of being wrong can be determined.[44] Social threats are constructed, not natural.

Consider an example. Would we assume, a priori, that we were about to be attacked if we are ever contacted by members of an alien civilization? I think not. We would be highly alert, of course, but whether we placed our military forces on alert or launched an attack would depend on how we interpreted the import of their first gesture for our security—if only to avoid making an immediate enemy out of what may be a dangerous adversary. The possibility of error, in other words, does not force us to act on the assumption that the aliens are threatening: action depends on the probabilities we assign, and these are in key part a function of what the aliens do; prior to their gesture, we have no systemic basis for assigning probabilities. If their first gesture is to appear with a thousand spaceships and destroy New York, we will define the situation as threatening and respond accordingly. But if they appear with one spaceship, saying what seems to be "we come in peace," we will feel "reassured" and will probably respond with a gesture intended to reassure them, even if this gesture is not necessarily interpreted by them as such.[45]

This process of signaling, interpreting, and responding completes a "social act" and begins the process of creating intersubjective meanings. It advances the same way. The first social act creates expectations on both sides about each other's future behavior: potentially mistaken and certainly tentative, but expectations nonetheless. Based on this tentative knowledge, ego makes a new gesture, again signifying the basis on which it will respond to alter, and again alter responds, adding to the pool of knowledge each has about the other, and so on over time. The mechanism here is reinforcement; interaction rewards actors for holding certain ideas about each other and discourages them from holding others. If repeated long enough, these "reciprocal typifications" will create relatively stable concepts of self and other regarding the issue at stake in the interaction.[46]

It is through reciprocal interaction, in other words, that we create and instantiate the relatively enduring social structures in terms of which we define our identities and interests. Jeff

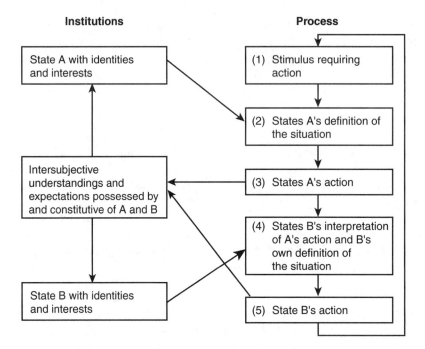

FIGURE 1   The Codetermination of Institutions and Process

Coulter sums up the ontological dependence of structure on process this way: "The parameters of social organization themselves are reproduced only in and through the orientations and practices of members engaged in social interactions over time. . . . Social configurations are not 'objective' like mountains or forests, but neither are they 'subjective' like dreams or flights of speculative fancy. They are, as most social scientists concede at the theoretical level, intersubjective constructions."[47]

The simple overall model of identity- and interest-formation proposed in Figure 1 applies to competitive institutions no less than to cooperative ones. Self-help security systems evolve from cycles of interaction in which each party acts in ways that the other feels are threatening to the self, creating expectations that the other is not to be trusted. Competitive or egoistic identities are caused by such insecurity; if the other is threatening, the self is forced to "mirror" such behavior in its conception of the self's relationship to that other. Being treated as an object for the gratification of others precludes the positive identification with others necessary for collective security; conversely, being treated by others in ways that are empathic with respect to the security of the self permits such identification.

Competitive systems of interaction are prone to security "dilemmas," in which the efforts of actors to enhance their security unilaterally threatens the security of the others, perpetuating distrust and alienation. The forms of identity and interest that constitute such dilemmas, however, are themselves ongoing effects of, not exogenous to, the interaction; identities are produced in and through "situated activity."[48] We do not *begin* our relationship with the aliens in a security dilemma; security dilemmas are not given by anarchy or nature. Of course, once institutionalized such a dilemma may be hard to change (I return to this below), but the point remains: identities and interests are constituted by collective meanings that are always in process. As Sheldon Stryker emphasizes, "The social process is one of constructing and reconstructing self and social relationships."[49] If states find themselves in a self-help system, this is because their practices made it that way. Changing the practices will change the intersubjective knowledge that constitutes the system.

Predator States and Anarchy as Permissive Cause

The mirror theory of identity-formation is a crude account of how the process of creating identities and interests might work, but it does not tell us why a system of states—such as, arguably, our own—would have ended up with self-regarding and not collective identities. In this section, I examine an efficient cause, predation, which, in conjunction with anarchy as a permissive cause, may generate a self-help system. In so doing, however, I show the key role that the structure of identities and interests plays in mediating anarchy's explanatory role.

The predator argument is straightforward and compelling. For whatever reasons—biology, domestic politics, or systemic victimization—some states may become predisposed toward aggression. The aggressive behavior of these predators or "bad apples" forces other states to engage in competitive power politics, to meet fire with fire, since failure to do so may degrade or destroy them. One predator will best a hundred pacifists because anarchy provides no guarantees. This argument is powerful in part because it is so weak: rather than making the strong assumption that all states are inherently power-seeking (a purely reductionist theory of power politics), it assumes that just one is power-seeking and that the others have to follow suit because anarchy permits the one to exploit them.

In making this argument, it is important to reiterate that the possibility of predation does not in itself force states to anticipate it a priori with competitive power politics of their own. The possibility of predation does not mean that "war may at any moment occur"; it may in fact be extremely unlikely. Once a predator emerges, however, it may condition identity- and interest-formation in the following manner.

In an anarchy of two, if ego is predatory, alter must either define its security in self-help terms or pay the price. This follows directly from the above argument, in which conceptions of self mirror treatment by the other. In an anarchy of many, however, the effect of predation also depends on the level of collective identity already attained in the system. If predation occurs right after the first encounter in the state of nature, it will force others with whom it comes in contact to defend themselves, first individually and then collectively *if* they come to perceive a common threat. The emergence of such a defensive alliance will be seriously inhibited if the structure of identities and interests has already evolved into a Hobbesian world of maximum insecurity, since potential allies will strongly distrust each other and face intense collective action problems; such insecure allies are also more likely to fall out amongst themselves once the predator is removed. If collective security identity is high, however, the emergence of a predator may do much less damage. If the predator attacks any member of the collective, the latter will come to the victim's defense on the principle of "all for one, one for all," even if the predator is not presently a threat to other members of the collective. If the predator is not strong enough to withstand the collective, it will be defeated and collective security will obtain. But if it is strong enough, the logic of the two-actor case (now predator and collective) will activate, and balance-of-power politics will reestablish itself.

The timing of the emergence of predation relative to the history of identity-formation in the community is therefore crucial to anarchy's explanatory role as a permissive cause. Predation will always lead victims to defend themselves, but whether defense will be collective or not depends on the history of interaction within the potential collective as much as on the ambitions of the predator. Will the disappearance of the Soviet threat renew old insecurities among the members of the North Atlantic Treaty Organization? Perhaps, but not if they have reasons independent of that threat for identifying their security with one another. Identities and interests are relationship-specific, not intrinsic attributes of a "portfolio"; states may be competitive in some relationships and solidary in others. "Mature" anarchies are less likely than "immature" ones to be reduced by predation to a Hobbesian condition, and maturity, which is a proxy for structures of identity and interest, is a function of process.[50]

The source of predation also matters. If it stems from unit-level causes that are immune to systemic impacts (causes such as human nature or domestic politics taken in isolation), then it functions in a manner analogous to a "genetic trait" in the constructed world of the state system. Even if successful, this trait does not select for other predators in an evolutionary sense so much as it teaches other states to respond in kind, but since traits cannot be unlearned, the other states will continue competitive behavior until the predator is either destroyed or transformed from within. However, in the more likely event that predation stems at least in part from prior systemic interaction—perhaps as a result of being victimized in the past (one thinks here of Nazi Germany or the Soviet Union)— then it is more a response to a learned identity and, as such, might be transformed by future social interaction in the form of appeasement, reassurances that security needs will be met, systemic effects on domestic politics, and so on. In this case, in other words, there is more hope that process can transform a bad apple into a good one.

The role of predation in generating a self-help system, then, is consistent with a systematic focus on process. Even if the source of predation is entirely exogenous to the system, it is what states *do* that determines the quality of their interactions under anarchy. In this respect, it is not surprising that it is classical realists rather than structural realists who emphasize this sort of argument. The former's emphasis on unit-level causes of power politics leads more easily to a permissive view of anarchy's explanatory role (and therefore to a processual view of international relations) than does the latter's emphasis on anarchy as a "structural cause";[51] neorealists do not need predation because the system is given as self-help.

This raises anew the question of exactly how much and what kind of role human nature and domestic politics play in world politics. The greater and more destructive this role, the more significant predation will be, and the less amenable anarchy will be to formation of collective identities. Classical realists, of course, assumed that human nature was possessed by an inherent lust for power or glory. My argument suggests that assumptions such as this were made for a reason: an unchanging Hobbesian man provides the powerful efficient cause necessary for a relentless pessimism about world politics that anarchic structure alone, or even structure plus intermittent predation, cannot supply. One can be skeptical of such an essentialist assumption, as I am, but it does produce determinate results at the expense of systemic theory. A concern with systemic process over structure suggests that perhaps it is time to revisit the debate over the relative importance of first-, second-, and third-image theories of state identity-formation.[52]

Assuming for now that systemic theories of identity-formation in world politics are worth pursuing, let me conclude by suggesting that the realist-rationalist alliance "reifies" self-help in the sense of treating it as something separate from the practices by which it is produced and sustained. Peter Berger and Thomas Luckmann define reification as follows: "[It] is the apprehension of the products of human activity *as if* they were something else than human products—such as facts of nature, results of cosmic laws, or manifestations of divine will. Reification implies that man is capable of forgetting his own authorship of the human world, and further, that the dialectic between man, the producer, and his products is lost to consciousness. The reified world is . . . experienced by man as a strange facticity, an *opus alienum* over which he has no control rather than as the *opus proprium* of his own productive activity."[53] By denying or bracketing states' collective authorship of their identities and interests, in other words, the realist-rationalist alliance denies or brackets the fact that competitive power politics help create the very "problem of order" they are supposed to solve—that realism is a self-fulfilling prophecy. Far from being exogenously given, the intersubjective knowledge that constitutes competitive identities and interests is constructed every day by processes of "social will formation."[54] It is what states have made of themselves.

Institutional Transformations of Power Politics

Let us assume that processes of identity- and interest-formation have created a world in which states do not recognize rights to territory or existence—a war of all against all. In this world, anarchy has a "realist" meaning for state action: be insecure and concerned with relative power. Anarchy has this meaning only in virtue of collective, insecurity-producing practices, but if those practices are relatively stable, they do constitute a system that may resist change. The fact that worlds of power politics are socially constructed, in other words, does not guarantee they are malleable, for at least two reasons.

The first reason is that once constituted, any social system confronts each of its members as an objective social fact that reinforces certain behaviors and discourages others. Self-help systems, for example, tend to reward competition

and punish altruism. The possibility of change depends on whether the exigencies of such competition leave room for actions that deviate from the prescribed script. If they do not, the system will be reproduced and deviant actors will not.

The second reason is that systemic change may also be inhibited by actors' interests in maintaining relatively stable role identities. Such interests are rooted not only in the desire to minimize uncertainty and anxiety, manifested in efforts to confirm existing beliefs about the social world, but also in the desire to avoid the expected costs of breaking commitments made to others—notably domestic constituencies and foreign allies in the case of states—as part of past practices. The level of resistance that these commitments induce will depend on the "salience" of particular role identities to the actor.[55] The United States, for example, is more likely to resist threats to its identity as "leader of anticommunist crusades" than to its identity as "promoter of human rights." But for almost any role identity, practices and information that challenge it are likely to create cognitive dissonance and even perceptions of threat, and these may cause resistance to transformations of the self and thus to social change.

For both systemic and "psychological" reasons, then, intersubjective understandings and expectations may have a self-perpetuating quality, constituting path-dependencies that new ideas about self and other must transcend. This does not change the fact that through practice agents are continuously producing and reproducing identities and interests, continuously "choosing now the preferences [they] will have later."[56] But it does mean that choices may not be experienced with meaningful degrees of freedom. This could be a constructivist justification for the realist position that only simple learning is possible in self-help systems. The realist might concede that such systems are socially constructed and still argue that after the corresponding identities and interests have become institutionalized, they are almost impossible to transform.

In the remainder of this article, I examine three institutional transformations of identity and security interest through which states might escape a Hobbesian world of their own making. In so doing, I seek to clarify what it means to say that "institutions transform identities and interests," emphasizing that the key to such transformations is relatively stable practice.

Sovereignty, Recognition, and Security

In a Hobbesian state of nature, states are individuated by the domestic processes that constitute them as states and by their material capacity to deter threats from other states. In this world, even if free momentarily from the predations of others, state security does not have any basis in social recognition—in intersubjective understandings or norms that a state has a right to its existence, territory, and subjects. Security is a matter of national power, nothing more.

The principle of sovereignty transforms this situation by providing a social basis for the individuality and security of states. Sovereignty is an institution, and so it exists only in virtue of certain intersubjective understandings and expectations; there is no sovereignty without an other. These understandings and expectations not only constitute a particular kind of state—the "sovereign" state—but also constitute a particular form of community, since identities are relational. The essence of this community is a mutual recognition of one another's right to exercise exclusive political authority within territorial limits. These reciprocal "permissions"[57] constitute a spatially rather than functionally differentiated world—a world in which fields of practice constitute and are organized around "domestic" and "international" spaces rather than around the performance of particular activities.[58] The location of the boundaries between these spaces is of course sometimes contested, war being one practice through which states negotiate the terms of their individuality. But this does not change the fact that it is only in virtue of mutual recognition that states have

"territorial property rights."[59] This recognition functions as a form of "social closure" that disempowers nonstate actor and empowers and helps stabilize interaction among states.[60]

Sovereignty norms are now so taken for granted, so natural, that it is easy to overlook the extent to which they are both presupposed by an ongoing artifact of practice. When states tax "their" "citizens" and not others, when they "protect" their markets against foreign "imports," when they kill thousands of Iraqis in one kind of war and then refuse to "intervene" to kill even one person in another kind, a "civil" war, and when they fight a global war against a regime that sought to destroy the institution of sovereignty and then give Germany back to the Germans, they are acting against the background of, and thereby reproduced, shared norms about what it means to be a sovereign state.

If states stopped acting on those norms, their identity as "sovereigns" (if not necessarily as "states") would disappear. The sovereign state is an ongoing accomplishment of practice, not a once-and-for-all creation of norms that somehow exist apart from practice.[61] Thus, saying that "the institution of sovereignty transforms identities" is shorthand for saying that "regular practices produce mutually constituting sovereign identities (agents) and their associated institutional norms (structures)." Practice is the core of constructivist resolutions of the agent-structure problem. This ongoing process may not be politically problematic in particular historical contexts and, indeed, once a community of mutual recognition is constituted, its members—even the disadvantaged ones—may have a vested interest in reproducing it. In fact, this is part of what having an identity means. But this identity and institution remain dependent on what actors do: removing those practices will remove their intersubjective conditions of existence.

This may tell us something about how institutions of sovereign states are reproduced through social interaction, but it does not tell us why such a structure of identity and interest would arise in the first place. Two conditions would seem necessary for this to happen: (1) the density and regularity of interactions must be sufficiently high and (2) actors must be dissatisfied with preexisting forms of identity and interaction. Given these conditions, a norm of mutual recognition is relatively undemanding in terms of social trust, having the form of an assurance game in which a player will acknowledge the sovereignty of the others as long as they will in turn acknowledge that player's own sovereignty. Articulating international legal principles such as those embodied in the Peace of Augsburg (1555) and the Peace of Westphalia (1648) may also help by establishing explicit criteria for determining violations of the nascent social consensus.[62] But whether such a consensus holds depends on what states do. If they treat each other as if they were sovereign, then over time they will institutionalize that mode of subjectivity; if they do not, then that mode will not become the norm.

Practices of sovereignty will transform understandings of security and power politics in at least three ways. First, states will come to define their (and our) security in terms of preserving their "property rights" over particular territories. We now see this as natural, but the preservation of territorial frontiers is not, in fact, equivalent to the survival of the state or its people. Indeed, some states would probably be more secure if they would relinquish certain territories—the "Soviet Union" of some minority republics, "Yugoslavia" of Croatia and Slovenia, Israel of the West Bank, and so on. The fact that sovereignty practices have historically been oriented toward producing distinct territorial spaces, in other words, affects states' conceptualization of what they must "secure" to function in that identity, a process that may help account for the "hardening" of territorial boundaries over the centuries.[63]

Second, to the extent that states successfully internalize sovereignty norms, they will be more respectful toward the territorial rights of others. This restraint is *not* primarily because of the costs of violating sovereignty norms, although when violators do get punished (as in the Gulf War) it reminds everyone of what these costs can be, but because part of what it means to be a "sovereign" state is that one does not violate the territorial rights of others without "just cause." A clear example of such an institutional effect, convincingly argued by David Strang, is the markedly different treatment that weak states receive within and outside communities of mutual recognition.[64] What keeps the United States from conquering the Bahamas, or Nigeria from seizing Togo, or Australia from occupying Vanuatu? Clearly, power is not the issue, and in these cases even the cost of sanctions would probably be negligible. One might argue that great powers simply have no "interest" in these conquests, and this might be so, but this lack of interest can only be understood in terms of their recognition of weak states' sovereignty. I have no interest in exploiting my friends, not because of the relative costs and benefits of such action but because they are my friends. The absence of recognition, in turn, helps explain the Western states' practices of territorial conquest, enslavement, and genocide against Native American and African peoples. It is in *that* world that only power matters, not the world of today.

Finally, to the extent that their ongoing socialization teaches states that their sovereignty depends on recognition by other states, they can afford to rely more on the institutional fabric of international society and less on individual national means—especially military power—to protect their security. The intersubjective understandings embodied in the institution of sovereignty, in other words, may redefine the meaning of others' power for the security of the self. In policy terms, this means that states can be less worried about short-term survival and relative power and can thus shift their resources accordingly. Ironically, it is the great powers, the states with the greatest national means, that may have the hardest time learning this lesson; small powers do not have the luxury of relying on national means and may therefore learn faster that collective recognition is a cornerstone of security.

None of this is to say that power becomes irrelevant in a community of sovereign states. Sometimes states *are* threatened by others that do not recognize their existence or particular territorial claims, that resent the externalities from their economic policies, and so on. But most of the time, these threats are played out within the terms of the sovereignty game. The fates of Napoleon and Hitler show what happens when they are not.

Cooperation among Egoists and Transformations of Identity

We began this section with a Hobbesian state of nature. Cooperation for joint gain is extremely difficult in this context, since trust is lacking, time horizons are short, and relative power concerns are high. Life is "nasty, brutish, and short." Sovereignty transforms this system into a Lockean world of (mostly) mutually recognized property rights and (mostly) egoistic rather than competitive conceptions of security, reducing the fear that what states already have will be seized at any moment by potential collaborators, thereby enabling them to contemplate more direct forms of cooperation. A necessary condition for such cooperation is that outcomes be positively interdependent in the sense that potential gains exist which cannot be realized by unilateral action. States such as Brazil and Botswana may recognize each other's sovereignty, but they need further incentives to engage in joint action. One important source of incentives is the growing "dynamic density" of interaction among states in a world with new communications technology, nuclear weapons, externalities from industrial development, and so on.[65] Unfortunately, growing dynamic density does not ensure that states will in fact realize joint gains; interdependence also entails vulnerability and the risk of being "the sucker," which if exploited will become a source of conflict rather than cooperation.

This is the rationale for the familiar assumption that egoistic states will often find themselves facing prisoners' dilemma, a game in which the dominant strategy, if played only once, is to defect. As Michael Taylor and Robert Axelrod have shown, however, given iteration and a sufficient shadow of the future, egoists using a tit-for-tat strategy can escape this result and build cooperative institutions.[66] The story they tell about this process on the surface seems quite similar to George Herbert Mead's constructivist analysis of interaction, part of which is also told in terms of "games."[67] Cooperation is a gesture indicating ego's willingness to cooperate; if alter defects, ego does likewise, signaling its unwillingness to be exploited; over time and through reciprocal play, each learns to form relatively stable expectations about the other's behavior, and through these, habits of cooperation (or defection) form. Despite similar concerns with communication, learning, and habit-formation, however, there is an important difference between the game-theoretic and constructivist analysis of interaction that bears on how we conceptualize the causal powers of institutions.

In the traditional game-theoretic analysis of cooperation, even an iterated one, the structure of the game—of identities of interests—is exogenous to interaction and, as such, does not change.[68] A "black box" is put around identity- and interest-formation, and analysis focuses instead on the relationship between expectations and behavior. The norms that evolve from interaction are treated as rules and behavioral regularities which are external to the actors and which resist change because of the transaction costs of creating new ones. The game-theoretic analysis of cooperation among egoists is at base behavioral.

A constructivist analysis of cooperation, in contrast, would concentrate on how the expectations produced by behavior affect identities and interests. The process of creating institutions is one of internalizing new understandings of self and other, of acquiring new role identities, not just of creating external constraints on the behavior of exogenously constituted actors.[69] Even if not intended as such, in other words, the process by which egoists learn to cooperate is at the same time a process of reconstructing their interests in terms of shared commitments to social norms. Over time, this will tend to transform a positive interdependence of *outcomes* into a positive interdependence of *utilities* or collective interest organized around the norms in question. These norms will resist change because they are tied to actors' commitments to their identities and interests, not merely because of transaction costs. A constructivist analysis of "the cooperation problem," in other words, is at base cognitive rather than behavioral, since it treats the intersubjective knowledge that defines the structure of identities and interests, of the "game," as endogenous to and instantiated by interaction itself.

The debate over the future of collective security in Western Europe may illustrate the significance of this difference. A weak liberal or rationalist analysis would assume that the European states' "portfolio" of interests has not fundamentally changed and that the emergence of new factors, such as the collapse of the Soviet threat and the rise of Germany, would alter their cost-benefit ratios for pursuing current arrangements, thereby causing existing institutions to break down. The European states formed collaborative institutions for good, exogenously constituted egoistic reasons, and the same reasons may lead them to reject those institutions; the game of European power politics has not changed. A strong liberal or constructivist analysis of this problem would suggest that four decades of cooperation may have transformed a positive interdependence of outcomes into a collective "European identity" in terms of which states increasingly define their "self"-interests.[70] Even if egoistic reasons were its starting point, the process of cooperating tends to redefine those reasons by reconstituting identities and interests in terms of new intersubjective understandings and commitments. Changes in the distribution of power during the late twentieth

century are undoubtedly a challenge to these new understandings, but it is not as if West European states have some inherent, exogenously given interest in abandoning collective security if the price is right. Their identities and security interests are continuously in process, and if collective identities become "embedded," they will be as resistant to change as egoistic ones.[71] Through participation in new forms of social knowledge, in other words, the European states of 1990 might no longer be the states of 1950.

Critical Strategic Theory and Collective Security

The transformation of identity and interest through an "evolution of cooperation" faces two important constraints. The first is that the process is incremental and slow. Actors' objectives in such a process are typically to realize joint gains within what they take to be a relatively stable context, and they are therefore unlikely to engage in substantial reflection about how to change the parameters of that context (including the structure of identities and interests) and unlikely to pursue policies specifically designed to bring about such changes. Learning to cooperate may change those parameters, but this occurs as an unintended consequence of policies pursued for other reasons rather than as a result of intentional efforts to transcend existing institutions.

A second, more fundamental, constraint is that the evolution of cooperation story presupposes that actors do not identify negatively with one another. Actors must be concerned primarily with absolute gains; to the extent that antipathy and distrust lead them to define their security in relativistic terms, it will be hard to accept the vulnerabilities that attend cooperation.[72] This is important because it is precisely the "central balance" in the state system that seems to be so often afflicted with such competitive thinking, and realists can therefore argue that the possibility of cooperation within one "pole" (for example, the West) is parasitic on the dominance of competition between poles (the East–West conflict). Relations between the poles may be amenable to some positive reciprocity in areas such as arms control, but the atmosphere of distrust leaves little room for such cooperation and its transformative consequences.[73] The conditions of negative identification that make an "evolution of cooperation" most needed work precisely against such a logic.

This seemingly intractable situation may nevertheless be amenable to quite a different logic of transformation, one driven more by self-conscious efforts to change structures of identity and interest than by unintended consequences. Such voluntarism may seem to contradict the spirit of constructivism, since would-be revolutionaries are presumably themselves effects of socialization to structures of identity and interest. How can they think about changing that to which they owe their identity? The possibility lies in the distinction between the social determination of the self and the personal determination of choice, between what Mead called the "me" and the "I."[74] The "me" is that part of subjectivity which is defined in terms of others; the character and behavioral expectations of a person's role identity as "professor," or of the United States as "leader of the alliance," for example, are socially constituted. Roles are not played in mechanical fashion according to precise scripts, however, but are "taken" and adapted in idiosyncratic ways by each actor.[75] Even in the most constrained situations, role performance involves a choice by the actor. The "I" is the part of subjectivity in which this appropriation and reaction to roles and its corresponding existential freedom lie.

The fact that roles are "taken" means that, in principle, actors always have a capacity for "character planning"—for engaging in critical self-reflection and choices designed to bring about changes in their lives.[76] But when or under what conditions can this creative capacity be exercised? Clearly, much of the time it cannot: if actors were constantly reinventing their identities, social order would be impossible, and the relative stability of identities and interests in the real world is indicative of our propensity for habitual rather than creative action. The exceptional, conscious choosing to transform or transcend roles has at least two preconditions. First, there must be a reason to think of oneself in novel terms. This would most likely stem from the presence of new social situations that cannot be managed in terms of preexisting self-conceptions. Second, the expected costs of intentional role change—the sanctions imposed by others with whom one interacted in previous roles—cannot be greater than its rewards.

When these conditions are present, actors can engage in self-reflection and practice specifically designed to transform their identities and interests and thus to "change the games" in which they are embedded. Such "critical" strategic theory and practice has not received the attention it merits from students of world politics (another legacy of exogenously given interests perhaps), particularly given that one of the most important phenomena in [recent] world politics, Mikhail Gorbachev's policy of "New Thinking," [was] arguably precisely that.[77] Let me therefore use this policy as an example of how states might transform a competitive security system into a cooperative one, dividing the transformative process into four stages.

The first stage in intentional transformation is the breakdown of consensus about identity commitments. In the Soviet case, identity commitments centered on the Leninist theory of imperialism, with its belief that relations between capitalist and socialist states are inherently conflictual, and on the alliance patterns that this belief engendered. In the 1980s, the consensus within the Soviet Union over the Leninist theory broke down for a variety of reasons, principal among which seem to have been the state's inability to meet the economic-technological-military challenge from the West, the government's decline of political legitimacy at home, and the reassurance from the West that it did not intend to invade the Soviet Union, a reassurance that reduced the external costs of role change.[78] These factors paved the way for a radical leadership transition and for a subsequent "unfreezing of conflict schemas" concerning relations with the West.[79]

The breakdown of consensus makes possible a second stage of critical examination of old ideas about self and other and, by extension, of the structures of interaction by which the ideas have been sustained. In periods of relatively stable role identities, ideas and structures may become reified and thus treated as things that exist independently of social action. If so, the second stage is one of denaturalization, of identifying the practices that reproduce seemingly inevitable ideas about self and other; to that extent, it is a form of "critical" rather than "problem-solving" theory.[80] The result of such a critique should be an identification of new "possible selves" and aspirations.[81] New Thinking [embodies] such critical theorizing. Gorbachev [wanted] to free the Soviet Union from the coercive social logic of the cold war and engage the West in far-reaching cooperation. Toward this end, he . . . rejected the Leninist belief in the inherent conflict of interest between socialist and capitalist states and, perhaps more important, . . . recognized the crucial role that Soviet aggressive practices played in sustaining that conflict.

Such rethinking paves the way for a third stage of new practice. In most cases, it is not enough to rethink one's own ideas about self and other, since old identities have been sustained by systems of interaction with *other* actors, the practices of which remain a social fact for the transformative agent. In order to change the self, then, it is often necessary to change the identities and interests of the others that help sustain those systems of interaction. The vehicle for inducing such change is one's own practice and, in particular, the practice of "altercasting"—a technique of interactor control in which ego uses tactics of self-presentation and stage management in an attempt to frame alter's definitions of social situations in ways that create the role which ego desires alter to play.[82] In effect, in altercasting ego tries to induce alter to take on a new identity (and thereby enlist alter in ego's effort to change itself) by treating alter *as if* it already had that identity. The logic of this follows directly from the mirror theory of identity-formation, in which alter's identity is a reflection of ego's practices; change those practices and ego begins to change alter's conception of itself.

What these practices should consist of depends on the logic by which the preexisting identities were sustained. Competitive security systems are sustained by practices that create insecurity and distrust. In this case, transformative practices should attempt to teach other states that one's own state can be trusted and should not be viewed as a threat to their security. The fastest way to do this is to make unilateral initiatives and self-binding commitments of sufficient significance that another state is faced with "an offer it cannot refuse."[83] Gorbachev . . . tried to do this by withdrawing from Afghanistan and Eastern Europe, implementing asymmetric cuts in nuclear and conventional forces, calling for "defensive defense," and so on. In addition, he . . . skillfully cast the West in the role of being morally required to give aid and comfort to the Soviet Union, . . . emphasized the bonds of common fate between the Soviet Union and the West, and . . . indicated that further progress in East–West relations is contingent upon the West assuming the identity being projected onto it. These actions are all dimensions of altercasting, the intention of which is to take away the Western "excuse" for distrusting the Soviet Union, which, in Gorbachev's view, . . . helped sustain competitive identities in the past.

Yet by themselves such practices cannot transform a competitive security system, since if they are not reciprocated by alter, they will expose ego to a "sucker" payoff and quickly wither on the vine. In order for critical strategic practice to transform competitive identities, it must be "rewarded" by alter, which will encourage more such practice by ego, and so on.[84] Over time, this will institutionalize a positive rather than a negative identification between the security of self and other and will thereby provide a firm intersubjective basis for what were initially tentative commitments to new identities and interests.

Notwithstanding . . . rhetoric about the end of the cold war, skeptics may still doubt whether Gorbachev (or some future leader) will succeed in building an intersubjective basis for a new Soviet (or Russian) role identity. There are important domestic, bureaucratic, and cognitive-ideological sources of resistance in both East and West to such a change, not the least of which is the shakiness of the democratic forces' domestic position. But if my argument about the role of intersubjective knowledge in creating competitive structures of identity and interest is right, then at least New Thinking shows a greater appreciation—conscious or not—for the deep structure of power politics than we are accustomed to in international relations practice.

Conclusion

All theories of international relations are based on social theories of the relationship between *agency, process,* and *social structure.* Social theories do not determine the content of our international theorizing, but they do structure the questions we ask about world politics and our approaches to answering those questions. The substantive issue at stake in debates about social theory is what kind of foundation offers the most fruitful set of questions and research strategies for explaining the revolutionary changes that seem to be occurring in the late twentieth century international system. Put simply, what should systemic theories of international relations look like? How should they conceptualize

the relationship between structure and process? Should they be based exclusively on "microeconomic" analogies in which identities and interests are exogenously given by structure and process is reduced to interactions within those parameters? Or should they also be based on "sociological" and "social psychological" analogies in which identities and interests and therefore the meaning of structure are endogenous to process? Should a behavioral-individualism or a cognitive-constructivism be the basis for systemic theories of world politics?

This article notwithstanding, this question is ultimately an empirical one in two respects. First, its answer depends in part on how important interaction among states is for the constitution of their identities and interests. On the one hand, it may be that domestic or genetic factors, which I have systematically bracketed, are in fact much more important determinants of states' identities and interests than are systemic factors. To the extent that this is true, the individualism of a rationalist approach and the inherent privileging of structure over process in this approach become more substantively appropriate for systemic theory (if not for first- and second-image theory), since identities and interests are *in fact* largely exogenous to interaction among states. On the other hand, if the bracketed factors are relatively unimportant or if the importance of the international system varies historically (perhaps with the level of dynamic density and interdependence in the system), then such a framework would not be appropriate as an exclusive foundation for general systemic theory.

Second, the answer to the question about what systemic theories should look like also depends on how easily state identities and interests can change as a result of systemic interaction. Even if interaction is initially important in constructing identities and interests, once institutionalized its logic may make transformation extremely difficult. If the meaning of structure for state action changes so slowly that it becomes a de facto parameter within which process takes place, then it may again be substantively appropriate to adopt the rationalist assumption that identities and interests are given (although again, this may vary historically).

We cannot address these empirical issues, however, unless we have a framework for doing systemic research that makes state identity and interest an issue for both theoretical and empirical inquiry. Let me emphasize that this is *not* to say we should never treat identities and interests as given. The framing of problems and research strategies should be question-driven rather than method-driven, and if we are not interested in identity- and interest-formation, we may find the assumptions of a rationalist discourse perfectly reasonable. Nothing in this article, in other words, should be taken as an attack on rationalism per se. By the same token, however, we should not let this legitimate analytical stance become a de facto ontological stance with respect to the content of third-image theory, at least not until after we have determined that systemic interaction does not play an important role in processes of state identity- and interest-formation. We should not choose our philosophical anthropologies and social theories prematurely. By arguing that we cannot derive a self-help structure of identity and interest from the principle of anarchy alone—by arguing that anarchy is what states make of it—this article has challenged one important justification for ignoring processes of identity- and interest-formation in world politics. As such, it helps set the stage for inquiry into the empirical issues raised above and thus for a debate about whether communitarian or individualist assumptions are a better foundation for systemic theory.

I have tried to indicate by crude example what such a research agenda might look like. Its objective should be to assess the causal relationship between practice and interaction (as independent variable) and the cognitive structures at the level of individual states and of systems of states which constitute identities and interests (as dependent variable)—that is, the relation-

ship between what actors *do* and what they *are*. We may have some a priori notion that state actors and systemic structures are "mutually constitutive," but this tells us little in the absence of an understanding of how the mechanics of dyadic, triadic, and *n*-actor interaction shape and are in turn shaped by "stocks of knowledge" that collectively constitute identities and interests and, more broadly, constitute the structures of international life. Particularly important in this respect is the role of practice in shaping attitudes toward the "giveness" of these structures. How and why do actors reify social structures, and under what conditions do they denaturalize such reifications?

The state-centrism of this agenda may strike some, particularly postmodernists, as "depressingly familiar."[85] The significance of states relative to multinational corporations, new social movements, transnationals, and intergovernmental organizations is clearly declining, and "postmodern" forms of world politics merit more research attention than they have received. But I also believe, with realists, that in the medium run sovereign states will remain the dominant political actors in the international system. Any transition to new structures of global political authority and identity—to "postinternational" politics—will be mediated by and path-dependent on the particular institutional resolution of the tension between unity and diversity, or particularism and universality, that is the sovereign state.[86] In such a world there should continue to be a place for theories of anarchic interstate politics, alongside other forms of international theory; to that extent, I am a statist and a realist. I have argued in this article, however, that statism need not be bound by realist ideas about what "state" must mean. State identities and interests can be collectively transformed within an anarchic context by many factors—individual, domestic, systemic, or transnational—and as such are an important dependent variable. Such a reconstruction of state-centric international theory is necessary if we are to theorize adequately about the emerging forms of transnational political identity that sovereign states will help bring into being. To that extent, I hope that statism, like the state, can be historically progressive.

I have argued that the proponents of strong liberalism and the constructivists can and should join forces in contributing to a process-oriented international theory. Each group has characteristic weaknesses that are complemented by the other's strengths. In part because of the decision to adopt a choice-theoretic approach to theory construction, neoliberals have been unable to translate their work on institution-building and complex learning into a systemic theory that escapes the explanatory priority of realism's concern with structure. Their weakness, in other words, is a lingering unwillingness to transcend, at the level of systemic theory, the individualist assumption that identities and interests are exogenously given. Constructivists bring to this lack of resolution a systematic communitarian ontology in which intersubjective knowledge constitutes identities and interests. For their part, however, constructivists have often devoted too much effort to questions of ontology and constitution and not enough effort to the causal and empirical questions of how identities and interests are produced by practice in anarchic conditions. As a result, they have not taken on board neoliberal insights into learning and social cognition.

An attempt to use a structurationist–symbolic interactionist discourse to bridge the two research traditions, neither of which subscribes to such a discourse, will probably please no one. But in part this is because the two "sides" have become hung up on differences over the epistemological status of social science. The state of the social sciences and, in particular, of international relations, is such that epistemological prescriptions and conclusions are at best premature. Different questions involve different standards of inference; to reject certain questions because their answers cannot conform to the standards of clas-

sical physics is to fall into the trap of method-driven rather than question-driven social science. By the same token, however, giving up the artificial restrictions of logical positivist conceptions of inquiry does not force us to give up on "Science." Beyond this, there is little reason to attach so much importance to epistemology. Neither positivism, nor scientific realism, nor poststructuralism tells us about the structure and dynamics of international life. Philosophies of science are not theories of international relations. The good news is that strong liberals and modern and postmodern constructivists are asking broadly similar questions about the substance of international relations that differentiate both groups from the neorealist-rationalist alliance. Strong liberals and constructivists have much to learn from each other if they can come to see this through the smoke and heat of epistemology.

Notes

1. See, for example, Joseph Grieco, "Anarchy and the Limits of Cooperation: A Realist Critique of the Newest Liberal Institutionalism," *International Organization* 42 (Summer 1988), pp. 485–507; Joseph Nye, "Neorealism and Neoliberalism," *World Politics* 40 (January 1988), pp. 235–51; Robert Keohane, "Neoliberal Institutionalism: A Perspective on World Politics," in his collection of essays entitled *International Institutions and State Power* (Boulder, Colo.: Westview Press, 1989), pp. 1–20; John Mearsheimer, "Back to the Future: Instability in Europe After the Cold War," *International Security* 13 (Summer 1990), pp. 5–56, along with subsequent published correspondence regarding Mearsheimer's article; and Emerson Niou and Peter Ordeshook, "Realism Versus Neoliberalism: A Formulation," *American Journal of Political Science* 35 (May 1991), pp. 481–511.

2. See Robert Keohane, "International Institutions: Two Approaches," *International Studies Quarterly* 32 (December 1988), pp. 379–96.

3. Behavioral and rationalist models of man and institutions share a common intellectual heritage in the materialist individualism of Hobbes, Locke, and Bentham. On the relationship between the two models, see Jonathan Turner, *A Theory of Social Interaction* (Stanford, Calif.: Stanford University Press, 1988), pp. 24–31; and George Homans, "Rational Choice Theory and Behavioral Psychology," in Craig Calhoun et al., eds.,

Structures of Power and Constraint (Cambridge: Cambridge University Press, 1991), pp. 77–89.

4. On neorealist conceptions of learning, see Philip Tetlock, "Learning in U.S. and Soviet Foreign Policy," in George Breslauer and Philip Tetlock, eds., *Learning in U.S. and Soviet Foreign Policy* (Boulder, Colo.: Westview Press, 1991), pp. 24–27. On the difference between behavioral and cognitive learning, see ibid., pp. 20–61; Joseph Nye, "Nuclear Learning and U.S.–Soviet Security Regimes," *International Organization* 41 (Summer 1987), pp. 371–402; and Ernst Haas, *When Knowledge Is Power* (Berkeley: University of California Press, 1990), pp. 17–49.

5. See Stephen Krasner, "Regimes and the Limits of Realism: Regimes as Autonomous Variables," in Stephen Krasner, ed., *International Regimes* (Ithaca, N.Y.: Cornell University Press, 1983), pp. 355–68.

6. See Nye, "Nuclear Learning and U.S.–Soviet Security Regimes"; Robert Jervis, "Realism, Game Theory, and Cooperation," *World Politics* 40 (April 1988), pp. 340–44; and Robert Keohane, "International Liberalism Reconsidered," in John Dunn, ed., *The Economic Limits to Modern Politics* (Cambridge: Cambridge University Press, 1990), p. 183.

7. Friedrich Kratochwil and John Ruggie, "International Organization: A State of the Art on an Art of the State," *International Organization* 40 (Autumn 1986), pp. 753–75.

8. Keohane, "International Institutions."

9. See Nicholas Onuf, *World of Our Making* (Columbia: University of South Carolina Press, 1989).

10. On Science, see Keohane, "International Institutions"; and Robert Keohane, "International Relations Theory: Contributions of a Feminist Standpoint," *Millennium* 18 (Summer 1989), pp. 245–53. On Dissent, see R. B. J. Walker, "History and Structure in the Theory of International Relations," *Millennium* 18 (Summer 1989), pp. 163–83; and Richard Ashley and R. B. J. Walker, "Reading Dissidence/Writing the Discipline: Crisis and the Question of Sovereignty in International Studies," *International Studies Quarterly* 34 (September 1990), pp. 367–416. For an excellent critical assessment of these debates, see Yosef Lapid, "The Third Debate: On the Prospects of International Theory in a Post-Positivist Era," *International Studies Quarterly* 33 (September 1989), pp. 235–54.

11. The fact that I draw on these approaches aligns me with modernist constructivists, even though I also draw freely on the substantive work of postmodernists, especially Richard Ashley and Rob Walker. For a defense of this practice and a discussion of its epistemological basis, see my earlier article, "The Agent-Structure Problem in International Relations Theory," *International Organization* 41 (Summer 1987), pp. 335–70; and Ian Shapiro and Alexander Wendt, "The Difference That Realism Makes: Social Science and the Politics of Consent," . . . in *Politics and Society*. Among modernist constructivists, my argument is particularly indebted to the published work of Emanuel Adler, Friedrich Kratochwil, and John Ruggie, as well as to an unpublished paper by Naeem Inayatullah and David Levine entitled "Politics and Economics in Contemporary International Relations Theory," Syracuse University, Syracuse, N.Y., 1990.

12. See Viktor Gecas, "Rekindling the Sociological Imagination in Social Psychology," *Journal for the Theory of Social Behavior* 19 (March 1989), pp. 97–115.

13. Kenneth Waltz, *Man, the State, and War* (New York: Columbia University Press, 1959), p. 232.

14. Ibid., pp. 169–70.

15. Ibid., p. 232. This point is made by Hidemi Suganami in "Bringing Order to the Causes of War Debates," *Millennium* 19 (Spring 1990), p. 34, fn. 11.

16. Kenneth Waltz, *Theory of International Politics* (Boston: Addison-Wesley, 1979).

17. The neorealist description is not unproblematic. For a powerful critique, see David Lumsdaine, *Ideals and Interests: The Foreign Aid Regime, 1949–1989* (Princeton, N.J.: Princeton University Press).

18. Waltz, *Theory of International Politics*, pp. 79–101.

19. Stephen Walt, *The Origins of Alliances* (Ithaca, N.Y.: Cornell University Press, 1987).

20. See, for example, Herbert Blumer, "The Methodological Position of Symbolic Interactionism," in his *Symbolic Interactionism: Perspective and Method* (Englewood Cliffs, N.J.: Prentice-Hall, 1969), p. 2. Throughout this article, I assume that a theoretically productive analogy can be made between individuals and states. . . .

21. The phrase "distribution of knowledge" is Barry Barnes's, as discussed in his work *The Nature of Power* (Cambridge: Polity Press, 1988); see also Peter Berger and Thomas Luckmann, *The Social Construction of Reality* (New York: Anchor Books, 1966). The concern of recent international relations scholarship on "epistemic communities" with the cause-and-effect understandings of the world held by scientists, experts, and policymakers is an important aspect of the role of knowledge in world politics; see Peter Haas, "Do Regimes Matter? Epistemic Communities and Mediterranean Pollution Control," *International Organization* 43 (Summer 1989), pp. 377–404; and Ernst Haas, *When Knowledge Is Power*. My constructivist approach would merely add to this an equal emphasis on how such knowledge also *constitutes* the structures and subjects of social life.

22. For an excellent short statement of how collective meanings constitute identities, see Peter Berger, "Identity as a Problem in the Sociology of Knowledge," *European Journal of Sociology*, vol. 7, no. 1, 1966, pp. 32–40. . . .

23. Berger, "Identity as a Problem in the Sociology of Knowledge," p. 111.

24. While not normally cast in such terms, foreign policy scholarship on national role conceptions could be adapted to such identity language. See Kal Holsti, "National Role Conceptions in the Study of Foreign Policy," *International Studies Quarterly* 14 (September 1970), pp. 233–309; and Stephen Walker, ed., *Role Theory and Foreign Policy Analysis* (Durham, N.C.: Duke University Press, 1987). . . .

25. On the "portfolio" conception of interests, see Barry Hindess, *Political Choice and Social Structure* (Aldershot, U.K.: Edward Elgar, 1989), pp. 2–3. The "definition of the situation" is a central concept in interactionist theory.

26. Nelson Foote, "Identification as the Basis for a Theory of Motivation," *American Sociological Review* 16 (February 1951), p. 15.

27. In neo-Durkheimian parlance, institutions are "social representations." See Serge Moscovici, "The Phenomenon of Social Representations," in Rob Farr and Serge Moscovici, eds., *Social Representations* (Cambridge: Cambridge University Press, 1984), pp. 3–69. See also Barnes, *The Nature of Power*. . . .

28. Berger and Luckmann, *The Social Construction of Reality*, p. 58.

29. See Giddens, *Central Problems in Social Theory;* and Alexander Wendt and Raymond Duvall, "Institutions and International Order," in Ernst-Otto Czempiel and James Rosenau, eds., *Global Changes and Theoretical Challenges* (Lexington, Mass.: Lexington Books, 1989), pp. 51–74.

30. Security systems might also vary in the extent to which there is a functional differentiation or a hierarchical relationship between patron and client, with the patron playing a hegemonic role within its sphere of influence in defining the security interests of its clients. I do not examine this dimension here; for preliminary discussion, see Alexander Wendt, "The States System and Global Militarization," Ph.D. diss., University of Minnesota, Minneapolis, 1989; and Alexander Wendt and Michael Barnett, "The International System and Third World Militarization," unpublished manuscript, 1991.

31. This amounts to an "internationalization of the state." For a discussion of this subject, see Raymond Duvall and Alexander Wendt, "The International Capital Regime and the Internationalization of the State," unpublished manuscript, 1987. See also R. B. J. Walker, "Sovereignty, Identity, Community: Reflections on the Horizons of Contemporary Political Practice," in R. B. J. Walker and Saul Mendlovitz, eds., *Contending Sovereignties* (Boulder, Colo.: Lynne Rienner, 1990), pp. 159–85.

32. On the spectrum of cooperative security arrangements, see Charles Kupchan and Clifford Kupchan, "Concerts, Collective Security, and the Future of Europe," *International Security* 16 (Summer 1991), pp. 114–61; and Richard Smoke, "A Theory of Mutual Security," in Richard Smoke and Andrei Kortunov, eds., *Mutual Security* (New York: St. Martin's Press, 1991), pp. 59–111. These may be usefully set alongside Christopher Jencks' "Varieties of Altruism," in Jane Mansbridge, ed., *Beyond Self-Interest* (Chicago: University of Chicago Press, 1990), pp. 53–67.

33. Waltz, *Theory of International Politics,* p. 91.

34. See Waltz, *Man, the State, and War;* and Robert Jervis, "Cooperation Under the Security Dilemma," *World Politics* 30 (January 1978), pp. 167–214.

35. My argument here parallels Rousseau's critique of Hobbes. For an excellent critique of realist appropriations of Rousseau, see Michael Williams, "Rousseau, Realism, and Realpolitik," *Millennium* 18 (Summer 1989), pp. 188–204. Williams argues that far from being a fundamental starting point in the state of nature, for Rousseau the stag hunt represented a stage in man's fall. On p. 190, Williams cites Rousseau's description of man prior to leaving the state of nature: "Man only knows himself; he does not see his own well-being to be identified with or contrary to that of anyone else; he neither hates anything nor loves anything; but limited to no more than physical instinct, he is no one, he is an animal." For another critique of Hobbes on the state of nature that parallels my constructivist reading of anarchy, see Charles Landesman, "Reflections on Hobbes: Anarchy and Human Nature," in Peter Caws, ed., *The Causes of Quarrel* (Boston: Beacon, 1989), pp. 139–48.

36. Waltz, *Theory of International Politics,* pp. 74–77.

37. See James Morrow, "Social Choice and System Structure in World Politics," *World Politics* 41 (October 1988), p. 89. Waltz's behavioral treatment of socialization may be usefully contrasted with the more cognitive approach taken by Ikenberry and the Kupchans in the following articles: G. John Ikenberry and Charles Kupchan, "Socialization and Hegemonic Power," *International Organization* 44 (Summer 1989), pp. 283–316; and Kupchan and Kupchan, "Concerts, Collective Security, and the Future of Europe." Their approach is close to my own, but they define socialization as an elite strategy to induce value change in others, rather than as a ubiquitous feature of interaction in terms of which all identities and interests get produced and reproduced.

38. Regarding individualism, see Richard Ashley, "The Poverty of Neorealism," *International Organization* 38 (Spring 1984), pp. 225–86; Wendt, "The Agent-Structure Problem in International Relations Theory"; and David Dessler, "What's at Stake in the Agent-Structure Debate?" *International Organization* 43 (Summer 1989), pp. 441–74. Regarding structuralism, see R. B. J. Walker, "Realism, Change, and International Political Theory," *International Studies Quarterly* 31 (March 1987), pp. 65–86; and Martin Hollis and Steven Smith, *Explaining*

and *Understanding International Relations* (Oxford: Clarendon Press, 1989). The behavioralism evident in neorealist theory also explains how neorealists can reconcile their structuralism with the individualism of rational choice theory. On the behavioral-structural character of the latter, see Spiro Latsis, "Situational Determinism in Economics," *British Journal for the Philosophy of Science* 23 (August 1972), pp. 207–45.

39. The importance of the distinction between constitutive and causal explanations is not sufficiently appreciated in constructivist discourse. See Wendt, "The Agent-Structure Problem in International Relations Theory," pp. 362–65; Wendt, "The States System and Global Militarization," pp. 110–13; and Wendt, "Bridging the Theory/Meta-Theory Gap in International Relations," *Review of International Studies* 17 (October 1991), p. 390.

40. See Blumer, "The Methodological Position of Symbolic Interactionism," pp. 2–4.

41. See Robert Grafstein, "Rational Choice: Theory and Institutions," in Kristen Monroe, ed., *The Economic Approach to Politics* (New York: Harper Collins, 1991), pp. 263–64. A good example of the promise and limits of transaction cost approaches to institutional analysis is offered by Robert Keohane in his *After Hegemony* (Princeton, N.J.: Princeton University Press, 1984).

42. Mead's analysis of gestures remains definitive. See Mead's *Mind, Self, and Society*. See also the discussion of the role of signaling in the "mechanics of interaction" in Turner's *A Theory of Social Interaction,* pp. 74–79 and 92–115.

43. On the role of attribution processes in the interactionist account of identity-formation, see Sheldon Stryker and Avid Gottlieb, "Attribution Theory and Symbolic Interactionism," in John Harvey et al., eds., *New Directions in Attribution Research,* vol. 3 (Hillsdale, N.J.: Lawrence Erlbaum, 1981), pp. 425–58; and Kathleen Crittenden, "Sociological Aspects of Attribution," *Annual Review of Sociology,* vol. 9, 1983, pp. 425–46. On attributional processes in international relations, see Shawn Rosenberg and Gary Wolfsfeld, "International Conflict and the Problem of Attribution," *Journal of Conflict Resolution* 21 (March 1977), pp. 75–103.

44. This discussion of the role of possibilities and probabilities in threat perception owes much to Stewart Johnson's comments on an earlier draft of my article.

45. On the role of "reassurance" in threat situations, see Richard Ned Lebow and Janice Gross Stein, "Beyond Deterrence," *Journal of Social Issues,* vol. 43, no. 4, 1987, pp. 5–72.

46. On "reciprocal typifications," see Berger and Luckmann, *The Social Construction of Reality,* pp. 54–58.

47. Jeff Coulter, "Remarks on the Conceptualization of Social Structure," *Philosophy of the Social Sciences* 12 (March 1982), pp. 42–43.

48. See C. Norman Alexander and Mary Glenn Wiley, "Situated Activity and Identity Formation," in Morris Rosenberg and Ralph Turner, eds., *Social Psychology: Sociological Perspectives* (New York: Basic Books, 1981), pp. 269–89.

49. Sheldon Stryker, "The Vitalization of Symbolic Interactionism," *Social Psychology Quarterly* 50 (March 1987), p. 93.

50. On the "maturity" of anarchies, see Barry Buzan, *People, States, and Fear* (Chapel Hill: University of North Carolina Press, 1983).

51. A similar intuition may lie behind Ashley's effort to reappropriate classical realist discourse for critical international relations theory. See Richard Ashley, "Political Realism and Human Interests," *International Studies Quarterly* 38 (June 1981), pp. 204–36.

52. Waltz has himself helped open up such a debate with his recognition that systemic factors condition but do not determine state actions. See Kenneth Waltz, "Reflections on *Theory of International Politics:* A Response to My Critics," in Robert Keohane, ed., *Neorealism and Its Critics* (New York: Columbia University Press, 1986), pp. 322–45. The growing literature on the observation that "democracies do not fight each other" is relevant to this question, as are two other studies that break important ground toward a "reductionist" theory of state identity: William Bloom's *Personal Identity, National Identity and International Relations* (Cambridge: Cambridge University Press, 1990) and Lumsdaine's *Ideals and Interests.*

53. See Berger and Luckmann, *The Social Construction of Reality,* p. 89. See also Douglas Maynard and Thomas Wilson, "On the Reification of Social Structure," in Scott McNall and Gary Howe, eds., *Current Perspectives in Social Theory,* vol. 1 (Greenwich, Conn.: JAI Press, 1980), pp. 287–322.

54. See Richard Ashley, "Social Will and International Anarchy," in Hayward Alker and Richard Ashley, eds., *After Realism,* work in progress, Massachusetts Institute of Technology, Cambridge, and Arizona State University, Tempe, 1992.

55. On the relationship between commitment and identity, see Foote, "Identification as the Basis for a Theory of Motivation"; Howard Becker, "Notes on the Concept of Commitment," *American Journal of Sociology* 66 (July 1960), pp. 32–40; and Stryker, *Symbolic Interactionism.* On role salience, see Stryker, ibid.

56. James March, "Bounded Rationality, Ambiguity, and the Engineering of Choice," *Bell Journal of Economics* 9 (Autumn 1978), p. 600.

57. Haskel Fain, *Normative Politics and the Community of Nations* (Philadelphia: Temple University Press, 1987).

58. This is the intersubjective basis for the principle of functional nondifferentiation among states, which

"drops out" of Waltz's definition of structure because the latter has no explicit intersubjective basis. In international relations scholarship, the social production of territorial space has been emphasized primarily by post-structuralists. See, for example, Richard Ashley, "The Geopolitics of Geopolitical Space: Toward a Critical Social Theory of International Politics," *Alternatives* 12 (October 1987), pp. 403–34; and Simon Dalby, *Creating the Second Cold War* (London: Pinter, 1990). But the idea of space as both product and constituent of practice is also prominent in structurationist discourse. See Giddens, *Central Problems in Social Theory;* and Derek Gregory and John Urry, eds., *Social Relations and Spatial Structures* (London: Macmillan, 1985).

59. See John Ruggie, "Continuity and Transformation in the World Polity: Toward a Neorealist Synthesis," *World Politics* 35 (January 1983), pp. 261–85.

60. For a definition and discussion of "social closure," see Raymond Murphy, *Social Closure* (Oxford: Clarendon Press, 1988).

61. See Richard Ashley, "Untying the Sovereign State: A Double Reading of the Anarchy Problematique," *Millennium* 17 (Summer 1988), pp. 227–62.

62. See William Coplin, "International Law and Assumptions About the State System," *World Politics* 17 (July 1965), pp. 615–34.

63. See Anthony Smith, "States and Homelands: The Social and Geopolitical Implications of National Territory," *Millennium* 10 (Autumn 1981), pp. 187–202.

64. David Strang, "Anomaly and Commonplace in European Expansion: Realist and Institutional Accounts," *International Organization* 45 (Spring 1991), pp. 143–62.

65. On "dynamic density," see Ruggie, "Continuity and Transformation in the World Polity"; and Waltz, "Reflections on *Theory of International Politics*." The role of interdependence in conditioning the speed and depth of social learning is much greater than the attention to which I have paid it. On the consequences of interdependence under anarchy, see Helen Milner, "The Assumption of Anarchy in International Relations Theory: A Critique," *Review of International Studies* 17 (January 1991), pp. 67–85.

66. See Michael Taylor, *Anarchy and Cooperation* (New York: Wiley, 1976); and Robert Axelrod, *The Evolution of Cooperation* (New York: Basic Books, 1984).

67. Mead, *Mind, Self, and Society.*

68. Strictly speaking, this is not true, since in iterated games the addition of future benefits to current ones changes the payoff structure of the game at T1, in this case from prisoners' dilemma to an assurance game. This transformation of interest takes place entirely within the actor, however, and as such is not a function of interaction with the other.

69. In fairness to Axelrod, he does point out that internationalization of norms is a real possibility that may increase the resilience of institutions. My point is that this important idea cannot be derived from an approach to theory that takes identities and interests as exogenously given.

70. On "European identity," see Barry Buzan et al., eds., *The European Security Order Recast* (London: Pinter, 1990), pp. 45–63.

71. On "embeddedness," see John Ruggie, "International Regimes, Transactions, and Change: Embedded Liberalism in a Postwar Economic Order," in Krasner, *International Regimes,* pp. 195–232.

72. See Grieco, "Anarchy and the Limits of Cooperation."

73. On the difficulties of creating cooperative security regimes given competitive interests, see Robert Jervis, "Security Regimes," in Krasner, *International Regimes,* pp. 173–94; and Charles Lipson, "International Cooperation in Economic and Security Affairs," *World Politics* 37 (October 1984), pp. 1–23.

74. See Mead, *Mind, Self, and Society.* . . .

75. Turner, "Role-Taking."

76. On "character planning," see Jon Elster, *Sour Grapes: Studies in the Subversion of Rationality* (Cambridge: Cambridge University Press, 1983), p. 117. . . .

77. For useful overviews of New Thinking, see Mikhail Gorbachev, *Perestroika: New Thinking for Our Country and the World* (New York: Harper & Row, 1987); Vendulka Kubalkova and Albert Cruickshank, *Thinking New About Soviet "New Thinking"* (Berkeley: Institute of International Studies. 1989); and Allen Lynch, *Gorbachev's International Outlook: Intellectual Origins and Political Consequences* (New York: Institute for East–West Security Studies, 1989). . . .

78. For useful overviews of these factors, see Jack Snyder, "The Gorbachev Revolution: A Waning of Soviet Expansionism?" *World Politics* 12 (Winter 1987–88), pp. 93–121; and Stephen Meyer, "The Sources and Prospects of Gorbachev's New Political Thinking on Security," *International Security* 13 (Fall 1988), pp. 124–63.

79. See Daniel Bar-Tal et al., "Conflict Termination: An Epistemological Analysis of International Cases," *Political Psychology* 10 (June 1989), pp. 233–55. . . .

80. See Robert Cox, "Social Forces, States and World Orders: Beyond International Relations Theory," In Keohane, *Neorealism and Its Critics,* pp. 204–55. See also Brian Fay, *Critical Social Science* (Ithaca, N.Y.: Cornell University Press, 1987).

81. Hazel Markus and Paula Nurius, "Possible Selves," *American Psychologist* 41 (September 1986), pp. 954–69.

82. See Goffman, *The Presentation of Self in Everyday Life;* Eugene Weinstein and Paul Deutschberger, "Some Dimensions of Altercasting," *Sociometry* 26 (December

1963), pp. 454–66; and Walter Earle, "International Relations and the Psychology of Control: Alternative Control Strategies and Their Consequences," *Political Psychology* 7 (June 1986), pp. 369–75.

83. See Volker Boge and Peter Wilke, "Peace Movements and Unilateral Disarmament: Old Concepts in a New Light," *Arms Control* 7 (September 1986), pp. 156–70; Zeev Maoz and Daniel Felsenthal, "Self-Binding Commitments, the Inducement of Trust, Social Choice, and the Theory of International Cooperation," *International Studies Quarterly* 31 (June 1987), pp. 177–200; and V. Sakamoto, "Unilateral Initiative as an Alternative Strategy," *World Futures*, vol. 24, nos. 1–4, 1987, pp. 107–34.

84. On rewards, see Thomas Milburn and Daniel Christie, "Rewarding in International Politics," *Political Psychology* 10 (December 1989), pp. 625–45.

85. Yale Ferguson and Richard Mansbach, "Between Celebration and Despair: Constructive Suggestions for Future International Theory," *International Studies Quarterly* 35 (December 1991), 375.

86. For excellent discussions of this tension, see Walker, "Sovereignty, Identity, Community"; and R. B. J. Walker, "Security, Sovereignty, and the Challenge of World Politics," *Alternatives* 15 (Winter 1990), pp. 3–27. On institutional path dependencies, see Stephen Krasner, "Sovereignty: An Institutional Perspective," *Comparative Political Studies* 21 (April 1988), pp. 66–94.

Turbulent Change

JAMES N. ROSENAU

In this article, excerpted from his book Turbulence in World Politics, *Professor Rosenau identifies two competing "worlds"—state-centric and multicentric. He focuses on both micro- and macro-level factors as he explores a world marked by the uncertainties associated with turbulence. Change is being propelled by the dynamics of technology, the emergence of complex issues, the reduced capacity of states to deal effectively with many contemporary problems, and the emergence of "subgroupism" and individuals who are analytically ever more capable and diverse in orientation.*

Doubtless every era seems chaotic to the people who live through it, and the last decades of the twentieth century are no exception. It is as if Spaceship Earth daily encounters squalls, downdrafts, and wind shears as it careens into changing and unchartered realms of experience. Sometimes the turbulence is furiously evident as thunderclouds of war gather or the lightning of a crisis streaks across the global sky; but often the turbulence is of a clear-air kind, the havoc it wreaks unrecognized until after its challenges have been met or its damage done.

In seeking here to account for this turbulence in world politics and the changes that it both reflects and promotes, the analysis will focus on the underlying and enduring dynamics out of which daily events and current issues flow. Some of the dynamics are located at micro levels, where individuals learn and groups cohere; others originate at macro levels, where new technologies are operative and collectivities conflict; and still others derive from clashes between opposing forces at the two levels— between continuity and change, between the pulls of the past and the lures of the future, between the requirements of interdependence and the demands for independence, between centralizing and decentralizing tendencies within and among nations.

While equating the turbulence of world affairs to stormy weather captures well the current human condition, its use here as a metaphor may divert from my larger purpose. The goal in identifying a hitherto unimaginable scheme is to facilitate empirical explanation rather than to provide poetic expression. What is needed is a conception of turbulence that denotes the tensions and changes that ensue when the structures and processes that normally sustain world politics are unsettled and appear to be undergoing rearrangements. Turbulence is thus more than the commotion that accompanies shifts in major variables. Such fluctuations make up the day-to-day life of any system, be it social or meteorological. Just as shifts from cloudiness to showers to sunshine constitute normal weather patterns, so do electoral shifts from right to center to left or industrial shifts from high to moderate to low productivity form standard political and economic patterns, thereby allowing the analysis of such shifts to proceed by treating the system's boundaries as constant and the range within which the variables fluctuate as a measure of underlying stability. When the system's boundaries no longer contain the fluctuations of the variables, however, anomalies arise and irregularities set in as structures waver, new processes evolve, outcomes become transitory, and the system enters a period of prolonged disequilibrium. These are the hallmarks of turbulence. Meteorologically, it appears in the form of hurricanes, tornadoes, tidal waves, droughts, and other "abnormalities" of nature that transform the terrain across which they sweep. Socially, it is manifested in technological breakthroughs, authority crises, consensus breakdowns, revolutionary upheavals, generational conflicts, and other forces that restructure the human landscape in which they erupt.

It follows that uncertainty is a prime characteristic of turbulent politics. While the fluctuations of variables usually adhere to recognizable patterns, regularities disappear when turbulence sets in. At such times, the structures and processes of world politics enter a realm without prior rules or boundaries. Anything may happen, or so it seems, as demands are intensified, tensions exacerbated, relationships transformed, policymaking paralyzed, or outcomes otherwise rendered less certain and the future more obscure.

Closely related to the uncertainties associated with political turbulence is the pace at which it moves. Unlike conventional diplomatic or organizational situations, which evolve in the context of formal procedures, cautious bargaining, and bureaucratic inertia, those beset by turbulent conditions develop rapidly as the repercussions of the various participants' actions cascade through their networks of interdependence. Sustained by the complexity and dynamism of diverse actors whose goals and activities are inextricably linked to each other, and facilitated by technologies that transmit information almost instantaneously, turbulent situations tend to be marked by quick responses, insistent demands, temporary coalitions, and policy reversals, all of which propel the course of events swiftly if erratically along the fault lines of conflict and cooperation.

Viewed in this context, it is not surprising that . . . protests and uprisings [have] followed quickly upon each other in Soviet Armenia, the West Bank, Poland, Burma, and Yugoslavia, or that the same time span was marked by regimes being shaken up in the Soviet Union, Chile, Haiti, and Lebanon. Likewise, and no less conspicuous, [the world has] witnessed cascades of cooperation: within weeks of each other, negotiations to end wars were initiated in Afghanistan, Angola, Central America, Cambodia, the Western Sahara, and the Persian Gulf.[1] The winds of turbulence, in short, can propel postinternational politics in many directions, through the world's diplomatic and legislative chambers, where compromises are reached, no less than through its streets and battlefields, where conflicts are joined.

But how to extend the analysis beyond a suggestive metaphor? How to employ turbulence as a serious and systematic analytic concept that helps to account for the emergence of postinternational politics? ... [A]n answer is found in the field of organizational theory, where the concept of turbulence is well developed and widely used. In particular, reliance is placed on a model of organizations that identifies turbulence as the condition they face when their environments are marked by high degrees of complexity and dynamism. In this formulation, high complexity is not a synonym for events and trends that are difficult to understand. It refers, rather, to such an inordinate number of actors in the environment, and such an extensive degree of interdependence among them, that the environment is dense (rather than thin) with causal layers. This density is conceived to be so great as to enable any event to give rise to a restless commotion, which reverberates in fast-paced and unexpected ways throughout the environment and its diverse systems. When the dynamism of the environment is also high—i.e., when great variability marks the conduct of its actors—the interdependence of its many parts is bound to be greatly affected by the volatility that accompanies large-scale social transformations.

It could be argued that high complexity and high dynamism are not new to world politics, that global wars, revolutions, and depressions reflect such conditions, and accordingly, that change has always been at work in world politics. In order to differentiate the familiar and commonplace changes from the profound kind of transformations that seem to be occurring today, one other attribute of political turbulence needs to be noted—namely, it involves *parametric* change. Only when the basic parameters of world politics, those boundary constraints that shape and confine the fluctuations of its variables, are engulfed by high complexity and high dynamism is turbulence considered to have set in. Being boundaries, parameters are normally stable. They make possible the continuities of political life, the ability of individual and collective actors to get from one day to the next and from one era to the next. Hence, when the orientations, skills, relationships, and structures that have sustained the parameters of world politics begin to crumble—i.e., when the complexity and the dynamism of the parameters reach a point where the existing rules of conduct no longer serve to constrain behavior and outcomes—the course of events is bound to turn turbulent.

Three dimensions of world politics are conceptualized as its main parameters. One of these operates at the micro level of individuals, one functions at the macro level of collectivities, and the third involves a mix of the two levels. The micro parameter consists of the orientations and skills by which citizens of states and members of nonstate organizations link themselves to the macro world of global politics. I refer to this set of boundary constraints as the *orientational* or *skill* parameter. The macro parameter is here designated the *structural* parameter, and it refers to the constraints embedded in the distribution of power among and within the collectivities of the global system. The mixed parameter is called the *relational* one; it focuses on the nature of the authority relations that prevail between individuals at the micro level and their macro collectivities.

All three of these parameters are judged to be undergoing such a thoroughgoing transformation today as to bring about the first turbulence in world politics since comparable shifts culminated in the Treaty of Westphalia in 1648.[2] At first glance, it doubtless seems excessive to argue that the turbulence of the present era is the first in more than three hundred years. Clearly, the history of most countries is marked by periods of turmoil. As already noted, however, the claim being made here pertains to turbulence in the international system and not to the upheavals experienced within national systems, to the transformation of three specific parametric patterns and not to the commotion that attends the waging of wars or the fluctuation of economies. In the case of the structural parameter, the transformation is marked by a bifurcation in which the state-centric system now coexists with an equally powerful, though more decentralized, multi-centric system. Although these two worlds of world politics have overlapping elements and concerns, their norms, structures, and processes tend to be mutually exclusive, thus giving rise to a set of global arrangements that are new and possibly enduring, as well as extremely complex and dynamic.[3] In the case of the relational parameter, the long-standing pattern whereby compliance with authority tends to be unquestioning and automatic is conceived to have been replaced by a more elaborate set of norms that make the successful exercise of authority much more problematic, thus fostering leadership and followership conflicts within and among state and nonstate collectivities that can fairly be judged as amounting to a series of authority crises which, in both their pervasiveness and their scale, are new and global in scope. Lastly, at the micro level, the analytic skills of individuals have increased to a point where they now play a different and significant role in world politics, a role which has intensified both the processes of structural bifurcation and the breakdown of authority relations.

It is the simultaneity and interaction of these parametric changes that distinguish the present period from the previous three centuries. By virtue of their newly acquired skills, people are more able and ready to question authority, and in turn the new authority relationships have facilitated the development of new, more decentralized global structures. But the causal flows also move from the macro to the micro level as the centralized structures invite the formation of new authority relationships, which then serve to refine further the skills and orientations through which individuals link themselves to their collectivities. Earlier eras have witnessed wars that shifted global structures from multipolar to bipolar foundations and revolutions that undermined the prevailing authority relationships; but not since the seventeenth century have circumstances arisen in which the values of all three of these fundamental parameters underwent reinforcing realignments.

Between Peace and War

The turbulent conditions of postinternational politics should not be equated to those of violence. While uncertainty may promote the possibility of armed conflict in world politics, there is no one-to-one relationship between them. Turbulence can prevail within communities, markets, organizations, and alliances without their conflicts bringing on a resort to armed force. To study turbulence is to analyze responses to uncertainty, to the changes wrought by technology and an ever-expanding global interdependence, and war is but one of those responses. What follows, therefore, is only incidentally an analysis of violence in world politics. Indeed, . . . there are good reasons to anticipate that responses involving force will diminish as world politics becomes more turbulent.

In some important respects, in fact, war is free of the uncertainties that accompany turbulence. When war breaks out, adversarial relationships become clear, the goals of policy making self-evident, and the tasks ahead unmistakable. Viewed in this way, turbulence may be more a prewar or postwar condition than a mark of wartime. And of course it is not a characteristic of peacetime, if by the latter is meant stable circumstances in which parameters remain essentially fixed.

In both peace and war, in other words, the day-to-day fluctuations are familiar. They are within the range of variations that have occurred before, that people know how to cope with and adjust to. Under turbulent conditions, on the other hand, even the slightest fluctuation can seem portentous, with each shift confirming that change is the norm, that patterns are fragile, and that expectations can be frustrated.

The Sources of Change

What are the forces at work toward the end of the twentieth century that drive these parametric transformations? Five seem particularly relevant. One involves the shift from an industrial to a postindustrial order and focuses on the dynamics of technology, particularly on those technologies associated with the microelectronic revolution that have made social, economic, and political distances so much shorter, the movement of ideas, pictures, currencies, and information so much faster, and thus the interdependence of people and events so much greater.[4] A second engine of global change is the emergence of issues—such as atmospheric pollution, terrorism, the drug trade, currency crises, and AIDS—that are the direct products of new technologies or of the world's greater interdependence and are distinguished from traditional political issues by virtue of being transnational rather than national or local in scope. A third dynamic is the reduced capability of states and governments to provide satisfactory solutions to the major issues on their political agendas, partly because the new issues are not wholly within their jurisdiction, partly because the old issues are also increasingly intertwined with significant international components (e.g., agricultural markets and labor productivity), and partly because the compliance of their citizenries can no longer be taken for granted. Fourth, with the weakening of whole systems, subsystems have acquired a correspondingly greater coherence and effectiveness, thereby fostering tendencies toward decentralization (what I call *subgroupism*) at all organizational levels that are in stark contrast to the centralizing tendencies (here regarded as

nation-statism or *transnationalism*) that marked the early decades of this century and those that preceded it. Finally, there is the feedback of the consequences of all the foregoing for the skills and orientations of the world's adults who comprise the groups, states, and other collectivities that have had to cope with the new issues of interdependence and adjust to the new technologies of the postindustrial order; with their analytic skills enlarged and their orientations toward authority more self-conscious, today's persons-in-the-street are no longer as uninvolved, ignorant, and manipulable with respect to world affairs as were their forebears.

The hypothesized interactions among these five sources of change, and an indication of the historical setting in which they accelerated, are presented diagrammatically in Figure 1. This causal model involves more than a simple identification of five prime sources of global turbulence and a presumption that they are highly interactive. One of the five dynamics, the shift in micro capabilities and orientations, is deemed to be more powerful than the other four, so much so as to be a requisite to the expansivity and intensity of the other four. That is, although world politics would not be on a new course today if the microelectronic and other technological revolutions had not occurred, if the new interdependence issues had not arisen, if states and governments had not become weaker, and if subgroupism had not mushroomed, none of these dynamics would have produced parametric change if adults in every country and in all walks of life had remained essentially unskilled and detached with respect to global affairs. To be sure, these shifts in skills and orientations have been hastened and refined by the other dynamics, and in this sense the latter can also be viewed as necessary determinants of the turbulence. Without the micro transformations, however, none of the others could have emerged on a worldwide scale, and in this sense the enlargements of the capacities of citizens is the primary prerequisite for global turbulence.

The analysis, then, is not based on a single-cause model. Nor does it presume that the micro changes preceded the others in time. On the contrary, all of them are seen as being initially responses to the technological upheavals that underlay the ever-growing interdependencies of economic, political, and social life. Once the micro level shifts began, however, alterations in the status of states, governments, and subgroups were bound to follow, as people became receptive to the decentralizing consequences inherent in their growing capacity to locate their own interests more clearly in the flow of events. The subtlety of these interactive processes is perhaps most clearly evident in the links between the expansion of citizen skills and the technologies made available by the microelectronic revolution. If one asks what the advent of instantaneous communications and information retrieval—of satellites bringing pictures of ongoing events into homes everywhere and of computers storing, processing, and disseminating information heretofore unknown and ungatherable—may be doing to individuals as actors on the global stage, the answer seems inescapable that the new technologies have had a profound, if not always desirable, impact upon how individuals perceive, comprehend, judge, enter, avoid, or otherwise interact with the world beyond their workplace and home. For example, the new electronic technologies have so greatly collapsed the time in which organizations and movements can be mobilized that the competence of citizens feeds on itself, in the sense that they can virtually "see" their skills and orientations being cumulated into larger aggregates that have consequence for the course of events. No longer does the translation of commitment into action await word brought by stagecoach that like-minded citizens are banding together or that leaders discern an opportunity for effective participation. Today, events and the words about them are, in effect, simultaneous occurrences. Unlike any prior time in history, therefore, citizens are now able to intrude themselves readily into a situation anywhere in the world, because information about its latest twists and turns is immediately at hand.

Indeed, even if the ensuing analysis exaggerates the extent to which the skills and orientations of citizens have enlarged, the ability to mobilize those skills and orientations is so much greater and speedier than in the past that the practical effect is an expanded capacity for identifying and articulating self-interests and participating effectively in collective action. And if, as seems likely, those who head organizations recognize the effects of this capacity on their leadership circumstances, then their sensitivities to the wishes and demands of their followers will intensify and lend further credence to the perception of citizens as undergoing an expansion and redirection of their skills and orientations.

The Technological Dynamic

Given the conception of turbulence as a process of parameter realignment, a further question arises as to the sources of turbulence. Except for the dynamics unleashed by technological innovations, those noted so far are embraced by the three parameters of the global political system and are thus endogenous to it. But there may be exogenous sources in addition to those that derive from technological developments. That is, while turbulence partly feeds on itself, as each parametric alteration gives rise to circumstances that exert pressure for further alterations, political systems are also subject to a broad array of changes originating in the economy and society, all of which are also sufficiently dynamic to spur still further changes once they have been absorbed by the polity.

Following the insightful formulation of Choucri and North, three dynamics are conceived to be especially relevant as exogenous sources of global turbulence.[5] As indicated in Figure 1, one is the pressures created by extensive changes in the structure and size of populations in recent decades. A second involves the shifting availability and distribution of natural resources, especially those related to the generation of energy. The third derives from the previously mentioned consequences of technologies in all fields of human endeavor, from information processing to medicine, biogenetics and agriculture.

Since it has also contributed to the shifts in population and natural resources, technology is perhaps the most powerful of the exogenous dynamics. For it is technological developments, those combinations of human ingenuity and material nature, that have transformed the industrial order and brought into being the age of information, the post-industrial society, the technocratic era, the microelectronic revolution—whatever one may wish to call the emergent arrangements by which people move toward goals, satisfy needs, and otherwise conduct their affairs. Technology has expanded the capacity to generate and manipulate information and knowledge even more than the ability to produce material goods, leading to a situation in which the service industries have come to replace the manufacturing industries as the cutting edge of societal life. It is technology, too, that has so greatly diminished geographic and social distances through the jet-powered airliner, the computer, the orbiting satellite, and the many other innovations that now move people, ideas, and goods more rapidly and surely across space and time than ever before. It is technology that has profoundly altered the scale on which human affairs take place, allowing more people to do more things in less time and with wider repercussions than could have been imagined in earlier eras. It is technology, in short, that has fostered an interdependence of local, national, and international communities that is far greater than any previously experienced.[6]

The impact of these technology-driven exogenous dynamics on societies, economies, and polities has been imaginatively and fully recorded by students of national systems. One needs only read the works of Daniel Bell, Peter Drucker, John Naisbitt, and Daniel Yankelovich —to mention a few of the many observers who have focused on the social consequences of modern technology—to appreciate the extraordinary transformations through which the world is passing.[7] They convincingly demonstrate that families, marriages, acquaintanceships, work, unions, businesses, leisure, agriculture, productivity, housing, travel, electoral politics, and every other aspect of life have recently undergone, and still continue to undergo, changes of great magnitude.

Yet somehow, students of global politics have not begun to take account of the transformations at work within societies. While they do not ignore the domestic sources of international relationships when internal conflicts, consensuses, or stalemates predominate, the dynamics of the postindustrial society tend to be taken for granted. That the world is considerably more interdependent is widely recognized, but the ways in which the sources of expanding interdependence sustain or alter the structures and processes of world politics have not been foci of intensive investigation.[8] The prevailing orientation seems, rather, to presume that the basic structures and processes of international politics remain intact even as change swirls through its component parts.

Likewise, students of the postindustrial society have not been especially concerned with the implications of their findings and insights for global politics. While Drucker, for example, does explore these implications for international economics, his analysis is limited to the problems of politically managing the world economy and does not get into the even larger question of management in world politics itself. Similarly, Bell anticipates "that the post-industrial society will involve *more* politics than ever before, for the very reason that choice becomes conscious and the decision-centers more visible,"[9] but his inquiry does not extend beyond the politics of who rules the community and society. The possibility that the global effects of the relatively few

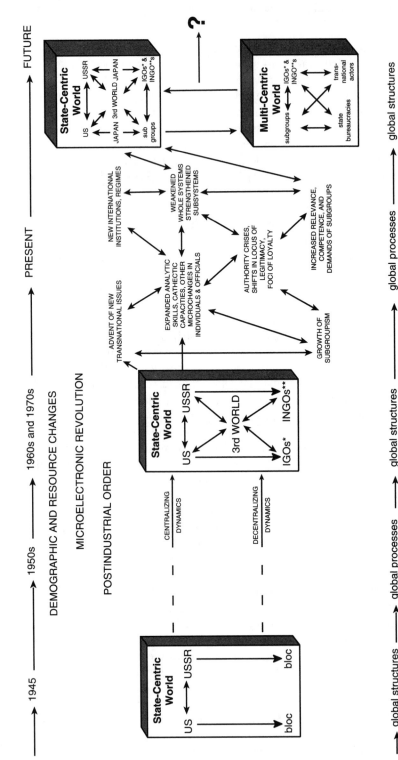

* IGOs – International Governmental Organizations
**INGOs – International Non-governmental Organizations

FIGURE 1   Evolution of the Two Worlds of World Politics

postindustrial societies might give rise to worldwide norms and practices that influence the development of preindustrial and industrial societies is not entertained.

An Overview

Political turbulence is not so powerful as to sweep away existing institutional arrangements and cultural patterns without resistance. If we are to comprehend the tensions inherent in the clash between the forces that sustain the prevailing order and those that promote transformation, we need to be clear about the concepts of turbulence and change as well as the procedures employed to analyze them. . . .

In sum, by exploring turbulence in world politics we are investigating a major analytic gap that needs to be filled. The gap is that nexus wherein politics on a global scale have been transformed by the diverse dynamics that have taken modern life beyond the rules and arrangements that prevailed throughout the industrial era. The need to fill the gap stems from the premise that it is inconceivable that so many great changes could occur within societies without major consequences for the conduct of affairs among them.

Notes

1. For an analysis of these developments, see James N. Rosenau, "Interdependence and the Simultaneity Puzzle: Notes on the Outbreak of Peace," in Charles W. Kegley, Jr., ed., *The Long Postwar Peace: The Sources of Great Power Stability* (forthcoming), chapter 15.

2. The Treaty of Westphalia is generally recognized as the beginning of the modern system of nation-states. However, this is not a unanimous view. Wight, for example, argues that the start of the French-Spanish struggle over Italy in 1494 marked the origin of the modern system, noting that "at Westphalia the state system does not come into existence; it comes of age." M. Wight, *Systems of States* (Leicester: Leicester University Press, 1977), p. 152.

3. . . . It seems appropriate to treat the state- and multicentric systems as separate "worlds," a formulation not to be confused with the generic label "world politics" that is used throughout to designate structures and processes of global scope. The frequent references to the "two worlds of world politics" (or, occasionally, to the "two-world political universe") are intended to serve as a continual reminder that the global system has structure even though it lacks unity, having entered a period of far-reaching (and possibly irreversible) bifurcation.

4. For a thorough exploration of the diverse dimensions of the microelectronic revolution, see Rob van Tulder and Gerd Junne, *European Multinationals in Core Technologies* (Chichester: John Wiley, 1988).

5. Nazli Choucri and Robert C. North, *Nations in Conflict: National Growth and International Violence* (San Francisco: W. H. Freeman, 1975).

6. For a succinct and cogent discussion of the diverse ways in which new electronic technologies have changed the face of politics at all levels, see Walter B. Wriston, "Technology and Sovereignty," *Foreign Affairs* 67 (Winter 1988/89): 63–75.

7. These authors have each written more than one work on the dynamics of change in the late twentieth century, but their views can be readily grasped in Bell, *Coming of Post-Industrial Society;* Peter Drucker, *Managing in Turbulent Times* (New York: Harper & Row, 1980); John Naisbitt, *Megatrends: Ten New Directions Transforming Our Lives* (New York: Warner Books, 1982); and Daniel Yankelovich, *New Rules: Searching for Self-Fulfillment in A World Turned Upside Down* (New York: Random House, 1981).

8. Exceptions to this generalization can be found in James N. Danziger, "Computing and the Political World," *Computers and the Social Sciences* 2 (1986): 183–200, and Robert Gilpin, "The Computer and World Affairs," in M. L. Dertouzos and J. Moses, eds., *The Computer Age: A Twenty-Year View* (Cambridge, Mass.: MIT Press, 1979), pp. 229–53.

9. Bell, *Coming of Post-Industrial Society,* p. 263 (italics in original).

GLOSSARY

abstraction A general idea, principle, or concept without physical or tangible quality. International relations theorists sometimes write of systems, interdependence, the balance of power, and equilibrium—examples of abstractions that may be useful to the theorist who wishes to explain or account for political or other phenomena.

action A movement or physical act, as when the state or its decisionmakers take some concrete step in a given situation. An action is the practical expression of policy. See also **policy, interaction**.

actor A participant or player. The state is considered by realists to be the principal actor in international relations; other nonstate actors include transnational actors such as multinational corporations and banks. See also **rational, unitary, transnational**, and **transgovernmental** actors.

agency, agent A voluntarist, non-determinist focus on the role played by human beings and human institutions in effecting outcomes; human beings matter and what they think and do matter. See **social constructivism**.

aggregation The bringing together of parts into a single whole, as when the state is understood to be a *unitary* actor. Pluralists tend to see the state not as a single, unitary whole but as many parts, thus disaggregating or breaking the state apart into its component institutions, groups, and individual persons.

amoral Morally neutral; without moral content. See also **moral**.

anarchic See **anarchy**.

anarchy The absence of political authority. International politics or the international system are said to be anarchic in that there is no central or superordinate authority over states.

anthropology The scientific study of humankind, including its physical, social, and cultural origins and development.

appeasement The policy of allowing another state to have what it wants—an attempt to avoid aggression by that state; for an example, see **learning**.

assumption A premise or statement taken to be true without empirical or factual proof. The theorist typically makes assumptions as the starting point in developing a given theory. For example, some balance-of-power theorists make assumptions about the state as principal, unitary, and rational actor.

asymmetry, asymmetric Not symmetrical; lacking precise correspondence or relation between or among components. An interdependence relation is said to be asymmetric if Party *A* is more dependent on Party *B* than Party *B* is on Party *A*.

autarky An independent posture of self-sufficiency without dependence on other actors. Autarky occurs when a state attempts as a matter of policy to exist in economic isolation from other states.

authority A legitimate right to direct or command and to make, decide, and enforce rules. The term *authority* has a moral or legal quality and, as such, can be distinguished from control by brute force or by coercion. See also **power**.

autonomous development See **development**.

balance of payments Accounting concept by which the international economic transactions (inflows and outflows) of states and their corporate and private elements are tracked. Balance of payments includes export and import of goods and services (balance of trade), capital investment and other "invisible" or financial flows, and gold or other financial reserve transactions. "Balance" is achieved when gold or other financial reserves flow in or out to cover differences in the other accounts as when a country exporting more than it imports receives foreign currency that it can hold as a financial reserve.

balance of power A key concept among realists that refers to a condition of equilibrium among states. Realists differ on whether the equilibrium or balance among states is (a) created by statesmen or (b) occurs quite apart from the will of statesmen as an inherent characteristic of international politics. Balance-of-power considerations may be used by decisionmakers as justification for a given foreign policy. Some critics have noted that the multiple definitions or meanings of balance of power diminish its utility as a concept in international relations theory.

behavior The actions and interactions among units; the behavior of policymakers or of states. **Behavioralism** refers to a way to study politics or other social phenomena that focuses on the actions and interactions among units by using scientific methods of observation to include quantification of variables whenever possible. A practitioner of *behavioralism* is often referred to as a *behavioralist*. *Behaviorism* refers to the ideas held by those behavioral scientists who consider only observed behavior as relevant to the scientific enterprise and who reject what they consider to be metaphysical notions of "mind" or "consciousness."

behavioralism See **behavior**.

bipolar, bipolarity The condition of having two poles as when the distribution of power or capabilities in international politics is said to be *bipolar*. Some theorists consider the Cold War international political system to have had a bipolar *structure*—the United States and the former Soviet Union. Others consider it today to be unipolar, multipolar or to conform to some other characterization. See also **structure**.

bourgeoisie The capitalist (and, at the time of its emergence, the "middle") class. The class defined in Marxian terms by its relation to the means of production—its ownership of capital, including factories and other machinery of production in a capitalist economic mode. A member of this class is sometimes referred to as a *bourgeois*.

bureaucracy The administrative arm of government staffed primarily by appointed, non-elected officials. A given governmental agency may be referred to as a bureaucracy, whereas the generic category of such agencies may be referred to as the bureaucracy. An individual member of a bureaucracy or administrator is sometimes referred to as a *bureaucrat*. Bureaucracy, bureaucrat, and bureaucratic are words sometimes used to convey negative connotations about government, but most academic usage is merely descriptive of the governmental administrative function.

bureaucratic politics   The formulation of policy is a function of the competition among opposing individuals who represent diverse governmental institutions. Coalitions and counter-coalitions typically form as a part of the process of bureaucratic politics. See also **organizational process.**

capitalism   An economic system or mode of production that emphasizes private ownership of the means of production and a free market. One who owns the means of production is a capitalist, or *bourgeois*. See also **bourgeoisie.**

capitalist world-system   An approach to international relations that emphasizes the impact of the worldwide spread of capitalism; a focus on class and economic relations and the division of the world into a core, periphery, and semi-periphery. See also **core, periphery, semi-periphery, class.**

categorical imperative   Concept associated with the work of Immanuel Kant—that one ought to act "according to the maxim that you can at the same time will [such conduct] to be a universal law" and that one should treat others "as an end as well as a means, never merely as a means."

causality   B occurs on account of A, which precedes it in time. A produces or is responsible for the subsequent occurrence of B. In this sequence, A is the *cause* and B is the *effect*. Some causes have multiple effects, as when A causes B, C, and D. Some effects have multiple causes, as when effect T is caused by Q, R, and S. Some causes may be *necessary*, but not *sufficient* to produce a given effect, as when A is necessary to cause D but will not do so unless B or C is also present (thus, A and B or A and C are *necessary and sufficient* causes of D). Some causes are sufficient in themselves to produce a given effect, as when the presence of A always produces B. An *efficient* cause is the factor immediately responsible for a given effect, whereas a *permissive* cause may refer to an underlying condition that allows a certain effect to be produced (Kenneth Waltz, for example, argues that international anarchy is the permissive cause of—the absence of any obstacle to—war whereas other factors proximate to a particular situation, such as misperception in a crisis, are among the efficient causes of a given war). Some theorists reject causality as an abstract or metaphysical notion: One can observe B as coming after or following A in terms of time, but that does not prove that A is a "cause" of B.

causal modeling   The depiction, such as by a computer simulation or diagram, of sequential relations among two or more variables and how they result in a particular event, action, or outcome, including the relative importance or "weight" of each variable in producing a particular outcome. Causal models depict cause–effect relations, as in a model of an arms race that hypothesizes a causal connection between the decision of the former Soviet Union to increase the level of its military expenditure and an increase in the later military expenditure of the United States in an action–reaction sequence. The Soviet Union's actions, it may be hypothesized, caused the United States to react in a similar fashion, resulting in an overall increase in the amount of money devoted to military expenditures and producing, in turn, similar reaction by the Soviet Union—in effect, an arms race spiral.

center   The term used especially by many dependency theorists to refer to First World or the industrialized countries in the global political economy—Japan and the countries in Europe and North America with advanced industrial or post-industrial economies. Also sometimes used to refer to the elites or dominant classes. See also **core** and **periphery.**

city-state   A political entity composed of a city and its surrounding territory as in the city-states of ancient Greece (Sparta, Athens, Corinth, etc.) or Renaissance Italy (Florence, Venice, Padua, etc.).

class   A stratum of society with an identifiable characteristic or set of characteristics that differentiate it from another stratum. In Marxian usage, the term is defined by relations to the means of production. Under capitalism the *bourgeoisie* is defined by its ownership of capital (not only money but, significantly, the factories and machinery that are the means of production), and the *proletariat*, or working class, is defined by its labor. Under feudalism, the *aristocracy* is defined by its ownership of land, and the *serfs*, or peasants, by their labor.

class conflict   A concept associated with Marxism that emphasizes the inevitable clash of interests between strata, or classes, defined in terms of their relations to the means of production (i.e., how goods are produced). Marx, for example, analyzed the conflict between the *bourgeoisie* (owners of capital, especially factories and machinery of production) and the *proletariat*, or workers, who were being exploited by the bourgeoisie. Marx argued that eventually exploitation would reach the point at which a proletarian revolution would occur and the power of the bourgeoisie would be broken. See **proletarian revolution, Marxism.**

coalition   A combination or alliance of individuals, factions, or states, including both temporary and more enduring groupings of actors around a common interest or purpose.

cognition   The process by which human beings come to know or acquire knowledge through perception, reasoning, and (some would say) intuition. The term *cognitive* refers to this process.

cognitive dissonance   A concept developed by Leon Festinger wherein human beings tend not to perceive what is contrary to their preconceived or previously held perspectives. To avoid cognitive dissonance, individuals either (a) unconsciously screen out information or evidence that contradicts what they already believe to be true, or (b) interpret such discordant information in such a way as to support their preconceptions.

collective goods theory   Relates to the allocation of, and payment for, goods that, once provided, cannot easily be denied to others and whose use does not deny their use to others. Providing national security or international security through alliances has been described by some theorists as collective goods. Collective goods are referred to by some as public goods. See also **public choice theory.**

colonialism   See **imperialism.**

communism   A mode of production in Marxist thought that is to be achieved after the passing of capitalism and a socialist transition period. Communism is a classless society in which each person produces according to his or her ability and receives or consumes according to need. In Marxist thought, given the absence of classes, the state as an instrument of class domination ceases to exist.

communist   An individual committed to the eventual attainment of communism, particularly through revolutionary means that would lead to the overthrow of capitalism.

comparative advantage   The concept that holds that countries specialize in the production of those goods and services which they produce more efficiently. In a free trade environment there would be, according to theory, a global specialization or division of labor with aggregate productivity maximized. As critics point out, however, free trade theory does not address such matters as equity in the distribution of wealth. Some dependency theorists see free trade theory as the vehicle by which Third World countries are kept in a status of dependency and precluded from development.

complex interdependence   A term developed by Robert Keohane and Joseph Nye that refers to the multiple transnational channels that connect societies, including interstate, transgovernmental, and transnational relations. The resulting relations are extremely complex, with economic interests assuming far greater importance than in classic realism. See also **interdependence**.

comprador class   A term referring originally to the stratum of native businessmen in various Asian countries (including China) who served as local agents for foreign, colonial business interests. In contemporary usage, it refers to the aggregate of business elites in a Third World country or countries who maintain close links with their counterparts in the industrial countries of the First World. Particularly in Marxist usage, the term is used to explain relations of exploitation by the bourgeoisie of Third World workers and peasants.

compromise   Reaching accommodation or settlement between or among parties. A process typically involving give-and-take and concessions by one or more of the parties.

concept   An idea of a general or abstract nature; sometimes referred to as a *construct*. Such concepts as *power, interdependence, order, justice,* and *peace* are used in the construction of international relations theories.

conceptual   See **conceptualization**.

condition   A set of circumstances or state of being. An underlying condition of international politics, for example, is the absence of a single or central source of authority. When a given population has established a sense of community, this can be described as a condition.

conflict   Disagreement; the opposition or clash of units. Conflicts may be nonviolent or at varying degrees or levels of violence. Some theorists see the management of conflicts that cannot be resolved as being central to maintaining peace. Conflict of interest among states or other actors is a widely used concept.

constant   A factor that does not vary. See **variable.**

constitutionalism   The liberal idea that individual freedom is served by constraining the power or authority of government and setting formal limits, whether written or unwritten.

construct   Used synonymously with *concept*. A construct can be understood as an abstraction created or put together often out of simpler elements. See **concept.**

constructivism   See **social constructivism.**

core   A term sometimes used synonymously with *center*, a reference to the industrialized countries in the global political economy. The term is also sometimes used to refer to the elites or dominant classes. See also **center** and **periphery.**

correlation   An association between two, or among more than two, variables, of such a nature that a change in one seems to be tied or related to a change in another. A correlation among variables does not necessarily mean that they are causally linked. See also **causality, variable**.

cost   A loss as opposed to a benefit; something paid as opposed to something received. The concept is central to rational choice or game theory, including coalition and alliance formation. Costs may be distributed asymmetrically or unevenly among the actors in interdependence relations.

counterintuitive   Against, or contrary to, what is thought to be true. See **intuition, intuitive**.

crisis   A situation characterized by surprise, high threat to values or interests, and short decision time.

critical theory   Associated with Jürgen Habermas and the "Frankfurt School" in Germany that offered a theory of social reality based on the dialectic of knowledge and power, arguing that theory must be connected to practice. This also entailed a critique of positivist–empiricist approaches to knowledge, with critical theorists claiming all knowledge is historical and political in nature. Current "dissidents" in the field of international relations have also drawn, among others, from Antonio Gramsci's own version of critical theory, Ludwig Wittgenstein's work on linguistics and hermeneutics, and the post-structuralist perspective of such writers as Michel Foucault. Critical theory challenges the stated and unstated assumptions and alleged objectivity of mainstream social science. Ideologies that represent particular interests, while masquerading as "theories," are especially suspect. Such theories are depicted deceptively as if they were objective portrayals of sociopolitical time and space. Critical theorists reject the pretense to objective knowledge—the logical positivism of the "Vienna Circle" advanced in the interwar period and followed by many social scientists in subsequent decades. The rigid division between normative and empirical theory is illusory. Moreover, what we think we know really is a function of language and sociopolitical context. Critical theory calls for interpretive understanding of time and space, an insight drawn originally from Max Weber's work in social science methodology.

customary international law   Established practice by states over time gives a customary base for international law. For example, centuries of practice had established immunities and other diplomatic rights long before they were codified formally in a treaty.

decision   Making a choice among often competing alternatives or options; making a judgment or drawing a conclusion. A *rational* decision-making process is one in which alternative means to achieve certain objectives are evaluated and the option or options best (or at least satisfactorily) leading to the attainment of these objectives are selected. See also **policy**, which can be understood as being composed of both *decisions* and *actions*.

decision making   See **decision**.

deconstruct   See **post-modernism**.

deduction   Conclusions drawn logically and necessarily from specified premises.

deductive-nomological   Formal approach to scientific explanation often associated with Carl Hempel's work that relies on *covering laws* that relate the *explanans* (explanatory sentences) to the *explanandum* (what is to be explained). See also **deduction, nomology, nomothetic**.

dependency   A situation in which the economies of Third World countries are conditioned by and subordinate to the economic development, expansion, and contraction of the economies of advanced capitalist states. It is a situation of exploitation and is examined in a historical context. Domestic constraints and structures (such as land tenure patterns) are also critical in inhibiting balanced economic development.

dependent variable   The thing that is to be explained or accounted for. Some theorists have tried to explain, or find the causes of, war, which is their dependent variable. See also **variable, independent variable**.

description   A verbal statement that provides an understanding or meaning. Description is often differentiated from *explanation* or *prediction*, which are understood to be *theoretical* tasks. Thus, *theory* is considered to be different from mere *description*. From this perspective, description is a necessary but pretheoretical task.

détente   An easing or relaxation of tensions as when the relations between major powers are said to be less tense. The Cold War was said to have given way in the late 1960s and 1970s to a period of détente.

determinism, deterministic   A philosophical view that what we observe inevitably occurs as the consequence of factors over which human beings have no volition or control. Most social theorists who accept the characterization or who can be labeled as *determinists* do not reject totally the role of human will, as the strict definition of determinism would imply, but they do allow much less freedom of action for individuals to affect outcomes than those theorists labeled as *voluntarists* or *social constructivists*. The determinism–voluntarism issue among social science theorists has its analog in theological disputes over determinism or predestination on the one hand and free will on the other. Critics consider *structural realists* and *Marxist class analysts* to be overly deterministic, but this claim is often rejected by these theorists. See also **voluntarism.**

deterrence   Psychological effect on an opponent that results in a decision not to take some act such as attacking or starting a war. Deterrence is thought to be achieved either through fear of retaliatory punishment or through rational calculation that taking this action will not succeed in achieving intended objectives or that the costs of doing so will be too high.

development   The process associated with the industrialization of societies. *Modernization* is a term sometimes used synonymously with *development*, but some theorists differentiate between the two. For some, *modernization* refers to societal values and processes that undergo major changes from preindustrial traditional society, including the effects of industrialization, whereas *development* refers to the building of societal or governmental administrative infrastructure more capable of coping with increasing demands brought on by the modernization process. *Autonomous* development occurs in isolation, or independent of what is going on outside of a given country, a circumstance more difficult to achieve in the contemporary period than may have been true in the nineteenth century. *Reflexive* development, when and if it occurs, is responsive to external economic conditions and may well be dependent on them.

diachronic   Refers to a study over a period of time; sometimes referred to as a *longitudinal* study, as in a study of the causes of war between 1815 and 1945. See also **synchronic.**

dialectic, dialectical   A form of reasoning or argument that juxtaposes contradictory ideas with the goal of resolving the contradiction and thus moving closer to the truth. The term is associated with the ancient Greek philosophers, the German philosopher Hegel, and Karl Marx. Marx substituted materially based class conflict and the contradictions between means and modes of production for the clash of ideas. Whereas Hegel argued that the dialectical clash of ideas moved history forward, Marx focused on the importance of material forces. See also **class conflict, proletarian revolution, Marxism, means of production, modes of production.**

diffuse   Dispersed widely; not concentrated or narrowly focused. When a state is said to be a functionally diffuse actor, it performs a multitude of functions. The opposite of functionally diffuse is to be functionally specific or more narrowly focused.

diplomacy   The process or art of communication among states and their statesmen in international relations, negotiation, including positive inducements or persuasive tactics, compromise, threats, or other measures understood to be part (or tools) of diplomacy. Diplomacy is the state's political or policy element in the conduct of its foreign relations. The terms *diplomat* and *diplomatic* have a positive connotation, referring in common parlance to peaceful, nonwarlike approaches. As a technical term, *diplomacy* includes the threat or imposition of punishment or sanctions as tactics that may be employed by the diplomat in addition to (or in place of) more positive inducements.

disaggregation   See **aggregation**.

dissuade, dissuasion   From a position of strength to persuade other states not to do something they might otherwise do; dissuasion is usually seen as using both positive and negative measures to persuade. See also **deterrence**.

distributive justice   The question of the rightness of (or moral criteria associated with) the allocation of scarce resources, particularly material or economic resources. The rightness of a particular distribution of wealth or profit could be subject to normative standards of distributive justice. See also **justice, normative**.

dyad, dyadic   As between two units. See **interdependence**.

East   During the Cold War years, *East* referred to the Soviet Union and other Marxist-Leninist countries, mainly those in Eastern Europe. A more traditional meaning is the Orient or countries of Asia. Variants are the Far East (the countries of East Asia, including China, Japan, and the Koreas), the Middle East (originally referring to such south Asian countries as India and Pakistan, but now more commonly used to refer to Egypt, Israel, Jordan, Syria, Saudia Arabia, and neighboring countries), and the Near East (originally referring to countries in North Africa and Arabia; now more commonly referred to as the Middle East). See also **East–West**.

East–West   During the Cold War years, *East–West* referred to conflict between capitalist, industrial democracies of the First World or West (including West Europe, North America, and paradoxically even Japan) and the Marxist-Leninist countries of the Second World, or East (including the former USSR and other Marxist-Leninist countries, mainly those in Eastern Europe, but sometimes including China, particularly in the Maoist years). The more traditional meaning of East–West refers to Europe and the Americas as "West" and Asia as "East"—the meaning in Kipling's observation that East is East and West is West and never the twain shall meet. See also **East** and **West.**

EC   See **European Communities, European Union.**

econometrics   Quantitative techniques used in economic analysis.

economic development   The sustained expansion of production in an economy such that the standard or level of living is raised for the citizenry. See also **development**.

efficient cause   See **causality**.

elite   The upper stratum or strata of a society.

empirical, empirically   Factual or known through observation. Propositions or hypotheses may be subject to empirical or factual test to determine whether observed "facts" are consistent with what is predicted.

empiricism, empiricist   Consistent with the philosophical view of knowledge as rooted in experience, empiricists adopt a scientific focus on observation of facts and hypothesis testing as the virtually exclusive source of knowledge.

endogenous factor   See **system**.

English school   Scholars influenced by the earlier work of Martin Wight, Hedley Bull, F. H. Hinsley and others. The school focuses on the societal aspects of international relations rather than seeing politics in purely abstract, systemic terms. Power, law or rules based on enlightened self-interest, and emergent global norms are all part of an anarchical international society.

epistemology   Refers to the study of how one knows or how one acquires knowledge.

equilibrium   When various elements of a system are in balance. When disturbed, some systems are said to have an inherent tendency to restore this balance or equilibrium. For example, when a state or group of states upset the balance of power, other states respond in opposition, restoring the balance.

ethnocentrism   An inward-looking tendency or favorable disposition toward the people or nation with which one identifies, particularly when it is seen as superior to others.

E.U.   See **European Union**.

European Communities (EC)   Refers to European collaborative activity or international organization in several issue areas—the European Coal and Steel Community (ECSC), The European Economic Community (EEC), and the European Atomic Energy Community (EURATOM). See **European Union.**

European Union (EU)   Decision taken at Maastricht in 1991 to go beyond customs union and common market to achieve economic and monetary union and coordinated foreign policy goals resulted in adopting a new name—European Union—for the EC countries.

exogenous factor   See **system**.

expected utility, expected utility theory (model)   Rational-choice concept in which actors compare the relative attractiveness of options and choose the alternative that maximizes expected gains or minimizes expected losses. Concept used by Bruce Bueno de Mesquita and others concerning conflict situations that may lead to war. The expected utility model also addresses how policy positions emerge in the presence of competing interests, leading to predictions and strategic opportunities for altering them. See **rational choice theory**.

explanation   See **theory**.

explanans   See **deductive = nomological**.

explanandum   See **deductive-nomological**.

externality   When an international actor takes an action that has an intended or unintended impact (positive or negative) on another actor.

factor analysis   A quantitative technique by which the analyst tries to identify underlying and related elements or factors (usually as part of a causal explanation of some observed phenomenon or phenomena).

falsifiability   Associated with Karl Popper's thought, to be "scientific" propositions or hypotheses have to be stated in a form that, if they are false, they can be shown to be false through empirical test. When empirical tests fail to show a proposition or hypothesis is false, we gain greater confidence that it may be true.

federalism   See **world federalism**.

feedback   A concept in systems theory and communication theory (or cybernetics) by which responses to decisions or actions taken are returned by affected elements to the sender or taker of these decisions or actions, thus allowing for corrective actions.

feminism, feminist   An approach to theory that takes into account the constructive and collaborative potential of human beings, often rejecting such cold, abstract analysis as found in neorealist and other structural explanations; the focus is more on multilateral relations rather than unilateral or hegemonic dominance. In the policy realm, feminism also seeks the empowerment of women, putting women on an equal plain with men.

feudal, feudalism   A system of political, social, and economic organization that existed in Europe from approximately the ninth to approximately the fifteenth centuries. Reciprocal rights and duties were expected between the lord and his vassals—for example, protection of the vassal by the lord in return for the vassal's giving up a percentage of his crops. Feudalism is viewed in Marxist usage as a mode of production dominant in the Middle Ages and that preceded capitalism. See also **modes of production**.

First World   See **Third World**.

force   Usually refers to efforts undertaken by states in an attempt to compel others to take a certain course of action or to cease an action. The term usually means the use of armed or military force.

foreign policy   Refers to external affairs, particularly to decisions and actions taken by states in their dealings with other states or such "external" actors as international organizations, multinational corporations, and other transnational or non-state actors.

functionalism, functionalist   A focus on purposes or tasks, particularly those performed by organizations. Some theorists have explained the growth of organizations, particularly international organizations, as a response to an increase in the number of purposes or tasks demanding attention. *Neofunctionalism* as a theory of regional integration emphasizes the political calculation and payoff by or to elites who agree to collaborate in the performance of certain tasks. See also **integration, spillover**.

functionally diffuse   See **diffuse**.

fungibility   The condition that exists when one element or unit has no unique identity and can easily be exchanged or replaced by another of like nature. Money is said to be fungible (for example, funds in a national budget can easily be shifted from one account to another when cuts are made in one area of the budget to fund increases in another). Whether the power of states, like money, is fungible and can readily be transferred from one issue area to another is a point of some dispute among international relations theorists.

game theory   A decision-making approach based on the assumption of actor rationality in a situation of competition. Each actor tries to maximize gains or minimize losses often under conditions of uncertainty and incomplete information, which requires each actor to rank order preferences, estimate probabilities, and try to discern what the other actor is going to do. In a two-person *zero-sum* game, what one actor wins the other loses; if *A* wins 5, *B* loses 5, and the sum is zero. In a two-person, *non-zero-sum* or *variable sum* game, gains and losses are not necessarily equal; it is possible that both sides may gain. This is sometimes referred to as a *positive-sum* game. In some games, both parties can lose, and by different amounts or to a different degree. So-called *n-person* games include more than two actors or sides. Game theory has contributed to the development of models of deterrence and arms race spirals, but it is also the basis for work concerning the question of how collaboration among competitive states in an anarchic world can be achieved: The central problem is that the rational decision for an individual actor such as a state may be to "defect" and go it alone as opposed to taking a chance on collaboration with another state actor. Dealing with this problem is a central concern of much of the literature on international regimes, regional integration, and conflict resolution. See also **anarchy, rational, rational choice theory, theory.**

general theory   See **theory.**

global civil society   The network of relationships among people around the world that are not associated with the state *per se*; organizations that aggregate individual interests below the level of the state, but operate across the border of any single state. (Non-governmental organizations (NGOs) are an example.) Institutions and norms associated with the pluralist image of international relations.

globalism, globalist   As used in this volume, *globalism* refers to an image of politics different from *realism* and *pluralism* (or *liberalism*). Globalism focuses on the importance of economy, especially capitalist relations of dominance or exploitation, to understanding world politics. The globalist image is influenced by Marxist analyses of exploitative relations, although not all globalists are Marxists. Dependency theory, whether understood in Marxist or non-Marxist terms, is categorized here as part of the globalist image. Also included is the view that international relations are best understood if one sees them as occurring within a capitalist world-system. See also **image.**

government   The lawmaking, judicial, administrative, and enforcement apparatus of a state.

Grotian   Refers to the influence of Hugo Grotius, seventeenth-century Dutch scholar usually identified as the father of international law. The Grotian view is that international relations, although lacking central authority, can be subject to rules or norms, some of which have the binding character of law, that are expressly or tacitly agreed to by states.

groupthink   According to Irving Janis: a "mode of thinking that people engage in when they are deeply involved in a cohesive in-group, when the members' strivings for unanimity override their motivation to realistically appraise alternative courses of action." Indicators of groupthink include social pressure to enforce conformity, limiting discussion to a few alternatives, failing to reexamine initial decisions, and making little attempt to seek information from outside experts who may challenge a preferred policy.

hegemony, hegemon   Relations of dominance as when a major power exercises hegemony over countries within its sphere of influence. A state exercising hegemony is sometimes referred to as a *hegemon*. An alternative characterization reflecting preeminent position for a state, but not necessarily implying dominance, is to refer to it as a leader exercising leadership of other states within its sphere. The difference between hegemony and leadership is often a subtle distinction and perhaps more a matter of nuance or connotation intended by the user of the terms. See also **hegemonic stability.**

hegemonic stability   The view that stability in international relations stems from the presence of hegemony or dominance. The absence of hegemony or hegemons would imply a lack of order in the relations among states whether in commercial activities (trade, the exchange of money, and investment), social issues, or security concerns. See also **hegemony.**

hermeneutics   A field of study owing much to Ludwig Wittgenstein's work on how human beings interpret or draw meanings as is reflected in the language they construct and use.

heuristic   Refers to the illustrative value of some device or schematic presentation. Such a presentation is not intended as an actual or precise, empirically verified representation of relations among variables in a model, but it is useful for gaining a better understanding of some concept or set of concepts under investigation.

high politics   Refers to matters of security, particularly the strategic interests of states. Realists have tended traditionally to draw a distinction between such high political concerns and those dealing with socioeconomic or welfare issues of lesser interest to statesmen—the so-called *low politics*.

Hobbesian (or Hobbist)   Deriving from the influence of Thomas Hobbes, seventeenth-century English philosopher, who characterized anarchic politics—the absence of a sovereign or central authority—as producing grave threat to individual security. The absence of central authority in international relations in this Hobbesian view poses a security threat to all states to which they may respond internally by strengthening their power positions, or externally by forming alliances. International security in the Hobbesian view rests, therefore, more on power and the balance of power than on law and other rules or norms.

human rights   Regardless of culture, national, state, or other identity human beings possess certain rights by virtue of being human. Many of these rights have been codified in treaties and conventions. See **natural rights**.

hypothesis, hypotheses (plural)   A proposition usually relating two or more variables (such as "Arms races cause wars") but subject to empirical or factual test. In one view, hypotheses may be verified or confirmed to the extent that tests do not show the hypothesis to be false. Repeated tests, including *replication* of earlier work, increase confidence in the correctness of the original hypothesis, although it is always subject to being shown to be false in subsequent tests and thus can never be confirmed with 100 percent certainty. A *null* hypothesis, the starting point, is a proposition in which no relation between or among variables is specified (as in "There is no relation between arms races and the onset of war") in contrast to a *working* hypothesis in which such a relation is specified. If one's empirical tests show no relation, then the null hypothesis is retained and the working hypothesis is rejected.

idealist   One who sees such values or human preferences as justice or a desire for world peace as potentially decisive and capable of overcoming obstacles to their realization. Referred to by critics as utopian in that the idealist does not understand the political or other realities that constrain human choice. An idealist considers ideas as having important causal effects as opposed to others who see power or material factors as being the determinants of political outcomes.

ideal (pure) type   A concept developed by the German sociologist Max Weber to describe an extreme, or pure, case that is not found in this form anywhere but that serves as an analytical benchmark useful in comparing real-world cases. Strictly defined, ideal types for democracy or modern and traditional societies are constructed by theorists even though the actual cases they examine are, at best, only approximations of the conditions they specify.

ideology   A belief system or set of ideas or values usually held as a matter of conviction. Ideological views are usually not subjected to the same standards of empirical test as are theories and associated hypotheses. Marxism–Leninism as ideology offers not only explanation and prediction of world politics but also a means for interpreting social relations. Liberalism as ideology leads some to advocate free or open trade and commerce.

idiographic   A detailed study of a particular case or event. See also **nomothetic**.

IGO   An abbreviation used to designate international, governmental organizations in which membership is composed of states—for example, the United Nations and its affiliated agencies. See also **INGO, NGO**.

image   As used in this book, an image refers to a general perspective of international relations and world politics that consists of certain assumptions about actors and processes. See also **realism, pluralism, globalism**.

imperalism   In its classic meaning, a position or policy of preeminence or dominance with respect to foreign elements, as in the Roman, Ottoman, or British empires. Imperialism in earlier centuries involved the establishment of colonies, which led to so-called *colonialism*. Although most of these colonies have become formally independent states, the relations of economic, social, cultural, and even political dominance by the former colonial power remain—so-called *neocolonialism*. Some theorists also contend that contemporary imperialism involves economic and other forms of exploitation or dominance by multinational corporations in less developed countries. Marxist theories of imperialism tend to emphasize the economic dynamics of capitalism and associated class relations.

incrementalism   A step-by-step rather than a comprehensive, all-encompassing, sweeping approach. In an incremental decision-making process, decisions are often deferred until information on which to base a choice has been maximized (or until not making a decision would foreclose certain options and thus, in effect, be a decision in itself).

independent variable   A factor used to explain some outcome. See also **variable, dependent variable**.

indeterminacy   The degree to which an outcome cannot be predicted with a reasonable degree of confidence or is subject to seemingly random influences. There may be a great deal of indeterminacy in voluntarist theories that maximize the effect of human choice or volition. See also **determinism, voluntarism**.

indeterminate solution   Refers to problems in which the outcome cannot be predicted with much, if any, confidence, as when the influence of variables appears to have random effect. See also **indeterminacy**.

individualism   Associated with *liberalism*, individuals have particular value in themselves and for what they can do—that people as individuals have more importance than the groups, tribes, communities, or societies to which they may belong. See **liberalism**.

induction   Logical and inferential process by which we posit general statements based on observation of only a part or sample of a class of facts; the general statement is an answer to the question posed in this text by James Rosenau: "Of what is this an instance?" Induction lacks the logical certainty of deduction. See **deduction**.

INGO   An abbreviation used to designate international, nongovernmental organizations, those in which membership is composed of private individuals and groups, but usually *not* states or their governments. Examples are the International Red Cross and the World Council of Churches. See also **IGO, NGO**.

institution, institutionalism   See **neoliberal institutionalism**.

integration   The coming together of separate states or other political units under a common authority. Integration may occur as an international or regional phenomenon with varying degrees of authority given to institutions established to deal with common issues or problems facing member states. Integration can be viewed either as *process* or as *outcome* that reflects and encourages cooperation among states operating under conditions of international anarchy (i.e., lack of common government). Research on integration has tended to focus on the assignment of economic and social tasks to regional or international authorities. Earlier theories of regional integration saw political union as a possible outcome of collaboration in economic or social issues. See also **functionalism, ramification, spillover.**

interaction   An exchange between two, or among more than two, units as in the *interactions* of states, groups, classes, or individuals. By contrast, *actions* do not refer to the back-and-forth of an exchange but to steps or measures taken by a state, group, class, individual, or other unit. See also **action.**

interdependence, interdependent   A relation or relations between two (a *dyadic* relation) or among more than two units in which one is *sensitive* or *vulnerable* to the decisions or actions of the other or others. The flow of capital or money to or from one country may respond to (or be *sensitive* to) changes in the interest rates in other countries—so-called *sensitivity interdependence*. To the extent that one unit may be adversely affected by decisions or actions of another, it is said to be *vulnerable* to the other unit or units, as when State *A* depends on State *B* as the principal source of its oil supply and thus is vulnerable or would be adversely affected by its cutoff. To many theorists, such *vulnerability interdependence* is to be minimized or avoided altogether. Interdependence may be *symmetric* (affecting both or all sides equally), but it is more likely to be *asymmetric* (with effects varying from actor to actor). State *A* may be more dependent on a supply of oil from State *B* than State *B* is on the security of its investments in State *A*. See also **complex interdependence, balance of power.**

interest   That which is of importance to a unit (state, class, group, or individual), usually including, as a minimum, its survival. *National* interest refers to matters of importance to a state. Some theorists have found the concept of national interest to be too vague; they prefer to substitute the notion that states do formulate certain objectives that can be identified more easily. Others view the national interest as little more than what leaders say it is.

interest group liberalism   An approach to politics that emphasizes competing groups or institutions. Not only is interest group liberalism thought to be an accurate description of democratic politics, particularly in the United States, but it is also thought by many to be the way politics *should* be conducted. See also **liberalism.**

international   Specifically, relations between or among states. More loosely, it is a reference to matters outside a state, which has led to the synonymous usage by many persons of the terms *international politics* and *world politics*.

International Court of Justice   Located in the Hague; a principal organ of the United Nations. See **international law.**

international governmental or inter-governmental organizations (IGOs)   See **international organizations.**

international law   A body of rules considered to be binding on states and other actors even though there is no central enforcement authority to assure compliance. Sources of international law include treaties or covenants made by states, customary practice, generally accepted principles, and the writings of jurists. International courts such as the International Court of Justice interpret international law and apply it to individual cases brought by states. National courts and enforcement systems (those of individual states) are the primary mechanisms for dealing with international law. International law (particularly that based on treaty commitments) may have precedence over domestic laws that conflict with such international obligations.

international law of war, international law of armed conflicts   International law governing warfare and the use of force in international relations requires legitimate reasons for using force and places specific limitations on the actual use of force. See **just war**.

international organization   An institution composed of states as members (for example, the United Nations [UN], European Union [EU], and the North Atlantic Treaty Organization [NATO]). More broadly, the term refers to patterns of behavior or structures and actors that cross or go beyond national frontiers.

international politics   The *political* focus is on choices made by actors with authority to do so on issues external to states or that cross the frontiers or boundaries of state jurisdiction. *International politics* is often used synonymously with *world politics* or *international relations*, although these terms do have separate, more precise meanings. See also **international relations**.

international regimes   See **regime**.

international relations   The total of political, social, economic, cultural, and other interactions among states (and even nonstate) actors. *International politics* can be understood to be a part (or subset) of international relations, although the terms *international relations, world politics*, and *international politics* are often used synonymously. See also **international politics**.

international security   In its narrowest construction, the term refers to defense matters among states and their respective societies. In a broadest sense, it encompasses a very wide range of issues that affect the welfare of human beings—not just defense, but also economics, health, environment, human rights, and other social questions that cross national boundaries. Critics of broad definitions argue that if *security* as a concept can be construed to mean so many things, then as a practical matter does it really mean anything? Their preference is to retain the more traditional distinction that sees *security* and related defense issues as separate from *welfare* issues.

international system   An aggregation of similar or diverse entities united by regular interaction that sets them apart from other systems; e.g., the *interstate* or *international* system of states or *world politics* understood as a system composed of both state and non-state actors. See **system**.

interpretive understanding   That concepts are constructs defined by the meanings we give them, a view that owes much to the thinking of Max Weber that gave *Verstehen* or understanding a deeper meaning.

intervention   Interference in the domestic affairs of another state by diplomatic, economic, military, or other means.

intuition, intuitive   That which is held, assumed, or seems to be true *a priori* (beforehand). The term refers to a view that usually has not been subject to formal or empirical test but merely seems to make sense. See also **counterintuitive**.

jus ad bellum   See **just war**.

jus in bello   See **just war**.

justice   In common usage, that which is right, fair, or equitable for (or pertaining to relations among) individuals, groups, classes, states, or other units. See also **distributive justice, just war.**

just war   Normative theory referring to conditions under which (1) states rightfully go to war (*jus ad bellum*) with just cause, as in self-defense in response to aggression, when the decision to go to war is made by legitimate authority in the state, as a last resort after exhausting peaceful remedies, *and* with some reasonable hope of achieving legitimate objectives; (2) states exercise right conduct in war (*jus in bello*) when the means employed are proportional to the ends sought, when noncombatants are spared, when weapons or other means that are immoral in themselves are not used (typically those that are indiscriminate or cause needless suffering), *and* when actions are taken with a *right intention* to accomplish legitimate military objectives and to minimize collateral death and destruction. Many of these principles of just war are part of the body of international law and thus are legally binding on states and their agents.

Kantian   Deriving from the influence of Immanuel Kant, eighteenth-century East Prussian philosopher whose ethical writings emphasized certain *categorical imperatives* as being universal, morally binding norms such as the obligation to treat other human beings as ends important in themselves and not merely as means. In normative international relations theory, the Kantian preference was for a cosmopolitan world society, perhaps a world federation based on universal values in which perpetual peace would be maintained.

laissez faire   The classical liberal idea that governments ought not intervene in markets—that they should be left alone because competitive markets are understood to be self-regulating.

law   In domestic and international politics, the term refers to authoritative rules that are binding on those subordinate to them. In the natural sciences, the term refers to a general statement that specifies some regularity, as in Newton's second law of motion that force is equal to the time derivative of momentum: $F = d(mv)/dt = m(dv/dt) = ma$. Such specificity of relations among variables and constants has been elusive in the social sciences, and theorists have had to be content with identifying tendencies and generating what are at best "lawlike" statements.

LDC   Abbreviation for *less*-developed country. In some usages, LDC refers to *lesser*-developed country. See also **Third World, South.**

learning   Inferences or lessons drawn from the experiences of states (and statesmen) that guide future policy choices. For example, correctly or incorrectly (the inference is disputed by some), statesmen "learned" that appeasement of aggressors does not make such states less aggressive but may actually whet their appetites for more aggressive behavior (the case usually cited is appeasement of Hitler's Germany in 1938 when diplomats, meeting in Munich and wishing to avoid war, allowed the Germans to annex that portion of western Czechoslovakia inhabited primarily by Germanic peoples). Statesmen may "learn" the benefits of international collaboration as opposed to going it alone, an inference that might lead them to create new and expand existing international organizations.

legitimacy   The implication of the existence of *right*, as when a government is said to have, or to have been granted, a right to govern based on such criteria as its popular acceptance, the legal or constitutional processes that brought it to, or maintains it in, a position of authority, traditional grounds as in the divine right of kings, or the charismatic quality of its leadership that commands a following and thus contributes to its popular acceptance. See also **authority.**

less-developed country, lesser-developed country (LDC)   A country in Latin America, Africa, Asia, or the Pacific that is in the early stages of industrialization or that has not yet industrialized to the extent that Japan and most of the countries in Europe and North America have. See also **North–South**.

levels of analysis   Individuals, groups, state and society, or international system as separate points of focus. Such levels help scholars to be systematic in their approach to understanding international relations. In explaining a phenomenon such as war, for example, the theorist may identify possible causes as being some characteristic or characteristics of the international system; states and their societies, groups or individuals. In accounting for or explaining such a phenomenon, one may look both within a unit such as a state, as well as how the unit relates to its external environment, which are different levels of analysis. In current usage, "unit level" factors such as state, society, interest groups, bureaucracies, and individuals are contrasted to structural factors operating at the system level. See **structure, system**.

Leviathan   The biblical beast of gargantuan proportions used as a metaphor by Thomas Hobbes to refer to the state—the supreme authority that provides order and security to individuals living under its sway; also the title of Hobbes's classic work. See also **Hobbesian**.

liberal institutionalism   See **neoliberal institutionalism**.

liberalism   Political philosophy (sometimes referred to as an ideology) with origins in the seventeenth and eighteenth centuries that emphasizes individual liberty to be achieved through a minimal state. A *laissez-faire* government, one that provides for law and order (sometimes referred to as a "night watchman" state) but otherwise constrained or not granted authority to infringe on the rights of individuals, is said to be a liberal government. In both domestic and international economy, this classic liberalism implies commitment to free market principles without government intervention, including free trade policies and unconstrained commercial activities both at home and abroad. In contemporary American political usage, influenced by President Franklin Roosevelt and those who have followed him, *liberalism* usually means enhancing individual rights and well-being through government action or government programs—a substantial departure from the *laissez-faire* of classic liberalism. See also **interest group liberalism, ideology**.

linkage   Coupling among units or issues as in ties that cross state boundaries and thus link internationally or transnationally the domestic elements (corporations, groups, individuals, etc.) of various states. In another sense, various policies may be tied to one another in such a way that international trade policy is affected by changes in international monetary policy (linkages sometimes referred to as "policy interdependence"). The term *linkage* has also been used to describe foreign policy connections, as when a government ties negotiations with another government in one field (such as progress in arms control) to behavior by that government in another field (such as demonstration that it will not intervene in the affairs of some third state).

logical positivism   Pursuit of a pure science that would separate fact from value and achieve the precision of mathematics, a perspective identified with scholars in the "Vienna circle" of the 1930s.

longitudinal   See **diachronic**.

low politics   See **high politics**.

Machiavellian, Machiavellianism, Machiavellism   Deriving from the influence of Niccolò Machiavelli, the sixteenth-century Florentine political philosopher. In its pejorative meaning, the term refers to unprincipled behavior by statesmen or other state agents who aim to achieve certain objectives deemed to be in the state's interest. In this view, the ends of the state (its survival and its continuing security) may justify means or actions taken for these purposes, even though the same means might otherwise be considered immoral or illegal.

macrotheory   See **theory**.

Madisonian   Deriving from the influence of James Madison, often referred to as the "father of the U.S. Constitution." Madison's ideas (along with those of such other Federalists as Alexander Hamilton and John Jay) on the separation of powers among various branches of government and the division of powers between central and state governments were central to framing the U.S. Constitution.

Marxism   A body of thought inspired by the German Karl Marx. It emphasizes the *dialectical* unfolding of historical states. It stresses the importance of economic and material forces and *class analysis*. It predicts that contradictions inherent in each historical epoch eventually lead to the rise of a new dominant class. The era of capitalism, according to Marx, is dominated by the *bourgeoisie* and will give way to a *proletarian*, or working class, revolution and an era of *socialism* in which the workers own the *means of production* and move toward a classless, *communist* society in which the state, historically a tool of the dominant class, will wither away. A number of contemporary theorists have drawn on Marxian insights and categories of analysis—an influence most evident in work on *dependency* and the *capitalist world-system*. See also **dialectic, means of production, proletarian revolution, class, capitalist world-system, bourgeoisie, socialism**.

means of production   A concept particularly associated with Marxist analyses that refers to factors essential to the production of goods—combinations of land, labor, and capital. Classes are defined in Marxian terms as relations to the means of production: The feudal aristocracy owned land, the bourgeoisie owns capital (including factories and machines), and the proletariat is defined by its labor. See also **class, modes of production**.

mercantilism, mercantile   A theory in early capitalism that saw the wealth of a nation as a function of the amount of gold and other treasure that could be accumulated. Accordingly, running trade surpluses (exports more than imports), while finding new gold in mines or accepting it in payment for goods or services sold became national economic policy. In his *Wealth of Nations* (1776) Adam Smith challenged this view, arguing that the true wealth of a nation was to be found in its productive capacity, not its treasure. Present-day *neomercantilist* policies pursued by some states try to maximize trade surplus, accumulating large monetary-reserve balances.

methodology   The approach one takes to an academic study; modes of research and analysis, as in the use of historical case and comparative case studies, or the use of statistics as in formal hypothesis testing or causal modeling of variables. See also **causal modeling**.

microtheory   See **theory**.

minimum winning coalition   The smallest number of actors needed to agree to a policy or course of action in order to put it into effect. See also **game theory**.

MNC   See **multinational corporation**.

modernism, modernist   See **post-modernism**.

modernization   See **development**.

modes of production   The organization of the economy for the production of goods, as in such historical epochs identified by Marx as slavery, feudalism, and capitalism. According to Marx, as technology has advanced, the mode of production has also changed—feudalism being a more productive mode than slavery and capitalism being more productive than feudalism.

monopoly   Occurs when a firm has solitary or complete control of a market. Marx noted an increasing concentration of capital or a tendency toward monopoly in advanced capitalism.

moral   Principles of right and wrong in one's behavior.

multinational corporation (MNC)   A firm usually with headquarters in one country but with production facilities in more than one country. Because they operate across national borders, MNCs are among those units referred to as transnational actors. See also **transnational**.

multipolar, multipolarity   A distribution of power in the international system with more than two centers or "poles," such as a world in which there are five principal or major powers.

nation   A group of people with a common identity. A nation coterminous with state boundaries is referred to as a *nation-state*, although in common language the terms *nation, state*, and *nation-state* are often used synonymously. It is possible for there to be a nation without a single state—for example, a *nonstate nation* such as the Palestinian and Kurdish peoples in the Middle East. Some states such as India contain more than one nation and are sometimes referred to as multinational states.

nation-state   See **nation**.

national interest   See **interest**.

national security   Issues dealing with the survival, welfare, and protection of a state.

national self-determination   The view that a people with a common identity have the right to be independent from outside control, as in establishing a state for such a national group. National self-determination has been an important rallying cry for Third World countries that have demanded an end to colonial rule.

nationalism   Promoting national identity usually to the exclusion of other, competing identities and legitimizing actions of a state taken for national purposes. Nations without states often solidify movements to establish a nation-state around nationalist themes.

NATO   The North Atlantic Treaty Organization; a mutual defense organization founded in 1949 by the United States, Canada, and Western European countries. There are currently nineteen members.

natural law, universal law   A philosophical view dating back at least to the time of the ancient Greeks that posits there are laws inherent in nature that transcend any laws made by mere mortals. All leaders and all forms of government, it is argued, are bound by these laws, and they should not be violated. Some scholars have dealt with natural law as a means to develop a body of international law to govern the relations among states.

natural rights   Reference is to a theory that finds human rights in nature which can be discovered through reason. Social-contract theorists such as Locke and Rousseau saw rights in this naturalist understanding; however, utilitarians such as Bentham and Mill argued that human rights rested on other grounds also discoverable through reason—the greatest good or happiness for the greatest number. See **human rights, utilitarian**.

neocolonialism   See **imperialism**.

neofunctionalism   See **functionalism, spillover**.

neoliberal institutionalism   Like realism, neoliberal institutionalism as advanced by Robert Keohane and others is utilitarian and rational in orientation—states are treated as rational egoists and interstate cooperation occurs when states have significant interests in common. The goal is to discover how, and under what conditions, institutions matter. As such, neoliberal institutionalism addresses both security and nonsecurity or welfare issues. In this regard, institutions provide information, reduce transaction costs, make commitments more credible, establish focal points for coordination, and aid in the operation of reciprocity and multilateralism among states. The term *institution* may also refer not just to organizations, but also to such accepted patterns of recurrent or institutionalized relations as *multilateralism*—a meaning advanced by John Ruggie and others.

neoliberalism, neoliberal   Critical of pluralist (or "liberal") theories that discount the relative importance of states, the neoliberal position is that states also matter alongside a wide array of non-state actors. See **neoliberal institutionalism**.

neorealism   A label applied to **structural realists** or those realists who are interested in explaining state behavior under conditions of anarchy and who emphasize the importance of the structure of the international system and how this influences and constrains state behavior. The term may also have negative connotations in the eyes of some critics who claim that the neorealists have neglected the importance of values and norms as stressed by earlier realists such as Hans Morgenthau and E. H. Carr. Neorealists deny the validity of such charges, and some even reject the neorealist label. See also **structure, structural determinist, structural realist**.

neutrality, neutral   States that announce they do not take sides in an international dispute or war nor join an alliance. Some like Switzerland claim *permanent* neutrality. Others choose to be neutral, perhaps more accurately, *nonaligned* as a tactical choice that serves its interest at a particular time.

newly industrializing country (NIC)   Countries such as Taiwan, Singapore, South Korea, or Malaysia whose rapid economic growth over the past 30 years made the label *Third World* inappropriate. All such countries exhibited strong *market* orientations, developed industrially, and heavily emphasized *exports*.

NIC   Newly industrializing country.

nomology   Study relating to discoverable scientific laws that contribute to human understanding. See also **deductive-nomological**.

nomothetic   Related to finding general or universal laws as in the study of numerous, different cases over time. See also **idiographic**.

nongovernmental organization (NGO)   Transnational organizations have a standing independent of governments, often with diversified members that work to fulfill specific political, social, or economic objectives that may benefit or have some positive or negative impact on a wide-range of persons. Examples include human rights organizations; multinational corporations and banks; labor unions; privately owned telecommunications, newspaper, and other print media firms; churches and other religious organizations; etc. See also **international organization**.

nonstate actors   International actors other than governments, such as international organizations, multinational corporations, international banks, terrorist groups, and the Red Cross. Pluralists with a transnationalist perspective on international relations emphasize the importance of such nonstate actors. See also **transnational**.

non-zero-sum   See **game theory**.

normative, norm   A principle of right action; a standard to guide behavior, as in norms or obligations governing the conduct of war, transit on the high seas, diplomacy, trade and commerce. Normative judgments are often equated to value judgments and the idea of what *ought* to be; some norms may have the binding character of international law.

normative theory   Value-oriented or philosophical theory that focuses on what ought to be. As such it is usually differentiated from *empirical* theories that try to explain the way things are or predict what they will be.

North   See **North–South**.

North–South   Terms meant to distinguish between the advanced industrialized states of the northern hemisphere and the poorer states of the southern hemisphere. The South is also referred to as the Third World. Some authors include the former Soviet Union and Eastern Europe as part of the North, but most others restrict the definitions to Western Europe, Japan, and North America. Debate and discussion revolve around the question of how the North–South economic gap can be bridged and what, if any, obligation the North has toward the South.

n-person game   See **game theory**.

oligopoly   An economic market in which a few firms control the production (or distribution) of certain goods or services. Marx and Lenin argued that capitalism tended to move toward greater concentration of capital, resulting in oligopolies or monopolies. See **monopoly**.

ontology   Philosophical term referring to the study of existence or being or, in Kant's terms, "the more general properties of things." Thus, dialectical materialism as universal law or set of laws with historical implications for humanity is an example of a materialist ontology central to Marxist thought.

operationalize, operationalization   See **variable**.

operational code   The world view or belief system of foreign policy elites. The pathbreaking work was by Nathan Leites on the Bolsheviks and was later developed by Alexander George and others.

optimal   In the context of decision making, the best possible outcome.

organizational process   A model developed by Graham Allison to distinguish *bureaucratic politics* from organizational process—the institutional perspectives, routines, standard procedures, and processes of particular bureaucracies.

pacta sunt servanda   Latin for "treaties are binding"; the idea that treaties or formal covenants are legally binding even in the absence of a central authority to enforce adherence to them.

paradigm   A pattern, model, or perspective that helps one organize and guide research. A paradigm may include key assumptions about the world and the best way to go about understanding it. The concept was central in Thomas Kuhn's influential *The Structure of Scientific*

Revolutions (1962) and has since been applied to the social sciences. According to Kuhn, a scientific era is characterized by a dominant paradigm that represents "normal science"; the majority of scholars work within this paradigm, often accepting the assumptions of the paradigm in an unquestioning manner. These assumptions have an impact on how research is conducted and the resultant scholarly work.

parsimonious theory   A theory that contains only a few elements yet can explain or predict a wide variety of phenomena. See also **theory, hypothesis**.

partial theory   See **theory**.

peace   A wide variety of definitions exist, including the absence of war; a situation of security, order, or stability; harmonious relations among states. For some theorists, it means worldwide collaboration to solve common global problems.

perception, perceptual   Awareness of the world through the medium of the senses. In international relations, the literature on deterrence and crisis situations, for example, often deals with the importance of perception and misperception.

periphery   The less-developed countries or areas of Asia, Latin America, and Africa. In the dependency literature, the periphery is dominated by the *center*, which consists of the economically and politically dominant countries of the world (usually viewed as those in North America, Europe, and Japan). The literature on the capitalist world-system has applied the concept of periphery back to the origins of capitalism in Europe. The periphery plays a subordinate but important role in a worldwide capitalist division of labor by providing raw materials and cheap labor. As capitalism expanded, countries that at one time were part of the center slipped into peripheral or semiperipheral status. See also **semiperiphery, core**, and **center**.

permissive cause   See **causality**.

phenomenology   A philosophical term with various complex meanings, one of which is the classification and description of phenomena, including identification of the formal structures of phenomena as part of an attempt to establish their scientific foundations. Following Edmund Husserl and others, the focus is on carefully describing the phenomena we experience—an interpretive approach to human understanding and the categories of understanding we construct.

phenomenon, phenomena (plural)   An observed or observable occurrence.

pluralism, pluralist   As used in this book, pluralism refers to an image of international relations that assumes that nonstate actors are important entities in international relations. The state is not necessarily a rational and unitary actor but is composed of a multitude of competing bureaucracies, individuals, and groups. The agenda of world politics is extensive and goes well beyond security concerns. Much of the work on decision making and transnationalism falls within the pluralist image as the result of a focus on a multiplicity of factors and actors. The term **liberalism** is often used to refer to this pluralist image. See also **image**.

policy   A decision or a course of action chosen from alternatives.

politburo   The supreme policy and decision-making body of the former Soviet Union and other Marxist-Leninist states; an organ of the Communist Party.

political culture   Those norms, values, and orientations of a society's culture that are politically relevant; e.g., many societies have a tradition of deferring to political authorities in the making of domestic and foreign policies. Other, more participant political cultures reflect a public interest in political matters and attempt to influence political decisions.

political economy   There are at least two major ways in which this term is used in international relations research: (1) the view that politics and economies are inextricably linked, leading one to study the interrelations of political and economic variables, and (2) the use of economic models of rationality to explain political actions. For example, some theorists use economic models of rationality in order to determine under what conditions international collaboration can be achieved among states.

politics, political   Numerous definitions have been offered including the processes that determine who gets what, when, and how (Harold Lasswell), the authoritative allocation of values (David Easton), or simply authoritative choice.

polity   In common usage, a political system such as the American polity or the Canadian polity. In the original Aristotelian usage, the term referred to an ideal form of government.

positive-sum game   See **game theory**.

positivist   The view that laws stem only from the actions of those having the political authority to make them rather than being the derivation of divine or natural law. In science, the view that knowledge comes from empirical testing of propositions or hypotheses against evidence or facts.

post-modernism, post-modernist   A rejection of scientific or "modernist" epistemology, post-modernism *deconstructs* or takes apart the meanings embedded in what we say and write, looking for underlying meanings or *subtexts*; in the extreme, some post-modernists adopt a purely relativist position—that no knowledge or truth is possible apart from the motivations and purposes people put into their construction. See also **critical theory, hermeneutics**.

power   Capabilities, or the relative capabilities, of actors such as states. The ability to control or influence outcomes or the actions of others. Central to realist works on international relations. For more detailed discussion, see the text.

prediction   See **theory**.

proletarian   See **proletarian revolution, proletariat**.

proletarian revolution   A Marxist concept referring to the rising up of the working class, or proletariat, and the overthrow of the capitalist system dominated by the bourgeoisie who own capital—the factories, industries, and banks. The revolution is, theoretically, the result of contradictions internal to the nature of capitalism.

proletariat   A Marxist concept referring to a particular class or stratum of people, in this case the working class. The proletariat is usually viewed as being in opposition to the bourgeois class, which owns the means of production. See also **Marxism, means of production**.

prophecy   See **self-fulfilling prophecy**.

psychohistory   The study of historically significant individuals through the analysis of what is known about their personality and psychological development.

psychology   The study of the mind and its impact on individual behavior. See also **social psychology**.

public choice theory   The use of economic methods to analyze what are essentially political problems (issues involving choices or decisions by political authorities). See also **collective goods theory, rational choice theory**.

pure type   See **ideal type**.

ramification   A concept developed by David Mitrany in his work on functionalist integration: Successful collaboration by states in one particular technical area would encourage the expansion of collaboration into other areas. Mitrany hypothesized that if states became increasingly integrated in a number of technical or functional areas, the cost of breaking these ties (such as by going to war) would be high enough to prevent such actions from occurring in the first place. See also **functionalism, spillover**.

rational   To act rationally requires a rank ordering of preferred goals, consideration of all feasible alternatives to attain those goals in the light of existing capabilities, and consideration of the costs and benefits associated with using particular methods to attain particular goals. The assumption is often made in international relations research that actors do indeed act rationally. The assumption is made in order to develop hypotheses and to produce insights on world politics. See **decision, action, policy, rational choice theory**.

rational choice theory   Theory that assumes actor rationality in economics and politics, focusing on that rational dimension—maximizing interest or utility—in the development of explanatory and predictive theories. See also **collective goods theory, decision, expected utility, game theory, rational**.

rationality   See **rational**.

realism, realist   A perspective on international relations that focuses on the state as unitary and rational actor and on the actions and interactions of states. Realists attempt to understand patterns of conflict and collaboration under conditions of anarchy or lack of common government. Security issues are usually the most important for realists. *National interest* or objectives, *power*, and *balance of power* are key concepts for most realists. See also **image**.

Realpolitik   A German term referring to power politics. It emphasizes policies based more on practical power considerations and less on moral or ethical considerations. The attainment and maintenance of state security in a hostile world through power or balance-of-power politics is viewed as the primary goal of leaders.

reductionism   An analytic approach leading to oversimplification and incompleteness of explanation. In some usages, the term refers to explanations that look only within a unit, such as state or individual, ignoring the environment within which the unit is immersed and the interaction of that unit with elements in its environment. Reducing the explanation of some phenomenon such as war among states to something deep within the human psyche (as being, for example, at the level of synapses between nerve endings) is an extreme example of *reductio ad absurdum*—explanation reduced to an absurd degree of oversimplification and incompleteness—as if one could explain the recurrence of war among states purely in neurological terms. Similarly, theorists who have tried to explain revolution solely in social or social-psychological terms, ignoring economic, political, and other factors, have been criticized for reductionism.

reflectivism, reflectivist   As opposed to a purely rationalist view as in abstract cost-benefit calculations, reflectivists take into account the ideas and understandings in relation to interests that influence the decisions we make and the actions we take. See **cognition**.

reformism   The idea that revolution or the violent overthrow of an existing capitalist political-economic order is not necessary, but that change can occur incrementally and nonviolently. The possibility of evolving toward socialism by peaceful means such as parliamentary methods or the creation of trade unions is a tenet of reformism. The issue of reformism is one reason the socialist movement split in the late nineteenth and early twentieth centuries. V. I. Lenin and Rosa Luxemburg argued that the reformist policies of Karl Kautsky, Eduard Bernstein, and others were wrong. Lenin believed that capitalism could not be reformed to benefit the working class, that a revolution was required. See **proletarian revolution.**

regime, international regime   In its domestic context, an existing governmental or constitutional order defined in terms of sets of rules and institutions established to govern relations among individuals, groups, or classes within a state. In its international context, the term is defined as voluntarily agreed-upon sets of principles, norms, rules, and procedures around which actor expectations converge in a given area of international relations. The literature on international regimes blossomed in the 1970s. Scholars argued that international collaboration was obviously not restricted to formal international organizations such as the United Nations—cooperation was necessary in monetary and trade areas, telecommunications, air traffic control, and a whole host of areas of greater and lesser importance.

reified, reification   Giving a concrete reality to what is in fact an abstract concept of analysis. For example, some critics claim that realists have reified the state, attributing to it human characteristics such as rationality, or treating the state as if it operated in the international arena like an actual human being. The concept of system, used by some realist, pluralist, and globalist theorists, has also been criticized on similar grounds.

relativist, relativism   A view that what is true varies from individual to individual, group to group, and context to context. See **natural law.**

satisficing   A less-than-optimal choice that does not completely maximize the values or goals one is pursuing but is good enough; work on decision making shows that people often choose the first viable option that is minimally acceptable.

scientific proposition   See **falsifiability.**

Second World   See **Third World.**

security   For realists, the basic survival and protection of the state. Pluralists have a more expansive definition, also applying the concept to individuals and groups of people. In fact, from this perspective the state may not even be a provider of security, but rather a threat to the security of many people.

security dilemma   A term coined by John Herz: In an anarchic international system, State *A* may sincerely increase its level of defense spending only for defensive purposes and self-preservation, but it is rational for other states to assume the worst and impute aggressive intentions to State *A*. They therefore also increase their level of arms, leading State *A* to feel insecure and contemplate a further increase in military spending. Hence, by initially trying to enhance its own security, State *A* sets in motion a process that results ironically in its feeling less secure. In another usage, the term merely refers to the security problem faced by all states in a world without central authority or lack of common government among states. See also **anarchy, self-help.**

self-fulfilling prophecy   To predict a particular outcome and then choose policies or actions that help to bring about the predicted outcome even though this is not the intended effect. For example, predicting that State *B* will increase support for a war of national liberation against an ally of State *A*, State *A* provides its ally with more military assistance to combat rebels, resulting in State *B*'s feeling it is necessary to increase its support for the guerrillas. State *A*'s prophecy that State *B* will increase support for the guerrillas hence becomes self-fulfilling.

self-help   In the international arena, there is no superordinate authority, world government, or "Leviathan" to ensure order or to see that all parties to an agreement keep their end of a bargain. Each state must look after its own security and not assume the help of other states. See also **anarchy**.

semi-periphery   As used by capitalist world-system theorists (see Chapter 4), term refers to those countries or regions that occupy an intermediate position between core and peripheral areas. The semi-pheriphery is engaged in a mix of activities, some associated with the core and some with the periphery. It serves as an outlet for investment when wages, and thus the cost of production, in core areas become too high. The semiperiphery may at one time have been a core or peripheral area, or it may be moving into either status. See also **bourgeoisie, class conflict**.

sensitivity interdependence   See **interdependence**.

social constructivism   Social theories that attempt to explain the formation and transformation of identities and interests, in particular those of states. The fundamental structures of international politics are social rather than strictly material or capabilities as neorealists would have it. These social structures shape actors' identities and interests, not just their behavior. According to Alexander Wendt, social structures are made up of shared knowledge and material resources and practices. What makes ideas (and thus structure) "social" is their intersubjective quality. Material resources only acquire meaning for human action through the structure of shared knowledge. Social structures are to be found in practices or process. Wendt argues that collective meanings constitute the structures that organize our actions.

social contract   A philosophical idea used by theorists such as Thomas Hobbes, John Locke, and Jean-Jacques Rousseau to justify their preference for a particular type of political order. Living in an imaginary "state of nature"—a condition without any social or political structure—individuals contract with one another to create a political community or society governed by certain rules. For Hobbes, the social contract resulted in the establishment of a sovereign or central authority who is given the task of maintaining order. In international relations, however, no such sovereign exists. See also **self-help, security dilemma**.

socialism   Ownership of the means of production and distribution of goods by the society or the people as a whole (the public) rather than by private individuals. In a more limited form of socialism, only major industries and utilities are publicly owned. In some usages, socialism refers not only to public ownership of the means of production; it also includes public welfare programs and government acts in the name of the people in carrying out these programs. In Marxist thought, socialism is a stage or mode of production between capitalism and communism.

social psychology   The study of the mental processes of individuals and how they relate to their environment, especially to other individuals and groups. Behavior is explained by the interaction of individual and environment, not solely by elements within an individual's psyche.

society of states   The view that at certain times in history states have agreed upon basic rules, norms, and international laws to govern their relations. The 19th-century Concert of Europe is one example. See also **English school**.

sociology The study of society, particularly social groups and classes and relations among them.

South See **North–South**.

sovereign, sovereignty The supreme, independent, and final authority. The attribute of a state that refers to its right to exercise complete jurisdiction over its own territory. In international relations, states as sovereign units have a right to be independent or autonomous with respect to other states. States may differ in their power, but as sovereign entities all are legal equals.

spillover In the regional integration literature, a concept referring to a process whereby successful collaboration by states in one technical area leads to the realization by state authorities that it is in their rational self-interest to expand collaboration into related fields. Thus, progress in reducing barriers to trade may depend on, and lead to, further progress in rules facilitating the exchange of money among states. As used by Ernst Haas, the term refers to a process whereby states upgrade or collaborate in issue areas of common interest, similar to the concept of ramifications. See also **ramification**.

stability, destabilizing An attribute of a system. Some theorists compare unipolar, bipolar, and multipolar international systems in terms of which is more or less stable. Stable deterrence relations are said to depend on maintaining second-strike capabilities that would allow either party to absorb a first strike prior to choosing whether and how to retaliate. By contrast, when one party fears it has lost (or will lose) its second-strike capability, this may be *destabilizing* because it may be prone in a crisis to launch first or to launch on warning of an attack even before it has confirmed that an attack has actually taken place. See also **system, equilibrium, deterrence**.

state A legal entity composed of territory, a population, and an administration or government. It possesses sovereignty and recognition by other states. See also **government, sovereignty**.

state of nature A philosophical construct referring to a time prior to the creation of civil society—a world without governmental authority. An analogy to the *anarchic* structure of the international system. An important concept, particularly for realists who follow the thinking of Hobbes, as it raises the issue of how order and stability can be achieved in an international system of states competing for power and prestige.

structural See **structure**.

structural determinist One who believes that the structure of the international system largely determines the behavior of individual states and that there is very little effective choice for leaders of states. The term is usually used in a negative or critical sense against realists, neorealists, and some Marxists. Few, if any, theorists would admit to complete structural determinism in their theories, but some do assign greater weight to structure as a determinant of the behavior of states and other actors. See also **system, structure, neorealism, realism, Marxism, structural realism**.

structural realism, structural realist A term preferred by Kenneth Waltz and other neorealists because in their view it more accurately describes neorealism's focus on structure as a principal determinant of the behavior of states, the principal units in the international system. See **neorealism**.

structure The arrangement of parts of a whole, as in the structure of the international system being defined in terms of the distribution of capabilities or power among states. The international system structure, following this usage, may be bipolar, multipolar, or unipolar. Some theorists look for underlying structure associated with the anarchy of the system—the lack of central authority. For others, structure refers to observed patterns of behavior as among states, although still others contend that such a definition confuses underlying *structure* with *behavior*, or the interactions of states—concepts that are, and should be, kept analytically separate. Some theorists of dependency and the capitalist world-system use the term *structure* to describe relations or mechanisms of dominance, dependence, and exploitation. *Note:* One can also apply the term "structure" to the state–society level of analysis—such as the Federalist structure of the United States—and deduce expected behavior on the part of actors. For social constructivists, structure is made up of shared knowledge and practices as well as material resources. See also **system, behavior, bipolar, multipolar, structural determinist, structural realism**.

suboptimal   Less than the best choice or outcome, although it may be deemed good enough. See also **optimal**.

subtext   See **post-modernism**.

supranational   Beyond or above the state. For example, a world government would be a supranational authority that governs the relations among states.

surplus value   In Marxist usage, the value of goods and services produced comes from the labor put into their production. After paying wages (which tend toward subsistence or minimum levels) and other costs, the remainder is *surplus* that can be pocketed or invested by the owners of land or capital.

sustainable development   Increased economic production puts increasing pressure on resources and adds pollution effects that can undermine continued development. Rapid population growth adds further strain. For economic development to continue or be sustained over the long term requires attention be paid to these resource, environmental, and demographic constraints.

synchronic   Refers to a study of phenomena at a given point in time as opposed to over a period of time. See also **diachronic**.

synthesis   Putting together parts to make a whole.

system   A set of interrelated parts or an arrangement of units connected in such a way as to form a unity or whole; an abstract concept used by many theorists to bring order to their work. The use of the term varies. For example, some theorists see the *international* system as being composed of states and other actors, whereas some authors see world capitalism as a system composed of classes with conflicting interests. Some systems are said to be *open* to external influences, whereas others are *closed* systems. Factors external to a system that may affect it are *exogenous*, whereas those internal to the system are often referred to as *endogenous* factors. Some systems are said to have certain inherent qualities or attributes, such as a tendency toward balance or equilibrium, although not all systems theorists assign such automaticity to systems. Some theorists use systems merely as taxonomies, or frameworks, for organizing research and analysis.

systemic   See **system**.

taxonomy, taxonomies   A classification as in a categorization of states as democratic, socialist, or fascist.

teleology, teleological   That phenomena are to be explained by the purposes they serve. In systems theory, for example, it is teleological to argue that the need for a system to return to some natural state of equilibrium causes units within the system to behave the way they do. It may be that unit interactions within a system have a tendency to produce equilibrium, but it is teleological in effect to reverse the causal flow and argue that this systemic purpose (equilibrium) somehow causes the behavior of actors within the system to occur so as to achieve this result. Similarly, some functionalist theories have been criticized to the extent that they are also teleological.

terms of trade   The ratio of a country's average export prices to its average import prices, especially regarding merchandise trade. When import prices rise faster than export prices, the terms of trade worsen. This is said to be the case for most less-developed countries since the 1950s; the prices of raw materials have generally lagged behind the prices of imported manufactured goods from developed countries.

theory   A set of interrelated propositions that aims to *explain* or *predict* phenomena, thereby attempting to make the world more intelligible. *Explanation* involves accounting for, or understanding causes of, such phenomena as war, arms races, and regional integration. In a loose sense, *prediction* amounts merely to forecasting, but in a strict sense it implies explanation sufficient to anticipate outcomes, given the presence of certain variables or conditions (for example, theories that would predict war as the outcome of arms races). *General* theories attempt a comprehensive or complete explanation of some phenomenon, whereas *partial* theories are often understood as initial steps or attempts to explain narrower aspects of the phenomenon under investigation. There are considerable differences about the use of the terms *microtheory* and *macrotheory*. Most theorists use the term *microtheory* to refer to partial theories and *macrotheory* to refer to grand theory that would, for example, explain all of international relations. For a more extensive discussion, see the text. See also **parsimonious theory, hypothesis.**

Third World   The economically less-developed (or underdeveloped) states of Asia, Africa, and Latin America. The *First World* includes the more industrially developed states in North America, Europe, Japan, Australia, and New Zealand; the *Second World* consists of the few remaining Marxist-Leninist countries. Some theorists have identified the poorest of the less-developed countries as constituting a *Fourth World*. See also **North–South, East, West,** and **East–West.**

traditionalism   A mode of thinking about international relations that emphasizes the studying of such disciplines as diplomatic history, international law, and philosophy in an attempt to develop better insights. Traditionalists tend to be skeptical of behavioralist approaches that are confined to strict scientific standards that include formal hypothesis testing and, usually, the use of statistical analysis. See also **behavior, methodology.**

transformation, system transformation   A *fundamental* change in the system, as in a shift from a multipolar to a bipolar world or vice versa. The creation of a world government to replace an anarchic system of sovereign states would be such a system transformation. In a domestic context, the overthrow of the bourgeoisie by the proletariat would be considered a transformation of the political, social, and economic order.

transgovernmental   Relations involving links, ties, or even coalitions among bureaucratic or other official actors of different states. To the extent that these are effective, they may be a means for bypassing central government authorities in each state, although some theorists consider such circumvention of authority more an exception to the usual pattern in which the state remains unitary and speaks with one voice. See also **transnational**.

transnational, transnationalism   Interactions and coalitions across state boundaries that involve such diverse nongovernmental actors as multinational corporations and banks, church groups, and terrorist networks. In some usages, transnationalism includes both nongovernmental as well as *transgovernmental* links. The term *transnational* is used both to label the actor (for example, a transnational actor) or a pattern of behavior (for example, an international organization that acts *transnationally*—operates across state borders). Theorists focusing on transnationalism often deemphasize the state as primary and unitary actor. See also **transgovernmental**.

uneven development   A concept used by Marxists and other theorists that emphasizes capitalism's unequal spread of global economic benefits. In Lenin's *Imperialism*, for example, he argued that the increasing concentration of capital in advanced capitalist states led to monopolies and cartels that sought foreign investments once national markets were exhausted. This spread of capitalism inevitably resulted in the exploitation of colonies. In the present period, uneven development continues to characterize not only individual national economies but the capitalist world as a whole. Both domestically and internationally, benefits accrue to the few.

unipolar, unipolarity   See **structure**.

unitary   Undivided, whole. In many realist analyses, states are viewed as unitary actors that speak ultimately with one voice.

units of analysis   That which is being studied, such as a state.

utilitarians, utilitarianism   A doctrine developed in the nineteenth century that postulated that the greatest happiness of the greatest number should be the aim of all action. The term can also mean a belief that the value of anything is determined solely by its utility. Utilitarian thinking as applied to theory building tends to emphasize a rational decision-making process in which actors seek to maximize benefit or minimize cost.

utopian   See **idealist**.

values   Refers to the way things *ought* to be quite apart from the way things *are*. Political values would include preferences with respect to liberty, equality, order, and so on. A value is an estimate made of the worth or goodness of a goal or action. Also refers to measures as in numerical values. See also **normative**.

variable   A characteristic of an object or class of objects that may take on different values. The variable may be quantitative (such as height) or qualitative (such as marital status). In international relations research, for example, the class of objects may be states and the variable military power. Researchers wish to *operationalize* a variable, which means finding a way to measure the variable. Military power may be operationalized, for example, by using such indicators as number of nuclear weapons, amount of the gross national product devoted to military expenditures, or number of persons under arms. A *dependent variable* is simply what one is trying to explain, such as the frequency and intensity of war since 1800. *Independent variables* are factors that may help to explain or predict the dependent variable.

variable sum game   See **game theory**.

Verstehen   See **interpretive understanding**.

voluntarism, voluntarist   A philosophical position that reality is created by human will; that humans can affect, if not control, their destinies. In international relations, it generally means that decisionmakers have effective choice and are able to influence outcomes. As used in this volume, voluntarism is in opposition to the philosophical idea of determinism. *Social constructivism*, for example, is a voluntarist formulation. See also **determinism, social constructivism.**

vulnerability interdependence   See **interdependence.**

war   To engage in hostilities and military operations, usually for some political purpose. War among states is *interstate* war; war between opposing parties within a state is *civil* war; war involving irregulars and unconventional tactics is *guerrilla* war. The explanation of war is traditionally the primary concern of many realist scholars of international relations.

welfare issues   Socioeconomic and other issues associated with improving the living conditions and standards of people.

West   Generally, the countries of North America, Europe, and, paradoxically, Japan because of its level of industrial development and its links to other advanced capitalist states. See **East–West.**

world federalism   The goal of individuals favoring a world government that would have authority in certain areas over constituent states.

world politics   See **international relations.**

zero-sum game   See **game theory.**

INDEX